THE EXTERNALISATION

OF

THE HIERARCHY

BOOKS BY ALICE A. BAILEY

THE EXTERNALISATION

OF

THE HIERARCHY

by

ALICE A. BAILEY

LUCIS PUBLISHING COMPANY
113 University Place, 11th Floor
P.O. Box 722, Cooper Station
New York, N.Y. 10276

LUCIS PRESS LTD.
Suite 54
3 Whitehall Court
London SW1A 2EF
England

First Printing 1957

Sixth Printing 1981

Eighth Printing 1989 (4th Paperback Edition)

ISBN 0-85330-106-9

The publication of this book is financed by the Tibetan Book Fund which is established for the perpetuation of the teachings of the Tibetan and Alice A. Bailey.

This Fund is controlled by the Lucis Trust, a tax exempt, religious, educational corporation.

The Lucis Publishing Company is a non-profit organisation owned by the Lucis Trust. No royalties are paid on this book.

This title is also available in a
clothbound edition.

This title is also available in Dutch, French, German, Italian and Spanish. Translation into other languages is proceeding.

MANUFACTURED IN THE UNITED STATES OF AMERICA
By Fort Orange Press, Inc., Albany, N.Y.

THE GREAT INVOCATIONS

Let the Forces of Light bring illumination to mankind.
Let the Spirit of Peace be spread abroad.
May men of goodwill everywhere meet in a spirit of cooperation.
May forgiveness on the part of all men be the keynote at this time.
Let power attend the efforts of the Great Ones.
So let it be, and help us to do our part.   1935

* * * * *

Let the Lords of Liberation issue forth.
Let Them bring succour to the sons of men.
Let the Rider from the Secret Place come forth,
And coming, save.
Come forth, O Mighty One.

Let the souls of men awaken to the Light,
And may they stand with massed intent.
Let the fiat of the Lord go forth:
The end of woe has come!
Come forth, O Mighty One.
The hour of service of the Saving Force has now arrived.
Let it be spread abroad, O Mighty One.

Let Light and Love and Power and Death
Fulfil the purpose of the Coming One.
The WILL to save is here.
The LOVE to carry forth the work is widely spread abroad.
The ACTIVE AID of all who know the truth is also here.
Come forth, O Mighty One and blend these three.
Construct a great defending wall.
The rule of evil *now* must end.   1940

* * * * *

From the point of Light within the Mind of God
    Let light stream forth into the minds of men.
        Let Light descend on Earth.

From the point of Love within the Heart of God
    Let love stream forth into the hearts of men.
        May Christ return to Earth.

From the centre where the Will of God is known
    Let purpose guide the little wills of men—
        The purpose which the Masters know and serve.

From the centre which we call the race of men
    Let the Plan of Love and Light work out.
        And may it seal the door where evil dwells.

Let Light and Love and Power restore the Plan on Earth.
                                                          1945

THE GREAT INVOCATION

From the point of Light within the Mind of God
    Let light stream forth into the minds of men.
    Let Light descend on Earth.

From the point of Love within the Heart of God
    Let love stream forth into the hearts of men.
    May Christ return to Earth.

From the centre where the Will of God is known
    Let purpose guide the little wills of men —
    The purpose which the Masters know and serve.

From the centre which we call the race of men
    Let the Plan of Love and Light work out
    And may it seal the door where evil dwells.

Let Light and Love and Power restore the Plan on Earth.

"The above Invocation or Prayer does not belong to any person or group but to all humanity. The beauty and the strength of this Invocation lies in its simplicity, and in its expression of certain central truths which all men, innately and normally, accept — the truth of the existence of a basic Intelligence to Whom we vaguely give the name of God; the truth that behind all outer seeming, the motivating power of the universe is Love; the truth that a great Individuality came to earth, called by Christians, the Christ, and embodied that love so that we could understand; the truth that both love and intelligence are effects of what is called the Will of God; and finally the self-evident truth that only through *humanity* itself can the Divine Plan work out."

ALICE A. BAILEY

EXTRACT FROM A STATEMENT BY THE TIBETAN

Suffice it to say, that I am a Tibetan disciple of a certain degree, and this tells you but little, for all are disciples from the humblest aspirant up to, and beyond, the Christ Himself. I live in a physical body like other men, on the borders of Tibet, and at times (from the exoteric standpoint) preside over a large group of Tibetan lamas, when my other duties permit. It is this fact that has caused it to be reported that I am an abbot of this particular lamasery. Those associated with me in the work of the Hierarchy (and all true disciples are associated in this work) know me by still another name and office. A.A.B. knows who I am and recognises me by two of my names.

I am a brother of yours, who has travelled a little longer upon the Path than has the average student, and has therefore incurred greater responsibilities. I am one who has wrestled and fought his way into a greater measure of light than has the aspirant who will read this article, and I must therefore act as a transmitter of the light, no matter what the cost. I am not an old man, as age counts among the teachers, yet I am not young or inexperienced. My work is to teach and spread the knowledge of the Ageless Wisdom wherever I can find a response, and I have been doing this for many years. I seek also to help the Master M. and the Master K.H. whenever opportunity offers, for I have been long connected with Them and with Their work. In all the above, I have told you much; yet at the same time I have told you nothing which would lead you to offer me that blind obedience and the foolish devotion which the emotional aspirant offers to the Guru and Master Whom he is as yet unable to contact. Nor will he make that desired contact until he has transmuted emotional devotion into unselfish service to humanity,—not to the Master.

The books that I have written are sent out with no claim for their acceptance. They may, or may not, be correct, true

vii

and useful. It is for you to ascertain their truth by right practice and by the exercise of the intuition. Neither I nor A.A.B. is the least interested in having them acclaimed as inspired writings, or in having anyone speak of them (with bated breath) as being the work of one of the Masters. If they present truth in such a way that it follows sequentially upon that already offered in the world teachings, if the information given raises the aspiration and the will-to-serve from the plane of the emotions to that of the mind (the plane whereon the Masters *can* be found) then they will have served their purpose. If the teaching conveyed calls forth a response from the illumined mind of the worker in the world, and brings a flashing forth of his intuition, then let that teaching be accepted. But not otherwise. If the statements meet with eventual corroboration, or are deemed true under the test of the Law of Correspondences, then that is well and good. But should this not be so, let not the student accept what is said.

AUGUST 1934

TABLE OF CONTENTS

Table of Contents

Table of Contents

INTRODUCTORY REMARKS

THE PERIOD OF TRANSITION

March 1934

One of the results of the world condition at this time is the speeding up of all the atomic lives upon and within the planet. This necessarily involves the increased vibratory activity of the human mechanism, with a consequent effect upon the psychic nature, producing an abnormal sensitivity and psychic awareness. It would be of value here to remember that the condition of humanity at this time is not the result of simply one factor, but of several—all of them being active simultaneously, because this period marks the close of one age and the inauguration of the new.

The factors to which I refer are, primarily, three in number:

1. This is a transition period between the passing out of the Piscean Age, with its emphasis upon authority and belief, and the coming in of the Aquarian Age, with its emphasis upon individual understanding and direct knowledge. The activity of these forces, characteristic of the two signs, produces in the atoms of the human body a corresponding activity. We are on the verge of new knowledges and the atoms of the body are being tuned up for reception. Those atoms which are predominantly Piscean are beginning to slow down their activity and to be "occultly withdrawn," as it is called, or abstracted, whilst those which are responsive to the New Age tendencies are, in their turn, being stimulated and their vibratory activity increased.

2.   The world war marked a climax in the history of mankind, and its subjective effect was far more potent than has hitherto been grasped. Through the power of prolonged sound, carried forward as a great experiment on the battlefields all over the world during a period of four years (1914-1918), and through the intense emotional strain of the entire planetary populace, the web of etheric matter (called the "veil of the temple") which separates the physical and astral planes was rent or torn asunder, and the amazing process of unifying the two worlds of physical plane living and of astral plane experience was begun and is now slowly going on. It will be obvious, therefore, that this must bring about vast changes and alterations in the human consciousness. Whilst it will usher in the age of understanding, of brotherhood and of illumination, it will also bring about states of reaction and the letting loose of psychic forces which today menace the uncontrolled and ignorant, and warrant the sounding of a note of warning and of caution.

3.   A third factor is as follows. It has been known for a long time by the mystics of all the world religions and by esoteric students everywhere, that certain members of the planetary Hierarchy are approaching closer to the earth at this time. By this I want you to infer that the thought, or the mental attention, of the Christ and of certain of His great disciples, the Masters of the Wisdom, is directed or focussed at this time on human affairs, and that some of Them are also preparing to break Their long silence and may appear later among men. This necessarily has a potent effect, first of all upon Their disciples and on those who are attuned to and synchronized with Their Minds, and secondly, it should be remembered that the energy which flows through these focal points of the Divine Will will have a dual effect and be destructive as well as constructive, according to the quality of the bodies which react to it. Different types of men respond distinctively to any inflow of energy, and a tremendous psychic stimulation is at this time going on, with results both divinely beneficent and sadly destructive.

It might be added also that certain astrological relationships between the constellations are releasing new types of force which are playing through our solar system and on to our planet and thereby making possible developments hitherto frustrated in expression, and bringing about the demonstration of latent powers and the manifestation of new knowledges. All this must be most carefully borne in mind by the worker in the field of human affairs if the present crisis is to be rightly appreciated and its splendid opportunities rightly employed. I have felt it wise to write a few words concerning the condition to be found in the world today especially in connection with esoteric, occult and mystical groups and the spiritualistic movement.

All true spiritual thinkers and workers are much concerned at this time about the growth of crime on every hand, by the display of the lower psychic powers, by the apparent deterioration of the physical body, as shown in the spread of disease, and by the extraordinary increase in insanity, neurotic conditions and mental unbalance. All this is the result of the tearing of the planetary web, and at the same time it is a part of the evolutionary plan and the providing of the opportunity whereby humanity may take its next step forward. The Hierarchy of Adepts has been divided in opinion (if so unsuitable a word can be applied to a group of souls and brothers who know no sense of separateness, but only differ over problems of "skill in action") over the present world condition. Some believe it to be premature and consequently undesirable and providing a difficult situation, whilst others take Their stand upon the basic soundness of humanity and regard the present crisis as inevitable and brought about by the developments in man himself; They look upon the condition as educational and as constituting only a temporary problem which—as it is solved—will lead mankind on the way to a still more glorious future. But there is, at the same time, no denying the fact that great and frequently devastating forces have been let loose upon the earth, and that the effect is a cause of grave concern to all the Masters, Their disciples and workers.

The difficulty can, in the main, be traced back to the overstimulation and the undue strain placed upon the mechanism of the bodies, which the world of souls (in physical incarnation) have to employ as they seek to manifest on the physical plane and so respond to their environment. The flow of energy, pouring through from the astral plane and (in a lesser degree) from the lower mental plane, is brought in contact with bodies that are unresponsive at first, and over-responsive later; it pours into brain cells which, from lack of use, are unaccustomed to the powerful rhythm imposed upon them; and humanity's equipment of knowledge is so poor that the majority have not sense enough to proceed with caution and to progress slowly. Therefore, they are soon in danger and difficulty; their natures are oft so impure or so selfish that the new powers which are beginning to make their presence felt, and so opening up new avenues of awareness and contact, are subordinated to purely selfish ends and prostituted to mundane objectives. The glimpses vouchsafed to the man of that which lies behind the veil are misinterpreted and the information gained is misused and distorted by wrong motives. But whether a person is unintentionally a victim of force or brings himself in touch with it deliberately, he pays the price of his ignorance or temerity in the physical body, even though his soul may "go marching on."

It is of no use at this time to close one's eyes to the immediate problem or to endeavour to lay the blame for the sad failures, the occult wrecks, for the half-demented psychics, the hallucinated mystics and the feeble-minded dabblers in esotericism at the door of their own stupidity, or upon the backs of some teachers, groups or organisations. Much blame can indeed be placed here and there, but it is the part of wisdom to face facts and to realise the cause of that which is everywhere transpiring and which can be stated as follows.

The cause of the growth of the lower psychism and of the increasing sensitivity of humanity at this time is the sudden inflow of a new form of astral energy through the rent veil which has, until a short while ago, safeguarded the many. Add to this the inadequacy of the mass of human vehicles to meet the newly imposed strain and some idea of the problem can be grasped.

Let it not be forgotten, however, that there is another side to the picture. The inflow of this energy has brought many hundreds of people into a new and deeper spiritual realisation; it has opened a door through which many will pass before long and take their second initiation, and it has let a flood of light into the world—a light which will go on increasing for the next thirty years, bringing assurance of immortality and a fresh revelation of the divine potencies in the human being. Thus is the New Age dawning. Access to levels of inspiration, hitherto untouched, has been facilitated. The stimulation of the higher faculties (and this on a large scale) is now possible, and the coordination of the personality with the soul and the right use of energy can go forward with renewed understanding and enterprise. Ever the race is to the strong, and always the many are called and the few chosen. This is the occult law.

We are now in a period of tremendous spiritual potency and of opportunity to all upon the probationary path and the path of discipleship. It is the hour wherein a clarion call goes forth to man to be of good cheer and of goodwill, for deliverance is on the way. But it is also the hour of danger and of menace for the unwary and the unready, for the ambitious, the ignorant, and for those who selfishly seek the Way and who refuse to tread the path of service with pure motive. Lest this widespread upheaval and consequent disaster to so many should seem to you unfair, let me remind you that this one life is but a second of time in the larger and wider existence of the soul, and that those who fail and are disrupted by the impact of the powerful forces now flooding our earth will nevertheless have their vibration "stepped up" to better things along with the mass of those who achieve, even if their physical vehicles are destroyed in the process. The destruction of the body is not the worst disaster that can overcome a man.

It is not my purpose to cover the whole ground possible

in relation to the situation in the field of psychism caused by the inflow of astral energy at this time. I seek to confine myself to the effect of this inflow on aspirants and sensitives. These two words—aspirants and sensitives—are employed by me in this article to distinguish the awakened seeker after control and mastery from the lower type of psychic, who is controlled and mastered. It is necessary here to remind you that psychism, so-called, can be divided into the following two groups:

Higher Psychism	*Lower Psychism*
Divine	Animal
Controlled	Uncontrolled
Positive	Negative
Intelligently applied	Automatic
Mediatorship	Mediumship

These distinctions are little understood, nor is the fact appreciated that both groups of qualities indicate our divinity. All are expressions of God.

There are certain psychic powers which men share in common with the animals; these powers are inherent in the animal body and are instinctual, but they have, for the vast majority, dropped below the threshold of consciousness and are unrealised and therefore useless. These are the powers, for instance, of astral clairvoyance and clairaudience, and the seeing of colours and similar phenomena. Clairvoyance and clairaudience are also possible on mental levels, and we then call it telepathy, and the seeing of symbols, for all visioning of geometrical forms is mental clairvoyance. All these powers are, however, tied up with the human mechanism or response apparatus, and serve to put the man in touch with aspects of the phenomenal world for which the response mechanism, which we call the personality, exists. They are the product of the activity of the divine soul in man, which takes the form of what we call "the animal soul," which really corresponds to the Holy Ghost aspect in the human microcosmic trinity. All these powers have their higher spiritual correspondences, which manifest when the soul becomes consciously active and controls its mechanism through the mind and the brain. When astral clairvoyance and clairaudience are *not* below the threshold of consciousness, but are actively used and functioning, it means that the solar plexus centre is open and active. When the corresponding mental faculties are present in consciousness, then it means that the throat centre and the centre between the eyebrows are becoming "awake" and active. But the higher psychic powers, such as spiritual perception with its infallible knowledge, the intuition with its unerring judgment, and psychometry of the higher kind with its power to reveal the past and the future, are the prerogatives of the divine soul. These higher powers come into play when the head and heart centres, as well as the throat centre, are brought into activity as the result of meditation and service. Let the student, however, remember two things:

That the greater can always include the lesser, but the purely animal psychic does not include the higher.

That between the lowest type of negative mediumship and the highest type of inspired teacher and seer are found a vast diversity of grades, and that the centres are not uniformly developed in humanity.

The complexity of the subject is great, but the general situation can be grasped, the significance of the opportunity proffered can be understood, and the right use of knowledge be employed to bring good out of the present critical period, and thus the psychic and spiritual growth of man be fostered and nurtured.

Two questions should, I believe, at this time engross the attention of all workers in the field of esotericism and those who are engaged with the training of students and aspirants.

I. How shall we train our sensitives and psychics so that the dangers can be avoided and men can go safely forward to their new and glorious heritage?

II.   How can esoteric schools or "disciplines," as they are
sometimes called, make right use of the opportunity?

Let us speak first of the training and safeguarding of
our psychics and sensitives.

I. The Training of Psychics

The first thing to be borne in mind is that negative,
unintelligent mediumship and psychism reduces its exponent to the level of an automaton; it is dangerous and
inadvisable because it deprives man of his free will and his
positivity, and militates against his acting as a free intelligent
human being. The man is not acting in these cases as a
channel for his own soul, but is little better than an instinctual animal, if he is not literally an empty shell, which
an obsessing entity can occupy and use. When speaking
thus I am dealing with the very lowest type of animal
mediumship of which there is far too much these days, and
which is the cause of concern to the best minds in all the
movements which foster mediumship. A mediumship which
is entered into with a fully conscious focussed attitude and
in which the medium, knowingly and intelligently, vacates
his body to an entering entity of whom he is fully aware
and who takes possession with his conscious permission in
order to serve some spiritual end and help his fellowmen can
be right and good. But how often is this type of mediumship to be seen? Few mediums know the technique governing the passing in or out of an informing entity, nor do they
know how to carry on this work in such a way that never
for a moment are they unaware of what they themselves
are doing and the purpose of their activity. Definitely and
with purpose they lend their body temporarily to another
soul for service, preserving their own integrity all the time.
The highest expression of this type of activity was the giving
of his body by the disciple Jesus for the use of the Christ.
It is in the word *service* that the whole story lies, and the
safeguard. When this true mediumship is better understood,
we shall have the medium passing out of his body in full

waking consciousness through the orifice at the top of his head, and not, as is now the case in the majority of instances, through the solar plexus, with no preservation of awareness of the transaction, nor any recollection of what has transpired.

We shall then have the temporary entrance of a new tenant along the line of a synchronous vibration through the entrance in the head, and the subsequent use of the instrument of the loaned body in service of some kind or another. But this procedure will never be followed in order to satisfy idle curiosity, or an equally idle grief, based on personal loneliness and self-pity. At present many of the lower kind of mediums are exploited by the curious or unhappy public, and those peculiar human beings whose consciousness is centred entirely below the diaphragm and whose solar plexus is indeed their brain (as it is the brain of the animal) are forced to act as mediums to satisfy the love of sensation or desire for comfort of their almost equally unintelligent fellowmen.

At the same time, there are mediums of a very much higher order whose lives are offered in service to advanced souls on the other side of the veil and who give themselves so that their fellowmen may learn of them; thus, on both sides of the veil of separation, are souls aided and given opportunity to hear or serve. But these, too, would profit by a more intelligent training and by a more accurate understanding of the technique of their work and the organisation of their bodies. They would then be better channels and more dependable intermediaries.

Above all, let the psychics in the world today grasp the necessity of controlling and of not being controlled; let them realise that all that they do can be done by any trained disciple of the Ageless Wisdom should the occasion warrant it, and circumstances justify such an expenditure of force. Psychics are easily deceived. For example, it is of course obvious that on the astral plane there is a thoughtform of myself, your Tibetan brother. All who have received the disciples' degree monthly instructions, all who read the books which I have sent out into the world with the aid of A.A.B., also all who are working in my personal group of disciples have naturally and automatically aided in the construction of this astral thoughtform. It is not me, nor is it linked to me, nor do I use it. I have definitely disassociated myself from it and do not employ it as a means of contacting those I teach, for I work from choice entirely on mental levels thereby undoubtedly limiting my range of contacts but increasing the effectiveness of my work. This astral thoughtform is a distortion of me and my work, needless to say, and resembles an animated and galvanised shell.

Because there is in this form much emotional substance and also a certain amount of mental substance, it can make a wide appeal and its validity is such that like all shells, for instance, which are contacted in the seance room, it masquerades as myself and where the intuition is unawakened the illusion is complete and real. Devotees can therefore tune in with great facility on this illusory form and be completely deceived. Its vibration is of a relatively high order. Its mental effect is like a beautiful parody of myself and serves to place the deluded devotees in touch with the scroll of the astral light, which is the reflection of the akashic records. These latter are the eternal scroll whereon the plan for our world is inscribed and from which those of us who teach gather our data and much of our information. This, the astral light distorts and steps down. Because this is a distorted image and functions in the three worlds of form and has no source of validity higher than those of form, it has in it the seeds of separativeness and of disaster. Forms of flattery are sent out from it, ideas of separateness, those thoughts which feed ambition and which foster love of power, and those germs of desire and personal longing (which divide groups) emerge from contact with it. The results to those who are deceived thereby are sad.

I would like to point out also that trance mediumship, as it is called, must inevitably be superseded by that mediumship which is offered by the man or woman who is clairvoyant or clairaudient on the astral plane, and who therefore in full waking consciousness and with the physical brain alert and active can offer himself as an intermediary between men in physical plane bodies (and therefore blind and deaf on the subtler levels) and those who, having discarded their bodies, are cut off from physical communication. This type of psychic can communicate with both groups and their value and their usefulness as mediums is beyond computation when they are singleminded, unselfish, pure and dedicated to service. But in the training to which they subject themselves they must avoid the present negative methods, and instead of "sitting for development" in a blank and waiting silence, they should endeavour to work positively as souls, remaining in conscious and intelligent possession of the lower mechanism of their bodies; they must know which centre in that body they use whilst working psychically, and they must learn to look out, *as souls,* upon the world of illusion in which they are undertaking to work; from their high and pure position let them see clearly, hear truly and report accurately, and so serve their age and generation, and make the astral plane a familiar and well-known place of activity, accustoming mankind to a state of existence wherein are found their fellowmen, experiencing, living and following the Path.

I cannot here write concerning the technique of that training. The subject is too vast for a brief article. I do say, with emphasis, that a more careful and wise training is needed and a more intelligent use of the knowledge which is available, if sought after. I appeal to all who are interested in the growth of psychic knowledge to study, and think, and experiment, and teach, and learn until such time as the entire level of psychic phenomena has been lifted out of its present ignorant, speculative and negative position to one of potent assurance, proved technique, and spiritual expression. I appeal to such movements as the Psychical Research Societies in the world and the vast Spiritualistic Movement to lay the emphasis on divine expression and not so much on phenomena; let them approach the subject from the angle of service and carry their researches into the realm of energy, and cease to pander so much to the public. The opportunity offered them is great and the need of their work is vital. The service rendered has been real and essential, but if these movements are to avail themselves of the coming inflow of spiritual energy, they must shift their attention into the realm of true values. The training of the intellect and the presenting to the world of a group of intelligent psychics should be a main objective, and the astral plane will then be, for them, only a stage on the way to that world wherein all the spiritual Guides and Masters are found, and from whence all souls go forth to incarnation and all souls return from the place of experience and of experiment.

It might be asked what ground this training should cover. I would suggest that teaching should be given as to the nature of man and the purpose and objectives of the soul; training can be offered as to the technique of expression, and careful instruction also given as to the use of the centres in the etheric body and in the development of the ability to preserve inviolate the attitude of the positive on-looker, who is always the directing, controlling factor. There will have to be careful analysis of the type and character of the psychic, and then the application of differentiated and suitable methods so that he may progress with the least hindrance. Training schools and classes which seek to de-velop the student must be graded according to his point in evolution, and his passing into a group, optimistically hop-ing that something will happen to him whilst in it, will have to cease.

The goal for the low-grade negative psychic should be the training of the mind and the closing of the solar plexus until such time as he can function as a true mediator; if this involves the temporary cessation of his mediumistic powers (and consequently of his commercial exploitation), then so much the better for him, viewing him as an im-mortal soul, with a spiritual destiny and usefulness.

The instruction given to the intelligent medium and psychic should lead him to a full understanding of himself and of his powers; it should develop those powers without risk and with care, and he should be stabilised in the position of the positive controlling factor. His clairvoyant and clair-audient powers should gradually be perfected, and the right interpretation of what he sees and contacts on the plane of illusion, the astral plane, should be cultivated.

Thus we shall gradually find emerging in the world a large body of trained psychics whose powers are understood and who function on the astral plane with as much intelligence as they function on the physical plane, and who are preparing themselves for the expression of the higher psychic powers—spiritual perception and telepathy. These people will constitute eventually a body of linking souls, mediating between those who cannot see and hear on the astral plane because they are the prisoners of the physical body and those who are equally the prisoners of the astral plane, lacking the physical response apparatus.

The great need, therefore, is not that we should cease to consult and train our psychics and mediums, but that we should train them rightly and guard them intelligently and so link, through their means, the two worlds of the physical and the astral.*

II. Esoteric Schools and Disciplines

Our second question relates to the work of the esoteric schools or "disciplines," as they are sometimes called, and the training and safeguarding of the aspirants found working in them.

I would like first of all to make one point clear. The great hindrance to the work of the majority of the esoteric schools at this time is their sense of separateness and their intolerance of other schools and methods. The leaders of these schools need to absorb the following fact. All schools which recognise the influence of the trans-Himalayan Lodge and whose workers are linked, consciously or unconsciously, with such Masters of the Wisdom as the Master Morya or the Master K.H., form one school and are part of one "discipline." There is therefore no essential conflict of interests, and on

---

* *A Treatise on the Seven Rays*, Vol. II (*Esoteric Psychology*), pp. 555-598.

the inner side—if they are in any way functioning effectively —the various schools and presentations are regarded as a unity. There is no basic difference in teaching, even if the terminology used may vary, and the technique of work is fundamentally identical. If the work of the Great Ones is to go forward as desired in these days of stress and of world need, it is imperative that these various groups should begin to recognise their real unity in goal, guidance and technique, and that their leaders should realise that it is fear of other leaders and the desire that their group should be numerically the most important which prompts the frequent use of the words, "This is a different discipline," or, "Their work is not the same as ours." It is this attitude which is hindering the true growth of spiritual life and understanding among the many students gathered into the many outer organisations. At this time, the "great heresy of separateness" taints them. The leaders and members talk in terms of "our" and "your," of this "discipline" and that, and of this method being right (usually their own) and the other method which may be right, but it is probably doubtful, if not positively wrong. Each regards their own group as specifically pledged to them and to their mode of instruction, and threaten their members with dire results if they cooperate with the membership of other groups. Instead, they should recognise that all students in analogous schools and working under the same spiritual impulses are members of the *one school* and are linked together in a basic subjective unity. The time must come when these various (and at present) separative esoteric bodies will have to proclaim their identity, when the leaders and workers and secretaries will meet with each other and learn to know and understand each other. Some day this recognition and understanding will bring them to the point where they will endeavour to supplement each other's efforts, exchange ideas with each other, and so in truth and in deed constitute one great college of esotericism in the world, with varying classes and grades but all occupied with the work of training aspirants and preparing them for discipleship, or superintending the work of disciples as they prepare themselves to take initiation. Then will cease the present attempts to hinder each other's work by comparison of methods and of techniques, by criticism and defamation, by warning and the cult of fear, and the insistence on exclusiveness. It is these attitudes and methods which at this time are hindering the entrance of the pure light of truth.

Aspirants in these schools present a different problem from that of ordinary psychism and mediumship. These men and women have offered themselves for intellectual training and have subjected themselves to a forcing process which is intended to bring the full flower of the soul into *premature* blossoming, and this in order more rapidly and effectively to *serve* the race, and to cooperate with the plan of the Hierarchy. Such students thereby lay themselves open to dangers and difficulties which would have been avoided had they chosen to go the slower and equally sure way. This fact should be realised by all workers in such schools and the problem carefully explained to the entering aspirant, so that he may be on his guard and adhere with care to the rules and instructions. He should not be permitted to be afraid or to refuse to subject himself to this forcing process, but he should enter upon it with his eyes wide open and should be taught to avail himself of the safeguards offered and the experience of the older students.

The emphasis in all esoteric schools is necessarily, and rightly, laid upon meditation. Technically speaking, meditation is the process whereby the head centre is awakened, brought under control and used. When this is the case, the soul and the personality are coordinated and fused, and at-one-ment takes place, producing in the aspirant a tremendous inflow of spiritual energy, galvanising his whole being into activity, and bringing to the surface the latent good and also evil. Herein lies much of the problem and much of the danger. Hence also the stress laid in such true schools upon the need of purity and truth. Over-emphasis has been laid upon the need for physical purity, and not sufficient emphasis laid upon the avoidance of all fanaticism and intolerance. These two qualities hinder the student far more than can wrong diet, and they feed the fires of separativeness more than any other one factor.

Meditation involves the living of a one-pointed life always and every day. This perforce puts an undue strain on the brain cells for it brings quiescent cells into activity and awakens the brain consciousness to the light of the soul. This process of ordered meditation, when carried forward over a period of years and supplemented by meditative living and one-pointed service, will successfully arouse the entire system, and bring the lower man under the influence and control of the spiritual man; it will awaken also the centres of force in the etheric body and stimulate into activity that mysterious stream of energy which sleeps at the base of the spinal column. When this process is carried forward with care and due safeguards, and under direction, and when the process is spread over a long period of time there is little risk of danger, and the awakening will take place normally and under the law of being itself. If, however, the tuning up and awakening is forced, or is brought about by exercises of various kinds before the student is ready and before the bodies are coordinated and developed, then the aspirant is headed towards disaster. Breathing exercises or pranayama training should never be undertaken without expert guidance and only after years of spiritual application, devotion and service; concentration upon the centres in the force body (with a view to their awakening) is ever to be avoided; it will cause overstimulation and the opening of doors on to the astral plane which the student may have difficulty in closing. I cannot impress too strongly upon aspirants in all occult schools that the yoga for this transition period is the yoga of one-pointed intent, of directed purpose, of a constant practice of the Presence of God, and of ordered regular meditation carried forward systematically and steadily over years of effort.

When this is done with detachment and is paralleled by a life of loving service, the awakening of the centres and the raising of the sleeping fire of kundalini will go forward with safety and sanity and the whole system will be brought to the requisite stage of "aliveness." I cannot too strongly advise students against the following of intensive meditation processes for hours at a time, or against practices which have for their objective the arousing of the fires of the body, the awakening of a particular centre and the moving of the serpent fire. The general world stimulation is so great at this time and the average aspirant is so sensitive and finely organised that excessive meditation, a fanatical diet, the curtailing of the hours of sleep or undue interest in and emphasis upon psychic experience will upset the mental balance and often do irretrievable harm.

Let the students in esoteric schools settle down to steady, quiet, unemotional work. Let them refrain from prolonged hours of study and of meditation. Their bodies are as yet incapable of the requisite tension, and they only damage themselves. Let them lead normal busy lives, remembering in the press of daily duties and service who they are essentially and what are their goal and objectives. Let them meditate regularly every morning, beginning with a period of fifteen minutes and never exceeding forty minutes. Let them forget themselves in service, and let them not concentrate their interest upon their own psychic development. Let them train their minds with a normal measure of study and learn to think intelligently, so that their minds can balance their emotions and enable them to interpret correctly that which they contact as their measure of awareness increases and their consciousness expands.

Students need to remember that devotion to the Path or to the Master is not enough. The Great Ones are looking for *intelligent* cooperators and workers more than They are looking for devotion to Their Personalities, and a student who is walking independently in the light of his own soul is regarded by Them as a more dependable instrument than a devoted fanatic. The light of his soul will reveal to the earnest aspirant the unity underlying all groups, and enable him to eliminate the poison of intolerance which taints and hinders so many; it will cause him to recognise the spiritual fundamentals which guide the steps of humanity; it will force him to overlook the intolerance and the fanaticism and separativeness which characterise the small mind and the beginner upon the Path, and help him so to love them that they will begin to see more truly and enlarge their horizon; it will enable him to estimate truly the esoteric value of service and teach him above all to practice that *harmlessness* which is the outstanding quality of every son of God. A harmlessness that speaks no word that can damage another person, that thinks no thought which could poison or produce misunderstanding, and which does no action which could hurt the least of his brethren—this is the main virtue which will enable the esoteric student to tread with safety the difficult path of development. Where the emphasis is laid upon service to one's fellowmen and the trend of the life force is outward to the world, then there is freedom from danger and the aspirant can safely meditate and aspire and work. His motive is pure, and he is seeking to decentralise his personality and shift the focus of his attention away from himself to the group. Thus the life of the soul can pour through him, and express itself as love to all beings. He knows himself to be a part of a whole and the life of that whole can flow through him consciously, leading him to a realisation of brotherhood and of his oneness in relation to all manifested lives.

The Present Urgency

October 10, 1934

I have somewhat to say to those who are the recipients of my words as embodied in my books and pamphlets and who, with mental interest and devotion, follow out as far as may be my line of thought.

I have for years—ever since 1919—sought to aid you to the best of my ability. The Hierarchy (a name covering the working disciples of all degrees) has for hundreds of generations sought to aid humanity, and since the fifteenth century has steadily approached closer to the physical plane and sought to make a deeper impact on the human consciousness. This has resulted in a recognition which has in it (at this time) the *seeds of world salvation*. Until the fifteenth century, the pull and the magnetic appeal was from the side of the watching Elder Brothers. Today, so numerous are the inner and outer disciples, and so many are the world aspirants, the pull and the magnetic appeal are largely equalised, and what will happen in the world unfoldment and in the recognitions by the races will be the result of mutual interplay of the two intents (I am choosing my words with care) —the intent of the Masters to help humanity, and that of the world aspirants and disciples to aid in that helping.

Esoterically speaking, a point of contact, a moment of "spiritual intercourse," is imminent, and *out of that moment a new world can be born.*

If that can be brought about, then there can be re-established on earth the condition which was brought to an end in earlier days, when the Hierarchy (in order to further man's mental development) withdrew behind the scenes for a period. If this spiritual contact can be brought about, it means that the Hierarchy will no longer be hidden and unknown, but will be recognised as present upon the physical plane. This would at first be necessarily on a small scale, and the recognition will be confined to the aspirants and disciples. Increasingly the new group of world servers will be active in every nation and found functioning throughout the entire world.

The two thoughts which I seek to impress upon your minds are, first, the re-establishing of this closer relation, and secondly, the work of a practical kind that each of you can do to bring about this general recognition. I seek to emphasise the point that the final activity which will bring about this spiritual event *must* come from the outer plane of physical life. All of us who are occupied with the Plan for "the next three years" are seeking earnestly for those who can help us and to whom appeal can be made for the putting forth of that final last effort which *will* bring the desired and anticipated result.

I would preface what I have to say with the reminder that I only *make a suggestion* and that naught that I say carries with it the slightest weight of authority; and also that I am aware of the frequent futility of such appeals for co-operation. The history of the world of thought evidences the fact that men are oft thrilled and enlightened and aided by ideas and by the promise of a developing future, but that when their aid is sought in the materialising of the idea, then their hope and interest fade out on the mental plane, or— if it reaches the world of emotion and of strong desire—the sacrifice required to bring the hope to birth on the physical plane is lacking or too feeble to produce the longed-for result.

What I have to say as a result of the urgency upon me to bring about a more intensive cooperation upon the part of those who read with interest the pamphlet *The Next Three Years*,* carries not the smallest fraction of authority. I only appeal to you in the hope of intensifying your effort for the space of the next two years (one has already passed), because after the early autumn of 1936, any effort along this particular line will either have failed or will no longer be required in this particular form.

My sole responsibility is to put the opportunity before the world aspirants, to point out to them the inherent possibilities of this particular situation, to indicate lines of helpful activity, and then (having so done) to withdraw the power of my mind and thought, and so leave each aspirant free to come to his own decisions.

The pamphlet *The Next Three Years* is going forth to-day upon its mission. Its objective is to educate public opinion. It carries both inspiration and the power to produce cleavages in the life—cleavages which will *produce new activities and the cessation of old attitudes of mind.* A possible happening is indicated—the formation upon the physical plane of that group of aspirants and disciples which,

---

* *A Treatise on White Magic*, pp. 401-433.
    A Treatise on the Seven Rays, Vol. I (*Esoteric Psychology*), pp. 170-189.

given time and opportunity, can *salvage a distressed world and bring light and understanding to humanity.* As to this, I need say no more.

All of you have read the plan as it is embodied in the pamphlet, and the challenge to faith and the appeal to your service is before you. The next two years will see the decision as to whether the fusion of the inner and the outer groups of world servers can be made, or whether more time must elapse before the earlier ancient cooperation between the Hierarchy and humanity can be re-established.

I speak with love and almost anxiety, and with a wider knowledge of the present urgency than you can possibly have. I couch what I have to say to you in the form of certain questions, which I ask that you should put to yourselves with quietness and sincerity.

1.   Do I really and in truth desire the establishment of this closer interplay between the inner and outer worlds? If so, what am I prepared to do in order to bring this about?

2.   Is there any way in which I can make a definite contribution towards this desired end? Recognising my special circumstances what more can I give in
  a. Meditation
  b. Understanding of the Plan
  c. Love of my fellowmen?
Forget not that *meditation* clarifies the mind as to the fact and nature of the Plan, that *understanding* brings that Plan into the world of desire, and that *love* releases the form which will make the Plan materialise upon the physical plane. To these three expressions of your soul I call you. All of you, without exception, can serve in these three ways, if you so desire.

3.   The objective of all the work to be done at this time is to educate public opinion and to familiarise the thinking people of the world with the urgency and the opportunity of the next two years. If this is indeed so, what am I doing to make this possible? To elaborate this question:

a. Have I spoken to all I could in my environment, or have I been held back by fear?
b. Have I made possible the wide distribution of the pamphlet on this subject? Its distribution in its present form is possible only until the fall of 1936, and the time is therefore short.
c. Have I aided in a material and financial way as far as is possible? Can I do more than I have done so far to help to meet this requirement?
d. What more of my time can I give to help this work, to aid those who are distributing the pamphlet, or to gather people together for discussion? Can I not dedicate some time every day to this definite idea and service?

Responding to my appeal will involve sacrifice, but all who grasp the Plan are today spending themselves in the effort to lift humanity up to another rung of the ladder and into greater light. Their hands need strengthening, their work needs helping, and there is not one of you who cannot do more than you are doing, through the aid of meditation, money and thought, to salvage the world, to educate public opinion and so bring in the New Day.

A Challenging Opportunity

April 1935

During the Wesak Festival this year, Those Who are seeking to lift humanity nearer to the Light and to expand the consciousness of mankind, will be gathering Their forces for a renewed approach with its inevitable consequences. These consequences are the stimulation of the human family to a fresh spiritual effort; the process and the exalted Personnel involved have been described by me in my previous message (*A Treatise on the Seven Rays,* Vol. II, *Esoteric Psychology* pp. 683-688) ; They will also bring about the strengthening of the new group of world servers so that they can work with greater effectiveness, vision the Plan with greater clarity and—within themselves as a group—bring about greater integration. Thus they can aid in carrying out the plans of the Council of the Hierarchy to meet the immediate human emergency. As I told you before, the plans for humanity are *not* laid down, for humanity determines its own destiny; the effort is directed towards establishing a closer relationship between humanity and the Hierarchy.

It is possible for all aspirants and disciples to participate in this effort to the extent of rendering the task of the Masters easier by their clarity of thinking, their renewed spiritual effort, and the rededication of themselves to the task of service. To this effort I call you. It is a continuing effort which will be spread over many years. The opportunity will be offered to all true servers and aspirants and, above all, to the new group of world servers to participate in the establishing of the necessary momentum in the immediate cycle.

I call you, therefore, to a month of inner silence, of introspective thought, of self control and of meditation, to self-forgetfulness and attentiveness to opportunity and not to your own inner aspiration to achieve. I call you to concentrate upon the world need for peace, mutual understanding and illumination and to forget utterly your own needs— mental, emotional and physical. I call you to prayer and to fasting, though along what lines your abstinence should go is for you to decide. For the five days of meditation, I call you to a more complete 'fasting,' to a grave silence, to an inner focalisation, to a purity of thought and to an active spirit of loving kindness which will make you a pure channel. Thus will the work of the Hierarchy be facilitated and the door opened to the regenerative forces of Those extraplanetary Beings Who offer Their help at this time and particularly during 1936. The response of this Festival will submit a gauge of opportunity for the guidance of the Great Ones. (This theme is developed in the book, *A Treatise on the Seven Rays,* Vol. II, *Esoteric Psychology,* pp. 629-751, which contains the writings from May, 1935 to April, 1938, inclusive.)

One practical thing also I will ask of you. Will you say, each night and morning, with all your heart's desire and with the attention of your mind as well, the following words. Their united saying will set up a rhythm and a momentum of great potency.

> Let the Forces of Light bring illumination to mankind.
> Let the Spirit of Peace be spread abroad.
> May men of goodwill everywhere meet in a spirit of cooperation.
> May forgiveness on the part of all men be the keynote at this time.
> Let power attend the efforts of the Great Ones.
> So let it be, and help us to do our part.

These words sound simple, but the "Forces of Light" is the name for certain new Powers which are being invoked by the Hierarchy at this time, Whose potencies can be brought into great activity at the May full moon if due effort is made. The Spirit of Peace which is invoked is an inter-planetary Agent of great power Whose cooperation has been promised if all aspirants and disciples can cooperate to break through the shell of separation and hatred which holds our planet in thrall.

May I therefore close with these simple words: Please give us your aid, my brothers.

SEED GROUPS IN THE NEW AGE

July 1937

Earlier I gave you some thoughts anent the new groups which come into functioning activity under The Law of Group Progress. This law has a peculiarly close relation to the new Aquarian Age.*

Groups have always existed in the world, as for instance the family group unit, but they have been predominantly third ray groups with, therefore, a dominant outer expression and control, and originating as the result of desire.

---

* *A Treatise on the Seven Rays,* Vol. II (*Esoteric Psychology*), pp. 174-194.

Their focus has been outstandingly material, and that has been part of the intended plan. Right objectivity and expression has been the goal, and still is, of the evolutionary process. But the groups now forming are a second ray activity and are *building groups*—building the forms of expression in the new age. They are not the result of desire, as the term is usually understood, for they are founded basically on a mental impulse. They are subjective in fact and not objective in nature. They are distinguished by *quality* more than by form. That they may eventually produce potent objective effects is to be desired and such is their intent in our minds, but—at the present stage which is that of germination—they are subjective and (occultly speaking) they are "working in the dark." At some distant date, groups will emerge which will be first ray groups, animated by the will aspect and consequently still more subjective in nature and more esoteric in origin, but with these we need not concern ourselves.

These seed groups are embryonic and therefore, like germinating seeds, their activity is at present dual. Every seed demonstrates its life by putting out two outward evidences of its internal life and activity, and these seed groups are no exception to this universal law. Their activity is evidenced in a relation to the Hierarchy and their relation to each other. Not yet have they succeeded in emerging into outer plane activity. Their inner life is not adequately strong, but they are, as says the scripture, "taking root downwards" in order to "bear fruit upwards."

Should these groups develop as intended, should the corporate life of the members persist in right integral relation and should *continuance* be their keynote, then these seed groups, tiny as they may be, will come to flower, and—through an eventual "scattering of the seed," succeed finally in "covering the earth with verdure." I am speaking here in the language of symbolism which is, as you well know, the language of truth. One small plant which, in its turn, succeeds in producing a seed, through rightful fruition can thus reproduce itself in multiple order. Be not therefore unduly impressed by the smallness of the effort. A tiny seed is a potent force—if duly tended, rightly nurtured and ripened by sun and water within the soil—its potencies are unpredictable.

Certain germ ideas are emerging into the human consciousness. These differ peculiarly from those of the past, and it is these widely different ideas which are the distinctive characteristics of the new age, the Aquarian Age. Hitherto the great ideas which succeeded finally in controlling a race in any age have been the gift of the intuitive sons of men to their generation. Advanced human beings have then seized upon the intuited idea, subordinated it to the process of mentation, made it desirable, and then have seen it come into being through the "agency of recognition," as it is occultly called. One illumined mind would sense the divine idea, needed for the growth of the racial consciousness, and then would give it form; the few would recognise it and thus foster its growth; the many would eventually desire it and it then could manifest experimentally and sporadically all over the civilised world of any age, wherever culture of any kind made itself felt. Thus the idea was manifested.

Two ways in which these determining ideas in the past came into being and played their part in leading the race onward might be mentioned. One was through the teaching of some teacher who founded a school of thought, thus working through the minds of a chosen few, and through them eventually coloured the thoughts of the men of his time. Of such a teacher, Plato, Aristotle, Socrates and many others are outstanding examples. Another method was the evocation of the desire of the masses for that which is deemed desirable and their mass reorientation towards a fuller life expression. This life expression, founded on some voiced idea, was embodied in an ideal life. Thus the work of the Saviours of the world came into expression, and this brought about the emergence of a world religion.

The first method was strictly mental, and even today remains so; the masses, for instance, know little of Plato and his theories in spite of the fact that he has moulded human minds—either through acquiescence in his theories or through refutation of them—down the ages. The other method is strictly emotional and so more easily colours the mass consciousness. An instance of this was the message of the love of God which Christ enunciated and the emotional reaction of the masses to His life, His message, and His sacrifice. Thus the need of the mental few and the emotional many has been met down the ages. In every case, the origin of the work effected and the medium whereby the race has been guided has been a human-divine consciousness; the medium has been a Personality Who knew and felt and was at-one with the world of ideas, with the inner world order, and with God's plan. The result of these two techniques of activity has been the emanation of a stream of force, coming from some layer or level of the world consciousness—the mental or the emotional planes—which are aspects of the consciousness of the manifesting deity. This impact of force has evoked a response from those who function upon one or other of these levels of awareness. Today, as the integration of the human family proceeds and as the mental level of contact becomes more potent, there is to be found a powerful human reaction to schools of thought and a lessened reaction to the methods of orthodox religion. This is due to the fact that the trend of the human consciousness is (if I might so express it) away from the emotional to the mental levels of consciousness, and this, as far as the masses are concerned, will go on increasing.

The time has now come when there are enough people to be found who—having themselves made the religious and the mental approaches to truth definite factors in their consciousness in some small measure, and having established enough soul contact so that they can begin to touch the world of ideas (upon the intuitional levels of consciousness) —can employ a new technique. *Together and as a group* they can become sensitive to the incoming new ideas which it is intended should condition the new age that is upon us; *together and as a group* they can establish the ideals and develop the techniques and methods of the new schools of thought which will determine the new culture; together and as a group they can bring these ideas and ideals into the consciousness of the masses, so that schools of thought and world religions can be blended into one, and the new civilisation can emerge. It will be the product of the mental and emotional fusion of the techniques of the Piscean Age, and it will thus produce an eventual manifestation upon the physical plane of the plan of God for the immediate future. This is the vision which lies behind the experiment being carried on in the new seed groups.

Looking at the whole problem from another angle, it might be stated that the effort of the past has been to raise the consciousness of humanity through the pioneering efforts of its foremost sons. The effort of the future will be to bring down into manifestation the consciousness of the soul through the pioneering efforts of certain groups. It has therefore, as you will readily understand, to be *a group effort* because the soul is group conscious and not individually conscious; *the newer truths of the Aquarian Age can only be grasped as a result of group endeavour.* This is relatively a new thing. In the past, a man had a vision and sought to materialise it with the aid of those whom he could impress and influence to think as he did; a man sensed an idea or intuited an idea and then tried to give it form, later calling in the help of those who saw his idea as an ideal; a man had a great ambition which was, in reality, a dim grasping of a part of God's general plan, and he then became a group leader or a ruler, with the assistance of those who succumbed to his power or to his right to guide, lead and dominate them. And so, progressively, the race has been led from point to point and from stage to stage of unfoldment until today many are seeing the vision, sensing the plan, and dreaming dreams which they can work out together. This they can do because they recognise each other, because they are beginning to know themselves and each other as souls, because their understanding is united and because (and this is of prime importance) the light of the intellect, the light of knowledge, the light of the intuition and the light of understanding is evoked within them; it enters *not* from without; and in that light, together, they see Light. It is a group activity, a group recognition, and the result of group at-one-ment.

All this is, however, so new and relatively so rare that these groups remain as yet in an embryonic stage. We call them the seed groups of the new age. There are many such, as I told you before, but all as yet so small and so undeveloped that the success of their effort remains for the future to decide. This applies also to the groups which I began to build in 1931 (*Discipleship in the New Age,* Vols. I and II).

It will be apparent to you therefore why it was necessary for the initial or first group to lay the emphasis upon telepathic rapport, because upon that rapport, understandingly cultivated and developed, the success of these seed groups must depend. It does not mean that their success depends upon the established success of the first group, but upon the comprehension by all the groups of the meaning and purpose and techniques of telepathy. (See *Telepathy and the Etheric Vehicle*)

The founding upon the inner planes of a school of telepathy to which humanity can become sensitive, even if unconsciously so, is part of the task which the first group, the Telepathic Communicators, has undertaken. They are the custodians of the group purpose, and work on mental levels. The second group, the Trained Observers, has the objective to see clearly through the use of the intuition; they serve on astral levels. The third group, the Magnetic Healers, has the objective of working with forces on the physical plane. The other six groups will be mentioned later.

You have become somewhat accustomed to the concept of these groups. The novelty is dying out and you are apt to ask yourselves whether there is, in the last analysis, anything really new in them. I will give you further on three reasons for the fact of their being a step in advance of anything hitherto possible on the physical plane. This may re-establish their importance in your minds and enable you to carry forward your work with fresh ardour. I have stated that these groups constitute an experiment and that they are connected paramountly with the work of the new age as it will express itself through the coming civilisation and the future culture. It might be of value here if I pointed out the distinction which exists between a civilisation and a culture.

A *civilisation* is an expression of a mass level of consciousness as that consciousness works out in physical plane awareness, physical plane adjustments, relationships and methods of living. A *culture* is essentially an expression of the intellectually and vitally mental significances and the state of consciousness of the mentally polarised people of the race, of the intelligentsia or of those who constitute the link between the inner world of soul life and the outer world of tangible phenomena. In those words the *raison d'être* of the mental plane is concisely stated. Its function in this connection will be increasingly understood during the next few decades.

The masses are negative to the plane of desire and of feeling, and the civilisation of any age is largely the exteriorisation of that particular level of consciousness. The intelligentsia are positive and their positive mental orientation produces the culture of their time, or their race or their community. We have therefore in the human family:

Masses . . . **Negative** . . . responsive to desire . . . Civilisation

Intellectuals . . . Positive . . . responsive to mind . . . Culture

In these you have the two poles which distinguish the race, and it is through the interplay between these two that human activity, progress and development is generated and carried forward.

There is another grouping which should not be overlooked. The spiritually minded people of the world are negative to the higher spiritual world as it expresses itself through or calls forth the higher type of desire which we call aspiration. This produces those exponents of the spiritual nature who constitute—in the aggregate—the Church of Christ or the world religions in the exoteric sense and in any race or time. Positive to this group and giving them the key-note of the culture of their particular age on this higher turn of the spiral are the esotericists and aspirants throughout the world. These are responsive to the mind aspect. In this way the spiritual culture and the resultant civilisation comes into being and to it the lower becomes responsive. You have, therefore, the masses and the intellectuals together negative in their turn to the positive impression of the deeper civilisation and culture as it is expressed through the religions of the world and the groups of idealistic esoteric seekers after reality. These latter are the glory of every age and the positive germ of the subjective unfolding impulse which is basically the source of all current phenomenal appearance.

This group of religionists and esoteric aspirants in their turn constitute the negative pole to the positive impression and energy of the planetary or occult Hierarchy. Consequently, we have:

Negative Groups	Positive Groups
The Masses	The Intelligentsia
The Churches and religions	The Esotericists, aspirants and occultists
The Esotericists, in their turn	The Planetary Hierarchy

Broadly speaking, these groups divide themselves into the extroverted groups and the introverted groups, into the objective and the subjective levels of consciousness, and into the major divisions of the phenomenal world and the world of spiritual realities.

The problem before the Hierarchy at the beginning of the new or Aquarian Age was how to fuse and blend these two distinct groups, attitudes or states of consciousness so that from their fusion a third group could emerge which would be exterior in its activity and yet consciously alive to the interior values; they should be able to function upon the outer plane of appearances and, at the same time, be equally awake and active upon the inner plane of reality and of spiritual living.

This type of dual functioning is the easiest activity for

the Members of the Hierarchy and constitutes the *sine qua
non* prior to association with that Hierarchy. It was realised
that many people could be trained in the appreciation of
this possibility and slowly developed to the point where
theory could pass into practice. Yet these people would
not be equipped throughout their natures in such a way
that they were ready to become part of the occult Hierarchy,
even in the stage of accepted disciples.

It was the realisation of the need for a bridging group
which would be neither entirely negative nor entirely positive which prompted some of the Masters (Who are connected with the Hierarchy) to form the New Group of
World Servers. These people belong to neither group and
yet they can function more or less in relation to both. This,
as you well know, has been done with quite a measure of
success and this large group now exists and is magnetic
enough to draw forth response from the mass of world
aspirants and servers (who represent the current civilisation
and current culture) and at the same time to absorb and thus
transmit knowledge, wisdom, force and light from the
Planetary Hierarchy.

It has now been deemed possible to form groups within
the new group of world servers whose members can begin
to prepare themselves to express both the phenomenal and
the impulsive, the negative and the positive, the material
and the spiritual with such a measure of success that, in due
time, there can exist on earth a replica of the Hierarchy,
its methods and techniques of work. Such is the purpose of
the groups which I have formed, and of other groups
throughout the world who—in a different way and form, and
employing perchance a different phraseology—yet are motivated and actuated as are the seed groups for which I have
made myself responsible.

The three reasons for their importance might therefore
be stated as follows:

1. They constitute the germ of life which will result
   in the emergence of the Hierarchy at a later date

upon earth, coming forth from the seclusion of the ages to function again in the light of physical day.

2. They are a bridging group, bridging between the negative mass of mankind and the positive agency of the Hierarchy. That is the reason why, in these groups, emphasis is laid upon *service* because that embodies response to the mass and its need, and upon *soul contact* because that embodies response to the world of souls, as typified for us in the occult Hierarchy.

3. They also hold within themselves *as a group* the seeds of the coming civilisation and the germ of the new culture. The germ of the life of the new age is there, within the husk of the old age and the old forms. Hence the opportunity, the service and the problems of these groups.

Let me endeavour to indicate to you in what manner these groups can measure up to the threefold demand or opportunity mentioned above.

1. They conceal and nurture the germ or seed of the new civilisation of the Aquarian Age.

2. They bridge between the old groups and the new group, between the mass of men (of whom the foremost find their way into the new group of world servers) and the Planetary Hierarchy.

3. They will constitute in the future an aspect of the Hierarchy and its work upon the outer physical plane.

You will note that the first opportunity concerns *the spirit aspect* or the vital impulsive life aspect of divinity; that the second concerns *the soul aspect* or the subjective consciousness aspect of divinity; whilst the third concerns *the body aspect* or the physical expression, through consciousness, of the divine life. The first three groups which I have formed are intended to be small reflections of these three aspects from the angle of modern need and the meeting of that need.

I have indicated somewhat the intended work of the first group from the angle of telepathic interplay (*Telepathy and the Etheric Vehicle*). The method of communication between the Members of the Hierarchy has to be externalised, eventually, upon earth and this is one of the tasks of the group. It might be of service to you if I outlined a little more clearly what is the purpose of the new seed groups, in terms of the new age civilisation and culture so that the practical results might be visioned with clarity and some new ideals emerge as to the quality of the coming new world order.

The second group, the trained observers, will inaugurate the era of light and of a free control of the astral plane, with its quality of freedom from illusion and glamour. This freedom will be brought about when "right observation" takes the place of the disturbed vision of the present, and glamour will be dissipated through the "right direction" of the light of the soul throughout the plane of illusion. The Aquarian Age will be predominantly the age of synthesis and light.

The third group carries the initial impulse through "into the light of day" and will bring the physical world into a condition whereby "the healing of the nations through the arising of the sun of righteousness" will become possible, because the laws of healing (which are basic and fundamental) can be applied and worked out in all departments of life upon the outer levels of appearance—for disease is only found in the world of phenomena.

As regards telepathic communication between the Members of the Hierarchy: within itself, the Hierarchy functions practically entirely on the plane of mind. This is necessarily essential and for two reasons:

1. The members of the Hierarchy have freed themselves from the limitations of brain activity and brain consciousness. They can, therefore, in their essential Selves and when they so choose, carry on simultaneously two different lines of activity—both

of real import. They can pursue their normal avocations upon the physical plane (if functioning in physical bodies) and when so doing are conditioned in the performance of those activities by the brain limitations of time consciousness and space consciousness. But they can also work upon the mental plane with the chitta or mind stuff, and can do this at the same time as they are conditioned and limited by their physical mechanism. They are then entirely freed from the time consciousness and from any such limitations as space relations within the solar system.

2. The focus of their polarisation is on the mental plane and they function there as sons of mind or of manas. Their normal mode of intercourse is through the medium of telepathic understanding. This is the normal technique of a divine and free manasaputra.

This is all made possible when a human being has polarised himself in the soul consciousness, when the egoic lotus is unfolding and when, therefore, the mental method of working is that of mental relationship or telepathy.

I earlier told you that, as the race achieves increasingly a mental polarisation through the developing attractive power of the mental principle, the use of language for the conveying of thoughts between equals or of communicating with superiors will fall into disuse. It will continue to be used in reaching the masses and those not functioning on the plane of mind. Already voiceless prayer and aspiration and worship are deemed of higher value than the pleadings and proclamations of voiced expression. It is for this stage in the unfoldment of the race for which preparation must be made, and the laws, techniques and processes of telepathic communication must be made plain so that they can be intelligently and theoretically understood. The method of communication between members of the Hierarchy is a tenfold process, and only in the contribution of the ten groups (the nine and the synthesising tenth) will their share in the externalising process, as it is to take place in the world, be completed.

From certain angles the work of the second group (the Trained Observers) is exceedingly hard, harder perhaps than that of any other group—except that which is engaged in political work. In the latter field the work of the first Ray of Will or Power is beginning to make its presence felt, and hence the great difficulty. The energy which works out in political activity is not yet understood. The work of the Destroyer Aspect has been kept relatively in the background and only during the past half century has it become definitely active. This became possible because the whole world, practically speaking, was involved and *only in the region or realm of synthesis* can the first Ray function. This is a point to be remembered and one that is little grasped as yet. I wonder if you can appreciate the importance of the two statements anent the first Ray found in this short paragraph? I oft give you so much real information of which you remain oblivious.

The second group is wrestling with glamour. The processes of light and their relation to group glamour and to individual glamour form a very close connection. Right illumination—which is another name or aspect of right direction—will take the place of glamour, and the objective (personally considered) of this group of disciples is to bring "light into dark places" and illumination into their lives. It is not my intention here to deal with the problem of glamour. With that I have concerned myself in the instructions to this group (*Glamour: A World Problem*).

The task of this group of disciples is closely connected with the astral task of the Hierarchy. This is, at this time, the dissipation of the world illusion. That has been its problem since Atlantean times, and the climaxing of its effort is imminent and immediate. It takes the form (for all illusions take to themselves form of some kind or other) of the "pouring in of light," esoterically understood. This is an illusion and at the same time a great and significant spiritual fact. Hence we have today upon the physical plane the emergence of much light everywhere; we have festivals of illumination, and a consistent endeavour on the part of all spiritual workers to enlighten mankind, and a great deal of talk on the part of educators anent illumination of a mental kind. The keynote of this effort to eliminate world glamour was sounded by Christ when He said (following the example of Hermes, Who initiated the process of enlightenment for our race, the Aryan), "I am the Light of the World."

Disciples must learn the significance of illumination, received in meditation, and the necessity to work with light *as a group* for the dissipation of glamour. Hermes and Christ undertook this work of astral enlightenment and are constantly occupied with this task. Their work in the new age is to be aided by the intensive activity of certain groups of which this second group is one. Later, when the new civilisation is nearing appearance, these groups will all have in them two key persons or points of energy through which the forces of Hermes and the will of Christ will be focussed, and through which They will be enabled to work. When this takes place, the task of dissipating the world glamour will be much more rapid than it is today. In the meantime groups of disciples can "nurture and conceal," thus protecting from trouble the germ or seed of the new Aquarian culture and civilisation along this particular line of freedom. Again, I repeat, they must do this along with other groups, working along similar lines, either consciously or unconsciously.

The second task of this group of disciples is to act as a bridge for forces which are seeking etheric expression and which emanate from soul levels, via the mind. I have earlier pointed out in *A Treatise on White Magic* that the astral plane is itself an illusion. When the first task of the groups working with world glamour is accomplished this will be evident. I can give you as yet no real idea of the underlying meaning, for you are all working in some measure upon the plane of illusion and of glamour, and for you the world illusion exists and the astral plane is for you a fact. But this I can say: for the initiate members of the Great White Lodge the astral plane does not exist. They do not work on that level of consciousness, for the astral plane is a definite state of awareness even if (from the spiritual angle) it has no true being. It embodies the great creative work of humanity down the ages, and is the product of the 'false' imagination and the work of the lower psychic nature. Its instrument of creative work is the sacral and the solar plexus centres. When the energies, finding expression through these two centres, have been transmuted and carried to the throat and heart by advancing humanity, then the foremost people of the race will know that the astral plane has no true existence; they will then work free from its impression, and the task of freeing humanity from the thralldom of its own creation will proceed apace. In the meantime a group of disciples is being slowly built up (of which this second group is a part and in which it can play an important function, and occupy a key position), which can gradually aid in the task of dispelling the great illusion and can act also as a bridging group so that those who are freeing themselves from glamour can find their way into the vortex of influence wielded by the group, empowered thus to work. Then three things can happen:

1. Those who thus approach the group will find their efforts to live free from glamour greatly helped and intensified by the group assistance.
2. They will swell the number of those so working and hasten the processes of dissipation.
3. The Hierarchy will be enabled then to work more closely upon earth and to approach much nearer to mankind.

The third function of this second group lies in a more distant future. The Hierarchy has necessarily a department of workers whose major task it is to work solely in the world of illusion and with astral matter. This department came into being in Atlantean days when the great controversy took place between those who embodied the consciousness or soul aspect of deity and those who were similarly representative of the matter aspect of deity. Symbolically speaking, the left-hand and the right-hand paths came into being; white and black magic were brought into conflict with each other and the pairs of opposites (always existent in manifestation) became active factors in the consciousness of advanced humanity. The battle of discrimination was opened, and humanity became active upon the field of Kurukshetra. Where there is no conscious response to a condition and no registered awareness, there is no problem of responsibility, as far as the soul is concerned. In Atlantean times, this condition was evoked and hence the problem facing the race today; hence the task of the Hierarchy to free the souls of men from the surrounding glamour and to enable them to achieve liberation. The culmination of the issue and the controversy, then initiated, is now upon us.

The third function, therefore, of the group can be grasped at this time, and eventually this branch of the hierarchical effort can find due expression upon earth.

From the above analysis of opportunity it is evident how the groups have a definite place in the plans of the Hierarchy. By developing spiritual sensitivity, and achieving freedom from glamour, the disciples who are members of these groups can raise the racial consciousness and bring in illumination. It should be remembered that it is *inspiration* which is the goal of all true telepathic work, and *illumination* which is the reward of effort and the real instrument for the dissipation of world glamour. Thus these groups can nurture the germ of the future culture, act also as bridging units, and externalise certain departmental activities of the planetary Hierarchy—the next great desire of its Members.

Turning now to the work of the third group, we find ourselves concerned with the task of the magnetic healers of the world. This has been dealt with elsewhere (*Esoteric Healing*). I will here refer to one or two points of more general interest, and to their threefold opportunity. It is of interest to note that the work of this group is perhaps one of the hardest to carry through, although from another angle it is far easier than the task of most of the other groups, because the consciousness of the bulk of humanity is found to be predominantly upon the plane of illusion and therefore, as the *Old Commentary* says:

> "They who work to bring in light and yet are surrounded by the maya of the senses, work from the point of present being and need not to move out or in, or up or down. They simply stand."

The healers of the world upon the physical plane have to work upon that plane and their task is that of bringing through the energies of life, emanating from the soul plane, via the mind, but excluding the emotional. These energies have to be brought through into physical consciousness and, from the physical level, do their necessary and magnetic work. The task of the healers, if successful, involves:

1. The bringing through of healing divine energy.
2. The exclusion of the astral world, and therefore illusion.
3. The utilisation of the healing energy in full waking consciousness upon the physical plane.

Most of the healers in the world are working as follows:

1. As purely physical healers, dealing with the vital forces of the physical body, and with their own consciousness polarised in the etheric body.

2. As emotional astral psychics, with the consciousness polarized upon the astral plane, and utilising the astral body and working in and with glamour and illusion. The effect of their work, if successful (and I would have you note that "if," for I deal with the idea of relative permanency) may be one of two things:

a. They may cure the physical ills in the patient which are of such a nature that the inner astral desire (and therefore the lower desire) has eventuated in physical disease, experienced in some aspect or organ of the physical body.

b. They may intensify the effect of the illusion of desire in the physical brain consciousness and cause such a violent increase of the active energies that death may occur before so very long. This is quite a frequent happening. Nevertheless death is a cure, remember this.

Under these two categories the bulk of the world healers are found—sometimes doing good, oft doing harm, even if not realising it, and even if (as is usually the case) of good intention. There are three other categories of healers, however, to add to the two above:

3. Mental healers in the true sense of the word. Most mental healers unduly flatter themselves and work not with their minds at all. They have much mental theory and astral methods. Desire is the motivating power and not mental impulse. The true mental healer only brings about his results when he knows something of illumination in the technical and academic sense, and of the power of light to dispel illusion. Disease is not an illusion; it is a definite effect of a real cause from the standpoint of average humanity. When healers can work mentally, they deal with the causes of disease and not with the effects.

4. Those healers whose soul contact is established and who work through the souls of people, enabling them therefore:

a. To stand in spiritual being
b. To work, free from illusion
c. To achieve true perspective upon the physical plane
d. To coordinate the personality and the soul so that the will of the inner spiritual man can work out upon the physical plane.

5. Those who can work (as is eventually intended that this third group should work) definitely as outposts of the con-

sciousness of the Hierarchy of Masters. This work will be done in group formation and with a united synthesised effort. The personal effect of such healers is therefore:

a. To coordinate the personality of the patient. They are themselves coordinated.
b. To bring about contact with the soul, on the part of the patient. They are themselves vitally in contact.
c. To fuse and blend the personality and the soul and thus provide an instrument for the distribution of spiritual energy. They are themselves thus fused.
d. To understand and use the laws of true spiritual healing through intelligent activity upon the mental plane, through freedom from glamour, and through such a right use of force that the instrument of the soul (the personality) becomes vitally magnetic.

I would remind you that such effort in the early stages (and those stages are the present ones) results inevitably in the development of a critical spirit through the intelligent effort being made and the discriminative recognition of glamour in many cases, because only through such an effort can analysis of a right kind eventually be achieved and criticism be eliminated. In the meantime, those thus in training are oft a difficulty and a problem both to themselves and to their friends and co-workers. But this phase is temporary and leads to a more lasting relationship and to the emergence of that true magnetic link and love which must heal and lift and stimulate all that it may contact.

In the coming Aquarian Age we shall see humanity producing a culture which is sensitive to the finer and higher spiritual values, a civilisation which is free from glamour and from much of the illusion which today colours the Aryan peoples, and a racial life which will be embodied in those forms which will bridge the gap at present existing; it will be free from what we now know as disease of the worst kind, though death and certain forms of bodily breakdown which may eventually end in death will, of course, still be prevalent. The overcoming of death is not contingent upon the elimination of bodily ills, but upon the establishing of that continuity of consciousness which carries over from the physical plane of life to the inner subjective existence. Of this state of being, groups such as this third group can be the custodian and their problem is therefore:

1. To establish that state of personality development which will lead to magnetic living upon the physical plane.
2. To study the laws of life, which are the laws of health and of right relationship.
3. To develop that continuity of consciousness which will "open the doors of life and dispel the fear of the known and of that which disappears."

From the angle of the work of the world healers, the above is a statement of opportunity. This they face as the nucleus or one of the germs or seeds of the new civilisation and the coming culture. It embodies the objective of all their work, and their contribution to the united work of the groups.

Equally so, they can bridge the gap at present existing in the racial consciousness between

1. Life and death.

2. The sick and the well. This is between
   a. The physically sick and the inwardly well, which is the case with a few—a very few—of the advanced people, or the disciples of the world and the senior aspirants.
   b. The physically well and the psychically sick, which is sometimes the case, but of singular rarity.
   c. The physically sick, the psychologically sick, and the overshadowing soul. This situation is often found today.

3. The physical plane and the world of souls, because of the development of a sound instrument and the dissipation of those causes which work out as effects in the physical body as disease, and act as barriers to the inflow of soul energy and the entrance of soul awareness into the brain activity.

This bridging work, when it occurs today, is often simply a fortunate but fortuitous happening and is not the result of a consciously planned bridging work. But it is the intent of the Hierarchy that the groups which will be later formed, and which are today in process of forming (including this third group of mine) can aid in this process, if such is the will of the constituent parts.

Finally, every initiate is a magnetic healer. This is a statement of fact. Though the members of the Hierarchy have each of Them Their duly appointed functions and Their planned activity (dependent upon Ray, upon race and upon dedication) there is one activity which They share in common and that is the power to heal. Their ability to act as magnetic healers works out in various ways, predominantly in the realm of psychological readjustments and psychic disentanglements, and—only incidentally and as a result of the two above activities—in the processes of bodily healing. You will note from the above, that the healing work done by the initiate members of the Great White Lodge is threefold—*psychological,* bringing in the soul; *psychic,* releasing the lower psychic nature from illusion so that the psyche or soul can have full sway; *physical,* as the result of the inner psychological and psychic adjustments.

This triple healing activity is intended to be the objective of all groups working as this third group, the magnetic healers, should work; thus will be brought about an emergence of hierarchical effort into outer activity. Thus you will note, my brother, that the work of the first three groups just discussed, and viewing them as constituting one unit, produces a synthetic endeavour in the three worlds, and leads from the plane of the soul to the plane of outer expression.

The Work of the Seed Groups

January 1938

We have been endeavouring to apprehend a little more intelligently the work of the new age seed groups, their interrelation and their work as part of the new age "set-up," if I might employ such a term. We considered with some care the three major groups. We saw that each of them had three tasks to perform and we attempted a slight analysis of their planned undertakings. Now we can do the same with the remaining groups, particularly with the fourth and fifth which have education and political work as their projects. And then we will only briefly indicate the triple intended purpose of the sixth, seventh, eighth and ninth groups. We will not take time to consider the tenth, which will be composed of the key people in the other groups, beyond stating that when its twenty-seven members (three from each group) are chosen and put in rapport with each other, there should come to all the groups such a quickening of their life that they will become one living vibrant organism.

The fourth group has ahead of it a rich and most interesting course of study and an illuminating objective. Its instructions (See *Education in the New Age*) will evoke more interested response from a larger group of readers than perhaps will be the case in the instructions of any of the other groups, except those of the sixth whose subject is religion in the new age, and the third (See *Esoteric Healing*). I give them in the order of their importance. They will be more definitely popular and meet a more general need. The interest which the teaching on education will evoke will be owing to the fact that education is today widely recognised as the major moulding factor, next to economic pressure and circumstance, and there is a widespread interest in progressive education and in the new ideals which should —and will—eventually govern educators.

There is a definite stirring among the masses and the life of the mind (note that phrase) is now more active and potent than ever before. For this there is an occult reason of a most interesting nature.

Those of you who have studied *The Secret Doctrine* will remember that in that momentous period wherein animal-man made the great transition into the human family and humanity came into being, developing the germ of individuality, the seed of self-consciousness and embryo intellect, we are told that this event was brought about in three ways:

1.   The seed of mind was implanted in some of the aspiring animal-men by the Hierarchy, and these animal men became human beings, of a very low order to be sure, but still men. They were "sparked," if I might so express it, and a point of light appeared where before there was none. Before there was only a diffused atomic light but no central point of light within the head, and no indication of the higher centres. These individuals, along with the more advanced humanity which came to the planet in Atlantean times (having individualised elsewhere), constitute the most advanced humanity of our present period. They represent culture and understanding, no matter where it is found, or in what class or race.

2.   The instinctual nature of animal-man (found active among those who had not reached the stage of any conscious aspiration) was suddenly stimulated or vitalised by the coming into expression of the first group and the directed attention of the Hierarchy, working under the ancient Law that "energy follows thought." Thus gradually, with a remarkable rapidity, instinct became blended into, or resolved into, its higher expression—the intellect. Thus in due course of time a large group of animal-men became human beings. They today represent civilisation and the masses of ordinary intelligent people, educated under the mass systems of the present time, able occasionally to think and rise to mental emergencies, yet not highly cultured. They constitute the so-called general public which we designate by the words "upper and lower middle class" people, the professional classes and the bourgeoisie everywhere.

3.   At the same time there is to be found a vast number of people who are human beings but who are not the result of either of these two processes. They are the product of the slow moving influences of life itself, of what we are apt to call the evolutionary urge, innate in matter itself. They

have painfully and with infinitely slow processes evolved
out of the animal condition into that of human beings, with
an awakening conscience, an urge to betterment, and an
embryonic mind of such a nature that it can respond to
simple educational processes, when available, and is so responding. They are the illiterate masses, the still savage
races and the low grade human beings who are met with
in their millions on our planet.

The cause for the momentous situation which calls for
a re-alignment of our educational systems and processes, and
for a readjustment of our present concepts of education, is
to be found in the fact that the light of knowledge and the
benefits which accrue from it have penetrated to the lowest
grades of these slowly evolving people; all three groups are
now strictly human and not simply the first two. The highest
of them is therefore nearing the stage of demonstrating that
which is superhuman and the lowest is separating itself (by
almost imperceptible stages) from the animal condition.
This necessarily causes a cleavage but it is one of which the
highest group and the Hierarchy itself is cognisant, and
which they "heal by their own inclusiveness." Forget not,
that the greater can always include the lesser and thus bridge
all gaps.

It is the education of these three groups which will
be considered by the fourth group which has as its project
education in the new age. Here again we touch the threefold purpose which each group has to hold before itself
and which in the present instance consists of:

1.   The educating of the lowest of these groups into which
humanity divides itself, so that they can become strictly and
consciously human. This was the objective of the impulse
which inspired the Renaissance and which lay behind the
work of Rousseau, that great initiate, and this is the impulse
which is today responsible for modern Humanism with its
apparent materialism and yet its deeply spiritual subjective
programme and purpose. This eventually produces civilisation by the inflow of the light of knowledge.

2. The education of the second group so that it may be stimulated by the inflow of the light of wisdom and thus constitute a bridging group between the other two, being—as it is—strictly human and self-conscious. This process will make of its members cultural aspirants, with a new sense of values, with a recognition of spiritual objectives and with a developed ability to make them the moulders of public opinion. They will then be the most important group, expressing the culture of the new age. They will set the standard of values for the masses.

3. The education of the advanced thinkers, of the aspirants and world disciples in *applied* knowledge, expressed wisdom and occult understanding. This group synthesises all that is available in the other two groups and thus forms the nucleus of the Kingdom of God, of the fifth kingdom which is so rapidly coming into being.

I cannot do more than indicate these points, for their proper theme and their elucidation will be dealt with in the group's instructions. What I have stated, however, will serve to indicate to you the general theme of the new education and point the way to some of the considerations which are prompting my handling of this subject.

The work to be done (political service) by the fifth group of disciples is by far the most difficult of any for it is in many ways far less advanced. This is due to two facts:

1. The masses of men are, as yet, relatively so little evolved that the task of this group of workers must therefore necessarily be dependent upon the success of the educational work of the world, as it will eventually be exemplified by the ideals and point of view of the fourth group and similar groups everywhere.

2. So few truly first ray people are manifesting on the planet at this time and, when they do, their work perforce proves destructive, owing to the unevolved condition of the masses of men. That is why revolu-

tions so seldom, if ever, can be carried out without bloodshed, for the intended ideas have to be *imposed* upon the masses and are not immediately *recognised* and *adopted* by those masses; they evoke counter responses which arouse those in authority to wrong activity. The above ideas should arouse you to careful thought.

Let it not be forgotten that the objective of all true governmental control is right synthesis, leading to right national and interior group activity. The problem resolves itself into a dual one. First of all, we have the problem of the type of authority which should be recognised by the peoples; and secondly, we have the problem of the methods which should be employed, so that the chosen authoritative measures will proceed either by the method of enforced control, or would be of such a nature that they will evoke a generously rendered and recognised cooperation. Between these two ways of working, many changes can be rung, though the system of cooperation, willingly rendered by an intelligent majority, has never yet been seen. But we are moving towards such a condition of world consciousness and are on our way towards experimenting with it.

Let me here briefly indicate to you some of the modes of government which have been tried out, or will be tried out in the future.

1. *Government by a recognised Spiritual Hierarchy.* This Hierarchy will be related to the masses of the people by a chain of developed men and women who will act as the intermediaries between the ruling spiritual body and a people who are oriented to a world of right values. This form of world control lies indefinitely ahead. When it becomes possible so to govern, the planetary Hierarchy will have made a major Approach to earth, and there will then be thousands of men and women in touch with Their organisation because they will be developed enough to be sensitive to Its thoughts and ideas.

2.   *Government by an oligarchy of illumined minds,* recognised as such by the massed thinkers, and therefore chosen by them to rule. This they will do through the education of the thinkers of the race in group ideas and in their right application. The system of education, then prevalent, will be utilised as the medium of reaching the masses and swinging them into line with the major ideas and this will be done not by force, but through right understanding, through analysis, discussion and experiment. Curiously enough (from the point of view of many) the spiritual Hierarchy will then work largely through the world scientists who, being by that time convinced of the factual reality of the soul and wise in the uses of the forces of the soul and of nature, will constitute a linking body of occultists.

3.   *Government by a true democracy.* This again will be made possible through a right use of the systems of education and by a steady training of the people to recognise the finer values, the more correct point of view, the higher idealism, and the spirit of synthesis and of cooperative unity. Cooperative unity differs from an enforced unity in that the subjective spirit and the objective form are functioning towards one recognised end. Today, such a thing as a true democracy is unknown, and the mass of the people in the democratic countries are as much at the mercy of the politicians and of the financial forces as are the people under the rule of dictatorships, enlightened or unenlightened. These latter might be regarded as selfish idealists. But I would have you here note the word "idealist"! When, however, the world has in it more truly awakened people and more thinking men and women, we shall see a purification of the political field taking place, and a cleansing of our processes of representation instituted, as well as a more exacting accounting required from the people of those whom they have chosen to put in authority. There must eventually be a closer tie-up between the educational system, the legal system and the government, but it will all be directed to an effort to work out the best ideals of the thinkers of the

day. This period does not lie so far ahead as you might imagine, particularly if the first move in this direction is made by the new group of world servers.

This first move involves a right comprehension of goodwill. These three systems, which are the three major systems, correspond to the three major rays of synthesis, of idealism, and of intelligence, which are only other names for the rays of Will or Power, of Love-Wisdom and of Active Intelligence.

4. *Government by dictatorship.* This type of government divides itself into three parts:

    a. Rule by a monarchy, limited usually today by the will of the people, or rather by the politicians of the period, but symbolic of the ultimate rule of the Hierarchy under the Kingship of the Lord of the World.

    b. Rule by the leader of some democratic country, who is usually called a president, or by some statesman (no matter by what name he may choose to be called) who is frequently an idealist, though limited by his faulty human nature, by the period in which he lives, by his advisors, and by the widespread corruption and selfishness. A study of such men who have held office in this capacity, made by a fair-minded neutral, will usually demonstrate the fact that they held office under the influence of some idea, which was in itself intrinsically right (no matter how applied), which was forward-moving in its concept, and belonged to the then new age. This relates them to the second ray.

    c. Rule by dictators, whose animating principle is not one of the new age ideals, emerging in their particular time, but an idealism of a more material kind—a generally recognised *present* idealism. They are not usually reactionary nor are they found among the intuitive workers of their age, but they take what is grounded, settled and easily available—made so by the thinkers of their time—and then give it a material, national and selfish twist and objective, and so force it on the masses by fear, warlike means and material promises. They belong, therefore, more practically to the third ray methods of work, for they are intelligent, expedient, and materially constructive. True idealism, involving as it must the new age patterns, and religious incentives are lacking in their techniques. Nevertheless, they do lead the race on another step, for they have a mass effect in evoking thought, and sometimes eventual resistance, as the result of that thought.

Later we shall study these and other ways of governing, and analyse their ordinary modern expressions and future spiritual correspondences. These will some day appear on earth as a result of the many experiments today going on. Remember this.

As I earlier said, the processes of education, of law and of government are so closely allied and so definitely related that if ever the work of this fifth group reaches a stage where it is indeed a germ of a new age organism (and many such groups will necessarily appear in the different countries of the world), it will be found that they will act as a clearing house or a linking body between the educators of the time, those whose task it is to enforce the law, and the statesmen who are chosen by the educated masses to formulate the laws whereby they should be governed. It will be apparent, therefore, along what three lines of study and work the members of this fifth group will proceed. These I will not further elaborate in this place.

In view of the steady progress towards religious unity which has proceeded apace during the past 150 years, the work of the sixth group (religion in the new age), as is also the case with the first group (telepathic communication) promises rapid results. This is, however, necessarily dependent upon the "skill in action" and the willingness of the group members and allied groups to proceed with slowness and tact.

The moment any idea enters the religious field, it gains immediate momentum from the fact that the outstanding characteristic of the human consciousness is the sense of the Innermost or the Real, a recognition of subjective destiny, and an innate knowledge of and reaching out to the Unknown God. Therefore, any truth or presentation of truth or method which has in it the possibility of producing a nearer approach to divinity or a more rapid understanding of the "deeper Being" evokes an immediate response and reaction. There is consequently much need for caution and considered action.

I have already indicated to you the form that the religion of the new age will take (See *The Reappearance of the Christ*). It will be built around the periods of the Full Moon, wherein certain great Approaches will be made to the world of reality, also around two periods of massed Approaches to be made at the time of the major eclipse of the moon and of the sun during the year. The two major Full Moon Approaches will be those of the Wesak Full Moon and the Full Moon of June—one hitherto consecrated to the Buddha Who embodied the wisdom of God, and the other to the Bodhisattva (known to Christians as the Christ) Who embodied the love of God.

The platform of the new world religion will have in it three major presentations of truth, or three major doctrines, if such an undesirable word can be permitted. It is with the elaboration of these three points of view, or evocations of truth, that the work of the sixth group of disciples will be concerned. They are:

1. The fact of the Spirit of God, both transcendent and immanent, will be demonstrated, and also a similar fact in relation to man. The mode of their approach to each other, via the soul, will be indicated. This aspect of the emerging truth might be called *Transcendental Mysticism*.

2. The fact of the divine quality of the Forces in nature and in man and the method of their utilisation for divine purposes by man. This might be called *Transcendental Occultism*.

3. The fact, implied in the first, that Humanity, as a *Whole*, is an expression of divinity, a complete expression, plus the allied fact of the divine nature and work of the planetary Hierarchy, and the mode of the Approach of these two groups, in group form, to each other. This might be called *Transcendental Religion*.

More than this I will not here indicate as I seek to touch briefly upon the remaining three groups. I will, however, point out that we shall elaborate somewhat the Technique of the Presence of God, approaching it from a new angle, that of the Group, and also upon the Technique of Light. Two lesser Techniques I have at times called to your attention and with these we will later deal, for they are in the nature of approaches to the other two—the Technique of Indifference and the Technique of Service (See *Glamour: A World Problem*). As we study the divine Approaches, we shall see that they involve two parties or two groups—those found on the objective and those on the subjective side of life.

The work of the seventh group, which is in the field of science, is closely allied to that of the seventh ray and is one with a most practical physical purpose. It is strictly magical in its technique, and this technique is intended to produce a synthesis between the three aspects of divinity upon the physical plane, or between life, the solar energies and the lunar forces. This involves a difficult task and much understanding; the work to be done is not easy to comprehend. It will be carried forward by first ray workers, assisted by seventh ray aspirants, but using fifth ray methods. They will thus combine, in their personnel, the work of the destroyer of outgrown forms, the findings of the scientists who penetrated behind the outer form to its motivating energy, and the practical work of the magician who—under the law—creates the new forms, as expressions of the inflowing life.

This group of disciples will make a close study of the problem of evil, and they will bring about a better understanding of the *purpose* existing in matter or substance, and the inflowing enlightened and different purpose of the soul aspect. That is why (in my earlier discussion of the subject) I linked the results of religion and of science together; religion is concerned with the awakening to conscious purpose of the soul in man or form, whilst science is concerned with the activity of the outer form as it lives its own life, yet slowly becomes subservient to that purpose and to soul impress. This is the thought contained in the words "scientific service" as used by me. The work of this group is therefore a triple one:

1. They will take the most advanced inferences of the workers in the field of science, and will then formulate the new hypotheses upon which the next immediate steps forward in any particular scientific field will be founded.

2. They will avail themselves of the sensitive reactions which the new spiritual Approaches (as taught by the world religion of the time) will have made possible and—utilising the inferences thus made available in connection with the inner world of spirit—will outline the nature of the incoming forces which will determine and motivate the culture of the time.

3. Taking the substance or material, and the spiritual inferences and the scientific hypotheses, they will formulate those forms of service on the physical plane which will precipitate with rapidity the Plan for the immediate present. They will release through this blend of scientific knowledge and intuitive idealism, those energies which will further human interests, relate the subhuman to the human through a right interplay of forces, and thus clear the way of those intellectual impediments which will (and always have) blocked man's approach to the superhuman world.

I doubt that it will be possible to do much in connection with the forming of this group, and this for several reasons.

The first is that such a group cannot be formed until a certain scientific discovery has been made of such moment that our present scientific inhibition in recognising the fact of the soul as a creative factor, will disappear. This discovery will be part of the acknowledged "facts of science" by the year 1975. Secondly, A.A.B. has not the necessary scientific knowledge to do more than grasp the broader outlines of the intended work, and then only primarily from the angle of the more mystical and philosophical approaches. Nor, my brothers, have I. It will take a fifth or seventh ray initiate to deal with this matter, and though I could invoke the assistance of such a brother, it does not seem to me a profitable expenditure of force at this time. The sigh of relief from A.A.B. as she grasps the fact that there is one less group to tackle on my and your behalf would almost warrant my making this a major reason!

Let us now pass on to a brief indication of the work of the eighth group, which is psychological service. In this field the work will be lifted out of the realm of the strictly human and will concern itself with wider issues—for, my brothers—there *are* wider issues than those which concern the human family alone. The work of these disciples will cover the following three issues:

1.   The relation of the human soul to the subhuman kingdoms in nature and the place of the human kingdom as an intermediary between the three higher kingdoms and the three lower.

2.   The quality of the soul in the three subhuman kingdoms, with particular emphasis upon the animal and the vegetable kingdoms. The consciousness of the mineral kingdom is so far removed from the human that it is not possible for us to formulate anything about it in words, or to identify ourselves with it until after the expansion of consciousness which takes place after the third initiation—that of the Transfiguration.

3.   A study of the Plan, as it appears at this time to be working out in the five kingdoms in nature. It will be apparent to you that the teaching connected with this group will be more definitely and academically occult in its significance than will be the case in the others, for it will be based upon information contained in *The Secret Doctrine* and in *A Treatise on Cosmic Fire*. It will be founded upon certain premises contained in those volumes. Therefore, the members of this group of disciples will be of the more orthodox persuasion; they will be theosophists by nature, and academic by disposition.

The nature of the anima mundi, the fact of the subjective consciousness found in all forms without exception, and the existence of an interplay between these forms, through the medium of the soul, will be the major theme. Soul sensitivity and reaction to the energy in any form will be the *training* objective of the group members. Owing to the difficulty of this task, the members of this eighth group will be chosen from the personnel of the other groups, for they will have had a fair measure of training in their preliminary work. Two groups will then be interlocking groups—that which is formed of the key people in all the groups, and this one.

The ninth group, whose project is financial service, will be one of the most practical and interesting from the standpoint of the present world situation and modern conditions. I may begin to organise this group before long, provided some of my disciples show me the subjective signs for which I look, which involves a right understanding and spiritual appreciation of money. By this I do not mean that any of you who do show such signs will be in this group, but you will provide the right conditions which will make its inception possible; one or two of the key people, however, may form part of the financial service group if the plan works out as hoped and intended.

The task to be undertaken by this group is to study the significance of money as *directed and appropriated energy*. This direction of force produces concretisation, and the work is then in the field of magical endeavour. As with the work of the other groups, the task to be carried out falls into three categories of endeavour:

1.   The effort to understand the nature of prana or of vital etheric energy, and the three qualities which distinguish it; these are (as you well know) inertia, activity and rhythm or—giving them their Hindu names—tamas, rajas and sattva. When the mineral wealth of the world was undiscovered and unused, we had the stage of tamas at its deepest and most inert point. Much concerning money today is related to the karma and destiny of the mineral kingdom. With this, however, we need not here concern ourselves. The processes of the pranic life were originally carried out in the realm of barter and the exchange of that which is found upon the surface of the earth and later went down into the depths, thus bringing into fluidity the deepest and densest expression (from the human standpoint) of divinity. This is a point to be remembered.

Today the process is being reversed and money is connected with the produce of the vegetable kingdom in the form of paper money, founded upon the mineral wealth of the world. This is an interesting subjective reality to have in mind.

2.   A study of the processes whereby money has been steadily deflected from personal uses, both in the good and in the evil sense.

I do not, however, intend to write a treatise upon finance. It would largely be a record of man's dire selfishness, but I seek to deal with money as the Hierarchy sees the problem, and to consider it as a form of energy, prostituted at this time to material ends or to the selfish aspirations and ambitions of well-meaning servers. They are limited in their view and need to get a picture of the possibilities inherent in the present situation which could deflect much of this form of concretised divine energy into constructive channels and "ways of light."

3. A study of the Law of Supply and Demand, so that there can be made available for the Masters' work through the medium of the world disciples (of pure motive and skill in action and tried responsibility) that which is needed, and, my brothers, sorely needed by Them.

Money has been deflected into entirely material ends, even in its philanthropic objectives. The most spiritual use now to be found in the world is the application of money to the purposes of education. When it is turned away from the construction of the form side and the bringing about solely of material well-being of humanity and deflected from its present channels into truly spiritual foundations much good will be done, the philanthropic ends and the educational objectives will not suffer, and a step forward will be made. This time is not yet, but the spiritualising of money and its massing in quantities for the work of the Great Ones, the Disciples of the Christ, is part of a much needed world service and can now make a satisfactory beginning; but it must be carried forward with spiritual insight, right technique and true understanding. Purity of motive and selflessness are taken for granted.

The Immediate Task

September 28, 1938

The Hierarchy is deeply concerned over world events. I am asked to request you to continue with the goodwill work at all costs and in the face of all obstacles. The nucleus already formed must be preserved. The new group of world servers must preserve its integrity and work undismayed. All is not yet lost. The steadiness of those who know God's Plan will help humanity and aid the efforts of the Elder Brothers. They are those who love and do not hate and who work for unity—both subjective and spiritual.

This is all I can say at this time, for the Hierarchy itself knows not which forces will prevail. They know that good must ultimately triumph but They do not know what

the immediate future holds for humanity because men determine their own courses. The Law of Cause and Effect can
seldom be offset. In those cases where it has been offset, it
has required the intervention of Forces greater than those
available at this time upon the planet. Those greater Forces
can intervene if the world aspirants make their voices penetrate. Will this be possible? The forces of destruction, militating against the Forces of good, have (to use your American
phrase) "cornered" the money assets of the world and have
turned the tide of prana—which automatically crystallises
into money and in the financial wealth of the world—towards
entirely material, separative and personal ends. It is not
easily available, therefore, for the spread and culture of
goodwill and this applies equally to the money which is in
the hands of aspirants, as in the hands of those who are
purely selfishly minded. So many aspirants have not learnt
to give with sacrifice. If you can reach some of the financial
abundance and deflect it towards the ends of the Great
White Lodge of which the Christ is the Master, it will be,
at this time, one of the most constructive things you can do
to help.

In this time of stress and strain, my brothers, I would
remind all aspirants and disciples that there is no need for
the sense of futility or for the registration of littleness. The
seed groups that will function in the new age are, at this
time, in the dark and growing stage and in the process of
expansion, working silently. This stage is, however, most
important for according to the healthiness of the seeds and
their ability to cast strong roots downwards and to penetrate
slowly and steadily upwards into the light, so will be the
adequacy of their contribution to the new age which is
upon us. I would emphasise that fact to you. The New Age
is upon us and we are witnessing the birth pangs of the
new culture and the new civilisation. This is now in progress.
That which is old and undesirable must go and of these
undesirable things, hatred and the spirit of separation must
be the first to go.

I told you before that accidents to individuals are the

result, usually, of an explosion of force and that these explosions are caused by the hatreds and the unkind thoughts and the critical words of those involved in the accident. The world situation today is *not* caused by the ambitions of any one person or race, or by the materialism, aggression and pride of any particular nation. It is not basically the result of the wrong economic conditions existing in the world at this time. It is caused entirely by the widespread hatred in the world—hatred of people and of races, hatred of individuals and of those in power, or of influence, and hatred of ideas and of religious beliefs. Fundamentally, it is caused by the separative attitudes of all peoples and races who, down the centuries and also today, have hated each other and loved themselves. It is caused by people in every country, who have sought to cast the blame for conditions on everyone except themselves, and who have diligently sought for scapegoats whereby they may feel personal immunity for their share in the wrong thinking, the wrong speaking and the wrong doing.

This fact should be grasped and faced by all aspirants and disciples, including the members of the seed groups. They are not immune from the prevalent failings and many of them have sought to apportion the blame for world conditions and to criticise those who are seeking, in their own way and fashion, to deal with the situation. Clear thinking, a clear appraisal of causes and a loving outgoing to all, should distinguish all disciples at this time. Where this attitude does not exist, there is ever the danger of absorption into the vortex of hatred and separativeness and the divorcing of the person by this (even if only temporarily) from the vortex of love. This spells danger and glamour. The very fact that disciples are all so pronouncedly individual, intensifies their reactions, good and bad.

I stand almost bewildered (did I not know and love human nature so well) at the little advance in loving thinking that some disciples have shown. It is time now, in the face of the difficulty and seeming inadequacy, to begin the intended group work, if such a beginning is ever to be made.

Each group has been organised to fulfill a specific task. This united group work has not yet been started. That task must be begun.

Group One can telepathically influence leading people and speak to their minds so that they may be impressed with the need which has been described by one of the Great Ones as "the loving salvage of the world." They must be led to realise that their policies must be determined by world good. The success that the group had in helping . . . indicated their ability to be constructively useful.

Group Two can work, if they are willing, in a constructive fashion to end some of the world glamour. This they can do because several of the group members have successfully fought glamour in their lives.

Group Three can begin group healing under direction, once certain interior adjustments have been made.

Group Four can attempt to aid in the building of the world antahkarana, working of course in group formation. This they can do if they divorce themselves, as individuals, from all separative ideas and learn to work in the spirit of love and with a conscious decentralisation of their personalities.

There are, my brothers, weaknesses to be found in all the group members. Personality tendencies and errors exist and the mistakes which involve, primarily, a man's own interests and his own internal life; but these constitute no serious detriment to group work, for they can be overcome or rendered entirely superficial with a very little effort. Impatience with the results already achieved, a feeling of smug superiority, certain physical failings and personal ambitions of a superficial kind are present in several members in all of the groups. And in each group, at this time, there is one member whose difficulties are of a more serious nature, because they constitute a true detriment to the group life, providing (as they do) entrance for forces which do, most definitely, hold back the flow of spiritual life and prevent the work of a group nature moving forward to accomplishment. In these cases, what can I do?

First of all, I must exert infinite patience and give to each person full time for change. This I have done—for years in some cases, and have thereby taxed the patience of the group members who were not implicated in the particular situation and weakness, and who longed to begin group work. The lesson of patience has not been lost and I would remind the group members that if they ever hope to have hierarchical standing, they must learn that love and that patience which can *wait*—thinking no evil and fostering only good.

I made clear to you this year that a drastic reorganisation might be in order and that the groups might have to be rearranged somewhat before the united group work could be carried forward. This reorganisation seems now to me to be unavoidable. It is not final. It does not touch the enduring, unchanging relation which has been established and which will persist among all of you eternally. Nothing can basically separate you.

The objective of the work of these seed groups is to familiarise people with the hierarchical Plan as it is working out today in this time of crisis. In these last three words you have the theme which is of paramount importance to you at this time. Is it? Your work is partly to dispel illusion, but primarily to impress the Plan upon the consciousness of the leading people in the world. It has seemed to us that this crisis is more keenly realised by worldly people than it is by world aspirants, who do have a slight vision of the objectives. Those who are not oriented to the spiritual Hierarchy and to the Path are now largely dedicated to activities of a world nature (either good or what you call bad) and this is *not* true of the world aspirants. They, instead of working actively to bring about the accomplishment of the ends indicated by the Plan (which are of a spiritual nature and unifying in their effect, breeding not hatred and separativeness, but world understanding and fusion) spend their time in speculation, in criticism of the various world leaders and in fearful foreboding—none of which is in the least helpful and, in the last analysis, is definitely harmful. This harmfulness is due to a powerfully directed thoughtform, constructed by men and women of a certain aptitude in spiritual advancement.

The responsibility of thought is little grasped as yet by those who are numbered among the world aspirants; yet their thought-making activity is now either definitely constructive or potentially destructive. I hesitate to enlarge upon this theme, owing to the probable personality reactions which those who read these words may generate. I am, therefore, speaking here of the world in general and not so specifically of the world aspirants and pledged workers.

SECTION TWO

THE GENERAL WORLD PICTURE

THE GENERAL WORLD PICTURE

The Causes of the World Difficulty

September 1938

In giving these Instructions I am anxious for you clearly to comprehend the end I have in view. Sincere students and disciples must hold ever before them the idea of Service; in connection with our present theme this is political service—along the line of world planning and world government. This teaching will carry to the general public some idea of the trend of human destiny where nations and larger groups are concerned, and should give a conviction of hierarchical potency and a sense of illumination. It will, however, do this far more easily if the ideas I attempt to convey are backed by the understanding thought, and the intelligent mental cooperation of a group of people who have pondered deeply on the theme.

What is our theme? A study and an analysis, *from the esoteric angle,* of the social organisation of humanity. I seek to have you grasp some of the universal implications which the signs of the times portray and not be entirely engrossed with the immediate situation (or dilemma; too close a perception and too near a point of view does not tend to true understanding. It fails, for one thing, to indicate the particular place in the general world picture which the immediate happenings outline.

It is a platitude and a truism to state that humanity is today passing through a crisis of immense proportions. The causes of this crisis must be sought in many factors. They lie in the past; in the growth, through evolution, of certain

basic tendencies in man; in past mistakes, present opportunities, and the powerful activity of the Hierarchy of Love.
The future is of great promise, provided man can learn
the lessons of the present which have been closely presented
to him; he must accept them and understand clearly the
nature of his problem and of the crisis with its many
ramifications and various implications.

The seething turmoil in which the masses of the people
are now living and the emergence of one or two key people
in every nation have a close relationship. These key people
make their voices heard and evoke attention; their ideas are
followed, rightly or wrongly, with attention, appreciation
or distrust. The slow and careful formation of the New
Group of World Servers is indicative of the crisis. They are
overseeing or ushering in the New Age, and are present
at the birthpangs of the new civilisation, and the coming
into manifestation of a new race, a new culture and a new
world outlook. The work is necessarily slow and those of
you who are immersed in the problems and the pains, find
it hard to view the future with assurance or to interpret
the present with clarity.

I have listed some of the reasons for the present world
unrest in another book (*Education in the New Age,* pp.
116-125) reminding you that some of the causes lie in so
remote a past that history knows nothing of them. You
would find it useful to re-read those few pages at this point,
for in them I sought to give some insight into the essential
situation which confronts mankind due to certain evolutionary developments:

1. The point reached by humanity itself
2. The emergence of the new racial type
3. The ending of the Piscean Age
4. The coming in of the Aquarian Age.

We barely touched upon the fourth point and I am not
enlarging at length upon it here either, fascinating as
speculation might be, because I am anxious to have its
major characteristics—those of unity and synthesis—stand

out with clarity in your minds. It gives the clue to all that is happening today in the world of politics and international governments, and accounts for the trend toward synthesis, amalgamation and affiliation.

The remaining four causes which we will consider later might be enumerated as follows:

5. The time of the end. The judgment of people. This period of judgment is a group interlude to the full emergence of the New Age influences.

6. The levelling of all classes and distinctions so that the spiritual values may appear and the spiritual Hierarchy manifest on earth.

7. The fact of the Approach of the Hierarchy towards external contact with humanity. I would suggest that you read my earlier writings on the Great Approaches.*

8. The power and significance, politically considered, of the Great Invocation.

THE HIDDEN SOURCE OF THE OUTER TURMOIL

January 1939

Another angle from which the world situation can be viewed with profit is to look for the hidden source of the outer turmoil. This is seldom what men think it is, for the source lies in the realm of energies and forces. As I explained elsewhere (*The Destiny of the Nations,* pages 3-47), there are three great streams of energy working powerfully in the world at this time and two others are also struggling for expression, making the five that—together—will determine the trend of world affairs. To repeat briefly:

1. The first and the most powerful force is that pouring into the world from *Shamballa,* the planetary centre where the Will of God is known. Only twice in our planetary

---

* *Esoteric Psychology (Vol. II A Treatise on the Seven Rays),* pages 268-283, 701-751.

history has this Shamballa energy made its presence felt *directly:* the first time, when the great human crisis occurred at the individualisation of man in ancient Lemuria; the second time, in Atlantean days in the great struggle between the Lords of Light and the Lords of Material Form, also called the Dark Forces. Today, this force streams out from the Holy Centre; it embodies the Will aspect of the present world crisis and its two subsidiary effects or qualities are:

a. The destruction of that which is undesirable and hindering in the present world forms (in government, religion and society).
b. The synthesising force which binds together that which has hitherto been separated.

The Shamballa force is so new and so unrecognised that it is hard for humanity to know it for what it is—the demonstration of the *beneficent Will of God* in new and potent livingness.

2.   The second major force which is potently making itself felt today is that of the spiritual *Hierarchy,* the planetary centre where the Love of God holds sway, as it swings into one of its major cyclic approaches to the earth. The problem before the Hierarchy at this time is so to direct and control all five of the powerful energies that the Divine Plan can materialise, and the close of this century see the Purpose of God for humanity assuming right direction and proportion.

3.   *Humanity* itself is the third major planetary centre through which one of the three divine aspects, Intelligence, is expressing itself, producing its world effects.

These three centres are closely interrelated and must be thought of as expressions of divine livingness, as embodying three stages in the unfoldment of God's Plan, and as constituting the three major centres—Head, Heart, Throat— in the body of the One in Whom we live and move and have our being. Students can relate these three centres to the three solar systems, referred to in *A Treatise on Cosmic Fire*. In the first solar system, the centre which is Humanity was prepared and the principle of intelligence came into manifestation. In the second solar system, the Hierarchy of Love made its appearance and must come into full manifestation, thereby enabling the love of God to be seen. In the next solar system, the centre which we today call Shamballa, will manifest the Will aspect of Deity intelligently through love. It is interesting to note that it is only through human beings, that these three centres ever come into true functioning activity; and likewise that the three major ideologies (the totalitarian, the democratic, the communistic) may be the response—distorted and yet responsive—to the forces playing from the two higher centres on to the human. This we discussed earlier (*The Destiny of the Nations*, page 22).

Those of you who are seeking to serve humanity and to join in the Hierarchical effort to bring healing to a world in pain, must learn to penetrate behind appearances, behind the methods and schemes, the results and effects on the physical plane and endeavour to contact the forces of Shamballa or of the Hierarchy, plus the human need which has produced these modes of expression and thus see them for what they are—not worn out systems and childish efforts at improvement but embryonic plans whereby, eventually, may come release and the culture and civilisation of the New Age. If you are seeking to bring illumination into the dark places of the earth (which means into the minds of men), then you must yourselves see clearly and relate the abstract and the concrete in such a manner that, in your own lives, a working idealism may be seen; only so can a working idealism of a national, racial and human nature also be seen. The head as well as the heart must be used, and this many earnest people are apt to forget. Can you possibly work at high tension in this endeavour—*a tension produced by the interrelation of the head and the heart, working out creatively through the throat centre,* esoterically understood? In this last sentence I have expressed for disciples the nature of the effort they need to make.

It is in the recognition of what is happening to mankind *as a whole* and behind the scenes, that the thinkers of the world and the new group of world servers can best serve; it is the unfoldment of the human consciousness in response to the presented conditions in any country or countries that is of moment; the "human state of mind" is just beginning to focus itself on the things that matter and to express itself in a living fashion. The thinkers and servers must learn to concentrate upon the awakening consciousness and not upon the superficial movements. This awakening goes on apace and, my brothers, satisfactorily. The form or forms may suffer but the intrinsic awareness of man is becoming, during this century, expressively divine.

The two other forces which tend to increase the already prevalent tension in the world are:

4.   The forces of materialism, streaming out into the three worlds from the so-called "Dark Forces" or Black Lodge, and from those groups of lives and workers which are the antithesis of the Great White Lodge.

5.   The force emanating from that section of humanity which is found in every part of the world and which we call the Jewish people. What I say here has no specific reference to any individual; I am considering the world problem, centering around the Jews as a whole.

These two forces greatly complicate the problem by which humanity and the Hierarchy are faced, but it should be remembered that they also produce that balancing which is ever needed for the production of right conditions.

There is little that I can tell you about the Dark Forces. They are not the problems of humanity but that of the Hierarchy. The task of these Forces is the preservation of the form life and the working out of methods and aims which are inherent in the processes of manifestation. The Black Lodge, so-called, is occupied with the form aspect of manifestation; the White Lodge, with the consciousness aspect. It might, therefore, be stated that:

1. Shamballa is occupied with the life aspect in its graded impulses.
2. The Hierarchy is occupied with the consciousness aspect in its graded series of expansions.
3. The Black Lodge is occupied with the matter aspect in its multiplicity of forms.

Again, light may come to you, if you relate this triple statement to the three solar systems and to the three aspects of divinity. Evil or wrong, therefore, exists only when the emphasis is retained in the wrong aspect from the point of view of the unfoldment attained or when that which has been used and developed to the necessary point, holds the life or consciousness too long. Hence, my brothers, the beneficent nature of death.

The Forces of Darkness are powerful energies, working to preserve that which is ancient and material; hence they are pre-eminently the forces of crystallisation, of form preservation, of the attractiveness of matter, and of the lure of that which is existent in the form life of the three worlds. They consequently block deliberately the inflow of that which is new and life-giving; they work to prevent the understanding of that which is of the New Age; they endeavour to preserve that which is familiar and old, to counteract the effects of the oncoming culture and civilisation, to bring blindness to the peoples and to feed steadily the existing fires of hate, of separateness, of criticism and of cruelty. These forces, as far as the intelligent peoples of the world are concerned, work insidiously and cloak their effort in fair words, leading even disciples to express hatred of persons and ideologies, fostering the hidden seeds of hatred found in many human beings. They fan to fury the fear and hate of the world in an effort to preserve that which is old and make the unknown appear undesirable, and they hold back the forces of evolution and of progress for their own ends. These ends are as inscrutable to you as are the plans of the Ruler of Shamballa.

These are forces which it is well for you to recognise as existing, but there is little that you, as individuals or as groups, can do about them beyond seeing to it that there is nothing in you which could make you—unimportant as you are—a focal point for their efforts or an agent for the distribution of their peculiar type of energy—the energy of focussed and directed hate, of separation, of fear and pride. With them we who are connected directly with the Hierarchy have to deal, but you can aid more than you know through the regulation of thoughts and ideas, through the cultivation of a loving spirit and through the general use of the Great Invocation.

We come now, for a brief moment, to a consideration of the Jewish question. Remember that it is an interesting fact that the Jews are found in every land without exception, that their influence is potent and widespread (far more so than they themselves are willing to recognise), and that they wield most potently that peculiar concretisation of energy which we call money. They constitute, in a strange manner, a unique and distinctly separated world centre of energy. The reason for this is that they represent the energy and the life of the previous solar system. You have often been told how, at the close of this solar system, a certain percentage of the human family will fail to make the grade and will then be held in pralaya, or in solution, until the time for the manifestation of the next and third solar system comes around. Then they will constitute the advanced guard and the symbol of the coming humanity of that system. The same thing occurred in the system before this one and those whom we now call the Jews (a purely modern name and distinction, as I tried to show in the last few pages of *A Treatise on the Seven Rays*, Vol. I, *Esoteric Psychology*), are the descendants of that earlier group which was held in pralaya between the first and second solar systems. If you will remember that the third ray governed that system and also governs the Jewish race, if you bear in mind that that system was occupied with the divine aspects of matter only and with external conditions, and that the Jews were the highest product of that system you can come to an understanding of the Jew, his separateness, his desire for racial purity and his interest in that which is commercial and tangible. The Jew, down the ages, has insisted upon being separated from all other races but he brought over from the previous system the knowledge (necessary then but obsolete now) that his race was the "chosen people." The "Wandering Jew" has wandered from System One to this where he must learn the lesson of absorption and cease his wandering. He has insisted upon racial purity, for that was his major problem in early Lemurian times when the race came into a world that had in it no human beings, for it was before the coming of the Lords of Flame; this insistence has been carried down the ages and has governed the rules of marriage and the preparation of food instead of being dropped (as it should have been) thousands of years ago. It is these facts (unknown to the modern Jew) which has militated against him down the years and made it possible for the forces of separativeness and of hate, to use the Jewish race to stir up world difficulty, and thus bring to a crisis the basic human problem of separation. When humanity has solved the Jewish problem (with the understanding cooperation of the Jew) and overcome ancient antipathies and hatreds, it will do so by fusing the problem in one vast humanitarian situation. When that happens, the problem will be rapidly solved and one of the major difficulties will disappear off the face of the earth. Racial fusion will then be possible. Our earth humanity and the group of human beings who are far more ancient in their origin than we are, will form one humanity and then there will be peace on earth.

Why our planet and this solar system should have been constituted the nursery for the seeds of separativeness and why this remnant of humanity, far more advanced than ours, should have been destined to work out its future on our earth, is hid in the knowledge of the Lord of Shamballa, and is unattainable knowledge for you and, indeed, for many in the Hierarchy. It is simply a fact to be accepted by you. The solution will come, as I said, when the races regard the Jewish problem as a humanitarian problem but also when the Jew does his share of understanding, love and right action. This he does not yet do, speaking racially. He must let go of his own separative tendencies and of his deep sense of persecution. He will do this latter with great facility, when he grasps, as a race, the significance and inevitability of the Law of Karma, and from a close study of the Old Testament and of the acts and deeds there claimed by him as his racial acts and deeds (conquest, terrorism and cruelty), realises that the law is working out and incidentally releasing him for a greater future. There must, at the same time, be a realisation by the Jew and Gentile of equal responsibility and equal liability for the present world difficulty.

The two forces to which I have been referring must, therefore, be taken into account by all disciples as they seek to serve in this critical cycle; these two forces must also be taken into your calculations as you start this new group work or your wrong idealisms and thoughts may hinder the group work. You must recognise theoretically the five forces (three major and two minor) which meet and clash in the human family at this time. It has been necessary for me to bring these facts to your attention. If disciples are to do group work together on mental levels, they must clear their minds of prejudice, hatreds and any tendency to superiority and criticism. You cannot work, as a group, if these ideas and thoughts are present, and I am preparing now to teach you some of the first stages of group work and usefulness. It would not have been necessary for me to deal with these world problems if you had been immune from emotional reactions to them, but very few of you have your minds clear from prejudice and free from hatred. Those few make the work possible and it is also possible for the rest of you to detach your minds from undue influence and wrong ideas.

I ask you, in this work, to concentrate upon the Shamballa and the Hierarchical forces. I ask you to regard yourselves as pure and unclogged channels and to seek only to be linked with the soul of each and all, whose nature is pure love, realised synthesis and divine potency.

It is essential, however, in spite of the work to which I have called these groups and which—as you know—is intended to lay the basis for the work of the esoteric schools of the future, that the members of all the groups realise that exoteric group work must also be undertaken. Too many in these groups are satisfied with the significance of their own group work and permit it to usurp the place of objective service.

If it is so hard, my brothers, to arouse aspirants, such as yourselves, to urgent service and a full sense of responsibility; if men and women with all the information that you possess cannot be aroused to sacrificing effort, you can gain some idea of the magnitude of the task with which the Hierarchy is confronted at this time. You can realise, perhaps, the sense almost of frustration which could sweep over me (if I were limited by any time concept) when, for instance, those to whom I look for cooperation, are preoccupied with their own affairs, have no sense of immediacy and prefer to concentrate upon their own development, their own families, their own problems, rather than achieve the larger world view which would lead to full cooperation. The averting of a world debacle is the aim of our effort and towards this aim I have asked your help.

THE SPIRITUAL TREND OF HUMAN DESTINY

Wesak, May 1939

In this hour of crisis, anxiety and suspense, it has seemed that there are certain things which you would do well to remember, and certain things which you should endeavour to do.

The first thing, therefore, of which I would like to remind you is that *The Hierarchy stands.* Behind all that is going on today, the same group of spiritual Forces and the same Elder Brothers and Masters are to be found as here-tofore, guiding humanity along the path of life and bringing us safely and satisfactorily to our present point of development. The Buddha, Whose festival we are celebrating, and the Christ, Who expresses to us the unchanging love of God, are still with us, and the Hierarchy stands as a bulwark of strength between us and possible disaster; this centre of spiritual life is "like the shadow of a great rock in a weary land".

The second thing I would have you all remember is that mankind has marched steadily forward from a state of blind ignorance and unawareness to one of an intelligent pre-occupation with life and a growing sense of responsibility. This sense of responsibility, which is awakening in all of you, is—on its present large scale—relatively new and is one of the factors definitely increasing the distress and pain you are all feeling. You ask yourselves, where, as a race, have we failed and what can we do to rectify our mistakes? In spite of everything, however, men have gone from stage to stage of intelligent and spiritual unfoldment and no matter what the outer happenings have been or may be, the race has made real progress. There has been no turning back, and there will be none. Mankind has weathered many storms and survived many difficulties; men have emerged from periods of crisis better and stronger, purified "so as by fire" and definitely nearer the goal.

I would remind you also of the integrity and solidarity of the human family. We are one people—one in our rela-tionships, and capacities and desires, our origin and our goal. It is this essential and recognisable integrity which is emerg-ing at this time powerfully in the human consciousness. You are apt to think that this may not be so, that your position in believing this is somewhat unique and that you stand somewhat alone. But this is your error and is not true to the facts of the case. In every land and among widely dif-fering peoples, the same desire exists for understanding, for the establishing of right and peaceful relations, and for the expression of that basic goodwill which is one of the deepest human characteristics and our divine inheritance.

These are the things which, it seems to me, are important at this time, and which all of us would do well to remember. Will you try to do so? No matter what may take place in the world—whether war or peace, strife and aggression or understanding conciliation and conference—we face a difficult period of adjustment, and for this we must be prepared. The next three years are critical, and this we have often been told.

Much will depend upon what you and all men of goodwill and disciples think and what they do. I would like to remind you of another most encouraging thing, and that is that the power wielded by those who are seeking to live as souls and in touch with the soul and the world of spiritual realities is out of all proportion to their registered sense of power and usefulness. You are, as you endeavour to wield spiritual force constructively and selflessly, far more potent than you realise. If you add to this realisation the recognition that you are not alone in this, but that people with a vision similar to yours and with the same ideals and spiritual aspiration are to be found in every country without exception of any kind, in every religion, group and organisation, then indeed you can go forward with courage and with hopeful faith. If this is a statement of fact (and I believe it to be so) then let us go forward in unison with our brothers everywhere, conscious of opportunity, of strength, of responsibility and of the joy of service.

As regards some of the things which you can do, I would suggest the following. Refuse to allow yourselves to be swept by any fear psychosis or to be stampeded into any attitude through which the anxiety and unrest and distress in the world can overwhelm you. Strive to stand in spiritual being. Each morning, in your meditation, seek to take that attitude with a new and fresh definiteness and to hold it during the hours of service which lie ahead each day. This will not be an easy thing to do, but it can be done if you can get quiet enough for five minutes each morning—completely and interiorly quiet—and if you fill your days with vital occupation and true service, guarding with care all thought and speech.

Between now and the Wesak Festival in 1940 let each of you gain that control of speech which has often been your goal but seldom your achievement, and remember that the most powerful factor in the control of speech is a loving heart. Wild and fearful talk, hateful gossip, cruel innuendo, suspicion, the ascribing of wrong and wicked motives to persons and peoples, and the divergences of attitude which have separated the many different nations in the world are rampant today and have brought the world to its present distressing situation. It is so easy to drift into the same habits of speech and thought which we find around us and to discover ourselves participating in attack and the spirit of hate. Guard yourselves strenuously against this and say nothing which could inflame hate and suspicion in connection with any race, any person, any group or any leaders of groups and nations. You will have to guard yourselves with care, so that even in defense of that which you may personally or nationally approve you do not find yourselves full of hate and breaking the law of love—the only law which can truly save the world. Perhaps the key to your success along this line will be *the silence of a loving heart.*

It will be good also to cultivate the joy that brings strength. This is not the time for gloom, despair or depression. If you give way to these, you become negative and destructive focal points in your environment. If you truly believe that the spiritual life is fundamental in the world today, if you do believe that divinity guides the world, if you truly grasp the fact that all men are your brothers and that we are all the children of the One Father, and if you are convinced that the heart of humanity is sound—are these not adequately potent ideas to hold us joyously steady in the midst of a changing world?

Will you, therefore, carry with you the following ideas?

First, that the Hierarchy of spiritual Forces stands in spiritual Being.

Second, that we too can stand steady in spiritual Being.

Third, that the silence of a loving heart should be our keynote for the coming year.

Fourth, that strength to stand is the result of a joyous attitude and a true orientation to the soul.

CONFLICT BETWEEN FORCES OF ANCIENT ORIGIN

August 1939

I have already written anent the fivefold stream of energy which is today in conflict with world forces or with the forces of light or darkness, so called. (I would remind you that there would be no darkness without the light and no light without the dark. Ponder on this.) I would ask you to realise that the organised efforts of the Great White Lodge are directed toward lifting the organised forces of materialism to a higher and spiritual plane. Today, gold and separativeness, materialism and selfishness are in conflict with spiritual energy and with the spirit of cooperation or understanding fusion. The law which will determine the results can be expressed in the words that have been often used: by holding, man loses; by relinquishing, he gains; by seeking to grasp that which he has, it must and will inevitably disappear. Reflect upon this law.

The method whereby the forces of separation and of selfishness work are by competitive cooperation. Throughout the world, groups are already formed (or are in process of forming) to bring about the attainment of various materialistic goals, the achievement of personal or national ambitions, and the imposition of intellectual plans and concepts (the so-called ideologies) upon the mass of the people. Parties, organisations, groups, societies, associations and alliances exist for the furtherance of political and sociological aims and to carry forward the projects of many peoples and the many and differing points of view, plus the many attitudes toward life and its arrangement and re-arrangement. I am not here dealing with the churches, the

great religions or the religious organisations. I am concerned with the determining factors which are today conditioning the material life of the planet. Speaking broadly,
these forces and groups are occupied with material values
and mental ideas. They are not principally occupied with
the more subtle values, though these are incidentally present. The emphasis is upon the economic situation; upon
the possession of land or cultural predispositions and tendencies and with the relations between people and nations;
these latter are based fundamentally, as you know, on that
which is tangible and objective, guarded, defended or gained
and procured by definitely tangible means which are in
themselves separative and divided. This statement, I think,
the people of every nation would regard as true. The basic
underlying methods employed are those of organisational
arrangement (large, as in nations, or smaller, as in the
groups within the nations), propaganda, the imposition of
favoured ideas through the use of the spoken and written
word in every country, group loyalty, group adherence to
the leader, and group methods. Success depends upon the
gained group cohesion, the group willingness to sacrifice,
plus loyalty and allegiance to some directing personality.

Behind these many groups stand the forces of ancient
origin which are pledged either to the material or the
spiritual values. Because many ages have gone by in the
building up of the material values, to the development of
the personality consciousness, and to the achievement of a
tangible and objective civilisation, the forces of materialism
are apparently far stronger and more potent than the forces
of the spirit or of the intangible worlds. Up to the present
this has *not* been wrong, though it has been accompanied by
much that has been undesirable and which has led to a one-
sided evolution. But the time has now come for the shift
of the human consciousness into the world of true and
spiritual understanding and of the intangible and more
desirable standards of living.

Pouring through the chaos of offensive and defensive
groups and through the many warring organisations (polit-

ical for the most part, or religious), and affecting both the reactionary bodies and those who stand for the new ideals and the coming civilisation and culture, are the five streams above mentioned—streams of energy.

At this point I would remind you that *the effect of the impact of energy is dependent upon the nature of the vehicle of response.* According to his equipment and the nature of his bodies, so will man react to the inflowing energies. This is a fundamental statement. It is a law and should be most carefully considered. The effects of a Master or initiate upon men are widely different, because each man brings to the impact of His vibration a type of physical body, an astral or emotional nature, and a mind which are in each case different from all the others. The use each makes of the stimulating energy will be different; the focus of his consciousness is very different; his type of mind is quite different; his centres, their activity and their internal organisation are different. And it is the same for groups, organisations and nations.

Nations, for instance, have seven centres, as have all forms of existence from the human and animal upwards, and it is an interesting study to discover these centres and note the type of energy which flows through them. In connection with the United States of America, Chicago is the solar plexus centre, whilst New York is the throat centre and Washington the head centre. The heart centre is Los Angeles. The heart centre of Germany is Munich, and its head centre is Nuremberg, whilst Berlin is the throat centre. London is, of course, the heart centre for Great Britain (and temporarily it is also the head centre, though this will not always be the case), whilst Ottawa is the throat centre and Sydney is the solar plexus centre of the British Empire. Some day I may indicate to you the centres through which the forces of manifestation have to work for the various nations. This information constitutes one of the major hierarchical sciences and indicates to us who know it the possibilities latent in any nation, the point of attainment and the opportunities for work and advancement, or the obstacles to progress; this is gauged by the light in the centres and the heightening and the obscuration of their vibration. It is this that makes possible or hinders the growth of what is called spirituality in individuals and in nations, and this science will later be recognised. It is by means of this science that the Hierarchy can form its larger plans and know in what manner individual nations will react to stimulation and to progress of the desired kind. This is the modern form of the ancient Atlantean laya-yoga, or the yoga of the centres.

According, therefore, to the condition of the sensitive bodies of the planet, of nations and of individuals, so will be their reaction to the five kinds of inflowing forces. The Shamballa force, for instance, in making its impact upon first ray types, and upon the other ray types on that line of major energy—the third, fifth and seventh ray types—evokes widely differing results than when it makes an impact upon the second ray line of energy; the results of the impact of Shamballa energy upon the first ray individuals and nations can be potent in the extreme. This impact, being relatively a new one to humanity, evokes in the world today all the political and organisational changes which are so prevalent and so disturbing. There is little that humanity can do about this except endeavor to balance this first ray display of energy with second ray or hierarchical force. This latter energy—working through the world religions and the men and women who respond to the love influence—can change methods (though not the purpose or the direction) by pouring in the love force.

Again, that force which we regard as emanating from the strictly human centre, the third ray type of energy, is of the third or creative order; and in these three energies you have, in reality, the expression of the three major centres of the planetary Logos. The first or will energy is, as you know, focussed in Sanat Kumara, the Ancient of Days (as He is called in the Christian Bible), the Lord of Shamballa, Who is the embodiment of the Personality of the planetary Logos. The love force is focussed through the two great spiritual Lords of the Hierarchy, the Buddha and the

Christ, Who are both embodiments of the heart centre of the planetary Logos, for the Buddha represents the twelve-petalled lotus in the head, of which the Christ represents the counterpart, the twelve-petalled lotus of the heart centre. This is a fact seldom grasped or even mentioned. The petals of the throat centre are represented at this time by certain of the leading world rulers, whose activity is responsible for the rapid creation of the new world with its rapidly altering civilisations and culture. These thoughts will provide much that you would do well to consider.

The fourth type of force, which is responsible for the state of world affairs at this time, is that of the Jews; they, as a whole, constitute the solar plexus of the planetary Logos; their problem is being used today to focus, qualify and condition the world feeling-nature and the emotional reactions of the sensitive nature of humanity and of the planetary Logos. Forget not that the Personality of our planetary Logos is not yet perfect, hence the fact that His body of manifestation, the planet, is not reckoned as being one of the sacred planets. Through the Jewish people throughout the world, feeling—sympathetic or antagonistic, expressive of love or conditioned by hate—is being gathered to a focus in the planetary solar plexus centre, preparatory to a great and permanent change. It is for this reason that I have said to some of my pupils that when humanity will have solved correctly the Jewish problem, and when it has been resolved in a humanitarian and sound manner, then the energy of the planetary solar plexus centre will have been raised to the heart and a great transmutation will have taken place.

The Dark or Materialistic Forces correspond in their entirety to the energies of the sacral centre of the planet, dealing with the generation of forms, and their work is to keep the direction of planetary interest upon the form side of divine expression. They are concerned with the life of matter itself, with its magical usage, and with that which is regarded as dark because, for humanity at its present stage of development, that divine aspect should have lost its major hold and should lie behind "in the darkness of that which has been outgrown and which has no further hold upon the son of God". You therefore have the following tabulation expressing what I have sought above to make clear to you.

I would point out here that the fourth energy, focussed in the Jewish problem, is definitely producing cleavage as a part of the divine plan. The Jews are instruments in the working out of the Plan for the production of certain syntheses and to bring humanity to certain realisations and decisions. A close study of this tabulation will bring you much of knowledge. However, it only expresses the *present situation* in this interim period between the old Piscean age which is passing and the new Aquarian age which is coming in. It depicts this present world cycle. The emphasis of the rays changes in connection with the last two types of energy expressions quite constantly, because they are symbolic (in this day and age) of the personality nature in its physical and emotional forms.

I wonder whether you can grasp the implications of this paragraph. When the mind aspect (the third aspect of the personality) is more fully developed, then the focus of the effort of the Dark Forces will change and the problem of the Jews will disappear. Mankind is not yet handling its problems intelligently. Thus the forces and energies of the creative process are exceedingly active at this time in preparing what I might call the "material of the world" and the substance of all the four kingdoms in nature for the coming changes. As the ploughman turns the soil of his field and harrows it, and so brings that which is underneath to eventual fruition, so a similar process is taking place in the world today, and all is preparatory for the sowing and its resultant effects. These effects will constitute the new Aquarian culture and civilisation. In this process the Hierarchy is taking a definite and influential part and is working more uniquely and specifically than ever before in the history of the world, under instruction and vital aid from Shamballa.

I. *The Shamballa energy*........Planetary head centre...........First Ray.................Will
   The divine purpose.   Conditioning the life of nations. Determining.
                                                                   THE PLAN.

   Expression:
   Sanat Kumara.   Politics. Esotericism.   New.   Destroys.

II. *Hierarchical energy*.........Planetary heart centre...........Second Ray.............Love-Wisdom
    Divine love-wisdom.   Conditioning the soul.   Inspiring.
    Expressions:
    Buddha and Christ.   Religious. Spiritual.   Permanent.   Builds.

III. *Humanity's energy*..........Planetary throat centre..........Third Ray.............Intellect
     Divine intelligence.   Conditioning the mind.   Creative
     Expression:
     Many people today.   Educational.

IV. *The Jewish force*............Planetary solar plexus...........Seventh Ray aspect of Third Ray...Magic
    Temporary.   Conditioning world emotion.   Money
    Producing separation.   Sensitivity.

V. *The materialistic forces*.....Planetary sacral centre..........Fifth Ray aspect of First Ray......Mind
   The Matter aspect.   Conditioning substance.
                                 Generation.

Seed groups are in process of being "esoterically anchored" in the field of the world, having in them those who can respond to the subtler forces and who can—through the strength of their clear thought at this stage of the proceedings—produce those conditions (within the present existing world trends and world groups) which will enable the new sciences, the new approaches to divinity, the new education, and the new modes of handling the economic situation and the political problems, to precipitate and further the growth of the Kingdom of God in such a manner that this fifth kingdom in nature may be a tangible, factual and objective occurrence upon the Earth.

In the founding of the fourth kingdom in nature, the human kingdom, the process is spoken of in the ancient books and archives in the library of the Hierarchy in the following terms which are (some of them) paraphrased and expanded in *The Secret Doctrine:*

"Seven men appeared, the prisoners of the Prajapatis and the prisoners also of the earthly Barhishads . . . Seven men of seven colours . . . Seven men, each on his own lot and related to the eighth. They spoke and knew each other. They saw and they desired that which then appeared. They sensed the first, the second and the third. They were themselves the fourth, but of the fifth they had as yet no knowledge for they were prisoners of the world and the fifth could not appear. The fires which were forty-nine in number proceeded then to do their work, and the prison bars grew firm as steel . . . But time persisted and the seven— each on his own lot—began to grow too large for the confining bars."

This parable will be apparent to esotericists. The clue to what I have to say comes later in the same ancient writing, and here I will roughly paraphrase or freely translate it for you.

"The seven—each on his own lot—acquired knowledge. The knowledge was the same, but the soil within the lots differed. Nevertheless, the goal of reaching towards the heavens was the same as in the second (a reference to the vegetable kingdom and its symbolically skyward aspiration) . . . No further do they reach. Upon the lot of each, nine points of light appear, reflected in the heavens; they brought to seeding point that human seed which has within it that which is not of man. The light produced the germination and thus the new and better forms of life. And yet the form remains and yet its quality is changed. (I can find no better word than 'quality' wherewith to translate the ancient symbol). Some things are lost and disappear and rightly so. Some newer modes of life and what life builds appear, and thus the fifth is seen on earth like to the second and nurtured by the fourth. Within it are the one, the two, the three and then the fifth. And thus the glory of the One is seen."

One meaning is obvious if you study with care the implications and relate it to the kingdoms of nature. There are of course several meanings to these ancient writings.

I have referred above to the five streams of energy and have related them to the five centres. Let me extend the idea somewhat by pointing out that these five energies are related to the centres or the lotuses to which I referred in *A Treatise on Cosmic Fire,* or to the dynamic point within the lotus, through which the central life of the lotus flows; in the case of the first three energies (of Shamballa, the Hierarchy and Humanity) you have the permanent point of life, light and activity in the lotus; in the case of that potent energy connected with the Jews, you have a very temporary inflow of energy, and in the case of the Forces of Materialism, you have a relatively temporary—though apparently permanent—focal point of reactionary energy.

In connection with the petals of the lotus, you will find a close connection with the forces of the five kingdoms in nature; therefore, to the tabulation which was earlier given I would add the following for your consideration:

1. 5th Kingdom............Intuition.................spiritual soul...................head centre
2. 4th Kingdom............. Intelligence.............human soul...................throat centre
3. 3rd Kingdom.............Instinct...............animal soul.................solar plexus
4. 2nd Kingdom............. Sentiency...............feeling consciousness............heart centre
5. 1st Kingdom............. Response.................sub-consciousness.............. base of spine

To this you may add the following:

1. Shamballa............Head Lotus.............Kingdom of God.........   1st Ray.......Will
   Quality of Will

2. Hierarchy...........Heart Centre............Kingdom of Souls.......   2nd Ray......Love
   Quality of Giving .. Love

3. Humanity..........Throat Centre...........Kingdom of man.........   4th Ray.......Harmony through Conflict
   Quality of Acquisitiveness

4. The Jews..........Solar Plexus Centre....Kingdom of man ....   3rd Ray......Active Intelligence
   Quality of Separativeness

These can be linked up with the kingdoms in nature, but in this particular cycle it is not possible to fit them in such a way that the correspondence will appear to you as accurate. The mineral kingdom and the Forces of Materialism do not really coincide today, for the one works through the sacral centre at this time, and the other through the centre at the base of the spine. Esoteric students must always remember that no correspondences are correct and entirely accurate in their parallelism in this solar system of changing forces, shifting cycles and constant mutation directed towards the inscrutable ends of Deity—inscrutable as far as the human consciousness is concerned. They remain inscrutable to humanity, because the three major ends or purposes which affect you, for instance, as members of the fourth kingdom in nature are:

1. The direction in which the solar Logos is going upon the Cosmic Path.
   Esoterically........The Way towards the Central Spiritual Sun.
2. The plans of the planetary Logos upon the Systemic Path.
   Esoterically........The Way towards the Heart of the Sun.
3. The purpose ahead for the human family upon the Path of Light.
   Esoterically........The Way of the Sun.

I put this in here only to show you how vague and uncertain are your very highest speculations. Be content with your duty and the immediate service which will lead you a step further upon the way to which you are ordained, and this way you can travel rapidly and with eager feet or slowly and with lagging steps.

The above enumerated forces are, however, part of the temporary interlocking of energies which is going on between the many expressions of the creative process at this time. They are likewise conditioned by the incoming Aquarian force and "measured" by the outgoing Piscean forces. I would have you note here my use of the word "forces" and "force," for not idly have I made them singular and plural.

In this process of founding the kingdom of heaven upon earth, the same procedure is being followed as was used in the earlier stage of founding the fourth kingdom. The "seven men, each on his own lot," reach a moment of tension and of creative power wherein the seeds of life, which they contain within themselves, can come to fruition, and groups of such appearing seeds can appear in the world "on their own lot." Putting it more simply and in terms symbolic, and therefore more easy of understanding, we might state that the seven rays, expressing themselves in the human family through the seven ray types, are now at the stage of unfoldment where the process can be carried forward into the formation of the seven ray groups, and these in their totality will express the Kingdom of God. Groups will be formed which will be outstandingly of a particular ray type but which will work in all the nine major fields of human expression. These I outlined when indicating the work of the nine groups planned by me. However, let me here point out that the groups which I planned are not in themselves the coming groups nor are they the only evidences of the emergence of these ray groups in the world. There are several similar experiments going on at this time upon the various streams of ray energy and under the direction of various Masters of the Wisdom. The groups for which I have made myself responsible are second ray groups essentially and are in the nature of a tentative move to see if the time is really ripe for the distribution of such seed groups throughout the entire world. Will the response of humanity and the reaction of these groups be such that a network of them may be started on a large scale everywhere —groups which will be characterised by vision, cohesion, love, impersonality, sacrifice, persistency and creative ability? These are the questions which we, the teachers on the inner side, are today asking ourselves as we study the problem of the best way of helping the human family through this crisis.

Bear in mind that the objective before these groups is

to relate the Hierarchy, and that for which it stands, to humanity; to bring into a close rapport the two centres whose energy must eventually be fused and blended into one whole. Perhaps you will grasp the underlying idea with greater clarity if you will remember the personal work which you should be endeavoring to do with yourself. This is, is it not, the effort to fuse and blend the personality and the soul, or the higher Self and the lower selves. To do this you have to realise that the illumination of the mind is a vital and essential factor. There are, therefore, three points to consider: the Soul, the illumined Mind and the Personality. To these three you have to add a consecrated and awakened heart, full of love to all, vibrant with compassion and with understanding. Bear, therefore, these four factors in mind:

1. The dedicated oriented man........the personality
2. The overshadowing, spiritual man.........the soul
3. The illumined mind.......the medium of relation
4. The consecrated, loving heart.......the expression of these three.

This is the personality and individual correspondence to the broader picture and the world factors and the wider undertakings with which humanity is at this time faced. Just as in the life of the individual a man is confronted with the opportunity to function as a disciple in training with a view to initiation, so today humanity is faced in the same way with a similar situation and possibilities. The higher correspondence with which the Hierarchy is occupied at this time, and of which the outline just given is an inadequate analogy, is as follows:

1. The intellectual centre, Humanity, receptive, ready and expectant.
2. The spiritual centre, the Hierarchy, positive, deliberate and munificent—ready and waiting to bestow that which is desired, reached for and claimed.

3. The New Group of World Servers. They are the more advanced members of the human family, sensitive to hierarchical inspiration and to human need and to spiritual unfoldment as a determining factor in world affairs.

4. Small groups which correspond to the illumined minds of the individuals—intuitional and acting as a cohesive element and a fusing factor between humanity and the Hierarchy. They are gathered out of the New Group of World Servers.

Let me now present you with another vital consideration. Looking back over your individual lives, you will be conscious that it was the points of crisis and the cycles of tension which constituted for you the major opportunities and the moments of "moving forward." Of these opportunities you either profited or—by neglecting them—you temporarily failed. This same critical factor (if I might call it so) acts also in the world of men and in groups and masses; today the point of tension for humanity in such a situation, similar to that to be found in the individual life, can be noted. The Hierarchy stands also at a point of extreme and scientific tension—scientific because induced and directed; you can, if you so choose, picture these two great groups as facing each other. The Hierarchy is aware of the need, of the purpose of the dual tension, and desirous of bringing this tension to such a "crisis of precipitation" that the fusion of the two groups will be inevitable, whilst the other group, humanity, unaware generally of the implications of the situation, is suffering, bewildered and full of fear. Between these two groups stands the New Group of World Servers, constituted today of two bodies of people:

1. Those who are aware of the Plan, are subject to and sensitive to hierarchical impression and dedicated to the task of bringing about the desired fusion or group at-one-ment. These are the consecrated servers of the world who are free from all taint of separativeness, full of love to all men and eager for the

spread of understanding goodwill. They correspond to the "consecrated loving heart," mentioned above.

2. A small minority who have emerged out of the New Group of World Servers and who can (in every country) function in group formation if they choose, and so bring about the fusion for which the New Group of World Servers is working and for which the point of tension in humanity and in the Hierarchy predisposes and has prepared the hearts of men. Their opportunity and responsibility is great, because they know the Plan, they are in touch with the guiding teachers on the inner side—and are sensitive to the higher impression. They correspond to the points of illumination, and so to the "illumined minds," referred to above.

Here is the picture of these esoteric interrelations, and here you can note the position which you could hold, for these groups have a definite opportunity to bring about this world fusion and so precipitate the "crisis of love" to which I have so oft referred. The Great Approach upon the side of humanity is now going on, with the tension induced thereby growing momentarily; this will increase with growing speed and tension until 1942 when either the first stage of fusion will have been made upon earth, resulting in widespread goodwill and world understanding or in postponement—with sad results to the human family and an inevitable break in the tension which will take a form that will cause much real suffering and widespread disaster. This disaster can take many forms, but upon them we will not speculate, except to realise the urgency and the need for immediate action which is demanded at this time.

There are two points to remember in connection with these seed groups, and these are in line with, but also expansions of, analogous conditions in the "seeds" which fructified—after implantation and development—in animal-man, producing the living self-conscious individual and, in their totality, the fourth kingdom in nature. The first point has reference to *the quality* of the implanted seed, and the second to *the method* of its implantation.

The quality of the "seed of the sons of God" which was effectual in producing the human family was intellectual, and the self-conscious self-directed man was the result. The fruit of this quality, plus the livingness of the seed itself, can be seen today in the more advanced and cultured thinking people and in those who are in any sense of the word personalities.

The method employed was the gift of mind to the more advanced among the animal-men in a majority of cases, the stimulation of the instinctual faculty in others, whilst a third method was the leaving of a minority to the ordinary course of evolution. These latter today constitute the least developed and the most backward of the races upon the Earth. They are, in fact, a very small number indeed.

In connection with the "seed-groups" which are fusing and blending in humanity at this time, and which—in their totality—constitute the nucleus of the fifth kingdom, the distinguishing quality is the ability to respond intuitionally to higher impression and to present the mind (with which humanity was endowed in the earlier process) to the light of the intuition and hence to illumination. This intuition is a blend of the two divine qualities of buddhi-manas, or intuitive spiritual understanding (involving interpretation and identification) and the higher abstract mind, which is essentially the power to comprehend that which is not concrete or tangible but which is, in reality, an innate recognition of the lower aspects of the divine Plan as it must affect life in the three worlds. Humanity, being still primarily self-conscious and self-centered, regards this Plan as the divine Plan for man, but—as the seed groups grow and develop— the narrowness of this partial view will become increasingly apparent. God's Plan is all-embracing and His purposes are inclusive of all forms of life and their relationships. This quality of the seed groups is described in current esoteric literature as love-wisdom (the heart nature and the higher mind), and this is descriptive of the future groups; it is *not* love, however, as usually understood, or wisdom as man generally defines it. This is free of emotion and of the astralism which is distinctive of the solar plexus life which most people live; love, esoterically and in reality, is perceptive understanding, the ability to recognise that which has produced an existing situation, and a consequent freedom from criticism; it involves that beneficent silence which carries healing in its wings and which is only expressive when the inhibition aspect of silence is absent and the man no longer has to still his lower nature and quiet the voices of his own ideas in order to understand and achieve identification with that which *must* be loved. Can you follow the beauty of this concept and comprehend the nature of this silent depth of true understanding?

Wisdom is the sublimation of the intellect, but this involves the sublimation of the higher as well as of the lower aspects of the mind. It is a blend of intuition, spiritual perception, cooperation with the plan and spontaneous intellectual appreciation of that which is contacted, and all this is fused and blended with and by the love which I have defined above, plus that esoteric sense which must be unfolded before the second initiation can be taken. I call this especially to your attention. Seek to understand and perceive the subtle evidences of the esoteric sense, and then define it and explain its processes and evidences, invoking as you do so the higher sensibilities.

And now, as to *the methods* to be employed in creating these groups. The primary method is the presentation of the more advanced ideas (which are stimulating in their effects upon the minds which are receptive) and the presentation of the vision, which is evocative in its influence and produces amazing results. Ponder on this.

The basic method employed, which lay behind the three methods outlined in *The Secret Doctrine* and referred to above, was the presentation (very dimly and vaguely) of the concept of the self, of the lower integrated self and its correlated inner implications of self-centeredness and self-direction. The presentation made today to self-conscious man and to this self-directed individual is the revelation of the larger Whole of which the individual is a part. To this Whole the self must dedicate its life, love and light. Those are the three gifts which the fourth kingdom in nature has finally and consciously to make to the planet—gifts of definitely directed energies producing peculiar and equally definite relations of forces; they are not the gift of strength, kindness and knowledge, which is man's feeble interpretation of the divine energies with which he will some day salvage the planetary life.

The presentation of this vision to the aspirants and disciples of the world has had a dual effect; first of all, it has produced an immediate responsive cohesion among them which resulted in the appearance of the New Group of World Servers, and secondly, it led to the formation along the line of the seven rays throughout the world of small groups (within the New Group of World Servers) who were dedicated to the production of this innate synthesis and subjective fusion and to the expression of this blended dedicated consciousness. These latter groups, a small minority, correspond to the earlier and first method of mind-implantation in animal man, whilst the New Group of World Servers corresponds to the second method of general stimulation.

In both of these embryonic activities, which will eventually be responsible for producing the manifestation of the Kingdom of God on earth, the two great necessities are vision, plus living organisation. The vision has to be sensed, sought and discovered individually by each group member, and it is this personal knowledge and this personal dedication to the revelation which leads next to the organisation of the group life and relation, or to a determined process of correlation with the life and purpose of the Whole. The individual who has for himself seen the vision relates himself to the group which is conscious of this vision along with him, and then follows the relating of this "visioning group" to the kingdom of God as it exists on the subtler planes, in the effort to exteriorise it and make the vision a fact upon the plane of manifestation. It is a process of vision, activity and precipitation.

It is in connection with vision that much of the group difficulty lies. Let me be specific and illustrate. I, your Tibetan brother, friend and teacher, have a vision of the Plan; I am aware (because of my status as an initiate of a certain degree) of the nature of the purpose for this particular cycle and what its conditioning activities should be and to what end they are directed, for there is an esoteric distinction between the Plan as it exists for humanity and for the planet, and the purpose of the present world situation. Upon this, reflection would be profitable. Through the cooperation of A.A.B. I put this plan—as far as was possible—before you, calling your attention to the New Group of World Servers. As far as I could and dared I put it before the world aspirants and called attention to the general *trend* of world events from the spiritual and subjective angles. This evoked from all of you an immediate and gratifying response; but it is possible, is it not, that this response has remained subjective, intellectually perceived and aspirationally desired, but that the Plan and the purposes of the kingdom of God are not yet truly a part of your life pattern and do not yet thoroughly condition your brain and your life activity.

Perhaps, therefore, the vision is not a part of your life and so integrated into your consciousness that you attach yourself to it as you have, in the past, attached yourself to individuals; the vision is a vision of group work, of group relationships, of group objectives, and of the group fusion to the larger Whole. When this is realised, then the vision determines your life incentives, tendencies and work, and when it is thus truly a part of your mental equipment, your emotional aspiration and your activities, and when there are sufficient groups thus actuated, then the Kingdom of God will function objectively upon the earth. This is not yet the case, because the needed conditions are not fulfilled.

The early seeds sown among animal-men were imbued with, or qualified by, *separateness*—a necessary quality for the unfoldment of self-consciousness, but one which must now be superseded.

The seed groups now in process of forming will be distinguished by the quality of *fusion,* and this should be as inevitable a development as is the separative and protective nature of the ordinary human consciousness. It is this sense of union and of at-one-ment which is the protective and essential characteristic of the fifth kingdom, and it is this latent, yet actively present, factor which leads unerringly and inevitably to the organisation—interior and subjective—of the seed groups, to their radiatory activity, and to the magnetic pull they evidence when duly organised. Thus they produce fusion and blending.

I am here putting new ideals and possibilities into as simple language as possible; I seek not to veil and obscure their simplicity and truth by many explanatory paragraphs. What I have here said must be read with the eye of vision and the understanding of the heart. Disciples must have these two faculties as part of their usable equipment. Have you got them, or are you trying to cultivate and unfold them, my brothers?

Another of the aspects of this group work is that its influence is pervasive, and not at the beginning dynamic. The force which it later exerts will be due to constant pervasive pressures and the steady spreading of the group influence and ideals. It is therefore ultimately very far-reaching in its effectiveness, providing the work is done as indicated. This will be due eventually to two factors: one, the power of the groups upon the subtler planes of thought and desire, and finally upon egoic levels; this will become steadily more potent; secondly, to the activity of those who form part of the key groups; they will themselves form corresponding groups of nine, or seven or five, and thus there will be a gradual spreading throughout the world of an esoteric network. For this the majority are not yet ready, but I would have you bear it in mind. True interest and acceptance of that which is indicated as essential to the disciple and to the work must first of all be patiently evidenced.

I have used the word "subjective" a great deal in my writings; I have done this in an effort to shift the focus of attention to that which lies below the surface. This refers, in the case of aspirants, to the subjective synthesis in the three worlds and not to the astral and mental planes per se, or specifically to egoic levels. If the inner kingdom of divine realities is to demonstrate upon earth, it will come through the emergence of the inner synthesis on to the physical plane, and this is brought about by vital recognition and an expression of the realities and laws governing that kingdom. The organisation which follows the Vision is entirely subjective in nature and pervasive in quality. It is a process of germination, but if that which germinates does not eventually appear in objective manifestation the activity is then abortive.

The influence of these new groups is due to the close inner relation demonstrated through uniform thinking and a recognised unity of purpose. It is for this reason (a truly scientific one in its nature) that I have emphasised so strongly the ordinary characteristics of the trained disciple, which are non-criticism, sensitivity and love. Where these are lacking, this simultaneous oneness and directed thought and this "group aroma" (as it is esoterically called, though the word I am attempting to translate is more adequate than the above) become impossible. I have not been interested in the elimination of hindering faults for the individual's sake, but for the carrying forward of the desired group purposes. The need is for group thinking of a powerful nature along the indicated lines; for visualisation of the Vision of such a clear nature that it becomes a fact for the individual; for the development and functioning of the imagination, applied to the lines of outcome and results, and functioning so creatively that the results are seen with clarity and must inevitably materialise. It involves also the holding of the inner subjective link with each other with such firmness that potent centres of force and of creative energy—working under inspiration from the Hierarchy, via the focussed minds of group members who are definitely en rapport with their souls and with each other—may function so successfully that the new civilisation and the new culture can be rapidly established. As this has to be founded on a basis of loving goodwill and upon nondestruction, and as its methods lead to right relations between men and nations, it is essential that the establishing groups should themselves express the subtler aspects of these desired virtues.

The emphasis upon the work which serving groups must seek to develop is that of an organised, scientific activity. Esoterically, this involves an understanding of the basic science of occultism, which is that of energy. The qualities, characteristics and activity upon which you should be engaged are definitely the expression and understanding of energy along some line; hitherto, for the majority, force has been used and its impact on other forces has been noted and recorded as force impacting force, leading thus to forceful results. But I seek to have you, as esotericists, deal with *energy and the result of its impact upon forces.* This is the scientific aspect of the occult life.

The world is today full of forces in conflict and in wrong relation with each other, and this produces the present chaos. *The new order will be brought into expression by the play of the spiritual energy upon the forces in the three worlds, and this will be the task of the New Groups when organised and functioning correctly.* In these words, I have summed up one of the first and most important objectives of the group work with which I and others of the workers upon the spiritual side of life are at this time occupied. Some small understanding of the significance of these words can be gained if you will watch the effect that you produce in your environment during those times when you do succeed in living as souls, and are therefore expressing soul energy, and are thus counteracting the personality forces in yourselves and in those around you.

The desire of the Hierarchy at this time is to fill the world of striving forces with points of spiritual energy, and to distribute everywhere those who are affiliated with spiritual groups and are therefore linked subjectively to their group brothers in all lands, so that a pervasive, intelligent influence can ceaselessly make its impact felt upon the minds of men and produce finally the needed good feeling, good will and good lives.

THE WORLD CRISIS

September 1939

Humanity is passing through an acute crisis and its karma or fate is heavy upon it. Being so close to events, it is not easy for humanity to see them in their true perspective and it is in order that you may see more clearly that I write today. A broader vision and a wider horizon may help you to understand, and it may be of profit to you if you can be helped to see the picture as it appears to us, the teachers on the inner side, and also in relation to its background.

There are two outstanding and important points which are present in the consciousness of the Hierarchy as it looks on at mankind going through the present stupendous struggle. The first is that humanity is today and on a large scale aware that what is happening is entirely its own doing and the result of humanity's own mistakes. Men either feel responsible for what is occurring or they are shifting the responsibility openly and deliberately on to shoulders other than their own. Of these endless and age-old mistakes, the Versailles Treaty is only the symbol and the practical focal point.

The second fact is that in spite of war and separation, of cruelty and of passions and selfishness running wild, there is nevertheless, today, more true understanding, more good-will and more outgoing love than at any previous time in the history of the race. I say this with deliberation and because I have the hierarchical knowledge available to my hand. Be not deceived, therefore, by the outer clamour of war. I tell you that men's hearts everywhere are full of compassion both for themselves and for all other men; the wide scope and the vast extent of the conflict is indicative of an inner unity and a subjective interrelation of which all are somewhat conscious and which the conflict itself does not negate. Is this a hard saying? I seek to indicate to you its basic truth if you will but ponder upon what I say with an open mind. The task of all aspirants and of all men of good-will everywhere is to see that prolonged suffering does not undermine the present right and essential attitudes and that the chaos and clamour does not shut out response to the voice of the soul which has been speaking with increasing clarity for the past fourteen years. The stimulation which was set up and the light which was permitted to creep through after the last hierarchical conclave in 1925 has been real and effective. That meeting of the Masters of the Wisdom upon spiritual levels led to three results or happenings, and these we are today experiencing.

The first was a fresh inflow of the Christ principle of spiritual or true love which is ever free from emotionalism and selfish intent. This inflow resulted in the immediate and rapid growth of all movements towards peace, world understanding, goodwill, philanthropic effort and the awakening of the masses of men to the issues of brotherhood.

The second was the stimulation of the principle of relationship and this led to the growth and the perfecting of all sources of inter-communication such as the press, the radio and travel. The inner objective of all this was to bring human beings closer together upon the outer plane of existence and thus parallel objectively the developing inner, spiritual unity.

The third was the inflow of the force of *will or power* from the Shamballa centre. This, as previously explained, is the most powerful force in the world today, and only twice before in the history of mankind has this Shamballa energy made its appearance and caused its presence to be felt through the tremendous changes which were brought about. Let us recapitulate briefly.

The first time was during the great human crisis which occurred at the time of the individualisation of men in ancient Lemuria.

The second time was at the time of the struggle in Atlantean days between the "Lords of Light and the Lords of Material Expression."

This little known divine energy now streams out from Shamballa. It embodies in itself the energy which lies behind the world crisis of the moment. It is the Will of God to produce certain racial and momentous changes in the consciousness of the race which will completely alter man's attitude to life and his grasp of the spiritual, esoteric and subjective essentials of living. It is this force which will bring about (in conjunction with the energy of love) that tremendous crisis—imminent in the human consciousness—which we call the second crisis, the *initiation* of the race into the Mystery of the Ages, into that which has been hid from the beginning.

It might be of value here if we considered the three great planetary centres and their relationships in tabular form and thus get the general idea more clearly in mind.

1. SHAMBALLA .....Will or Power ....Planetary Head centre
   The Holy City ......Purpose..Plan ....spiritual pineal gland

   Life Aspect
   Ruler : Sanat Kumara, the Lord of the World
   The Ancient of Days
   Melchizedek

2. THE HIERARCHY. Love-Wisdom ....Planetary Heart centre
   The New Jerusalem . Unity ....At-one-ment

   Group Consciousness
   Ruler : The Christ
   The World Saviour

3. HUMANITY ......Active Intelligence .....Planetary Throat Centre
   The City, standing
   foursquare ....Creativity

   Self-consciousness
   Ruler : Lucifer
   Son of the Morning
   The Prodigal Son

This Shamballa energy now for the first time is making its impact upon humanity directly and is not stepped down, as has hitherto been the case, through transmission via the Hierarchy of Masters. This change of direction constituted a somewhat dangerous experiment as it necessarily stimulated the personalities of men, particularly those whose personalities were along the line of will or power and in whom the love aspect of divinity was not sufficiently expressing itself; it was, however, permitted because it was realised that it would not affect the man in the street or the masses who would remain unresponsive to it, though it might greatly stimulate and intensify the mental and more potent type of man.

The effects of this widespread stimulation have been all that was anticipated and the so-called "evil results" of the Shamballa force upon ambitious and powerful personalities in all countries and all schools of thought have, nevertheless, been offset to some extent by the growth of the sense of relationship everywhere and by the spread of the Christ energy which generates at-one-ment, loving understanding and goodwill.

You might here rightly enquire how this can be so when humanity is overwhelmed by a ghastly world war at this time. I would remind you that the Hierarchy is guided in its conclusions by the mass light and by the inner subjective oft unexpressed reactions of the multitude and never by the outer happenings upon the physical plane. The fate of the form life and of outer organisations is deemed of small importance compared with the sensed inner spiritual development. That development must necessarily outrun the outer manifestation. Humanity is today further advanced spiritually and mentally than might appear from external happenings. The first result of such development is eventually the destruction of the outer form because it is proving inadequate to the pulsing, inner, spiritual life; then, secondly, comes the building of the new and more adequate outer expression. This accounts for the world crisis at this time. The cause is based upon four major factors upon which I would like somewhat to enlarge:

1. Upon the point achieved in racial evolution. This today warrants the building of a better vehicle for human and racial expression.

2. Upon the karmic causes which—as far as present humanity is concerned—can be traced back to an ancient conflict upon old Atlantis.

3. Upon the coming into incarnation of certain potent personalities whose dharma or destiny it is to bring about great evolutionary changes.

4. Upon certain planetary happenings, connected with the life of the One "in Whom we live and move and have our being." These involve the impact upon our planet of Forces and Energies which will be instrumental in altering the existing civilisation and culture, in climaxing karmic necessity and in thus engineering release, presenting humanity with that stage in the experience of the disciple which we call "the meeting of the Dweller on the Threshold with the Angel of the Presence," and inducing as a consequence a certain planetary initiation.

These four stages of the Law of Cause and Effect (as it affects humanity at this time) might be called:

1. The *perfecting* of form expression .Law of Evolution

2. The *precipitation* of karma . . . . . .Law of Cause and Effect

3. The achievement of *personality* Law of Polar (The Dweller on the Threshold). . Opposites

4. The attainment of *planetary* Law of initiation . . . . Initiation

You may perhaps think at this point that I am being academic and that the world stress at this time is such that love, sympathy and kind words are needed far more than learned, historical retrospection and suggested hypotheses. I seek, however, to foster in you the spirit of understanding. Such true comprehension necessitates head knowledge as well as heart reaction. The disciples of the world today must endeavour to see why and to what end the present terrible happenings have occurred. A clear expression and statement of causes is needed—free from emotional bias and partisan emphasis. What is happening today is not the result of immediate occurrences. When I say "immediate," I refer to all happenings which have occurred within the Christian era. I want you to attempt to regard the present crisis as being caused or initiated by events which are of so ancient an origin that modern, orthodox historians have no record of them.

Only two points of view will serve truly to clarify what is happening at this time.

First of all, a recognition that modern academic history constitutes only one page in a vast historical record and that the initiating events of which we are in search and which are working out as effects in the planetary life at this time belong to an age so distant that no modern historian recognises its episodes. Information anent this ancient period must be sought in the many world Scriptures, in ancient monuments, in the science of symbols, in the racial myths, and in inherited and transmitted legends.

Secondly, that a study of the microcosm, man, will be found to hold, as always, the key to the study of human affairs as a whole. Just as the aspirants and disciples are at this time being tested and tried and subjected to the working out of inexplicable conflicts and drastic changes in their lives, so the same is true of the world aspirant, Humanity.

To the above two reasons another might perhaps be added which will have significance and meaning to esotericists and to all who have in any way grasped the teaching I have attempted to give you in my books anent the three world centres—Humanity, the Hierarchy and Shamballa. This world crisis is related to the approach or the relation of the Hierarchy to Humanity. That great spiritual centre of force, the Human Kingdom, has now reached a point of such potency and of such a high vibratory activity that it is shaken to its very depths; all its evolutionary grades and groups are responding to the stimulation, generated within the centre itself and also stimulated by Forces emanating from the hierarchical centre and from Shamballa.

This precipitates a crisis which has had no parallel in human history but which finds a faint reflection in the crisis which overtook the animal kingdom and which resulted in the formation of a new kingdom in nature—the human. As I have earlier told you, this present world crisis, if met correctly and rightly controlled, will result in the manifestation of the fifth or spiritual kingdom upon earth. This (as you know) will be brought about by the at-one-ing of the two centres—the human centre and the Hierarchy. One of the major planetary syntheses is taking place or, perhaps I should say, can take place. (I am wording this with care and would call your attention to my wording.)

It might serve a useful purpose if I enlarged somewhat upon the four stages of the early causes, mentioned above. In so doing, I can give you some idea of the underlying purpose of all the present happenings and some understanding of the predisposing conditions which are to be found, lying far back in the night of time. If I can do this adequately and if you can read and study with understanding and an open mind, some of your natural bewilderment may disappear and you may then be able to help others to live calmly through this crisis and to preserve an attitude of patience, goodwill, balance and compassion. Let us, therefore, consider these four points because, in so doing, we shall cover the field sufficiently—I believe—to bring at least some measure of light to you. Later I will try to explain the significance of the Great Invocation and to give you some idea of the nature of the Forces invoked and of the esoteric meaning which these words (used so frequently by you) are intended to convey.

The Cause of the Present Crisis

It is well known to you that the great Law of Rebirth is the controlling and major law in all the processes of manifestation. It governs the exoteric expression of a solar Logos or of a human being, and the object of this constantly recurring process is to bring an increasingly perfect form to the expanding service of the soul. For the first time since its inception, the human family is in a position to note for itself the processes of the rebirth of a civilisation as an expression of spiritual culture at a particular point in evolution. Hence the magnitude of this crisis as it assumes its place in the human consciousness. Many lesser crises, initiating specific tribal, national and racial experiments in the renewal of form have gone on and have been registered by some group within a nation or by a nation itself (if advanced enough). Such a national registration took place for the first time in connection with the French Revolution. Such registrations of evolutionary intent have taken place with increasing clarity and understanding during the past two hundred years. Such crises have taken place in practically every nation in modern times and have been recognised to some degree, and upon them historians have enlarged and philosophers speculated. But the crisis today is far vaster, embracing as it does the majority of nations in both hemispheres. No nation remains at this time unaffected and the results are and must be registered in some aspect of the national life.

Owing to the factual interrelation between nations everywhere and to the rapidity of intercommunication, the present crisis is the first major international crisis in human affairs and covers a period of twenty-eight years (from 1914 till 1942). These are interesting numbers, for 28 is 4 x 7, which are the years of a complete personality cycle. I do not wish you to infer from the above that the period of active combat and conflict must necessarily be prolonged until 1942. Such is *not* the case. The early termination of the conflict or its indefinite extension lies in the keeping of humanity itself; men must increasingly determine their own fate as they emerge from the stage of adolescence into that of maturity, responsibility and achievement. This period of twenty-eight years is, however, of paramount importance and upon the next three years much depends.

Again I tell you that even the Hierarchy itself, with all its knowledge, vision and understanding and with all its resources, cannot coerce and cannot forecast what mankind will do. It can and does stimulate to right action; it can and does indicate possibility and responsibility; it can and does send out its teachers and disciples to educate and lead the race; but at no point and in no situation does it command or assume control. It can and does bring good out of evil, illuminating situations and indicating the solution of a problem, but further than this the Hierarchy cannot go. If it assumed authoritative control, a race of automatons would be developed and not a race of responsible, self-directed, aspiring men. This must surely be apparent to you and may serve to answer the question which is uppermost in the minds of the unthinking, occult students today: Why could not the Hierarchy have prevented this catastrophe? Unquestionably the Masters of the Wisdom with Their knowledge and Their command of forces could have interfered, but in so doing They would have broken an occult law and hindered the true development of mankind. This They will never do. At all costs, man must learn to stand and act alone. Instead, having done all that was permissible, They now stand beside suffering and bewildered humanity and—with the deepest compassion and love—will help men to right the wrongs they have initiated, to learn the needed lessons and to come through this crisis (which they have themselves precipitated) enriched thereby, and purified in the fires of adversity. These are not platitudes but eternal truths.

This world crisis, with all its horror and suffering, is—in the last analysis—the result of successful evolutionary processes. We are ready to recognise that when a man's life cycle has been run and he has learnt the lessons which the experience of any particular life has been intended to teach, his physical body and the inner form aspects (making the sum total of his personality expression) will begin to deteriorate; destructive agencies within the form itself will become active and eventually death will take place, resulting in the liberation of the indwelling life in order that a new and better form may be built. This, we perforce accept either blindly or intelligently, regarding it as a natural and unavoidable process, but normal and inevitable. We are apt, however, to forget that what is true of the individual is true of humanity. Cycles of civilisation such as that we call our modern civilisation are analogous to a particular, individual, human incarnation with its inception, its progress and growth, its useful maturity and its ensuing deterioration and subsequent death or the passing away of the form.

Forms are ever open to attack. A strong subjective life and spiritual detachment are the two safeguards. Where the form is more potent than the life, danger is imminent; where attachment to the material aspect or organisation is present, spiritual values are lost.

Today we are watching the death of a civilisation or cycle of incarnation of humanity. In all fields of human expression, crystallisation and deterioration had set in. Worn-out religious dogmas and the grip of theology and the orthodox churches have no longer sufficed to hold the allegiance of the potent, inner, spiritual life; humanity is deeply spiritual and innately religious but needs today a new form with which to clothe the ancient verities. Old political schools have been deemed inadequate and new ideologies bear witness to the strength of the life which is seeking more adequate expression; the educational systems, having served their purpose, are fast being recognised as inadequate to meet the need of the demanding life of the race; there is everywhere a cry for change and for those new forms in the religious, political, educational and economic life of the race which will allow of freer and better spiritual expression. Such a change is rapidly coming and is regarded by some as death—terrible and to be avoided if possible. It is indeed death but it is beneficent and needed. It is this realisation of the passing of a civilisation which gives rise to the recurrent and foreboding cry, "This is the death of civilisation; it must not be"; "This is the end of the order, and the old order must be saved"; "This is the destruction of the old and loved values, and it must not be permitted."

That humanity is bringing about this needed change in unnecessary, cruel and painful ways is indeed true, just as it is true today that human beings by their wrong thinking, foolish habits of physical living and undesirable emotional attitudes do precipitate a final, physical breakdown and eventually death. Nevertheless, for the progress of the soul of the individual and the soul of humanity, death is inevitable, good and necessary; it is also a practice with which we are all most familiar in our own experience and in watching it in others. But we need to remember that the worst death of all (as far as humanity is concerned) would be if a form of civilisation or a body form became static and eternal; if the old order never altered and the old values were never transmuted into higher and better ones, that would indeed be a disaster.

We need to bear in mind also that the forces of destruction or death are two-fold: first, the rapidly emerging and developing life with its demand for more room for expression and fuller experience, and its spiritual aspiration for change and progress; and secondly, the reactionary forces and the conservative attitudes which adhere to the well-known and the familiar, and which hate the new, the untried and the unknown. Both of these produce the great and divine transition from the past into the future, and from the old into the new, from experience into fruition and then into experience again. The realities are eternal and undying; the forms are ephemeral and temporary; the soul is persistent and deathless; the form is changing and doomed to die. The processes of evolution have in the past and will in the future prove successful in bringing forms to birth, to maturity and to death.

But (and this is the interesting and significant point)

humanity is for the first time *aware of process*. It has for the first time chosen intelligently to observe what is going on and to relate it to experience and to environment. This in itself indicates a stage of true and much to be desired development. Reasoning, analysis and the presentation of differing viewpoints are going on in every country on a large scale with varying results, based on differences of temperament, of tradition, of development and of training.

This stage of death and of birth (for the two are proceeding simultaneously) can be easily grasped by the esotericist as he studies the world war in its two distinctive periods: 1914 to 1918, and 1939 until 1942. The first stage (if you could see the situation as it truly is) was most definitely the death stage; the second stage, in which we now find ourselves, is literally the stage of birth—the birth pangs of the new order and of the new civilisation through which humanity's sense of life can express itself. The mother dies in order that the child may live; the form is sacrificed to the life. But today, the form aspect, the Mother or matter aspect, is dying consciously, and just as consciously the child, the infant civilisation, is coming into being. This is the new thing and it is in this that we are all participating. It is the *death of the personality of humanity and the coming in of the soul*.

Such a dying is ever a painful process. Pain has always been the purifying agent, employed by the Lords of Destiny, to bring about liberation. The accumulated pain of the present war and the inherited pain of the earlier stage (begun in 1914) is bringing about a salutary and changing world consciousness. The Lord of Pain has descended from His throne and is treading the ways of earth today, bringing distress, agony and terror to those who cannot interpret His ends, but bringing also a re-stimulation of the instinct to self-preservation which—in its higher aspect—is the instinct to immortality; it tends to focus humanity's attention upon the life aspect and not upon the form. The names of the Lords of Karma signify, symbolically and from the angle of their inner meaning, Relationship, Enlightenment, Pain and Return. Ponder on this. They are all peculiarly active at this time, and in their activity lies the hope of humanity.

Ancient Karmic Events

It is not my intention to explain or elaborate the subject of Karma. This occult yet fundamentally exoteric theme, the Law of Cause and Effect, evokes a general recognition when called by this name. When called the Law of Karma, it is immediately regarded as mysterious, Oriental and new. Called (as it sometimes is) the Law of Retribution, an entirely erroneous connotation has become attached to it. Today, the karma of humanity is descending upon it. I would remind you, however, that the continuous emphasis laid upon the malevolent aspects of karma conveys a wrong impression and negates the full grasp of the truth. There is as much good karma as there is bad; even in the present world situation, the good karma emanating from the soul of humanity balances the evil which comes from the material aspect and is continuously over-emphasised. It is the rhythm of matter in contradistinction to the rhythm of the soul, and these constitute the initiating causes of the present conflict, both in individual lives and in the general world situation. When this is properly grasped, the true picture may emerge in your hearts and minds with greater clarity.

In my effort to make clear the picture, I shall have to overlook many essential details; I shall also be forced to take the always debatable position of making statements which cannot be checked and which find their sole arguments (as far as the average thinker is concerned) in deduction from the effects produced by causes that do not appear to the occultly unenlightened. In time to come, man will develop that mental attitude which will consider causes of greater importance than effects; he will then learn to consider with care the first steps taken in initiating any line of action, pondering upon and deducing the probable effects before committing himself to any specific deed. Only through pain, error and consequent price-paying will this salutary stage be reached.

Today, all that is taking place is due, first of all, to the essential duality of man; in the second place, it is due to certain major lines of cleavage which were brought about by this essential dualism in an early stage of human history, and thirdly, to the growing tendency towards synthesis which the inflow of the Shamballa force is producing at this time. This is the simplest statement I find it possible to make anent this complex problem. With broad generalities I cover the past, indicate the effects which are now being experienced in the present, and forecast the future.

It was the coming into incarnation of the spiritually self-conscious human being which is the inciting cause of the present conflict. Had the sons of God not "come in unto the daughters of men" (which is the Biblical and symbolic way of expressing the great relationship between spirit and matter which was established in the human kingdom), had the spiritual entities which are humanity itself not taken unto themselves material forms, and had the positive spiritual element not attached itself to the negative material aspect, the present world conflict would not be taking place. But the divine plan of evolution was based upon the production of this relationship between spiritually conscious man and the form aspect, and thus the great Law of Duality came into action, bringing about the "fall of the angels," as they descended from their sinless and free state of existence in order to develop full divine awareness upon earth, through the medium of material incarnation and the use of the principle of mind. This was the divine plan, emanating from the Mind of God and swept into activity and progressive unfoldment by an act of His Will. At its inception, there took place the original "war in the heavens," when the sons of God who responded to the divine urge to experience, to serve and to sacrifice, separated themselves from the sons of God who responded to no such inspiration but who chose to stay in their original and high state of being. To this truth, Christ Himself bore witness in the story of the Prodigal Son and his relationship to his elder brother, who had not left the Father's home. It is obvious, is it not, from this parable, where the approbation of the Father lay; a careful study of this story and an intuitive understanding of its implications may evoke some day a response to the "sin of experience," as it has been called, and a comprehension of the two major laws governing the process: the Law of Evolution and the Law of Rebirth. Here lies the prime initiating cause of what is taking place today.

The second cause arose slowly out of the first. Matter and spirit, focussed in the human family and expressing their basic qualities and essential nature, were eternally in conflict. In the early stages and during the long Lemurian cycle, infant humanity steadily evolved and yet in spite of this the lines of cleavage, though present, were not recognised. The latent spark of mind served only to bring a relative enlightenment to the five senses and their purely physical application. The physical life was strong; the deductive or self-registering life was practically nil. The life of humanity was then focussed within the physical body, thus fortifying and stimulating the animal nature and developing the physical organism and the various internal organs through the unfoldment of the five senses; man became primarily a selfish and a fighting animal with, however, at times, vague tendencies towards something dimly sensed as better and with moments of high grade desire which was not aspiration and the urge to progress, as we know it, but their embryonic forms.

It is not possible for modern man to vision or understand such a state of consciousness, for he has left it too far behind. The focus of the life force was also in the region of the adrenal glands, producing animal courage and resistance to shock. But the dualism of man's essential nature was, as always, present and the lines of cleavage gradually appeared; slowly yet steadily, the pioneering souls (a very small minority) shifted their consciousness gradually higher into the solar plexus and a recognition of the factor of desire for that which was material and a capacity for emotional reaction began to develop. Hitherto, in Lemurian times, desire and instinct were identical. Ponder on this, for it is interesting because it concerns a state of consciousness of which modern man knows practically nothing. But, in Atlantean times, the lines of demarcation between what constituted purely physical life and that which—though still material—could be the goal of effort and thus acquired, began to control the purely animal nature; man began to be acquisitive and to surround himself with that which he wanted. The lines of cleavage between the instinctual animal and acquisitive man began to be more clearly defined.

Gradually the mental element unfolded among these pioneers just as the intuitive element is today unfolding among the mental types; men began to acquire some form of mental perception and to bring what little mind they had to the processes of increasing their material possessions. The stage of civilisation (which is basically a recognition of group relation) began. A period of urban existence superseded that of a pure nomadic and agricultural existence. Men began to congregate together for their greater material comfort and protection, and the rhythmic processes of concentration and their world-wide extension began. These cycles are similar to the inbreathing and the outbreathing of the physical organism of man. Some day a study will be made of these basic and controlling factors of human existence, dispersion or decentralisation, and community life or the expression of the herd instinct on a higher or lower turn of the spiral of existence. The past few hundred years have seen a major problem arise in the present tendency of humanity to collect together in great cities and to congregate in vast herds, leaving the countryside denuded of its population and creating serious problems of sustenance, of health and also of crime. Right before our eyes this rhythm is today changing and a serious problem is being solved; cities are being evacuated and—as men and women are driven forth for one reason or another into the country —the lords of evolution are forcing the breaking up of the rhythm of concentration and substituting for it the rhythm of dispersion. This will do much for the race and will facilitate the unfoldment of a subjective synthesis which will greatly enrich humanity and give new values to living.

The lines of cleavage between the animal, instinctual nature and some form of desire (embryonic aspiration) steadily grew during Atlantean times and this early civilisation began to demonstrate its own note and to set new standards of material comfort and of selfish control on an increasingly large scale as the urban existence developed. It is perhaps difficult for us to visualise a world as densely populated then as is the modern world but so it was. The animal nature, being dominant, the tendency was towards sexual relationship and the production of large families, just as it is among the lower orders in our civilised areas today, for the peasantry and the slum dwellers produce more children than do the intelligentsia. In those far-off times, the only people who had any true measure of intelligence were the disciples and initiates; they guided and guarded infant humanity, much as modern parents guide and guard their children, and as the state assumes responsibility for the welfare of the nation. The Hierarchy was, in those days, present upon the earth as the priest-kings and they acted as focal points of attractive energy, drawing to themselves those in whom the more intangible values were slowly assuming a vague control, thus making the lines of cleavage between materialism and spirituality still more clear and definite.

We must remember that the spirituality of that time was of a very different quality from that which now goes under that name. It was in the nature of an aspiration towards a sensed hereafter, for a satisfying beauty and for emotional completion. There was no thought—as we know thought—in this attitude but only a reaching out after a sensed *unattainable* and for that which was desirable. This was fostered in the people by the Hierarchy through the gift of various inventions and by the use of the instinctual masses of men in building great and beautiful cities and stupendous structures, the remnants of which persist until today. This was done under the expert guidance of the initiates and adepts who employed their knowledge of the nature of matter and energy to produce much that today man is gropingly endeavouring to discover and make possible. All that the modern processes of civilisation have made possible, and much more than that which today comes under the name of scientific discovery were known in old Atlantis, but they were not developed by men themselves but given to them as a free gift, much as people today give to a child beautiful and wonderful things which the child uses and enjoys but which he does not understand in any way. Great and beautiful cities, full of temples and great buildings (of which the Chaldean and Babylonian remains are the degenerate remnants, and the modern skyscraper the child) were everywhere to be found. Most of our modern scientific knowledge was possessed by these priest-kings and constituted in the eyes of the masses a form of wonderful magic. Sanitation, hygiene, means of transportation and air machines were developed and of a very high order; these were not the result however of man's achievement but gifts from the Hierarchy, developed or constructed under a wise guidance. There was command of air and water because the guides of the race knew how to control and master the forces of nature and of the elements, but none of it was the result of human understanding, knowledge or effort. The minds of men were undeveloped and not adequate to such a task, any more than is the mind of a little child.

The cleavage between the two groups (the one expressing the forces of materialism and the other the energy of light) grew gradually wider until towards the close of the Atlantean Age it was so wide, and the lines of demarcation between the two schools of life and thought were so clear, that a crisis was precipitated in the then civilised world of which the present conflict is a definite effect. Let us also hope that it constitutes a climax which will never again occur. Then took place the great war between the Lords of Form and the Lords of Being, or between the Forces of Matter and the Great White Lodge. A careful study of volume two of *The Secret Doctrine* will prove enlightening to students, if they will study with particular care pages 275-466. To our understanding, this account may seem vague and obscure, but the issues at the time were clear. The Forces of Light triumphed because the Hierarchy was forced to intervene potently, and, with the aid of certain great Lives extraneous to our planetary life, They brought the Atlantean civilisation to an abrupt end after a long period of chaos and disaster. This took place through the medium of a culminating catastrophe which wiped hundreds of thousands of human beings off the face of the earth. This historical event has been preserved for us in the universal legend of the great flood.

Those who survived are symbolically spoken of in the Bible as those who were saved in Noah's ark, and in the ancient writings it is expressed in the following terms:

"Like as a dragon snake uncoils slowly its body, so the sons of men, led on by the Sons of Wisdom, opened their folds and spreading out like a running stream of sweet waters . . . . Many of the faint-hearted among them perished on their way. But most were saved."

A close study of the tale as given in *The Secret Doctrine* will reveal the state of immature development (from the angle of our modern standards) and of the basically emotional and physical focus of the humanity of the period; it will show also man's magical ability to subdue and control the subhuman kingdoms and the elemental forces of the planet. These are two angles which have been but little studied.

Emphasis has, however, been rightly placed upon divine interference and intervention; this succeeded in salvaging an ethically sound minority (the word "spiritual" would not yet apply, except relatively) and in destroying those who were wrongly focussed or oriented and, therefore, dedicated to the life of material aspiration and perception.

This nucleus which was saved, formed the basis of our present root race, the Aryan. The whole theme of the *Old Testament* is built around the development and growth of this nucleus. Symbolically speaking, the inhabitants of the ark and their descendants and the Jewish race stand for the salvaged remnant of humanity—salvaged in spite of themselves and in face of stupendous difficulties by the Great White Lodge.

Two points warrant attention here. The first and least important from the standpoint of the soul is the disappearance off the earth of practically all signs of the wonderful Atlantean civilisation except for those few archeological treasures which intrigue and interest modern research workers, plus those dim memories of ancient scientific achievement which lead the modern student to investigation and invention, and which incite him to discovery and the production of what we call the triumphs of modern science.

The second point is that for the good of humanity, the Hierarchy withdrew into the background, leaving man to find his own way out of the mirage and illusion of materialism in right ways and eventually to bring to an end the ancient cleavages. War must be brought to its final consummation and expression with a view to its final discarding as a means of arriving at desired ends.

The Modern Era

I would like to pause here and remind you of one or two points which should be recognised as we approach this modern era in which all these culminating effects are taking place. Let me state them concisely and clearly.

The lines of cleavage between materialism and spirituality (as we now understand the terms) have become increasingly clear. Two things have tended to bring this about. First, the pronouncement of the Ten Commandments. These, though negative in their form and dogmatic in their attitude, have made the issues and the required attitudes adequately clear. Owing to the relatively low stage of the universal human intelligence at the time that they were given (for the Biblical dates are not correct and the date of their pronouncement is far older than is thought) they were expressed by the formula, "Thou shalt not," thus turning human attention to the material expression of material tendencies. In days to come, the Ten Commandments will be expressed in a reversed form of which the Sermon on the Mount and the Beatitudes are the embryonic form.

Second, the Hierarchy withdrew in order that humanity, on reaching maturity and years of discretion, should not be handicapped and hindered by coercion and undue safeguarding but should express its major divine characteristics. Of these, free will and the discriminating use of the mind are the outstanding qualities. There was no free will in Atlantean days. There is a tendency to free will (note that term) today and we call it liberty and independence, freedom of thought and the right of the individual to determine the issues which control or should control the group of which he is a part. These are all attributes and qualities of free will but not the divine principle of free will per se. Of that we know as yet but little. Only the disciples of the world and the initiates know the true significance and implications of freedom of choice, and the right use of the will, and this because they are motivated by group good and the need of the majority.

The test to which humanity was to be subjected and which is today the controlling factor was whether—given mental development and knowledge—it would consecrate that knowledge and its scientific and mental attainment to group good or to selfish ends, to material issues or to spiritual incentives and impulses. This ancient conflict has now been carried through into another field of human expression, that of the mind and—as the race has progressed and the personalities of human beings have reached a high stage of integration and achievement—the conflict has become acute, the issues clearer and the ranging of the opponents into two clearly defined groups is now so complete that the final struggle has become possible.

Intelligent appreciation of the situation and a general capacity to present to the mind the underlying conditions has now been achieved by the bulk of the intelligent people upon the planet and, though the point of view is necessarily coloured by national traditions, inherited ideas and policies as well as by environmental control and bias, the race has gone a long way towards its final emancipation. There is, therefore, a certain measure of free will displayed, and this constitutes an entirely new factor and a most satisfactory development. But I would remind you of a most important point and that is that the masses of the people—the middle classes, the bourgeoisie and the proletariat (I use these words in their general sense and simply because of their significance and meaning)—are still victims of authority, of control, and remain relatively unthinking and childlike. This means that the true conflict is between a small minority to whom the issues are illuminatingly clear and who have definitely ranged themselves on one side or other of the embattled forces. A mere handful of men, the direct descendants or rather the reincarnations of the leaders in the ancient Atlantean conflict, are now on earth, directing the forces of light or of darkness and bringing into being a direct line-up of millions of men whose will is that of their leaders.

The lines of cleavage have grown steadily until now they can be expressed in terms of a humanity which is oriented towards the higher spiritual and altruistic values and whose keynotes are sacrifice, group good and world understanding, and those whose focus is predominantly material and whose aims are selfish, animated by ambition and the spirit of acquisition.

It was the acuteness of this situation, and the wide extent of the cleavage, which induced the watching Hierarchy to permit a direct inflow of the Shamballa force (in spite of its attendant risks) to pour into the world. The objective was to stimulate the free will of the masses; the result upon them has been relatively good as it has led to the formulation and expression of the great world ideologies—Fascism,

Democracy and Communism as well as that peculiarly distorted blend of Fascism and Communism which goes by the name of Hitlerism or Nazism. All these ideologies are fostered by the desire of the masses for the betterment of the condition in which the populace in any country lives and it has become focussed, expressive and creative by the force of the Shamballa influence. But another result of this inflow of the will-to-power has been to stimulate a certain group of outstanding personalities in many lands so that they have assumed control of the masses and can thus determine the policies and methods—religious, political and social —of the different nations. In every nation a relatively small group of people decide all important issues and determine all major national activities. This they do either by force, terror and deception or by persuasion, fair words and the application of ideological motives. Of this situation in the world the Lords of Destiny are availing themselves in order to bring the ancient conflict to an end and so enable humanity to pass into the new Aquarian Age relatively free and with a clearer understanding of right human aims, right relationships and man's predestined future.

It will serve no purpose for me to trace the relation of the present world conflict and the present world leaders to the conflict and the leaders in Atlantean times. Suffice it to say that many of the same personalities (on a higher turn of the spiral) are again playing their various parts in the great drama. It is no service to you and to your mental grip upon the situation for me to emphasise the details of that great war and its modern correspondences; it is of no value for me ·to compare the old methods and the modern usages whereby one side or the other carries forward the struggle for supremacy. You are in no position to verify what I say or to check the accuracy of my statements. The point which is, however, of major importance is for you to arrive at a clear understanding of what is at stake and a just appreciation of the values involved and also a correct grasp of the ideals animating the two groups of opponents.

In Atlantean days, it was stated that the battle was between the Forces of Darkness (the so-called "Black Lodge of Adepts") and the Forces of Light (the so-called Great White Lodge, the Hierarchy of Masters). That was then approximately true, for the conflict was between two small groups and the masses of the people were simply the blind and miserable victims of the fight and of the situation.

Today, it is not possible to make such a clear distinction between the forces engaged, nor is it properly admissible. No nation or group of nations can be classed in a broad generalisation as either black or white. Bear this in mind. Only those with no vision and an intolerant and prejudiced spirit will speak thus. All nations have within them those who belong in their thousands to the category of those who are swayed by the Forces of Light and who, therefore, respond normally and easily to the concept of goodwill, to the desire for right relationship between all men and to the ideal of true international and world understanding. In all nations there are those to whom this position makes no appeal at all and they are still in darkness and blinded to the true issues. This is a statement of fact. Those who seek to see the establishment of goodwill and understanding are in the majority but are—as I pointed out in earlier writings —relatively futile to control the situation as yet or to force their leaders to follow the mass will-to-good. They are either inspired or protected by the Hierarchy of Light and it is with them that the task of stimulating the free expression of this goodwill must be carried forward when the conflict ends.

As for the other group, they are those who through inclination or ancient karma are the descendants of the Lords of darkness; their actions and ideals make possible the activity of the forces of materialism. I would have you note that phrasing. Even the most dangerous of them are nevertheless conscious of some form or another of idealism, but they are misguided and full of response to the will-to-power (power upon the physical plane and through the medium of form activity). This is stimulated by the inflow of the Shamballa energy. Because of these reactions and tendencies, they constitute focal points for those Lives and

Energies which are inherent in matter itself and whose influence and work are dedicated to the preservation of form, and of *that which is*. They endeavour constantly to negate the new and to hold back the evolution and development of the human consciousness. Forget not that the real issue is in the field of consciousness and that the struggle is between form and the life within the form, and between progress, leading to the liberation of the human spirit, and reactionary activity, leading to the imprisonment of the human consciousness and the restriction of its free expression.

I would pause here and solemnly beg you not to make the lines of cleavage wider by placing yourself, and all who follow your form of ideology, upon the side of the Forces of Light and all other people and their ideologies, with which you may not agree, upon the side of the Forces of Darkness. The issue is, in the last analysis, the right to express the will-to-good, the right to express human relationships, untrammelled by territorial barriers and national habits of thought; it involves the right and the felt necessity to shew love to all beings and thus stamp out all hate and separateness. It concerns the right of all nations to live at peace with their neighbours and harmoniously with each other and to express the true and subjective synthesis of humanity, and not place national possessions, frontiers, culture, power and ambition before the general good and the happiness of the world of men. This is the real and underlying issue. All the national challenges and patriotic calls are simply the attempts of the leaders everywhere to hold the people to a particular line of thought and of action. To make the world safe for democracy, to gain room to live, to defend the rights of little nations, to preserve the balance of power, to meet force with force, to restore ancient and historical boundaries, to impose some culture deemed desirable, to prevent economic destruction, to conserve national stakes and interests are all the talking points of the leaders today. But the real issue is the intangible one of Direction. Which way will humanity go?

Will it go the way of selflessness, expressed in a willingness to act always in the interests of all, thus promoting world understanding and world unity, or the way of selfishness and aggression, expressed in an intense nationalism, thus sacrificing the true and larger values of liberty, independence and freedom to think. This *selfishness may show itself through active aggression or an active neutrality.* Those nations who participate in no way in this struggle will lose much and—enhancing their own selfish struggle and clouding the real issue in beautiful words—will help to prolong the struggle and hold back their own people from useful opportunity.

I would point out here also that as in all families, business and organisations there are those who are the focal points of authority and the designers of the planned activities, so within that group or organised body which goes by the name of humanity there are similar focal points or those who plan, direct and produce the outer happenings and events. They are in the period of *personality* achievement—that time in which human beings, having achieved integration and a blended expression of feeling and perception and mind, are actively and effectively working upon the physical plane. These focal points are used to bring about two major changes in the world; the first is the fusion and blending of peoples and minorities so that co-ordinated empires and cultural nations are appearing everywhere and, secondly, the changing of frontiers and the altering of boundaries so that a complete re-adjustment of the map of the world in Asia, Europe and Africa can take place.

It will be apparent to you that three major methods or modes of producing these fusions can be noted. Great Britain, the United States of America and the Union of Socialist Soviet Republics (the U.S.S.R.) are working out the principle of federation, of relation and of the fusion of bodies into concentrated wholes, responding to the same inspiration but employing their own specialised methods to bring about the desired ends. Be not surprised by my including Russia in this triplicity. Their ideology is fundamentally as sound as that in the other groups, but the difference lies in the factors of personality and the mode of applying the ideology. The control of powerful and dangerous personalities, and the use of the methods of force and cruelty have been avoided in the first two groups of nations, and the reason is based upon the different source of the inspiration producing the effects. Another reason is to be found in the placing of power in the hands of those who are historically unprepared to rule and of those whose past unfoldment has as yet brought them only to the nursery stage of evolution.

Nevertheless in these three groups there is much of interest to be noted. One of them, Great Britain, represents a fusion, the foundations of which have been laid in a long historical *past* of preparation for government; another, that of the U.S.A. represents a fusion which is unfolding and developing in *the present* which is new in its experiments, though employing factors from every nation in Europe; the U.S.S.R. in its turn represents a coming fusion or *future* synthesis. In these three, you have an interesting and immediate expression of the three divine aspects, each of which inspires and colours the embryonic civilisation. Great Britain expresses the will-to-power but on account of age and experience, dearly bought, this is today mellowed by justice and a growing understanding of human need. This, in its turn, is the result of the control for many centuries in the past by *the aristocracy*, with its paternalism, conservatism and its method of slow adjustment. The U.S.A. expresses the will-to-love, which shows itself in an ability to absorb vastly divergent elements and yet to present equal opportunity to all. This is brought about very largely because the control is, in this federation of states, in the hands of *the bourgeoisie*, with its financial goals, its power to determine living conditions, and its quick and sympathetic touch upon life. Its method is not that of slow adjustment but of quick assimilation. It is in that country also that people are most sensitive to the influence of the Hierarchy. The U.S.S.R. expresses the will-to-create and to produce new conditions and a new order—planned and determined and foreseen. This has been brought about through cruelty very often, by a willingness to compromise and to change or lower the original ideal. This, in its turn, is brought about by the activity of *the proletariat* with its inability to govern, its desire to retaliate, and its ignorance of tradition and of inherited procedures.

A most interesting experiment is, therefore, working out in these three groups of interrelated elements and differing national ideals. The U.S.S.R. will eventually place its emphasis and direct its major interest upon Asia, bringing about great changes on that continent, as far as the Pacific The other, Great Britain, through its successful demonstration of the principle of federation, can affect major changes in Europe if there is an awakened insight, a true and sympathetic justice and wise patience. The U.S.A. has a similar task to perform for the Americas, calling for statesmanship of a high order and a spirit of understanding.

It will also be apparent to you if you have rightly understood the above suggestions that the *Shamballa* force is working through that community of federated nations called the British Empire and is expressing the will-towards-synthesis and the will to just and legal procedure. It is the force of the *Hierarchy* which can express itself increasingly through the United States of America, for an intuitive recognition of subjective realities and a real sense of the higher values can and frequently do control the impulses governing this group of federated states. The will-to-be of *Humanity* with its almost extravagant emphasis upon human values and the will-to-rule creatively is the contribution of the U.S.S.R., that great federation of republics. Thus the influence of the three great world centres about which I have earlier written can be seen expressing itself through these three groups of nations. At the same time, the Shamballa force is active in all of them, for it produces federation and synthesis. Its first great expression or demonstration of the spirit of fusion took place in the 18th and 19th centuries, and led to the formation of such countries as Italy and Germany which were created out of many smaller states, duchies and kingdoms. A history of the trend towards fusion in the modern world would prove a most illuminating study. It would be found that the first faint indications were felt around 1575 A.D. This was due to the fact that permission for the inflow of this force was given when demanded at the Centennial Conference of the Hierarchy, held in 1425. I referred to this conference in my earlier writings.*

In the second group of changing ideologies and of reaction to mass need, you will find France, Germany, Italy, Spain and Portugal, all of whom have altered their ancient policies, changed their forms of government and reacted gradually and slowly to the Shamballa force. They have, however, reacted to that force through the medium of certain great and outstanding personalities who were peculiarly sensitive to the will-to-power and the will-to-change and who (during the past 150 years) have altered the character of their national life, and emphasised increasingly the wider human values. The men who inspired the initiating French revolution; the great conqueror, Napoleon; Bismarck, the creator of a nation; Mussolini, the regenerator of his people; Hitler who lifted a distressed people upon his shoulders; Lenin, the idealist, Stalin and Franco are all expressions of the Shamballa force and of certain little understood energies. These have wrought significant changes in their day and generation and altered the face of Europe, incidentally affecting Asia and conditioning attitudes and policies in America.

The results even when dangerous and terrible, have developed two vital characteristics in humanity. One has been the widespread development of the discriminating faculty, and secondly, a tendency to dispersion with its

* *A Treatise on White Magic,* pp. 401-433.
   A Treatise on the Seven Rays, Vol. I (*Esoteric Psychology*), pp. 170-189.

consequences of diffusing civilised and cultural values and the diverse gifts of the many people to the world soul. The drift of people to the colonies from Great Britain, the drift of the people from every nation in Europe to America, North and South, the dispersal of people within national boundaries as the result of war and expediency such as the evacuation of cities has brought about today, the removal of people out of Italy and of groups of people within Russia, and the constant moving onwards of the wandering Jews indicate a breaking down, upon a world-wide scale, of all outer boundaries and the institution of a process of blending and amalgamation such as the world has never seen before. It constitutes an educational system of untold value, leading as it does to the constant necessity to readjust viewpoints, to change modes of living, to intermarriage and so-called illicit relations. The outer change is producing an inner synthesis and outer dispersion, and cleavages are working out interiorly in closer relations and a more tolerant spirit of understanding. The power to consider, to choose, to think and to discriminate is rapidly developing among all classes everywhere as a result of the many cataclysmic happenings, the presentation of many changing circumstances and the many points of view and theories of government and of religion; these grow naturally out of new contacts and the rapid presentation of events through the medium of the press and the radio.

It is this that is of importance from the standpoint of evolution and the growth of the world consciousness. The physical plane happenings are incidental and of no permanent lasting power.

The physical plane events and precipitations are carried forward and made possible through focal points of energy who are the world dictators, the world statesmen, and the outstanding human beings in all lands as well as by groups which are actively working in every country for their own ends or—as is more often the case—under the influence of some group ideal or wisdom plus personal ambition, personal will-to-power and personal aggrandisement. We call these people dictators, demagogues, inspired leaders, or just and wise men, according to our peculiar ideology, tradition, attitudes to our fellowmen and our particular political, economic and religious training. But all these leaders are simply human beings and like other men— idealistic, mistaken, lovers of their country, egoists, impressionable, foolish, cunning, powerful, focussed on some goal or ambition, with clear vision and at the same time myopic reactions, cruel or wise as the case may be—but, in the last analysis, highly developed personalities. They are being used to engineer great and needed changes and to alter the face of civilisation. The wrong methods employed and the evil things done are the fault of humanity as a whole, and of the habits of thought which have made mankind selfish and cruel and cause this great and universal spirit of the will-to-change to manifest so powerfully and cruelly.

Blame not the personalities involved or the men who produce these events before which we stand today bewildered and appalled. They are only the product of the past and the victims of the present. At the same time, they are the agents of destiny, the creators of the new order and the initiators of the new civilisation; they are the destroyers of what must be destroyed before humanity can go forward along the Lighted Way. *They are the embodiment of the personality of humanity.* Blame yourselves, therefore, for what is today transpiring and seek not to evade responsibility by placing it upon the shoulders of spectacular men or any statesmen, dictator or upon any group. Look not to one person or to one group of persons and accuse them of causing the present world condition. Look not also to any one person or group to bring liberation or to find a solution of the world problem. That is for humanity itself to do. Humanity must take action and will do so, when the right time comes. To recognise joint responsibility, joint mistakes, ancient errors of judgment, wrong attitudes and habits of thought, world-wide selfish purpose and intent, a universal spirit of aggression which, down the ages, has influenced first one nation and then another, the tendency last century to crystallise and become static, the reactionary forces on every hand—these are universal qualities and no nation and no race is free of guilt or has entirely clean hands. Also, no one national group is purely wrong and evil or purely good and unselfish. There are mixed motives everywhere. Nationalism, aggression, selfishness and cruelty in all countries face a desire for world understanding, peaceful relations, and an unselfish and beneficent spirit also in all countries. The Forces of Light find their adherents and their workers in every country though some are subjected to greater handicaps in expression than others. So also do the Forces of Materialism. And in between these two great groups stand the masses—waiting for the emergence of fresh opportunity and new revelations.

It is the universality of these conditions and the clearcut issues that have made this period one of planetary opportunity and planetary initiation. Initiation is essentially a moving out from under ancient controls into the control of more spiritual and increasingly higher values. Initiation is an expansion of consciousness which leads to a growing recognition of the inner realities. It is equally the recognition of a renewed sense of the need for change and the wise engineering of these needed changes so that real progress can be made; the consciousness is expanded and becomes more generously and divinely inclusive and there is a fresh and more potent control by the soul as it assumes increasingly the direction of the life of the individual, of a nation and of the world.

In the last analysis, and from the standpoint of the Hierarchy, the present conflict between the personality of humanity (expressing the material values as the dominating factor in life experience) and the soul of humanity (expressing the spiritual values as the dominating factor in human affairs) is identical with the conflict which takes place within a human being's consciousness when he has reached the stage of discipleship and is faced with the problem of the pairs of opposites. This conflict is expressed in many ways according to the point of view and the background of thought. It can be called the conflict between Christ and anti-Christ but not as those who usually employ those phrases understand them. No one nation is expressive of the spirit of anti-Christ, just as no one nation expresses the spirit of Christ. Christ and anti-Christ are the dualities of spirituality and materialism, both in the individual and in humanity as a whole. Or you can speak of God and the Devil with the same basic implications. For what is man himself but an expression of divinity (God) in a material form (the Devil), and what is matter but the medium through which divinity must eventually manifest in all its glory? But when that takes place, matter will no longer be a controlling factor but simply a medium of expression.

The battle is therefore on between the form side of life and the soul. The Dweller on the Threshold (the threshold of divinity, my brothers) is humanity itself with its ancient habits of thought, its selfishness and greed. Humanity today stands face to face with the Angel of the Presence—the Soul Whose nature is love and light and inclusive understanding. The great problem today is which of these two will emerge the victor out of the conflict, and which of these two great agencies of life will determine humanity's future and indicate the way which humanity will decide to go.

The issues at stake are clear to all right-thinking people. Intolerance and an intense national pride and self-satisfaction can blind men to the facts of the case today, but there are enough people thinking clearly to make the future of right decision more probable than at any previous time in the history of the race.

Preparation for World Goodwill

The causes of the present war are ancient. This historical sequence of the predisposing factors can be clearly traced in the exoteric records of all nations as well as in the esoteric records of the Hierarchy. The inherent human qualities which have led to the development of the present war are well known. All who are conscious of and observers of the war within their own natures, between personality selfishness and the selflessness of the soul, are aware of the implications and the correspondences. Where then lies the solution? What must be done to arrest the fires of hate and of aggression, of revenge and of fear? What also must be done to prepare for that time when the rebuilding of the world of men and the inauguration of the new and better civilisation arrives? With this we might now briefly deal.

As regards active participation in the work to be done in preparing the world for the expression of goodwill, there is little to be done of an active exoteric nature at this time; it is necessary to wait with patience and to see what is going to happen and along what lines the activity of the nations will run. But there is very much to be done of an esoteric and a preparatory nature and it is this which I seek to impress upon your minds.

Up to date and in spite of appearances, the Forces of Light are victorious and are definitely holding things steady. It is for this reason that nothing has yet quenched the spirit of goodwill and of sympathetic understanding which exists among the peoples of all nations, not excluding Germany; this has been the outstanding significant characteristic of the present conflict. There is little hate or vindictiveness to be found, and this fact constitutes the difference between this war and the last, in 1914. It indicates a triumph for the Forces of Light and in it lies the hope of the future. It is here, however, that the time factor must be considered, for a prolonged war may cause a change in this desirable attitude, and much drastic experience may produce deep psychological and unavoidable changes in human thought and action. This must be consciously offset. It has not yet occurred but it could happen and if it does much pain, terror, fearful anticipation, suffering and the agony entailed by the sight of suffering might eventually turn this goodwill into a dynamic spirit of hate and revenge unless it is definitely and consciously offset. Groups who are adhering to the principles of the Forces of Light, who are bending every effort to end the spirit of aggression and to rid the world of the focal points for material influence and power, must yet carry forward the task of binding men and women of every nation together in a spirit of loving understanding; they must interpret nation to nation in terms of brotherhood and of the new order.

This is no easy thing to do at this time. The astral or emotional bodies of human beings (which constitute the astral body of humanity as a whole) are today in a state of chaos, and are swept by ancient desires, ancient and deep-seated selfish attitudes and by ancient hatreds. The task is also complicated by the activity of the mental processes of man which is characterised by pronounced and developed illusions, by separative attitudes and by specious arguments. But there are, at the same time, enough people in the world who are responsive to the spirit of goodwill, of tolerant understanding, and animated by a desire for permanent right human relations.

I have earlier suggested to you * that it should be possible to have—at a later date—a world-wide recognition of a Day of Forgetfulness, of Forgiveness and of Fulfilment of the Biblical injunction to "forget the things which lie behind and to press forward" into the New Age, the new relationships and the new civilisation. For that time we can all begin to plan, and to work for that psychological moment wherein this idea can be presented. It will come immediately after the cessation of hostilities. But today and in every land, where possible, the peoples must be educated in this expression of human synthesis and human interrelation.

It involves, however, an emphasising of the values to which I have referred earlier in this article. This is human-

---

* *A Treatise on the Seven Rays*, Vol. II (*Esoteric Psychology*), page 647.

ity's joint responsibility because of humanity's general mistakes, and the ancient wrong attitudes and controls. It involves, consequently, a stepping down from the position of critics and assigners of responsibility to that of a joint shouldering of the stupendous task of changing present conditions and of instituting those reversals of policy which will make a united world order possible and beautiful. This is no easy task. It is one which calls all men and women of goodwill in the world today and challenges them to prepare whilst the conflict is on for what can be done when it is over.

I have given much in the past which can provide a platform of objectives and of methods. Nothing that I have outlined is now abrogated; only fulfilment is postponed. For seven critical years, it lay in the hands of the spiritually minded men of the world, in the hands of the Churches in all lands and of the men of goodwill and of the world aspirants so to work that the present conflict could have been avoided. But the spirit of Christ was lost in clerical organisation; emphasis has been laid upon technical theology; the spirit of goodwill was not expressed dynamically and practically, but theoretically and negatively; the aspirants of the world had no true sense of values but were content to give a little time to the spiritual life and to other people, but much time was lost in individual, personal aims. A spirit of inertia settled down upon the better inclined and upon the more understanding people; nothing that we could do served to arouse them to powerful action or to sacrifice personal temporary values to the lasting and universal values. The individual remained more important to himself than did the good of the whole.

Be not over-distressed, my brothers. You are not alone in this but part of a vast number, if that is to you any real satisfaction.

But a renewed opportunity lies in front of you and it is of a practical nature, falling into definite spheres of work and of planned activity. You are asked, first of all, to prepare for the great opportunity which will come at the close of this conflict, and

1. To explain clearly to all people the cause which produces the opportunity and which is dedicated to the ending of the present state of affairs.
2. To engineer some dramatic and universal event which will serve as the inspiration and the inauguration of the new era of goodwill and of right human relations.

Secondly, to keep up a steady process of right thought, right interpretation of current events and a right preparation whilst the war lasts, so that any weakening of the gained spirit of goodwill can be immediately offset, and so that understanding can grow in potency and not suffer obscuration. In order to bring this about, the following activities are suggested beginning with those which concern the individual worker.

1. A close personal watch over every word said or written, so that nothing said or written by any of you will have in it hate or bias of the wrong kind and your minds and hearts will be kept clear of all undesirable reactions. This is the personal and practical thing to do and the difficult task set before each of you who read my words.

2. Study and apprehend clearly the issues which lie behind this conflict, so that there is no inner wavering as to the rightness of the side on which your interests lie—the side of the Forces of Light. Parallel this with an understanding appreciation of the problem of those who are bewildered by the emphasis and the dynamic activities of those through whom the Forces of materialism are working. At the same time, also, kill out all hateful criticism in your minds.

3. Endeavour to use the following formula or mantram every day. It is a modernised and mystically worded ver-

sion of the one which was used widely in Atlantean days during the period of the ancient conflict of which the present is an effect. For many of you this mantram will be in the nature of a recovery of an old and well-known form of words:

"The sons of men are one and I am one with them. I seek to love not hate: I seek to serve and not exact due service. I seek to heal, not hurt.

"Let pain bring due reward of light and love. Let the soul control the outer form and life and all events, and bring to light the love which underlies the happenings of the time. Let vision come and insight; let the future stand revealed. Let inner union demonstrate and outer cleavages be gone. Let love prevail. Let all men love."

These words may seem inadequate, but said with power and an understanding of their significance and with the potency of the mind and heart behind them, they can prove unbelievably potent in the life of the one who says them. They will produce also an effect in his environment, and the accumulated effects in the world, as you spread the knowledge of the formula, will be great and effective. It will change attitudes, enlighten the vision and lead the aspirant to fuller service and to a wider cooperation based upon sacrifice. My brothers, you cannot evade the sacrifice in the long run, even if you have evaded it until now.

4.   Then apply yourselves to the spreading of the use of the Great Invocation and help to carry forward the plan for distribution. The Great Invocation, as you will see in the next article which I am writing for your information, is a potent solar instrument designed to bring about changes and needed readjustments. It is so powerful that when it was suggested for general use in the world of men some opposition was evoked among the members of the Hierarchy because They feared its potent effects upon the unready, and undeveloped people. Its use has, however, been justi-

fied and it is desired that its usefulness should be very greatly increased and its use far more widely spread.

5.   I would have you in your own way prepare for a major spiritual effort which is to take place when this conflict has worn itself out and some measure of peace and calm has come about. Each of you has your own sphere of influence and of contacts and each of you is in touch with similarly minded or enquiring people, with groups and churches, clubs, organisations and societies which are pledged to some form of effort towards human betterment, of goodwill effort, and of endeavour of some kind towards human welfare. Now is the time for much work to be done with the leaders and senior workers in such groups and with people who can be prepared by each of you for active effort when the right time comes. To this task I call each of you. Later you can swing these people into active goodwill work and to effort which will tend to world understanding and fusion. You can with them bring about the healing of the wounds of humanity which will be greatly needed and for which you can now prepare. You can get in touch with such people, keep records of names and addresses and capacity to serve and help, establish group contacts and so systematise your work that when the call goes out (as it did in 1936) there will be found available to the organisers a wealth of ready contacts and of interested and prepared people who will then work intelligently to establish the new order.

6.   The instructions in my earlier pamphlets remain as before and should be carefully followed in preparation for a campaign at the close of hostilities. Mailing lists can be gradually brought alive by judicious correspondence and new lists can be compiled; the Great Invocation can be increasingly used if the method outlined by me is studied and rightly organised by each of you, and so the goodwill already present in the world can be brought to a point of dynamic livingness, ready for later use. But, my brothers, nothing can be done unless you do it.

THE GREAT INVOCATION

Stanza One

Let the Forces of Light bring illumination to all mankind.
Let the Spirit of Peace be spread abroad.
May men of goodwill everywhere meet in a spirit of cooperation.
May forgiveness on the part of all men be the keynote at this time.
Let power attend the efforts of the Great Ones.
So let it be and help us to do our part.

October 1939

In my last article, I suggested giving you some facts anent the Great Invocation and some explanation of its significance and meanings. These may enable the occult students in the world today to use it with greater fervor and with greater understanding and, consequently, with greater success.

There are several such mantric formulas and Words of Power in use by such students but they fail to accomplish very much because the person using them has no real understanding of their import and purpose and is usually so focussed in his emotional, aspirational, astral nature that all that he says and does (in connection with such Words of Power) is entirely innocuous and futile. Words of Power, ancient mantrams (such as the Lord's Prayer) and the Great Invocation are only effective if used upon the mental plane and with the power of a controlled mind—focussed on their intent and meaning—behind the spoken effort. They then become potent. When said with the power of the soul as well as with the directed attention of the mind, they automatically become dynamically effective.

Students all the world over have for years used the Sacred Word, and have sounded the O.M. with great diligence. I would like here to ask: With what results? I myself will reply. With practically no results except a slight stimulation of the aspiration and a small awakening of the creative imagination. This means that the results achieved have had effect *only within the aura of the person concerned* and have not penetrated into his environment or produced any recognisable effects. The O.M. is potent and dynamically effective when rightly used and will produce changes, destroy that which must be eliminated or ended, and will build in, by attraction and consolidation that which is desired into the fabric of *the group life,* producing incidentally (though none the less certainly) needed changes and the wise reconstruction of the individual life. Ponder upon this.

If the above is true of the O.M. and of its group effects, it is infinitely more true of the Great Invocation. Words of Power (and this is true also of the O.M.) are all of second ray origin. This is the ray of the manifestation of consciousness. They are, therefore, intended for *soul use* because the soul is the expression of the second aspect of divinity, and only the soul can really employ these Words and sounds and thus produce the desired results which are always in line with the divine Plan. It is frequently forgotten that they must be used by the soul in a dynamic manner, involving the serious recognition of the *will aspect.* The Great Invocation, the O.M. and all such Words of Power must go forth from the soul (whose nature is love and whose purpose is solely group good), backed by or "occultly propelled forth" (to use a translation of an almost untranslatable occult idea) by the dynamic will aspect, and carried outwards as an integrated thoughtform upon a stream of living, illumined mental substance. This process therefore brings into activity the will, the love and the intelligence of the man who is using these words and formulas. Frequently, however, an hiatus occurs even when a man has integrated these three controlling factors within himself as far as he is able to do so at his particular point in evolution. All that he has succeeded in doing is the retaining of the created thoughtform upon the mental plane; he fails to make its presence felt upon the physical plane and to achieve the desired results because his brain (the lower receiving and distributing centre within the head) is incapable of the needed dual activity—retaining awareness of the intent, meaning and purpose of the formula being used and, at the same time, carrying on the task of sending forth the potency, hidden yet conveyed by the Words or sounds. These two activities must be carried on simultaneously by the soul on its own plane through the medium of the mind and the brain. Here again is one of the objectives of all meditation work but one which is not emphasised as it is a sequential happening and not an objective. Effectiveness is, therefore, dependent upon a grasp of the above facts and a developed and trained integration between soul, mind, desire, brain and the spoken Word or sound.

What I am here telling you refers not only to the use of the Great Invocation but also to the daily and constant use of the Sacred Word by occult students and aspirants in their daily meditation. They could change their lives, re-orient their life purpose and focus, and achieve spiritual unfoldment and expansion if they could use the OM as it should be used. The Great Invocation, rightly used by the many hundred thousand people who have already attempted to use it, could reorient the consciousness of humanity, stabilise men in spiritual being, disrupt and rebuild the planetary thoughtform which men have created in the past and which has had (and is having) such disastrous and cata-clysmic results, and open the door into the New Age, thus ushering in the new and better civilisation. This could be done so rapidly, that the needed changes would come about almost overnight; the present reign of horror would end and the race of men could settle down to a life of group good-will, individual harmlessness and right human relations.

Nevertheless, for your encouragement, I would state that the use of it has materially hastened world events, even though it has definitely stirred up a great deal of the trouble and brought it into manifestation upon the physical plane. The basically selfish purpose (even if unrecognised) of those who have used the Great Invocation has served to stimulate the selfish purposes of the forces of materialism. I would ask you: How many used the Great Invocation in a purely detached, spiritually potent and fully understanding manner? The merest handful. How many sent forth the Great Invocation in a spirit of pure love and with a com-

pletely unbiased attitude? Very few indeed. How many
sounded it out through the medium of a controlled mind,
with a recognition and deep belief that it embodied the will
of the planetary Logos and must, therefore, become dynamically effective upon the physical plane? Hardly more than
a tiny handful. Most of those who used it were intrigued
by its novelty, or felt it to be comprehensive though in an
unrealisable manner, or considered it must be occultly effective because they heard that it emanated from a member of
the Hierarchy, was used by the occult Hierarchy of the
planet, and was endorsed by those they trusted, or because—
foremost reason of all—anything that could make the world
nicer, more comfortable, happier and provide eventually
easier living conditions must be at least tried; it did not
take long to say and was probably well worth doing. But
the dynamic power behind the effort in individual cases has
often been personal self-interest, distress at the existing terrible and unhappy world conditions and an emotional reaction at pain and horror and fear. In many ways, this has been
a normal reaction to world tension and was to be expected.
The standard that I have indicated above is, I well know,
too high and too impossible for the average aspirant, and
most people are average. But the world need is such that
they must now swing out of the normal and, for the sake
of service, heighten their consciousness and work more definitely from a higher plane of awareness.

I am seeking today all over the world for a group of
aspirants and disciples who can and will use the Great
Invocation in the right way and who will be willing, consequently, to be trained to do so. In this way there will
be a group upon the physical plane and in everyday life
who will be able to combine their efforts with those of the
Hierarchy and thus produce an effective use of the Great
Invocation with its stupendous results.

I would remind you that for the purpose of developing
human will and human freedom of action, motivated by
group consciousness, the Hierarchy chooses to produce the
desired unfoldments and changes upon the physical plane

only through the medium of a conscious and awakening humanity. Such a humanity (and it is rapidly coming to this state of awareness through joint pain and suffering) will be impressed by and responsive to the directed thought of the guiding Elder Brothers of the race, but will be free at all times to reject that impression and to proceed as they personally may choose. There is no authoritative control over the minds of men assumed or cultivated by the Hier-archy; all aspirants and disciples are free to·choose a dif-ferent way to the one suggested if they so prefer, or if they are unconvinced of the advisability of the indicated method of work, or fear the arduous task of carrying forward the stage of the plan which has been indicated to them, or if they shirk the discipline implied and required by those who seek to make man correctly responsive to spiritual contact and teaching and so able rightly to interpret the intent of the Hierarchy.

Ability to use the Great Invocation so that it may be effective can be developed if those who are working along the lines of true meditation can make a beginning by the right use of the Sacred Word, which does not require such a sustained effort in occult concentration. They must learn to breathe it forth in the manner I have indicated above when speaking of the Great Invocation, and must also learn to gauge its results in their individual lives, thus viewing those lives from the angle of the trained spiritual Observer.

I would like to touch briefly and for a few minutes upon the significance of the entire process and method of invocation.

Much has been said and written in the past by the curious investigator and by those engaged in magical work of any kind anent the use of invocation as it applies to elemental forces and subhuman agents, with the consequent evocation of active agents and responsible energies of some kind or another upon the physical plane. What is oft for-gotten is that this process consists entirely of the production of contact and subsequent control of the forces of earth, water, fire and air. This is one of the aims of the magical workers but it concerns material nature and the control of substance and, in the realm of the lower occultism, is allied to the invocation and evocation of money, good health and the tangible material results as practised in the realm of mysticism by many schools of thought. Note this, for it holds a clue to the relation of occultism and mysticism upon the lower levels of consciousness and indicates the need of both groups to shift their focus of interest and their emphasis on to the higher and more spiritual values. The control of the natural forces and the evocation of the desired material rewards will arrive normally and inevitably but as secondary effects; they will depend also upon the karma or destiny of man recognised and considered, and the man will escape the danger of being himself controlled and motivated by the forces of materialism, letting in—as this condition must— much that is evil and dangerous.

The invocation, evocation and resultant activity of the Hierarchy and of those Forces, Energies and Beings Who are not controlled by matter in any way, or by substance (the lower pole of manifestation) but Who are related to the positive spiritual pole is a new activity, and as yet relatively an untried experiment on the part of humanity and the formulas unknown. Of what use was it to impart the formulas to humanity when it was as yet controlled by the lower values and unable to lay hold upon the soul aspect and to function on that level of consciousness whereon the soul is found. Only those can use the formulas effectively who live, work, think and feel as souls, which means ever in group terms.

Today, however, there are those in every land who are rapidly becoming aware of the soul as a controlling factor in consciousness, who respond to world affairs and conditions increasingly as souls, and who can, therefore, be trained to work upon the physical plane. When this is so, it becomes possible to impart certain of these Words of Power and mantrams and to institute that new and potent activity which will bring the Hierarchy and Humanity into conscious and direct cooperation, as well as Shamballa and certain great

Forces which are interplanetary or solar, and also great cosmic Energies. It is now possible to discover those who—being free within themselves and who are learning rapidly to be detached and selfless—can institute and carry forward the task of invoking these higher spiritual forces, thus reinforcing the efforts of the Great White Lodge. It is this process of spiritual invocation which will motivate the new and coming world religion. This is not magical invocation, as man understands it, and which is concerned with the invocation and control of the substantial and elemental forces of the manifested world, but the invocation which will evoke contact with the spiritual Lives and the divine embodied Energies as well as with the Hierarchy (which is Their intermediary) in order to bring about the manifestation on earth of the soul of humanity and the qualities of the subjective and inner divine life which all outer forms veil. This is now for the first time possible in the life of the planet.

The objective of these processes of invocation is threefold:

1.   To invoke the soul of humanity and so bring about its freer expression upon the physical plane. This can be brought about in two ways:

  a. The stimulation of the souls of men everywhere by the increased inflow of the Christ principle of love, which will express itself in world understanding, goodwill, cooperation, and peace.
  b. The setting up of a vibration within humanity itself of such potency that it will magnetically attract a response from the waiting, watching Hierarchy and bring about a much closer and likewise *conscious* rapport between the two planetary centres, the Hierarchy and Humanity.

This is called the invocation of the Great White Lodge. Much of this invocation of the Christ principle is carried forward by true believers in all lands (Christian and non-Christian) who address themselves to the Christ, no matter under what name they recognise Him and then, with love in their hearts to Him and their fellowmen, seek to ameliorate world conditions, end hatred and misery and demonstrate goodwill everywhere. This refers to the first stage of evoking the response to love and understanding in human hearts and minds as the result of the invocation of the Christ and of the Christ principle. Ponder on these words and see on every hand the process going forward. Esoteric students are apt to overestimate the effectiveness of the work that *they* are doing. The focussed aspiration and the unselfish struggle to serve which characterises millions of people in the world who do pray to, follow and seek to invoke the great spiritual head of the Hierarchy, the Master of all Masters, the Christ, has now reached a point of true and real effectiveness. It may be, and usually is, untinged by much mental activity or intellectual perception of the implications or the scientific nature of their procedure but is, for that very reason, potent. Esoteric and occult students demonstrate almost unavoidably a divided focus, owing to the activity of the mind and their failure as yet to blend perfectly both soul and personality. This leads to the dissipation of energy and oft renders their good intent futile. But, out of these groups are rapidly emerging those who can work in the right way and the results will be increasingly effective.

The evocation of the Hierarchy through right invocation is proceeding also rapidly, producing much activity and response from the Hierarchy of Light.

2.   To set up a closer relation with the third, major divine centre on our planet, Shamballa. From that centre, the will of God goes forth and the power of God becomes the messenger of His will. Hitherto that highest form of spiritual energy has only reached humanity (as I have before told you) via the Hierarchy. Today, it is deemed desirable that it should be ascertained whether there are enough selfless and group-conscious people upon the planet to warrant a direct inflow of that higher energy to humanity, thus producing upon the physical plane a hastening of the divine plan and a more rapid working out of that which is to be. This direct contact can be produced if the Great Invocation

is used by the world aspirants and disciples in collaboration with the Hierarchy. Hence the emphasis I have laid upon all of you using this Great Invocation as souls and as those who are in touch in some small measure with the Hierarchy. When the note of humanity and the note of the Hierarchy are synchronised by the use of the Great Invocation, there will come a dynamic and immediate response from Shamballa, and that will rapidly take place which the Hierarchy and the world disciples desire to see.

The primary result of the correct use of the Great Invocation (as far as humanity is concerned) is acceleration. As I have also earlier pointed out, such an acceleration carries with it its own risks, and consequently we have the appearance of the truly terrific problems and the dire happenings which have for many years overtaken the aspirants and the disciples in the world. They are by this process learning the work of world salvage and becoming gradually fitted for the post of world saviour and to be absorbers of evil karma. You might here quite correctly point out that all the world is now suffering and that the past twenty-five years have been those of a general and most unhappy world karma. Wherein then lies the distinction between the pain and suffering of the world in general and that of aspirants and disciples in particular? I would reply that aspirants and disciples are conscious of this karma and its results in all three vehicles simultaneously—in the mind as well as in the emotional body with resultant physical reactions. This produces an intensification, retrospection and anticipation which the larger group does not register, involving as it does the entire personality. To this, in the case of the disciple in particular, must be added sensitivity and the ability to tune in and to absorb world pain, world reactions, and world conditions, thereby greatly increasing that which they may have individually to bear. The capacity to shoulder and register group pain as well as to bear his own personal karma greatly aggravates the disciple's task.

When, therefore, I call the world aspirants and disciples to the use of the Great Invocation, I call them also to the "fellowship of Christ's sufferings"; this is ever preliminary to the resurrection or to the release of the human consciousness into higher realms of spiritual awareness. The Forces which are contacted by the use of this Great Invocation, in conjunction with trained hierarchical effort, are thereby attracted or magnetically impelled to respond and then potent energies can be sent direct to the waiting planetary centre, Humanity. Two effects of an immediate nature are consequently induced over a specific period of time:

a. The energy of the Will of God serves to awaken the illumined but latent will-to-good in men and this, once dynamically awakened, will flower forth as goodwill. There is so much of this which remains latent and unexpressed because the will to demonstrate goodwill activity has not been aroused; it will be automatically aroused in the general public once the world disciples have invoked and evoked the inflow of this higher dynamic energy. Humanity awaits this and its arrival is dependent upon the efforts of those who know what should be done and who should now make their spiritual theories facts in outer expression. Nothing can arrest the eventual progress of this will-to-good and its planned activity any more than a bud which has started to unfold its petals in the light of the sun and subject to the proper stimulation can revert again to the condition of a tightly closed bud, potential but unexpressed. The expression of what has been potential will be the result of the impact of first ray force, of the will-to-good at this time, induced by the efforts of the world disciples.
b. The second effect will be the forming or constitution of a planetary triangle or recognisable triad which will be the correspondence between the three planetary centres to the spiritual triad of Monad, Soul and Personality (the atma-buddhi-manas of the theosophical literature). Hitherto the word *alignment* has best described the planetary situation; there has been a straight line along which energy has poured from Shamballa to the

Hierarchy and from the Hierarchy to Humanity, but this has meant no direct interplay between Humanity and Shamballa. If the Great Invocation can be rendered effective, humanity can then set up a direct relationship with Shamballa. The resultant triangle of force-relationship will promote the circulation of spiritual energies between the three centres from point to point so that there will be a triple relation. A planetary process of give and take between all three will then be established, and the emphasis upon *giving* will be far more pronounced.

You will now see a little of the occult objective which lay behind the words which I asked you all to repeat in connection with the Great Invocation:

> *We know, O Lord of Life and Love,*
> *about the need;*
> *Touch our hearts anew with love,*
> *that we too may love and give.*

It is this thought of the free circulation of energy between the three world centres which motivates this mantric sentence. A study of this will show you how the implication and significance of apparently simple words may be far deeper and far more wide-reaching in effect than you have been able to conceive. A recognition of this and a creative impassioned use of the imagination may serve to add greater potency to your thought and to your personal will-to-good as you use the Great Invocation and its subsidiary mantram. The keynote of the first aspect is Sacrifice, and of the second, Love. The words therefore "that we too may love and give" can produce a contact between the two.

A clue also to the significance of pain and of suffering will gradually emerge in the world consciousness as study is made of the above statements. Suffering is the most effective and most rapid way of evoking world understanding and of burning away the barriers which human beings have set up to the expression of the will-to-good. One of the most beneficent results of the inflow of the Shamballa force through the focussed demand of the aspirants and world disciples will be the intelligent recognition of the uses of pain and suffering. It is this truth—distorted and selfishly misapplied and interpreted—which has led certain types of people and certain types of governing bodies among the nations to take the position that the greater the suffering inflicted (as, for instance, in war time) and the greater the process of terrorism, the quicker the end which is desirable and right; they hold often that the more dire the effects of planned conditions, the more rapidly will the correct consummation be achieved. It is not, however, the duty or right of man to turn first ray force to selfish ends or material objectives; responsibility cannot be veiled behind specious and distorted half truths and evil cannot be done in order that good may come. What is applied by the Lord of the World in Shamballa under the motivation of love, wisdom and selflessness with a sure touch and a judgment as to times and seasons cannot be so used by those motivated by personality objectives, either on an individual or a personality scale (for nations as well as individuals have personalities). Ponder on this and seek enlightenment from the soul.

3. When the Great Invocation is thus rightly used and the world centres are consequently consciously interrelated, then certain extra-planetary Energies can be called in by the Ruler of Shamballa to aid in the re-adjustments required for the New Age and its coming civilisation. These Forces— spiritual and potent in nature—exist in two categories: solar Forces which are inter-planetary and cosmic Forces which enter into our solar system via Jupiter as the transmitter of divine energies from Virgo and Aquarius which Jupiter *esoterically* governs. Virgo is esoterically the mother of the Christ child and is, therefore, the emanator of energies which nourish and aid the growth of the Christ consciousness; Aquarius is the coming expression of the group consciousness which is the first and immediate revelation of the ever present Christ consciousness on a large scale in humanity. Jupiter also, exoterically and from the angle of orthodox

astrology, rules Sagittarius, the sign of discipleship, and also Pisces, the sign of the world saviours. The implications will, therefore, be obvious to real students.

In considering these great Energies, there is little you can do beyond accepting—if you care to do so—my statements anent them, regarding them as interesting and simply explanatory hypotheses. There is little that you can do (or I either) to arrive at first hand knowledge of the facts along this line. Few even of the Members of the Hierarchy are conscious of the impact of force from extra-solar centres or reservoirs of spiritual force. Only the group of Contemplatives in the Hierarchy which are given the exoteric name of Nirmanakayas are responsive to Their influence in any conscious manner and then only when that influence has been stepped down by certain powerful agencies in Shamballa. It is not necessary for me or for you to say more anent Them though I shall touch upon Them again later in this article.

Prior to taking up the Great Invocation sentence by sentence, I would like briefly to touch upon the needed procedure as you attempt to say it correctly and effectively:

Forget not, first of all, the necessary process of alignment wherein you do two things:

1. Endeavour consciously (which for most of you at present means imaginatively) to align or link soul, mind and brain so that there is a direct and free inflow from the higher Self to the lower.
2. Endeavour to realise or register your relation to the Hierarchy, via your own group of disciples (if you know which it is) or in relation to whichever one of the Great Ones or Masters appeals the most to your heart and mind. If neither makes any appeal to your consciousness, the same results will be achieved if you seek to link up with the Christ.

I might here point out that the difference between the linking up that you can effectively do and that which is done by a Member of the Hierarchy itself is that you link up via the Hierarchy and then through the medium of the Great Invocation reach forth to Shamballa whereas the initiates and the Masters link Themselves directly with Shamballa and use the Great Invocation in a manner totally different to that in which you use it. There is for you and the average aspirant no direct contact, and that is definitely fortunate for you. I may not further elucidate.

The second thing which you do is then to focus yourself in as high a consciousness as you are capable of achieving. Then you aim at complete self-forgetfulness and when that has been gained you direct your attention to the dual activity of the true disciple to which I earlier referred, i.e., the task of emphasising a significant understanding of the implications and meanings of the words said and of the results to be achieved. There comes next the sending forth of the words with their hidden potency and this must be done by you *as a soul,* using the mind and the brain as agents.

Integration, conscious activity, and the expression of the work to be done upon the physical plane will cover the entire story. These rightly carried forward will prove effective. Would it clarify matters for you if I state that:

1. *Integration* is a correspondence in consciousness to the Inhalation of the breath. This is the withdrawing of the consciousness to as high a point as possible.
2. *Conscious activity* corresponds to the right use of the Interlude between inhalation and exhalation. It involves the recognition of the forces contacted and their purpose.
3. *Right expression* corresponds to the period of Exhalation. This is the sending forth of the forces contacted by an act of the will in order that they may produce the desired ends.

Forget not that this has to be a group endeavour and must be carried forward in cooperation with the Hierarchy. It involves also the recognition that the soul is one and that there is no such thing as my soul—only our soul.

In considering the five sentences which form what might

be called the mandate of the Great Invocation (see page 144), I would like, first of all, to point out a few underlying and basic ideas.

This Great Invocation has been used by the Hierarchy ever since the year 1425 A.D. though it is thousands of years older than that. Owing, however, to the unreadiness of humanity to cooperate in its use, the results have been delayed and are regarded as "hovering." I know not how else to express the results already achieved. Today, they can precipitate, if right cooperation can be extended by humanity, and such cooperation now seems immediately possible.

The first phase, *Let the Forces of Light bring illumination to mankind,* definitely invokes potencies which are to be found upon monadic levels of consciousness and upon what is occultly called the second plane of divine manifestation. These Forces include the Lord of the World and the Representatives of the seven sacred planets Who are spoken of in the Christian Bible as the "seven Spirits before the Throne of God." They include also the three Agents of the Divine Triplicity Who are known, esoterically and in the East as the three Kumaras, or the three Buddhas of Activity.

What do these names and these great Individualities mean to you and to average humanity? Nothing at all and this is necessarily so. They remain but names and possible hypothetical expressions of divinity until after the third initiation when the conscious recognition of the Monad becomes possible; then Forces and Energies, personified for us in these great and stupendous Lives, can be demonstrated as having true existence. On the way to these fundamental recognitions, Their three Representatives within the limits of the Hierarchy must be accepted and known to be correspondingly functioning Activities. These Three are, the Manu, the focal point of the first Ray of Will or Power; the Christ, the head of the Hierarchy and the representative of the second Ray of Love-Wisdom; and the Lord of Civilisation, the expression of the third Ray of Active Intelligence. This knowledge is achieved during the process of training for the first three initiations. Therefore, all that I here tell you must be regarded as possible of verification, and as being testified to by all the world Scriptures and by the initiates of all lands, but it must necessarily remain personally unverified by you until a much later date in your unfoldment.

The Spirit of Peace Who is invoked in the second phrase, *Let the Spirit of Peace be spread abroad,* is that mysterious and divine Entity with Whom the Christ came into touch and Whose influence played through Him at the time that He earned the right to be called the "Prince of Peace." As I have elsewhere told you in my earlier writings, the Christ embodied in Himself the cosmic principle of love, the expression of which in manifestation will work out as "glory to God, peace on earth and goodwill towards men." To this the angels testified at His birth. When He expressed this principle of love in His life and world service, He definitely linked up our planet and humanity (in particular) with the Source of the light, love and life to which we refer in this second phrase. This was the world salvation which He brought—a fact which is as yet little realised and which will not be widely recognised until this powerful Invocation has taken due effect.

When the world aspirants and disciples use this Invocation, the first phrase takes the consciousness to the Hierarchy of Light, which is the intermediate centre between Humanity and Shamballa. It serves then to emphasise and establish a close rapport, blending and fusing the human and the hierarchical centres. When this has taken place, the Hierarchy can then use this Great Invocation with greater potency and can carry the relation to a higher state still and produce a blending with the Shamballa centre, where the Forces of Light are found as embodied Presences and where Their focussed energy serves to provide great reservoirs of light and love. These have hitherto not been made available for planetary distribution, owing to the lack of established relation between the three centres: Humanity, Hierarchy and

Shamballa. That relation is now becoming somewhat established; the inflow of light and love to humanity is now possible if the disciples and aspirants of the world can be led to make the needed effort to stand in spiritual being and, from that poised attentive attitude, to invoke these great Entities. It was to this possibility that the story in the New Testament refers where reference is made to the pool which was stirred at times by the Angel and thus a condition was produced which led to the healing of the sick. The Angel of the Presence, the soul of humanity, as embodied in the Hierarchy and those who are consciously endeavouring to function as souls can now stir these reservoirs of force and light upon etheric levels in Shamballa so that a definite "healing of the nations" can take place.

When the thought behind the Great Invocation can be carried high enough in the consciousness of those using it through a joint effort of the world disciples and the Hierarchy of Light—as well as being reinforced by the Forces of Light—then the Spirit of Peace can be invoked.

On a lower turn of the spiral, you will note that the Wesak Festival enacts a similar invocation and process. It is a re-enacting and training process. There and at that time, the three Representatives of Shamballa within the Hierarchy—the Manu, the Christ and the Mahachohan—invoke the Buddha, Who in His turn is the transmitter of still higher Forces. He is invoked by a special mantram and transmits the appeal to the One Whose agent He is. If this Great Invocation which we are studying can be rightly said, the three great planetary centres can be related in a similar manner. The Lord of Civilisation, the Master R—, representing humanity, the Christ representing the Hierarchy and the Lord of the World, linked through the Manu and representing Shamballa can be brought into a close relation so that the result will be the setting up of such a potent vibration and note that the Spirit of Peace will be invoked and contacted. By the voiced appeal His attention will be forced to turn itself towards our planet. The consequences will be significant and potent but as to the form which they will take it is impossible for me to say. Perhaps it will lead to some peculiar and powerful demonstration of the meaning of peace as the expression of universal and planetary love; perhaps it will produce the sending of an Avatar or Messenger of Peace to lead the nations to right action; perhaps some happening will take place of such significance that its import will be immediately recognised by humanity as a whole, leading them to take all the needed steps to restore right human relations. The nature of the activities which the Spirit of Peace will institute is not our responsibility. Our duty is to learn rightly to contact the Hierarchy, via our own souls; rightly to use the Great Invocation as souls, and rightly to render ourselves responsive to and sensitive to the resultant effects. Ponder on the above.

It might, therefore, be noted that the Forces of Light express Themselves through the Hierarchy of Light and Their major effect is the illumination of the minds of men with love and light. This precipitates upon the mental plane. The personality or the form aspect of humanity is thereby pervaded and illumined. Thus the third great planetary centre, Humanity, becomes creative and magnetic, and two divine aspects—intelligence and love—will reach fruition upon the physical plane, making it possible for the first aspect and the will of God (understood by humanity as the Plan) to be consciously carried forward on earth in conformity with the activity instituted at Shamballa. The will of God is *purpose* and this is, for the first time, to be recognised consciously by man.

The Spirit of Peace will, when the right time comes, vitalise the responsiveness of humanity, via the influence of the Hierarchy, to the will of God which has for basic intent the bringing of peace on earth. What is peace? It is essentially the establishing of right human relations, of synthetic rapport with its resultant cooperation, of correct interplay between the three planetary centres and an illumined, loving understanding of the will of God as it affects humanity and works out divine intent. It is for this reason that the Christ, Who established for the first time in planetary history a contact between the Hierarchy, Humanity, Shamballa and the Spirit of Peace in His Own high place, in His first recorded utterance said that He must be about His Father's business and then at the end of His life, reiterated the same thought in the words: "Father, not my will but Thine be done," thus carrying the thought up to the highest plane for He addressed the Father, the first Aspect of Divinity. He then focussed in Himself the two major divine attributes and aspects—will and love (atma-buddhi)—and because of this, His consciousness became extra-planetary as is the consciousness of the Lord of the World, and He could then touch certain heights of awareness and contact certain solar Agencies which had never before been contacted by man. This achievement enabled Him to put Humanity in touch with the Spirit of Peace. He thus Himself became the Light of the World and the Prince of Peace.

In this manner, Shamballa and the Hierarchy were brought into a close relationship and two great streams of force were blended and a definite interplay set up between them. The Buddha, through His achievement of illumination, established the first major link with the Forces of Light. The Christ, through His ability to express the will of God in love and as world salvage, established the first major link with the Spirit of Peace.

If you will study the above information with care, you will find that the importance of the Wesak Festival at the time of the full moon of May will assume increasing importance in your minds. It is the festival at which three factors of importance to humanity are brought into relation:

1. The Buddha, the embodiment or agent of the Forces of Light can then be contacted and that which They seek to transmit to humanity can be consciously appropriated.

2. The Christ, the embodiment of the love and the will of God and the agent of the Spirit of Peace, can also be contacted and humanity can be trained to appropriate this extra-planetary type of energy.

3. Through the Christ and the Buddha, humanity can now establish a close relationship with Shamballa and then make its own contribution—as a world centre—to the planetary life. Pervaded by light and controlled by the Spirit of Peace, the expression of humanity's will-to-good can emanate powerfully from this third planetary centre. Humanity will then for the first time enter upon its destined task as the intelligent, loving intermediary between the higher states of planetary consciousness, the super-human states and the sub-human kingdoms. Thus humanity will become eventually the planetary saviour.

If you will have these thoughts in mind, the first three phrases of the Great Invocation will assume great significance. Let me put some of these significances in tabular form:

Let the Forces of Light bring illumination to mankind

Intermediary ....The Hierarchy. Soul consciousness
Agent ....The Buddha
Expression ....Light. Understanding. The illumined mind
Planes of emphasis ...The second or monadic plane
                      The buddhic or intuitional plane
                      The mental plane
Focal point ....The head centre
Planetary centre .....The Hierarchy

Let the Spirit of Peace be spread abroad

Intermediary ....Shamballa. Spiritual consciousness
Agent ....The Christ
Expression ....The will of God as love and peace
                      Sentient response
Planes of emphasis ...The logoic or first plane
                      The buddhic, or intuitional plane
                      The astral or emotional plane
Focal point ....The heart centre
Planetary centre .....Shamballa

May men of goodwill everywhere meet in a spirit of cooperation

Intermediary . . . . Humanity itself. Self-consciousness

Agent . . . . The Lord of Civilisation

Expression . . . . Intelligent love, dedicated to the Plan
                             Creativity
                             The will-to-good

Planes of emphasis . . . The atmic or plane of spiritual will
                             The mental plane
                             The physical plane

Focal point . . . . The throat centre

Planetary centre . . . . . Humanity

Thus all the great centres are linked and all the planes are interrelated; the past has contributed its finished work; the present is evoking its just and right development; the future of wonder and of divine possibility appears—its results contingent upon a spirit of right understanding and invocation. Three statements in the New Testament begin now to demonstrate their profound esoteric significance and their amazing living potency:

I am the Light of the World . . The Forces of Light
                               Phrase 1. 2nd Aspect

My peace I give unto you . . . . The Spirit of Peace
                               Phrase 2. 1st Aspect

Love thy neighbor as thyself . . The Men of Goodwill
                               Phrase 3. 3rd Aspect

The three aspects of divinity in man achieve practical expression through the influence of the Great Invocation, both in living usefulness and true comprehension—true at least in so far as man's present point in evolution permits of his correct apprehension of significance. *Goodwill,* as the practical and possible expression of love demonstrates on earth, evoking right relationship; *light,* as the expression of the Hierarchy pours into the human consciousness, irradiating all dark places and evoking a response from all forms of life in the three worlds of manifestation, and in the three subhuman kingdoms through the medium of the human; *peace,* as the expression of the will of Shamballa produces balance, equilibrium, synthesis and understanding, plus a spirit of invocation which is basically an action, producing reaction. This demonstrates as the first great creative and magical work of which humanity is capable, swinging, as it does, all the three divine aspects into a simultaneous activity in line with the will of God.

We come now to the last two phrases which summarise the effects—synthetic and eternal (and consequently lasting) which the establishment of direct relationship with Shamballa will produce in the two other planetary centres, the Hierarchy and Humanity. I refer to effects which will express themselves as a group activity, motivated by the essential values of selflessness and persistent effort (which is sustained concentration, in the last analysis) and thereby producing conditions for which the Lord of the World, the Ancient of Days, has long waited. The patience and sustaining love of Shamballa is infinite.

The fourth phrase runs: *May forgiveness on the part of all men be the keynote at this time.* As you know, the word "forgiveness" is a curious and unusual one and signifies (according to the best derivative sources) simply "to give for." Forgiveness is *not* therefore, a synonym for pardon though the word has been distorted in theological circles to mean this, so little has the Church understood the basic, motivating power behind divine expression in our solar system. Theologians ever think in terms of the human mind and not in terms of the divine mind. Forgiveness is sacrifice, and is the *giving* up of one's self, even of one's very life, for the sake of others and for the good of the whole group. This spirit of sacrifice is ever found when the Shamballa force is rightly contacted, even in the smallest degree, and the underlying impulse behind the loving will of God is sensed and understood, accompanied as this always is with the desire to participate in that will and its spirit of divine sacrifice. Manifestation is itself the Great Forgiveness. The stupendous Lives—outside manifested existence—entered into manifestation in order to give Themselves for the lesser lives and forms of existence in order that these lesser lives might be enabled to proceed onward towards a goal which is known to Deity alone, and thus eventually reach high places of spiritual expression. Achievement is ever followed by sacrifice and the giving of the greater for the lesser. This is an aspect of the Law of Evolution. Such is the note and theme of the entire creative process and is the basic meaning of the phrase, "God is Love," for love signifies giving and sacrifice, at least in this solar system.

It is for this reason that the esoteric teaching emphasises the fact that the soul of man is a Lord of Sacrifice and of loving persistent Devotion—the two outstanding qualities of the Shamballa Lives, sustaining life and giving. This is lasting devotion to the good of the whole or the expression of the spirit of synthesis and sacrifice in order again that all lesser lives (such as those embodied in the personality of man) may rise to the "resurrection which is in Christ," through the crucifixion or sacrifice of the soul upon the Cross of Matter.

It is this thought again which gives significance to the life of Christ on earth for He re-enacted for us an eternal process, externalising it in such a way that it became the symbol of the motive of the entire manifested universe and the impulse which should direct each of us—crucifixion and death, resurrection and life, and the consequent salvation of the whole.

It is this thought which is embodied in the challenge of this fourth phrase of the Great Invocation, and means literally, "May all men everywhere respond to the keynote of the universe and give themselves for others."

And, is not this in a faint and dim manner, the present keynote of human effort? In spite of a real inability to think truly, effectively and intuitively, the mass of men in all lands are responding clearly and definitely to this note of sacrifice. Leaders of the great nations everywhere are using this note and call to sacrifice in their appeals at this time to

their peoples. Men in Germany were called to battle by
their leaders with the challenge of sacrifice and told that
they must give their lives in order that Germany may live.
A study of the speeches by the German leaders will be found
to contain this note. The other group, whom you call the
Allies (because they stand more specifically for the good
of the whole and not for the good of the separated nation
or unit) are also calling the masses of their people to fight
for the good of civilisation and for the preservation of those
values which are next upon the evolutionary scale and essential to the general good. The wording of these calls and
the objectives expressed may differ in formulation but the
theme is the same and the effect is to call forth the spirit
of sacrifice in the nations. Though the motives behind such
a call may be mixed and the leaders guided as much by
expediency and selfish, national interests as by the general
good, yet they know that the note which will evoke an immediate response from the unit and the individual is fundamentally the good of the larger unit (the nation or the
group of nations). Therefore, forgiveness or sacrifice in
order to save others is increasingly the recognised needed
keynote at this time and in this recognition lies much to justify the sorry story of past evolutionary processes and methods.
When it is recognised that the "giving-for" involves *right
living* upon the physical plane and not (as is so often
thought) the *dying* of the physical body then we shall see
a revitalised world. It is the living Christ (the *living* world
Saviour) Who saves humanity. It is the sacrifice, day by
day, in the process of daily living which can save the world
of men—the sacrifice of selfish personal interests for the good
of the whole and the giving up of one's practical life to the
salvage of the world. It is living in order that others too
may live which is the theme of the New Testament. When,
therefore, the mode of sacrifice enters into the realm of the
subtler and subjective values and the true meaning of forgiveness is intellectually, practically and spiritually comprehended, the New Age will be abundantly realised with its
truly human civilisation and a culture which will embody

the realities of the esoteric teaching, as well as the best of
the externalised past. Then and only then will the new
esotericism be revealed to a race of men who have made
aspiration a fact in their outer experience. The attitude
of the masses in the present conflict is the guarantee of this
and the proof also of the success of Christ's mission.

The result of what is happening today must, sooner or
later, produce an at-one-ment between all nations and
peoples. At-one-ment is ever (under evolutionary law) the
consequence of sacrifice. Of this, Christ's sacrifice was the
symbol and the guarantee, impulsed as His life and activities
were by the Spirit of Peace. As He made "of twain, one
new man, so making peace" (Ephesians 2:15) so today
out of the duality of soul and body, humanity is achieving
the same ends and the result of this final stage of the Piscean
Age will be the *fusion in consciousness* of soul and body.
The Aquarian Age will demonstrate an increasing expression
of this at-one-ment, wrought out in the crucifixion of humanity at the present time. The difference between this coming
stage and that of the past is that, in the past, the soul has
sought this development and at-one-ment and (from the
angle of evolution) it has been slowly and gradually attained,
but in the future, it will be consciously sought, achieved
and recognised by man upon the physical plane as a result
of the present period of "giving-for" the whole, of the best
which the individual can give.

I would point out that just as the energies released by
use of the first three phrases of the Invocation relate   to
the Head, Shamballa; to the Heart, the Hierarchy; and
to the Throat centre, Humanity) ; so the right use of this
fourth phrase will bring into conscious, functioning activity the centre between the eyebrows, the ajna centre in
individual man and in humanity as whole. This centre
begins to become active and to function dynamically, governing and directing the individual energies, once any real
measure of personality integration has been achieved. It is,
as you know, the fourth centre found above the diaphragm

in the human body and the phrase which awakens it (both individually and in the group) is this fourth phrase. There is, therefore, a numerical relationship. When used wisely and intelligently by human beings, many of the blended potencies which the first three phrases have made available are invoked and so made available to the individual as well as to the group. They can then be focussed for his use in the ajna centre. In many ways, therefore, this fourth phrase of the Great Invocation is of paramount importance to the individual as well as to humanity, invoking as it does great and vital potencies and indicating process (Sacrifice) and purpose, plus the identification of the unit and the group with the basic intent of manifestation.

The fifth phrase, *Let power attend the efforts of the Great Ones,* is definitely related to the effect in the Hierarchy of a constructive use of the Great Invocation, just as the previous one is related to the effect in humanity. This effect in the Hierarchy is a relatively new one and is due to the participation of humanity in the process of invocation, thus producing new effects and contacts. It is the united effort of the two great centres which is of such paramount importance and upon which I desire to have you concentrate. Its utterance by man throws the weight of human appeal and desire behind the age-old efforts of the Hierarchy and this is now, for the first time, truly possible on a large scale. For aeons, the Hierarchy has struggled alone to help and lift humanity and to stimulate the potency of the human plane-tary centre so that its vibratory activity would eventually be sufficiently powerful to swing it into the radius or magnetic field of hierarchical activity. This long task has at last achieved success. The Hierarchy and humanity are at last en rapport. This is the higher reflection or correspondence to what goes on within the consciousness of a human being who—having reached the stage of discipleship—is at the point of blending the light of the personality (as it is expressed through the ajna centre and its externalisation, the pituitary body) and the light of the soul (as it is, in its turn, expressed by the light in the head, or by the head centre and its externalisation, the pineal gland).

You will, therefore, note afresh the *practical* significance of these fourth and fifth phrases of the Great Invocation. One serves to arouse humanity (as a planetary centre) to activity and realisation and the other serves to aid the Hierarchy in its ancient efforts so that the two are then related to each other's magnetic fields and produce a blending and a synthesis which will lead to a fuller expression of the soul of divinity through the medium of humanity. Ponder on this statement.

In the esoteric teaching, this takes place in the life of the individual when—by an act of the will—the centre at the base of the spine is aroused and the fire and the light of the personal threefold life (one aspect of which is often called the kundalini fire) is carried upwards and merged with the power and the light of the soul. The major approach of the two basic energies of form and soul (as an expression of spirit) are thereby related within the human being; the "marriage in the heavens" takes place and the task of the creative process of incarnation or individual manifestation is on the way to completion. Within the planetary life, the same process goes on. The life of humanity as a whole (which is intelligent form life) and the life of the Hierarchy (which is the life of the soul), under impulse from the Spirit or will aspect as symbolised in Shamballa, are fused and blended and then a new departure in the evolutionary process becomes possible. The kingdom of God, which is the kingdom of souls, and the human kingdom as mutually expressive and interrelated, are perfectly synthesised and anchored on earth. The glory of the One can then be faintly seen, which is the glory of Shamballa. The Dweller upon the threshold of divinity and the Angel of the Presence then stand face to face.

This is the situation today. Tomorrow they will blend and synthesise and the glory of God will appear on earth. The second great Approach will have been achieved.

CALL TO A UNITED ACT OF SERVICE

November 1939

The situation is serious. Sea and air and land are arrayed against the Forces of Light; they are the agents of material substance and can be used potently against the spiritual Forces. The forces of the air are, however, increasingly on our side. The Members of the Hierarchy are hard put to it to turn the tide in favour of that true and more spiritual civilisation which is on the way. This civilisation will be a combination of the best which has hitherto been produced and that which is new and, as yet, dimly sensed by the best of the world thinkers. The tide *must* be turned in favour of that which we call righteousness.

The seeds of evil are in every country; those who war against that which is good are numerous in every land, whether they war with aggressive and planned intent, whether they preserve an attitude of passivity and acceptance, or a planned neutrality, as in America, or are actively fighting for that which is against the material forces.

The World Crisis was, as you know, inevitable, but physical warfare could have been avoided if right psychological methods had been employed, and it could have been cured if a process of transmutation and of transference had been correctly carried forward, and if the spirit of sacrifice had also been demonstrated by the world aspirants. The need for group sacrifice has not met with adequate response, except in those cases where it has been imposed by governments upon their nationals. Such is the sorry history of what is taking place today.

What can be done at the present moment to arrest defeat and the overwhelming of the Forces of Light? Here I refer not to the outer physical victory. True victory will not be indicated unless the higher values which should govern human civilisation emerge with clarity and power. I would here like to emphasise the fact that the tide must be definitely turned before the close of the year if a prolonged conflict is to be avoided. I would ask you, therefore, to participate in the subjective focussing and rallying of the world thinkers, and particularly the heads of organisations, groups and churches of all kinds and temperaments who can swing their many adherents into a uniform and united activity.

The Masters of the Wisdom have no time today to do the task Themselves; Their hands are full, combating the forces of materialism. These forces are active in every country; the Hierarchy in its consciousness does not isolate Germany, even though these forces have chosen that sad land for their major point of departure and enterprise; in Germany They have Their people working as elsewhere. The Masters of the Wisdom are active in dispelling the depressions and terrors which settle down upon all Their workers in the arena of the world today, as these workers struggle to stand steady under the fierce impact of wrong thinking and of world-wide despair; these workers are likewise sensitive (owing to their point of integrated development) to the agony of mind, the tension of emotion and the ravages of physical pain which are felt by all those upon whom the War has had its dire effects, and upon whom it has laid the hand of suffering. Such a sensitivity and such a sympathetic response are apt to produce a condition of negativity and a psychic preoccupation with the immediate situation among all workers, and thus render them deaf to the call of their actual duty or else liable to become distraught by the dual effort of being effective in service, whilst at the same time fighting off emotional reactions. The capacity of the worker to respond, therefore, to the inner voices and to serve dispassionately and selflessly is seriously handicapped.

I challenge all workers and all members of the New Group of World Servers to leave their personal problems behind. This is a time of crisis and such problems must be solved through complete self-forgetfulness. I ask you to work anew with fresh ardour in *joyful* service, forgetting past weaknesses and failures in the urgency of that which I ask all to do for the world. There has been much lack of joy in the service rendered to the world lately. When I speak thus, I refer not to happiness, which is a personality reaction,

but to that joyous confidence in the law and in the Hierarchy which lies behind the Biblical words, "The joy of
the Lord is our strength." "Rise up and fight, Arjuna," preserving the flame of love intact, permitting no breath of
hate to disturb the serenity of love or upset that inner poise
which will enable you to sound forth the clarion note of
world understanding, that will rally all men and women of
goodwill to the aid of the Hierarchy. This will bring to an
end all hatred, separativeness and aggression, which are the
three major sins of humanity. All men have hated; all men
have been separative in both thought and action; all have
been and many still are materialistic, full of pride and the
desire to gain that which is not their own by right. This
spirit of acquisitiveness belongs to no one group; it has
been a universal and general fault, and has produced the
present disastrous economic situation, thus precipitating the
world into war, hate and cruelty.

The fusion of many minds into one directed activity is
today of supreme importance; this has been symbolised in
the union which now exists between two great nations,
France and Great Britain. Unity of directed thought and
purpose is the guarantee of inevitable and future success.
The power of massed thought is omnipotent. The potency
of focussed and directed mental activity is unpredictable. If
you accept this premise and this statement, then act upon it.

The Spirit of Peace is hovering close to humanity, seeking opportunity to make His Presence felt. The Spirit of
Peace is not an abstract concept but a potent Individual,
wielding forces hitherto unfamiliar to our planet. Great
Forces are awaiting the hour when They can function as
the Liberators and the Deliverers of mankind. But the door
to Their entrance must be opened by humanity itself and
it will be opened by *a united act of the will,* expressed
through some formula of words and expressed in sound. It
will be brought about by an activity performed simultaneously by all men and women of goodwill and by all the
world aspirants and disciples. The door will not open unless
the act of invocation is backed by the focussed will. The

directed determination of the man or the group who is using the suggested formula, prayer or invocation is essential.

I would ask you to call as many people as you can reach through the medium of every available channel to a definite activity upon the coming Christmas day, if possible, and again at the time of the full moon of January, thus making two great appeals to the Forces of Peace and Light, so that they may help humanity. I would ask you to get in touch with leaders and workers—important and unimportant—in every land, asking them to associate themselves in their own way and with their own people, and to do this on as large a scale as possible—as large, at least, as that of your effort in May, 1936.

The times are ripe for a response to these ideas; the recognised pain and distress of the world will open both hearts and purses. The idea of a Christmas appeal and call to prayer and to invocation of the Prince of Peace will be potent in evoking a desirable reaction, and will serve also to blend into closer unity all who recognise the work the Hierarchy is attempting to do. I would ask you to call for help from all sides, and to let these ideas work out into the world on the basis of their usefulness and opportuneness. Omit from this appeal none that you know, for through them millions can be reached and swung into the desired activity.

To those of you who can appreciate and use the Great Invocation, I would suggest its renewed and earnest use. This alternative invocation might, however, be suggested and found useful:

"O Lord of Light and Love, come forth and rule the world.
May the Prince of Peace appear and end the warring of the nations.
May the reign of Light and Love and Justice be begun.
Let there be peace on earth, and let it begin with us."

THE COMING WORLD ORDER

April 1940

This analysis of world conditions is being written in America, where there is, as yet, relative physical safety and

time for the re-adjustment of views, and the opportunity also
to give direction—along with embattled Britain and her
Allies—to a world sorely needing guidance and vision. There
is great confusion of voices. Those who know the least speak
ever the loudest and apportion the blame for events with
facility. There is much mental distress everywhere, occa-
sioned by the war and also by the desire of the well-intentioned to stress their particular solutions of the world
problem.

It is necessary, therefore, to speak with directness, to
indicate the inherent dangers of the present situation, to
present its amazing opportunity to bring about needed
changes, and to point out the lines of demarcation between
the right and the wrong ways of living, between a vision of
the new world order and the retrograde plans of the so-called
"new order" with which the totalitarian powers seek to
bewilder humanity.

We start with the premise that two opposing world
visions confront humanity and that two world orders are
presented to mankind. Between these man must choose, and
his choice will determine the future.

The years 1941 and 1942 will be years of crisis and of
tension. Those who perceive the risks, the opportunity, and
the important decision to be made are struggling with almost
frantic haste to awaken the masses to the uniqueness of this
moment. What mankind decides during the next twelve
months will condition the future as no other human decision
has ever before done in the history of mankind.

There have been points of crisis before in history, but
not one that involved the entire planetary population. There
have been periods of danger, difficulty, war, famine and
distress, but none which conditioned the lives of untold
millions as does the present. Time and again there has been
the emergence of leaders, conquerors, dictators and world
figures, but they have hitherto come at a time when their
influence was limited by world communications and by
national limitations; therefore their power was not universal
and their progress was arrested by the conditions of the

period in which they lived. Today, the entire planet is involved and all the nations of the world are definitely affected.

There is the setting up of barriers in a futile effort to keep out of trouble and avoid war; dominant groups are swinging many nations under their banners so that they are either associated with the totalitarian powers or with those nations which are opposing them. The nations which are not actually belligerents are equally active in the task of endeavouring to preserve their national integrity.

The conflict today is a world conflict. The following groups of people are involved:

1. The fighting aggressor nations, ruled by ambitious dictators.
2. The nations which are seeking to defend themselves and the liberties of humanity.
3. The neutral nations, seeing the issues involved and faced with the immediate necessity to take sides.

The momentum of this struggle is gaining daily. Fresh areas of the world are being swept into the conflict every week. The real issues, the impending economic results and the political implications are emerging with growing clarity in every land and—make no mistake—even in those lands which lie numbed and suffering under the heel of the conqueror. Among them there is a silent and at present voiceless revolt. The inner speechless revolt in itself constitutes a menace to world peace and, if evoked into full expression, may plunge the world still deeper into conflict.

Facing humanity today are two major dangers. These are: first, the conflict will be so prolonged that humanity will be completely exhausted, and thus a stalemate will be reached and a situation will arise which will bring to an end all civilised relationships and all hope of an ordered life of beauty, peace and culture. Secondly, the nations not yet involved will fail to see the realities of the situation and will not come to the assistance of those fighting for the preservation of national and individual freedom. If this should prove to be the case, then—without so intending and yet inevitably—they will stand on the side of evil and share in the responsibility of engineering world disaster.

Today, there are no more than two parties in the world—those who are on the side of right human relations and those who are on the side of selfish and cruel power politics. The totalitarian powers are on the march—ruthless, selfish, cruel and aggressive; the powers which are battling for human liberty and for the rights of the defenceless little nations are standing with their backs to the wall, facing the strongest display of human might that the world has ever seen. The nations which are not yet physically involved are preparing for some form of action and for defence—defence against the dictator powers but not against the fighting democracies.

The battle today is being fought out on the land, on the sea, and in the air. From the economic standpoint, every country is involved, and ruin stalks in the wake of war; the stopping of imports or of exports in many lands is bringing about the financial ruin of thousands; the pressure of economic disaster, the fear of famine and pestilence and the constant risk of becoming actively a part of the war faces every country not yet actually in the fighting line. The fear of defeat, of death and injury, and of the loss of all possessions is added to these problems, where the nations at war are concerned.

Humanity must face up to these facts. No matter how people may evade the truth, no matter how they may escape into a dream world of wishful thinking, the fact remains—inevitable and undeniable—that the world is at war and everyone is involved.

The Goodwill Work

Prior to September, 1939, the objectives of our worldwide work, over a period of nine years, were the spreading of world goodwill, the discovery of the men and women of goodwill throughout the world, and the endeavour to teach the meaning of the will-to-good. This is the main task of the new group of world servers. We inculcated a non-separative attitude and the need for right human relations. We endeavoured to make clear that differing forms of government and varying ideological systems were right and possible, provided that human beings lived together in goodwill and recognised their blood brotherhood.

Then humanity made its decision to fight, and the war broke out: one group, the instigators of the war, fighting to acquire material power, the glory of a nation and the subjugation of the defenceless; and the other, fighting to preserve its own liberty of action, the preservation of its integrity, the right of the little nations and the spiritual values. Immediately, the issue was abundantly clear in the minds of those who were in touch with human affairs; immediately certain nations took sides against the forces of aggression; immediately, other nations, biased by similar distorted ideologies and equally selfish purposes, stood with the aggressor nation; immediately, panic swept the remaining nations, who took refuge in short-sighted neutrality and defence programmes—a neutrality and programmes which have proved quite futile to protect them.

Where, then, should the new group of world servers stand? What should the men and women of goodwill do? Should they side with the totalitarian powers because in so doing they will bring the conflict more rapidly to an end, or should they stand on the side of the neutral powers, frantically pursuing ineffective peace programmes, policies of appeasement, and play into the hands of the totalitarian powers?

Humanity having decided to fight out the battle *physically*, there was nothing left to do but issue a challenge to the men and women of goodwill to take their stand on the side of such action as would release humanity through the destruction of the evil forces. These had determined to prove that might was right. Therefore, the forces fighting for progress and civilisation had to meet force with force.

The challenge was taken up by the democracies who

stand for human rights and liberty. Because of the decision to fight on the side of spiritual progress, the spiritual forces of the planet had no alternative but to align themselves on the side of the allied democracies, and endeavour to awaken the neutral nations to the issue. They ranged themselves against the leaders of the aggressor nations, though not against their poor deluded or subdued peoples. They too must be liberated by the allied democracies.

On the basis of an active will-to-good, the men and women of goodwill, acting under the inspiration of the New Group of World Servers, had no alternative but to take their stand with the spiritual forces and join the struggle for the liberation of humanity from totalitarian ambitions and the intentions of a group of evil men. But the spirit of goodwill must be, steadily and unchangingly, the motivating impulse. No hate must be allowed to enter in. The greatest good of the greatest number lies today in the release of the nations from the domination of the totalitarian powers.

The Pacifist Position

The second point upon which I would touch is the arguments brought out by the pacifists of the world. All true and good people are pacifically minded and all hate war. This is a fact which the academic idealist and pacifist often forgets. Such people tell us that two wrongs do not make a right; and to meet murder with murder (which is their definition of war) is sinful; that war is evil (which no one denies) and that one must not take part in it. They contend that thinking thoughts of peace and of love can put the world straight and end the war. Such people, fighting the existent fact of war, usually do little or nothing concrete to right the wrongs which are responsible for the war, and permit their defence—personal, municipal, national and international—to be undertaken by others. The sincerity of these people cannot be questioned.

It should be remembered, in countering these ideas and in justifying the fighting spirit of the Christian democracies, that it is *motive* that counts. War can be and is mass murder, where the motive is wrong. It can be sacrifice and right action, where the motive is right. The slaying of a man in the act of killing the defenceless is not regarded as murder. The principle remains the same, whether it is killing an individual who is murdering, or fighting a nation which is warring on the defenceless. The material means, which evil uses for selfish ends, can also be employed for good purposes. The death of the physical body is a lesser evil than the setting back of civilisation, the thwarting of the divine purposes of the human spirit, the negating of all spiritual teaching, and the control of men's minds and liberties. War is always evil, but it can be the lesser of two evils, as is the case today.

The present war, if carried forward to a successful completion by the defeat of the totalitarian powers, constitutes a far lesser evil than the subjugation of many nations to the unparalleled cupidity, the appalling educational process and the defiance of all recognised spiritual values by the Axis powers. If the totalitarian powers should conquer, it would mean years of turmoil and revolt; their victory would result in untold misery.

It is no doubt an undeniable spiritual truth that right thought can change and save the world, but it is also true that there are not enough people *able to think* to do this work. Also, there is not enough time in which to do it. The thoughts of peace are mainly founded upon a stubborn idealism that loves the ideal more than humanity. They are based also upon an unrecognised fear of war and upon an individual inertia which prefers the dream world of wishful thinking to the shouldering of responsibility for the security of humanity.

Thus briefly have I sought to make the position of the New Group of World Servers clear as it fights for the rights of man, for the spiritual future of humanity, and for the new world order. What I have now to say will fall into four parts:

I.   *The world as it exists today.* The present situation is the result of past tendencies, of underlying pressures and of human decisions.

II. *The new world order.* This we will contrast with the old order and with the so-called "new order" of the totalitarian powers.

III. *Some problems involved.* Four major world problems will call for discussion and these we must consider.

IV. *The task ahead.* We will then deal with the interlude until peace is achieved plus some suggestions for the coming period of reconstruction.

I. THE WORLD TODAY

What are the causes which have produced present world conditions? What are the underlying pressures which are producing the present chaos or those which can produce eventual order? Before there can be correction, there must be appreciation of error; there must be understanding of the predisposing causes producing the necessity; there must be realisation of the general guilt and a shared responsibility for the evil conditions; there must be determination to make restitution, and to cease from evil doing.

The tendency to fasten the war on Hitler and his gang of evil men should not blind us to the causes which have made his evil work possible. He is mainly a precipitating agency, for through him world selfishness and cruelty have been brought to a focus. But, as Christ has said: "Woe unto the world because of offences! for it must needs be that offences come; but woe to that man by whom the offence cometh." (Matthew 18:7.) The causes of this rampant evil are inherent in humanity itself.

Ancient and untrammeled selfishness has ever been a characteristic of man; the desire for power and for possession has ever motivated men and nations; cruelty, lust, and sacrifice of the higher values to the lower have been deeply rooted human habits for ages. Of these ancient habits of thought and behaviour all peoples and all nations are guilty. Steadily, as the world grew closer, the lines of cleavage and the antagonism of the nations increased, and thus the present war (beginning in 1914) is the inevitable result of wrong thought, selfish goals and ancient hatreds. Individualistic interest, separative aims and aggressive desire march towards their inevitable finale—war and chaos.

The economic situation also provides a symbol of this condition. The nations divide themselves into the "Haves" and the "Have Nots," and thus bring in the present era of gangsterism. Organised gangs in the United States came into being as an expression of these tendencies in national life. In the international world, three nations are now playing the same part. The allied nations and the United States are recognising the menace of national and international gangsterism and are endeavouring to crush it. But—and this is the point of importance—these conditions have been made possible by humanity as a whole.

Materialism and Spirituality

There are today three major human trends: First of all, a trend towards a spiritual and free way of life; secondly, a trend towards intellectual unfoldment; and lastly, a potent trend towards material living and aggression. At present, the last of these innate tendencies is in the saddle, with the second, the intellectual attitude, throwing its weight upon the side of the material goals. A relatively small group is throwing the weight of human aspiration upon the side of the spiritual values. The war between the pairs of opposites—materialism and spirituality—is raging fiercely. Only as men turn away from material aggression and towards spiritual objectives will the world situation change, and men—motivated by goodwill—force the aggressors back to their own place and release humanity from fear and force. We are today reaping the results of our own sowing. The recognition of the cause of the problem provides humanity with the opportunity to end it. The time has arrived in which it is possible to institute those changes in attitude which will bring an era of peace and goodwill, founded on right human relations.

These two forces—materialism and spirituality—face each other. What will be the outcome? Will men arrest the evil and initiate a period of understanding, cooperation and right relationship, or will they continue the process of selfish planning and of economic and militant competition? This question must be answered by the clear thinking of the masses and by the calm and unafraid challenges of the democracies.

On all sides the need for a new world order is being recognised. The totalitarian powers are talking of the "new order in Europe"; the idealists and thinkers are unfolding schemes and plans which vision entirely new conditions that will bring the old bad order to an end. There is a constant demand for the Allies to state their peace aims and indicate clearly what adjustments will be made after the war, because a vision of the future world policy will help humanity through the present crisis.

Historical Background

Throughout the Middle Ages, the rule of powerful monarchs, the spread of empires and the march of national conquerors were outstanding characteristics. A relatively small number of people were involved. The Church of the time had immense power in all European countries; it controlled the education of the people, but laid no foundation for right political thought. The history of the past is the history of many forms of government. Races and nations have come and gone. Political regimes and religious forms have played their part, have persisted or disappeared. The sorry history of humanity has been one of kings and potentates, rulers and warriors, presidents and dictators—rising into power at the expense of their own or other nations. Conquerors come and go—Akbar, Genghis Khan, the Pharaohs, Alexander the Great, Caesar, Charlemagne, William the Conqueror, Napoleon, Hitler and Mussolini. These have all upset the rhythm

184   THE EXTERNALISATION OF THE HIERARCHY

of their times and have come to power through aggression
and slaughter. As the nations grew more closely interrelated,
their influence and their field of expression increased. The
growing means of communication brought this about; Great
Britain knew nothing of the movements of Alexander; the
peoples of America knew naught about Genghis Khan; but
the sound of the marching armies of Napoleon was heard
over a far wider area, and the triumphs of Hitler—diplomatic
and military—are known throughout the world.

The totalitarian powers have turned the world into one
armed camp—for offence or defence. Motivating all these
conquerors was lust for gold, lust for land, lust for power,
lust for personal triumph. The modern dictators are no
exception. They bring nothing new.

World Anarchy

The history of the world has been built around the
theme of war; its points of crisis have been the great battles.
The thought of revenge motivates some nations; the demand
for the righting of ancient historical wrongs influences
others; the restitution of lands, earlier held, directs the acts
of others. For instance: the ancient glory of the Roman
Empire must be restored—at the expense of the helpless
little peoples; the culture of France must be paramount and
French security must outweigh all other considerations;
British imperialism has in the past outraged other nations;
German hegemony and "living space" must dominate
Europe, and the German superman must be the arbiter of
human life; American isolationism would leave humanity
defenceless in its hour of need and hand men over to the
rule of Hitler; Russia, in her silence, cannot be trusted;
Japan is upsetting the balance of power in Asia. Such is
the picture today. Anarchy rules the world; famine stalks
the inhabitants of Europe; the civilian population of cities,
the women and children, are in grave danger of injury and
death and are forced to live underground; pestilence appears; there is no safety on land or sea or in the air; the

nations are on the verge of financial ruin; science has turned to the invention of the instruments of death; the populations of cities and entire districts are shifted from one part of a country to another; families and homes are broken up; there is intense fear, hopeless looking into the future, bewildered questioning, suicide and murder; the smoke of countless fires blackens the skies; the seas are strewn with dead and with wrecked vessels; the thunder of guns and the noise of exploding bombs are heard in approximately twenty countries; war rises up from the waters, marches over the lands and descends from the skies.

It is to this situation that the old order has brought humanity. It is to this disaster that man's cruelty and selfishness have tended; no nations are exempt from this criticism, and all are more rapidly moved by selfish purpose than by the spirit of sacrifice.

Even idealistic America can only be aroused into action by an appeal to her self-interest and security.

For our encouragement let us recognise that the same humanity which has brought about these terrible conditions can also create the new world, the new order and the new way of life. The selfish, wicked past can give way to a future of understanding, of cooperation, of right human relations and of good. Separativeness must be superseded by unity. The combination of totalitarian aggressors, of allied democracies and of anxious neutral nations must be changed into a world which is characterised by one endeavour—the establishing of those relations which will produce the happiness and peace of the whole, and not only of the part.

II. THE NEW WORLD ORDER

I assume that my readers recognise some intelligent or spiritual direction of humanity. I care not by what name they call that guiding Purpose. Some may call it the Will of God; others, the inevitable trends of the evolutionary process; still others may believe in the spiritual forces of the planet; others may regard it as the spiritual Hierarchy of the planet, or the great White Lodge; many millions speak of the guidance of Christ and His disciples. Be that as it may, there is a universal recognition of a guiding Power, exerting pressure throughout the ages, which appears to be leading all towards an ultimate good.

Some definite direction has led man from the stage of primeval man to that evolutionary point where a Plato, a Shakespeare, a da Vinci, a Beethoven can appear. Some power has evoked man's capacity to formulate ideas, to produce systems of theology, of science and of government; some inner motivating power has given man the ability to create beauty, to discover the secrets of nature; some realisation of divine responsibility lies behind the philanthropy, the educational systems, and the welfare movements throughout the world. The progress of the human spirit has been one of irresistible unfoldment, of a developing appreciation of reality, beauty and wisdom. Instinct has developed into intellect; intellect is beginning to unfold into intuition. The significance of God, the registering of man's divine potentialities, and the increasing capacity to understand and to share in the thought processes of others—all these indicate progress and unfoldment.

This picture of the beauty of the human spirit must be placed beside the earlier picture of man's selfishness and cruelty, of man's inhumanity to man. Both pictures are true, but only the one of beauty is eternal; the other is but transient. Man is a composite of higher and lower expressions, and behind all the wars and difficulties which accompany man's progress through the ages lies this major factor—an ancient persistent fight between man's spiritual aspiration and his material desires. This condition is today brought to a focus in the conflict raging between the totalitarian powers and the nations which are fighting for the rights of the human spirit and for the freedom of humanity.

My use of the word *spiritual* has nothing to do with the use of this word as the orthodox religions use it, except in so far as the religious expression is a part of the general spirituality of mankind. Everything is spiritual which tends towards understanding, towards kindness, towards that which is productive of beauty and which can lead man on to a fuller expression of his divine potentialities. All is evil which drives man deeper into materialism, which omits the higher values of living, which endorses selfishness, which sets up barriers to the establishing of right human relations, and which feeds the spirit of separateness, of fear, of revenge.

On the basis of these distinctions, it is surely apparent that God is on the side of the allied nations, for it cannot be supposed that Christ is on the side of Hitler and the rule of cruel aggression. The spiritual Hierarchy of the planet is throwing the weight of its strength against the Axis powers just in so far as the spiritually minded peoples of the world can collaborate, for there can be no coercion of man's free will. No one is afraid of the allied nations; the situation has not been precipitated by the Allies; their methods are not the methods of lying propaganda and the terrorising of the weak and the defenceless. Facts prove these points, and it is this recognition which lies behind the constant aid of the United States. The way of living and the spiritual objects of the democracies are recognised by all, and it is these which are threatened by the totalitarian concepts of life. Through the democracies humanity speaks.

The Axis World Order

The totalitarian order must go because it is contrary to the spiritual vision. The world order, as visioned by Hitler, is based upon the subjection of the weak to the rule of a super-Germany; it is one in which the life of the little nations will be allowed to go on just in so far as they serve the need of Germany. The lesser Axis powers are permitted existence only because they benefit German aims—Italy, to give Germany scope in the Mediterranean; Japan, to handle the Asiatic problem which is too large for Germany to handle alone. It is an order whose intention is that the best of all industrial and agricultural products shall go to Germany and the unwanted residue to the little nations. It is an order in which the educational processes will be controlled by the dominant super-race. All departments of knowledge will be subordinated to the glorification of Germany. Germany will be portrayed as the seed of all world glory, and as the ruthless saviour of mankind; the beauties of war, of struggle and of physical strength will be emphasised, and these so-called admirable objectives of the human spirit will be developed to produce a race of men in whom the "effeminate" beauties of loving kindness and wise consideration for others will find no place.

I would call your attention to the teaching now being given to the German youth. Might is right. The German belongs to the super-race, and all other races are inferior. Only a chosen aristocracy should be permitted the privilege of education and of rule. The masses of the people are no more than cattle and exist only to be slaves of the superior race. War is to men what childbirth is to women. War is a natural process and therefore eternally right. All sources of supply must be controlled by Germany, and consequently even those nations at present neutral must be brought under the German sphere of influence. The totalitarian powers will dominate the economic system of the world and control all imports and exports. The standard of living in both hemispheres will be lowered; everything will be related to the good of Germany, and no other nation will be considered. Christian teaching and Christian ethics must necessarily be eliminated, because Germany regards Christianity and its divine Founder as effeminate and weak, as emphasising the softer qualities of human nature, and as responsible for the decadence of all nations, except Germany. Christianity must also be overthrown because it is based on Jewish sources; the rule of Christ must come to an end, because only the rule of force is right.

In the world order of the Axis powers, the individual has no rights; he has no freedom except in so far as he serves the state; there will be no liberty of thought or conscience, all issues will be decided by the state, and the private citizen will have no right to an opinion. Men will be drafted like slaves into the service of the state.

Such is the picture of the order which the Axis powers are preparing to impose upon the world, and to this their own words testify. Only insight into the true nature of this crisis, a determination to face the facts, and fearlessness will suffice to defeat Hitler. This conquering fearlessness must be based on a recognition of the spiritual values involved, on a belief in God, and on a commonsense which is determined to establish security, right human relations and liberty.

It is important that people face up to the facts immediately. They must realise what is the nature of the world order which Hitler is preparing to enforce, and what lies ahead of humanity if the Axis powers triumph. It is essential that the little children of the world be rescued from this overshadowing evil and from the false education to which they will be subjected if the totalitarian powers hold Europe in their grasp. The intensive culture given to the youth of Germany during the past twenty years has proved the effects of environing mental attitudes. These boys who roll their tanks and fly their planes over the countries of Europe and who wage war on women and children are the product of an educational system, and are therefore the victims of an evil process. The children of Germany must be rescued from the future which Hitler plans, as well as the children of other countries; the women of Germany must be set free from fear, as must the women in other lands; the population of Germany must also be liberated from the evil rule of Hitler. This is recognised by the allied nations. Make no mistake. The German is as dear to the heart of humanity, to God, to Christ and to all right thinking people as are any other people. The German must be rescued from Hitler's world order as much as the Pole, the Jew, the Czech or any captive nation. In effecting this freedom, the allied nations and the neutral powers must preserve the spirit of goodwill, even when using force, which is the only means of conquest the totalitarian powers understand.

Steps Towards the New World Order

In contradistinction to the totalitarian world order, what should the rest of the world plan? Towards what world objectives should the democracies work? Utopian schemes, idealistic forms of government and cultural living processes have ever been the playthings of the human mind, down through the centuries. But these Utopias have been so far ahead of possibility that their presentation seems useless. They are most of them wholly impractical.

Certain immediate possibilities and attainable objectives can, however, be worked out, given a definite will-to-good and patience on the part of humanity.

Certain major and spiritual premises should lie back of all efforts to formulate the new world order. Let me state some of them:

1. The new world order must meet *the immediate need* and not be an attempt to satisfy some distant, idealistic vision.

2. The new world order must be appropriate to a world which has passed through a destructive crisis and to a humanity which is badly shattered by the experience.

3. The new world order must lay the foundation for a future world order which will be possible only after a time of recovery, of reconstruction, and of rebuilding.

4. The new world order will be founded on the recognition that all men are equal in origin and goal but that all are at differing stages of evolutionary development; that personal integrity, intelligence, vision and experience, plus a marked goodwill, should indicate leadership. The domination of the proletariat over the aristocracy and bourgeoisie, as in Russia, or the domination of an entrenched aristocracy over the proletariat and middle classes, as has been until lately the case in Great Britain, must disappear. The control of labor by capital or the control of capital by labor must also go.

5. In the new world order, the governing body in any nation should be composed of those who work for the greatest good of the greatest number and who at the same time offer opportunity to all, seeing to it that the individual is left free. Today the men of vision are achieving recognition, thus making possible a right choice of leaders. It was not possible until this century.

6. The new world order will be founded on an active sense of responsibility. The rule will be "all for one and one for all." This attitude among nations will have to be developed. It is not yet present.

7. The new world order will not impose a uniform type of government, a synthetic religion and a system of standardisation upon the nations. The sovereign rights of each nation will be recognised and its peculiar genius, individual trends and racial qualities will be permitted full expression. In one particular only should there be an attempt to produce unity, and that will be in the field of education.

8. The new world order will recognise that the produce of the world, the natural resources of the planet and its riches, belong to no one nation but should be shared by all. There will be no nations under the category "haves" and others under the opposite category. A fair and properly organised distribution of the wheat, the oil and the mineral wealth of the world will be developed, based upon the needs of each nation, upon its own internal resources and the requirements of its people. All this will be worked out in relation to the whole.

9. In the preparatory period for the new world order there will be a steady and regulated disarmament. It will not be optional. No nation will be permitted to produce and organise any equipment for destructive purposes or to infringe the security of any other nation. One of the first tasks of any future peace conference will be to regulate this matter and gradually see to the disarming of the nations.

These are the simple and general premises upon which the new world order must begin its work. These preliminary stages must be kept fluid and experimental; the vision of possibility must never be lost, and the foundations must be preserved inviolate, but the intermediate processes and the experimentations must be carried forward by men who, having the best interests of the whole at heart, can change the detail of organisation whilst preserving the life of the organism.

Right Human Relations

The objective of their work can be summed up thus: the new world order will facilitate the establishing of right human relations, based on justice, on the recognition of inherited rights, on opportunity for all—irrespective of race, colour or creed—on the suppression of crime and selfishness through right education, and on the recognition of divine potentialities in man as well as the recognition of a divine directing Intelligence in Whom man lives, and moves and has his being.

The difficulties confronting the nations when the war is over may seem insuperable but—given vision, goodwill and patience—they can be solved. Assuming that humanity will not rest until the aggressor nations are subdued, it will be necessary for the conquering democracies to be generous, merciful, understanding and attentive to the voice of the people as a whole. It is that voice (usually sound in its pronouncements) which must be evoked, recognised and listened to, and not the voices of the separative exponents of any ideology, of any form of government, religion or party. The objective of those who are entrusted with the straightening out of the world is not the imposition of democracy upon the entire world or to force Christianity upon a world of diversified religions. It is surely to foster the best elements in any national government to which the people may subscribe, or which they intelligently endorse. Each nation should recognise that its form of government may be suited to it and quite unsuited to another nation; it should be taught that the function of each nation is the perfecting of its national life, rhythm and machinery, so that it can be an efficient co-partner with all other nations.

It is equally essential that the new world order should develop in humanity a sense of divinity and of relationship to God, yet with no emphasis upon racial theologies and separative creeds. The essentials of religious and political beliefs must be taught and a new simplicity of life inculcated. Today, these are lost in the emphasis laid upon material possession, upon *things* and upon money. The problem of money will have to be faced; the problem of the distribution of wealth—whether natural or human—will need careful handling and a compromise reached between those nations which possess unlimited resources and those who have few or none; the problem of the varying forms of national government must be faced with courage and insight; the restoration—psychological, spiritual and physical—of mankind must constitute a primary responsibility. The sense of security must be put on a firm basis—the basis of right relationship, and not the basis of force. Men must feel secure because they are seeking to develop international goodwill and can trust each other, and are not therefore dependent upon the strength of their armies and fleets.

The recognition of a spiritual Hierarchy which is working through the new group of world servers must steadily grow in some form or another. This will happen when the world statesmen and the rulers of the different nations and governing bodies—political and religious—are men of vision, spiritually motivated and selflessly inspired.

The future world order will be the effective expression of a fusion of the inner spiritual way of life and the outer civilised and cultural way of acting; this is a definite possibility because humanity, in its upper brackets, has already developed the power to live in the intellectual and physical worlds simultaneously. Many today are living in the spiritual world also. Tomorrow there will be many more.

III. SOME PROBLEMS INVOLVED

The new world order will be confronted with many problems. These problems will *not* be solved by the imposition of a solution by means of force, as in the Axis world order. They will be solved by right educational processes and by understanding the objectives of the true world order. They fall roughly into four categories: the racial problem, the economic problem, the problem of government, and the religious problem.

The Racial Problem

There is no way of solving the racial problem by legislation, segregation, or by the effort to produce national blocs, as in the case in Germany today when she proclaims Germany as the super-race. Such efforts will only produce insuperable barriers. With very few exceptions, there are no pure races. Germany in particular, by its place at the crossroads of Europe, is definitely the fusion of many strains. Tides of emigration, marching armies throughout the centuries, and modern travel have inextricably mixed and fused all the races. It may therefore be assumed that any attempt to isolate a race or to enforce so-called "racial purity" is foredoomed to failure. The only solution of this problem is the basic recognition that all men are brothers; that one blood pours through human veins; that we are all the children of the one Father and that our failure to recognise this fact is simply an indication of man's stupidity. Historical backgrounds, climatic conditions and widespread inter-marriage have made the different races what they are today. Essentially, however, humanity is one—the heir of the ages, the product of many fusions, conditioned by circumstances and enriched by the processes of evolutionary development. This basic unity must now be recognised.

The major racial problem has, for many centuries, been the Jewish, which has been brought to a critical point by Germany. This problem is also capable of solution if properly recognised for what it is, and if coupled with an effort by the Jews themselves to solve it, and to be cooperative in the world efforts to adjust their problem. This they have not yet done because the average Jew is lonely and unsettled, able to do little to put himself right before the world. Instinctively and intellectually, the Jew is separative; intuitively he has vision, but at the same time he possesses no sense of fusion with other peoples.

There is no scientific and hitherto unknown mode of solving racial problems. It is finally a question of right thinking, decent behaviour, and simple kindness. The question will not be solved by inter-marriage, or by isolating groups for occupation of special areas, or by any man-made ideas of superiority or inferiority. Right human relations will come by a mutual recognition of mistakes, by sorrow for wrong action in the past, and by restitution, if possible. It will come when nations can be educated to appreciate the good qualities of other nations and to comprehend the part they play in the whole picture. It will be developed when the sense of racial superiority is killed; when racial differences and racial quarrels are relegated to the unholy past and only a future of cooperation and of understanding is actively developed; it will make its presence felt when the living standards of right relation (sought by the enlightened people of every race) become the habitual attitude of the masses and when it is regarded as contrary to the best interests of any nation to spread those ideas which tend to erect racial or national barriers, arouse hatreds or foster differences and separation. Such a time will surely come. Humanity will master the problem of right human relations and attitudes.

It is inevitable that racial differences, national quarrels and caste distinction exist, but it is equally imperative that they disappear. The world is one world. Humanity is one unit in the evolutionary process. Differences are man-made and engender hatreds and separation. When the children of the various races are taught from their earliest years that there are no differences, that all men are brothers, and that the apparent distinctions are essentially superficial, then future generations will approach the problem of world inter-relations unhandicapped by prejudice, by pride of race, or by instilled historical resentments. By right education little children can be taught right attitudes and will respond, for a child sees and recognises no differences, and the truth of the Biblical promise that "a little child shall lead them" will be proven scientifically true. In the new world order this educational process will be started.

The Economic Problem

This problem is basically far less difficult of solution. Sound commonsense can solve it. There are adequate resources for the sustenance of human life, and these science can increase and develop. The mineral wealth of the world, the oil, the produce of the fields, the contribution of the animal kingdom, the riches of the sea, and the fruits and the flowers are all offering themselves to humanity. Man is the controller of it all, and they belong to everyone and are the property of no one group, nation or race. It is solely due to man's selfishness that (in these days of rapid transportation) thousands are starving whilst food is rotting or destroyed; it is solely due to the grasping schemes and the financial injustices of man's making that the resources of the planet are not universally available under some wise system of distribution. There is no justifiable excuse for the lack of the essentials of life in any part of the world. Such a state of lack argues short-sighted policy and the blocking of the free circulation of necessities for some reason or other. All these deplorable conditions are based on some national or group selfishness and on the failure to work out some wise impartial scheme for the supplying of human need throughout the world.

What then must be done, apart from the education of the coming generations in the need for *sharing,* for a free circulation of all the essential commodities? The cause of this evil way of living is very simple. It is a product of past wrong educational methods, of competition and the facility with which the helpless and weak can be exploited.

No one group is responsible as certain fanatical ideologists might lead the ignorant to suppose. Our period is simply one in which human selfishness has come to its climax and must either destroy humanity or be brought intelligently to an end.

Three things will end this condition of great luxury and extreme poverty, of gross over-feeding of the few and the starvation of the many, plus the centralisation of the world's produce under the control of a handful of people in each country. These are: first, the recognition that there is enough food, fuel, oil and minerals in the world to meet the need of the entire population. The problem, therefore, is basically one of distribution. Secondly, this premise of adequate supply handled through right distribution must be accepted, and the supplies which are essential to the health, security and happiness of mankind must be made available. Third, that the entire economic problem and the institution of the needed rules and distributing agencies should be handled by an *economic league of nations*. In this league, all the nations will have their place; they will know their national requirements (based on population and internal resources, etc.) and will know also what they can contribute to the family of nations; all will be animated by the will to the general good—a will-to-good that will probably at first be based on expediency and national need but which will be constructive in its working out.

Certain facts are obvious. The old order has failed. The resources of the world have fallen into the hands of the selfish, and there has been no just distribution. Some nations have had too much, and have exploited their surplus; other nations have had too little, and their national life and their financial situation have been crippled thereby. At the close of this war all the nations will be in financial difficulties. All nations will require re-building; all will have to attend actively to the settlement of the future economic life of the planet and its adjustment upon sounder lines.

This period of adjustment offers the opportunity to effect drastic and deeply needed changes and the establishing of a new economic order, based on the contribution of each nation to the whole, the sharing of the fundamental necessities of life and the wise pooling of all resources for the benefit of everybody, plus a wise system of distribution. Such a plan is feasible.

The solution here offered is so simple that, for that very reason, it may fail to make an appeal. The quality required by those engineering this change of economic focus is so simple also—the will-to-good—that again it may be overlooked, but without simplicity and goodwill little can be effected after the world war. The great need will be for men of vision, of wide sympathy, technical knowledge and cosmopolitan interest. They must possess also the confidence of the people. They must meet together and lay down the rules whereby the world can be adequately fed; they must determine the nature and extent of the contribution which any one nation must make; they must settle the nature and extent of the supplies which should be given to any nation, and so bring about those conditions which will keep the resources of the world circulating justly and engineer those preventive measures which will offset human selfishness and greed.

Can such a group of men be found? I believe it can. Everywhere there are deep students of human nature, scientific investigators with wide human sympathies, and conscientious men and women who have for long—under the old and cruel system—wrestled with the problem of human pain and need.

The new era of simplicity must come in. The new world order will inaugurate this simpler life based on adequate food, right thought, creative activity and happiness. These essentials are only possible under a right economic rule. This simplification and this wise distribution of the world's resources must embrace the high and the low, the rich and the poor, thus serving all men alike.

The Problem Of Government

Coming now to the realm of government, under the new world order, one is faced with a very complex situation.

Certain great ideological regimes have divided the world into opposing groups. There are the great democracies, under which certain of the few remaining monarchies find a place; there are the totalitarian powers in which the ancient dictatorships and autocracies of the past are summed up. There is nothing new in the Axis policies. They are essentially reactionary groups, for tyrants, cruelty and the exploitation of the weak are part of ancient history. The democracies, with all their present ineffectiveness, have in them the germ of that which is truly new, for they are the expression of an upward surging towards self-rule and self-mastery by humanity as a whole. There is also the communistic ideal which is a curious blend of individualism, dictatorship, the ancient conflict between labor and capital, the Sermon on the Mount, and the worst aspects of revolution and exploitation. The lines which it will follow, even in the immediate future, are unpredictable. There are other countries and peoples whose governments are conditioned by their environment and who at present play no real determining part in world events, except in so far as a greater power uses them. Again, there are peoples and tribes who still pursue their little lives, unaffected by the turmoil to be found in the more highly civilised parts of the world.

Behind all this diversity of governmental methods, certain clear outlines are emerging which indicate wider fusions and a tendency to bring about certain syntheses. Various basic trends of thought are appearing which, in the new world order, will unfold into that major synthesis so much desired by the spiritual Hierarchy of the planet, and which, whilst preserving the large national and racial outlines, will produce an underlying and subjective state of mind which will end the age of separateness. Desire is today being evoked for the Federated States of Europe, modelled on the lines of the British Commonwealth of Nations or the United States of America; there is talk of a new order in Asia, of the Good Neighbor policy in America, of a Federal Union of the democratic nations; there is also the steady spread of the Soviet Socialist Republics. Certain major groupings would seem possible and probably advisable. They might be divided as follows:

1.   A Federal Union of the great democracies after the war. This might include the British Empire as a whole, the United States, the Scandinavian countries and certain northern European nations, including Germany.

2.   A Union of the Latin countries, including France, Spain, all the Mediterranean countries, the Balkan countries (except one or two which might be absorbed into the U.S.S.R.), and South America.

3.   The United Soviet Socialist Republics and certain Asiatic nations working in collaboration with them, such as China, and later Japan.

These three great blocs would not be antagonistic blocs but simply geographical spheres of influence. They would all three work in the closest unity and economic relation. Each nation within the three blocs would preserve its sovereign independence, but between these independent nations and between these blocs there would be identity of purpose, unity of effort and the recognition of the economic control of a league of nations. This league, being formed of the representatives of all the nations and its inner governing body being chosen by the three blocs, would control all sources of supply, distribute all such supplies and determine all economic policies.

With the details of these future adjustments I shall not deal. They must be wrought out by the men and women of goodwill in the crucible of experiment and experience. Only universal disaster could have brought men to a state of mind wherein such propositions and solutions could be presented. The general recognition that the old order has lamentably failed is most valuable.

The Religious Problem

When we come to consider religion in the new world order, we are faced with a far more complicated problem and yet, at the same time, with a far easier one. The reason for this is that the subject of religion is one which is studied and somewhat understood by the majority of men. On theological interpretations there are wide differences; on a widespread recognition of a universal divine Intelligence or of God (by whatever name the all-embracing Life may be called) there is a general similarity of reaction. Forms of religion are so different, and the theological adherents are so fierce in their loyalties and partisanships, that the emergence of a world religion is necessarily of profound difficulty. But that emergence is very close at hand and the differences are relatively superficial. The new world religion is nearer than many think, and this is due to two things: first, the theological quarrels are mainly over non-essentials, and secondly, the younger generation is basically spiritual but quite uninterested in theology.

The intelligent youth of all countries are rapidly repudiating orthodox theology, state ecclesiasticism and the control of the church. They are neither interested in man-made interpretations of truth nor in past quarrels between the major world religions. At the same time, they *are* profoundly interested in the spiritual values and are earnestly seeking verification of their deep-seated unvoiced recognitions. They look to no bible or system of so-called inspired spiritual knowledge and revelation, but their eyes are on the undefined larger wholes in which they seek to merge and lose themselves, such as the state, an ideology, or humanity itself. In this expression of the spirit of self-abnegation may be seen the appearance of the deepest truth of all religion and the justification of the Christian message. Christ, in His high place, cares not whether men accept the theological interpretations of scholars and churchmen, but He does care whether the keynote of His life of sacrifice and service is reproduced among men; it is immaterial to Him whether the emphasis laid upon the detail and the veracity of the Gospel story is recognised and accepted, for He is more interested that the search for truth and for subjective spiritual experience should persist; He knows that within each human heart is found that which responds instinctively to God, and that the hope of ultimate glory lies hid in the Christ-consciousness.

Therefore, in the new world order, spirituality will supersede theology; living experience will take the place of theological acceptances. The spiritual realities will emerge with increasing clarity and the form aspect will recede into the background; dynamic, expressive truth will be the key-note of the new world religion. The living Christ will assume His rightful place in human consciousness and see the fruition of His plans, sacrifice and service, but the hold of the ecclesiastical orders will weaken and disappear. Only those will remain as guides and leaders of the human spirit who speak from living experience, and who know no creedal barriers; they will recognise the onward march of revelation and the new emerging truths. These truths will be founded on the ancient realities but will be adapted to modern need and will manifest progressively the revelation of the divine nature and quality. God is now known as Intelligence and Love. That the past has given us. He must be known as Will and Purpose, and that the future will reveal.

When the racial problem has disappeared through the recognition of the one Life, when the economic problem has been solved by the nations working cooperatively to-gether, when the problem of right government within each nation has been determined by the free will of their respec-tive peoples, and the spirit of true religion is unobstructed by ancient forms and interpretations, then we shall see a world in process of right experience, right human relations and a spiritual moving forward to reality.

A study of these four lines of human living will show how truly Germany is today the focal point of the world situation. In that unhappy nation, the racial problem has attained such importance that the entire world is affected. From the economic angle, Hitler has said that Germany has been forced to fight in order to preserve the life, economically speaking, of her people; factually, the economic life of Germany was not as critically threatened as that of many smaller nations. The problem of government has also been brought to a critical point by German activity and conquest and by the emphasis laid by the Axis powers upon the relation of the state to the individual. The attitude of the German rulers to religion is recognised as one of pronounced antagonism. *Thus the four major world problems are today being precipitated by Germany into the arena of action;* they are evoking enquiry everywhere; the attention of men in every land is now focussed on these problems, and solution is inevitable when the war is over. When these problems are rightly approached by the men and women of goodwill, then we shall see a "world planning" for the production of harmonious living such as never before has been possible.

It is for humanity to solve its serious problems on the basis of brotherhood, and so bring in a way of living which will provide adequate supply of the necessities of life through the proper organising of time, labor and goods. This will lead to an interplay between the citizen and the state which will evoke the service of the individual and the right protection of the state. Humanity will then be free for the experiment of spiritual living, and this will express itself through awakened human lives. Can more be asked for or expected than this? Such a way of life can be made possible if the men and women of goodwill, of intelligence and of idealism can begin the task of inaugurating the new world order.

IV. The Task Ahead

This brings us now to the practical aspects of the subject and to the answering of the following question: Given the possibility of the new world order, what can be done to bring it into being at this time, in the midst of the conflict?

The period into which we are now entering divides itself into two parts:

1. The present period of the war itself, until the defeat of Germany and the end of the actual fighting.

2. The period after the guns have ceased roaring. The needed peace, reconstruction and rebuilding will then have to be determined.

It is with these periods that we must concern ourselves. They are, and will be, times of great difficulty and of painful conflict and adjustment. The task of restoring the world to harmony and order is a stupendous one. The educating of people everywhere in the necessity for new ideals of right living, for the new rhythms and the new "sharing" will not be easy. The work of healing the wounds of humanity, of rebuilding the shattered civilisation, of instituting disarmament, of recognising national, material and psychological needs, and of rescuing and restoring the happiness of the little children of the world and planning their future security will take the best that is in the men and women of goodwill; it will call for the wise guidance of the new group of world servers and will engage the attention of intelligent people and understanding minds in every nation.

The first preliminary is for the men and women of goodwill to decide once and for all with which of the two forces, battling together, they will take their stand, mentally and spiritually, even if they are not called upon by their country to do so physically. I write at this time for those who take their stand on the side of the constructive forces which are fighting for the democratic values and the freedom of the peoples. I would here remind you that among the people in Germany and Italy there are thousands who also silently take their stand with those struggling for victory over the Axis powers. This must never be forgotten, for such people exist in their multitudes under totalitarian rule. The Forces of Light are found in every land but are at present only able to express themselves effectively in the countries ranged against Germany.

The men and women of goodwill, associated with the new group of world servers, should seek intelligently to understand the current problem, and to study the world situation from all possible angles. Intelligent understanding, love of one's fellowmen and sound commonsense are pre-requisities of all demanded service. Men should cultivate these qualities, divorcing them from all sentimental emotion and dealing factually with circumstance and environing conditions. It must be realised that the task to be done will take time, and the men and women of goodwill must brace themselves for sustained effort, for opposition, and for that dead lethargy and sick inertia which afflicts the masses of the people in every land. The immediate activities are two in number:

1. The finding of those people in every country who react to the vision of the new world order and who are the men and women of goodwill.
2. The presentation of the future possibilities, by them, to the masses of people in all lands.

I would here remind you that members of the new group of world servers and men and women of goodwill must be sought for in every department of life. They will be found among the adherents of all the current ideologies and in political and scientific circles, among the world educators and philanthropists, among the creative workers, the industrialists, in ordinary homes and in the ranks of labour.

The New Group of World Servers

The new group of world servers is not a new organisation which is forming in the world. It is simply a loose linking together of all men of constructive peace aims and goodwill who lay the emphasis upon the prior need of establishing right human relations before any lasting peace is possible. This group in no way interferes with the allegiance and loyalties of any man. It is a banding together of all who seek to express *the spirit of Christ* and who are free from the spirit of hatred and revenge. The challenge of this group to the world is to drop all antagonisms and antipathies, all hatred and racial differences, and attempt to live in terms of the one family, the one life, and the one humanity.

The new group of world servers believes that (through the agency of goodwill) the new world order can be firmly established on Earth. Today, in the interim period of the war, preparation for reconstruction can go forward simultaneously with the effort to defeat the totalitarian powers.

The men and women of goodwill must not be energised into activity with the note of sacrifice. The war has exacted much of that from them. The clarion note of joy through goodwill activity must be sent out. Let the beauty of what can be, the glory of the vision and the spiritual, scientific and physical rebuilding of humanity be held before them, inspiring them to renewed effort.

Through the work earlier done all over the world by the men of vision and of goodwill, there exist today many thousands of people in Europe, America and elsewhere who are waiting for the guidance which will start them into right activity. In every land the men and women of goodwill are to be found, ready to respond to a clear call and intelligent organisation in the service of reconstruction. Let them be found.

The message to be taught prior to any future peace consists of the following three clear and practical truths:

1. That the errors and mistakes of past centuries, culminating in the present world war, are the joint errors and mistakes of humanity as a whole. This recognition will lead to the establishing of *the principle of sharing*, so needed in the world today.

2. That there are no problems and conditions which cannot be solved by the will-to-good. Goodwill nourishes the spirit of understanding and fosters the manifestation of *the principle of cooperation*. This cooperative spirit is the secret of all right human relations and the enemy of competition.

3. That there is a blood relationship between men which, when recognised, dissolves all barriers and ends the spirit of separativeness and hate. The peace and happiness of each is the concern, therefore, of all.

This develops *the principle of responsibility* and lays the foundation of right corporate action.

These are the basic beliefs of the men and women of goodwill and provide the incentive to all service and action. These three practical and scientific truths embody the three basic facts and the initial acceptance of all world servers. They are contrary to no world position, subversive of no government or religious attitude and are innate in the consciousness of all men, evoking immediate response. Their acceptance will "heal" international sores.

I call on all the men and women of goodwill in the world to study the principles of the new world order. I call upon them, as they fight for justice and the rights of the little nations and the future of the children of all nations, to begin to educate those whom they can reach, in right attitudes and in that foresighted vision which will make the mistakes of the past impossible in the future.

One basic divine attribute is not yet as strong as it should be in humanity—the attribute of forgiveness. It is still associated with magnanimity. It is not seen to be essentially a condition of future relation between all nations, based upon a recognition of our common humanity. Germany, under her misguided and evil rulers, needs forgiveness. All the great Powers have also sinned in some degree and all have grievously erred in the past. Germany has precipitated the evil which has come upon the world, but she has within herself the seeds of her own punishment; these seeds will not come to fruition if excessive punishment is inflicted from outside.

Three recognitions will save the world when the guns cease firing:

1. The recognition of joint responsibility for past world conditions. The truth that "all have sinned" must be faced.
2. The recognition that, though the German people weakly acquiesced in the rule of Hitler, they are basically the victims of an organised deception. Since

1914 they have been told only lies. The future new world order will inaugurate an era of truthful propaganda and national and international information.

3. The recognition that the past has gone with all its evils, and that a future of unlimited possibilities for good and for constructive changes lies ahead. The future must be developed by all nations in the closest collaboration.

These three points must be constantly presented to the public in the simplest language, because it is the inert mass of unthinking people who will constitute the hardest problem. Appeal must be made to the best that is in them, because the immediate task ahead is the development of those right attitudes without which no peace can be lasting and justice will not be possible. Peace must not be *imposed* by those who hate war. Peace must be a natural outcome and expression of the human spirit, and of a determination to change the world attitude into one of right human relations.

This is no impossible idealistic dream, but an immediate possibility, given the spirit of forgiveness and goodwill. Patience will be required, because the nervous strain of war and pain and anxiety, fear and underfeeding will have to be reckoned with. Human beings will be the same as before the war, except for exhaustion and a willingness on the part of the majority to accept almost any terms which will allow them to live quietly again, free from the immediate fear of bombs and starvation and ruin. The great need will be for slow action, leaving time for the needed healing processes and adjustment before the final peace terms are settled by the nations, sitting in conclave. Nations will have to shift from a war footing to settled peace activities, and from the organised tensions of war to the comparative relaxations of peace. Disarmament must go forward as an initial move, but in such a manner that the question of unemployment is not unduly aggravated. The "turning of the cannon into ploughshares" must be carried out with judgment, and only wide international planning can take care of this stupendous process. The settling of national boundaries and spheres of influence will be one of the utmost difficulty and can only be satisfactorily determined if goodwill is *actively present and consciously used,* and when the wishes of the people involved are consulted in a non-partisan spirit. The emphasis upon past historical boundaries as a determining factor is ever dangerous. Wise and slow action will here be needed and proper consideration of population desires. It is not the restoration of the ancient landmarks which is desirable, but the restoration of national and racial spheres of influence in accordance with the present situation.

It is not the imposition of any particular ideology upon the world, or its removal, which is of importance, but the establishing of those world conditions which will give all the nations adequate food, the necessities of life, and opportunity then to express themselves, and to make their unique contribution to the welfare of the whole family of nations.

The working details will have to be developed by all peoples in the closest collaboration. Men of vision, and not just politicians; world servers, and not just military leaders; and humanitarians, and not just the rulers of nations, must determine these tremendous issues. As they do so they must be able to count upon the support of the men and women of goodwill in every land. To sum up:

The interim between the present time and the final adjustment falls into two major periods and the practical work in each can be clearly defined:

1. The interim between today and the cessation of war. This must be used in the following ways:

    a. To educate and stabilise all men and women of goodwill.

    b. To discover the workers, humanitarians and those men and women of understanding and vision who will respond to the principles here given.

    c. To prepare these men and women to work in unison for justice and right human relations in all countries after the cessation of the war.

2. The interim between the end of the physical fighting and the final peace settlement. It is to be hoped— for the sake of justice—that this interlude will cover several years of rehabilitation and education. During these interludes between the past and the new world order, the men and women of goodwill can actively aid the statesmen of all nations by intelligent cooperation, in the planned focussing of enlightened public opinion, and in defining and teaching the real meaning of right human relations.

It is with the first interlude that we are now concerned.

It is desirable to get into immediate touch with those whose names are already known to you, and set them to work and let them—in their turn—find others, and guide them also into the way of reconstruction. Let all these names and addresses be gathered together in central and national mailing lists, but let them also be kept in both New York and London, for it is the task of the English speaking peoples to rebuild the world with the help of all other nations. There must, therefore, be some measure of centralisation of the work and some way in which these people can be reached and swept into cooperative activity.

With goodwill to all, with a staunch belief in the divine possibilities of human beings and in the future resurrection of humanity, with an exalted recognition of God, with an acknowledgment of the fundamental values of Christ's teaching, and with a joyful determination to go forward with the work of reconstruction, I call upon those who respond to this vision immediately to set to work.

I call you to no organisational loyalties, but only to love your fellowmen, be they German, American, Jewish, British, French, Negro or Asiatic. I call you from your dreams of vague beauty, impossible Utopias and wishful thinking to *face life as it is today;* and then to begin, in the place where you are, to make it better. I call you to the experiment of right human relations, beginning with your own personal relations to your family and friends, and then to the task of educating those you contact so that they also start a similar work. It is the work of attaining right individual relations, right group relations, right intergroup relations, right national relations and right international relations. I call you to the realisation that in this work no one is futile or useless, but that all have a place of practical value. I call you to recognise that goodwill is a dynamic energy which can bring about world changes of a fundamental kind, and that its mode of expression is through the activity of the individual man and woman and through their massed intent. The massed power of goodwill, the dynamic effect of intelligent and active understanding, and the potency of a trained and alive public opinion which desires the greatest good of the greatest number, are beyond belief. This dynamic power has never been employed. It can, today, save the world.

THE WORLD CRISIS FROM HIERARCHICAL VIEWPOINT

April-May 1940

Another Wesak Festival will be close at hand when you receive this communication. Its urgency, imminence and finality prompt me again to attempt to awaken those of you who receive it to the present opportunity and to the spiritual urgency of this high moment in human affairs. The three Full Moon periods of April, May and June are most significant and determining, and upon what happens during the next few weeks, whilst the sun is still moving northwards, much will depend.

In this communication I would like to do two things: First of all, give you a better idea as to how the spiritual Hierarchy of our planet regards the present world crisis, and secondly, indicate to you certain major eventualities which are dependent upon three things:

1. A possible divine intervention which may be brought about through the aspiration of all right-minded people, plus the intelligent and constant use of the

Great Invocation, now being used in its tens of thousands by the world aspirants in every country.

2. The emergence of certain clear lines of demarcation between the activities of the Forces of Light and the forces of materialistic aggression.

3. The place which clear thinking, wise speech and skill in action should play in the attitude of the world disciples and the men and women of goodwill every where.

I shall endeavour to speak with a reasonable brevity and clarity, and I do so with complete freedom from what you call bias. I speak in terms of humanity—without distinction of race, colour or nation; I have no particular political views, because I know that all potential theories, ideologies and governments are temporary states and conditions, controlling different groups of human beings on their way from the human state to the divine. This is a point of view oft overlooked by many of you who—temporarily and oft fanatically—belong to one or other of these ephemeral states of mind and passing human attitudes. I have no particular religious preferences, knowing as I do that all roads lead to God and that the sense of divinity is so dominant and inherent in the human heart that naught at any time can crush it out; life, experience, trial, pain and instinctive human orientation lead all men finally back into the light of God. I can and do, therefore, love all men, irrespective of nationality and present ideas, as do all with whom I am associated. Looking upon the moving screen of time with a vision which reaches into the future and is inclusive of the past (for this is the prerogative of all trained world disciples) I know that present events will play their timely part, will give place to others in due time, and that—when the immediate processes of readjustment in human values, spiritual objectives and political schemes, religious orientations and territorial syntheses are completed—the world will settle down again to the processes of daily living. The immediate opportunity and situation in which we find ourselves will have proved dynamically useful or (such is the sad possibility) negatively futile. A fresh cycle of civilisation, culture and growth will have been inaugurated which will be coloured by the ancient hues of selfish desire and aggressive acquisitiveness, or by the newer and more beautiful colouring of happy and satisfactory international relationships, of religious understanding and of the much needed and demanded economic cooperation.

Such a dual possibility confronts us now. One—new, right and spiritually oriented; the other, ancient, evil and undesirable. Whether man will go forward into the better way of life or permit the perpetuation of the old ways and the domination of selfish personal, national and racial interests remains yet to be determined.

Two things are, however, obvious to us as we look at the present world situation; first, that the lines of demarcation between the two ways of living and the two objective attitudes are far more clearly defined than at any previous time in the history of humanity; secondly, that it is the muddled thinking of vast masses of well-meaning people (many of them not immediately implicated in the world conflict) which is largely responsible for the slowness of the final crisis and the postponement of the advancing decision.

For decades, we, the teachers of the race of men, have watched certain great world (or planetary) tendencies take shape, assume defined and pronounced outlines and become conditioning potencies. This shaping and definition was essential if the issue was to be presented with clarity to humanity, thus enabling a basic choice to be presented to the sons of men and the placing in their hands of certain determinations which could, if rightly directed, carve out for them a new and better future. Such a presentation has never before been possible, because never before has mankind been at the stage where it could grasp the situation intelligently, or been so closely and rapidly interrelated by the radio, telephone, the press and the telegraph. The needed choices can now be made in cooperation, in consultation and with open eyes. The choice is clearly before the thinking people in every country, and upon their decision rests the fate of the less intelligent masses. Hence the present responsibility of the national leaders, of the representatives of the people in the governments, of the churches, and of the intelligentsia in all lands, without exception. There should be no shirking or evasion of responsibility. There is, however, much.

In past communications I have oft spoken of the Forces of Light and the Forces of Materialism, meaning by these terms the controlling trends towards brotherhood, right human relations and selfless purpose, and those which reverse these higher tendencies and bring into human affairs selfish acquisitiveness, emphasis upon material interests, brutal aggression and cruelty. The two positions are clear to the unprejudiced onlooker.

To these two groups I would add a third. This third group is taking shape in the world today with extreme definiteness and is composed of those who throw the weight of their influence and of their action on neither side; theoretically, they may advocate the higher way, but practically they do nothing to further its interests. This third group is formed internally of two groups: first, those people who are potentially weak and are therefore ridden by fear and terror, feeling that they dare not move in any way against the forces of aggression, and secondly, an intrinsically powerful group who, through selfish material interests, plus a sense of separative superiority, or distance from the seat of trouble and the domination of false values, hold aloof from the situation and shirk their evident responsibility as members of the human family. This latter group includes, among others, a number of powerful democracies and re-publics. Fear, terror and a sense of helpless futility govern the reactions of the one, and who can criticise? Selfishness and separativeness control the other group.

You have, therefore, in the world at this time three groups of people who embody the three major views of the whole of humanity, plus the unthinking masses, swayed by propaganda, controlled by their governments, and the prey of the loudest voices. It is of value to you to get this picture clearly in your minds, and I would like again to define them.

1. The ancient entrenched forces of aggression, of material acquisition and pure selfishness, working through a pronounced cruelty which reaches out and grasps what it wants, irrespective of any other rights, historical and legal possessions or the will of anyone.

2. The forces of spiritual purpose, embodied in the will to protect the rights of others, along with individual rights; to end aggression and its consequent fear, and to throw the weight of their combined influence on to the side of the most spiritual values, of human freedom, of the right to think, and of kindness. I use the word "kindness" advisedly because it embodies the idea of kin-ship, of brotherhood and of right human relations. It is world goodwill in expression, just as the will-to-good is the basis of any possible peace—a goodwill which would negate any premature peace at this time, because the latter would give time for the Forces of Materialism to consolidate their gains and prepare the way for further aggression. Kindness, the will-to-good and peace— such should be the practical expression and the formulated intention of those who are conditioned by the Forces of Light.

3. The force of mass negativity, as expressed today by the dominated people in the strongholds of aggression and by the neutrally minded people everywhere. They are all coloured by racial fear, by the instinct to self-preservation, and by short-sighted selfish interest.

The problem is one of exceeding difficulty because, even though the lines of demarcation are becoming steadily more distinct, yet the exponents of these three groups are to be found in every land and among all people—in every church and in every home. No nation or group is exempt from this triplicity. *It is rooted in human attitudes, and that is why this conflict is a strictly human conflict and not a European war.* Every nation has its selfish, aggressive people, who believe that might is right and that men must be governed by the law of the jungle, taking what they want, no matter at what cost to others. Every nation has those within its borders who see the vision of right human relations, who seek to live by the law of brotherhood, who respond to the influence of the Forces of Light and of the spiritual Hierarchy, and who desire peace, kindness and goodwill to rule world affairs and control the policies of the governments. Every nation has also within it those neutrally-minded people who fail to think clearly, who seek to place the blame upon the shoulders of all except themselves, who theorise and speculate, advise, and assign responsibility, but who refrain from any active participation in the processes of adjustment, from reasons of pride or unwillingness to pay the price. Many of them are *group* conscientious objectors who will eventually profit by the victory of the Forces of Light but who refuse to share in the struggle, reserving themselves for the future peace settlements, longing for the conflict to end, but doing nothing to bring that about. Many are entirely sincere, but their thinking needs adjusting.

If you will rightly grasp the reality of the statements made above, you will do your share in the mental clarification which is going on in the world. These three groups *are* functioning today and are in conflict. The neutrally-minded group is definitely hindering the work of the Forces of Light. These three world attitudes *are* to be found in every nation, as well as in the consciousness of every single individual. The realisation of this may enable you to grasp and shoulder your individual responsibility better. You will realise the need to ascertain for yourself where you stand and will refuse to be conditioned by other people's points of view and the world-wide propaganda; you will appreciate where your nation stands and on which side, and where you, as a soul, stand. You will then be able—if you are sincere and clear-thinking—to work for that group within the whole which seems to you to embody the highest possible activity and aims, and you will relinquish that attitude of futile negativity, smug neutrality or bewildered confusion which may distinguish you. You will then emerge from the glamour of propaganda and of world illusion into the clear light of your own soul, whose essential nature is love and selflessness and whose major aspiration is to bring peace and goodwill among men and to see the consummation of the mission of Christ.

This will lead eventually to the disappearance of so-called neutrality upon earth—a neutrality in act, for there is never neutrality in thought.

One of the things which the spiritual leaders of humanity have sought to do is to bring clearly to the attention of men the basic duality which is found in the world today—the duality of selfish, material living and that of unselfish spiritual objectives. This is now clearly defined. The second stage of their task now lies ahead, and that is so to stimulate the vision of men everywhere that—beginning with the intelligentsia—they can consciously take their stand under one or other of the two banners, and so know what they are doing and why. The neutrally-minded waver between the two and, to date, do nothing.

I would like in this connection to deal with one problem which has somewhat disturbed the least clear-thinking among those whom I have for some time taught. I have for years sought to develop in the world a group of men and women who would stand for the spiritual values, who would love all men, who would foster the spirit of goodwill, and who would stand to humanity (as far as they could) as the Hierarchy of Light, as Christ and His disciples seek to do. This has been interpreted by some of you as meaning that you must refrain from rebelling against the evil thing in your midst, and from all criticism and partisanship. You seem unable to love with steadfastness the offender and yet to rid the world of the offence. The situation might clarify if you answered to yourself one or two questions:

Do you believe that the Hierarchy of Light, under the leadership of Christ, is on the side of cruelty, aggression and the slaughter of the defenceless?

Do you believe that the world can be saved by a refusal to think and by the shirking of individual responsibility, thus ignoring a situation which does exist?

Do you feel that there are no issues and principles which are worth fighting for and dying for, if need be?

Do you stand with the Forces of Light or with the Forces of Materialism?

What are you doing to aid the side which claims your allegiance, loyalty and idealism?

Are you governed by a sense of individual futility—that weapon which the Forces of Materialism are using now so potently to stun possible opponents into helplessness?

A clear and searching analysis of the spiritual objectives of humanity will enable you to answer these questions. If you do not need to answer them because your position is clear in your mind, the study of the questions may enable you to serve your day and generation more ably and to present the situation more clearly to the bewildered.

A horror of war and a longing for peace are no excuse for slack thinking, nor do they provide an alibi or the opportunity to shirk individual or national responsibility. The conflict is on. It is of ancient lineage. The issues are clearly marked between right and wrong, between cruelty and kindness, between aggression and freedom. To evade responsibility because of past national mistakes and historical sins and failures is an unwarranted alibi; the shirking of due participation in the struggle because every nation has certain materialistic objectives is wrong; a nation is but the sumtotal of its people. To refuse to think because of the general condition of fatigue in which you share is no excuse, and is unworthy of the world disciples and aspirants.

The Hierarchy of Light is seeking to arouse men everywhere to the basic dualism underlying this conflict and to the essential significance of the issues with which humanity is faced. Hence the emphasis which I am laying upon the need to face the problem, to think clearly and intelligently about what is going on around you, and to take right and cooperative action. The whole world problem will be clarified and the end of the conflict more rapidly reached when there are only two parties and not three. The recognition of this underlying dualism is necessary prior to the shifting of humanity's consciousness away from its major preoccupation—acquisitive material desire, aggressively obtained—into soul consciousness, with its correlations, group interests, the meeting of group need, and the functioning of a steady group cooperation on a world scale. This is true of individuals, of nations and of races; as you, an individual, work out your own problem in your daily life, you are helping to solve the world problem.

This is the situation as the Hierarchy sees it today and with which it challenges all men and women of goodwill. They ask you to share in the conflict in some way, and remind you of the occult significance of those oft misunderstood words of Christ, "He that is not with me, is against me."

In closing these remarks upon clear thinking I would add two more. There is some confusion arising out of the basic idealism which underlies the activities of many people in many countries. It is the importance of the somewhat new ideal of the good of the state as a whole versus the good of the individual and the good of humanity. The state becomes almost a divine entity in the consciousness of the idealist. This is necessarily part of the evolutionary plan, but in so far as it constitutes a problem, is too big for the individual to solve alone and unaided. Of one fundamental truth I can, however, assure you. When men everywhere—within the boundaries of their particular state and whilst upholding its authority and its civilisation—begin to think in terms of mankind, then public opinion will become so potent and so right in its inclusiveness that state policies must inevitably conform to the larger ideal, and the sacrifice of the individual and of humanity in large numbers to the individual state will no longer be possible. The part will be seen in its proper relation to the larger whole. It is this arousing of public opinion to world rights, to inclusive human interests and to international cooperation that is the true goal of all present spiritual endeavour. Eventually it will be realised that the responsibility for what governments do rests squarely upon the shoulders of the individual citizens who put governments in their position of power. This is a responsibility from which no citizens of any nation are or should be exempt, and to this all national thinking of the right kind is fortunately awakening.

The second point I would briefly add is that, with the precipitation of the present world situation, the citizens of all nations are involved in a condition from which there is no escape except through right action and wide vision on their part; to this world situation they must conform their lives temporarily, patterning their activities upon the needs of their own particular nation. For those who are swept into the world conflict under one or other of the clearly defined banners, their immediate action is clear—participation in the national emergency. This is, however, wholly compatible with a subjective process of right and clear thinking, which must run parallel to the demanded outer activity and which will lay a foundation for the increasingly right action as time elapses. This will involve right action on the part of those who are fighting under the Forces of Light, and will lead to an eventual right and just peace; it will involve also right action upon the part of those who have been swept into a bewildered activity under the Forces of Materialism, leading finally to a revolt against that which is wrong and evil—for the hearts of all men and the springs of the divine life are not to be permanently directed into wrong channels of activity. The responsibility for the immediate world moves and the present gigantic national enterprises is now out of the hands and the control of the individual; the responsibility for the future, nevertheless, still lies in his hands. This shouldering of right responsibility must be preceded, however, by an interlude of clear thinking plus right action as a citizen.

The problem of those living in neutral countries is different, and along what lines it should be solved I have earlier indicated.

As for the world disciples and aspirants (among whom you range yourselves), the entire problem can be seen along still wider and more comprehensive lines. You are forced by circumstance and karma, and by the free decision of your souls, to work under one or other of the two banners or in some one of the neutral and negative countries. Your problem in all three cases is to see clearly the spiritual focus of this world crisis, to swing the weight of any influence you may have—objective or subjective, spiritual, emotional or mental—on to the side of the Forces of Light. As you do so, you must preserve an understanding attitude of steadfast love (not sentiment or emotional reaction) to men and women everywhere, without any exception or reservations in your consciousness. That action has to be taken, at times, which hurts or damages the form side of life or the physical forms, is entirely compatible with the constant preservation of soul love—a thing which it is hard for the disciple to learn and master, but which is nevertheless a governing principle in evolution. This world crisis and the present world war will, it is hoped, awaken men to the realisation that the form side of manifestation, with its aggressive selfishness, its cruel emphases and its separative tendencies, carries inevitably with it the seeds of its own eventual elimination and the unavoidable results of pain, suffering, war, disease and death. This situation is therefore of man's own making and the result of his material nature and lack of soul control. But—the soul is eternal; its nature is inclusive love; and the whole aim of the present crisis is to shift the focus of human awareness out of the form and the material aspect of living, into the consciousness of the soul, and to do this at any cost to the hindering forms. It is against this transference of emphasis that the Forces of Materialism are today fighting.

For this reason, humanity is swept into a vortex of conflict, and the issue depends upon the clear thinking, wise speech and selfless intent of the world disciples, working in collaboration with all the forces for good in the world today, doing their duty as citizens of their own country but cultivating ceaselessly and unrelentingly a world-consciousness.

Let me now enlarge somewhat upon the possibility of divine intervention.

Hovering today within the aura of our planet are certain great spiritual Forces and Entities, awaiting the opportunity to participate actively in the work of world redemption, re-adjustment and reconstruction. Their Presence is sensed at times by the spiritually-minded people of the world, and Their reality is recognised by the mystics and occultists working in every land. Men and women express this recognition according to the trend of their religious and psychological training and their particular mental or emotional bias. The advent of Christ, or His "second coming," is anxiously anticipated by many orthodox Christians, who regard this world war as indicating the end of the world and as preparatory to the appearance of the Christ, to bring peace on earth. Others, more orientally minded, await the appearance of an Avatar Who will transmit from God the needed world message or new type of energy. Prophecy and astrology indicate a Coming One and their many differing opinions seem to converge on Him; occultists invoke everywhere the Forces of Light and call for the appearance of that extra-planetary Potency to Whom they give the title, "Spirit of Peace." Those with no religious or metaphysical bias recognise, however, that all times of emergency seem ever to evoke some Liberator or some man or group of men who are capable of changing world affairs and inaugurating— under the stress and strain of the times—the new and needed fresh cycle of civilisation and culture. Many refrain from specification of the requirements of such a Coming One today, because of the magnitude and planetary nature of His task, but they secretly hope and pray for His appearing. Still others regard such an idea and hope as simply a psychological fulfilment and the embodiment of the wish-life of the people—this time of humanity as a whole, for the first time in racial history. Such people are apt to feel that this embodiment has no true substance or place in the life of mankind, but wish that it had. They forget that when a thoughtform has been constructed of sufficient potency and has been built over a long period of time by the people of the world, a further and final stage becomes ever possible. The form can be rendered so magnetic that it can attract an Energy which will inform it and give it active potency; it can then become a vital link between the subjective world of energy and the objective world of forces and a thing of power, of impelling and guiding activity, and therefore the expression of a Life. This thoughtform, duly informed, becomes a mediating factor, constructed by humanity but animated by the will-to-good of some great and spiritual Entity. That thoughtforms, embodying evil lives can be and are constructed is equally true, but with these we are not at this time dealing.

We come now to the significant point of what I have to say today in this connection.

A great and vital thoughtform is in process of construction upon our planet and within our planetary aura. It is being built by the power of sound, by the magnetic pull of invocation leading to eventual evocation, and by the force of desire-substance, animated by the power of thought. It is being constructed by the united efforts of the Hierarchy, of the world disciples and aspirants, of the men and women of goodwill in all nations, and also through the inchoate longings of men everywhere, of all religious beliefs, political views and group loyalties. It is safely anchored upon the physical plane, is of vast proportions upon the astral or emotional plane, but lacks vitality and power upon the mental plane. It is here, within the realm of thought substance, that the weakness of the structure of this thoughtform becomes apparent. It is already potent spiritually, owing to the scientific work of the occult Hierarchy and Their trained helpers. This spiritual life relates the thoughtform to the waiting extra-planetary Forces and can make Their work possible and effective. It is potent physically and emotionally through the work of the lovers of humanity, the well-meaning efforts of the emotionally oriented people and the agonised longings of the masses, who hate war, desire quiet, and demand peace and good living conditions.

There is, however, a gap or hiatus upon the mental plane, for the minds of men are not functioning correctly. The disciples and world aspirants are not thinking with clarity, nor are they working in unity. They are evading issues or are thinking separatively or nationally or fanatically; they are not convinced of the potency of invocation or of prayer; they are failing to realise that it is possible to work ardently for those conditions which will lead to peace, and yet fight simultaneously so that those conditions may be available; they fail to love all men without exception in their longing to see their own loyalties emerge triumphant; they work doubtingly, hoping for the best but believing in the worst; they use the method of prayer and of invocation because such methods seem to have been successful in the past, and because they are told that "faith can move mountains," but they feel inwardly quite hopeless and uninspired and are not at all sure what faith intrinsically is; they realise that a united front and a spirit of joyous certainty are psychological assets of well-nigh invincible potency, but they feel unable to arouse within themselves the slightest enthusiasm.

It is this negative and lukewarm attitude, this mental uncertainty and this failure to link up the spiritual and the physical worlds in a positive relationship which is holding back the Forces of Light and the actual presence of the Spirit of Peace, and thus negativing a possible divine intervention. It is the test of group work. The faith of many individuals is real and deep, but they stand alone; the knowledge that the few have of the nature of the waiting Forces of intervention is being negated by the faithlessness of the world disciples and aspirants, weighed down by world karma, by their own physical fatigue and by their horror of the present situation, plus the difficulties of individual circumstance.

The problem can be most simply stated. Either the spiritual Hierarchy exists, with all its potencies of love, wisdom and skill in action, or for ages humanity has suffered from hallucinations; either Christ and His group of Masters, initiates and disciples are facts in the natural processes of evolution, historically proven and known through Their spiritual activity down the ages, or men have been victims during those ages of a gigantic fraud—emanating from what and where? Either the consistency of the evolving presentation of the spiritual effort of the Hierarchy is a witness to a great reality or mankind has developed a mentality which is an instrument for the fabrication of non-existent facts, and this is in itself so paradoxical as to give the lie to the inference. Either the spiritual worlds and the three worlds of human endeavour can be related, or there is nothing to past beliefs, to ancient stories of manifesting divinity and to the constantly recurring periods of divine intervention.

I would here face you with these alternatives and would ask you to consider your own position in these matters. Does the story of Easter and of the living Christ carry no truth, and is it not possible for that Risen Christ to express His power on Earth through His chosen instruments? Is there no foundation for the myth of the annual return of the Buddha, holding the door open between Shamballa and the Hierarchy so that, at need, intervention may be possible through that open door? Is it only a silly dream and a fantasy that at the time of the June Full Moon, Christ—in the closest cooperation with the Buddha—links the Hierarchy with Humanity? Is it quite impossible that when humanity awakens to the fact of this mediatorship and can then avail itself of the straight line of ascent and descent through the doors held open by the Buddha and the Christ, some stupendous appearing may be imminent and suddenly take place? May it not be possible that through the ascent of man's aspiration and spiritual desire, and through the descent of the waiting Potencies, certain great changes may take place, for which all the past has been only preparatory and through which the Aquarian Age of brotherhood and understanding may make itself felt by virtue of these great Potencies?

The two Full Moons of May and June present to you

a new opportunity to participate in the release of the planetary Life from the thralldom of the Forces of Materialism. If you are to do your share in this work of salvage, it will necessitate certain attitudes and activities on your part which I would like briefly to touch upon, leaving you to take right and appropriate action and to follow, with all other disciples and aspirants, the indicated stages:

1. Study with care and answer with sincerity and to your own complete satisfaction the questions I put to you earlier in this communication. When you have done this, you will know where you personally stand.

2. For the entire week prior to the May Full Moon and the June Full Moon endeavour to do the following things:

   a. Link up with all disciples, aspirants and men and women of goodwill throughout the world and in all nations, using the creative imagination.
   b. Eliminate out of your consciousness all negativity, seeing yourself clearly as ranged on the side of the Forces of Light; you are, therefore, not neutral in thought. See to it also that when taking right action in the conflict against the forces of materialism you preserve ever a spirit of love for all individuals who have been swept into the vortex of their potency.
   c. When meditating and invoking the Forces of Light, endeavour to forget entirely all your own personal difficulties, tragedies and problems. Disciples have to learn to carry forward their work for humanity in spite of personality stresses, strains and limitations.
   d. Prepare yourselves thus for the work of the two Full Moons, keeping your objective clearly in mind and submitting yourselves to an adequate temporary discipline.

3. For the two days prior to the Full Moon, on the day of the Full Moon itself, and for the two succeeding days (five days) endeavour at sunrise, at noon, at five o'clock P.M., and at sunset, plus the exact time of the Full Moon in your own

land, to say the Great Invocation with the intent to invoke, precipitate and anchor in outer manifestation the waiting Potencies. Do this aloud when possible, and in group formation whenever feasible. It is the focussed power of your unemotional thought which will bridge the present existing gap and link more closely the two worlds of spiritual activity and of human demonstration.

4. Repeat this activity for three days each and every month—the day prior to the Full Moon, the day of the Full Moon, and the succeeding day. As a preliminary exercise to these three days, you could take an earlier three days of preparation, and thus increase the effectiveness of your effort.

Many people the world over have for years been trained to recognise two things. First, the importance of the Wesak Festival at the time of the Full Moon of May, because it not only objectively links the major Eastern religion with the major Western faith, but because it esoterically provides the key to the open door between Shamballa and the Hierarchy, between the purpose of God (still unidentified by man, owing to his relatively low stage of evolution which makes it beyond human comprehension at present) and the method of God, which is love; it provides also the link between the Buddha, temporarily embodying will-wisdom, and the Christ, embodying love-wisdom, and also between humanity, focussed in consciousness through the Christ, and the Hierarchy, focussed in consciousness through the Buddha. Owing to the stress of humanity today and the urgency of the response which that distress evokes in the Hierarchy, the synthesis of these two reactions to the world crisis can prove adequate to bring in that outside assistance which could end the conflict along right lines and bring not only relief, but illumination to the human consciousness. But again—speaking here to a representative body of aspirants and disciples—I would state that the focus and the emphasis is not yet adequate to guarantee this extra-planetary response.

Nevertheless, it could be if, in your own life of medita-

tion and of discipline, in your speech with others and in
the general tone of your intercourse with your environment,
you can eliminate the negative and more selfish reactions
and (for the sake of human welfare) temporarily, at least,
live at your highest point of aspiration.

Secondly, you have been trained in the belief that all
the information which I have given out anent the relation
of the Buddha and the Christ, and of the Hierarchy, Humanity and Shamballa, will form part of the coming new world
religion and that the theme of the Great Approaches will
constitute the basic fundamentals of the future spiritual
teaching. This too you must have in mind, for the work you
are asked to do at the coming two Full Moons, and during
the less important full moons of the year, is not only related
to the present emergency, but is also constructively related
to the future faith of humanity. Bear this also in mind.

You will note that what I have said concerns your
mental attitudes and your emotional reactions to present
world affairs. It concerns also your soul tension, your willingness to undergo soul tension, and your capacity to stand
as part of the great chain of intermediaries who are today
being called to the service of the race in an hour of urgency.
It concerns the organising of yourself as an integrated personality in relation to your soul and to humanity; it involves
the recognition of the work which you *can* do from the
point of integration. I would ask you to ponder with care
upon this paragraph, stating the possibilities of your task.

I call you to a period of clear thinking. I seek not to
mould your political approach to life, but I do seek to aid
you to see humanity and its welfare—not only in terms of
your own nation or your own political group—but in terms
of the whole, and as we, the teachers on the inner side, are
forced to see it. I seek to see you free yourselves from the
condition where you are swayed by propaganda of a political,
national or religious kind, and deciding for yourself where
you, as a soul, must stand in this world crisis and on which
side you will place the emphasis of any influence you may
wield; I would have you note where your highest ideals

will lead you and whether the springs of your life's decisions and attitudes are truly pure and unadulterated.

I seek to draw your attention away from the many minor issues, the many clamouring voices, and from the widespread concentration upon the unworthy pasts and the undesirable aspects of all nations (without exception) , and help you to see with clarity the major dualism which underlies the present world conflict—might against right, materialism against the higher values, freedom against imprisonment, cruelty against fair dealing, liberty and safety against fear and aggression. Then, having balanced these pairs of opposites within your consciousness, decide where your loyalty, your interest and your ability to serve will be placed, and then go forward to further the ends of one or other of the two groups, at no matter what cost, but knowing where you stand and why you stand there.

That the will of Shamballa may be enabled to express itself through love and through the meditation of the Hierarchy, working through all disciples, aspirants and men and women of goodwill, is the earnest prayer of your fellow-disciple and co-worker.

THE WORLD CRISIS TODAY

June 30, 1940

Events and situations change with such rapidity at this time, as humanity takes action or refrains from action (which latter course is just as determining for good or evil as is the former) , that I feel again the need of writing on the world crisis, as I did last autumn, thus carrying forward my theme. I write as one who is working on the inner side today, sensing and seeing what is hidden from many of you. The exoteric outer history of events is known to all of you, and with its detail I need not deal. The action taken by the combatant nations, or withheld by the neutral nations, is also registered in your consciousness. The implications of such activity can only be truly known and appreciated by those people who today think *in terms of humanity as a whole,* and not in terms of a particular nation, such as the good of Germany or the destiny of America. Few disciples there are at this time who can thus think synthetically or who see the vision as a whole, precipitating as that which will condition eventually the entire human family. Many there are who are awakening to the need so to do and who are finding, in their processes of readjustment, many bewildering problems. For these sincere but bewildered people, I write. I find that there is little that I can say to the provincially minded or to those with the purely parochial point of view. Their limitations of vision lie within themselves and only dire events and strenuous emergency will enable them finally to transcend the petty quibbling and quality of their lower mind, with its concrete tendency to hark back to the past and its fear to venture with faith into the future.

I have been interested in the response to my earlier article, written in April, 1940. The majority of those whom I sought to reach and with whom I have communicated for many years accepted my premises without much questioning but refrained from positive action or the use of any influence. A few resented the implications of the existent divisions between the Forces of Light (focussed through the allied nations) and the Forces of Aggression (focussed through Germany). They embody a true, but erroneously interpreted, idea of human unity. They fail to understand that— as the New Age is ushered in—there must inevitably come a judgment day (speaking symbolically) and the emergence of a clear line of demarcation between that which is new and that which is of the old age; there must appear the distinction between exoteric happenings and esoteric attitudes and between those who see a new world order, developed and brought to functioning activity by the Forces of Light, through cooperation, coordination and understanding, and a world order which will be imposed by terror, through dictatorial government, by the suppression of liberty of conscience, and by the enthronement of a race whose values are, at this time, anti-spiritual and anti-social. This judgment day is now upon humanity, and the final decision will be arrived at by those whose normal inclinations and natural tendencies are on the side of law and order, and whose will-to-good is directed towards right human relations and true human welfare. These enlightened people will back their judgment with a focussed will to bring in the era wherein these values will dominate, and they are also willing to take the necessary measures to make these values possible.

I would like to deal openly and frankly with the problems with which you are being confronted when you face the world as it is today and the world as it may be tomorrow—a world whose fate is still unsettled. I would present possibilities with a definite application to the reactions of such empires as those of Great Britain, France and Holland, and with indication as to how the United States of America should be expected to respond. I write as one who represents the Hierarchy, as a member of a certain standing in its ranks, and as one also who works day and night for the success of those nations in the human family who, with their backs to a wall of misunderstanding, vilification and dislike, are strenuously opposing Germany and her satellite, Italy. I refer to that group of Allies who today stand with their purpose focussed in Great Britain, driven there by the trend of events. I do this because the basic hope of right human relations, of true and lasting peace, of liberty of conscience and of free and happy homes rests upon their triumphing; they are, at this time, the point of positive attack by the Forces of Evil. It is not possible for us as yet to reach the soul of the German people within that unhappy land, so complete is the glamour under which they are labouring. The day will come when again they will be reached, and this responsibility rests upon those Germans who remain free from glamour in other lands; it will come when the forces acting through the medium of a band of evil-intentioned men have been removed. With their disappearance will come the dissipation of the clouds of evil propaganda, lying information and distorted imputations and interpretations with which the masses of people, even in neutral lands, have been deluged.

Would you have me at this time of planetary crisis refrain from direct speech, have me withhold from you who read my words the truth—a truth which is already apparent to those who ponder the signs of the times with an unprejudiced mind, unbiased thought and a true love of humanity? This last quality, a *true love of humanity,* constitutes a basic test of wrong or right action. It is phenomenally clarifying if applied at this time to the combatants. Would you have me deal with pleasant platitudes anent a future happy world, when perhaps the very possibility of such a world trembles in the balance? Would you have me present the attitude of the Hierarchy as that of a placid band of onlookers, ready to help the world when the conflict is over, but at present insulated from all action and simply waiting till the dust and clamour of battle settle, to stimulate in men's minds the vision of a new world order wherein everyone will have a good time, where there will be no unemployment, wherein fear and terror will find no place and everyone will be happy, well fed and reasonably intelligent? Would you have me picture to you the great band of disciples, initiates and aspirants as a band of pacifists, cherishing the form side of life, afraid of death and remaining passive in the face of the death struggle of human liberty, of life, conscience and mind?

I tell you that this I cannot do. The Hierarchy is very different from this. Pacifism, as interpreted by you, has no place in its ranks. The destruction of form in battle (which causes so much fear to many of you) is of small importance to those who *know* that reincarnation is a basic law of nature and that *there is no death.* The forces of death are abroad today, but it is the death of liberty, the death of free speech, the death of freedom in human action, the death of truth and of the higher spiritual values. *These* are the vital factors in the life of humanity; the death of the physical form is a negligible factor in relation to these, and one easily righted again through the processes of rebirth and fresh opportunity.

I would say to those who preach a passive attitude in the face of evil and human suffering and who endorse a pacifism which involves no risks: With what do you propose to fight the forces of aggression, of treachery, evil and destruction which are today stalking over our planet? What weapons do you bring to this combat? How will you begin to stem the onslaught and arrest the whirlwind? Will you use prayers for peace, and then patiently wait for the forces of good to fight your battle and for God to do the work? I tell you that your prayers and your wishes are unavailing when divorced from right and potent action. Your prayers and petitions may reach the throne of God, symbolically speaking, but then the reply comes forth: The Forces of Light will strengthen your arms and turn the tide in your favour *if* you stand up and fight for that which you desire. Who will arrest the progress of aggressive selfishness if the men and women of goodwill rest back upon their idealism and do naught that is practical to justify their hope or aid in the materialisation of the desired ideal.

There are those in the world today who (despite past national selfishness and wrong) are fearlessly and with true insight fighting humanity's battle, and with them the Hierarchy stands, as it has ever stood on the side of liberty, right understanding and correct attitudes in human affairs. I would say to those who cry, "Peace, peace when there is no peace": Are you going to profit by their death and sacrifice when the ultimate triumph of the Forces of Light comes to pass? Are you going to take the position that you can then live in a safe world because others gave their lives that you might do so? Are you going to issue forth from the safe security of your pacifist alibi and gratefully acknowledge what they have done and grasp your share of the gains which they have purchased at such a cost? I would warn you not to be glamoured by the false premise that you must stand by your hard-earned convictions, even at the expense of other peoples' lives and the downfall of nations, forgetting that fear and false pride will make this argument of importance to you. Are the peace-minded people of the world going to reap the benefits of a peace for which they have paid no price? It is the people who value peace above all

234 THE EXTERNALISATION OF THE HIERARCHY

else who are today seeking by every possible method to stop Germany.

Let me tell you something about the peace for which the Hierarchy works and which the spiritually minded people of the world envisage *even whilst they fight,* and for which they are ready to pay the ultimate price. Peace, when it comes, will be the result of right world conditions and right human relationships. It is an effect and not a cause; it is the effect of certain subjective attitudes which are not yet present in the world on a sufficiently wide scale. Against these emerging conditions Germany has assembled her potent war machine, after years of scientific and planned preparation. Today the Allies stand waiting the opportunity for the final struggle with that potent nation, prepared to institute afterwards those conditions which will guarantee peace. There is no peace on the planet anywhere today. There is no peace in the questioning hearts of those who are not actively sharing in the struggle against evil. There is no peace in any field of human endeavour. It is not to be found in the economic field, torn as it is by the conflict between labour and capital, and between great schools of economic thought; it is not to be found in the religious field, where the struggle is going on between authority (tainted with old world churchianity) and experimental religion; it is not to be found in the social order, where class is ranged against class, poor against rich, and man against his brother; it is certainly not in the political field, where party strife controls and blinds the warring groups, hiding the wider vision of world affairs and the needs of humanity as a whole. There is no peace, and peace will not come through an applied and fanatical pacifism or through the loud talking and wishful thinking of those who hate war and who at the same time swell the tide of conquest and delay true victory by their violently uttered opposing views.

I tell you that all nations hate and oppose war; even Germany, behind the imposed terror, shrinks in horror at what is being done. The same love of peace which inspires the ordinary pacifist inspires those who are today fighting in order that peace may be the result of their sacrifice and the effect of the establishing of those right conditions which Germany is set to prevent. Yet many neutrally minded and pacifist people are unwilling to pay any price for what they profess so much to cherish. A complete refusal to fight on the part of the Allies and of those who are seeing with clarity the issues at stake would open the door to the world domination of the Forces of Materialism and Aggression. It is upon this that these evil forces count when they face the greatest neutral of all, the United States of America, and for which they are preparing as they disseminate their lying propaganda and plant their agents in every country and every state—preparatory to a peaceful conquest of a people who refuse sufficiently to value the spiritual issues at stake to take positive action.

And we, the teachers on the inner side, who for aeons have aided in the preparation of humanity for the coming age of peaceful cooperation and brotherhood, see all this future hope imperilled. Aggression and the rape of peaceful nations go steadily forward, as nation after nation crumbles under the iron heel of Germany, grinding the peoples of the world and sweeping them into slavery on a scale of serfdom and cruelty that the world has never before seen. As those who sought to arrest German progress succumb to treachery and pain and desert their comrades, the machine of evil marches on; neutral nations, resting back upon their peaceful intent and the claims of civilisation, are absorbed by the forces which impose the German demand for living space, and are thus denuded of liberty, of territory, and of all economic resources. And, at the same time, the greatest and most powerful neutral nation in the world *arms for defence of its territorial rights, but refuses to arm for the defence of human liberty.*

Do I speak too strongly to those of you who are not participating in this planetary war? I speak with clarity because I seek to arouse you to the true issues whilst there is yet time. I seek to arrest in you the idea that the western hemisphere is the seat of all civilisation, the custodian of the best that there is in humanity, and that the spiritual future of humanity lies in the cherished land of liberty. Liberty is a thing of the human soul and is found throughout the entire human race. Civilisation is a universal human right and not the prerogative of one nation. I tell you that humanity is everywhere spiritually minded and that the new race, the coming civilisation, and the new age culture will be found throughout the world—the universal inheritance of the human race. But everywhere humanity is the victim of propaganda—a propaganda which can only be seen in its true light when men think in terms of human liberty; when they *together* take the needed steps to ensure human happiness, and learn in so doing to face world conditions *as they are,* not hiding their heads in a dream world of their own making. The world of the future, of which men in all lands dream, is more than a possibility if men will shoulder their just responsibilities and together make it a fact in human experience. But such a world will not be possible for many long years if Europe goes down in the crash of battle and under the impact of the German war machine. It will emerge into realisation when there are enough people in the world who think clearly, see the vision truly, act intelligently, and meet force with force, which is the only method which the forces of aggression can understand.

Today the forces of evil have swept over France, Belgium, Holland, Norway, Poland, Finland and Roumania. Nothing has arrested their progress—neither truth nor armed might nor sacrifice. Today Great Britain stands with a handful of her allies upholding the banner of human liberty. With her stand France (for France is still loyal in her thousands to truth and liberty), Poland, Holland, Norway and Belgium—all represented in that small fortress of the Forces of Light which is the British Isles. Behind stand their great empires with their resources as yet untouched. Behind them again stand the spiritually minded peoples in every nation, and behind them all stands the Hierarchy of Light. In this interlude prior to the final struggle I write to those who are looking on with sympathy but without sacrifice and I ask you: Where do you stand?

I bring to you some of the contrasts in this war, in all simplicity and in an effort to enable you to choose right action.

The first great contrast might be called the way of appeasement and the way of aggression. The method of peaceful discussion was tried by the peace-loving peoples of France and Great Britain, and the way of aggression, developed for many years, is the way of Germany, of Russia, and in a lesser degree of Italy. I would remind you that it is to the eternal credit of the Allies (e'en though it lacked worldly common sense) that their preparations for war proved inadequate in the face of German preparedness. They were not one-pointed in their war effort, for the higher value of world civilisation engrossed them and the activities of their empires, which live at peace within themselves. They have made many grievous errors in the past (as have all peoples), but the way of expiation and of sacrifice is theirs, willingly accepted, and their reward is the freedom of humanity.

I will give you another contrast, growing out of the above. This is the emphasis upon a new world order within a rapidly changing world. The Allies uphold one point of view; the Germans, another. It is for this new and better world and the bringing in of the conditions wherein peace can be possible and the new world order developed that today the men of vision fight and die. The contrast is the enforced world order, emphasised by the so-called "German super-race," which will centralise the world around Germany, for the aggrandisement of Germany, for the expansion of the German living space and the supply of Germany's economic need—an order enforced by terror, by cruelty and death, ignoring the needs of humanity as a whole and the rights of all other nations, and sacrificing the whole world, if need be, to the glory of Germany. With this German-enforced rule and order, her greed for territorial expansion and her ruthless acquisition of the goods and pos-

session of other nations, I would ask you to contrast the
expressed aim of the Allies, reiterated again and again in
the speeches of the statesmen of both France and Great
Britain and summed up in the words of a great Englishman,
a government official and an aspirant to right and truth:

> "We shall use all our influence when the time
> comes in the *building of a new world* in which the
> nations will not permit insane armed rivalry to
> deny their hopes of fuller life and future confidence
> nor be forever overborne by grim foreboding of
> disaster. The new world that we seek will enlist
> the *cooperation of all peoples* on a basis of human
> equality, self-respect and mutual tolerance. We shall
> have to think out many things that lie on the route
> of international contacts—social, political and eco-
> nomic—and find means of reconciling the necessity
> of change in a constantly changing world with se-
> curity against the disturbance of the general peace
> through resort to violence. To this order that we
> shall create, *all nations have their contribution to
> make,* and a great responsibility both in thought
> and action will rest upon our people. We, not less
> than others, have our lesson to learn from past
> failures and disappointments."

I would have you note the recognition, by this spokes-
man for the Allies, of the need of change, the realisation
of the coming world order and the humble statement anent
past mistakes.

I would call your attention very briefly also to the
contrast in the methods employed: cruelty versus kindness,
merciless bombing and machine gunning on the one side,
and the constant refraining from attack upon the enemy
by the Allies, for fear of killing the defenceless; I would
call your attention to the broadcast from Great Britain,
warning the Germans to take cover when they hear the
British planes over Germany. I would call your attention
to the reticent but truthful propaganda which lays no

emphasis upon that which could stir up hate, and the lying information from Berlin and conquered cities. It is not my purpose to do more than indicate these contrasts which grow out of a widely differing subjective attitude to humanity. It is, however, of value for us all to face them in the process of clarifying issues. The basic contrast between freedom of speech, thought and action which distinguishes the democracies, and the cruel suppression of all liberty of thought and personal activity which controls the masses in Germany today, is too well known to require emphasising by me. But I bring these contrasts to your attention, asking you to recognise your responsibility to stand behind those who fight for liberty and to end the activity of those who are the enemies of all human freedom.

I would ask you to exercise your imagination in an effort to visualise a world in which there is a complete defeat of the Allies, expressing as they do the ideals for which the Forces of Light have ever stood. I would remind you of two things: First, that these Forces were defeated in the earlier phase of the conflict thousands of years ago, and secondly that—if They again go down to defeat—it will be largely due to the unpreparedness and to the pacific attitude of the neutrals of the world. Had the Allies been ready (and that in itself would have indicated attitudes similar to those now being expressed by Germany) and had the neutrals stood together from the outbreak of hostilities and proclaimed as one voice: This thing must not be—Germany would then have been arrested in her triumphant progress.

The Allies, however, were not prepared for the onslaught of the forces of evil; on the physical plane, their position was not impregnable. The neutrals at the same time have chosen and are still choosing the negative and weak way; and through fear, a misplaced idealism, or a separative spirit, plus the failure to grasp the acuteness of the world crisis and its significant implications, have placed humanity in a position of imminent though not inevitable disaster. These are points which require careful consideration and consequent readjustment of the attitude of those who are doing nothing to further the efforts of the Forces of Light and of the men of goodwill throughout the world.

What shall be done to stop the progress of aggression, of selfish nationalism and cruel attack upon the weak and the defenceless? These qualities are rampant in Germany. They are to be found in a lesser extent in many other nations and selfish nationalism is to be found in all to some degree, even when unaccompanied by militancy or paralleled by a true idealism. It is self-interest, short vision, and prejudice that basically govern neutrality and make the neutral nations, including the Americas, arm for defence but refuse to fight for human welfare. How, then, shall we awaken the world to the realities of the situation and so focus and direct a great world effort to throw off the yoke of the dictators as they seek to dominate the lands outside their own? How shall we free humanity to take its next step forward, without fear and terror and only conditioned by a world which is seeking unitedly to do that which is best for the whole, and not simply that which is best materially for the part? These are the questions with which we are today confronted. Desperately and fearfully, men are seeking a solution and turning hither and thither for help and comfort. Shall the demand, so widely prevalent at this time, for divine intervention, rise so strongly to heaven that it will perforce draw forth a response and, at the same time, deprive mankind of its right to settle its own affairs, decide its own issues and make progress by the method of trial and error, by the success of its own clear vision and its firm determination to find the right way out of the situation? Such intervention is possible, but it is not deemed desirable by the Forces of spiritual knowledge. They are therefore holding Their hand, feeling that this time humanity must be encouraged to battle to the end on behalf of its hope and its vision. Men pray for peace but will not pay the price of peace. Calmly praying and leaving the work to other men, forces or God, is the easy way, satisfying the emotional nature, but not involving clear thinking. Humanity has come of age; the child stage is over, and for

weal or woe, for good or ill, men must decide for themselves the way that the world, their governments and their
social order must go.

A new world order is possible, and there are certain
steps which need to be taken if the vision of this new world
is to enter into the realm of accomplished fact. Certain
angles of the vision I can—with the greatest brevity—point
out to you; I can indicate the sign posts on the way to the
future world order. I shall find myself in the position of
assuring you at the same time that every step of that way
will entail a fight, the overturning of that which is old and
loved and the destruction of that which is inhuman, selfish
and cruel; I shall have to impress upon you the prime and
initial necessity to overthrow the entrenched forces of aggression as they function today through the medium of the
totalitarian powers.

First, I would ask you all to ponder on the vision of
this new world order, preserving an open mind and realising
that this new mode of living hovers over humanity and will
materialise when selfishness is defeated, right human relations are correctly envisaged, and the ideal of this new
world order is divorced from all nationalistic concepts and
aspirations. It will not be an American world, or a French
world, or a British world, or a totalitarian world. It will be
the outcome of the civilisation which is passing and the
culture which is the flower of that civilisation, but at the
same time it will be neither of them. It will be a human
world, based on right understanding of correct human relations, upon the recognition of equal educational opportunities for all men, for all races and all nations, and upon
the fundamental realisation that "God hath made of one
blood all the peoples upon the earth." It will be a world
in which racial distinctions and national unities will be
recognised as enriching the whole and as contributing to
the significance of humanity. Such distinctions and nationalities will be preserved and cultured, not in a separative
isolation, but in the realisation that the many aspects of
human unfoldment and differentiation produce one noble

whole, and that all the parts of this whole are interdependent. All will comprehend their relation to each other in one progressive, synthetic, human endeavour, and the enterprise of united living will produce an interior work which will flower forth in the production of a beauty and a richness which will distinguish humanity as a whole. In this all will share, with wisdom and a planned efficiency, offering to the planetary life and to each other that which they have to contribute. This will be made possible because the whole of mankind will be recognised as the essential unit and as being of greater spiritual importance than the part.

This is no idle and visionary dream. It is already happening. Embryonic movements toward this world synthesis are already being made. There is a dream of federation, of economic interdependence and of religious unity, plus social and national interrelation which is rapidly taking form, first in the minds of men, and then in experiments. There is a tie of united purpose, felt by many in the political and economic fields, which is no wish fulfillment or fantasy but indicative of an emerging reality. It is felt and recognised by thinkers everywhere, and has worked out in the field of government through the medium of the federation of the British Dominions and their relation to Great Britain, and in the federation of the United States of America. It finds itself distorted and parodied in the concept of the superstate with which the dictators of the world glamour their peoples. But the links are being forged which will draw down the vision and precipitate on earth the pattern of things as they should be in this next world cycle.

When this vision of the new world order has been grasped by the men and women of goodwill throughout the nations, and has become part of the life and mind of every disciple and aspirant, then the next step will be to study the factors which are hindering its materialisation. For this a broad tolerance and an unprejudiced mind are essential, and these qualities are rare in the average student and the small town man. Past national mistakes must be faced;

selfishness in the spheres of both capital and labour must be recognised; blindness, nationalistic ambitions, adherence to ancient territorial demands and assumed rights, inherited possessiveness, the refusal to relinquish past gains, disturbances in the religious and social areas of consciousness, uncertainty as to the realities of subjective and spiritual life, and the insincerities which are based on glamour and fear— all these factors are woven into the life pattern of every nation, without exception, and are exploited by the evil forces and evaded by the well-meaning but weak people of the world. These must all be seen in their true perspective. The eyes of the people who seek to work under the Forces of Light must be lifted from the world of effects into the realm of causes; there must be appreciation of the factors which have made and conditioned the modern world, and these predisposing factors must be recognised for what they are. This sizing up of the situation and this recognition of blame and responsibility must preface every attempt to bring down into active being the new world order.

This new world will not come as an answer to prayer or by the passive wishful thinking and expectation of the peace-loving idealist and mystical visionary. They point the way and indicate the needed objective. It will come when the mystic and the man of vision awakens to the need of the hour and comes down from the world of dreams, of theories, and of words into the hard arena of daily and public life. He must be willing to fight for that which he desires and knows to be good and true and right, and must stand firm against those who seek to distort the vision and to arrest its appearance, arming for battle so that final disarmament may be possible.

A clear vision of the future world order (in broad and general outline but not in detail), an intelligent recognition of the hindrances and impediments which block its appearance, and a willingness to take the necessary steps upon the physical plane and to pay the required price and tender the demanded sacrifices are essential attitudes, prior to the elimination of the hindrances which stand in the way of the coming new world. It is a practical vision—long desired, much discussed and clearly outlined. The hindrances appear to be many, but they can all be summed up in the one word *Selfishness*—national, racial, political, religious and individual selfishness.

The practical aspect of the mode of elimination of the hindrances can also be simply stated. The vision will appear as fact on Earth when individuals willingly submerge their personal interests in the good of the group; when the group or groups merge their interests in the national good, when nations give up their selfish purposes and aims for international good, and when this international right relation is based upon the total good of humanity itself. Thus the individual can play his part in the bigger whole, and his help is needed, and thus the sense of individual futility is negated. To the most unimportant man in the most unimportant national unit there comes the call for sacrifice and service to the group of which he is part. Eventually humanity itself is thus swung—again as an integral unit—into the service of the Planetary Life.

In the above you have an attempt to portray the wider vision with its demanded, practical effort, and also an indication of the larger possibility which faces humanity. It is in truth for this the Allies fight and against which Germany today rallies her war machine.

What now of the immediate present, and what can the individual do to aid the cause of humanity and arrest the tide of evil? If he is fighting already upon the side of the Forces of Light and of the Allies, he knows his destiny and service. But what of those who question what they can do, and yet are eager to see clearly and to play their part when right vision is theirs? To them I would say the following things:

1. Eliminate prejudice, national pride, and religious antipathies out of your consciousness. The past mistakes of the Allies, as history gives them, are facts which they themselves do not deny. They stand not alone in selfishness, for

the same faults taint every national record. But they stand today for a new and spiritual order, based on a desire for synthesis, right methods of government and the good of the people. The unhappy past of all nations is today used as an alibi by those who do not choose to shoulder responsibility, or to sacrifice anything for the cause of humanity. A recognition of our own shortcomings and a spirit of tolerance and forgiveness are needed by all today.

2. Refuse to be afraid of any results of right and positive action. Fear lies behind much of the dissenting attitudes today, and fear kills truth, hides the vision and arrests right action. The great Leader of this Christian era has warned us not to be afraid of those who kill the body, but to fear only those who seek to kill the soul. The forces of aggression are slowly and ruthlessly killing out love and hope (qualities of the soul) in the conquered lands and in Germany. This, along with the great humanitarian plea, is sufficient reason to impel all men of goodwill to take up arms on the side of the Forces of Light. I would commend this to your imaginative attention. To put it even more practically, I would ask you if you would care to have your children subjected to the educational processes of the Nazi regime—with its crushing of all humanity, its emphasis upon pride of race and its cult of cruelty? Can you then stand idly by or simply resort to prayer and talk about the beauties of peace when the little children in the appropriated lands come under the soul-killing system of Germany? Refuse, then, in their interests, to be afraid.

3. Having sensed the vision, recognised the hindrances, and dealt with innate prejudice and fear, it will then become apparent to you what (in the face of this dangerous crisis) you must do. It is not for me to tell you what it is. The details are for you to decide; the methods which you must employ will become clear to you; the humanitarian issues will become increasingly plain to you; you will then range yourself on the side of the Forces of Light, and will uphold the hands of those who are *fighting* for world peace and security, preparatory to the inauguration of the new world

order. This you will do with no thought of self. You will face life truly and sincerely, with a fully dedicated sacrifice of time, self, money and, if need be, of life. You will realise dynamically that the attitude of the passive onlooker is not that of the agent of the Forces of Light or of a lover of humanity.

4. You will also learn to keep your mind free from hate, refusing to hate the deluded sinner even when imposing upon him the penalty of his sin. Hate and separation must cease, and they *will* cease as the individual aspirant stamps them out in his own life. The great error of the neutrally minded and of the pacifist is his refusal to identify himself constructively with human pain. Even when he reacts with violent emotion over the suffering, for instance, of little children in this great war, and of the defenceless refugee, he does not truly care enough to do anything about the situation, involving as it does sacrifice. This sounds harsh, but is a needed statement of fact. *Sympathy which does not produce positive action of some kind becomes a festering sore.*

Thus, by thought and word and deed, the lover of humanity will enter the battle against evil; with complete self-forgetfulness, he will take up the cause of humanity, hiding not behind the sense of futility and seeking no alibi in a misinterpreted idealism. He will face the facts of the present situation in the light which streams from the vision itself. He will then press forward into the age of right human relations, of spiritual unity and shared resources with complete confidence because his sense of values is adjusted. He knows that humanity has a divine mission which must be carried out on the wings of love, through understanding action, selfless service and the willingness to die in battle if that is the only way in which his brother can be served and freed.

Having now presented the attitude towards the present world crisis which seems to me consistent with all that I have taught in the past and in line with the teaching of the

Hierarchy, and having made clear the basic dualism which underlies this conflict, and pointed out the lines of demarcation which are clearly emerging, I now call upon all of you to stand with the Forces of Light.

These are difficult and terrible days. Men and women are needed who have the courage and the insight to stand with steadfastness and to take the steps which are needed—no matter what they may be—to bring this war to an end. Vast sections of humanity can do no more than acquiesce in the unhappy fate which has overtaken them. They are unable to think or pray or even to summon faith to their aid. They feel without hope. For them, you must think; for them, you must pray; for them, you must have faith and—above all else at this time—for them you must act. The work of reconstruction lies in the future. The demand today is for the building of a bulwark of defence around humanity; then—having fulfilled every physical plane requirement—to *stand* immovable. But you must stand with faces turned towards the enemy of the souls of men, ready to do battle, literally and physically, ready to take every needed step to drive the enemy back, and ready to sacrifice to the uttermost so that he may advance no further.

Your work will, therefore, be of a threefold nature. On the levels of mental consciousness, your vision of the need and of the future will be clear, inspiring you and enabling you to be a source of strength to all around you; your faith will see behind the obvious to the "substance of things hoped for, the evidence of things not seen," as the initiate, Paul, expresses it; your thought will then be anchored in right action, soul directed. On the emotional side of life, you will find no time for idle tears or for vague, sympathetic talk, because you will be completely identified with what is going on and all emotional energy will be directed to the pursuit of every available mode of practically alleviating the pain. The heart energy will be occupied with the task of giving understanding help so that there is no scope for the usual emotional solar plexus reactions. On the physical plane you will not be occupied with the problem of what to do, because every physical effort, time, and personality emphasis will be directed to the shouldering of your due share in arresting the forces of aggression from any further advance. This might mean fighting in the ranks of the Allied Armies, or it might mean driving an ambulance under Red Cross auspices; raising funds to succor the refugees; speaking on public platforms or to groups upon the issues at stake, or participating in some form of national effort to bring aid and strength to the Allies. Whatever it is, it will call for all that is in you and all that you are, integrated and directed to a sustained, substantial, one-pointed effort.

It will throw your will-to-good behind every attempt to frustrate the activites of the evil alliance which you may find in your environment; it will lead you to work with watchfulness for the good of your own country, whilst at the same time swelling the tide of the national effort to end war through the tangible victory of the Forces of Light. Ponder on these words.

The goodwill effort of the world, which I sought earlier to inaugurate and to synthesise, has passed through a negative stage and through an interlude wherein it was not possible to work actively. The needs of the new group of world servers calls it now into a renewed positive activity. The rediscovery and the immediate sustaining of the members of this group must be undertaken anew. In all lands they must be reached, if possible, and rehabilitated with wisdom, and re-established subjectively. They must be aided objectively and again inspired to work in order that they may form the nucleus of the *Forces of Reconstruction* when the Forces of Light have won the victory over the forces of aggression. This is the first point which I would ask you to consider doing.

The second thing is to begin the dynamic use of another Stanza of the Great Invocation. That which you have hitherto used has now served its immediate purpose, though it can again be called into use after the war is over. I give you now another set of phrases which can (if rightly used) invoke the Forces of the Divine Will on to the side of the

Forces of Light. It is not easy to give an adequate translation or paraphrase of this power-mantram, nor is it easy to step it down sufficiently so that it can be safely used by all, yet at the same time preserve its challenging, dynamic quality. The following sentences will suffice, however, and if used by you with focussed intention and with the attitude of a sacrificial personality (held silently dedicated in the light of the soul), much power may be generated. Along the lines of power which you may thus succeed in setting up may come that which is needed to release humanity from the thralldom of evil, provided the nature of the sacrificial will is somewhat understood by you.

Let the Lords of Liberation issue forth.
Let Them bring succor to the sons of men.
Let the Rider from the secret Place come forth,
And coming, save.
Come forth, O Mighty One.

Let the souls of men awaken to the Light,
And may they stand with massed intent.
Let the fiat of the Lord go forth:
The end of woe has come!
Come forth, O Mighty One.
The hour of service of the Saving Force has now arrived.
Let it be spread abroad, O Mighty One.

Let Light and Love and Power and Death
Fulfill the purpose of the Coming One.
The Will to save is here,
The Love to carry forth the work is widely spread abroad.
The Active Aid of all who know the truth is also here.
Come forth, O Mighty One and blend these three.
Construct a great defending wall.
The rule of evil *now* must end.

If, therefore, you will say these three stanzas with a focussed affirmative will, a great potency may be released for the salvaging of humanity and the immediate defeat of the forces of aggression. But I would reiterate that the use of these words must be accompanied by the dedication of your personality life to the cause of humanity, and by the transmutation of your personal will into the sacrificial will of the soul.

Finally, I would ask you to get in touch as soon as you can with the headquarters of the goodwill work and indicate also your willingness to cooperate to the fullest extent with the Forces of Light. This will serve practically to focus your effort. I would ask you also to make it possible to disseminate this article on the widest scale that is possible, so that the use of the new Invocation may be widespread. There are many to whom it could be sent, and it would arouse them anew to fresh activity and hopeful effort. I would ask you to use this new Invocation with faith, for it blends into a magnetic unity the forces of the divine Will-to-Good, the Love which underlies the efforts of the Hierarchy, and the Intelligent Activity of humanity, thus creating a reservoir of power into which the energy of the three divine centres can pour and upon which the Forces of Light can draw. The saying of this Invocation is not a substitute for the physical plane effort on your part; it is complementary to that, and the more you are serving upon the physical plane, the more effective will be your use of the new Invocation.

I said earlier that the war could have been averted from expression on the physical plane had the disciples and aspirants of the world measured up to their opportunity and responsibilities. The Great Invocation was rendered relatively powerless, from the angle of dynamic usefulness, because the majority of those who used it turned it into a peace prayer. It was instead a great spiritually militant invocative demand. This must not happen with this Stanza of Invocation. It is a demand; it is also an authoritative affirmation of existent fact; it sets in motion agencies and forces hitherto quiescent, and these can change the face of the world battlefield; it invokes the Prince of Peace, but He

carries a sword, and the effects of His activity may prove sur-
prising to those who see only the needs of the form aspect of
humanity.

That strength and enlightenment may be yours and the
power to stand and the ability to fight for the release of
humanity is the prayer and the appeal of your brother, the
Tibetan.

THE GREAT INVOCATION
Stanza Two

September 1940

It has seemed to me after due thought that it would
serve a most useful purpose if I elucidated somewhat the
theme of the new Invocation and dealt also with the idea
of divine intervention. There is much loose thinking in
this connection, due to the truth as well as the misinterpretation of the Christian teaching anent the return of the Christ.
Men's theological, analytical minds have distorted God's
revelation, and I would like to do something to produce a
wiser attitude to the reality of this inevitable return. This
loose thinking prevents much intelligent and cooperative
work. I would remind you that the success of invocation
and the true efficacy of prayer are dependent upon clear
thinking and not upon emotional desire or a powerful wish
complex. They are dependent, too, upon a certain dynamic
freshness and enthusiasm which it is hard to attain in a
time of stress and strain. The present time is peculiarly
hard. Perhaps a clearer understanding of the nature and
purpose of divine intervention may clarify somewhat the
issue.

To the casual thinker and the untrained occult student
it might appear that—given an almighty Deity or Planetary
Logos—He could with little trouble and much usefulness
and compassion intervene in this sad world situation and
bring to an end the warring of the nations through the
medium of some spectacular happening, some dramatic cataclysm of natural process or some supreme appearing which

would work much good. It might, it could be argued, con-
clusively convince the attacking, aggressive groups that their
day is ended and that their efforts had better be drawn to
an immediate finish. Would that it were so relatively simple
a matter; but the laws of nature, the free will of humanity
itself and the inevitability of karma combine to prevent
an intervention in just these terms. This does not mean
that some form of intervention may not be possible but it
must conform to law; it must not interfere with humanity's
right to handle its own affairs, and it must be timed in such
a way that the best and maximum results can be attained.

I would like first of all to touch upon the three points
which I have made above—natural law, free will and karma.
In so doing I may succeed in clearing up some of the confused thinking of many students.

Natural law is the inevitable working out upon the
physical plane of forces and energies which have long been
generated. People are apt to think that these must lie
outside of human control and constitute part of the inscrutable will of God, and that with them man has naught
to do. When it is realised that certain aspects of natural
law are concerned purely with the forces—subterranean,
superficial and aerial—of our planet, the premise will be seen
as correct in the present condition of the mental attitudes
of the race and will remain so for a very long time. There
are, nevertheless, causes and effects which can come under
the category of natural law which are yet not so far removed
from human control. For ages man has generated energies
which must inevitably produce events upon the physical
plane, evoke response upon the plane of the emotions,
and induce mental reactions. It is here that natural law
and the law of karma meet and interact upon each other.

There are many people today who find an alibi for
themselves in the present world situation, and a consequent
release from definite action and responsibility, by saying
that what is today happening is simply karma or the working out of cause and effect, and that there is nothing, therefore, that they can do about it; they take the position that

it is not their affair, and that in due course of time the process will be worked out and everything will be all right again. The slate will then be cleaner and incidentally they will not have been embroiled, but will have safely (even if uncomfortably) looked on. In so doing they overlook the third aspect of this same law, to which we have given the name of free will. It is the right use of free will and its understanding expression which must eventually straighten out and adjust the working out of karma and transmute that which now works such evil and havoc in the world into a demonstration of good and of the successful foundation for the pursuit of true happiness. Therefore, those who are looking on at the tragic sufferings of humanity and who refuse to be implicated, and thus succeed in evading responsibility as an integral part of the human family, are definitely storing up for themselves much evil karma. In some way they must learn participation, because the present situation has in it the seeds of release for humanity when the nature of evil is somewhat grasped, and above all when the oneness of humanity and the rights of human beings are truly recognised. Those who war against the race of men and who seek to wrest from them their God-given goal of freedom must be driven back from whence they came. Those who refuse to share in that struggle for freedom will be left out of the gains of freedom, even if it only means within their own home limits, in their life habits and in their private circumstances. When I here speak of "being driven back from whence they came" I am using phrases in both the simple and the occult sense.

It is therefore the free will and the will-to-good of humanity which must actively end the present conflict. One of these, the first, concerns man's responsibility to man; the other, rightly understood, concerns the right relationship of man to divine purpose, his right orientation to the divine goodwill, and his correct participation in its expression. Where these conditions exist, there can be drawn forth an act of divine intervention.

Natural law is today producing great changes in nature

through the effects of aerial and physical combat, through the results of the fluid movement of whole sections of the world population and through the effects of vast economic changes and processes. Conditions have been set in motion which must now work out to their predestined end, and it is the task of those who guide humanity spiritually to see that out of the surface evil and material activity good may eventuate, and that out of the wicked, materialistic intent lying behind the present aggressive activity of certain groups ultimate good may be engineered and the evil activity ended. But this possible good will be the result of the spiritual activity of those who know the law and who understand the purpose of the will of God; it will be wrought out in spite of, and not because of, the brute force and the selfish goals of the world aggressors; these embody and ensoul the materialistic forces of the planet in a manner utterly new in expression.

Free will involves a basic understanding of the lines of world cleavage; it concerns right choice and consequent correct action for the group and is determined every time by that which is right for the whole and not so much by that which is right for the part. Humanity is only now reaching the point where free will can be of significant importance. There has been little free will to date. This is definitely the needed demonstration at this moment. It is the lack of true free will which is today holding up the final activity. This is a statement of importance and it is here that the great and free neutrals can give a right lead to human affairs. Aggression, fear, terror, foreboding and the numbness that comes from undue and ceaseless mental and physical pain are stultifying and negating free will in many sections of the world at this time. There is no free will in many parts of Europe today.

Prejudice, the misinterpretation of presented facts, false and overemphasised idealism, racial and nationalistic thoughtforms and the withdrawing fear of responsibility are hindering the expression of free will in the less damaged parts of the world. Moral unpreparedness and the refusal to relinquish the many and differing misinterpretations of truth or of Christ's teaching are hindering many people today. Release for humanity will come when the so-called good people of the world give up their pet theories and their beloved ideals and grasp the essential fact that entry into the Kingdom of Heaven and into the new age will take place when mankind is truly loved and selflessly served, and when the true, divine purpose is seen and humanity is found to be one indivisible whole. Then petty nationalisms, religious differences and selfish idealisms (for that is what they often are as most people are idealists because they seek to save their own souls) are subordinated to human need, human good and the future happiness of the whole. The simplification of the attitude of men is the crying need at this time. Ideologies must go; old ideals must be relinquished; petty political, religious and social schemes must be discarded, and the one driving purpose and the one outstanding determination must be the release of humanity from the imposition of fear, from enforced slavery and the reinstatement of men in freedom and with due opportunity to express themselves through right human relations. This is not as yet possible and it is the appalling situation of terror, of slavery and of imposed and penalising rule which is breaking the heart of humanity and causing deep distress and questioning in those whose hearts are not yet so broken.

As to *Karma*, what man has made he can unmake. This is oft forgotten. Karma is not a hard and fast rule. It is changeable, according to man's attitude and desire. It is the presenting of the opportunity to change; this grows out of past activities, and these rightly met and correctly handled lay the foundation for future happiness and progress. The present situation is the fault of all peoples in all countries (particularly the more intelligent) and includes also the great neutrals if the Law of Rebirth and of joint responsibility means anything at all. Karma is not all that is bad and evil. Men make it so through their stupidities. There are today great forces of evil seeking expression in the world;

these emerge out of the past and seek to determine and bring about a very evil future wherein selfishness, material objectives, and the good and well-being of one race out of the many must be imposed upon the world—a world which innately revolts against such an imposition and distortion of reality. The force of evil example is shown in the fact that two other races seek abjectly to copy or aid the forces of aggression, focussed at this time through the aggressor race.

At the same time, the forces of good are seeking to offset this imposition of material selfishness and are now at bay with the issue still undecided—except upon the mental plane. It has yet to work out as the triumph of good upon the physical plane. When those who are not so drastically implicated in the present conflict relinquish their selfish-ness, their prejudices and their interpretations and see the basic duality of this conflict in its true light, they will throw the weight of their influence increasingly on the side of good-will and right human relations; then the bad karma which they apparently placidly accept for others and reject for themselves will be changed into the good karma which is the true destiny of humanity and will usher in the new era of joy and of peace and spiritual synthesis—that syn-thesis which we call brotherhood.

It is because of the delay in right understanding, and the slowness of many to appreciate the true situation, that Those Who guide the race and work on the spiritual side of life have been unable to do much up to date except spiritually strengthen the hands of the workers with the Forces of Light. The faith of many has kept the door ajar, yet even these have forgotten frequently that "faith without works is dead." It is only when faith finds active expression upon the physical plane in right cooperation and sacrifice (even unto death) that the door can be forced wide open and divine intervention become possible. It is only when the vision and dream of peace—which beguiles so many well-meaning people—gives way to the determination to take every possible means to achieve that peace in practical ways upon the physical plane that the inner spiritual forces will be enabled to work also more actively on earth.

Curiously enough, they are often hindered today by the idealists, who love their ideals more than they love humanity and who cling to their special interpretations of what they think Christ meant, at the same time excluding that real love which characterised His every act and which would drive them into active, selfless service to the Forces of Light. They do nothing to bring the conflict to an end because they are preoccupied with their own dreams, ideals and interpretations; when they can let these go because of love of humanity, then the new vision will come and the world will be saved; the Forces of Light will find potent expression and the forces of aggression will go down to defeat.

Given, therefore, an eventual fusing of vision and physical plane activity (the major need at this time), what form is it possible for the hoped-for divine intervention to take? I make no prophecies. All that I seek to show is that the blocking or hindrance is to be found today on the side of humanity. It does not lie on the side of the forces of light, life and love; it is not to be found on the side of Christ and His disciples or of the Masters of Wisdom, as these (under diverse names) constitute the spiritual Hierarchy of the planet. Call Them by what name you choose, the most cherished belief of humanity is that there exists in the world always and for ever a hidden Reality, Those Who have conquered death, Who possess illimitable powers to help, and Who can be reached by prayer and invocation.

It is the potency and grasp of things material and *the fact of undivided focus* upon the physical plane that has given the forces of aggression so much success up to the present time. These forces, through their very potency, have fused and blended together a group of seven men who personify in themselves great and specific aspects of material forces (connected with the seven types of energy in their lowest and most material expressions) and their manifestations—war, fear and cruelty. They are united by one point of view and by one goal, and hence their success. (It is interesting that, again in their case, there appears inevitably an initiatory seven—the base and dark parallel of the initiating Seven who lead human beings into light and who are symbolised in the seven Masons who constitute a Lodge of Masons.) They are the custodians of forces which control them and over which they themselves have no slightest control. You ask who these seven are: Hitler, von Ribbentrop, Goebbels, Goering, Hess, Himmler and Streicher—names well-known to you all. These men embody and personify the forces of aggression and rule by fear not only the enslaved nations but also their few allies who are not by any means in the same category of power—fortunately for them.

When those who are on the side of the Forces of Light and of non-aggression can see their goal with equal clarity and are equally and uniformly united with the objective of ending oppression and slavery and of freeing humanity, then we shall see also an embodiment of spiritual force which will bring disaster to these potent seven. Such a unification of objective and of purpose is possible and needed; and when it does take place, the force generated and the power let loose upon the physical plane will be of so stupendous a nature that human liberation will rapidly be brought about.

It is for this that I have worked and for this I have sought to arouse all of you. This spirit is growing among the allied forces, though the falling away of France was inevitable. France was animated by somewhat selfish purposes—the security and safety of France more than with the integrity and happiness of humanity, and this led to an inevitable collapse; France is learning, however, and its unshakable masses and its spiritual nucleus will save the day for the broken nation. The neutral powers are still selfish (though they seek by philanthropy to veil it), but they are rapidly awakening to the true issues, and when there is real synthesis of goal and of purpose and a true unification of vision upon the mental plane, of fixed and unalterable desire upon the emotional plane, and a dedication to practical effort upon the physical plane, then there will be hope that the embodiment of "the desire of all nations" will appear.

That embodiment is one mode in which divine intervention can take place. The Prince of Peace will lead His people—through war—to peace. Those who think only in terms of peace as they understand it and desire it are apt to forget the Biblical implication that the Prince of Peace takes a definite part in the battle of Armageddon (now in full progress). After achieving victory, He will then lead His triumphant cohorts through the gates into "Jerusalem," the city of peace. The symbolic and practical significance of this is becoming increasingly apparent. This notable event can and will take place when the free will of the people, blended by invocation and prayer, can make this possible.

Divine intervention could also take the form of a cataclysmic happening which would bring aggression to an end through destruction. It would probably be at such a cost of human life that there is definite hesitation over employing it by the custodians of natural law and the workers who understand divine purpose, apart from the fact that humanity has now reached the point in evolution where the expression of human free will is definitely possible. The use of cataclysm was the method employed in Atlantean days, as you well know from the tales of the flood; and through the flood there was almost complete destruction of the civilisation of that time. It is hoped that such a drastic step will not be needed today, though there are ancient prophecies which foretell the possibility of the destruction of this world at this time through fire—instead of flood. Which of the two methods—divine embodiment and natural cataclysm—will be employed will really be decided by humanity through its use or non-use of free will and understanding. If humanity fails to unite under the banner of the Forces of Light against the forces of material aggression and selfishness, then the "fiery ordeal" might be unavoidable.

There are also sleeping hosts which may be evoked for the aiding of the spiritual forces, and certain ancient prophecies hint at these, but as we study the new Invocation phrase by phrase, I may be able to make this matter clearer, for there are several significances and meanings behind each phrase. The one thing I seek to make clear in these opening remarks is that natural law, free will, and karma are becoming increasingly related and are all aspects of one great law, embodying divine purpose—a purpose which must work out through the medium of humanity itself if the present opportunity is to be met correctly and in line with divine purpose.

The stimulation of certain people to phenomenal action, and the instigation of others to emerge as dynamic and inspired leaders, is also another way in which divine intervention might find expression. Oft, down the ages, men have been overshadowed by divinity and inspired by God to accept positive leadership, and so make divine purpose a fact in conditioning world affairs. Had they not so responded to the influencing impression, and had they not accepted the responsibility imposed upon them, the course of world affairs and world events might have been very different. I refer not here specifically to spiritual leaders but also to leaders in other departments of human living—to such expressions of the divine will as Moses, the Lawgiver, Akbar, the warrior and student, Leonardo da Vinci, the inspired artist, and to other great and outstanding figures who have determined the basic trends of human civilisation; I refer also to the constructive forces which have guided mankind into the increasing light of knowledge and understanding. All these leaders have produced lasting effects upon the human consciousness and their work has lain therefore in the domain of the second aspect of divinity. Their activities parallel those of the workers who are, or have been, inspired by the material or matter aspect of manifestation, whose influence has been predominantly upon the physical plane, and whose effect has been outstandingly along selfish personal lines. This type of influence is felt predominantly upon the physical plane, and therefore, from certain angles, the present conflict might be regarded as one between the second aspect, the developed spiritual consciousness, and the material aspect of manifestation, with humanity constituting the great field of divine conflict at this time.

We have, therefore, hinted at the following forms of divine intervention:

1. Divine embodiments
2. Natural cataclysms
3. Evocation of slumbering Entities
4. Emergence of inspired leadership.

There still remains one mode of intervention which is still more mysterious, illimitably more powerful, and definitely more difficult both to evoke and subsequently to contact. This is the emergence, response, or appearing of great Sons of God Who dwell in sources far removed from our planetary life altogether; this involves the appearance of Lives of such stupendous and divine expression and potency that only the *massed* spiritual purpose of vast numbers of men can be potent enough and far-reaching enough to pierce beyond the veil which protects the Earth, to those far distant realms where They have Their natural and everlasting abode. They cannot be reached by prayer or even by well formulated desire—the expression of the wish life of the masses. They lie utterly beyond the realm of feeling (as humanity understands it) and dwell ever in that high place which can only be reached by intentionally directed, selfless thought.

Are there enough people in the world today whose focussed and illumined thought can be organised and directed towards these Lives in such a manner that They can be attracted and led to respond to human need for deliverance? Such is the problem. It is possible, but not, perhaps, probable. The problem of a blended demand from the spiritual Hierarchy and from humanity—simultaneously expressed—will have to be met, and this is by no means easy of accomplishment.

It is for this reason that these three stanzas from a very ancient invocation have been made available and put in your hands at this time. If you can use these phrases as *voiced demands* and *affirmed beliefs*—in unison with the

highest spiritual forces which claim your allegiance, no matter under what name—then there is just a chance that this
type of divine activity might be set in motion along a particular line, and this might lead to changes of so auspicious
a nature that a new heaven and a new earth might be rapidly precipitated. There is at least no harm in this attempt
and this effort at participation in hierarchical endeavour.
Planned collaboration with the work of the Christ at this
time is useful and needed; it will serve at least to elevate
humanity and its thought, and produce a permanent spiritual stabilisation. Great potencies and the expression of
ancient evil from the past are rampant upon earth at this
time, released through unusual human selfishness, cruelty
and error, and focussed through the medium of one unhappy
race and the power of certain dangerous men—men who
are easily subject to evil impression and influenced, obsessed,
by selfishness and evil—by forces of destruction. Is it possible to evoke at this time eternal good, latent in Lives
which would normally contact humanity in some far distant
future, and thus hasten the day of heightened and deepened
spiritual contact in the immediate present? Such is the question. If this can be done, the evil past and the glorious
future may perhaps be brought into contact in the unhappy
present, and an event take place which will produce stupendous changes.

I would remind you here that the evocation of this
divine contact will be, in itself, dangerous, disrupting and
destroying. The results are unpredictable for the human
being, for men are as yet unaccustomed to respond to Lives
and Influences of so high and divine a nature. There is
nevertheless a possibility that it might now be more safely
permitted *if* enough people can stand together spiritually
and selflessly, and so offer themselves as channels for these
new and unknown spiritual Forces. There are divine attributes, divine qualities and divine potencies which the most
enlightened humanity of all time have as yet failed even to
register, sense or vision—all three aspects escaping contact
with these potencies. Yet these powers exist, and the right

handling of the present crisis by spiritually oriented humanity may bring about the release of some of these higher energies and the establishing of a line of factual influence along
which They can move and consequently contact the Earth.
Ponder on this and limit not Deity through the rigidity and
finiteness of little minds.

The release of great impersonal forces is ever a critical
matter. The effects produced are dependent upon the quality
of the recipient aspects and the nature of the form quality
upon which they make their impact. In the world of chem-
istry, a catalyst, brought into contact with certain substances,
will produce something entirely new and bring about changes
not normally anticipated. These we are now beginning to
study and to understand. The intervention into the situation of certain potencies of stupendous gravity and unique
ness, and their effect upon the interacting Forces of Light
and forces of aggression, is still more unpredictable, and
only the grasp of the spiritually minded people of the world
and their steadfastness in sacrifice—plus their clarity of vision
and their *united* world focus—can make the situation safe
for humanity as a whole. Bear these thoughts in mind as
you use the great and new Invocation.

One other thought I would like to touch upon prior
to an analysis of the phrases of the Invocation.

It is a recognised truth today that all expression upon
the physical plane is the result, first of all, of thought, then
of desire, and finally of physical plane activity. A man sees
a vision and a possibility. He broods over it and it enters
then into the realm of mental invention. A thoughtform is
then organised, whether it is the thoughtform of a sewing
machine, of a political party, of an economic idea, or some
other type of organisation with some planned objective.
Much reflection and brooding will eventually produce a
magnetic field which will become so potent that desire will
enter in; then the dream or vision enters into a new stage
of vitalisation. In due time, when the processes of desire
have adequately developed, the vision will precipitate upon
the physical plane. Physical activity and concrete methods

of manifestation are then coordinated and gradually the thoughtform becomes an expressed reality, recognisable by all men.

Thought, desire, activity—such is the history of human vision and dream. Down the ages, from the very night of time, man has dreamed, expectant of divine revelation and of divine intervention. When all else seems to fail, men look to God. Again and again in the history of the race, the vision has taken form and the dream has materialised upon the wings of powerful desire and demand. Again and again, God has revealed and sent His Messengers and Representatives to aid and guide humanity. But this happens only when the demand is adequately voiced and the need has cried to high heaven. Never yet has the response failed. Again and again lately, the nations of the world have been called to prayer, and this proclaimed appeal of millions cannot be disregarded or remain negligible. An answer must be forthcoming, though it may not take the same form as of old, because man is today—in spite of appearances—more capable of handling his own affairs and determining consciously his own events. No matter how unrealised, back of all these demands and prayers in the many Christian countries, lies a subtle, deep-seated conviction that the return of Christ is imminent; there is widespread acceptance of the concept that the Presence of the Son of God *can* be evoked and that He *must* come to the assistance of His people. No matter what the dogmatic interpretation or the theological idealism, some form of this belief lies behind the cry of the millions.

Will this demand from the hearts of men induce the return of the Christ of Galilee? Will it bring about the emergence into manifestation of some great Son of God Who will embody perhaps another and unknown aspect of God's life and quality? Will it perhaps produce the embodiment of another divine revelation, and—just as the Buddha expressed the Wisdom of God and Christ revealed to us the Love of God—is it not possible that He Who may come will unfold to us the nature of the Will or Purpose of God, thus presenting that will-to-good which must be called into activity if the evil will-to-power is to be swept from the Earth. I present this possibility to your attention and would ask you to think about it. Thus, if this should prove the correct result of all invocation and prayer, we shall have the balancing of the personality will, of material selfishness and acquisitiveness, and the selfless will which seeks to aid the whole of humanity. The will of the lower self and the will of the Self or Soul will be brought into conflict with each other, with humanity throwing the weight of its influence upon one side or the other.

When I speak of throwing the weight of human influence upon one side or another, I refer not alone to thought power and to what so many euphemistically call "work on mental levels." I refer to the conscious activity of the whole man, working mentally, emotionally and most emphatically physically also. Only those, therefore, who are integrated personalities can work in this manner, and herein lies a difficulty. Those people today who work only mentally or who sit and send thoughts of love broadcast into the world, and who bask thus in the beauty of their own idealism (making frequently no adequate balancing physical effort to bring this present evil situation to an end through right choice, sacrifice and strenuous service), are in reality of no service at all to any except themselves. There are those who send thoughts of love to the group of evil men who are responsible for world disaster, believing thereby to influence them for good. I would remind them that love is essentially an impersonal potency or energy, dependent for its effect upon the type of form which it contacts and upon which it makes an impact. Pouring, therefore, upon the selfish materialistic nature, it will only enhance desire and promote increased acquisitive aggression, and thus foster the lower nature and distort the true expression of love, leading to increased evil activity. Pouring upon the selfless, the pure and the disinterested, it will foster reality and true love. These are points which should be remembered at this time by the well-intentioned but occultly ignorant server.

Let us now proceed to the analysis of the three stanzas or verses. The first of these refers to the waiting attentive group of spiritual Lives who seek to aid when right demand coincides with right time. The second stanza refers to humanity and its reactions, and to the possibility of interplay between the two groups—of spiritual Lives and men. The third indicates methods and results. We will take each phrase or expressed idea separately, for each carries its own import and all of them possess several significances. With all the meanings I cannot deal, but will present the simplest and the most important.

Let the Lords of Liberation issue forth. Let Them bring succour to the sons of men.

Who are the Lords of Liberation, and from whence do They come? All the ideas and concepts which control human life and have given rise to our civilisation have started as emanations from certain great Lives, Who are Themselves an expression of a divine Idea. The note They strike and the quality They emanate reaches out and makes an impact upon the most developed of the sons of men found at any particular time upon the Earth. These then proceed to make the sensed idea their own and to familiarise the thinkers of their time with the formulated concept. In this way great motivating, divine purposes become controlling factors in human progress. It is in this way that the basic urge to liberation and to freedom has slowly and consistently dominated human endeavour, leading first of all to the struggle for individual freedom and liberation (with the incidental ideal of heaven, of initiation and of spiritual attainment), and gradually moulding human thought to such an extent that the greater ideal takes shape. The freedom of humanity and the liberation of its power to be self-determining (which is an aspect of freedom) has become the dearest ideal and the best thought of the thinkers in all nations. In the last analysis, it is this interference with individual and group freedom which is the worst sin of the evil men who seek at this time to enslave the weaker nations and bend them to the rule of Germany, depriving them of their national assets and means of subsistence, and wresting from them—by force and fear—their dearest possessions, liberty of life and conscience.

All great ideas have their emanating Sources of life, therefore, and These are called in the ancient invocation with which we are occupied "Lords of Liberation." They are three in number, and one of Them is closer to the Earth and to humanity than are the other two, and it is He Who can be reached by those who comprehend the nature of freedom and who desire beyond all things to be liberated and to see all the oppressed and enslaved people of the world also liberated.

Every move of an enlightened consciousness (such as that of a Lord of Liberation) towards humanity produces a corresponding shift or move on the part of men. This in itself constitutes a definite problem, because no such move can be made by a Lord of Liberation unless humanity is ready to raise its ideal of freedom to a higher level of expression. Unless this world war has in it the seeds of a revelation of a higher human freedom, and unless humanity is ready to express this higher freedom to the best of its ability, it will not be possible for the Lords of Liberation to take action. They cannot be moved by prayer, demand and invocation alone. Such demand must have behind it the ideal of a newer freedom and a greater liberty for man. In the abrogation of the French idealism, summed up in the words —"Liberty, Equality, Fraternity"—the attention of the whole world was focussed on the theme of liberty, and the symbolism of the event is of far greater import than has yet been grasped. France has not relinquished the ideal of human liberty which she originally brought (on a large scale) to the attention of mankind. Her action, under the influence of the enemies of human freedom, simply focussed the danger with which humanity was confronted, and brought it emphatically to the attention of humanity, numbed by disaster, and bewildered by the accumulated weight of misery. By so doing, the problem was simplified for the untrained mind. It also produced, spiritually speaking, a direct line of communication between men who know the significance of freedom and long for human release, and the Lords of Liberation Who are responsible for implanting this innate desire in humanity.

The reason why these Lords of Liberation are the first mentioned in the stanza is that They are essentially related to *desire-will,* and are therefore the more easily contacted by man. The place from which They issue forth to the aiding of humanity is a certain area of the divine Consciousness which is open to the human sense of awareness, if sufficiently enlightened and selfless. You can see from the above remark how the effective use of invocation is therefore dependent upon the point of spiritual development of the one who seeks the aid of true prayer and invocation. One thing which should be grasped anent all these great Lives is that what is commonly called "worship" is abhorred by Them. Worship, the power to adore and the sense of awe (which is one of the highest aspects of fear) are *not* desired by Them. Such attitudes are emotional in origin and based upon the sense of duality, and therefore upon feeling. These Lives are embodiments of service and can be reached by true servers with the appeal of service. Bear this in mind. As man progresses upon the Path he forgets worship; he loses all sense of fear, and adoration fails to engross his attention. All these attitudes are obliterated by the realisation of an over-powering love and its consequent interplay and tendency to increase identification. The Lords of Liberation can be reached, therefore, by the call of the world servers, and They will then issue forth through the agency of One of Them, Who will unify the energies of all Three, and so produce those conditions which will bring about effective and recognised freedom. How They will do this is not for us to say; the most probable method will be through the overshadowing of some man, or some group of men, so that they will be inspired to bring about the victory of liberty.

Let the Rider from the secret place come forth and coming—save. Come forth, O Mighty One.

Here we come up against one of the oldest traditions

in the world and of the ancient East; one, too, which finds its counterpart in the New Testament, where the Coming One is seen coming forth to the rescue of the people "riding upon a white horse." In the Occident we have for long thought in terms of the "Lamb, slain from the foundations of the world," and in this statement lies a profound astrological truth. It refers to that great round of the zodiac (a period of approximately 25,000 years) in which the sun passes through all the twelve signs of the zodiac. The period to which reference is made started in the sign Aries, the ram. The Orient, however, harks still further back, to a much earlier period and to a still more ancient date, remote in the night of time, when the greater world cycle started in the sign Sagittarius, the Archer. The symbol of this is sometimes (towards the latter part of the cycle) depicted as an archer, riding on a horse and (in the early part of the cycle) as a centaur, half man and half horse. Both refer to an emerging revelation of the consciousness of Deity as revealed through some Great Divine Expression, through some manifesting Son of God. The point to bear in mind is that this Rider on the white horse is no extra-planetary Entity or Life, but is essentially One like unto ourselves—human and animal combined as are we all, but fused with divinity and inspired from on high, informed by some cosmic and divine Principle, as Christ was informed with the Love of God and carried the revelation of love to man. The Rider is one of our humanity Who has reached a pre-destined goal and Who—for very love and understanding of man—has remained for ages in the secret place of revelation (as it is esoterically called), waiting until His hour comes around again and He can then issue forth to lead His people to triumphant victory. This coming One is on the Path of a world Saviour just as the more potent Lives, the Lords of Liberation, are on the Path of world Service. They issue forth via that highest spiritual centre *wherein the Will of God* is held in solution or custody, for gradual release or revelation as humanity can arrive at the needed point of understanding response and receptivity. Though They can be reached relatively easily, it must be through the massed intent of the many focussed minds. The Rider on the white horse can be reached by the individual aspirant if he can raise his consciousness adequately high. This Rider comes forth (from the centre *wherein the Love of God* is held for distribution) as the human centre (which we call humanity) becomes attuned to true love and can identify itself with all men, responding freely and without any inhibition to divine Love—which is wisdom, understanding, and effective, skillful activity.

When this invocation is rightly used and voiced by an adequate number of people, those who can in some measure employ the enlightened will may succeed in reaching the Lords of Liberation and produce, as a result, a phenomenal intervention of some kind. Those who work more emotionally will reach the Rider from the secret place and may bring Him forth to save and lead the masses of people. Are there enough focussed minds and intense attentive hearts to reach the two centres where wait Those Who can aid at this time? That is the question. It will happen when the three centres—humanity, the spiritual Hierarchy of the planet, and the "place where the will of God lies hidden" (called in the ancient scriptures Shamballa)—are aligned and en rapport with each other. There will then be established a direct relation between all three, and a direct channel for the inflow of liberating force. This has happened only once before in the history of the race.

Owing to the fact that mankind is so weakened by pain, strain and suffering, the probability is that it will not be deemed wise for the Lords of Liberation *directly* to contact humanity. They will more probably do three things:

1.   Stand behind and strengthen the Rider on the white horse as He responds to the demand of the people everywhere, pouring through Him that dynamic energy which embodies the first divine aspect, the will aspect, the power expression. Thus They will enable Him to carry out the will of God in such a manner that humanity can grasp

what is being done. Mankind will then see the Love which animates the Will and Power of God. The true significance of liberty will then be revealed. It is not yet understood.

2. Pour Their strengthening will-to-good into the new group of world servers in all lands, so that there may be potent, simultaneous action in line with the purposes of the Rider from the secret place.

3. Stimulate and integrate into the minds of certain advanced disciples a number of new ideals which must govern the liberating process and find expression in the New Age. This was done in a small way at the time of the French Revolution when the three major concepts of freedom were expressed in the three words, Liberty, Equality, Fraternity, and were intellectually presented to the race. These have now been temporarily relinquished, and this in itself constitutes an important symbolic happening. It had to occur, because these three words stood for no factual truth but simply for a hope and for an academic concept; the events of the last few months reduced them to a farce. So they were deliberately withdrawn in order to enhance their importance, and will later be restored and will then assume a new and potent significance in the minds of all men. They are the three words which *must* govern the New Age.

Certain racial interpretations of ideals will also have to disappear in order to be succeeded by new and better ones. This applies even to man's understanding of the three words which we have been considering. "Liberty," as the Lords of Liberation may endorse it, is in reality the recognition of right human relations, freely adjusted, willingly undertaken and motivated by a sense of responsibility which will act as a protective wall; this will take place, not through coercive measures, but through correct interpretation and quick appreciation by the masses, who are apt to confound licence (personality freedom to do as the lower nature chooses) and liberty of soul and conscience. Yet this liberty is the easiest aspect of the divine will for humanity to grasp.

It is in reality the first revelation given to man of the nature of the Will of God and of the quality of Shamballa. "Equality" is that peculiar understanding which the Coming One will reveal and which is based on a right sense of proportion, correct Self-respect, and understanding of the spiritual, yet natural, laws of Rebirth and of Cause and Effect, and which will be founded in future centuries on the recognition of the age of a soul's experience and gained development, and not at all on the loud emphatic affirmation that "all men are equal." "Fraternity" is something that humanity itself will contribute as an expression of the third aspect of divinity, basing it on right contact and right reaction to contact. Thus there will be developed gradually the true life-theme of humanity, which is brotherhood, founded on divine origin (equality) and leading to a free and true expression of divinity (liberty).

Perhaps with these thoughts in mind, this first stanza of the new Invocation will assume more importance, and you will then be able intelligently to invoke Those Who can inspire to right action, thus bringing succour, and call forth the One Who can save the situation through right leadership.

On what level of consciousness He will ride, it is not for us to say. It is possible that He will not appear upon the physical plane at all. Who can say? But the sound of His coming will be known and, speaking symbolically, the thunder of His horse's hoofs will be heard. The influence which He will wield and the energy which He will transmit from the Lords of Liberation will inevitably be potently felt, evoking an immediate human response. This will prove an incontrovertible fact. That His radiation will reach forth and surround His disciples, struggling in the conflict with evil, is also certain and sure. This will enable them to make the supreme effort which will win the battle for humanity. That He will come in "the air" is a well-known prophecy from the New Testament, thus enabling "every eye to see Him." These words have more meaning today than when written nearly two thousand years ago, for this world conflict is outstandingly an aerial one. Students and those using this Invocation would be wise to bear this in mind or they may fail to see and recognise the Deliverer when He comes—a thing which has happened before.

We come now to the second stanza, with its direct references to human attitudes and recognitions. For decades, I, as one of the spiritual teachers, along with many others, have sought to awaken all to the fact of *Light*—light in the world, light coming from the plane of desire (called the astral plane quite often), light illumining science and human knowledge, the light of the soul, producing in due time the light in the head. You have been carefully taught that the right use of the mind in meditation and reflection will lead to the correct relation of soul and personality, and that when this has taken place, the light of the soul ignites or fosters the light in the head and the man reaches the stage of illumination. The reference in this second stanza is to the more extended idea of the relation of humanity (the kingdom of men) to the spiritual Hierarchy (the kingdom of God). When these two are more closely aligned and related, light will break out among the sons of men as a whole, just as light breaks out in the individual aspirant. This much-to-be-desired event can be brought about by the spiritually minded people in the world, by the men and women of goodwill, and by the world disciples, standing with "massed intent." This means with a uniform, united focus— a thing as yet rarely seen and much needed at this time. So many people are animated by wishful thinking, by hoping and by prayer; so few are motivated *by intention*. Intention here is that unbreakable, immovable determination that a situation shall be handled, that what is needed in order to release mankind assuredly must appear, for such is the *mental intention* of the focussed minds of many. I would ask you to give much thought to these words "massed intent" and to differentiate with care between intention and desire. When humanity has fulfilled the conditions through a focussed mental demand, based on correctly formulated mass intent, then will come the affirmation from the spiritual Forces.

Let the fiat of the Lord go forth: The end of woe has come.

The ending of the present evil situation is, therefore, a cooperative measure; and here, in this connection, we have the appearance of the Lord of Civilisation Who voices and engineers upon the physical plane the fiat of the Lord of Liberation and of the Rider from the secret place. He aids and makes possible, owing to His control, the precipitating upon the Earth and in the arena of combat, of the power generated by the Lords of Liberation, expressed by the coming One and focussed through Him as the hierarchical Representative in Europe. The work of the Master R. has always been recognised as of a peculiar nature and as concerned with the problems of civilisation, just as the work of the Christ, the Master of all the Masters, is concerned with the spiritual development of humanity, and the work of the Manu is occupied with the science of divine government, with politics and law. Thus the incoming focussed energy, called forth in response to right invocation, is stepped down still nearer to humanity, and the masses can then respond to the new impulses. You have, therefore:

1. The Lords of Liberation, reached by the advanced spiritual thinkers of the world whose minds are rightly focussed.
2. The Rider on the white horse or from the secret place, reached by those whose hearts are rightly touched.
3. The Lord of Civilisation, the Master R., reached by all who, with the first two groups, can stand with "massed intent."

On the united work of these Three, if humanity can succeed in calling Them forth, will come the alignment and the correct relation of three great spiritual centres of the planet, a thing which has never occurred before. Then:

1. The Lords of Liberation will receive and transmit to the Hierarchy energy from the centre *where God's Will is known and furthered.*
2. The Rider will receive this energy and take such action as will express it, plus the motivating energy from the centre *where God's Love is expressed.*
3. The Lord of Civilisation will stimulate and prepare the centre which we call humanity for right reception of this re-vitalising, stimulating and releasing force.

Thus Shamballa, the Hierarchy and Humanity will stand consciously related and dynamically in touch with each other. The Will of God, the Love of God and the Intelligence of God will thus fuse and blend on Earth and in relation to human problems. Conditions will consequently be brought about and energies will be set in motion which will end the rule of evil and bring war to an end through the victory of the Forces of Light, recognised and aided by Humanity.

This synthesis of the three energies, evoked through invocation and the response of certain divine Potencies, is esoterically given the name of "the saving Force." Of its exact nature and intended effects we know practically nothing. It has never before appeared in action on the physical plane, though it has been for some time active upon the mental plane. Though it is a blend of the energies of the three centres referred to above, it is primarily the energy of the divine Will, which will be its outstanding characteristic. One hint here I will give. Just as the externalisation of the materialistic lodge of seven men, to which I made reference above, has made its appearance and must be dealt with prior to the future externalisation of the lodge of spiritual Lives (the appearance of the kingdom of God on Earth) which we call the planetary Hierarchy, so the will-to-power of the forces of aggression has appeared on Earth and sought to gain control over humanity. Note that aim. This will-to-power can only be dissipated when the highest aspect of the same energy is given free rein among the sons of men. The divine and spiritual Will, carried on the impulse of selfless love, can and must be evoked for the destruction of the selfish and wicked will-to-power, rampant now on Earth under the direction of the focussed seven in Germany.

The "saving force" must, therefore, be spread abroad. For long ages men have prayed in the words of St. Paul: "Let the love of God be shed abroad *in our hearts.*" Today the need is for the spread of the "saving force" to take hold *of our minds* and to control from that directing centre, for it embodies the needed salvation at this time. It will take the united efforts of all the three focal points of divine expression on our planet to make this possible, but it can be done.

In the final stanzas (which we need not take phrase by phrase, as their significance is sufficiently clear) we have plainly put before us the methods whereby humanity can play its part and do its share in aiding all those who are cooperating with the Forces of Light to bring this planetary war to an end.

Look for a moment at the four words which embody the thought of what can be done by men to bring to fruition the mission of the Coming One, the Rider from the secret place. We are told that *Light and Love and Power and Death* must be invoked *to fulfill the purpose of the Coming One.* Here we come right down to the practical theme of man's individual part in the processes of liberation. Here we are concerned with that which—within humanity itself—needs evocation in order to produce right cooperation, right preparation and right understanding. Four potencies within the soul of man are available for his individual use in helping the Forces of Light—potencies he shares with all men to a greater or less degree, according to the expressive power of the soul. They are potencies which are not innate in the lower self, but only in the higher. The lower self reflects only distorted forms of the higher divine energies. This is a point to be carefully noted. Of Light and Love I can say but little to you. To esoteric students, these words are so familiar as to be somewhat meaningless, and only those who can walk in the light, and whose major reaction is love of humanity, will comprehend the significance and the inter-relation of these four words.

Light, with which to see the new vision, is needed by all. This will probably not be an intensification of any earlier vision, no matter how apparently spiritual, but something so entirely new that you will need all the light that is in you, and a trained insight, if you are to recognise it when contacted.

Love, which is not emotion or sentiment, and which is not related to feeling (which is a distortion of true love), but is the fixed determination to do what is best for the whole of humanity, or for the group (if the larger concept is not possible to you), and to do this at any personal cost and by means of the uttermost sacrifice. Only those who truly love their fellowmen can see the issues clear and can grasp the inevitability of the things which must be done to end the present rule of terror and so usher in the new rule of peace. Peace is *not* the goal for our race or time, no matter what many men think. This is a cycle of steadily growing activity, with the aim in view of establishing right human relations, intelligently carried forward. Such activity and intense change is not consonant with what is usually understood as peace. Peace has relation to the emotional side of life and was the goal in Atlantean days, where peace was a great spiritual issue. But peace and the love of peace can be a deadening soporific, and are so at this time. It is usually selfish in purpose, and people long for peace because they want to be happy. Happiness and peace will come when there are right human relations. Peace and war are not a true pair of opposites. Peace and change, peace and movement, are the real ones. War is but an aspect of change, and has its roots deep in matter. The peace usually desired and discussed concerns material peace, and in every case is related to the personality, whether it is the individual personality or that of humanity as a whole. Therefore I deal not with peace, but am concerned with love, which oft disturbs the equilibrium of matter and material circumstance, and can consequently work against so-called peace.

Power is something which has ever been of interest, down the ages, to advanced humanity and to those men who could respond to the will aspect through their mental unfoldment. It is today becoming of interest to the masses and to the more mediocre types of men, and is hence oft misused and turned to selfish purposes. The power here to be evoked out of the human soul, in this hour of need, is the ability to know the Plan and to work for its furtherance, thus cooperating with those forces which are endeavouring to re-establish order on Earth and to end the cycle of aggressive wickedness in which today we find ourselves.

The question arises here whether the cycle is susceptible to interference and whether it must not perforce run its appointed course. I would remind you that the law of cycles is the law governing the appearing and the disappearing of great and active energies which pass in and out of manifestation, fulfilling the purposes of Deity and yet limited and handicapped by the quality of the forms upon which they make their impact. If any intervention is possible and takes place, it will be an "intervention in time." Such an intervention is hinted at in the sacred scriptures, such as the New Testament, where it is foretold that "for the sake of the elect, the time shall be shortened." The real meaning of this (which is not apparent in the rather inadequate translation which we have) is *"because* of the elect or because of those who know and who take right action, the progress of evil can be arrested." This is encouraging, and I commend the thought to your attention. There is a power which such "elect" can wield—understanding its nature, preparatory and selfless.

And *Death*—to what does this refer? Not to the death of the body or form, for that is relatively unimportant; but to the "power to relinquish," which becomes in time the characteristic of the pledged disciple. The new era is coming; the new ideals, the new civilisation, the new modes of life, of education, of religious presentation and of government are slowly precipitating and naught can stop them. They can, however, be delayed by the reactionary types of people, by the ultra-conservative and closed minds, and by those who cling with adamantine determination to their beloved theories, their dreams and their visions, their interpretations and their peculiar and oft narrow understanding of the presented ideals. *They* are the ones who can and do hold back the hour of liberation. A spiritual fluidity, a willingness to let all preconceived ideas and ideals go, as well as all beloved tendencies, cultivated habits of thought and every determined effort to make the world conform to a pattern which seems to the individual the best because, to him, the most enticing—these must all be brought under the power of death. They can be relinquished with safety and security and no fear of results, if the motive of the life is a real and lasting love of humanity. Love, true spiritual love as the soul knows it, can ever be trusted with power and opportunity and will never betray that trust. It will bring all things into line with soul vision.

Again we have the energy of the three centres with which we are becoming familiar, and can see them being brought together and their triumphant relation being fused and blended. It thus becomes apparent that Those Who formulated this new and vital Invocation believed firmly in the power of humanity—upon its own levels of consciousness—to express the three divine potencies, Will, Love and Activity, in some measure. The demand goes forth to the Coming One to aid in the blending of the three upon Earth, so bringing them into physical plane expression, and thus unite the potencies of the human kingdom with the potencies which He will bring with Him for the saving of humanity. Only when humanity offers all that it has to give to the service of the sad, the suffering, and the oppressed, and will work actively and intelligently to bring about release, can that full cooperation be established between the inner and the outer potencies which is so deplorably needed at this time. Unless, for instance, those who can use this Invocation parallel its voiced expression with some form of definite physical plane service, and so aid constructively the Forces of Light, their efforts will prove negligible. It is humanity alone which can precipitate the new incoming energies from the Lords of Liberation and make possible Their activity of Earth. It is humanity alone which can open the door or to the physical plane for the Rider from the secret place The stupendous inner Potencies can reach certain levels of human activity and contact, such as the mental plane, but their further progress downward into outer expression, power and manifestation, is dependent upon the potent, magnetic *indrawing* power of man himself.

The thought lying behind the words *Construct a great defending wall* might be simply expressed in the words Thus far and no further. The limit of effectiveness of the evil expression and of the power of the aggressors has been reached *if* the disciples and the men of goodwill actually now play their proper part. Symbolically, they can put up an impregnable wall of spiritual light which will utterly confound the enemy of humanity. It will be a wall of energy—vibrating, protective, and at the same time of such power that it can repulse those who seek to pass in their pursuit of evil and wicked objectives. I speak in symbol but my meaning will be clear.

One point you need to grasp more clearly, and it is both an encouragement and a point difficult of belief. If the sons of men who are cooperating with the Forces of Light at this time stand with steadfastness, and if the "massed intent" of the men of goodwill is brought down from the mental plane (where most goodwill, desire, prayer and invocation becomes "frozen") and is carried away from its easy focus in the wish life of the aspirant, goodwill becomes active in expression and *in tangible deed* upon the physical plane, so that the work done through the means of invocation and prayer, plus the needed fighting for the right, is done by those who can truly coordinate and integrate on all three levels and thus function as a whole. This will mean the finish of the dominance of matter for all time. Such a desire able condition may come very slowly, from the standpoint of man's myopic vision, and may even not become apparent in its full significance to you in this life; nevertheless the victory will have been gained. Matter and materialistic interests will no longer rule the coming generation as they have ruled the last two. When the forces of aggression, of greed and cruelty are driven back, it will mean the conquest of selfish desire by unselfish love and sacrifice. This is the reward of those with whom we work, if reward is desired. This achieved situation will then bring into closer relation humanity and the spiritual Hierarchy; they will be en rapport in a manner new in history. The defeat of the oppressing nations and the liberation of the oppressed will be only the outer and visible sign of an inner and spiritual event—one for which all enlightened people are working. It will—after a period of adjustment, which will necessarily bring its own peculiar difficulties—usher in the new world, with all that is entailed in that phrase.

I have placed before you the possibility. I would reiterate, as I have in the past, that *it is humanity which determines its own fate.* Men have transcended the child stage and are now adult, though not mature. Maturity is achieved through self-engendered experience and decision, and for some time we who seek to guide have confined our efforts to reaching the intelligent people, impressing the spiritually minded, and in stimulating humanity to right action without encroaching upon man's growing expression of freewill. So the outcome is unpredictable, though we may see a certain measure of inevitability in future happenings. But man is free to choose the way that he shall go, and much of the responsibility for his choices rests upon the shoulders of the more instructed of the human family and upon those who have achieved some measure of vision.

With these thoughts upon the new Invocation I would leave you to work out these ideas in the recesses of your reflective consciousness. I would ask you to use the Invocation frequently, with dynamic intent and true understanding, and thus cooperate—by its use, by your love of humanity, and by your activity on the side of the Forces of Light—with those on the outer and inner planes who are seeking to drive aggression back to the place from whence it came, and to end the rule of hate and fear.

SECTION THREE

FORCES BEHIND THE EVOLUTIONARY
PROGRESS OF THE RACE

FORCES BEHIND THE EVOLUTIONARY PROGRESS OF THE RACE

THE DOCTRINE OF AVATARS

May 1941

As we enter the momentous month of May this year, I have asked myself if there is any way in which I can arouse the world aspirants and my disciples to a truer appreciation of the immanent significance of the presented opportunity, and also if there is any way in which I can simplify and make more real to you the Doctrine of the Coming One—linked as it is to the teaching of every great religion. In all of them, the idea of a subjective, spiritual Order, concerned with the developing welfare of humanity, is to be found.

This is an age of culminations. Such culminations appear today in the field of religion as well as in the field of science and politics. All the great lines of human approach to reality and to truth are passing out of the realm of the tangible and exoteric, into that of the intangible and esoteric. Science is rapidly becoming the science of the unseen and of the unprovable; religion has emerged from the realm of the mystical into the clearer atmosphere of the occult, and must now emphasise the reality of the unseen as the efficient cause of the seen; politics and governments are engaged with processes of thought and ideologies.

What then is the true inner structure of reality which will provide the needed strength for humanity at this time, thus sufficing to satisfy man's demand for truth and prove adequate to answer his ceaseless yet intelligent questions?

I would assert here that the great and satisfying reply

285

to all human questioning and human need is to be found in the doctrine of Avatars, and in the continuity of divine Revelations. This is the persistent belief—ineradicable and unalterable—that (at major moments of world need) God reveals Himself through Appearances, through a Coming One. This doctrine is found in all the basic world religions, in every time and age; it appears in the doctrine of the Avatars of the Hindu faith, in the teaching of the return of Maitreya Buddha or the Kalki Avatar, in the belief in the Western world in the return of Christ and His Advent or second Coming, and in the prophesied issuing forth of the divine Adventurer of the Moslem world. All this is tied up with the undying belief of mankind in the loving Heart of God, Who ever meets man's need. The witness of history is that always the appearance of man's necessity has been met with a divine Revelation.

The reason for this faith, innate in the human heart, is to be found in the fact of the nature of Deity itself. The Christian statement that "God is Love" is founded on that deepest, recognised, spiritual *fact*. The expression of this divine characteristic can be summed up in the words from *The Voice of the Silence:*

> Compassion is no attribute. It is the Law of *Laws*—eternal Harmony, Alaya's Self; a shoreless, universal essence, the light of everlasting right and fitness of things, the law of love eternal.

To this everlasting Compassion the cyclic appearance of the Sun Gods of the ancient myths, the World Saviours and the Avatars bear witness and are the guarantee.

The Wesak Festival

At the time of this Wesak Festival, I would call your attention to the fact that the annual return of the Buddha to bless His people everywhere and to convey the message of wisdom, light and love to humanity—coming as He does from the very Heart of Deity Itself—is the outer evidence and guarantee of inner divine guidance and revelation in this present world cycle of 2500 years. Year by year He returns. For a brief minute He reminds us that God exists and ever loves; that He is not unmindful of His people; that the heart of the universe is unalterable compassion, and that man is *not alone*. To bring this recognition about and to make this appearance possible, a living Triangle of Energy is created and focussed through three great spiritual Individuals, Who evoke recognition both in the East and in the West. They are known to believers of every faith and all nationalities. These Three are:

1. The Lord of the World, the Ancient of Days, Sanat Kumara, the planetary Logos, Melchizedek, He to Whom Christ referred when He said, "I and My Father are One."
2. The Buddha, the Illumined One, the Revealer of the light and the wisdom which come to us from sources far greater than our planetary Life, a Messenger of the Gods.
3. The Christ, the Son of the Father, the World Saviour, the Redeemer. He Who has remained with us and Who is gathering His sheep into His fold, the Lord of Love.

In these Three, Whose nature is radiant love and light, humanity can grasp in some measure the nature of divinity. They are greater than is known or realised; human intelligence and aspiration can only sense Their essential nature; Their spiritual potency has to be stepped down if mankind is to bear the pressure of the impact of the energy They wield and seek to transmit. It is this stepping down process which takes place at the time of the May Full Moon, and it is brought to a "focus of transmission" by the *massed intent* of the Hierarchy and the *massed demand* of the world aspirants and disciples—itself drawn forth by the *massed need* of the people of all lands.

Here, my brothers, is a simple statement of the facts which must be grasped by all of you who seek to participate intelligently in the Wesak Festival and who are anxious to act as transmitters of the spiritual energy which will, at that time, be poured out to suffering humanity. This Wesak Festival in 1941 can prove to be a "Changer of Conditions" and a major turning point in the life of mankind *if* every spiritually minded person can bring himself to the needed point of selflessness, disciplined purity and resultant receptivity.

There are certain fundamental truths which lie behind all revealed religions. They are essential to the spiritual growth and the progressive realisations of divinity by man. All else found under the term "doctrine" and allied phrases are but expansions of these fundamentals, explanatory in nature, expressive of human interpretations, and formulations of evolutionary recognitions. These are mainly additions and are in the nature of adornment, speculation and prediction; they are constantly subject to change, to rejection or development as man's intellect and spiritual perception unfolds; they are not basic or unalterable. It is the unalterable truths which must be discovered and recognised as the new world religion takes form on Earth and conditions human thought and consciousness in the coming New Age.

The Basic Truths To Date

These basic truths never change because they are related to the nature of Deity Itself and have become apparent to mankind through revelation, as evolution has proceeded and man has developed the needed perceptive faculties and the required persistence of search, plus the unfolding of the inner light of the soul. These truths, inherent in the divine nature, reveal the soul of God. They are:

1. *The Law of Compassion*. This is the truth of right relationship, of loving understanding, of actively expressed *Love*. It is the foundation of brotherhood and the expression of the inner unity.

2. *The Fact of God.* This is the truth that *Being* is God Immanent and God Transcendent; it involves the recognition of the great Whole and the related part; it is the knowledge of divinity, ascertained through right relationship and identity of origin. It is the revelation of the life of God, pervading all that is (God Immanent), and of that same life, providing that still greater cosmic relation (God Transcendent) which is the final guarantee of all progress and of progressive revelation. 'Having pervaded this whole universe with a fragment of Myself, I remain' is the challenge of Deity and the eternal hope of humanity. This is the answer of Life Itself to the demands of humanity, to the enquiries of science and to the whole world problem. God is here, present among us and in all forms of expression; He includes, pervades and remains beyond. He is greater than all appearance. He reveals Himself progressively and cyclically as man gets ready for further knowledge.

3. *The Continuity of Revelation.* Ever down the ages and at each human crisis, always in the hours of necessity, at the founding of a new race, or in the awakening of a prepared humanity to a new and wider vision, the Heart of God—impelled by the law of compassion—sends forth a Teacher, a World Saviour, an Illuminator, an Avatar. He gives the message which will heal, which will indicate the next step to be taken by the race, which will illumine a dark world problem and give to man an expression of a hitherto unrealised aspect of divinity. Upon this fact of the continuity of revelation and upon the sequence of this progressive manifestation of the divine nature is based the doctrine of Avatars, of divine Messengers, divine Appearances, and inspired Prophets. To all these history unmistakably testifies.

4. *The Inevitable Response of Humanity.* I have expressed in these simple words the instinctive spiritual reaction of man and of the undying human spirit to the three above foundational truths. This divine spirit in humanity must ever, and most surely does, respond to the divine Appearance. The witness to this is sure and proved. There is that in

mankind which is akin to God and which recognises its own when it appears. Such is the unshakable reality in the human heart, and recognition is the inevitable reward and result of revelation.

5. *Progress.* The reaction of the individual man and of the masses of men to the continuity of revelation—historically proved—cannot be denied. It is the basic fact of religion. The types of that revelation may vary but each new revelation—given in response to human need and demand—has ever led humanity onward towards a steadily brightening goal and a greater glory. The revelation may come on varying levels of the human consciousness. It may be the revelation of new lands to conquer, terrestrial or mental. Some person pointed the way. It may be the recognition of new laws and facts in nature, scientifically grasped and used; it may be the response of intelligent man to increased knowledge, producing a new type of civilisation. Some liberated spirit pointed the way. It may be the response of the human heart to the Heart of God, leading to the mystical beatitude, and to the recognition of spiritual Being. It may be the reaction of man to some new teaching, some further unfoldment, resulting in a new and enriched religious approach to the centre of life. Some Messenger pointed the way. But always it has meant progress, a moving forward, a rejection of some existing limitation, a repudiating of the undesirable and the evil. Always it involves the recognition of the possible, the ideal and the divine.

6. *Transcendence.* This means the innate capacity to pass beyond so-called natural law. This surmounting of limitation is ever taking place and this process of transcendence will call forth increasing recognition. It marks the next major phase in the manifestation of divinity in man; it signifies domination over physical law and humanity's imminent triumph over the forces which have for so long held him to earth. Of this transcendence the present mastery over the air is the symbol. Man is rapidly mastering the four elements. He cultivates the earth; he rides the waters; he

controls the electrical fires of the planet, and he flies triumphant through the air. The question now emerges: What, my brothers, next? Another transcendence lies ahead. It is one of the things which the coming Avatar will reveal.

With the lesser leaders, whom the human spirit evokes to its assistance, I shall not deal. I seek to unfold somewhat the Doctrine of Divine Messengers, of Avatars. From whence come They? What is Their nature? Who are They and what is Their relation to humanity, to the Hierarchy and to still greater groups of Lives? These are questions which normally arise and need clear answering.

An Avatar is a Being Who—having first developed His Own nature, human and divine, and then transcended it— is capable of reflecting some cosmic Principle or divine quality and energy which will produce the desired effect upon humanity, evoking a reaction, producing a needed stimulation and, as it is esoterically called, 'leading to the rending of a veil and the permeation of light.' This energy may be generated within the human family and focussed in a responsive Messenger; it may be generated within the planet itself and produce a planetary Avatar; it may be the expression of the life impulse and energy of the solar system, or of sources outside the solar system and therefore cosmic. But always it is focussed through a manifesting Entity, is called forth by a demand or massed appeal, and evokes response and consequent changes in the life activity, the culture and the civilisation of mankind.

The response or reaction of humanity to the divine Messenger establishes in due time the recognition of something transcendent, something to be desired and striven for, something which indicates a vision which is first a possibility and later an achievement. This is the historically proven process and testifies eventually to a *fact*. This new fact, when added to the facts established by other and earlier Avatars, enriches the spiritual content of the human consciousness, enhances the spiritual life of the race, and stimulates man to move a step forward into the world of reality

292 THE EXTERNALISATION OF THE HIERARCHY

and out of the world of illusion. Each revelation brings him nearer to the world of causes.

At the present time, the Avatars most easily recognised and known are the Buddha and the Christ, because Their messages are familiar to all and the fruits of Their lives and words have conditioned the thinking and the civilisations of both hemispheres; because They are divine-human Avatars and represent something which humanity can more easily understand; because They are of like nature to mankind, "flesh of our flesh and spirit of our spirit." They therefore mean more to us than any other Divine Emergence. They are known, loved and followed by countless millions. I would ask you to ponder on the potency of the nucleus of force which They have set up. The establishing of a nucleus of energy, spiritually positive, is the constant task of an Avatar. He focusses or anchors a dynamic truth, a potent thoughtform or a vortex of attractive energy in the three worlds of human living. Then, as the centuries pass, that truth and the effect of Their lives and words begin steadily to condition human thinking; the established thoughtform acts increasingly as a transmitter of divine energy as it expresses a divine idea, and this in time produces a civilisation, with its accompanying culture, religions, policies, governments and educational processes. Thus is history made. History is but the record of man's cyclic reaction to some inflowing divine energy, to some Avatar or some inspired Leader.

Divine Intervention

In considering the subject of Avatars I would like to point out that (from the standpoint of mankind at his present point in evolution) Avatars are of two kinds, as might be expected when the consciousness of humanity is subject to the control of the pairs of opposites. These two are:

1. Those Avatars Who are the embodiment of the Angel of the Presence, whether that Presence is the

soul in man, the planetary Logos, some extra-planetary Entity, some Cosmic Being, or an Expression of Cosmic Good.

2. Those Avatars who are embodiments of the Dweller on the Threshold, whether that Dweller is the human Dweller on the Threshold, planetary Forces of Materialism, or some Aspect of Cosmic Evil.

Let me attempt to make this analogy a little clearer. Just as in the case of individual man there comes a point in his life experience when the Angel of the Presence is sensed, known, seen and recognised as the revealer of divinity, so in the history of the race of men, the same great illumination may come. Revelation confronts the aspirant. Revelation confronts humanity. God is known within the human heart. God is known by mankind. This recognition of divinity in its varying aspects is naturally a progressive one—each stage and each life bringing its own revelation of the beauty of divinity and the glory of light more truly and clearly before the disciple. Similarly, there come cycles wherein the Dweller on the Threshold appears and confronts the aspirant, challenging his purpose and progress and blocking the door which leads to expanded life and liberation. The Dweller challenges the freedom of the human soul. So it is also in the life of a nation, a race, and humanity as a whole.

The Angel of the Presence indicates divine possibility, reveals to the attentive disciple the next step towards liberation which must be made, and throws light upon the immediate stage of the Path to Light which must be trodden. So does the Avatar Who reveals the Lighted Way to humanity.

The Dweller on the Threshold summarises in itself the evil tendencies, the accumulated limitations and the sum-total of the selfish habits and desires which are characteristic of the material nature of the disciple. The Angel of the Presence indicates *the future* possibility and the divine nature. So does the Avatar. The Dweller on the Threshold indicates *the past* with its limitations and evil habits. So do those Avatars Who from time to time appear as the embodiments of evil and of the lower nature of mankind. And, my brother, They do appear from age to age.

Some cycles in a disciple's life present one aspect of a "confrontation" and some another. In one life he may be entirely occupied with fighting the Dweller on the Threshold or with orienting himself to the Angel of the Presence and permitting the divine conditioning energy to flow into him; he may be succumbing to the influence of the dread sumtotal of his evil and material desires or he may be drawing gradually nearer to the Angel. But—and this is the point of importance—*it is he himself who evokes one or other of these manifestations.* So it is with humanity. The call of humanity's soul, or of humanity's material nature, must evoke response, and thus an Avatar can manifest. It is the magnetic appeal or the massed intent of the disciple or of humanity which produces the manifestation. In other lives, the disciple may simply swing between the two poles of his being, with no conscious effort, no direct confrontation and no clear understanding of life purpose. So does humanity.

Eventually, however, there comes a life wherein the disciple is confronted by both the Dweller and the Angel simultaneously and the major conflict of his experience takes place. So it is today in the world. The spiritual and the material are in conflict, and humanity itself is the battleground.

Again, a correspondence to the Doctrine of Avatars can be seen in the disciple's individual life. When he has achieved right desire and has made a true effort towards correct orientation, then—when the conflict between good and evil is at its height—there comes a moment when he demands more light, more power, more understanding, and liberation to take his next forward step. When he can make this demand with firm intent and can stand steady and unafraid, response will inevitably come from the very Presence Itself. A manifestation of light and love and power will stream forth. Recognition of need has then evoked response. The conflict ceases; the Dweller departs to his own place; the Path ahead lies clear; the disciple can move forward with assurance, and a better life dawns for him.

So it is for humanity. A demand rises to the very gates of Heaven; the massed intent of humanity is that evil must end and a better and truer life become possible. At the moment of greatest tension and of difficulty the demand goes forth. Response comes. The Avatar appears and light pours in, making the way clear. New hope awakens and fresh determinations are made. Strength to establish right relationships streams through the body of humanity, and mankind emerges into a more spacious life, conditioned by truer values. A fusion becomes possible between the outer world of daily living and the inner world of spiritual realities. A fresh influx of love and light is possible.

Today the moment of adequate tension in the life of humanity has been reached. The Angel of the Presence and the Dweller on the Threshold are at grips. Humanity stands apparently at its darkest hour. But the cry is going forth for aid, for relief, for revelation, for light, and for strength to shake off that which is evil. The massed intent of the world aspirants is directed towards the world of truer values, towards better human relations, more enlightened living and a better understanding between all men and peoples. With massed intent they stand, and their ranks are steadily increasing. With an increased focus of the will-to-good, with a clearer apprehension of future possibility, with a fixed determination that the world move forward in conformity with the divine pattern, and with an urgent cry for help, humanity stands expectant of relief. In every land there is a growing recognition that when mankind reaches the psychological point where, *having done all,* there is naught to do but stand, then some Expression of a divine determination to intervene will appear; there is a growing belief that human effort towards righteous action will be supplemented by the emergence of a divine Force, Person or Event which will bring the conflict to an end.

It might here be pointed out that in similar though somewhat less potent crises in the past, this divine intervention *superseded* human effort, but that it is hoped by Those Who are seeking to aid humanity that such intervention will today simply *supplement* human effort—a very different thing.

Therefore, humanity everywhere today awaits the Coming One. The Avatar is sensed as being on His way. The second Coming (according to prophecy) is imminent, and from the lips of disciples, mystics, aspirants and all enlightened people in all lands the cry goes up, "Let light and love and power and death fulfil the purpose of the Coming One." Those words are a demand, a consecration, a sacrifice, a statement of belief and a challenge to the Avatar Who waits in His High Place until the demand is adequate, and the cry clear enough to warrant His descent and His appearance.

Demand without paralleling action is useless, just as faith without works is dead. It is here that there is a break in the magnetic link which should unite the Avatar with the demand for His coming forth. His emergence must be caused by a fivefold chain or thread of energy: the focussed will of the people, the massed intent of the world disciples and aspirants, plus their desire, their active participation in the task of clearing the way for Him, and complete selflessness. Only when humanity has itself done everything possible to adjust that which is wrong and to end that which is evil, and has carried this effort even to the sacrifice of life itself, can He, the Desire of all nations, appear.

Today this is being attempted. The great event of the appearance of the Avatar can be made possible by a little increased effort. The mission of the Buddha at this particular Wesak Festival is to add that new impetus, that fresh illumination, and that added power and fixed purpose which will enable mankind to surmount this crisis. From the side of the spiritual Forces of the planet, everything will then have been done to make the appearance of the Avatar possible. From the side of humanity, I would ask you: What will be done?

Between the Source from which all Avatars come forth

and humanity, stands the Hierarchy of Love, stands Christ and His disciples, stand the Masters of the Wisdom. They are united, all of Them, in one stupendous effort to aid mankind at this time to surmount the Dweller on the Threshold and to come closer to the Angel. This necessitates some greater help and this help will be forthcoming when humanity and the Hierarchy in one fused and blended effort stand with massed intent, invoking that aid and expecting it also.

The Appearance of Avatars

Since the year 1400 (a date to which I referred earlier) there have been constant appearances of lesser avatars, called forth in response to minor crises, to national dilemmas and religious necessity. They have taken the form of those men and women who have championed successfully some truth or some right cause, some human right or correct human demand. All these people have worked actively upon the physical plane and seldom received recognition for what they truly were; only history, at a later date, laid emphasis upon their achievement. But they changed the current of men's thoughts; they pointed a way to a better life; they pioneered into new territories of human achievement. Such a one was Luther; another was Columbus; still others were Shakespeare and Leonardo da Vinci—to mention only four who so lived and thought and acted that they conditioned after events in some field of human living and are still recognised as pioneering souls, as leaders of men. With these disciples I shall not deal. They embodied ideas and made history—not the history of conquest but the history of progress. I seek to consider with you those still greater Appearances Who come forth from some hidden centre, remote from or near to humanity, and Who "release from crisis the sons of men." These fall mainly into four relatively minor groups:

1. *Racial Avatars.* These Appearances are evoked by the genius and destiny of a race. The *typical man* (in quality and consciousness, not necessarily physically) foreshadows

the nature of some race. Such a man was Abraham Lincoln, coming forth from the very soul of a people, and introducing and transmitting racial quality—a quality to be worked out later as the race unfolds. Coming forth correspondingly from the realm of cosmic evil, and responsible for the focus of materialism upon the planet today was Bismarck. Both men came forth within the same one hundred years, thus demonstrating the balance in nature and the constant interplay of the pairs of opposites. They are both types of the most powerful Avatars which humanity itself has as yet produced. They emerge along the lines of *government*, of the *first ray* and in the department of the Manu, and are very sensitive to Shamballa force. Such Avatars frequently emerge at the founding of a nation. This is true of both Bismarck and Lincoln.

2.   *Teaching Avatars.* These Appearances sound a new note in the realm of thought and of consciousness; they reveal the next needed truth; they pronounce those words and formulate those truths which throw light upon the spiritual development of humanity. Such Avatars were Plato, the first Patanjali and Sankaracharya; they emerge upon the *second ray* line of energy, in the department of the Christ and are expressions of hierarchical force. When I say the department of the Christ, I would remind you that the name "Christ" is that of an office—an office that has always had its Head. I do not mention the Christ or the Buddha as among these Avatars because They are Avatars of another class and of infinitely greater potency.

3.   *Ray Avatars.* These great Beings come forth at relatively long intervals when a ray is coming into manifestation. They embody the quality and the force of a particular ray. Next century, when the seventh ray has achieved complete manifestation and the Piscean influence is entirely removed, the *seventh ray* Avatar will appear. His work will demonstrate the law, order and rhythm of the creative process as it works out on the physical plane, blending spirit and matter. And as this ray is called the Ray of Ceremonial Order or Ritual,

He will be largely instrumental in producing those conditions which will permit of the reappearance upon Earth of the Mysteries of Initiation, of which the Hierarchy is the custodian. He is necessarily connected with the Great White Lodge on Sirius. This fact does not, however, concern us now, for we await the coming of a still greater Avatar.

4. *Transmitting Avatars.* These manifestations of divinity appear at those great cyclic moments of revelation when humanity needs the expression of a new truth or the expansion of an old one in order to progress still higher on the evolutionary ladder. These Avatars issue forth in response to demand and are not so much concerned with racial development as They are with the subjective unfoldment of consciousness and with the stimulation of humanity *as a whole.* Of these Avatars the Buddha and the Christ are outstanding examples. They were not only human-divine Avatars, and hence able to link humanity with the Hierarchy, but They were something far greater and more important. They had reached the point where They could act as Transmitters of certain cosmic principles which—focussed in Them in an extra-planetary sense—could stimulate the deeply hidden and latent corresponding principle in humanity. They transmitted and brought something from outside the planetary life—from the very Heart of God to the heart of man. The Buddha, because He achieved illumination, stimulated the light in the world, in humanity and in all forms. He served the soul of man. The Christ, because of His stupendous achievement—along the line of understanding—transmitted to humanity, for the first time in human history, an aspect and a potency of the nature of God Himself, the Love principle of the Deity. Prior to the advent of the Buddha, light, aspiration, and the recognition of God Transcendent had been the flickering expression of the human attitude to God. Then the Buddha came and demonstrated in His Own life the fact of God Immanent as well as God Transcendent; the idea of God in the universe and of God in humanity evolved. The Selfhood of Deity

and the Self in the heart of individual man became a factor in human consciousness. It was a relatively new truth to be grasped by humanity. It had always been known by disciples and initiates.

However, until Christ came and lived a life of love and service and gave mankind the new commandment to love, there had been very little emphasis upon God as Love in any of the world Scriptures. After He appeared as the Avatar of Love, then God became known as Love supernal, love as the goal and objective of creation, love as the basic principle of relationships, and love working throughout all manifestation towards a plan motivated by love. This divine quality Christ revealed, and thus altered all human living and human goals. At that time too there came a great impetus and extension to the work and growth of the Hierarchy, as there was in a lesser degree when the Buddha came. Many initiates became Masters; many Masters passed to still higher work, and many disciples took their places in the ranks of the initiates. There was numerically a great influx of aspirants into the ranks of accepted disciples.

I have considered some of these Avatars in my earlier writings under different names and categories. I deal with Them here simply in an effort to reach a wider public with the teaching on the doctrine of Avatars or of divine Appearances. The Bible is full of such Appearances, but little is really understood about Them. The above are the more familiar groupings.

In September 1940 I gave an interpretation of a new Stanza of the Great Invocation, and in that communication I spoke of Divine Embodiments as the highest type of Avatar for which humanity could look at this point in its evolution. I spoke of the activity of the Hierarchy and of Shamballa, should these two divine Agencies decide that intervention in the form of a widespread cataclysm (engulfing all peoples) was necessary, and I referred to the emergence of inspired leadership as another and lower aspect of divine guidance and participation.

Such inspired leadership is now being given to humanity by Winston Churchill and Franklin D. Roosevelt, in contra-distinction to the focussed leadership of the forces of ma-terialism through Hitler and another man in his group. But it is not with this form of leadership as expressive of the avataric principle that I deal here. Such leadership is called forth by elements present in humanity itself. I deal now with a fifth type of Avatar, greater than the other four. These Avatars have not, in this world cycle, experienced human life.

5. *Divine Embodiments.* These Avatars appear rarely; and when They do, the effectiveness and results of Their work are very great. They issue forth into manifestation via the centre at Shamballa, because They are an expression of the will nature of Deity; They embody divine purpose; the energy pouring through Them and transmitted by Them is focussed through the Lord of the World; They can only be reached by the united voices of the Hierarchy and of humanity speaking in unison; Their service is evoked only by realised need, and only after those who call Them forth have added to their faith strenuous action and have done their utmost, alone and unaided, to overcome evil.

They never descend lower than the mental plane, and the main emphasis and attention of Their work is directed to the Hierarchy; the Hierarchy is Their transmitting agency; They occasionally reach those thinking people, focussed on the mental plane, who have clear vision, potent resolve, directed will and open minds, plus of course, essen-tial purity of form. These Avatars express the Will of God, the energy of Shamballa, and the impulse lying behind divine purpose. When They do come forth, it will be the destroyer aspect of the first ray of power which They will express; They bring about death—the death of all old and limiting forms and of that which houses evil. Their work will, therefore, fall into two categories:

a. They will destroy the forces of evil, using the agency of the Forces of Light.

    b. They will reveal as much of the divine purpose as humanity is able to grasp through its best minds and most dedicated aspirants; They will clarify the vision of the world disciples and of all who have the disciplined will-to-know and who are dedicated to and expressive of the will-to-good. This knowledge and this will are needed in the coming period of readjustment.

How They will bring the present evil conditions to an end and how They will destroy the present evil state of materialistic aggression I may not reveal. It is not yet certain that human development and understanding and the massed intent of humanity will be adequate to the needed demand and strong enough to call Them forth. Time alone can determine that. God grant that the aspirants and disciples of the world will awaken to the opportunity and the imminent and waiting possibility. The plight of vast groups of people upon the planet today lies heavy upon the heart of the Hierarchy. But to bring release and the Appearance of the Power that can liberate, human cooperation is needed. Nowhere is this more desperately needed than among the German people in their unhappy land. God grant, therefore, that those Germans who have vision may join the forces of those who are seeking to free Germany and the German people from the imposed tyranny of the evil Lodge, working through their seven representatives in Germany. Once the Germans who are living free lives in other lands can think in terms of humanity as a whole and not in terms of national glamours, revenge or self-pity, then their voices will be added to those of the other free peoples and to those of the aspirants and disciples in all other nations.

    When the Avatar comes He will convey to humanity something for which we have as yet no true name. It is neither love nor will as we understand them. Only a phrase of several words can convey something of the significance and then only feebly. This phrase is *"the principle of directed purpose."* This principle involves three factors:

a. Understanding (intuitive and instinctual, but intelligently interpreted) of the plan as it can be worked out in the immediate future.

b. Focussed intention, based on the above and emphasising an aspect of the will, hitherto undeveloped in man.

c. Capacity to direct energy (through understanding and intent) towards a recognised and desired end, overcoming all obstacles and destroying all that stands in the way. This is not destruction of forms by force such as is now being imposed on the world, but a destruction brought about by the greatly strengthened life within the form. Only the next one hundred years will reveal the significance of this statement and then only if the massed intent of the people evokes this *Avatar of Synthesis* during the next twelve months. I have called this Being by this name because it expresses the quality and the objective of the force He brings and wields.

Another and lesser Avatar is also awaiting a call from humanity. He is esoterically related to the Avatar of Synthesis, being overshadowed by Him. This Avatar can descend on to the physical plane into outer expression and can thus step down and transmit the stimulation and quality of the force of the greater Avatar Who can come no nearer than the mental plane. Who this Coming One may be is not yet revealed. It may be the Christ, if His other work permits; it may be One chosen by Him to issue forth, overshadowed by the Avatar of Synthesis and directed in His activities by the Christ, the Lord of Love. In this way, the energies of both Shamballa and the Hierarchy will be focussed through the chosen Coming One. Thus a triangle of loving, purposeful energy will be created which may prove a more effective way of releasing energy and a safer way, than the focussed impact of one selected force might be.

I realise the difficulty of this subject and perhaps may simplify the matter by a brief summation:

1.   A great cosmic Avatar *can* come if the Hierarchy and humanity can stand together with massed intent.

a. He will descend into the three worlds of human endeavour, but no nearer than the mental plane.

b. He will transmit a cosmic energy whose quality is *Synthesis*. This will express itself through harmony and unity, producing necessarily understanding, promoting goodwill, and eventually ending the separative, isolating tendencies of mankind.

c. His note and vibration can only be sensed by those whose individual note is also synthesis and whose life objective is the will-to-good. These are consequently the Members of the Hierarchy, the disciples and aspirants of the world and a few of the men of goodwill.

2.   A Messenger or Avatar of equal rank to the Christ in the Hierarchy (or possibly Christ Himself) may come forth as the Representative of the Avatar of Synthesis and as His transmitting Agent.

a. This lesser Avatar works today as one of the senior Members of the Great White Lodge and is in close touch with the Christ, with the Manu and with the Lord of Civilisation, the Master R—; He will act as the Coordinator between the Hierarchy and Shamballa. He will fuse and blend in Himself, through the quality of His Own life, the three great energies:

   The will-to-spiritual power.
   The will-to-love in its spiritual connotation.
   The will-to-manifest spiritually.

b. The antiquity of the achievement of this Coming One is to be found in the name applied to Him, which is found in so many of the world Scriptures: The Rider on the White Horse. This refers to the time prior to the phrase so well-known in the Christian fields: "The Lamb slain from the foundation of the world." In the earlier cycle, the then initiates spoke of the "sacrificial horse, slain to all eternity." It conveys the same basic idea.

c. This Avatar can descend to the physical plane and there appear, to lead His people—as the Prince Who leads through war to peace.

d. The whole problem before the Hierarchy and humanity today, in connection with the coming Avatar, can be summed up in the following four questions:

Can He bring the energy of synthesis with Him, thereby bringing about rapid changes?

This depends upon His being overshadowed by the Avatar of Synthesis and upon that Avatar being evoked through the demand and the massed intent of humanity, aided by the Hierarchy.

Will the demand of the people be strong enough to evoke the higher potency, or will it be too feeble because of the failure of the world disciples and aspirants to focus this massed intent throughout the planet?

Will the higher overshadowing not take place and only the lesser Avatar come to institute a slower method of gradual reform?

This slower method will be necessitated only if and because humanity will have demonstrated its inability to call forth and receive the higher measure and more potent vibration of divine energy. It is entirely for the decision of the world disciples and aspirants; not the decision of poor bewildered, deluded humanity. Will the world disciples and aspirants appreciate the crisis and opportunity? They have not yet, as a whole, done so.

3.   The Hierarchy today stands with massed intent. The cry of the masses is rising up to the very gates of Shamballa. It is stronger far than the demand of the spiritually oriented people—the disciples, the aspirants, the men of goodwill. They seem—from the viewpoint of the Hierarchy—to be overcome by inertia, to be engrossed by their theories and idealisms, and to be blind to the issues at stake. Can they be aroused? Can they stand with focussed intent, strenuous

physical service and activity, and determined effort to struggle, even unto death, for the defeat of evil? Can they preserve the inner attitude of love and non-separateness? Can they relinquish all for love of humanity? Can they sacrifice everything for the cause of freedom and of righteousness? This is the problem confronting Those Who are working for the appearance of the Greater and the Lesser Avatars Who can at this time save humanity if humanity desires salvation and will take the needed steps.

The Needed Steps

These steps are various in kind though one in intent. The first step is to realise clearly what are the methods whereby the Avatar can come and so reach humanity. These are the same methods, whether it is the Avatar of Synthesis, working through the Hierarchy, or the Avatar of Coordination (as I might call Him), working through humanity and representing the greater Avatar upon the physical plane.

The methods whereby Avatars reach and influence Their agents or those who respond to Their note, vibration and message are three in number.

1. *Overshadowing.* Where there is kinship in quality, in objective and in nature, it is possible for the Avatar to overshadow some Member of the Hierarchy (as in the case of the Avatar of Synthesis) or some disciple or aspirant where humanity is concerned (in the case of a lesser Avatar). This is done through meditation, through a directed stream of thought energy, the presentation of a thoughtform and the evocation of the focussed will of the one who is overshadowed. All this proceeds rapidly where there is close cooperation between the latter (the sensitive responding disciple) and the Avatar. The Christ is today in very close rapport with the Avatar of Synthesis, and this rapport will continue, becoming closer and closer until the Full Moon of June; He is giving all possible aid, as is His Brother, the Buddha. It is this which makes the coming Full Moon of May of such supreme importance.

A group of Masters and initiates Who are specially related to the Christ's department, as well as a group working under the Master M., are endeavouring to respond to this overshadowing which is only possible—even to Them—when transmitted to Them by the Christ. (I talk here of mysteries.) It will therefore be apparent to you that, as They succeed and become increasingly sensitive to and aware of this overshadowing energy of the great Avatar, Their disciples on earth can also—in a dim and faint way—become responsive to the ideas that are formulated in the mind of their particular Master in response to avataric impression. Ponder on this.

2. *Inspiration.* This is more direct than overshadowing and more potent in results. Certain Members of the Hierarchy and, above all, the lesser Avatars, are inspired from "on high" by the cosmic Avatar and become at times direct expressions of His mind, His energy and His plans. This is the spiritual correspondence to obsession. In the case of obsession, a man is taken possession of and inspired by some evil entity; in inspiration, there is no possession but only what is called "identical response"—a very different thing. In the one case, the free will and intelligent understanding of the Master or the disciple is enlisted on the side of the spiritual Agent; the spiritual man, functioning as a soul, becomes the channel for forces, ideas and activities other than his own but to which he gives full intuitive assent. It is all carried forward with full understanding and consciousness of method, process and results. It is an act of free spiritual cooperation, for the good of humanity, in the work of a great spiritual Force or Being. The cooperation of the Master Jesus with the Christ is a case in point. In connection with the coming Avatar, it may involve the cooperation of the Christ or of a "kindred, equal soul" with a cosmic Being or Presence, taking place on still higher spiritual levels of consciousness and producing an incredibly focussed potency.

In the case of obsession, the evil force enslaves the personality which, in the majority of cases, is but a shell. Of this, Hitler is a case in point. This produces greater potency on the physical plane and on the astral plane; it is quicker and more immediate in results, but the lasting power is less and the effects are relatively temporary.

In the processes of inspiration, the lesser Avatar—through His life and contacts in the three worlds—will necessarily influence sensitive, spiritually oriented disciples and aspirants, and thus the inspiration coming from the cosmic Avatar becomes in time a *group inspiration,* and therefore can be more safely handled. This group inspiration can happen today. If it does, there will then be a simultaneous appearing of the cosmic Avatar, the World Saviour in the Person of the lesser Avatar, and—at the same time—a group saviour, composed of responsive disciples and world servers. Ponder again on this.

In this way, if you will note carefully, there is established a direct linked chain from humanity, via the Hierarchy, to Shamballa. The Hierarchy is working at the establishing of this chain, aided by Their disciples. The demand for the cooperation of all aspirants is now going forth, because the times are urgent. If this relationship can be established (and it will be a sad day for humanity if it cannot), then the third method of avataric expression becomes possible.

3. *Appearance or Manifestation.* Every possible step has been taken by the Hierarchy to enable the Avatar, the Coming One, to appear. What these steps are cannot be declared here. Only some questions, suggesting possibility, are permissible. Think you that His body of manifestation is already on Earth, waiting to be overshadowed, inspired and used at the right time, as was the vehicle of the Master Jesus by the Christ? There are those who say that it is waiting and has been waiting for 22 years. Is it possible that there will be a sudden descent of the Prince of Light and Peace to change present conditions by the effectiveness of His radiance and His message? There are those who look for Him to suddenly appear, and they number millions of expectant people. Some say He is already on His way. Is it possible that this Wesak Festival will see Him approach

nearer to the Hierarchy and make a contact with Them? Some say it will take place. Can the "massed intent" of humanity evoke response and lead to the appearance on Earth of the lesser Avatar? Some say nothing can stop it. Prophecy, expectation and the present time cycle testify to the opportunity. This possible dual event—the coming of the Avatar of Synthesis to the Hierarchy and of the lesser Avatar, His Representative, to humanity—can be a probable happening if the world disciples and aspirants measure up to the opportunity.

The Immediate Task

I enter upon my concluding remarks wondering if anything I can say will awaken disciples to the needed spiritual effort—a spiritual effort which must find expression in physical plane decisions and activity. A certain aspect of physical plane effort is already being undertaken by them through very force of circumstance: Red Cross activity in every land, response to urgent, surrounding, physical need, and the mobilisation of their time and resources by leaders in all countries are the keynotes of the time. But it is the inner spiritual activity and orientation (paralleling the outer activity) which is required. This is an activity which is preceded by clear factual thinking and decision. Can the world disciples and aspirants evidence this full life on all levels? Are they capable of an intensive inner life as well as of unflagging attention to outer duty and demands? This is the problem. Are they capable of laying aside their own pet theories and trifling ideals (trifling in the face of the appalling world situation) and focus every possible effort on fighting evil upon the physical plane, as well as on other levels, with every possible agency? Can they at the same time live that dynamic life of thought and inclusive comprehension which will find expression in the voiced appeal to the Avatar? It is feeling and fanatical adherence to a loved ideal which frequently stand between a disciple and effective service on the physical plane. It is old habits of thought and the determined effort to interpose some mystical dream between conditions as they are and conditions as they could be, if disciples took right action, which have prevented effective service.

But, my brother, all things have to become new and that means a new vision, a new idealism, and a new life technique. Past ideals, past dreams and past efforts to tread the Path and express brotherhood have produced most successfully a certain changed attitude in the race, a new orientation to the life of the spirit, and a focussed intention to move forward. That was the desired goal and that goal has now been reached.

The right attitude is now present in many people in every race, and it is the recognition of this which has called forth the activity of the Brothers of the Shadow at this time. They realise that the time of their power is shortening. The hold of the materialistic values over man is steadily becoming weaker. So far has man progressed that there are enough people in the world today to turn the tide *if* they can be aroused from their apathy.

I tried to arouse them to speed and clear thinking between the years 1932-1938 but though something was accomplished, it was not enough. The blindness, illusion, separativeness and inertia of the aspirants of the world today constitute one of the factors with which the Hierarchy has to contend. Aspirants are preoccupied with their own little affairs and with their own small efforts, instead of relinquishing everything in an endeavour to unite on the needed appeal and activity. They are contending for their own interpretations of truth, and for their pet ideals of peace, living or work and—like Nero—they "fiddle whilst Rome burns." All their lives they have fought for an ideal and a dream, and they love that more than they love humanity. Yet—all that is needed is such a deep love of humanity that it works out on all levels of activity and all life effort. If the idealists of the world would realise the situation *as it is*, they would relinquish all that they hold dear and come to the rescue of humanity, and thus snatch the helpless masses back from slavery and death. They would battle for the freedom of the human soul with every weapon in the armory of mankind. They would hold back the forces of aggression by force itself if need be. They would aim at clear thinking, and thus clear the channel for the inflow of spiritual force. The major pre-requisites today for true world service are an overwhelming love of humanity and a sense of proportion. The only requirements today for disciples and aspirants may be summed up as follows:

1.   The doing of everything possible to bring the war to an end. Every physical plane method must be used to drive the forces of evil and of cruelty back to their dark place. Physical plane methods, when motivated by unchanging love of humanity and under the direction of an enlightened soul, become agents of righteousness. There are worse things than the death of the physical body; there is the enslaving of the human soul.

2.   The focussing of the inner life towards the Hierarchy in radiant faith. The way of the Coming One must be made clear, and the life force must be dedicated to the outer life of compassion.

3.   The clarifying of the mental life in the pure light of the soul. Disciples live too much in the world of feeling; hence the clouding of their vision. When they have clarified their minds and see the situation whole, they can then appeal to the Avatar to make His appearance. This appeal must be made via the Christ.

4.   Disciples must endeavour to understand what are the objectives of the Avatar, and thus fit themselves to cooperate.

The second step is to understand clearly what is the task which must be undertaken in preparation for the Coming One. This entails four things:

1.   The effort to stand with all other disciples and aspirants in an attempt to call forth the Avatar, to reach Him by focussed intensive thought and to evoke His response. This

is the purpose of the new Invocation. It voices intent, makes demand and pledges cooperation.

2. The providing of a nucleus or group through which the Avatar of Synthesis can work when the lesser Avatar has come forth upon the physical plane. This involves individual activity, the sounding out of a clear note, based on clear mental perception, the recognition of those allied in the work and the development of conscious group work. In this group work the personality is subordinated and only the following determinations are dominant:

a. The determination to offer group service—as a group—to the world group.

b. The determination to establish right human relations upon the planet.

c. The determination to develop everywhere the spirit of goodwill.

d. The determination to withstand evil through planned group activity.

3. To construct a network of light and service in every land. This is begun in the individual environment of the server, and gradually extended throughout the world. It was with this idea in view that I suggested the forming of triangles of people, pledged to use the Invocation and to extend its use through the world. It is my specific plan to help *mass* world thought and thus evoke the Avatar, and likewise to provide a world group through which the new forces and energies can function, the new ideas can spread, and the coming world order find adherents.

4. To prepare the general public for the Coming One by pointing out the testimony of the past, the recognition of the universal need for divine intervention and the holding out of hope to the distressed, the doubting and the tortured. In His appearance lies hope, and history testifies that it has frequently happened at times of world crisis.

Such are the possibilities which I present to your understanding. I have told and taught you much in past years.

I have often asked for your cooperation and your help in world service. Some have responded and given help. Many have longed to aid. The majority have done little or nothing. In this moment of crisis (within the world crisis) I again ask for your cooperation and leave you to make your decision.

May the love of God and of your fellowmen inspire you; the light of your souls direct you and the strength of the group enable you to aid in bringing good out of the present evil by right action and clear thinking.

THE WORK OF RECONSTRUCTION

August 1941

As I have studied the world disciples during the present world crisis, I see them borne down by inertia—not the inertia that comes from selfishness and self-centredness, or the inertia due to lack of understanding of the nature of the crisis, or the inertia due to sheer laziness, but an inertia based upon a deep, inner depression, to a sense of human failure and to an introspectiveness which is natural but useless at this time. Some disciples (both on the probationary path and on the path of discipleship) take refuge in the perpetuation of the activities with which they were engaged when the war started; some take refuge in a determination to wait until the crisis is over, and appear to think that any work along the old lines of spiritual endeavour is of no real use; still others take refuge in a feverish outer occupation with things which the average man who is not spiritually oriented can do as well, if not better. Some disciples and aspirants are spending their time fighting a psychic sensitivity, evoked by world conditions; many are simply overwhelmed and stunned by humanity's pain and agony, by the horror of the moment, by anxiety over the future, and by anticipation of still worse happenings. Their imaginations are working over-time and quite uselessly. To some of these attitudes, all of you are susceptible.

I write today to call all world disciples and aspirants to an intensive period of preparation for future activity and work. From now until the Sun moves northward, I would ask each of you to do three things:

First, strengthen—through meditation, prayer and clear thinking—your faith, confidence and joy, and above all else, deepen your love of humanity, carrying the love of the soul through on to the physical plane and into all your human relations.

Secondly, eliminate out of your personality life, as far as you can or should, anything (mental, psychic, emotional or physical) which might hinder your future usefulness.

Thirdly, plan together for the work of the future. This work can be inaugurated shortly and must be started slowly, carefully, and with unreserved cooperation with me and with each other. It must be carried out steadily and undeviatingly, with no lost motion, once its outlines are determined, and it should be carried out *together*.

The major need today for each and all who must sponsor the work of the future that I am seeking to do with your cooperation and understanding, is to foster the growth of the *will* to love and work. This effort on your part will express itself in a steadily deepening love for humanity—for all men and for each other. It will demonstrate in a constant effort to invoke the spiritual will in self-discipline and persistence; it will show itself in the intelligent carrying forward of the plan as I shall seek progressively to outline it.

This work can only be carried forward by people who love their fellowmen enough and have sufficient illumination to enable them to work with me dependably for a period of five years in the face of anything which may happen; they must be people who will endeavour to permit no personality misunderstanding to hinder their usefulness and their group interrelation, and who—because they love enough—will ceaselessly subordinate everything to the task which must be done. The second thing I ask you to do is to gather out of all the past pamphlets and my later writings those plans and instructions on service which will be applicable to the changed conditions and in the immediate future. Study this carefully along with the requests and suggestions in this letter, so that you may know what I, your Tibetan teacher, feel could and should be done by you in the service of the immediate future. I would ask those of you who care to do so to meet together at the time of the Full Moon in October for fellowship, united meditation, consecration and consultation. I would ask those of you who live and work at more distant points to write briefly your reactions to the suggested endeavour, indicating how you feel you can best aid in the task. I would ask all of you who associate yourselves with me in the work of the future, each day to use the very brief meditation which I outline below. It is dynamic, affirmative and—if rightly used— should link head and heart, leading thus to intelligent loving service, and it should also serve to bind you all together in the closest spiritual unity. This will aid in the vitalising of the etheric bodies of all workers, and therefore in a group vitality which will be irresistible.

Suggested Meditation

Each morning, prior to starting the day's activities, achieve an inner quiet, see the Self as the soul, place yourself at the disposition of the soul, of humanity and of your group.

1.   Then say silently and with full dynamic intent:

> At the centre of all love I stand; from that centre, I the soul will outward move; from that centre, I the one who serves will work. May the love of the divine Self be shed abroad in my heart, through my group and throughout the world.

2.   Then, focussing your attention and dedication, see the group to which you belong as a great centre of love and light, irradiating the world of men, bringing relief, light, love and healing in increasing measure.

3.   Brood then upon the plan to be carried out and upon the indicated service for the coming day. Do this as the

soul, keeping the personal lower self in a waiting attitude, like a servant attentive for instruction.

4. Then say:
The joy of the divine Self is my strength.
The power of the spirit of man shall triumph.
The Forces of Light do control the forces of evil.
The work of the Great Ones must go on.
The Coming One is on the way. The Avatar approaches.
For this we must prepare.

5. Close with a minute of dynamic quiet.

I will ask you to do this meditation every day until January 1st, 1942, when I will give you another step in this Meditation of Preparation for the Coming One. Its aim is to prepare all of you interiorly. I would ask you also to read and re-read the instruction I gave you on Avatars. (pp. 285-313.)

You will constitute the initial group which I am asking to collaborate with me in the reconstruction work of the New Age. As time goes on, subsidiary groups will be indicated who can work in the various countries as focal points in the great network of light which is forming everywhere under the inspiration of the world disciples and aspirants in every land, as they work under instruction of the Hierarchy. Some of them are known to you. Many of them are not known to any of you. But they represent the working groups of all the Masters, and upon their shoulders rests the work of reconstruction, aided by the thousands and thousands of men and women of goodwill in every land.

The meeting upon the ocean of the two world disciples and leaders marked a crisis in world affairs. The Eight Points (see page 318) formulated by them constitute the basis of the coming world order. They were necessarily large in outline and without details as to application. It will be for a liberated humanity to work out these details, to make the necessary adjustments, and to so re-arrange human life that the higher spiritual values may prevail, a simpler mode of life may be instituted, a greater freedom be established, and a wider responsibility be shouldered by every man. This will take time. Some of you may not live to see the full clarification of the way that humanity must go (the "Lighted Way" of the future), but you can, all of you, aid materially in the important task of preparation, in indicating the needed world principles, in spreading the gospel of goodwill, and in establishing right human relations. The work done in thought, in love and in dedicated activity during the next three years is of paramount importance and will produce the stabilisation to take place in the last two years of the five mentioned by me above as your immediate time of cooperation.

You who are working in the midst of the chaos and conflict cannot and will not be able to judge accurately the measure of accomplishment. Only the Members of the Hierarchy (Masters, initiates and the disciples who are out of incarnation at this time) can get a true perspective. The working disciples in the forefront of the battle have to carry on their work in the midst of chaos, turmoil, questioning, pain, and distress. They cannot, therefore, see the picture whole. A few of the more advanced who can "live on the heights and in the valley and the depths" simultaneously can see truly, but their numbers are not large, and the Christ spoke a true word to His bewildered disciple when He said, "Blessed are they who have not seen and yet have believed." The following of the meditation, adherence to the instructions given, persistence in the face of difficulty, and a staunch belief in the beauty of the human spirit, in the love of God, in the victory of the Forces of Light and in the approach of the Coming One—these are the attitudes which we, the workers on the inner side, ask of those we choose to carry on our work upon the outer plane.

This letter deals with the forming of the group to carry out the plans for 1942-1945. It is being formed in the dark of the year, at the nadir point of human distress, at the most difficult moment in human history, at a point of crisis and—in the case of many of you as individuals—at the time of your deepest personal difficulty. I tell you that all of you, together, *are* equal to the task.

I will again write to you and will indicate the practical aspects of the work. In the meantime, ponder and reflect upon what I have written here; begin the meditation and endeavour to strengthen your link with your soul and with each other. Let love—not emotion and sentiment—control your thoughts, words and deeds. I would ask you also to study carefully the indications I have given in the past as to the work which must be done, and I would ask you also to study carefully the Eight Points outlined on the high seas, and the Four Freedoms so oft discussed throughout the world.

Let quietness and depth characterise your inner life.

THE EIGHT POINTS OF THE ATLANTIC CHARTER

August 14, 1941

The President of the United States of America, Franklin D. Roosevelt, and the Prime Minister, Mr. Churchill, representing His Majesty's Government in the United Kingdom, being met together, deem it right to make known certain common principles in the national policies of their respective countries on which they base their hopes for a better future for the world.

First, their countries seek no aggrandizement, territorial or other;

Second, they desire to see no territorial changes that do not accord with the freely expressed wishes of the peoples concerned;

Third, they respect the right of all peoples to choose the form of government under which they will live; and they wish to see sovereign rights and self-government restored to those who have been forcibly deprived of them;

Fourth, they will endeavor, with due respect for their existing obligations, to further the enjoyment by all States, great or small, victor or vanquished, of access, on equal terms, to the trade and to the raw materials of the world which are needed for their economic prosperity;

Fifth, they desire to bring about the fullest collaboration between all nations in the economic field with the object of securing, for all, improved labor standards, economic advancement and social security.

Sixth, after the final destruction of the Nazi tyranny, they hope to see established a peace which will afford to all nations the means of dwelling in safety within their own boundaries, and which will afford assurance that all the men in all the lands may live out their lives in freedom from fear and want;

Seventh, such a peace should enable all men to traverse the high seas and oceans without hindrance;

Eighth, they believe that all the nations of the world, for realistic as well as spiritual reasons, must come to the abandonment of the use of force. Since no future peace can be maintained if land, sea or air armaments continue to be employed by nations which threaten, or may threaten, aggression outside of their frontiers, they believe, pending the establishment of a wider and permanent system of general security, that the disarmament of such nations is essential. They will likewise aid and encourage all other practicable measures which will lighten for peace-loving peoples the crushing burden of armaments.

THE FOUR FREEDOMS

January 6, 1941

In the future days, which we seek to make secure, we look forward to a world founded upon four essential human freedoms.

The first is freedom of speech and expression—everywhere in the world.

The second is freedom of every person to worship God in his own way—everywhere in the world.

The third is freedom from want—which, translated into world terms, means economic understandings which will secure to every nation a healthy peacetime life for its inhabitants—everywhere in the world.

The fourth is freedom from fear—which, translated into world terms, means a worldwide reduction of armaments to such a point and in such a thorough fashion that no nation will be in a position to commit an act of physical aggression against any neighbor—anywhere in the world.

Franklin D. Roosevelt

PRACTICAL STEPS IN THE RECONSTRUCTION WORK

September 1941

It will be obvious to you that there is little that I can say as to exact procedure until such time as humanity itself has decided the future conditions of human living. I mean exactly that, my brother. The war is not yet decided. There is a widespread feeling that God (as we call the Central Power of Life itself) will or should intervene; there is a vague demand that right should triumph and a desperate hope that something unexpected will happen that will give victory to the arms of the Forces of Light. This attitude of painful expectancy is universal among the masses—both those in the fighting countries and the neutrals also. In the neutral countries (of which the United States is the largest and the most important) there are two factors conditioning the thinking of the people:

First, a deep-seated though not unnatural selfishness, which prompts the determination to take no real part in the war, except what can be done safely and at the least possible cost, and secondly, a steadily emerging cleavage between the relatively few who have vision and want actively to help the embattled Allies (the agents of the Forces of Light), and the selfish many who—for political, religious or personal reasons—will fight every effort to commit their country further than it is at this time committed, and who hope nevertheless to share in the benefits of victory.

In the last analysis, however, the world situation must be settled by humanity itself. The Hierarchy cannot interfere. Humanity has the privilege and the opportunity to take right action *now*. The Coming One Who is being so fervently invoked throughout the world, either by prayer, invocation or unvoiced demand, is concerned with readjustment, with the right fusion of forces and with the healing of the peoples. This worldwide invocative demand is largely prompted by a defeatist position or by a compassionate longing to see the long agony of man ended; it is seldom prompted by conviction, by the recognition of possibility or a paralleling decision to right the wrongs which lie back of the world situation and which constitute the alibi of the enemy of humanity—Hitler and his associates.

The Coming One will make His appearance when the tide of battle has definitely turned and the forces of evil are being driven back to their own place. I have made no pronouncement as to time, person or place. I have simply indicated that there is a possibility (subsequent to right action) of the appearing of the One for Whom the centuries have long waited, to Whom prophecy in all lands, the rapidly developing intuition of the people, and established precedent, all bear constant witness. His hour is near, provided the needed steps in preparation are taken, and it is for that that I have approached you. I have *not* indicated the place of His appearing, the nature of His emergence, or the country of His choice. These are the details which concern Him and not you. Your task is to get ready for His coming. This involves right understanding and increasing labour for humanity as a result of *the experience of love* within your own individual consciousness. This I emphasise.

I have suggested three preparatory steps to the group of aspirants with whom I am in touch:

1. The use of the great mantram or invocation—in two parts (see pp. 144, 249). The first was used in 1936 and the second in 1940, and is still in use. The first was intended to centralise human desire, and the second was intended to utilise what mental power was available to invoke Those Who (on the inner spiritual side of life) are waiting to help. This They cannot do unless the way is made possible for Them by humanity itself. Such is the law.

2. A general process of educating the public in the fact and use of goodwill. A great but undeveloped potency is still locked up in mankind which, if evoked by man himself, will prove adequate to do two things:

    a. Lay the foundation for a stable peace—active and positive because the result of active and positive action—*after* the Forces of Light have won the victory upon the physical plane.

    b. Provide the subjective synthesis or network of light,

embodying the force of goodwill as the expression of right human relations. This will guarantee a workable world order and not an imposed tyranny or a mystical and impossible dream.

3. The realisation of a general outline of that coming world order which will be in line with humanity's need, basic in its implications, and which will provide that structure of living interrelation which will foster latent love, intuitional understanding and the creative power in man.

Those are the three major objectives with which I have dealt in past communications. I have also made suggestion as to modes of activity which are practical—some of them of an exoteric nature, such as the compiling of mailing lists, in every country, of those who think and express goodwill; others, such as the creation of the network of light, through the formation of triangles. It is not for me to decide the details of your outer activities. That is for you to do, and for that I have called you to assist me.

Let me recapitulate a few of the things which have been undertaken in our joint work so that you can clearly see the background of our coming effort and grasp the work as a whole.

1. The first activity was the writing and distribution of the occult teachings through the medium of the books which A.A.B. has assisted me to write. These will serve (when the war is over) to lead humanity forward and nearer to the time when present day occultism will be the theme of world education in some modified form. The books which have been published can be stated—without any conceit—to have no competitors, and these, rightly distributed, will serve a useful part in carrying the consciousness of man to higher levels and in making clear the divine Plan for mankind. In them also the task immediately ahead at the close of the war is clearly indicated.

2. The founding and the work of the Arcane School. This was started by A.A.B. to train those ready for esoteric teaching and to prepare them for the stage and work of

Accepted Discipleship. The world today is full of groups occupied with the task of helping one or other of the groups of aspirants and seekers to be found everywhere, or with the more general undertaking of raising the mass consciousness. The Arcane School was therefore formed for two purposes:

a. Primarily to aid the Hierarchy in its work during the world crisis—a crisis for which the Hierarchy has been long prepared. The Arcane School was not and is not the only group with this objective, but it is definitely among the most influential.

b. To train probationary disciples to become accepted disciples, so that the Hierarchy could find those who could safely carry spiritual power and be channels of love and understanding to the world.

You can see, therefore, that the Arcane School is not so much engaged in helping the individual as in aiding the Hierarchy to salvage humanity. For this work, training is required, and the Arcane School provides this.

3. The fact of the existence of the New Group of World Servers was brought to the attention of the general public, and on quite a large scale. This group is composed of aspirants, disciples and initiates, and is intermediate between the spiritual Hierarchy and the intelligent public. Its members are to be found in every country, are un-organised except by their spiritual relation to the Hierarchy and to each other, and through their effort in every field of human consciousness to lead humanity into a more spiritual way of living. They aim to foster the growth of right human relations through goodwill, and this work is still going on.

4. The organising of the men and women of goodwill in every land so that eventually they can set the note of world goodwill for the new world order. Some of this work was started in 1934. Much lies ahead, demanding attention, and will have to be accomplished in a period much more difficult than the pre-war period. The nucleus of this group

exists, and among them the livingness of goodwill is still unimpaired.

5. The effort to utilise the power of sound and of thought combined was undertaken through the use of the two great invocations which you have—as a group—distributed throughout the world. Great world prayers have been used for ages; men have been driven by desire and spiritual aspiration to pray, and have recognised the power of the divine response. The art of invocation has been, however, relatively unknown, especially in the West. It employs the dynamic will and the focussed mind, and is intended to evoke response from the Forces which will condition the new world, which can come into being at the close of this war. A focussed will or intention, a convinced mind, a dedicated desire and a planned activity are essential to success.

6. The forming of triangles of light and goodwill, so that an inner network of people, pledged to goodwill, to the use of the power of invocation and to the growth of understanding throughout the world can be created; and a beginning has already been made. This is a potent and workable mode of procedure, once it is given an opportunity to spread.

7. The inauguration of an effort towards definite group work. This must be group work of a new order, wherein individual activity is subordinated to the group objective and the decisions of the group in conclave; it is not work carried forward through the imposition of some one will upon a group of weaker wills. The individual and his mode of working are not regarded as of importance in the group consciousness, because it is the will of the group—unitedly dedicated to a specific objective—which is the point of major importance. This is a new procedure and something to which you can apply yourselves. In this group which I have now formed, opportunity will arise to demonstrate the practicality of this new ideal in service methods.

These are a few of the undertakings in which we have for some years been engaged, and it is suggested that all of them be continued as a background to all future work and a fundamental platform.

You, as individuals, in this group (or in your relations with other groups) all have your personal problems. These problems are simply your participation in world karma and constitute your needed training ground and the field of your spiritual experimentation. With them I shall not deal, for you are all adult souls and progress by defined service, not by being helped. Your task is to aid the work which the Hierarchy plans to do, to find the ways and means whereby that service can be wisely rendered, to discover the manner in which world need (not your group need) can be met, to finance that share in the work of the Brotherhood to which you have been assigned by your soul, and to do your part in developing those human attitudes which are needed if true peace is to be found in the world by 1975. If this work is soundly done, then a world unity can be established which will produce right human relations, a sound world politic, a united spiritual effort and an economic "sharing" which will bring to an end all competition and the present uneven distribution of the necessities of life.

In the past I have outlined for you the general programme and the hoped-for objectives. I have given you much information and have indicated need and its possible solution. I have given you practical suggestions as to procedures and methods. I have asked—as I ask today—for your cooperation, and I ask it on behalf of the Forces of Light, of the spiritual Hierarchy and of distressed humanity.

The present world crisis could be shortened if the spiritually minded people lived up to their inner belief and knowledge. The task of unifying the men and women of goodwill is today infinitely more difficult than it was before the war. It can only be done if each servant of the Hierarchy thinks clearly, loves intelligently and serves to the utmost. I make no plea. I have pleaded much with all of you in the past, and the effort which resulted, though not a complete failure, was not adequately strong enough to off-set the forces of evil, focussed in Germany, Japan and—to a much smaller extent—in Italy.

This last statement (which I have made in other writings) has evoked resentment in the minds of those who believe that the Forces of Light must love so indiscriminately that their work on the side of evolution is negated, and that effort to promote the development of the human consciousness is rendered completely futile or should be held in abeyance until the fight is over. I would here point out that if the Forces of Light—aided by you—did nothing to influence the minds of men, the forces of materialism and of evil would triumph. Humanity would then be spiritually defeated and its evolution would be set back for an indefinite period. I would here call your attention to the words of my great Master and yours: "By their fruits ye shall know them." I would remind you that there would be no world war today if Germany had not marched on Poland. The cause of the widespread cruelty, terror, murder and agony rests squarely on the shoulders of the seven men in Germany.

Had the aspirants and the disciples of the world realised the situation earlier, and had they worked more wholeheartedly, the present catastrophe could have been held within bounds; it could have been retained and the problem worked out upon the inner planes of thought and desire, and could there have been transmuted and the needed readjustments made. But they failed to understand, and the storm broke upon the physical plane.

The next twelve months will be decisive in human affairs. By the end of 1942, chaos and difficulty will still be present, but the sound of the victor's trumpets will be heard. Will the victors be the Forces of Light, under whose banners fight the Allies, or will evil triumph and greed reap the profits of aggression? Will men be led into a darkness which —though not interminable—will engulf the human soul for decades? The answers to these questions lie in the decisions and the activities of humanity itself. The Hierarchy waits.

I have referred to the increased difficulty which will confront the men and women of goodwill (working under the

New Group of World Servers). What constitutes the difficulty, if we analyse the situation? Two major factors:

First, the steadily mounting feeling of intense resentment (amounting to hate in the case of some groups and
sections of suffering humanity), accompanied by a deep
fatigue, a shattered psychological integration as the result of
nerve strain, an acute fear of what the future may hold
(scientifically developed by the Axis powers), and a numb-
ing of the soul which is the result of death on every hand,
loss, separation and the sight of untold pain and suffering.

Secondly, the widespread physical destruction, wrought
by the invading and the defending armies—the destruction of
great cities with their accompaniments of civilised living,
the wholesale wiping out of industrial plants and the mechan-
ics of daily life, the sinking of the ships which distribute the
raw products of civilised living and the complete disorganisa-
tion of all human affairs in every country in the world—
directly or indirectly—and the breaking down of the structure of well-established financial relations, plus the disruption of the ordinary means of communication. Add to this
the monetary ruin of the masses of the people, and you have
a true and not a sensational picture of the world state. Out
of this wreckage of all that man has constructed during the
centuries and out of the spoliation of all existing culture
and civilisation, the new world order must be built. And, my
brother, it will be built, and you can help prepare for this
building of a more stable and beautiful way of life.

This creative process begins always in the realm of
intention, is impulsed by trained desire, and will be brought
into objective expression by the right direction of thought,
the inspiration of right ideals, and the educating of the
usually unthinking masses (who are, however, today thinking as never before), so that humanity *as a whole* will appropriate these ideals. They then can be trusted to take
the needed action. In this manner the desired conditions will
take form upon the physical levels of daily existence. There
are many enlightened thinkers working at this time upon
these problems; they are actively moulding public opinion;

free minds in all countries, or their representatives in the occupied lands, are already laying the foundations of freedom, more surely and soundly than ever before; groups everywhere are organising for the rebuilding (mentally, psychically and physically) of our world and for the reconstruction of our civilisation on saner lines and safer foundations. More intimate and understanding relations are being established between religion, politics and philanthropy, and the part which science, education and economics must play in the future is being brought increasingly into the forefront of human aspiration.

There is therefore no need for discouragement. There is only need for determined right action and sacrificing effort. This must be based on faith in the human spirit, on a conviction that good *must* ultimately triumph because it always has, and a knowledge that the New Age is dawning and that nothing can frustrate its establishment. To the advent of this new era the destruction itself bears witness, because—again quoting my Master, the Christ—you cannot put new wine in old bottles. To your share in the preparatory work for the future new world I call you; to renewed activity upon the outer plane of life I call you, and again I outline to you three years work, plus two years of activity which will grow out of the three years preparation.

Until May 1943, I suggest sound preparatory undertakings for future world activity. This must be accompanied by sound organisation, based on a long range vision of what must be done, and by experimental effort. This is the immediate work for this group and for those whom they may later choose as collaborators. Small groups must grow out of this group later, when it is duly established and functioning.

From May 1943, until November 1944, you should move outward into definite world experience and into a basic co-operation with any similar groups which are engaged in world salvage, primarily along the psychological line, for the psychological rehabilitation of humanity will be the major outstanding need, paralleling that of economic readjustment. These two must receive prior attention by all men and women of goodwill. This group must inspire, promote and strengthen wherever and whenever possible. Such a task can only be undertaken by people who have no religious bias, no political antagonisms and no sense of exclusiveness.

From then until the close of 1945 or the beginning of 1946, the work should consolidate, the men and women of goodwill will swing into increasing usefulness and the potency of their thought and attitude in moulding public opinion should make itself dynamically felt—if you all work as desired. It will be apparent, therefore, how important is the work that you can start now and stabilise during the next eighteen months. The major lines of action you already know, for the goodwill work done in 1936 still remains basic and its processes should be re-studied and employed. But I would make the following practical suggestions concerning the group and its planning.

1. Learn to know and trust each other, leaving each other free to work and plan within the group plan; develop *the experience of love* in your individual lives and in your group relation. Meet regularly for discussion, planning and united meditation—using the same meditation in this group as I have asked you to follow individually. Subordinate your own wishes and ideas to the group decision. *Let this be uniquely a group effort.*

2. Press forward with the Triangle work in every possible way and in every country open safely to contact. Plan this work along sound business lines, making a small group of you responsible for its functioning and success.

3. Discover, and where possible contact, all groups which are motivated by a true love for humanity, plus a groping after and understanding of the New Age ideals of freedom, cooperation and inclusiveness. I suggest a gradual compilation of a mailing list of such groups, accompanied with samples of their literature and an analysis of their ideas.

4.   Gather together all the many proposals that have been formulated by individuals, groups of world thinkers and specialists in the different fields of world endeavour as to the New Order. Find out what is being suggested in the many different nations as to the New World Order—both good and bad. This will involve the reading of books, their digesting and analysis, the forming of a small available library, and the study and accumulation of pamphlets on the subject. By doing this, a thoughtform of great potency can be built which will influence the minds of men.

5.   Keep in touch with people in all countries—occupied and unoccupied—who can later be swept into constructive activity. Thus this group will be ready to vitalise people and groups everywhere with whom they are in touch—some of which were formed prior to the war and are perforce inactive. The Units of Service in the occupied countries are a case in point. Therefore keep in touch objectively and subjectively with as many people as possible, all over the world.

6.   The organising of the needed financial equipment to carry forward this work must be the task of another group within this larger group of mine.

7.   Leaders of spiritual, religious and esoteric groups, as well as educational groups, should be approached in the interests of world unity. A letter should be prepared inviting such leaders into a comradeship of mutual friendship and cooperation—not of coordination or fusion. A "coming together" can thus be planned for united strengthening and advice. Such letters should always be the product of group effort and suggestion, after being formulated by the smaller group assigned to its production.

8.   A clear formulation of the objectives for which this group has been formed should be drawn up for general circulation; wise business organisation should be applied from the very start; right voluntary help should be enlisted; sound financial policies should be laid down.

9.   Definite work, preparatory to any work which future

necessity may indicate in Europe or elsewhere, must be undertaken. It is not possible for you to undertake the rehabilitation of the entire planet! There is, however, much that you can do along the line of interpretation of ideals, of unifying and of strengthening other groups. There are also three things possible to this group:

a. The discovery and aiding of the members of the New Group of World Servers in the occupied countries and elsewhere, giving spiritual and practical material aid.
b. Work for the rehabilitation and correct handling of the children in the devastated lands. This is an urgent need and has wide promise and great implications for the future world order. Concentration on this is desirable.
c. Continue with the work of finding and organising the men and women of goodwill throughout the world. It is they who will constitute the agents of this group and other New Age groups in the future. Work done by you prior to the war is thus to be continued, and along similar lines.

10. Make a close individual study of the Four Freedoms and the Eight Points of the Atlantic Pact, so that the members of this group can soundly envisage the freedoms of the New Age and can therefore think clearly, teach the new ideals correctly, and aid in this main world objective. This understanding is more important than you realise. Out of these suggestions your group plan can take shape. Having made them and having indicated to you the lines of hierarchical desire, I shall say no more. The responsibility is yours, and to you I leave the working out of these ideas. Move rapidly and as a united group with the Triangle work. It is basic in its usefulness and must be widely spread. Move with sureness, and more gradually, with the other aspects of the indicated work.

The strength and usefulness of this group will depend upon the inner union and love with which you work together, offsetting all personality reactions. You will help each other on all levels where help is needed. Let this group

work silently and as the Hierarchy works—impersonally be
hind the scenes. Let them draw upon all available spiritual
resources, dedicating all their mental, emotional and ma
terial reserves to the work of helping humanity, and let them
know (past all questioning) that *the Hierarchy stands.*

PREPARATION FOR FUTURE ACTIVITY AND WORK

October 1941

Certain questions arise in the minds of all disciples
anent the general position of the hierarchical effort, about
the possibility of materialising the Plan, and particularly
concerning the share in these plans which spiritual groups
can undertake. I would have you remember that disciples
learn to work with the plan by *working;* they learn to discover the inner expanding consciousness of humanity by the
development of an increasing sensitivity to it; and they find
their coworkers in the Plan by the old and tried method of
trial and error. The less evolved the disciple and worker, the
larger the number of trials and the greater the number of
errors.

But the system works, for it is an eliminating as well as
a perfecting process, and the residue which remains after
due effort, can be trusted. You have those, finally, who remain and who are worthy of trust. Why does this system
work? Because by its means the graces of humility, prompt
obedience to *soul* injunction, and inner integrity are unfolded and developed. Where these are present, there will
be found sureness of touch when humanity is contacted;
sensitivity to the impression of the Hierarchy when that
Hierarchy is seeking contact; and a right sense of proportion.

One of the difficulties which comes to the server immersed in the thick of the undertaking is that of preserving
contact with the vision. I refer to the vision itself and not to
its materialisation. Perhaps I can make my meaning clear
if I point out that, just as long as the contact is *a vertical one,*
the work is fairly simple, the next step is apparent and plain,
the line of activity to be followed is clear and the inspiration

is fresh and vital. But the moment that the consciousness of the disciple becomes *inclusive horizontally* (and that *must* take place), then the difficulty becomes great, and the disciple begins to understand—for the first time—the true significance of the words, "the Cross of the Saviour." Yet if he can train himself to stand where the four arms meet (I am here speaking symbolically) he will discover that he stands in the place of power, and at the "midway point." Then he can truly begin (again speaking symbolically) to look off to the four corners of the earth, both subjectively and objectively, and with reality; immediately the strain is terrific.

This is one of the difficulties confronting the new group of world servers at this time. You will remember that some little time back I spoke of the crisis with which the group is faced. How can I express in words the nature of this crisis? It is that of the invocation or the precipitation of the Plan, for those two words are synonymous. This necessarily involves a strain—the strain of prolonged inner contact and realisation, plus the effort to use skill in action and due physical plane executive ability. The new group of world servers is therefore today pulled two ways. Its effort must be to stand ready at the centre. The new group today stands at the very centre and must preserve and hold its position at all costs. That which signifies the most at this time is the spiritual poise and the spiritual sensitivity of the workers.

It is to this important condition that the group members must pay due attention. Disciples and spiritual workers must not be so occupied with the details of the Plan, with the production of that which will produce the externalisation of the ideas, that the spiritual training and strengthening of the workers is neglected. In the dust and turmoil and noise of the fight, grow not insensitive and hard, or so preoccupied that the needs of those with whom you work are forgotten or pass unnoticed. Let *love* be the keynote in all relationships, for the power which must salvage the world is the precipitation of love, and how shall that find its way onto the physical plane save through a group whose ears are attuned to its imminent emergence, and through the lives of those in the group who are irradiated by love itself? It is here that there is lack—not intentionally or because of the existence of its opposing quality—but simply through world pressure and strain. In the unfoldment of goodwill in the world at the close of the war—which will be one of the major tasks of the new group of world servers—let love be the active force among the senior members of the group. I would like to see more of it among all of you.

As the executive side of the group work grows, and the will aspect of humanity is contacted and its power used to evoke the emerging crisis of love, an increasing number of workers with first ray qualities will be drawn into the ranks of the new group of world servers. This constitutes the second difficulty, and it is here that I feel the need to utter a word of warning. This coming in will greatly strengthen the work but brings with it also great problems. Much of the work done hitherto has been second ray work; its quality is gentler, its technique is that of building and teaching, and its workers are magnetic and they present, when brought together, no great problems of cohesion and of group integration. Of this aspect of work, the Arcane School is an example.

When, however, first ray workers appear to aid in the expansion of the work and to carry it to the four quarters of the earth, then certain difficulties inevitably appear. It is the dynamic quality of the power aspect which must be guarded against, not in the sense that it must not be permitted expression, but in the sense that it must be motivated by love, harnessed to gentleness, and qualified by understanding.

The problem, therefore, will be to integrate first ray workers into the new group of world servers in such a manner that the destructive aspect of the ray will not cause difficulty, produce disruption or any obliteration of the dominant love note which should be the outstanding characteristic of all workers with the Plan at this time. Otherwise, the precipitation of the crisis of love will be hindered.

I would ask for an intensification of love between all of you, and a growth of real understanding. Forget not, at the same time, that love is the great attractive magnetic force, and will consequently draw to itself all that is needed at the present crisis and for the materialisation of the vision in due form on earth. This will require spiritual energy, sound business sense, skill in action and financial support. Remember that money is the consolidation of the loving, living energy of divinity, and that the greater the realisation and expression of love, the freer will be the inflow of that which is needed to carry forward the work. You are working with the energy of love and not with the energy of desire, the reflection or distortion of love. I think that if you will ponder on this, you will see the way more clearly. There are many first ray workers wielding the power of desire and thus materialising money. There are many first ray workers finding their way into the ranks of the workers among the new group of world servers. Unless these workers are swept by love, their first ray energy will wreck the work of the group. Yet they are needed at this time, for they have the strength to stand unmoved at the centre. It is the conjunction of the first and second ray workers which can carry the world through the coming crisis of Reconstruction, and it will be of value if this is borne in mind by all of you in all work connected with the new group. It is important integrating work.

You might ask me at this point to be specific and state if there is any significant hindrance which needs to be offset or changed, once realised. An understanding of all I have stated above will greatly help, for I have pointed out three difficulties. Add to this the realisation that a right handling of the broad issues will automatically tend to take care of the details. By this I mean that the establishing of sound inner group relations between all of the workers will produce that inner cohesion and one-pointed effort which must inevitably and surely produce the outer results and attract both the needed workers and the essential money.

See to it also that one department of the work is not over-emphasised in your minds to the exclusion of others, for that will produce strain, lack of balance and sometimes a sense of separation, leading if continued, to disruption. Let the consciousness be developed that there is one work being done by all, and that the whole group is concerned in the entire activity. This inclusive attitude should permeate the entire organisation, and thus the departmental spirit need not enter in.

One point I will touch upon for the clarification of your minds. The daily meditation, both personal and in relation to the group, would produce better results if the focus of attention were given to the attaining of the needed inner attitudes, the intensification of the inner spiritual life of understanding and the welding of all workers into one unity of service. A united attitude of love, of hopeful expectancy, of courage, of spiritual demand and of directed will is potent in results and will bring all that is required.

Has there not been too much attention in the past to aspects of physical plane effort, and to techniques of working? Has there not been too much consideration of *how* to do the work and too little consideration of the *spiritual dynamics* of the work itself? The need has been great and the problems many. The expansion of the work may seem necessarily to foster a departmental spirit. When such situations arise, it is necessary then to intensify the inner sense of unity. Differentiations are easy, for they follow the line of least resistance upon the physical plane. But the work is one work, and the workers constitute one group. The need now is fusion and group understanding.

Is it not true that a point of fusion achieved in the daily meditation by an individual brings about right expression in the daily life and a right handling of life conditions? A point of fusion achieved in group meditation will evoke the right results and produce an instrument of service of such power that its progress will be irresistible.

The strain of the past three years has been long and great. Many of the workers are feeling it, and the need for love and strength is great. The strain ahead will be no lighter, though it will register differently and bring different problems, but you are equal to it and to the task ahead.

Success can crown the efforts being made, and the new group of world servers can measure up to the need, if there is a more conscious and definite attempt to stand in the centre— the place of loving power—and an increased ability to think in terms of group synthesis and fusion, and to choose with wisdom those who (from inner development and outer ability, for these must go together) belong to the group.

AN IMPENDING CRUCIAL DECISION

December 1941

As the last month of the present sad year is upon us, I come to you with a message. The determination and the inner purpose of humanity will be so definite during the period when the Sun will begin to move northward—from December 25th until June 22nd, 1942—that the future of humanity for many hundreds of years will be decided. From that decision will date the coming New Age; on that decision, the Hierarchy will be able to make prediction and determine action; in that decision will be discovered the point in evolution of the mass of men. I urge you to face the future with strength, to free your minds from all vestiges of doubt, and to *know* (in your own life and for the race) that the forces of materialism and cruelty will *not* triumph. Again I say to you, *the Hierarchy stands.* Go forward with assurance.

A deeply rooted subjective process is taking place in the human consciousness which is evocative and producing definite effects. This needs to be recognised and the nature of invocation understood by all who seek to aid their fellow-men. As I explained elsewhere in detail (*Esoteric Astrology,* pages 570-575), this process of invocation falls into two stages in the life of the individual and also today in the life of humanity as a whole. The stage of *aspiration*, irregular and vague but gradually becoming focussed and assuming power; and the stage of *mysticism* with its uncomfortably recognised dualism; this merges into *occultism* which is the intelligent study of that which is hidden. It is because all these stages are actively present today that we have the dire and widespread crisis.

It was the need to give a constructive trend and to focus the invoked energies which led me, under instruction from the Hierarchy, to give out—at widely separated points of time—two Stanzas or parts of a great occult mantram, the first one to help focus the aspirants from whom it met with full response; the second was also offered to the masses, but was intended to be a test and a "decision in a time of crisis," hence made its appeal to the mentally focussed aspirants and disciples.

I am explaining this because world conditions today warrant the use of both Stanzas now. The Great Invocation, as earlier used, should again be made available to the masses. The second Stanza should be used by thinkers, occultists and disciples, and by all who respond to its note. In doing this there will be need on your part of great "skill in action," so that you may rightly and wisely distribute the two Invocations. The one will invoke the Rider from the secret place and aid in His evocation, for it is the Rider from the secret place Who is referred to and invoked in the first Invocation; the other will invoke the Lords of Liberation.

The blended invocation and the united call from the different levels of the human consciousness will bring a mighty appeal to bear upon the hidden Centres of the "Saving Force." It is this united appeal which must now be organised. Thus the mass of humanity will be stimulated to move forward into light, and the new world cycle, beginning in Aquarius, will be definitely inaugurated by humanity itself.

THE ONLY WAY TO VICTORY

April 1942

I have been working with A.A.B. as my amanuensis since November 1919. During that period the world has seen great and significant changes, and one of the most significant has been the growth—the phenomenal growth—

of spiritual perception. This shows itself in the fact that, in spite of the world catastrophe, in spite of the rampant horror and evil which is stalking our planet, and in spite of human pain, terror, suspense and uncertainty, there are today two factors present in the human consciousness: the vision of a better future and a fixed, unalterable determination to make that vision *fact* in human experience. This better world is to be a world in which the spiritual values will control, viewing those values as that which is good and right for the whole of humanity and not simply as religious and theological interpretations. Spiritual perception has become inclusive and now concerns the physical plane as well as the metaphysical.

It is not perhaps easy for you to realise the importance of this development which—again in the face of all contending forces—has enabled men to recognise that the Kingdom of God must function on Earth; that it must be externalised and that it need not be some distant point of wishful thinking but should condition man's daily life and control all his planning for the future. For this, men are today working and fighting. They call the vision by many names: better world conditions, the new world order, world reconstruction, the new civilisation, brotherhood, fellowship, world federation, international understanding—it matters not. It is the theme of betterment, of universal welfare, of general security, of widespread opportunity, irrespective of race, colour or creed. This is the factor of importance. The underlying purposes of God are working out, and with this note I seek to begin my Wesak communication to you.

This is the hopeful and most important side from the angle of the Hierarchy Who view all world events from the angle of the future. There is, however, the other side. It is not necessary for me to emphasise the seriousness of the present situation. The war is not yet won. At the time of writing, in spite of sporadic successes and the staying power of the Allied Nations, and in spite of a basic trend towards ultimate victory, the powers of evil have had things very much their own way. They have triumphantly moved forward, except in Russia. This was to be expected at first, because if evil is simply the dominance of matter and the negation of the spiritual values, it is obvious that on the material plane the line of least resistance is to be found for them. Their initial triumphing is, therefore, to be expected. The course of the war hitherto has demonstrated this. When the spiritually-minded people of the world, the men and women of goodwill, the idealists and the kindly, decent folk in every land can bring to bear upon the physical plane the same unified determination and the same united will-to-victory that the forces of evil have shewn, *then* the Forces of Light will assume the upper hand and control human affairs.

The difficulty with which the Hierarchy was confronted in the effort to bring this about was due to the fact that the condition of unity of objective, of method and of inter-relation had to be brought about without any infringement of the free will of the individual, group or nation. The occult law of spiritual freedom had to be recognised and protected. No such recognition or safeguarding hinders the activities of the forces of evil. The will-to-power and an organised, evil minority took control. Freedom of conscience and of action was removed, and the enforced submission of the majority to the will of a ruthless minority brought about a spurious but temporarily most effective unity. This has been lacking in the case of the United Nations, fighting for the Forces of Light and on behalf of human freedom.

Freedom, my brothers, can itself prove a limitation when it delays right action, when it centres attention upon the petty differences and the personality inclinations of people and when it serves to prevent that unity of action which can win the war. It has been necessary for the leaders of the peoples to take valuable time to bring them to a proper sense of values and to the realisation that individual and national differences and points of political and religious disagreement *must* all give place to the one supreme requirement—the winning of the war and the releasing of humanity from the threatened slavery, the steadily mounting fear, and the world domination of the Black Lodge.

As I have earlier told you, an ancient conflict is again in full swing and humanity has now the opportunity to settle it once and for all, and—for ever after—be free in a sense not hitherto known. This conflict falls into three stages:

1. The stage of physical warfare in which we are now engaged and from which there is no escape.

This requires the Will-to-victory.

2. The stage of reorganising world affairs when the war is over. This should properly fall into two phases:

   a. The establishing of right human relations during a prolonged armistice, if possible. This phase will prove in many ways as difficult as the war itself, but will work out on mental and emotional levels of warfare, instead of physical.
   b. The task of rehabilitation. This will be both physical and spiritual in scope and will embrace those activities which stretch all the way from the rebuilding of blasted cities, the restoration of the scorched earth, the psychological care of the youth, the sick in mind and the bewildered, and the re-enunciation of the essential spiritual values which *must* guide humanity in the future.

   This will involve the Will-to-good.

3. The stage wherein will come the recognition of the opportunities of peace, the right use of security, and the planned education of the youth of all lands in the principles of the new age.

This will involve the Will-to-organise.

Thus on all three levels of human living, mankind will be conditioned by a tendency towards the good, the beautiful and the true. Speaking esoterically, the personality of humanity will be integrated and reoriented towards the good

life, a new and better way. For the attainment of these objectives, I summon you today and all whom you can reach.

I should like to incorporate at this point part of what
I said elsewhere.

One thing you must constantly bear in mind. When
the war is over, when this time of acute trial and tribulation
has come to an end, a great spiritual awakening (of a quality
and a nature quite unpredictable now) will arrive. The
war will have taught humanity many lessons and will have
torn the veil of self away from many eyes. Values which
have been hitherto expressed and understood only by those
whose "eyes are on God," will be the goal and the desire
of untold thousands; true understanding between men and
between nations will be a longed-for objective, and what
humanity determines to have it ever succeeds in achieving.
This is an occult law, for desire is, as yet, the strongest force
in the world; *organised,* unified desire has been the basic
reason for the appalling Axis successes.

The only factor which can successfully oppose desire is
Will, using the word in its spiritual connotation and as an
expression of the first great divine aspect. There has been
but little of that organised, spiritual will shown by the
United Nations; the Allies are animated naturally by desire
for victory, desire for the arrival of the end of this all-en-
gulfing world cataclysm, by desire for peace and the return
of stability, the desire to end war once and for all and to
break its constantly recurring cycle, and a steadily mounting
desire to bring to a finish the terrible toll of suffering, of
cruelty, of death, of starvation and of fear which is gripping
humanity by the throat in the attempt to strangle out its life.

But all this determination is in most cases simply the
expression of a fixed and united desire. It is not the organised
use of the will. *The secret of the will lies in the recognition
of the divine nature of man.* Only this can evoke the true
expression of the will. It has in fact to be evoked by the
soul, as it dominates the human mind and controls the

personality. The secret of the will is also closely tied in with the recognition of the unconquerable nature of goodness and the inevitability of the ultimate triumph of good. This is not determination; it is not whipping up and stimulating desire so that it can be transmuted into will; it is not an implacable, unshakable, immovable focussing of all energies in *the need* to triumph (the enemies of the Forces of Light are adept at that). Victory for the United Nations does not lie in the effort to produce this focussing with better effect than the enemy. The use of the will is not expressed by an iron fixation to stand steady and not yield to evil forces. Determination, the focussing of energy and the demonstration of an all-out effort towards victory are only (where the United Nations are concerned) the expression of a one-pointed desire for peace and for an ending of the trouble. This type of effort is something which the masses can give, and which they do give on both sides in this conflict.

There is, however, a plus, a something else, which will swing the tide of victory on to the side of the United Nations. This will come through the effort to understand and express the quality of spiritual Will; it will be the manifestation of that energy which makes the first divine aspect of Will or Power what it is; it is that which is the distinctive feature of the Shamballa force; it is that peculiar and distinctive quality of divinity which is so different that even Christ Himself was unable to express it with facility and understanding. Hence we have the episode in Gethsemane. It is not easy for me to express its significance in words. Two thousand years have gone since Gethsemane and since Christ made His initial contact with the Shamballa force, and by this means and on behalf of humanity established a relationship which even after two thousand years is but a thin, frail line of connecting energy.

This Will force is nevertheless available for right usage, but the power to express it lies in its understanding (as far as may be possible at this midway point in human evolution), and in its *group* use. It is a unifying, synthetic force, but can be used as a regimenting, standardising force. May

I repeat those two key words to the use of this Shamballa energy: Group Use and Understanding.

Mankind has had much difficulty in comprehending the significance of Love. If that is so, the problem in relation to the Will will naturally be still more difficult. For the vast majority of men, true love is still only a theory. Love (as we usually interpret it) works out as kindness, but it is kindness to the form side of life, to the personalities of those around us, and fulfills itself usually in a desire to carry out our obligations and not to obstruct in any way those activities and relationships which tend to the well-being of our fellowmen. It expresses itself in a desire to end abuses and to bring about happier, material world conditions; it shows itself in mother love, in love among friends, but seldom as yet in love among groups and nations. It is the theme of the Christian teaching, just as Will, divinely expressed, will be the theme of the coming world religion, and has been the impulse lying behind much of the good work done in the fields of philanthropy and human welfare, but factually, true love has never yet been expressed—except by the Christ.

You might ask why, if this is so, do you emphasise this highest aspect? Why not wait until we know more about Love and how to manifest it in our environment? Because, in its true expression, the Will today is needed as a propelling, expulsive force, and also as a clarifying, purifying agent.

The Shamballa energy is therefore that which is related to the livingness (through consciousness and form) of humanity; we need not consider its relation to the rest of the manifested world; it concerns the establishing of right human relations and is that condition of being which eventually negates the power of death. It is therefore incentive and not impulse; it is realised purpose and not the expression of desire. Desire works from and through the material form *upwards;* Will works downwards into form, bending form consciously to divine purpose. The one is invocative and the other is evocative. Desire, when massed and focussed, can invoke will; will, when evoked, ends desire and becomes an immanent, propulsive, driving force, stabilising, clarifying, and finally destroying. It is much more than this, but this is all that man can grasp at this time and all for which he has, as yet, the mechanism of comprehension. It is this Will—aroused by invocation—which must be focussed in the light of the soul and dedicated to the purposes of light, and for the purpose of establishing right human relations; it must be used (in love) to destroy all that is hindering the free flow of human life and which is bringing death (spiritual and real) to humanity. This Will *must* be invoked and evoked.

There are two great handicaps to the free expression of the Will force in its true nature. One is the sensitivity of the lower nature to its impact, and its consequent prostitution to selfish ends, as in the case of the sensitive, negative German people and its use by the Axis nations for material objectives. The second is the blocking, hindering, muddled but massed opposition of the well-meaning people of the world who talk vaguely and beautifully about love but refuse to consider the techniques of the Will of God *in operation*. According to them, that Will is something with which they will personally have naught to do; they refuse to recognise that God works out His Will through men, just as He is ever seeking to express His Love through men; they will not believe that that Will could possibly express itself through the destruction of evil with all the material consequences of that evil. They cannot believe that a God of Love could possibly employ the first divine aspect to destroy the forms which are obstructing the free play of the divine Spirit; that Will must not infringe upon their interpretation of Love. Such people are individually of small moment and of no importance, but their massed negativity is a real detriment to the ending of this war, just as the massed negativity of the German people, and their inability to take right action when Hitler's purposes were disclosed, made possible the great inflow of ancient and focussed evil which has brought the present catastrophe to man. Such people are like a millstone around the neck of humanity, crippling true effort, murmuring, "Let us love God and each other," but doing nothing but murmur prayers and platitudes whilst humanity is dying.

You can easily appreciate the fact that the evocation of the energy of the Will and its effect upon the unprepared, materialistically minded person might and would prove a disaster. It would simply serve to focus and strengthen the lower self-will, which is the name we give to realised and determined desire. It could then create such a driving force, directed to selfish ends, that the person might become a monster of wickedness. In the history of the race, one or two advanced personalities have done this with dire results, both to themselves and to the people of their time. One such figure in ancient times was Nero; the modern example is Hitler. What, however, has made the latter so dangerously an enemy of the human family is that during the last two thousand years mankind has advanced to a point where it can also be responsive to certain aspects of this first ray force. Hitler therefore found associates and cooperators who added their receptivity to his so that an entire group became the responsive agents of the destructive energy, expressing itself in its lowest aspect. This is what has enabled them to work ruthlessly, powerfully, selfishly, cruelly, and successfully, at the destruction of all that attempted to impede their projects and desires.

There is only one way in which this focussed evil will which is responsive to the Shamballa force can be overcome, and that is by the opposition of an equally focussed spiritual Will, displayed by responsive men and women of goodwill who can train themselves to be sensitive to this type of new incoming energy and can learn how to invoke and evoke it.

You can consequently see why there was more than the casual use of a current word in my mind when I talked to all of you in terms of goodwill and of the will-to-good. All the time I had in my thoughts not just kindness and good intention, but the focussed will-to-good which can and must evoke the Shamballa energy, and use it for the arresting of the forces of evil.

THE SIGNIFICANCE OF THE WESAK FESTIVAL

May 1942

We have now reached the most important moment of the year. This year two such moments are brought together, reinforcing each other, the Full Moon of May and the Full Moon of June. I would have you bear in mind that time and energy are interchangeable terms upon the inner planes. Time is an event, and an event is a focussed expression of force of some type or kind. Two great streams of energy—one focussed through the Buddha and the other focussed through the Christ—are to be fused and blended and it is the task of the world disciples, the initiates and the accepted disciples to precipitate this combined energy on to the waiting world where its effective use will be largely dependent upon the sensitive response of the world aspirants. These are to be found in every country and their task is to react to the stream of directed energy. These are the points I would have you bear in mind as you endeavour to work through and in the ashram; in that ashram are to be found all types of disciples with all types and degrees of responsiveness.

There is an increasing emphasis being given in the West by esotericists to the Full Moon of May, which is the Festival of the Buddha and is held at the time when He makes His annual contact with humanity. This emphasis, which will continue to increase for years to come, has not been brought about in order to impose recognition of the Buddha upon the Occident. There have been two main reasons why, since 1900, this effort has been made. One was the desire on the part of the Hierarchy to bring to the attention of the public the fact of the *two* Avatars, the Buddha and the Christ, both upon the second Ray of Love-Wisdom, Who were the first of our humanity to come forth as human-divine Avatars and to embody in Themselves certain cosmic Principles and give them form. The Buddha embodied the Principle of Light, and because of this illumination, humanity was enabled to recognise Christ, Who embodied the still greater Principle

of Love. The point to be borne in mind is that light is substance, and the Buddha demonstrated the consummation of
substance-matter as the medium of Light, hence His title of
the "Illumined One." Christ embodied the underlying
energy of Consciousness. The one demonstrated the height
of the attainment of the third divine aspect; the other that of
the second aspect, and these two together present one perfect
Whole. The second reason was to initiate, as I have earlier
said, the theme of the new world religion. This theme will
eventually underlie all religious observances, colour all approaches to the divine centre of spiritual life, give the clue to
all healing processes, and—using light scientifically—govern
all techniques for bringing about conscious unity and relationship between a man and his soul, and between humanity
and the Hierarchy.

The first objective has been definitely reached. Today,
at the Full Moon of May, many millions everywhere will be
turning their thoughts towards the Buddha, seeking to come
under His influence and blessing and that of the Hierarchy
at His annual, though brief, return to bless humanity. This
recognition will grow until the time in the not too distant
future when His term of service will be over and He will
return no more, because the coming Avatar will take His
place in the minds and thoughts of the peoples of the world.
His task of reminding aspirants continuously of the possibility of illumination, and His work of keeping a channel
open for the light to irradiate men's minds by piercing annually through light substance to the Earth is nearly completed; the time has nearly come when "in that light we shall
see Light."

I would ask you to ponder on these two functions which
the Buddha has performed. There is a third which, in collaboration with the Christ, He has made possible; this is the
establishment of a more easily achieved relation between the
Hierarchy and Shamballa, thus facilitating the impress of the
Will of God upon the minds of men, through the medium of
the Hierarchy. This impress we interpret as yet in terms of
the divine Plan. This is expressing itself at present in the

keen recognition by men everywhere of the need to establish right human relations, culminating in the objectives for which the United Nations are fighting. These have been voiced for humanity by two great world disciples in terms of *The Four Freedoms* and *The Atlantic Pact*. These Four Freedoms relate basically to the four aspects of the lower self, the quaternary. Enough light has been permitted to penetrate by the efforts of the Buddha, to lead to a world-wide recognition of the desirability of these formulas; and there is enough love already in the world, released by the Christ, to make possible the working out of the formulas. Rest back on that assurance and—in full practice upon the physical plane—demonstrate its truth. I said "to make possible," for the working out lies in the hands of the new group of world servers and the men and women of goodwill. Will they prove adequate for the task? Will they brace themselves for the needed strenuous effort?

What now is the task which the Buddha has set Himself this coming Full Moon? As far as your comprehension is concerned, it is to evoke in humanity *the spirit of demand,* whilst holding open for them the channel whereby that demand can reach straight through to Shamballa. This is the point to have in mind as you prepare for the Wesak Festival and attempt to participate in the Full Moon blessing— blessing for the world and not for yourself. The Buddha comes this year, embodying the force which can stimulate men everywhere to focus their "massed intent" and thus reach symbolically "the ear and the heart" of the Avatar, wresting thus from the secret place of the Most High the aid, help, and directed recognition which will bring about a phenomenal event in due and proper time. Whilst He is attempting to do this, the Christ will join in the effort by focussing in Himself *the spirit of appeal* as it is evoked by the stimulation being applied by the Buddha. He will embody that appeal in a great Invocation, one which cannot be given to you, but which He is prepared to use *if* the appeal comes forth in sufficient strength from the people of the world. Will humanity respond to the evocation of the

Buddha? Will their massed intent be vital enough to enable
the Christ to become Himself, in a mysterious way, the very
Spirit of Invocation on their behalf? These are the possibilities with which we are confronted this Full Moon of May.

It is these which I would ask you to have in mind from
now until the Wesak Moon and on until after the June Full
Moon. It is at that Full Moon that the Christ can and will
use this Invocation, provided the will of the people permits.
At that time He will attempt to reach the Lords of Liberation and evoke Their response to the focussed will of the
spiritually minded people of the world, the aspirants, disciples and initiates; They, if evoked, can give the impetus
which will enable the Christ (as the Rider from the Secret
Place) to come forth in response to the "massed intent" of
the general public.

Do you see, therefore, the imminent and vital possibilities? Do you recognise the urgency of the opportunity?
The two Full Moons form one complete cycle of work and
should be prepared for in line with these statements of mine,
both now and in the years which will follow. As you prepare your own hearts, remember that the Full Moon of May
is the time in which the new group of world servers and all
the esotericists and spiritually oriented people of the world
must work in full cooperation with the Buddha, and that the
Full Moon of June is the opportunity for the men and
women of goodwill—aided by the new group of world servers
—to arouse people everywhere to make a great appeal, and
by this appeal enable the Christ to invoke for them the
needed aid.

One thing I would request. Set no dates for the appearing of the Coming One, the Avatar, or for any spectacular
aid. If the work is rightly done, He will come at the set and
appointed time and the needed aid will be forthcoming.
Modes and methods are none of your concern. Regard the
ancient prophecies as intrinsically right, true and correct, but
recognise that their phraseology is symbolic and not to be
taken literally. How the Lords of Liberation will work can
only be known to the Hierarchy. Their aid will be focussed

upon evoking in the Hierarchy those attitudes and capacities which will make possible the inflow of energy from Shamballa. Their work is with the Hierarchy, and the reaction of humanity to Their activity will come only from the new group of world servers, and may even then only be registered consciously by the senior disciples and initiates.

The work of the Avatar, the Rider from the Secret Place, will be primarily with humanity and will be for their relief and salvation.

The first half of this work, focussed through the Buddha, will begin in May 1942. The second half will be started by the Christ in June 1942, but only *if* the invocation of the new group of world servers and the massed intent of the men and women of goodwill is adequately strong and adequately focussed. It will consequently be a reciprocal process of invocation and evocation, facilitated by the extreme readiness to act and to respond on the part of Those invoked by humanity, but handicapped by the lack of sensitivity and the weakness of the will of those seeking aid. It is this inadequacy which the Buddha hopes to remove when He comes to His people in May. It is the strengthening and focussing of the will which the Christ is endeavouring to foster with a special effort in June.

These two Full Moons are therefore of paramount importance and should have a definite effect subconsciously upon *the minds* of the new group of world servers and upon *the hearts* of the men and women of goodwill in every land, nation and group. Let your meetings, your meditation and your individual thinking be steadily focussed upon these points, and endeavour to enter into the Full Moon exercises —both of May and June—with as clear an understanding of what is taking place as you can and a clear picture of the possibilities which can come as the result of right action. Both the Full Moons should be times of effective service. The Buddha does not require invoking. He will come. But the spirit of invocation needs evoking from the masses and it is this work that aspirants everywhere can aid the Buddha in bringing out, standing thus with Him and with the

Hierarchy. At the time of the Full Moon of June, and in preparation for the opportunity during the entire month of May, the point of focus for all servers must be the Christ and every effort must be directed to aiding His work as Representative for the people. He will endeavour to gather into Himself all that they have of appeal, prayer and demand —voiced or unvoiced—transmitting it in an act of spiritual intent to Shamballa.

A mobilising of the Forces of Light is going on upon the inner side of life. These Forces stand ready, but the word for action must come from the Christ, and He will give that word when the people give it to Him. We are the conditioners of our own destiny. Neither the Christ nor the Hierarchy may, at this stage in human evolution, take any step vitally affecting humanity unless released into this activity by humanity itself.

From April 15th till June 15th are critical weeks, spiritually and materially, and this is one of the important facts I want at this time to bring to your attention. I cannot detail to you what you should do or what should be your line of endeavour. I can give you a general idea of the hierarchical Approach and the nature of the human problem. The rest lies in your hands.

Even if the work done is entirely successful, the time of the Appearing and of divine intervention by the Forces of Light, through the medium of Their Agents, the Lords of Liberation and the Christ is dependent upon many factors beside that of right invocation. Of these you can know little, if anything. The question of right timing is one of deep esoteric significance and is basically involved here. The next three years are years of fulfillment and for that period the aspirants of the world are asked to stand steady in patient, yet convinced, expectancy. The task to be done by the Hierarchy involves not only the physical plane but also the inner planes of causes and impulses, of thought and desire. This all disciples know but are apt to forget. The critical situation upon the outer plane is only a reflection of still more critical inner conditions, and you can give acceptable help if you evoke your own will and control your emotions, disciplining your personality. Thus you will be able to present a tiny focal point through which the spiritual Forces can work. Through the agency of the many tiny points of light and will, much potency can be transmitted.

It is the will-to-victory that is demanded at this time; it is the will-to-invoke that which is needed; it is the will-to-focus and through this focussing to aid in the great act of invocation for which the Christ is at this time preparing Himself; it is the will-to-goodness, to self-control and to the evocation of right action for which the Hierarchy asks today. If humanity does its part, it will find that Hierarchy more than ready to respond and do its share in bringing about world release from the Forces of Evil.

Will you ponder on this and will you cooperate in every possible way? The plans may be laid, the vision may be seen but unless everyone recognises his essential contribution and his real usefulness, nothing can be done. There are no limitations when true esoteric work is undertaken. To this end, I seek to emphasise renewed application to meditation and a constant steady use of the Invocation, particularly the one which begins by invoking the Lords of Liberation.

"This work," Christ said, "goeth not forth save by prayer and fasting." I call you to prayer and to meditation for both are needed today, fusing as they do the emotional and mental bodies into one aspiring whole. I call you to discipline, for that is the meaning of fasting and to the constant effort to live at the highest possible point all the time; this is so often a dream but not often a fact. Today, in the hour of the world's need, aspirants and disciples who are willing to make at least consistent, persistent effort are needed by humanity and the Hierarchy.

My brothers, I have presented the picture; I have held before you for years the vision of opportunity, service and discipleship. I have outlined to you the mechanism of service which already is in existence and which can be galvanised into activity and world usefulness. I leave the matter in your hands, asking you to remember that the united interest, love, service and money of the many is far more potent than even the consecrated effort of the two or three. No one is futile or useless, unless he chooses so to be.

And in the meantime, paralleling your subjective work and externalising your inner endeavour must be your work for your country and for your fellowmen in humanity's hour of need. There must be steadiness, selflessness and silence, plus courage and confidence—confidence in the strength of your own souls, confidence in the watching Hierarchy and confidence in the Plan. The end of tribulation is not yet, but it is in sight. With this thought I leave you. May the blessing of the Masters rest upon you as a group and as individuals, and may the Holy Ones Whose pupils you seek to become show you the light you seek, give you the strong aid of Their compassion and Their wisdom until you stand where the One Initiator is invoked, until you see His star shine forth.

The Cause of the World Catastrophe

June 1942

We come now to the consideration of the present acute situation and world catastrophe which is rooted in world glamour, and will study the possibility of relief and cure. This possibility exists and is centred in the two great Avatars, the Buddha and the Christ.

It is difficult to write clearly about this matter of world glamour * because we are in the midst of its most concentrated expression—the worst the world has ever seen because glamour, incident to centuries of greed and selfishness, of aggression and materialism, has been focussed in a triplicity of nations. It is, therefore, easily to be seen and most effective in manifestation. Three nations express the three aspects of world glamour (illusion, glamour and maya) in an amazing manner, and their powerful assault upon the con-

---

* This message appears in the book *Glamour: A World Problem*. It is included here to preserve the historical sequence of the teaching in relation to world events.

sciousness of humanity is dependent not only upon the response of Germany, Japan and Italy to this ancient miasma but also upon the fact that every nation—the United Nations as well as the Totalitarian Nations—are tainted with this universal condition. The freedom of the world is consequently largely dependent upon those people in every nation who (within themselves) have moved forward out of one or other of these "glamourous illusions of mayavic impressions" of the human soul into a state of awareness wherein they can see the conflict in its wider terms, i.e., as that existing for them between the Dweller on the Threshold and the Angel of the Presence.

These people are the aspirants, the disciples and the initiates of the world.   They are aware of the dualism, the essential dualism, of the conflict and are not so pre-eminently conscious of the threefold nature and the differentiated condition of the situation which underlies the realised dualism. Their approach to the problem is therefore simpler and, because of this, world direction lies largely in their hands at this time.

It is right here that religion has, as a whole, gone astray. I refer to orthodox religion. It has been preoccupied with the Dweller on the Threshold and the eyes of the theologian have been held upon the material, phenomenal aspect of life through fear and its immediacy, and the fact of the Angel has been a theory and a point of wishful thinking. The balance is being adjusted by the humanitarian attitudes which are so largely coming into control, irrespective of any theological trend. These attitudes take their stand upon belief in the innate rightness of the human spirit, in the divinity of man and upon the indestructible nature of the soul of mankind. This inevitably brings in the concept of the PRESENCE, or of God Immanent and is the result of the needed revolt against the one-sidedness of the belief in God Transcendent. This spiritual revolution was entirely a balancing process and need cause no basic concern, for God Transcendent eternally exists, but can only be seen and known and correctly approached by God Immanent—immanent in individual man, in groups and nations, in organised forms and in religion, in humanity as a whole and in the planetary Life Itself. Humanity is today (and has been for ages) battling illusion, glamour and maya. Advanced thinkers, those upon the Probationary Path, upon the Path of Discipleship, and the Path of Initiation have reached the point where materialism and spirituality, the Dweller on the Threshold and the Angel of the Presence, and the basic dualism of manifestation can be seen clearly defined. Because of this clarity of demarcation, the issues underlying present world events, the objectives of the present world-wide struggle, the modes and methods of re-establishing the spiritual contact so prevalent in Atlantean days and so long lost, and the recognition of the techniques which can bring in the new world era and its cultural order can be clearly noted and appraised.

All generalisations admit of error. It might, however, be said that Germany has focussed in herself world glamour —the most potent and expressive of the three aspects of glamour. Japan is manifesting the force of maya—the crudest form of material force. Italy, individualistic and mentally polarised, is the expression of world illusion. The United Nations, with all their faults, limitations, weaknesses and nationalisms, are focussing the conflict between the Dweller and the Angel, and thus the three forms of glamour and the final form of the conflict between the spiritual ideal and its material opponent are appearing simultaneously. The United Nations are, however, gradually and most decisively throwing the weight of their effort and aspiration on to the side of the Angel, thus restoring the lost balance and slowly producing on a planetary scale those attitudes and conditions which will eventually dispel illusion, dissipate glamour and devitalise the prevalent maya. This they are doing by the increased clear thinking of the general public of all the nations, bound together to conquer the three Axis Powers, by their growing ability to conceive ideas in terms of the whole, in terms of a desirable world order or federation, and their capacity to discriminate between the Forces of Light and the potency of evil or materialism.

The work being done by those who see the world stage as the arena for the conflict between the Dweller on the Threshold and the Angel of the PRESENCE might be itemised as follows:

1. The producing of those world conditions in which the Forces of Light can overcome the Forces of Evil. This they do by the weight of their armed forces, plus their clear insight.

2. The educating of humanity in the distinction between

   a. Spirituality and materialism, pointing to the differing goals of the combatant forces.
   b. Sharing and greed, outlining a future world wherein *The Four Freedoms* will be dominant and all will have that which is needed for right living-processes.
   c. Light and dark, demonstrating the difference between an illumined future of liberty and opportunity and the dark future of slavery.
   d. Fellowship and separation, indicating a world order where racial hatreds, caste distinctions and religious differences will form no barrier to international understanding, and the Axis order of master races, determined religious attitudes, and enslaved peoples.
   e. The whole and the part, pointing to the time which is approaching (under the evolutionary urge of spirit) wherein the part or the point of life assumes its responsibility for the whole, and the whole exists for the good of the part. The dark aspect has been brought about by ages of glamour. The light is being emphasised and made clear by the world aspirants and disciples who by their attitudes, their actions, their writings and their utterances are bringing the light into dark places.

3. Preparing the way for the three spiritual energies which will sweep humanity into an era of comprehension, leading

to a focussed mental clarification of men's minds through-out the world. These three imminent energies are

a. *The energy of the intuition* which will gradually dispel world illusion, and produce automatically a great augmentation of the ranks of initiates.
b. The activity of light which will dissipate, by *the energy of illumination,* the world of glamour and bring many thousands on to the Path of Discipleship.
c. *The energy of inspiration* which will bring about, through the medium of its sweeping potency, the devitalisation or the removal, as by a wind, of the attractive power of maya or substance. This will release untold thousands on to the Path of Probation.

4.   Releasing new life into the planet through the medium of every possible agency. The first step towards this release is the proving that the power of materialism is broken by the complete defeat of the Axis powers and, secondly, by the ability of the United Nations to demonstrate (when this has been done) the potency of the spiritual values by their constructive undertakings to restore world order and to lay those foundations which will guarantee a better and more spiritual way of life. These constructive attitudes and undertakings must be assumed individually by every person, and by nations as collective wholes. The first is being undertaken at this time. The second remains as yet to be done.

5.   Bringing home to the nations of the world the truths taught by the Buddha, the Lord of Light, and the Christ, the Lord of Love. In this connection it might be pointed out that basically:

a. The Axis nations need to grasp the teaching of the Buddha as He enunciated it in the Four Noble Truths; they need to realise that the cause of all sorrow and woe is desire—desire for that which is material.
b. The United Nations need to learn to apply the Law of Love as enunciated in the life of Christ and to express the truth that "no man liveth unto himself" and no

nation either, and that the goal of all human effort is *loving understanding,* prompted by a programme of love for the whole.

If the lives and teachings of these two great Avatars can be comprehended and wrought out anew in the lives of men today, in the world of human affairs, in the realm of human thinking and in the arena of daily living, the present world order (which is today largely disorder) can be so modified and changed that a new world and a new race of men can gradually come into being. Renunciation and the use of the sacrificial will should be the keynote for the interim period after the war, prior to the inauguration of the New Age.

Students need to remember that all manifestations and every point of crisis are symbolised by the ancient symbol of the point within the circle, the focus of power within a sphere of influence or aura. So it is today with the entire problem of ending the world glamour and illusion which fundamentally lie behind the present acute situation and world catastrophe. The possibility of such a dispelling and dissipation is definitely centred in the two Avatars, the Buddha and the Christ.

Within the world of glamour—the world of the astral plane and of emotions—appeared a point of light. The Lord of Light, the Buddha, undertook to focus in Himself the illumination which would eventually make possible the dissipation of glamour. Within the world of illusion—the world of the mental plane—appeared the Christ, the Lord of Love Himself, Who embodied in Himself the power of the *attractive* will of God. He undertook to dispel illusion by drawing to Himself (by the potency of love) the hearts of all men, and stated this determination in the words, "And I, if I be lifted from the earth, will draw all men unto me." (John 12:32). From the point they then will have reached, the world of spiritual perception, of truth and of divine ideas will stand revealed. The result will be the disappearing of illusion.

The combined work of these two great Sons of God, concentrated through the world disciples and through Their initiates must and will inevitably shatter illusion and dispel glamour—the one by the intuitive recognition of reality by minds attuned to it, and the other by the pouring in of the light of reason. The Buddha made the first planetary effort to dissipate world glamour; the Christ made the first planetary effort towards the dispelling of illusion. Their work must now be intelligently carried forward by a humanity wise enough to recognise its dharma. Men are being rapidly disillusioned and will consequently see more clearly. The world glamour is being steadily removed from the ways of men. These two developments have been brought about by the incoming new ideas, focussed through the world intuitives and released to the general public by the world thinkers. It has been also largely aided by the well-nigh unconscious, but none the less real, recognition of the true meaning of these Four Noble Truths by the masses. Disillusioned and de-glamoured (if I may use such a term), humanity awaits the coming revelation. This revelation will be brought about by the combined efforts of the Buddha and the Christ. All that we can foresee or foretell anent that revelation is that some potent and far-reaching results will be achieved by the merging of light and love, and by the reaction of "lighted substance to the attractive power of love." In this sentence I have given those who can understand a profound and useful hint as to the method and purpose of the undertaking staged for the June Full Moon, 1942. I have also given a clue to the true understanding of the work of these Avatars—a thing hitherto quite unrealised. It might be added that when an appreciation of the meaning of the words "transfiguration of a human being" is gained, the realisation will come that when "the body is full of light" then "in that light shall we see Light." This means that when the personality has reached a point of purification, of dedication and of illumination, then the attractive power of the soul (whose nature is love and understanding) can function, and fusion of these two will take place. This is what the Christ proved and demonstrated.

When the work of the Buddha (or of the embodied buddhic principle) is consummated in the aspiring disciple and in his integrated personality, then the full expression of the work of the Christ (the embodied principle of love) can also be consummated and both these potencies—light and love—will find radiant expression in the transfigured disciple. What is true, therefore, of the individual is true also of humanity as a whole, and today humanity (having reached maturity) can "enter into realisation" and consciously take part in the work of enlightenment and of spiritual, loving activity. The practical effects of this process will be the dissipation of glamour and the release of the human spirit from the thralldom of matter; it will produce, also, the dispelling of illusion and the recognition of truth as it exists in the consciousness of those who are polarised in the "awareness of the Christ."

This is necessarily no rapid process but is an ordered and regulated procedure, sure in its eventual success but relatively slow also in its establishment and sequential process. This process was initiated upon the astral plane by the Buddha, and on the mental plane when Christ manifested on Earth. It indicated the approaching maturity of humanity. The process has been slowly gathering momentum as these two great Beings have gathered around Them Their disciples and initiates during the past two thousand years. It has reached a point of intensive usefulness as the channel of communication between Shamballa and the Hierarchy has been opened and enlarged, and as the contact between these two great Centres and Humanity has been more firmly established.

At the June Full Moon, 1942, will come the first test as to the *directness* of the communication between the Centre where the Will of God holds sway, the Centre where the Love of God rules and the Centre where there is intelligent expectancy. The medium of the test will be the united effort of the Christ, of the Buddha and of those who respond to

Their blended influence. This test has to be carried out in the midst of the terrific onslaught of the powers of evil and will be extended over the two weeks beginning on the day of the Full Moon (May 30th, 1942) and ending on June 15th, 1942. There is a great concentration of the Spiritual Forces at this time and the use of a special Invocation (one which humanity itself may not use), but the success or failure of the test, in the last analysis, will be determined by mankind itself.

You may feel, though wrongly, that not enough people know about or understand the nature of the opportunity or what is transpiring. But the success of such a test is not dependent upon the esoteric knowledge of the few, the relatively very few, to whom the facts and the information have been partially imparted. It is dependent also upon the tendency of the many who unconsciously aspire towards the spiritual realities, who seek for a new and better way of life for all, who desire the good of the whole and whose longing and desire is for a true experience of goodness, of right human relations and of spiritual enterprise among men. Their name is legion and they are to be found in every nation.

When the Will of God, expressed in Shamballa and focussed in the Buddha, the Love of God, expressed in the Hierarchy and focussed through the Christ, and the intelligent desire of humanity, focussed through the world disciples, the world aspirants and the men of goodwill are all brought into line—either consciously or unconsciously—then a great reorientation can and will take place. This event is something that *can* happen.

The first result will be the illumination of the astral plane and the beginning of the process which will dissipate glamour; the second result will be the irradiation of the mental plane and the dispelling of all past illusions and the gradual revelation of the new truths of which all past ideals and so-called formulations of truth have only been the signposts. Ponder on that statement. The sign-post indicates the way to go; it does not reveal the goal. It is indicative but not conclusive. So with all truth up to the present time.

The demand is, therefore, for knowers and for those whose minds and hearts are open; who are free from preconceived ideas fanatically held, and from ancient idealisms which must be recognised as only partial indications of great unrealised truths—truths which can be realised in great measure and for the first time *if* the lessons of the present world situation and the catastrophe of the war are duly learned and the sacrificial will is called into play.

I have made this practical application and this immediate illustration of teaching anent glamour, illusion and maya because the whole world problem has reached a crisis today and because its clarification will be the outstanding theme of all progress—educational, religious and economic—until 2025 A.D.

Today, as humanity awaits the revelation which will embody the thoughts and dreams and constructive goal of the New Age, the demand comes for the first time from a large group of intuitively inclined people. I said not intuitives, my brothers. This group is now so large and its focus is now so real and its demand so loud that it is succeeding in focussing the massed intent of the people. Therefore, whatever revelation may emerge in the immediate future will be better "protected by the spirit of understanding" than any previous one. This is the significance of the words in the *New Testament,* "Every eye shall see him"; humanity as a whole will recognise the *Revealing One.* In past ages the Messenger from on High was only recognised by and known to a mere handful of men, and it took decades and sometimes centuries for His message to penetrate into the hearts of humanity.

The stress of the times also and the development of the sense of proportion, plus an enforced return to simplicity of living and requirements may save the coming revelation from too swift and quick a submergence in the fire of the Great Illusion.

THE INTERLUDE BETWEEN WAR AND PEACE

August 1942

There is an insistent demand from the many thousands who in the past have read the pamphlets and articles which I have written, that I say something about the coming period of rehabilitation, and of what can be done (whilst the war is still in progress) to prepare for usefulness at that time. When the war broke out, I published an article entitled *The Present World Crisis*, and in it tried to trace the origins of the conflict and the factors which made this catastrophe possible. Later, another article appeared, called *The Coming World Order*, which sought to hold out to a suffering world a vision of a material and spiritual future which the hearts of men have long demanded. Thus an attempt was made to deal with both the past and the future.

More at that time was not possible, owing to the disunity existing among those nations which today form the United Nations. There was also a lack of understanding and a selfish perspective among those nations at that time neutral. Above everything else was the fact that the issues involved had to be settled by humanity itself and it was not then possible to foretell with any accuracy what humanity would do. Even the most enlightened of men and the spiritual leaders of the race could not judge what line mankind would take or whether there were enough clear-sighted people in the world who could and would sweep the mass of men into effective opposition to the Axis Powers. The question was: Would world fear and universal selfishness dominate, or would the spirit of freedom and the love of liberty be strong enough to weld the free nations into one united and steadfast whole?

Today the issue is clear and the end inevitable. The free nations and the defeated and enslaved little nations are subjectively and practically unified into one intense spiritual determination to win the war; the fate of the Axis Nations is therefore unalterably settled, even though, at this time of writing, they seem to be victorious all along the line. It is only the time of the final victory of right against might which remains as yet the factor of uncertainty, and this is owing to the enormous prepared strength of the aggressor nations and the unpreparedness of the democracies. This unpreparedness is being rapidly remedied.

This article is an attempt to indicate the problems, and perhaps some of the solutions, which must inevitably fill the interlude between the ending of the war and the coming world order. It will be necessary to deal with this subject in a broad and general way, for the subject is too vast for us to be intelligently specific. We can, however, consider the immediate work to be done in preparation for the cessation of war and indicate the first steps which can and should be taken to initiate sound reconstruction processes. The period of rehabilitation and of reconstruction should be the deep concern today of all who love their fellowmen.

There are those who will consider the study of the coming reconstruction period as premature. They believe (and rightly) that our first immediate concern is to win the war, and with this I am fully in agreement. The will-to-victory is the first and basic essential, for there will be no true reconstruction activity if the Axis nations triumph. But there are many today whose task is not that of fighting and whose place and function is perforce in the civilian aspects of the life of the nations. These can think, and talk, and work in preparation for the future. There are others who feel that only the trained expert in the fields of economic and political readjustment can approach this difficult problem with any hope of making a useful contribution. Still others feel that peace is the only thing that matters and that it should be followed by a long period of mental quiet in every country; they believe that people everywhere are too exhausted and unhappy to be ready as yet to undertake any work of rebuilding. Others again are so completely pessimistic that they despair of ever reclaiming the world, and they look sadly for a breakdown of all the civilised processes of living. There is some truth in all these points of view. The work of the experts will be sorely needed, but the understanding interest and the sustaining power of those whose hearts are aflame with love can alone make their work possible. It will not be the institutionalised activities and the financial enterprise of economic and social workers and government agents which will alone be needed, but above all else, the solution must be found in the uprising of goodwill in the hearts of men. This will provide the right compassionate incentive. Most certainly the world could be rehabilitated for purely commercial and selfish reasons, and because trade interchange, buying and selling capacity and the restoration of financial stability are important factors in world restoration. But these are not the basic motives which would restore humanity to self-respecting and secure living. They will provide the motive power for many men and groups, but not *the* motive which can produce true constructive rebuilding of the fabric of human life.

The work of reconstruction will be the work of the intelligent men and women of goodwill, and theirs will be the task to restore new life and happiness to humanity, and it is for them I write. Please bear this in mind. I am not writing for technical experts and trained advisors to the government, but to those who have goodwill in their hearts to all men, and who, because of it, want to do their share in bringing tranquility and peace to the world—a peace based on surer values than in the past and upon sounder planning. In the last analysis, it is not peace for which the men of goodwill are working, but for the growth of the spirit of understanding and cooperation; this alone will be strong enough to break down racial barriers, heal the wounds of war, and build a new world structure adequate to the intelligent demands of the masses.

In the earlier pamphlets, I sought (along with many other thinking people) to indicate the steps which might be taken to avert the impending cataclysm. Among the most important upon which emphasis was laid was the growth of world goodwill, for *goodwill is the active principle of peace*. I sought also to stress international understanding, a future of shared planetary resources, and a recognition of a general historically-proved guilt in relation to the war, plus those ideas which could—if developed—end the era of separativeness.

In spite of all the efforts of the men of goodwill, of all the peace organisations, and the enlightened work of the world thinkers, educators and leaders, two things happened which it had been hoped might be averted. The first was a definite and focussed precipitation of the spirit of evil and of materialism through the medium of the Axis nations, using the aggression of Japan as the initial focal point and expressing itself later in full force through Germany. The second was the failure of the neutral nations, in the early stages of the war, to take the needed steps to ally themselves actively with the nations fighting totalitarianism, and their inability to realise the full horror of what lay ahead for mankind. The selfishness of humanity was even more deep-seated than was grasped, and the United Nations came into cooperative activity only after two years of war and the planned rape of many of the neutral nations. The blindness of the neutral nations definitely upset the calculations of far-sighted workers for world good and seriously delayed the ending of the war.

The critical point is now passed, and the humanitarian grasp of the issues involved, and the unity existing among the Allied Nations, guarantee the inevitable defeat of the Axis Powers. Other factors also ensure the ultimate victory of the forces of right and the freedom of the world. There is not time to enlarge upon them, but they can be listed and people can then see how assuredly they guarantee the triumph of the free peoples of the world. These factors are:

1.   The will-to-victory is steadily growing. Appeasement, pacifism and uncertainty are as steadily dying out.

2.   The plight of humanity everywhere, as the result of Axis aggression, is definitely steadying public opinion and evoking an unalterable determination to end the evil initiated and carried forward by Germany and Japan, aided somewhat unwillingly by Italy.

3. The resources of the United Nations are vast and are now in process of mobilisation. Their massed use and their manufacturing potential are practically inexhaustible and are rapidly being organised. The man power and the resources of Germany and of her allies have reached their peak, bringing enormous present potency, but a steady decline is indicated for the future.

4. The issues in this war are being increasingly clearly realised; even the ignorant and the prejudiced recognise today that these issues can be grouped under three major positions, and this enables them to make a personal choice as to loyalties.

   a. The democratic position, with its emphasis upon the Four Freedoms and the Atlantic Charter, ensuring right human relations and the ending of aggression.
   b. The totalitarian position, with its emphasis upon world dictatorship, the slavery of the many conquered nations, its anti-racial bias and its blatant cruelty and terrorism.
   c. The appeasement and the pacifist attitudes—idealistic and impractical and finding their focus today in the attitude of Gandhi. He brings into clear perspective the uncompromising, fanatical attitude which is non-realistic and which will willingly sacrifice lives, nations and the future of humanity in order to attain its object. If Gandhi were to succeed in his objective *now*, it would precipitate civil war in India, sacrifice all immediate hope of freedom for that country, permit the Japanese to realise an easy conquest of India, bring about a slaughtering of countless thousands, and permit Germany to join hands with Japan across Asia, with the appalling probability of a totalitarian victory.

These three points of view are today being clearly realised by men everywhere, and their decisions as to loyalties and adherences are clarified.

5. The spirit of freedom is triumphing in every land (even in the conquered countries, much to the bewilderment of

Germany), and the beauty of the human spirit is emerging everywhere, both in the conquered lands and in the nations fighting, with their backs to the wall, for human liberty.

6.   An intense interest in after-war conditions is evidenced by the utterances of leaders, politicians, lecturers and the spiritually minded men everywhere; this is testified to by the articles, pamphlets, books, speeches and plans dealing with the new world order. The forces of rehabilitation and of goodwill are rapidly mobilising; they constitute a great army within all nations, and they are an invisible army, but one which is as yet inchoate, uncertain as to method and process, though clear as to goals and principles.

The above six factors ensure the defeat of the Forces of Evil and the triumph of the Forces of Light, and with these as the basis of optimism we can look ahead with sure hope to the ending of the war, to the demobilisation of the armies, to the tranquil passage of the seven seas and to the time when fear begins to die out.

What then will be the dangers to be offset? For what must we be prepared when the task of reconstruction confronts us? It might be useful to enumerate some of the dangers for which we must be prepared. Let us consider them in the order of their importance:

1.   *The danger of too prompt a peace settlement.* Let us work hard for a prolonged armistice, during which the heat of battle and the fires of revenge can have time to die down, the agony of mankind can be assuaged, and time be gained for calm, unhurried planning.

2.   *The danger of a return to so-called normality.* The outstanding disaster which faces humanity at this time is a return to the state of affairs prior to the outbreak of war, and the rehabilitation of the old familiar world, with its imperialism (whether of empire or finance) , its nationalisms and its distressed, exploited minorities, its vile distinctions and separative barriers between rich and poor, between

the oriental and the occidental, and between the castes and classes which are found in every land—without any exception.

3. *The dangers incident to the necessary adjustments between the nations.* Any adjustment made upon the basis of historical tradition or ancient boundaries will only serve to plunge the world again into war. These adjustments must be carried out on the basis of humanity itself; the will of free peoples must be the determining factor and not the will of technical, political experts, or of some ruling class or group. In the world which is coming, the human equation will take a predominant position; human beings will determine, as far as in them lies, their own destiny and men will exercise their free will in establishing the kind of world in which they choose to live. They will decide in which country they prefer to claim citizenship and the type of government to which they choose to give allegiance. This will necessarily all take time and must be an unhurried process. It will call for a planned education of the masses in every country; and the principles of freedom, and the distinction between freedom and license, will have to be carefully taught. A new world based upon the restoration of territorial limits, historically determined, will fail to end strife, aggression and fear. A new world based on human values and right human relations can institute (slowly to be sure, but inevitably) that new civilisation which men of goodwill demand for humanity as a whole.

4. *The dangers growing out of hate, revenge and pain.* These dangers will be the most difficult to avoid. A deep-seated hatred of the Nazi regime (and of the German nation as endorsing that regime) is steadily rising. This is almost inevitable, being based on the facts of Nazi activity. The task of the United Nations after the war will of necessity be—among other things—to protect the German people from the hate of those whom they have so appallingly abused. This will be no easy thing to do. Retribution and revenge must not be permitted, and yet at the same time *a just payment for evil action cannot, and should not, be*

avoided. The law ever works, and that law states that what-soever a man or nation sows, that shall it also reap. Germany has sown evil broadcast throughout the civilised world, and for some time to come her lot must be hard and she will have to pay in sweat and toil and tears for her evil deeds. But this payment should be part of the great work of rehabilitation and not a vengeful exaction, and if this is borne in mind, no serious mistakes will be made. The German people must work strenuously to put right the evil they have done, as far as in them lies, but the next generation—at present in the cradle or at school—must not be penalised. The little children and the babies of the German race—innocent of the wrong actions of their fathers and brothers—should not be implicated in the penalties exacted. The young men of today in Germany must, by the labour of their hands and the sweat of their brows, rebuild that which they have so ruthlessly destroyed, but the unoffending, though weak, elderly people, the little children and the adolescent boys and girls must be exempt and must be trained to be citizens of a better and a finer Germany than has ever yet existed—a Germany that is a constructive part of the whole and not a menace and a terror to all right-thinking men. *The arousing of the men of goodwill in every nation—men who see humanity as a whole and all men as brothers—is the only way in which this rising tide of hate can be stemmed.* It will not be stemmed by telling those who have suffered at the hands of the Axis nations that they must not hate, or by exhorting people who have been the victims of traitors that they must not bear ill-will to such men as Quisling and Laval. It will be offset by a great demonstration of practical love and understanding on the part of the United Nations—a love which will work out in the form of food for the hungry, nursing for the sick, the rebuilding of the ruined cities, and the restoration of the "scorched earth." The problems of hate and revenge will require the utmost skill in handling and will necessitate exceedingly wise action on the part of the free nations.

5. *The danger to humanity of the effects of war upon the children and the adolescents of the nations.* The children of today are the parents of the coming generations, and they have been through a shattering psychological experience. They can scarcely ever be truly normal again. They have seen the very depths of cruelty, wickedness, pain, horror, terror and uncertainty. They have been bombed, shell-shocked and machine-gunned. They have known no security and look forward today to no sure future. Millions have known no parental control; they have been separated by war from their families and frequently do not even know their own names. Even when the family unit has been preserved intact, their fathers are usually engaged in war work, either at home or abroad, and their mothers are working in factories or on the land; the children have therefore no home life or control. Malnutrition has weakened their stamina and rampant evil has undermined their morale and their standards of value. From the humanitarian and spiritual standpoint, the vital problem after the war will be the restoration of the children of the world to happiness, security, proper standards of life and conduct and some measure of understanding control. This is essentially a problem of education. Educators and psychologists of vision in every country must be mobilised and the "pattern of things to come" for the children must be intelligently determined. This will have to be done on an international scale and with the wisdom which comes from a grasp of immediate need and a far-sighted vision.

6. *The dangers of re-emergence of the nationalist spirit.* Intense nationalism was one of the prime movers in bringing about this war and no nation has been exempt from this spirit of national pride and from a nationalistic, separative outlook. Selfish interests have controlled the reasons for which every nation has entered this war; individual security has prompted the entry of even the most enlightened democratic nations. That to these selfish incentives they have added world need and the love of freedom is true and serves

to balance, though not offset, the selfish motives; that the instinct of self-preservation gave them no alternative is likewise true, but the fact remains that *there would have been no war if the democratic nations had been the determining factor.* That in itself gives rise to questions. Why did the powerful democracies, in the last analysis, permit this war when, united and banded together from the start, they might have arrested it in the initial stages? Also, given the existent aggressor nations, collective self-interest forced the democracies into combat, and yet this same self-interest should have made them take the steps which would have guaranteed the peace. National types, individual national interests, national cultures and national civilisations exist side by side, but instead of being regarded as contributory to one integrated whole, they have been zealously competitive and have been regarded as the peculiar and distinctive prerogatives of some one nation and as existing for the sole good of that nation. In the future, the contributory factor in life must be emphasised and developed, and the good of the entire family of nations must be substituted for the good of one nation or a group of nations. The education of the public in this ideal necessitates no loss of national identity or individual culture. That *must* remain and be developed to its highest spiritual goal for the enriching and the collective good of all. It is only the motive for the emphasis of any specific racial and national culture which must be changed.

The family of nations, viewed as a unit, its correct and proper interrelation, and the shouldering of responsibility for the *one,* or for the weak, must be the realised goal of *all* national enterprise; the resources of the entire planet must be shared collectively and it must be increasingly realised that the products of the earth, the gifts of the soil, the intellectual heritage of the nations, belong to the whole of mankind and to no one nation exclusively. No nation liveth unto itself, any more than any individual can happily so live; the nation or individual who attempts so to do must inevitably perish off the face of the earth. All nations have made this selfish attempt, as history, ancient and modern, goes to prove. Their tradition, their resources, their national genius, their past history, their mineral and agricultural products, their strategic position on the planet, have been used in past centuries for the benefit of the nation claiming them; they have been exploited for the increase of the power of that nation at the expense of the suffering of others. This is the sin which Germany is today committing, aided by Japan and feebly followed by Italy. Power politics, the exploitation of the weak, aggression, economic selfishness, ideals based on pure commercialism and materialistic and territorial goals colour all the past history of mankind in both hemispheres, and have laid the foundation for the present war.

Some nations, particularly the great democracies, like the British Commonwealth of Nations and the United States of America, now realise that these attitudes and activities must end and that the hope of the world lies in the spread of right human relations, in economic interchange, broad unselfish international politics and the growth of the spirit of cooperation. They believe unalterably, and as a basic national policy, in the rights of the individual and that the State exists for the benefit of that individual; to that they add the belief that the State also exists for the benefit of all other states and for humanity as a whole. Other nations, such as the Axis Powers, are violently crystallising the ancient viewpoints, emphasising the worst aspects of the old and evil order, and are aggressively grasping all that they can for themselves. They regard the individual as of no value and hold that he exists only for the benefit of the State; they believe that the State is the sole unit of importance, and that only their particular state counts. They divide the family of nations into a superstate for the control of Europe and another for Asia, and regard all other states as slave states; they would perpetuate the ancient evil of force and war and would and do resort to unheard-of cruelties in the effort to raise their state to supreme eminence.

This is the old order which must pass, but its dangers must be recognised. For its abolishing, the United Nations are fighting, but the difficulties are many, even though the spiritual strength of all good men is on their side and the Forces of Light are fighting to aid them. The nationalistic spirit is not dead as yet in any country. It must be helped to die. Minorities with historical backgrounds but no territorial rights are clamouring for a place to call their own and in which to build up a nation. The small nations are full of fear, wondering what place in the family of nations they will be permitted to hold, and whether the evil plans of the Germans will spare any of their citizens eventually to form a nation. The demand for national recognition is widespread; the emphasis upon *humanity* as the important unit is little heard.

Those nations impede the path of progress who live in the memory of their past history and boundaries and who look back upon what they call "a glorious past," resting upon the recollection of national or empire rule over the weak. This is a hard saying, but the nationalistic spirit constitutes a grave peril to the world; if perpetuated in any form, except as contributory to the good of humanity as a whole, it will throw the world (after the war) back into the dark ages and leave men no better off than they were, even though there have been twenty years of travail and agony.

We could take the nations, one by one, and observe how this nationalistic, separative or isolationist spirit, emerging out of an historical past, out of racial complexes, out of territorial position, out of revolt and out of possession of material resources, has brought about the present world crisis and cleavage and this global clash of interests and ideals. But it would profit not. The intelligent student of history (who has no nationalistic bias) knows well the facts and is deeply concerned today with the processes which must be brought to bear to end the world strife. He knows that the efforts to attain national aggrandisement, a place in the sun, *Lebensraum,* financial supremacy, economic control and power must end. At the same time he realises that if humanity is to get rid of these evil products of selfishness, certain basic values must be preserved. Past and present cultures and civilisations are of great value; the peculiar genius of each nation must be evoked for the enriching of the entire human family; the new civilisation must have its roots in and emerge out of the past; new ideals must come forth and be recognised, and for that the events and education of the past will have prepared the people. *Humanity itself must be the goal of interest and effort, and not any particular nation or empire.* All this has to be wrought out in a practical, realistic manner, divorced from visionary, mystical and impractical dreams, and all that is done must be founded on one basic recognition—human brotherhood, expressing itself in right human relations.

The revolt so widely prevalent against the "vague visionings" of humanitarian dreamers is based upon the fact that out of the welter of words and the plethora of plans, little of practical value has emerged and nothing sufficiently potent to end the old and horrid ways of life. Nothing really effective had been done, prior to the war, to offset the visible and shrieking evils. Palliative measures have been tried and compromises made for the sake of peace, but the basic evils of national ambition, economic disparity, and virulent class distinctions (hereditary or financial) still remained. Religious differences were rampant, racial hatreds widespread, and the economic and political orders remained corrupt, fostering party, social and national strife.

Today the war has cleared the air. The issues are clear and at least we know what has been wrong. In their demonstration of supreme selfishness, national ambition, racial hatred and utter barbarity and cruelty, plus their complete lack of all humanitarian feeling, the Axis Powers have served the race by showing us what must not, and shall not, be permitted. The democracies have awakened also to their weaknesses and to the realisation that true democracy does not as yet exist, owing to widespread political corruption, and to the ignorance and unpreparedness of the masses for rue self-government. Imperialistic powers, such as Great Britain, are publicly repudiating the old points of view and are forging ahead in the task of world reconstruction. The conservative reactionary is no longer popular. The small nations are realising their helplessness and their complete dependence upon their larger neighbours, and these in their turn, are recognising their responsibilities to the weak and small. People everywhere are waking up and beginning to think, and never again can they sink back into the negative condition of the past. There is faith on every hand that a new and better world order is possible and that it is even probable.

How can we simply and clearly express the goal of this hoped-for new world order and word briefly the objective which each person and nation should hold before itself when the war ends and opportunity faces each and all? It is surely that every nation, great and small (with the minorities given equal and proportionate rights) should pursue its own individual culture and work out its own salvation as seems best to it, but that each and all should develop the realisation that they are organic parts of one corporate whole and that they must contribute to that whole all they have and are. This concept is already present in the hearts of countless thousands and carries with it great responsibility. These realisations, when intelligently developed and wisely handled, will lead to right human relations, economic stability (based on the spirit of sharing) and to a fresh orientation of man to man, of nation to nation, and of all to that supreme power to which we give the name "God."

This is the vision and it is holding countless thousands steady in the path of duty, and for it many in every nation are prepared to work. In spite of the background of an evil past, in spite of the present world carnage, in spite of the almost overwhelming psychological problems confronting humanity, in spite of political machinations and old-time diplomacy, in spite of the improbability of any quick successes, there are thousands ready to start with the preparatory work. The number of men and women of vision and of goodwill is now so large (especially among the United Nations) that there *is* a chance of eventual success and it is possible today to make a start. The outline of the future world structure can already be dimly seen; the failure—complete, obvious and irremediable—of the old order and the old world is everywhere recognised. The will-to-good is growing. One of the interesting things which it is helpful to recognise is that this vision is more clearly seen by the man in the street and by the intelligentsia than it is by the exclusive classes. Through the material difficulties of life, and by resultant processes of thought, men know changed conditions are necessary and that there is no alternative.

The task ahead falls into two categories: First, directing mass thought and energy into right lines so that good motive and wise action can bring in the desired era of right human relations and eventual peace; secondly, educating those whose apathy and lack of vision impede progress. This latter phase of the work is well under way and a powerful, though small, group among the world leaders is voicing certain general propositions which must be regarded as imperative when world readjustment starts. Their demand is for a new governing principle in politics and in education, founded on universally recognised human rights, on the need for spiritual unity and the need to throw overboard all separative theological attitudes and dogmas in every field of thought. There is a mounting appeal not only for international understanding and cooperation, but also for *class* understanding. These demands are being expressed from every platform and pulpit and through the pen in every land, except in those sad lands where freedom of speech is not permitted.

The average man looks on at all of this and is frequently overwhelmed by the magnitude of the unfolding task, by the diversity of opinions expressed, by the many suggestions, plans and schemes for world betterment, and by a sense of his own utter unimportance and futility in the face of this gigantic human undertaking. He asks himself many questions. Of what use am I? What can I do? How can my little voice be heard, and of what use is it when heard? What part can I play in the vast arena of world affairs? How can I prove myself useful and constructive? How can I offset my ignorance of history, of society, of political and economic conditions in my own country, not to speak of other lands? Humanity is so immense, its numbers so vast and its races so many that he feels himself a helpless, insignificant unit. He has no academic or general training which would enable him really to grasp the problems or contribute to their solution. What, therefore, can the man in the street, the business man in his office, the woman in her home, and the average citizen everywhere contribute at this time and in the future to the helping of the world? It is for this type of person I write.

I would start by reminding the general public of one important fact. This is that *focussed, determined, enlightened public opinion is the most potent force in the world.* It has no equal but has been little used. The gullibility of the average citizen, his willingness to accept what is told him if it is said loudly enough and with sufficient plausible force, is well known. The well-turned phrases of the trained politician, intent on his selfish purposes, the arguments of the silver-tongued demagogue as he exploits some pet theory at the expense of the public, and the rantings of the man with a cause, a theory or an axe to grind, all find an easy audience. Mass psychology and mob determinations have been exploited down the ages, for the unthinking and the emotional are easily swayed in any direction, and hitherto this has been turned to their own advantage by those who do not have the best interests of humanity at heart. It has been used for selfish and evil ends far more often than for good. Of this tendency the negative and helpless attitude of the German people under the Nazi rulers is the outstanding example.

But this negative receptivity (which does not deserve the name of public opinion) can be as easily turned to good ends as bad, and to constructive measures as to destructive. A little planned direction and a wisely outlined programme with this in view can and will bring about the needed change and make a sound and intelligent public opinion one of the major factors in world reconstruction One of the most interesting features of this war period has been the direct contact which has been set up by some of the world leaders with the man in the street and the woman in the home, as witness the talks given by Roosevelt and Churchill. Those given by the Axis leaders are in a totally different category, for they have been directed to the male youth of their countries and to the man in uniform. Only the lesser leaders in Germany, for instance, talk to the people in their homes, and then only to give them orders, to foster hate and to misrepresent the truth. In all these cases, however, the value of mass opinion is recognised and the need to sway the mass mind, either bending it to the will of some leader, such as Hitler, or educating it in those principles which are of benefit to the whole.

The second point which needs to be grasped by the average citizen is that the mass is made up of individuals; that each of us, as an individual, is a definite and integral part of the whole. This is a basic and important fact and has a bearing on our subject. The first step in the rebuilding process which lies ahead of us is to reach the individual, show him his importance, indicate to him his very real sphere of influence, and then set him to work in that sphere and with what he has. In this way, his normal and natural sense of futility will disappear, and he will gradually realise that he is needed and can do much. Having grasped this for himself, he can then try to bring the same constructive attitude to those around him, and they will then do likewise.

May I point out here that the value of the individual is surely based on the inherent divinity of the human spirit and on the integrity of the whole. It is founded also on the knowledge, which must underlie all future reconstruction work, that at the very heart of the universe is a divine Power, call it what you will, and on the faith that love is the very law of life itself, in spite of all appearances and the record of the past.

It is essential that we be practical in our approach to

the subject and that the reconstruction plans involve steps which are possible and which the average man can take. The first practical attitude to be taken is to crush out hate because it is non-constructive and hindering. It blinds the vision and warps the judgment, and simply feeds the growth of fear and horror. But the love demanded of us is neither emotional nor sentimental. It is intensely practical, and expresses itself in service and cooperative activity. It seeks to aid all movements that benefit humanity and are in line with the new incoming era. Many people think that an emotional reaction and clamouring outcry of horror at what has overtaken the world indicates love and spiritual sensitivity. It is far more likely to indicate self-centredness and personal discomfort. True love has no time for these reactions, because the work of alleviation is entirely engrossing. The man who loves his fellowmen is mentally poised and intelligently working; he is mobilising all his forces for the service of the hour. A truly compassionate heart is *not* emotional.

Our second step, therefore, after the recognition of individual responsibility, is to replace emotion by practical love, expressed in selfless service. The third step is to reorganise our lives so that we have time for this needed service. Most people are not getting the maximum of results out of their daily lives, and this for several reasons. Frequently they do not really desire to make the sacrifices which such service demands; often they are under the delusion that their present output of service represents their utmost possibility; again, they fancy that their health could stand no more active work, or that they require time for themselves, or they waste many valuable hours doing those things which yield no real results. If, however, the need today is as great as we are led to believe, if this is the hour of man's extremity, if the issues are so great that the entire future of the race depends upon the outcome of the war, then the one thing that really matters is for man to play his part, to mobilise his time and all that he has and make that supreme effort which will release life and energy and make the winning of the war something immediately possible and the rebuilding era a success. This he must do at any cost, even that of life itself. A spiritual paradox becomes apparent. The individual is of supreme importance, and yet at the same time what happens to him as he serves and fights for human freedom is of no individual importance at all. A brief period of organised effort and, at the end, death, is of more vital usefulness today than a futile doing of the things a man feels like doing in a leisurely way, and then meandering feebly down the years.

Therefore, the development of a sense of individual responsibility, the expression of real love in service and the reorganising the life so as to get the utmost out of each day constitutes the preparatory stage for the man who seeks to participate in the reconstruction period.

Having then done this to the best of his ability (and many have already made a good beginning) he must develop in himself and evoke in others *the spirit of goodwill*. This will-to-good is of immediate effectiveness, because it governs a man's relation to his family and his household, his business or social associates, his casual acquaintances and all with whom he may come in contact. It enables him to begin the work of reconstruction right where he is and trains him in a familiar environment to practice right human relations. It is the major and potent factor which can enable the otherwise futile individual to become a focal point of constructive influence. He will then discover that, as a result of this, his sphere of constructive influence is continually enlarging.

These are the first four steps, and they are perhaps the most difficult, for they are non-spectacular and almost constitute spiritual platitudes. But they are the essential and unavoidable preliminaries for the man who wants to work wisely, usefully and intuitively in the future.

To the above he can then add the following efforts and attempt to impose upon himself this suggested programme:

1.   Study and reflect upon the many proposals which are being made by world leaders and thinkers as to the coming world rehabilitation. It will be necessary to plan your read-

ing and to know what is being discussed. Cultivate an intelligent opinion, based on goodwill and on what you, as a result of study, feel should be done. Then discuss the ideas in your home, among your friends and in your environment without fear or favour. It will help you to do so if you regard such discussions as a service and believe that your interests and enthusiasm cannot fail to have an effect.

2. If possible, gather people together to discuss and study the coming world order, or cooperate with those who are already doing so. Look upon this meeting together as a definite contribution to the moulding of public opinion and as a method of building up that reservoir of thought power which can be of use to those whose task it is to rebuild. If only two people cooperate with you in this matter, the effort will not be lost or futile, for you will be helping to change the content of world thought and impressing other minds, even if you do not know it.

3. Extend your interest to many countries and try to understand the diverse problems of those countries. Many know people in these foreign lands, and lists can be made of their names and addresses. As soon as the war is over and the lines of communication are again open, you can seek to reach these people, attempt to locate them through any available agencies, and then, when found, strengthen them with the knowledge of your goodwill or interest and by cooperating with them during the period of reconstruction. No matter how slight has been your contact with them in the past, foster it by thought and prayer, and later by direct communication. Thus a great network of relationship will be set up which will serve to weld a new world into one harmonious and understanding whole.

4. Pray constantly, and to your prayers add meditation and reflection. Behind the world pattern and structure stands its Originator, its Planner, its motivating Energy, its central Will, its living Creator, its God. Seek by prayer to reach that central Will and point of Life, thus blending yourself

with the sensed divine objective and identifying your will with the Divine Will. This central Will-to-Good can be reached by the man whose own will-to-good is a living, practical experience, and the more that goodwill is expressed, the more easily will you discover and cooperate with the divine Plan and follow the guiding hand of God in world affairs. The real work of reconstruction will be done by those who, in the silence of their own hearts, have walked with God and learnt His ways.

5.   Find two other people to work with you. There is a unique potency in this triple relationship. God Himself, so say all the world Scriptures, works as a Trinity of goodness, and you can, in your tiny sphere, do the same, finding two other people of like mind with you to form a goodwill triangle of light and spiritual interplay. Each of the two who cooperate with you can, in their turn, do the same, and thus a great *network of goodwill* can spread throughout the world. Through it the Forces of Light will be able to work and you, in your place and sphere, will have aided and helped.

6.   Find out and study the methods, techniques and objectives of the various groups and organisations which are interested in world reconstruction. You may not agree with all of them or with their plans and modes of working, but all are needed. The types of men are many, the races and conditions are varied, and the problems to be solved will call for innumerable ways of working. All can play their part if based on real goodwill and if fanaticism is absent. The fanatic is a danger wherever he is found, for he sees only one side of a question and is unable to appreciate the various points of view. He will not admit that all are needed. Cooperation is the key to expressed goodwill, and in the future period of rehabilitation *cooperation* will be the outstanding need. Keep a record of all such groups, their leaders, objectives and programmes. It will prove useful when the war is over. Establish helpful and friendly relations with them to the best of your ability.

7.   Find and keep a record also of the men and women of goodwill in your environment. Be spiritually aggressive in this matter and go out to discover them. When you have found them, then be interested in what they are doing, and also endeavour to have them cooperate with you in your lines of activity. Keep a register of the names and addresses of these people, adding also their capacities and functions if any, and thus build up a mailing list. You will then be aware of a group which can be depended upon to work in a spirit of goodwill and for world reconstruction. Later, these lists can be amalgamated, if deemed desirable, and form a vast mailing list of people in every country who will work along these indicated lines and who could be reached simultaneously. They will form a body of synchronised public opinion, sufficiently strong to mould ideas, influence the masses, and aid the world leaders to right and appropriate action.

8.   Above everything else and growing out of all the above suggestions, plan definitely for the rehabilitation—physical, psychological and spiritual—of the children of every country. They have been the victims of wickedness. Let them be the recipients of loving goodwill instead. The problems of economic rehabilitation, of territorial boundaries, of the demobilisation of armies and the subsequent re-employment of the demobilised, and of world rebuilding are profoundly important and will call for expert aid. But the problem of the children, as earlier pointed out, underlies the whole necessity for world rebuilding, is greater than all other problems, is above all racial and national barriers, and evokes the best in every human heart. The children have prior claim upon all men.

I would therefore appeal to all whom I can reach through this article to concentrate their major effort—mental, spiritual and practical—on preparing themselves to aid the children of Europe and the other countries which have suffered so much at the hands of the Axis Powers. This will take much time and careful planning; it will necessitate enlisting the cooperation of trained experts in the field of child welfare, doctors, surgeons, nurses, psychologists and educators; it will require much money to make the preparation effective, to send a trained personnel into the destitute and ruined countries and to carry forward the work whilst there; it will take also loving, compassionate action and long patience. It nevertheless constitutes the most important opportunity confronting the men and women of goodwill; it is the foundational activity of the new world order, for that order must be brought into being for the sake of the children of today. *They* will inhabit this new world, express the new ideals, and hand on to their children that for which we have fought and died, the best that we have inherited, and all that we have succeeded in salvaging for them. The thought of the children in the subjugated lands did not arrest the onward march of Hitler's soldiers; the sanctity of the home and the physical and moral needs of small children aroused no flicker of compassion in the young men trained under the Nazi system of education; the relationship of mother and child did not enter into the calculation of the German agents as they separated children from parents and set the child adrift in a world of carnage or in an institutionalised establishment. The planned cruelty must be remedied, and it must be remedied by the men and women of goodwill and loving hearts.

9.   Begin now to lay aside, no matter what the personality may demand, such small sums as can be spared and which can accumulate in preparation for the work of reconstruction. If we can all do this, it will enable us to take our share in the work without placing an undue load on others. Will you see to it that this sacrifice and its resulting fund be preserved inviolate in your own hands until such time in the future as you may choose to use it?

These are the practical suggestions which it would seem possible to make at this particular time. They are of a general nature and basically individual. The whole scheme of rebuilding is as yet in the formative thought stage. The process to be followed today is one of self-education and the awakening of all whom we can reach. It will demand the intelligent study and consideration of methods with which to meet this need, and the discovery of those who, irrespective of nationality or religion, can be depended upon to cooperate in the various phases of the work of reconstruction. In this work of preparation, all can share.

To this task we are all called, and to it there are many voices calling today; there are thousands who have dreamed the same dream, seen the same vision, believed in the divine possibilities which are latent in all human hearts and who know, past all controversy, that selfishness and universal greed have brought the world to its present desperate plight. They know also that selfless sharing and cooperative understanding between all men of goodwill everywhere can rebuild a new world, bring into being a more beautiful life, and restore that which humanity itself has destroyed. The best is yet to be. We can rest back upon the realisation that the history of the human race has been one of a steady moving forward down the ages and towards the light.

An Imminent Spiritual Event

March 1943

We are nearing the climax of the spiritual year. The greatest Approach of all time is imminent and possible. Much depends now upon the aspirants and disciples of the world, particularly those in physical incarnation today. A major contact between Shamballa and the Hierarchy, for which initiates and Masters have, for centuries, been preparing is in process of consummation. I shall very shortly be giving you some further information on the subject in an attempt to anchor on the earth that seed of the new world religion which an earlier instruction upon the Great Approaches * indicated might be founded, and lead to a true start of a universal faith which will serve the need of

---

* *A Treatise on the Seven Rays,* Vol. II (*Esoteric Psychology*), Pages 701-751.

humanity for a long time to come. All I ask of you today is to begin *now* a most careful preparation for the event which is impending at the time of the Full Moon of May, so that the energies then set in motion may be aided by your directed thought and you yourselves may come more fully into the current of the downpouring life.

At the coming Wesak Festival and until the Full Moon of June including the five days after that Full Moon I ask you to use both of the Invocations (pp. 144, 249), thus testifying greatly to the fusion of humanity into one great group of invocative appeal. Make a real effort to be present and in group formation at the exact time of the Full Moon of May, as far as you know it, using both Invocations and believing that you are voicing the unified will and desire of humanity itself. I will enlarge upon this in my Wesak message, but I seek to get this to you as early as possible so that my own group, in process of training, can lay the needed foundations of the work to be done.

Let me extend this concept a little further by pointing out that the invocative cry of humanity and of the Hierarchy, jointly sounded at the time of the Full Moons of May and June and particularly at the Wesak Festival, will be effective if the "cold light" of the aspirants and disciples of the world and of all selfless servers, no matter who or where they may be found, is united with the "clear light" of the initiates and of those who can function freely as souls—the Members of the Hierarchy and, to a lesser degree, all accepted disciples. This combination is the one that is desired and required. These people are relatively few in number, when compared with the world's population, but because they are to be found focussed at "the deep centre" and are distinguished by the quality of fusion and at-one-ment, they can be enormously potent. I would, therefore, ask all of you (during the weeks prior to the Full Moon of May and that of June and for five days thereafter) to seek to "dwell ever at the centre," to endeavour to blend the cold light of your personalities with the clear light of your soul, so as to work effectively for the five weeks of the desired period.

A SPECIAL WESAK FESTIVAL MESSAGE

April 1943

This communication is addressed to the members of the new group of world servers who can be reached (there are countless numbers of whom you have no knowledge) and to the men and women of goodwill everywhere. I would ask you to see that as many receive this as possible. We are nearing the climax of the spiritual year and the time that the Sun moves northward. The greatest Approach of all time is close and possible. Much however depends upon the aspirants and the disciples in the world at this time. The past year has been one of the world's worst experiences from the standpoint of agony and distress; the point of acutest suffering has been reached. It has, however, been the year in which the greatest spiritual Approach of all time has shown itself to be possible—an Approach for which the initiates and Masters have for centuries been preparing, and for which all the Wesak Festivals since the meeting of the Great Council in 1925 have been preparatory. I have, in past instructions, referred to the great meetings held at intervals by Those to Whom is entrusted the spiritual guidance of the planet and particularly of man. Certain facts must be assumed, such as the acceptance in the Western hemisphere of the existence of the Christ and in the Eastern, of the Buddha. It is, therefore, surely possible (given this acceptance) to assume that They and Their disciples must and do confer together upon the steps needed to guide mankind along the path of light, the path to God. To this all the world Scriptures bear witness and to this all spiritual knowers testify. I have not time today to enlarge upon this theme. I simply ask for your acceptance of the hypothesis (an hypothesis which is a fact to many millions and a proved event to many thousands) that spiritual guidance is accorded to mankind and that behind the veil which separates the visible from the invisible there stand Those Who are working strenuously—and, I might add, scientifically—to meet the present dire need.

Two things are occupying Their attention:

1. The need to bring the present strife and warfare to an end and so release mankind from an evil past and open the door to a better future.
2. The opportunity to lay the foundations for that new world religion which will suffice to meet man's need for many centuries ahead and for which all past world religions have prepared him.

Such, brother of mine, are two of the objectives lying before the Hierarchy at this time as it prepares for the Full Moons of May and June. Can the forces be so organised and the energies, pending distribution, so dispersed that the full measure of good can be evoked? Can the evocation of a new cycle of spiritual contact and of liberation be brought about by the action of the men and women of goodwill? Can the will-to-good of the spiritual Energies and the goodwill of humanity itself be brought together and produce those conditions in which the new world order—visioned by all who truly love their fellowmen—be enabled to function? Can the situation be so staged that the new world religion and the new approach of humanity to God are brought into being? These are the important questions which the Hierarchy is today attempting to answer.

The group of spiritual workers of whom I happen to be one is faced with two major problems: the problem of the war itself with its stupefying and stunning effect upon the masses everywhere, and the problem offered by the aspirants and disciples throughout the world. Can the suffering masses of men "stand with massed intent" and with eyes directed towards God so that their cry can mount to His ears? And will the spiritually minded people and the workers for humanity make that supreme effort (rendered from an adequate "point of tension") so that humanity may be focussed in its appeal and bring about a response from the highest available sources. Can the united effort of these two groups—one conscious of what is happening and the other unconscious—evoke reply?

In moments of extreme urgency or crisis, the story of the Christ brings to our attention the fact that He then came in touch with His Father in Heaven. God spoke to Him in terms of recognition; God testified to the fact that He knew Him for His beloved Son. To these basic facts of the historical record, we must add the realisation that "as He is, so are we in this world" and the assurance of Christ Himself that God is also our Father. Then the door of possibility opens. We can come then to the realisation that in times of intense human urgency, stress and crisis and when the soul of man is adequately aroused to the needed point of spiritual receptivity (as was ever the case with Christ) then there can likewise come a divine recognition from the highest possible source which will suffice to bring release and liberation and to give power—power to do the right, to take those steps which are demanded by the spiritual purpose and to proceed, consequently, along the path of evolution.

Let me here point out that where this is a group activity upon the physical plane there is—under the Law of Balance and of Action and Reaction—a paralleling spiritual activity. The entire world of men is today engaged in an intense activity in the material world—marching armies, factories working in shifts twenty-four hours a day, seething migrations and deportations of people, intense air activity and the organising and planned work of the hundreds of relief agencies in every country—to mention only a few of the myriad activities. The personalities of men everywhere are engaged and mentally, emotionally and physically they are all working at high pressure. The impact of circumstance and events has never been so potent. Alongside of this material activity of humanity is to be found the strenuous endeavour, the effort to think constructively, the focussed idealism, the registration of vision and the spiritual aspiration of the people of goodwill, of the disciples everywhere, plus the trained spiritual activity of the Hierarchy and of the spiritual leaders of the race upon the outer and the inner side of life. To this must be added the activity (the waiting activity, if I might use so paradoxical a phrase) of that centre of life where the will of God is focussed.

There are therefore, (speaking in terms of spiritual endeavour) the following groups whose massed intent is to bring about the liberation of humanity and who are to be found everywhere in the world:

1. The men and women of goodwill.
2. The idealists and the dreamers of dreams, the visioners of a future world.
3. The spiritually minded people whom we call the world aspirants.
4. Disciples throughout the planet.
5. The Members of the spiritual Hierarchy of the planet, either in or out of incarnation.
6. The Custodians of the Will or Purpose of God, holding Themselves in readiness at Shamballa and listening for the demand for succour as it rises from mankind.
7. Certain great Energies of extra-planetary significance Who stand ready to intervene should the spiritual invocation or the distress of humanity reach the pitch of evocation.

The problem is how to fuse and blend the first five groups so that the spiritual appeal can express a group integrated and united demand. Only such a united demand, focussing the "massed intent" of mankind will suffice to evoke an extra-planetary response.

Much of this task of unification lies in the hands of two groups: the planetary Hierarchy and the new group of world servers. With the work of the first group, mankind has little to do, for They can be depended upon to fulfil Their task and to shoulder Their responsibility to the full. With the work of the new group of world servers all of you have much to do and it is about this work that I write at this time.

I shall not waste time in defining the personnel of the group. Suffice it to say that all who truly love their fellow

men and who serve them with sacrifice and selfless understanding constitute this group. Along with the affiliated
body of men of goodwill, the members of the new group of
world servers must now prepare themselves for a great act
of service at the time of the May and June Full Moons and
throughout the weeks preceding those times.

The statements which I am now going to make, I will
put as briefly as possible, leaving you to ponder upon them
and trusting you to understand them. What I have now to
say will fall into three parts:

1. The work of the Hierarchy in the immediate future
   at these Full Moon periods
2. The task of the New Group of World Servers today
3. The New World Religion and its spiritual future.

It is necessary for you to understand the immediate spiritual
possibilities which confront humanity if those of you who
have vision and love humanity are to measure up to the
immediate opportunity. It is necessary that you should grasp
the immediate preparatory steps which you can take in relation to those possibilities and should also have a vision of
the principles which must govern the new world religion,
with its outstanding points of focus. I do not intend to
plead with you, as in the past, or ask you for cooperation
either to serve or sacrifice. I only seek to give you information, leaving you to make due application under the urge
of your own souls.

The Work of the Hierarchy in the Immediate Future

The past history of the relations existing between the
Hierarchy as a whole and humanity as a whole can be summarised in the idea of the carrying out of certain Great
Approaches between Those who express the spiritual attitude and those who are frankly material in their attitude.
By means of these Approaches, humanity has been brought
(in consciousness) increasingly nearer to the spiritual centres
of love and life and has been stimulated to make spiritual

progress, to awaken to the light within, to unfold the Christ consciousness and to find the Path of Light which leads to divinity. This steady trend towards increasing relationship has focussed itself throughout the historical record by means of certain great registered revelations—the result of these Approaches. Always in moments of crisis and tension, the cry of humanity has evoked response from the Hierarchy which has come, sometimes rapidly, sometimes more slowly, but always inevitably. In modern history, two such Approaches are recognised as existing on a broad human scale, i.e., the one which focussed through the coming of the Buddha to the Eastern civilisation and that which focussed through the Christ, coming to the West. Another Great Approach is now at hand but its date is dependent upon the activity of the New Group of World Servers and the spiritual tension which they can achieve.

A major preparatory period to this Approach took place in 1936 and in this preparation many of you participated; it culminated at the time of the Full Moon of May that year in a worldwide use of the first Invocation which I gave you. Now, seven years later, comes the opportunity to carry forward the work then started and to achieve results which may release spiritual tides of forces and these may turn the tide of battle. I refer not here to the battle in the physical sense. The war, from the physical angle, is already won though many months may elapse before the victory in the East and in the West is completely achieved. This you realise. But—again paralleling this physical achievement—must come a spiritual victory and this could be described as the gaining of a new spiritual orientation and a new attitude towards God, to express it very simply.

In reverse, I might point out that the reasons for a measure of failure in 1936 can be traced to two sources. The work was relatively so successful that it called forth a powerful paralleling activity upon the part of the Forces of Evil; these were potent enough to overwhelm temporarily the Forces of Light and to bring on the war with all its attendant horrors. Secondly, the New Group of World

Servers, the men and women of goodwill and the aspirants everywhere relaxed their efforts; they did not hold the tension gained but slipped back into negligence; the work did not go on and this in spite of the constant effort of a few. But they were too few.

Now again comes opportunity and the possibility of a Great Approach which can be the consummation of the work started in 1936. The battle is on between the *Forces of Light* and the *Forces of Evil.* To end this warfare rapidly, and with success, leaving a wide open door to a better world, the *Forces of Life* must be called in. It is this which is engaging the attention of the Hierarchy at this time. For aiding in this endeavour the Buddha is preparing Himself and for this the Christ stands ready, focussing in Himself the desire of Humanity for that "life more abundantly" which He promised when here before, and for liberation from evil and admission into good. One of the realisations emerging out of this war is the fact that humanity has now, as a whole, been able to see and grasp more clearly than ever before, the nature of evil. Men are recoiling in horror from this display of rampant evil and even the wicked man is shocked and arrested by the unleashed wickedness which is today stalking the Earth. That realisation is good and will help the needed reorientation of mankind towards God and good.

Putting it very simply, the Hierarchy is today getting ready for a Great Approach which will have two results:

1. It will bring about a closer relation between those great Lives Who embody the will of God and are the Custodians of the divine purpose, and Those Who embody the love of God and are the Custodians of the immediate Plan for humanity. This relationship can be established at the time of the May Full Moon at which time the Buddha will embody in Himself the powerful downpouring of energy—the dynamic energy of the divine will. The Christ, at the same time, will embody the outpouring dominant demand of the spiritual aspiration of mankind, plus

the demand of the Hierarchy for the needed aid at this time of crisis.

2. It will also bring about a closer relation between mankind and the Hierarchy. At the time of the June Full Moon, the Christ will focus in Himself the spiritual energies of the Hierarchy, plus the energy which the Buddha distributed at the time of the Wesak Festival; the New Group of World Servers will focus the spiritual demand for life and liberation, voicing the "massed intent" of humanity.

If both aspects of this one work can be satisfactorily carried forward, then a great release can be brought about. The Lords of Liberation could be successfuly invoked; the Spirit of Peace might appear as the "Rider from the Secret Place" and the new era of goodwill (based upon the will-to-good) might be inaugurated. I say "might be" because, my brothers, the success of all that could happen is dependent upon the work done by you and all men of goodwill, by the religious and spiritually minded people everywhere and by the world aspirants between the sacred season of May and June, 1943, and that of 1944.

Esoterically speaking, the work of the Hierarchy is to focus the divine will-to-good as it affects humanity. The work of spiritually minded men is to evoke that will-to-good on earth through as full an expression as possible of goodwill. It is the goodwill of the masses, focussed everywhere through the United Nations who are fighting for the liberation of mankind and through the New Group of World Servers, which is sufficient to invoke the will-to-good and only this is adequate. This is an important statement and one on which I would ask you to ponder.

During the past six years I have given you two Stanzas of a Great Invocation. The first one ran as follows:

Let the Forces of Light bring illumination to mankind.
Let the Spirit of Peace be spread abroad.
May men of goodwill everywhere meet in a spirit of cooperation.

May forgiveness on the part of all men be the keynote
at this time.
Let power attend the efforts of the Great Ones.
So let it be and help us to do our part.

This expressed the normal, largely unconscious, invocative
cry of humanity. It summed up in itself the desire of all men
everywhere for peace, for goodwill and cooperation. It was
generally popular and was and still is very widely used. It
was fairly easily understood and its outstanding note was
peace. It was used as a prayer by the majority and not as a
challenging demand as had been intended; it did not, therefore, prove adequately effective in arresting the onward march
of evil. It does, however, preserve the form which can and
will evoke eventually the Spirit of Peace. This evocation will
bring to humanity that stimulation and active desire to participate in the expression of goodwill which will render
world peace an effective outcome of wise action and the
establishment of right human relations. Just as the Great
Lord of Love and Son of God, the Christ, used as His
vehicle of expression on earth, the form of the Master Jesus,
so this great extra-planetary Life, the Spirit of Peace, can
be enabled, on a higher turn of the spiral, to use as His
vehicle of expression, the form of the Christ, the Prince
of Peace; thus His stupendous energies will be stepped
down through the medium of the Lord of Love and become
available to the mass of men.

I gave you later another Stanza of the Invocation, of
great power which was suited to the conditions of war—a
war which proved inevitable and unavoidable. This last
Invocation was not so popular and not nearly so easily understood and for this there was very good reason. It was an
invocation intended to evoke the Forces of Life just as the
previous one invoked the Forces of Light and Love. It could
only be successfully used by disciples, advanced thinkers and
the Hierarchy itself. It was, however, given out to the public
so as to familiarise them as far as possible with the concepts
of liberation and life and in an effort to anchor upon Earth

a new point of focus through which life could be made to flow. This effort has not been totally unsuccessful.

At the time of the Full Moon of May and of June, it will be advisable to use both these Invocations and thus to fuse and blend into one united invocation the massed intent of humanity as a whole and the enlightened purpose of the disciples and the Hierarchy. This fusion of the two groups—Humanity and the Hierarchy—may then suffice to sound out such a potent call that life may be released on Earth instead of death and the love of God play its active part in the reconstruction of world affairs. If this can be successfully accomplished, two great revelations may then be speeded on their way:

1. A revelation of light and understanding to humanity as a whole, leading them to knowledge and enabling men to see the cause of the present catastrophe, for "in that light shall we see Light." In that light, humanity will know what to do and how to rectify past errors.

2. A revelation of life and of "life more abundantly" as Christ promised when on earth. This revelation will give to the thinkers, idealists, true leaders and disciples working in the world today, that spiritual energy which leads to right activity, sound leadership and *inspired and inspiring living.*

Such is another of the goals confronting the Hierarchy at this time. Such is the will of God for humanity and such is the intent and purpose of Shamballa. When the massed purpose of the Custodians of the Will of God and the massed intent of the souls of men can be synchronised, then the Great Approach will become inevitable and the Great Release will automatically follow.

The Task of the New Group of World Servers Today

The immediate task of the new group of world servers is to focus the massed longing, aspiration, desire and intent of humanity so as to bring about the needed synchronisation at the time of the Full Moon of May and of June this year, and throughout the intervening weeks from the receipt of this communication (as far as you are concerned) until July first, approximately.

This they must do through their own clear thinking on current matters, by the cultivation of a receptive spirit, based on a willingness to learn, a readiness to let old preconceptions go and fixed ideas to disappear under the impact of new truths and new inspiration, and based also on a determination at all costs to recognise truth and presented spiritual developments.

I would ask all of you, therefore, to have an open mind, to redouble your belief in the fact of the spiritual realities, to have faith in the will-to-good of the divine purpose and to love your fellowmen; and—upon the plane of practical affairs and living—to do two things: Carry forward your due share in this physical plane war, aiding the armed forces of the United Nations to wage war to a successful finish, knowing that there are spiritual realities for which it is worth dying if need be, and that war on evil can be waged without hate and with right purpose; secondly, plan at the same time for those practical measures which, after the war is over, will aid the period of reconstruction and help rehabilitate humanity, and lead to a saner, better, truer way of living.

I would ask you also to take those measures in your individual life and in your environment, wherever possible, which will help make the work to be done at the time of the Full Moon in May and in June successful; to use both the Invocations constantly; do not use them as prayers or employing the energy of desire but as great challenging demands, employing the power of the will as you can muster it and focus it at a point of tension. At the time of the Full Moon gather people together for an act of fusion and of cooperation, thus aiding humanity and throwing your small individual effort behind that of the Hierarchy. I would ask you to recognise that, as a part of the new group of world servers and as a person of goodwill you *can* act as a mediating factor between humanity and the Hierarchy, bridging the gap between the mass of men (stunned by suffering, blind to the higher issues, and inert) and the spiritual Group which is seeking so earnestly to bring them help and life. I would have you use, with all the power which in you lies, the creative imagination as you endeavour to do this and to believe that the sincerity of your purpose and the love of your hearts can and will help make possible the Great Approach and so hasten the Great Release. I would have you (from the time you receive this communication) think deeply on what I have said, to walk silently in the light of your souls, to radiate love, to seek clarity of vision and then, when needed, to speak to others with power and understanding.

I would, finally, have you realise that in the work now being done and as a result of the Great Approach you can aid in the focussing or anchoring of the new world religion, that universal religion which will be founded on all the past, which will consummate the work of the Christ and which will open up a fresh stretch (if I may use such an expression) upon the Path of Light which leads to God.

The New World Religion

All past divine revelations have brought humanity to the point where (spiritually speaking) man's essential divinity is theologically recognised, where the brotherhood of man and the Fatherhood of God are recognised ideals and where science has demonstrated the fact of an unfolding purpose and the existence of a fundamental, intelligent Agent behind all phenomena. Step by step man has been led through prayer, the voice of desire, through worship, the recognition of deity, through affirmation of the fact of human identity of nature with the divine, to a belief in the divinity of man. Orthodox religion emphasises the divinity of the Christ, and He Himself has told us (and the *New Testament* in many places emphasises it) that we also are divine, all of us are the Sons of God and that as He is so are we in this world and that we are able to do still greater things than Christ did because He has shown us how. Such is the religious background of the spiritual thinking in the world. Therefore, taking our stand on these truths, acknowledging the fact of our divinity and recognising the glory of all past revelations and the still more glorious promise of the future, we can begin to realise that the time has now come for the presentation of the new step in this unfolding revelation. We can realise that to our past programmes of prayer, worship and affirmation, the new religion of Invocation and Evocation can be added, in which man will begin to use his divine power and come into closer touch with the spiritual sources of all life.

This new form of the one religion will be in fact the Religion of the Great Approaches—approaches between mankind and the great spiritual Centres which operate behind the scenes, between groups of workers on the physical plane and in the three worlds of human evolution and spiritual groups upon the inner planes, such as the Ashrams of the Masters and the egoic groups with which all human beings are in subjective—though usually unknown—relation.

The new religion will be one of Invocation and Evocation, of bringing together great spiritual energies and then stepping them down for the benefiting and the stimulation of the masses. The work of the new religion will be the distribution of spiritual energy and the protecting of humanity from energies and forces which they are not, at the particular time, fitted to receive. A little careful thought will show you how, at the coming Full Moon Festivals, these thoughts are present: the protection and liberation of humanity and the stimulation of mankind through the distribution and the transference of spiritual energy so that the right steps can be taken in any given period, leading mankind out of darkness into light, from death to immortality and from the unreal to the Real.

I would have you, therefore, add to your mental and spiritual activity the recognition that you are participating in the task of anchoring the basic tenets of the new world religion—the flower and fruition of the past and the hope of the future.

More along this line, I may not write at this time. Later I will elaborate for you the greater and the lesser festivals of the spiritual year as they will gradually supersede the festivals of the present world religions in the East and in the West. (See: *The Reappearance of the Christ,* Chapter VI.) Much that you have learnt and gradually absorbed will then be seen fitting into the general spiritual plan. You will find that the spiritual year is divided into two periods (symbolic of spirit and matter) ; the period in which the Sun moves northward and the period when it travels on the southern way. You will find that the month divides itself into two periods likewise, that of the waxing and the waning moon and you will find the future emphasis laid throughout the world upon the Easter Festival, the Festival of the Risen Christ; upon the Wesak Festival, the Festival of the Buddha or of Illumination; and the June Full Moon, the Festival of Unification carried forward by the Christ, the Master of all the Masters and the Teacher alike of angels and of men.

Today, however, I seek to focus your attention upon the immediate task of cooperation with the Hierarchy and strengthen you to play your part in world salvage.

THE NEW WORLD RELIGION

May 1943

In the first part of my message under this title (see: *The Reappearance of the Christ,* Chapter VI) I had much to say about *the form* into which the great world religions in the East and in the West have crystallised and its consequent deterioration. It will be essential, therefore, to look at and appreciate the fundamental truths which that form has preserved, even whilst hiding them. It will be valuable for us to realise that within the churches men of God and disciples of the Christ have ever worked, laboured and suffered. They have seen and agonised over the distortions and the misrepresentations. They have been hindered by the organisation, oft despised by the theologians, and have remained simple in the midst of learning. They have been loving and universal in their individual consciousness, among the separative and fanatical. They are the glory of the church—oft hated when alive and oft canonised after death. Their glory lies in the fact that they testify to the progress of the spiritual man and express in fullness what is in every evolving man; they are the flower of evolution and the tried representatives of God. In the indictment of the churches, given earlier, let us not forget the Christians found within those churches.

I would remind you that I write as one who believes in the great spiritual realities and who regards the unfolding spirit of man as the unshatterable evidence of the existence of "the One in Whom we live and move and have our being." I speak as one who believes in and loves the Christ and who knows Him to be the Master of all the Masters and the Teacher alike of angels and of men. I am one who looks to the Christ as the supreme expression of divinity upon Earth and who knows the extent of His sacrificial work for humanity, the wonder of the revelation which He brought, the imminence of His return and of His coming Assumption of spiritual rule in the hearts of men everywhere. I know that He has no pleasure in the great stone temples which man has built whilst His people are left without practical guidance or reasonable light upon their affairs; and I know too that He feels, with an aching heart, that the simplicity which He taught, and the simple Way to God which He emphasised have disappeared in the fogs of theology and the discussions of churchmen throughout the centuries. I know that He realises that the words He spoke have been lost in the labyrinths of the ecclesiastical minds which have sought to interpret them, and that the simple teaching of the Approach to God which He taught has been superseded by the pomp and ceremony of elaborate rituals.

To sum up: Because of the divergences of the many exoteric faiths, the multiplicity of the sects and cults in both the Orient and Occident, and the quarrels of theologians over words, phrases and interpretations, the sons of God—in process of development—are left without the needed help to contact the Christ and His great group of disciples, the spiritual leaders of humanity; the way to Christ, the living, loving Expression of God, is not made clear to the seeker. Together, the two great Sons of God present to mankind—the One in the East and the Other in the West—a complete and perfect representation of Deity; by Their lives and words They guarantee to man the possibilities always latent in the human spirit.

Today the Christ and the Buddha wait until the hour strikes. Then Their united effort, plus the invocative appeal of all who truly *know* and truly *love,* will bring humanity the new revelation for which they wait.

The new world religion must be based upon those truths which have stood the test of the ages. This I said elsewhere and enumerated four of those truths:

1. The Fact of God
2. Man's Relationship to God
3. The Fact of Immortality and Eternal Persistence
4. The Continuity of Revelation and the Divine Approaches.

These four facts are basic realities and truths which have conditioned the masses of men for aeons. Human unhappiness is founded primarily upon man's inability to live fully in the consciousness of these four fundamental realisations. But they are steadily taking shape in human thinking, and for them the United Nations fights.

Two more great and foundational facts are also part of the human state of awareness.

5. The fact of *our relationship with each other*. This is as much a foundational spiritual fact as is God Himself, because it is linked with our knowledge of Him as Father.

This relationship we call "brotherhood" and it expresses itself (or should I say, it will eventually express itself?) through human fellowship and right human relations. For this we work, and humanity is moving towards that relationship—and that in spite of the fact of war.

6. The fact of *the Path to God*. Awareness of this has been preserved for us down the ages by those who knew God and whom the world called mystics, occultists and saints. Opening out before aspiring men stretches the Way. The history of the human soul is the history of the search for that Way and its discovery by the persistent.

In every race and nation, in every climate and part of the world, and throughout the endless reaches of time itself, back into the limitless past, men have found the Path to God; they have trodden it and accepted its conditions, endured its disciplines, rested back in confidence upon its realities, received its rewards and found their goal. Arrived there, they have "entered into the joy of the Lord," participated in the mysteries of the kingdom of heaven, dwelt in the glory of the divine Presence, and then returned to the ways of men, to serve. The testimony to the existence of this Path is the priceless treasure of all the great religions and its witnesses are those who have transcended all forms and all theologies, and have penetrated into the world of meaning which all symbols veil.

These truths are part of all that the past gives to man. They are our eternal heritage, and connected with them there is no new revelation but only participation and understanding. These are the facts which the World Teachers have brought to us, suited to our need and capacity at any given time. They are the inner structure of the One Truth upon which all the world theologies have been built, including the Christian doctrines and dogmas built around the Person of Christ and His teaching.

Dimly sensed by the evolving human consciousness hovers another emerging truth of a larger nature—larger because related to the Whole and not just to individual man and his personal salvation. It is an extension of the individual approach to truth. Let us call it *the truth of the Great Cyclic Approaches of the divine to the human* of which all world Teachers and Saviours were the symbol and the guarantee. At certain great moments, down the ages, God drew nearer to His people and humanity (blindly and unconscious of their objective) at the same time made great efforts to draw near to God. On the part of God, this was intentional, conscious and deliberate; on the part of man, it was largely unconscious, forced upon him by the tragedy of circumstance, by desperate need and by the driving urge of the collective soul. These Great Approaches can be traced down the centuries, and each time one took place it meant a clearer understanding of divine purpose, a new and fresh revelation, the institution of some form of a new religion and the sounding of a note which produced a new civilisation and culture, or a fresh recognition of relationship between God and man or man and his brother.

A new definition of God was given us when the Buddha taught that *God was Light* and showed us the way of illumination, and when Christ revealed to us that *God was Love* through His life and service on earth. Today the knowledge aspect of illumination is being comprehended, but the inner meaning of love is only now dimly sensed. Yet light and love have been revealed to the world by two great Sons of God in two Approaches. A new Approach is on the Way, bringing us the next needed truth. We ask ourselves: What will it be? For it, the knowers and lovers of God and of their fellowmen are prepared; for it, the masses of men wait.

Some of these Approaches have been of a major nature, affecting humanity as a whole, and some of them are of less importance affecting only a relatively small part of mankind—a nation or a group. Those Who come as the Revealers of the love of God come from that spiritual centre to which the Christ gave the name "the Kingdom of God." Here dwell the "spirits of just men made perfect"; here the spiritual Guides of the race are to be found and here the spiritual Executives of God's plans live and work and oversee human and planetary affairs. It is called by many names by many people. It is spoken of as the Spiritual Hierachy, as the Abode of Light, as the centre where the Masters of the Wisdom are to be found, as the Great White Lodge. From it come those who act as Messengers of the Wisdom of God, Custodians of the truth as it is in Christ, and Those Whose task it is to save the world, to impart the next revelation and to demonstrate divinity. All the world Scriptures bear witness to the existence of this centre of spiritual energy. This spiritual Hierarchy has been steadily drawing nearer to humanity as men have become more conscious of divinity and more fitted for contact with the divine.

Behind this spiritual centre of Love and Light another centre is to be found, for which the West has no name but which is called in the East by the name Shamballa. Perhaps the Western name is Shangri-Lha—a name which is finding recognition everywhere and which stands for a centre of happiness and purpose. Shamballa or Shangri-Lha is the place where the Will of God is focussed and from which His divine purposes are directed. From it the great political movements and the destiny of races and nations and their progress are determined, just as the religious movements, the cultural unfoldments and spiritual ideas are sent forth from the hierarchical centre of Love and Light. Political and social ideologies and world religions, the Will of God and the Love of God, the Purpose of divinity and the plans whereby that purpose is brought into activity all focus through that centre of which we are each consciously a part, Humanity itself. There are, therefore, three great spiritual centres on the planet: Shamballa, the spiritual Hierarchy, and Humanity.

There is definite Biblical testimony to this highest of all centres, Shamballa. At moments of crisis in the earthly life of Christ we read that a Voice spoke to Him, the Voice of the Father was heard by Him, affirming His Sonship and setting the seal of approval upon His acts and work. At that moment a great fusion of the two spiritual centres—the Hierarchy and Shamballa, the Kingdom of God and the world of Spirit—was brought about, and thus spiritual energy was released on Earth. We need to remember that the work of all World Saviours and Teachers is to act primarily as distributors of divine energy and as channels for spiritual force. This outpouring manifests either as the impulse behind a world religion, the incentive behind some new political ideology, or the principle of some scientific discovery of importance to the growth of the human spirit. Thus do religions, governments and civilisations find their motivation. History has demonstrated that again and again these developments are the results of the appearance and the activity of some great man at an advanced stage of development. Those who come forth as Teachers, Saviours or Founders of a new religion come forth from the Hierarchy and are of the highest order of spiritual perfection. Those who convey to man the purposes of God through new ideological concepts are not as yet of so high an order, because man is not yet ready for the highest presentation. Much has yet to be learnt and mastered by man, and spiritual unfoldment always outpaces the outer expression of human relationships and the social order; hence the world religions come first and produce the conditions which make the work of the rulers possible. Those who come forth from the spiritual centre, Shamballa, are of great power, however, and the thread of Their influence can be traced throughout history in great declarations and pronouncements such as the Magna Charta, the Declaration of Independence and the Atlantic Charter. Those who come forth from Shamballa or the Hierarchy for the release and the guidance of humanity are evoked by human desire and demand, for there is a spiritual interplay existing between Humanity and the Hierarchy, and between both and Shamballa.

Such Messengers embody divine intention. The response of mankind to Their messages is dependent upon the point in evolution which has been attained by man. Back in the early history of the race these Approaches were rare indeed.

Countless ages passed between them. Today, owing to the greatly increased power of the human mind and the growing sensitivity of the human soul to the spiritual values as they express themselves through major world ideologies, these Approaches of the divine to the human can become more frequent and are taking on a new form. Man's inner realisation of his own innate spiritual potency and the unfoldment of his sense of relationship are bringing about an effort on his part—consciously undertaken—to make true progress towards the good, the true and the beautiful, and this in spite of the fact of the war and the misery and suffering present upon our Earth. It has therefore become possible to synchronise the Approach of the divine to the human and to instruct the masses of men in the technique of thus invoking the Approach. This attitude of humanity will lead to a new revelation, to the new world religion and to new attitudes in the relation of man to God (religion) and of man to man (government or social relationships).

Two major Approaches are to be found in the past history of the race, and both are of such significance that it would be well to note them here. They lie so far back in human history that we have only myth and monument to indicate their happening.

The first great Approach of the divine to man caused the appearance of the human soul and the adding of another kingdom in nature to the three (mineral, vegetable and animal) already existing. The kingdom of man appeared on Earth.

Aeons passed away whilst primitive man continued to evolve, and then the second great Approach took place and the Spiritual Hierarchy of our planet drew nearer to humanity; the spiritual Way to God was opened for those who consciously can move forward, who can definitely demonstrate the Christ spirit, and who earnestly seek enlightenment and liberation. The true appeal of Christ's words: "Ye shall know the truth and the truth shall make you free" urges them to move forward into the light, through the gate of initiation and on to that path which "shineth ever more and more until the perfect day." At the time of the second great Approach, the fact of the existence of the Spiritual Hierarchy, of the open door to initiation and of the Way of Sacrifice first dawned on the human consciousness; from that moment men have found the Way and have moved out of the human kingdom into the spiritual; they have transformed their human consciousness into divine awareness. The kingdom of man and the kingdom of God were brought into relationship. Religion became a factor in the development of the human spirit and God drew nearer to His Own. God Transcendent first conditioned man's concept of Deity. Then God as the national controller took possession of man's mind, and the Jehovah concept (as depicted in the Jewish dispensation) appeared; next God was seen as the perfected human being, and the divine God-man walked the Earth in the person of the Christ. Today, we have a rapidly growing emphasis on God Immanent in every human being. Such have been the results of the second great Approach and such have been the results of the work of the world Saviours and Teachers down the ages, culminating in the work of Christ, Who summed up in Himself the unfoldments of the past and the hope of the future.

A third great Approach is now possible and will take place once the world war is over and man—purified by fire and suffering—has set his house in order and is ready, therefore, for a new revelation. For this coming revelation the work of the Buddha and of the Christ has been preparatory. They embodied in Themselves two lesser Approaches, and through Their united effort, humanity throughout the world has been prepared to play its part in this third Approach.

The Buddha came embodying in Himself a great divine principle or quality. He was the Conveyor of Enlightenment to the world; He was the Lord of Light. As is always the case, He re-enacted in Himself, for the instruction of His disciples, the processes of illumination and became the "Illumined One." We are told in the scriptures of India that He achieved illumination *under the tree,* just as Christ achieved the liberation of the human spirit *upon the tree* set up on Golgotha. Light, wisdom, reason, as divine yet human attributes, were focussed in the Buddha. He proved the possibility of all men achieving this illumination and of walking in the light. He challenged the people to tread the Path of Illumination, of which wisdom, mental perception and intuition are the aspects.

Then came the next great Teacher, the Christ. He embodied in Himself a still greater divine principle or aspect, that of Love, whilst at the same time embracing within Himself all that the Buddha had of Light. Christ was the expression of both Light and Love.

Through Their work, therefore, there is now possible a deeper reaction to, and a broader comprehension of the work and influence of those great Lives Who are waiting today to help humanity. The work of these two Sons of God produced among many results the following:

1. They embodied in Themselves certain cosmic principles, and by Their work and sacrifice certain divine potencies poured through and upon the race, stimulating intelligence into wisdom and emotion into love. The Buddha, when He achieved illumination, "let in" a flood of light upon life and world problems. He formulated this revelation into the Four Truths. His group of disciples erected a structure of truth which (by the power of collective thought) has flooded mankind with light.

2. Through the message of the Buddha, man has for the first time grasped the cause of His constant distaste and dissatisfaction and has learnt that the Way of Release is to be found in detachment, dispassion and discrimination. Where these are present, there is rapid release from the wheel of rebirth.

3. Through the message of the Christ, three concepts emerge into the racial consciousness:

a. The value of the individual and the necessity for tensity of effort on his part.
b. The opportunity which was to be presented to humanity

to take a tremendous step forward and undergo the new birth or the first initiation.

c. The method whereby this next step could be taken in the new age, voiced for us in the words "love your neighbor as yourself." Individual effort, group opportunity and men's identification with each other—such is the message of the Christ.

In the message of the Buddha we have the three methods whereby the personality can be changed and prepared to be a conscious expression of divinity. Through *detachment*, the brain consciousness or state of awareness (embodying physical recognition of inner causes) is withdrawn or abstracted from the things of the senses and from the calls of the lower nature. Detachment is in reality the imposition of a new rhythm or habit reaction upon the cells of the brain which renders the brain unaware of the lure of the world of sensory perception. Through *dispassion*, the emotional nature is rendered immune from the appeal of the senses and desire fails to deter the soul from its rightful task. Through *discrimination*, the mind learns to select the good, the beautiful and the true, and to substitute these for the sense of "identification with the personality," which is so characteristic of the majority of men. Personality holds so many in thrall. This has to go. These three attitudes, when correctly and sanely held, will organise the personality, bring in the rule of wisdom, and prepare the disciple for initiation.

Then follows the work of the Christ, resulting in an understanding of the value of the individual and his self-initiated effort at release and illumination, with the objective of group goodwill. We learn to perfect ourselves in order to have somewhat to sacrifice to the group, and thus enrich the group with our individual contribution. This is the first result of the activity of the Christ Principle in the life of the individual. Personality fades out in the glory of the soul, which (like the rising sun) blots out the darkness and irradiates the lower nature. This is the second result, and is a group activity. The word goes forth to the initiates of the future: Lose sight of self in group endeavour. Forget the self in group activity. Pass through the portal to initiation in group formation and let the personality life be lost in the group life.

The final result of the work of the Christ is to be found in our identification with the whole: individuality, initiation, and identification—these are the terms in which the message of the Christ can be summarised. He said, when on Earth: "I and my Father are One," and in these words epitomised His entire message. I, the individual, through initiation, am identified with Deity. Therefore we have:

1. The Buddha..the method..Detachment, Dispassion, Discrimination.
2. The Christ..the result..Individualism, Initiation, Identification.

It is interesting to note that the work of the Buddha is expressed in words all beginning with the fourth letter of the alphabet, the letter D. The sense of personality is achieved; the quaternary is transcended, and the Buddha gave us the reason for this transmutation and the rules. The work of the Christ is expressed for us in words beginning with the ninth letter of the alphabet, the letter I, and this number is the number of initiation. These things happen not idly but all have their underlying purpose.

I have here very briefly and inadequately outlined the nature of two great Approaches and two minor. These have prepared humanity for the third great Approach which will bring the new revelation, with its realised consequences, of a new heaven and a new earth. I would ask the orthodox theologian how he interprets the words "a new heaven"? May it not signify an entirely new conception as to the world of spiritual realities and perhaps of the very nature of God Himself? May it not be possible that our present ideas of God as the Universal Mind, as Love and as Will, may be enriched by a new idea and quality for which we have as yet no name or word and of which we have as yet no faintest understanding? Each of the three present concepts as to the divine nature—the Trinity—have been entirely new when first sequentially presented to humanity.

What this third major Approach will bring to humanity we do not and cannot know. It will bring about as definite results as did the two earlier Approaches. For some years now the spiritual Hierarchy has been drawing nearer to mankind, and this is responsible for the great concepts of freedom which are so close to the hearts of men everywhere today and for which humanity is now fighting. As the Members of the Hierarchy approach closer to us, the dream of brotherhood, of fellowship, of world cooperation and of a peace (based upon right human relations) becomes clearer in our minds. As They draw nearer we vision a new and vital world religion, a universal faith, at-one in its basic idealism with the past but different in its mode of expression.

I have cited earlier the foundational truths upon which the new world religion will rest. I would suggest that the theme of the coming religion will be that of the great Approaches themselves; that it will emphasise anew God's love for man as evidenced in these divine Approaches, and also man's response to God as the word goes forth: "Draw near to God and He will draw near to you"; that it will—in its rites and ceremonies—be concerned with the invocative and evocative side of spiritual appeal.

Man invokes the divine Approach in two ways: by means of the inchoate, voiceless appeal or invocative cry of the masses, and also by the planned, defined invocation of the spiritually oriented aspirants, the intelligently convinced worker, disciple and initiate—by all, in fact, who form the New Group of World Servers.

The science of invocation and evocation will take the place of what we now call prayer and worship. Be not disturbed by the use of the word "science." It is not the cold and heartless intellectual thing so oft depicted. It is in reality the intelligent organisation of spiritual energy and of the forces of love, and when effective, will evoke the response of spiritual Beings Who can again walk openly among men and thus establish a close relation and a constant communication between humanity and the spiritual Hierarchy.

It will be obvious to you that as humanity, through its most advanced units, prepares for this next great Approach it must accept with faith and conviction (faith for the masses, and conviction for the knowers and the new group of world servers) the premises stated above:

1. The fact of God (God Transcendent)
2. Man's relationship to the divine (God Immanent)
3. The fact of immortality
4. The Brotherhood of man (God in expression)
5. The existence of the Way to God
6. The historicity of the two great Approaches and the possibility of a third and imminent Approach.

It is here that the churches, if regenerated, can concentrate their efforts, cease perpetuating the outer and visible form, and begin to deal with the reality underlying all dogmas and doctrines. Upon these inner assurances man must take his stand, and a study of them will reveal that the majority of the unthinking masses (an immense majority) do accept them hopefully and with desire, though without any definite understanding, and that a steadily increasing minority also accept them with a full convinced awareness—an awareness that is the result of the transformation of hope into self-proven fact. In between these two extremes is a large group of questioning people; they are not part of the unintelligent mass, nor are they yet either occultists, mystics or even aspirants. They question and seek conviction; they repudiate faith as unintelligent, but long for a substitute; they are constantly emerging out of the mass of men and constantly moving forward in consciousness through the following of spiritual techniques, eventually taking their stand among those who can say with St. Paul: "I *know* Whom I have believed." It is with these techniques that the true religious teaching should primarily concern itself.

As we look ahead into the world of tomorrow and begin

to question what structure the faith of humanity should assume and what building the skill of the knowers will erect to house the religious spirit of man, three more fundamental truths appear to be emerging as necessary adjuncts to the revealed body of truth:

1.   The *demonstrated* existence of a Spiritual Hierarchy, the life-purpose of which is the good of humanity. The Members of the Hierarchy are seen to be the Custodians of the divine Plan and expressions of the Love of God.

2.   The development of the Science of Invocation and Evocation as a means and method of approach to divinity. This will grow out of the ancient habits of prayer as used by the masses, and the practice of meditation as developed by the mystics and occultists. Prayer and meditation are the preliminary steps to this emerging science, and what is vaguely called "worship" is the group effort to establish some form of united approach to the spiritual Hierarchy, functioning under the guidance and control of the Christ and related to the highest spiritual centre, Shamballa, through its most advanced individuals, just as humanity is related to the Hierarchy by its spiritually minded people.

3.   The realisation that the starry heavens, the solar system and the planetary spheres are all of them the manifestations of great spiritual Lives and that the interrelation between these embodied Lives is as real and effectual as is the relation between members of the human family.

The spiritual Hierarchy of the planet, the ability of mankind to contact its Members and to work in cooperation with Them, and the existence of the greater Hierarchy of spiritual energies of which our tiny planetary sphere is a part—these are the three truths upon which the coming world religion may be based.

Relationship to God, through Christ, has ever been the teaching of the spiritual leaders of the world, no matter by what name they called Him. In the future we shall draw closer and more intelligently to the living substance of

Reality and be more definite in our apprehension of this hitherto vaguely sensed relationship. We shall know and see and understand. We shall not just believe, have hope and try to comprehend. We shall speak openly of the Hierarchy and of its Members and Their work. The hierarchical nature of all spiritual Lives, and the fact of the great "chain of hierarchies" stretching all the way up from the mineral kingdom through the human and the kingdom of God to apparently remote spiritual groups, will be emphasised. Then there will open for the spiritual Lives what has been called "the Way of the Higher Evolution." Much along these lines has been given out during the past two centuries. The fact of the existence of the Hierarchy is consciously recognised by hundreds of thousands today, though still denied by the orthodox; the general public are familiar with the idea of the existence of the Masters, and either gullibly accept the mass of futile and idiotic information handed out by many today or fight furiously against the spread of this teaching. Others are open-minded enough to investigate whether the teaching is true and to follow the techniques suggested, in the hope that hypothesis may turn to fact. This last group is steadily increasing in number and upon their accumulating evidence belief can be translated into knowledge. So many *know* the truth today; so many people of integrity and worth are cooperating *consciously* with Members of this Hierarchy that the very foundations of the ecclesiastical antagonisms and the belittling comments of the concrete minded are of no avail. What the orthodox theologian and the narrow doctrinaire have to offer no longer satisfies the intelligent seeker or suffices to answer his questions; he is shifting his allegiances into wider and more spiritual areas. He is moving out from under doctrinal authority into direct personal, spiritual experience and coming under the direct authority which contact with Christ and His disciples, the Masters, gives.

In considering our second point, the Science of Invocation and Evocation, we are also moving forward into the area of mental understanding. The grasping nature of many of the prayers of men, based as they are upon desire for something, has long disturbed the intelligent; the vagueness of the meditation taught and practised in the East and in the West, and its emphatically selfish note (personal liberation and personal knowledge) are likewise causing a revolt. The demand today is for group work, group good, group knowledge, group contact with the divine, group salvation, group understanding and group relationship to God and the Spiritual Hierarchy. All this indicates progress.

At this point it should be useful to repeat part of what I said elsewhere concerning future developments along this line. (*The Reappearance of the Christ,* pages 152-159.)

This new invocative work will be the keynote of the coming world religion and will fall into two parts. There will be the invocative work of the masses of the people, trained by the spiritually minded people of the world (working in the churches, whenever possible, under an enlightened clergy) to accept the fact of the approaching spiritual energies, focussed through the spiritual Hierarchy, and to voice their spiritual demand for light, liberation and understanding. There will also be the trained, scientific work of appeal and invocation as practised by those who have trained their minds through right meditation, who know the uses of sound, of formulas and of invocation, and who can work consciously, focussing the invocative cry of the masses and at the same time using certain great formulas of words which will later be given to the race, as *The Lord's Prayer* was given by the Christ and *The Great Invocation* has been given in this day and age.

This new religious science (for which prayer, meditation and ritual have laid the foundation) will train its students to present, at certain stated periods throughout the year, the voiced demand of the people of the world for relationship with God and with each other. This work, when rightly carried forward, will evoke response from the waiting Hierarchy; through this response, the belief of the masses will gradually be changed into the conviction of the knowers. In this way humanity will be transformed and spiritualised.

Then will begin, as the ages pass away, the regeneration of material nature, with the two spiritual centres—the Hierarchy and Humanity—working together in full consciousness and understanding. The Kingdom of God will be functioning on Earth.

It will be apparent to you that I can indicate only the broad general outlines of the new world religion. The expansion of the human consciousness which will take place as a result of the coming great Approach will enable man to grasp not only his relation to the spiritual Life of our planet, the "One in Whom we live and move and have our being," but will also give him a glimpse of the relation of our planet to the circle of planetary lives moving within the orbit of the Sun, and the still greater circle of spiritual Influences which contact our solar system as it pursues its orbit in the Heavens (the twelve constellations of the zodiac). Astronomical and astrological investigation has demonstrated this relationship and the influences exerted, but there is still speculation and much foolish claiming and interpretation. Yet the churches have ever recognised this relationship, and the Bible has testified to it. "The stars in their courses fought against Sisera"; "Who can withstand the sweet influences of the Pleiades?"; and many other passages bear out this contention of the Knowers. Many church festivals are fixed by reference to the moon or a zodiacal constellation. Investigation will prove this to be increasingly the case, and when the ritual of the new world religion is universally established this will be one of the important factors considered.

The establishing of certain major festivals in relation to the moon, and in a lesser degree to the zodiac, will bring a strengthening of the spirit of invocation and the resultant inflow of responsive influences. The truth lying behind all invocation is based upon the power of thought, particularly in its telepathic nature, rapport and aspect. The unified invocative thought of the masses and the focussed, directed thought of the New Group of World Servers constitute *an outgoing stream of energy*. This will reach telepathically those spiritual Beings Who are sensitive and responsive to such impacts. Their evoked response, sent out as spiritual energy, will in turn reach humanity, after having been stepped down into thought energy, and in that form will make its due impact upon the minds of men, convincing them and carrying inspiration and revelation. Thus has it ever been in the history of the spiritual unfoldment of the world and in the procedure followed in writing the world Scriptures.

Secondly, the establishing of a certain uniformity in the world religious rituals will aid men everywhere to strengthen each other's work and enhance powerfully the thought currents directed to the waiting Spiritual Lives. At present, the Christian religion has its great festivals, the Buddhist keeps his different set of spiritual events, and the Hindu has still another list of holy days. In the future world, when organised, all men of spiritual inclination and intention everywhere will keep the same holy days. This will bring about a pooling of spiritual resources and a united spiritual effort, plus a simultaneous spiritual invocation. The potency of this will be apparent.

Let me indicate the possibilities of such spiritual events, and prophesy the nature of the coming world-wide Festivals. There will be three such major Festivals each year, concentrated in three consecutive months, and leading therefore to a prolonged spiritual effort which will affect the remainder of the year. These will be:

1. *The Festival of Easter.* This is the festival of the risen, living Christ, the Teacher of all men and the Head of the Spiritual Hierarchy. He is the Expression of the Love of God. On this day the Spiritual Hierarchy which He guides and directs will be recognised, and the nature of God's love will be emphasised. This festival is determined always by the date of the first Full Moon of spring, and is the great Western and Christian festival.

2. *The Festival of Wesak.* This is the festival of the Buddha, the spiritual Intermediary between the highest

piritual centre, Shamballa, and the Hierarchy. The Buddha s the Expression of the Wisdom of God, the Embodiment of Light, and the Indicator of the divine Purpose. This will be fixed annually in relation to the Full Moon of May, as is at present the case. It is the great Eastern festival.

3. *The Festival of Goodwill.* This will be the festival of he spirit of humanity—aspiring towards God, seeking conformity with the Will of God and dedicated to the expression of right human relation. This will be fixed annually n relation to the Full Moon of June. It will be a day whereon the spiritual and divine nature of mankind will be recognised. On this festival, for two thousand years, he Christ has represented humanity and has stood before he Hierarchy and in the sight of Shamballa as the God-Man, the Leader of His people and "the Eldest in a great family of brothers" (Romans VIII:29). Each year at that ime He has preached the last sermon of the Buddha before he assembled Hierarchy. This will therefore be a festival of deep invocation and appeal, of a basic aspiration towards fellowship, of human and spiritual unity, and will represent he effect in the human consciousness of the work of the Buddha and of the Christ.

These three festivals are already being kept throughout he world, though they are not as yet related to each other, and as part of the unified spiritual Approach of humanity. The time is coming when all three festivals will be kept *simultaneously* throughout the world, and by their means a great spiritual unity will be achieved and the effects of he great Approach so close to us at this time will be stabilised by the united invocation of humanity throughout he planet.

The remaining full moons will constitute lesser festivals, but will be recognised to be also of vital importance. They will establish the divine attributes in the consciousness of man, just as the major festivals establish the three divine aspects. These aspects and qualities will be arrived at and determined by a close study of the nature of a particular constellation or constellations influencing those months. For instance, Capricorn (December) will call attention to the first initiation, the birth of the Christ in the cave of the heart, and indicate the training needed to bring about that great spiritual event in the life of the individual man. I give this one instance to you in order to indicate the possibilities for spiritual unfoldment that could be given through an understanding of these influences, and in order to revivify the ancient faiths by expanding them into their larger undying relationships.

We have, therefore, the following:

Shamballa ....the Will aspect of God...Wesak ....May Full Moon
                                                                     (Taurus)

Hierarchy ....the Love aspect of God...Easter ....April Full Moon
                                                                     (Aries)

Humanity .....divine Intelligence ......Goodwill ....June Full Moon
                                                                     (Gemini)

The remaining nine Full Moons will be concerned with the divine characteristics and their development in mankind.

Thus the twelve festivals will constitute a revelation of divinity. They will present a means of bringing about relationship, first of all during three months with the three great spiritual centres, the three expressions of the divine Trinity. The minor festivals will emphasise the inter-relation of the Whole, thus lifting the divine presentation out of the individual and the personal into that of the universal divine Purpose; the relationship of the Whole to the part and of the part to that Whole will be thereby fully expressed.

Humanity will therefore invoke the spiritual power of the Kingdom of God, the Hierarchy; the Hierarchy will respond, and God's plans will then be worked out on Earth. The Hierarchy, on a higher turn of the spiral, will invoke the centre of God's Will, Shamballa or Shangri-Lha, thus invoking the Purpose of God. Thus will the Will of God be implemented by Love and manifested intelligently; for this mankind is ready, and for this the Earth waits.

FACTORS IN THE WORLD SITUATION

April 1944

I have written to the world aspirants for many Wesaks now. I have again and again brought to your attention and theirs the close relation which is being established between the world of men and the world of souls. I have again and again pointed out that, under the Law of Evolution, certain great fusions, at-one-ments or great Approaches are taking place. I have indicated that the present activity of our planetary Logos is bringing certain major adjustments within the planetary sphere of influence and that these primarily affect the human kingdom. I have called to your notice the urgency of the incoming life, producing tension, spiritual recognitions of a far-reaching nature, the immediate overthrow of false Gods and standards, and the destruction of outworn and crystallised interpretations (called doctrines) of the spiritual realities. By these means, the way is cleared for a new and simple recognition of divinity which will satisfy not only the heart of the simplest person, but which will meet the need of the most intelligent. I have talked in terms of the union of Eastern and Western thought and of the need for the great civilisations—nurtured under the influence of Shri Krishna, the Buddha and the Christ—to be brought closer together. I have said (and I here re-affirm) that He Who comes will make this union possible and effective. This event will evoke world-wide recognition.

I have stated also that we are reaching a climaxing period in human history; in this period the Lords of Karma are unusually active; the Law of Cause and Effect is bringing the results of past activities, the subjective thinking and the secret impulses to the surface, and exacting penalty and the planned cleaning of the slate of human history. When He Whom all disciples serve was on Earth two thousand years ago, He said that secret things would be made plain; by this emergence of the good and of the bad into prominence, men will arrive at knowledge, at understanding, and will be forced to take those steps which will be needed to build a new and better world, based on the Law of Love and not on the Law of Separateness and hate. This is what is happening today.

I have said also that the Forces of Light are nearing the Earth and that the Hierarchy is coming steadily closer to mankind.

These basic events, these subjective happenings and these spiritual determinations—under the Law of Action and Reaction—have evoked a more rapid response from the Forces of Evil (present in our planetary life) than from humanity. Certain great Forces or embodied Energies of darkness and of evil organised themselves and took the needed steps (so they believed) to prevent humanity from stepping onward into light. They availed themselves of the weaknesses, the selfishness and the self-interest of man; just as good can stimulate the latent goodness in mankind into expression, so evil can evoke greater evil from those susceptible from innate weakness, and from the unthinking and emotional: the Forces of Light work only with men's souls. Lies, false teaching, evil propaganda, a war of nerves, the culture of fear, the organisation of groups and of isolated workers in every nation pledged to undermine righteousness and distort the truth, went rapidly forward. Great and fundamental truths were twisted to meet the ends of the evil workers.

The doctrine, for instance, of the super-race was interpreted to mean the superiority of the German nation and culture to all in the West, whilst the divinity of the Sons of Heaven (the Japanese race) was emphasised to all in the East. The bewildered peoples of both nations were led to believe that they had a great and spiritual mission to dominate the world.

This was the first result of the approach of the Kingdom of God to the earth, or rather to the physical plane. In that kingdom men of all races will demonstrate their divinity; the kingdom of souls will be recognised as the universal home and race of all men. Separative nationalities will, in that kingdom, have no place or recognition.

The Forces of Evil sought for those leaders and groups who are the materialistic correspondence to the spiritual leaders and those who seek to guide humanity along right lines. They took possession (and I use this word with deliberation) of the evil men who led the Axis Powers— Hitler, Tojo, Goebbels, Ribbentrop, Himmler and—to a much lesser degree—Mussolini, Hess, Goering and others. They completely overpowered the minds of these men, already distorted with ambition and sadistic inclinations. Who, you ask, do I mean by "they"? I mean those intelligent evil, unloving, hateful Individualities who are to the world of selfish and material focus what the Hierarchy of Masters, working under the Christ, are to struggling human aspirants. The power of these evil forces is enormous, for they recognise no restrictions or ordinary decent, human limitations; they work through violence, coercion, cruelty, hate, terror and lies; they aim to subjugate the human consciousness through the complete control of men's minds, through the withholding of good and the promulgation of evil. They stimulate the brains of men through the extent of their evil and magical knowledge; I mean this literally and physically. The Great White Lodge, working under the inspiration of the Christ and of Shamballa, functions necessarily under certain spiritual restrictions. Coercion is not permitted; the minds of men must be and are left free; the stimulation of the souls of men *is* permitted, because it results in the stimulation of the expression of love and of understanding, leading to right human relations. These spiritual restrictions greatly slow down the progress of the Forces of Light; it should interest you to remember that the length of the war was partly dependent upon the inability of the Armies of the Lord to commit the crimes for which the Axis Powers have been responsible. The physical activities of the Forces of Light do recognise certain limitations, and of this the Forces of Evil take constant advantage. The bombing of massed populations was started by Hitler and could have been ended by him immediately if he so chose.

There is another aspect of this matter to which I would like to call your attention. These restrictions which the Forces of Light recognise have also an undesirable effect where the unintelligent and well-meaning are concerned, and where those who are emotionally polarised interpret the Law of Love. The United Nations, working for human liberation and freedom (and therefore working under the Law of Love, rightly understood) is prevented from following the lines of indiscriminate cruelty which characterised the German and Japanese techniques: torture, starvation, lying propaganda, misuse of prisoners, the dissemination of a terror campaign. These are not permitted by the rules of the Brothers of Humanity. From a purely physical angle, this can be interpreted as putting the "Armies of the Lord" at a disadvantage. It is this right attitude on the part of the Forces of Light which has an undesirable effect upon the appeasers and pacifists of the world. These would, for humanitarian reasons and from love of the *forms* through which humanity functions, bring the war to an immediate end.

In their well-meaning blindness they would sacrifice the future of humanity and the lives of millions of people at a later date for a temporary cessation of hostilities. I would emphasise to you that the Forces of Evil must be defeated *now;* the evil leaders must be wrenched from their high place, and the complete defeat and annihilation of those responsible for launching this horror on humanity is an absolute necessity and bounden duty, if security, well-being and a new order of happier living is to be the lot of coming generations. A temporary ending of the war would only give time for the Forces of Evil to reorganise, and the future war would be infinitely worse than this one. This the intelligent humanitarian is saying, and this is the opinion of the Hierarchy. The Hierarchy stands firmly on the side of those who demand a war to a finish, and the reasons are the ultimate saving of millions of lives and the preservation of certain basic spiritual values.

The issue is far more serious spiritually than you know;

he work of the Hierarchy is handicapped not only by the restrictions under which the Forces of Light must work, but also by the work and utterances of the silly little men with small vision who see not the future possibilities if the war came to an inconclusive finish, and who (for the present comfort of the present generation) would sacrifice the children of tomorrow and later generations. The work of the Hierarchy is handicapped by the attitudes of men with no perspective and much selfishness, of no cruelty but of stupid thinking. These men—in the houses of legislature in the various United Nations, in Parliament, in Congress, and in the churches—plead for the cessation of the war before victory is won and before the enemies of humanity are beaten to their knees in supplication for mercy and in a demand for peace. They see the end of business as they have known it; they see the familiar landmarks of their comfortable world disappearing; they dislike the results of the war as it affects them; or they cannot bear the general suffering and prompted by pity they demand an immediate peace. Others are prompted by isolationism and the desire to withdraw from participation in the misery of war; others hate those whose duty it is to carry the war to a successful climax, or see their particular ambitions threatened by the conditionings of a changing world. They would sacrifice future generations, as I have said above, to their short-sighted policy and feeble judgment. They spread disunity, therefore, and shackle the hands of those administering· in high places. Their efforts prolong the war, dishearten the fighting forces, break down national and military morale, and lay a poor foundation for the work of the post-war world. There are many of these in every nation, there are too many in the United States of America; there are none in the U. S. S. R., and hence her triumphant march forward.

You have, consequently, in the world today:

1. *The Forces of Evil,* working through Germany and Japan. To date, they are holding their own and they are not yet defeated. They are terrorising the world. Within

their own national borders they do not possess enough people with courage, understanding, or with the ability to think clearly, who hate evil and who can hold to a vision. There is little in either nation to bring assistance to the Forces of Light. The Germans were deceived from the beginning, and a widespread national deception, backed by a terror campaign, argues a general weakness, lack of courage and a natural predilection for evil guidance. The tendency to be led along aggressive, selfish and evil lines has been characteristic of the German mentality for a great length of time. This negative nation, with its arrogant psychology (one of the great paradoxes of the ages), must be taught the ways of positive good, and a courageous championing of righteousness must take the place of the present negative acceptance of evil. With humility and intelligence must the German nation be taught to take a proper place in the community of nations. The Japanese nation, in spite of its great age, must go back into the nursery state; it must be taught, as children are taught, to be social and not anti-social, and it will be long before it will be safe to trust this nation. The Italian nation presents no greater problem than does any other nation in the world. It is normal, as are the United Nations; the German nation and the Japanese race are not normal, and must be brought back to normality by careful, kindly, but firm handling, and by applied educational processes.

2.   *The Forces of Light*. I would here correct an impression which exists among esotericists. By this phrase, (the Forces of Light), they are apt to mean that the Hierarchy is literally fighting against the Axis nations. This is not so in the physical sense. The Hierarchy works—as you well know—with the souls of men and with those minds which are so oriented and disposed that they react to soul impression. When I use the expression "the Forces of Light" I mean those enlightened nations upon whom the light of Freedom shines and who will refuse, at all costs, to relinquish that light. There is no freedom in Germany or in

Japan. In a lesser sense and for a brief time, there was no freedom in Italy, but Italy must be counted among the enlightened nations, for it could not be held in duress. The Forces of Light comprise those nations (working through their armies and in the diplomatic arena) who are today fighting for the freedom of humanity, for the eternal rights of man, for liberty of conscience, for the position of the individual in any nation, and for freedom of religion or the right of man's self-chosen approach to the spiritual realities. Behind these nations stands the Hierarchy. Freedom is the birthright of mankind, and free will is the highest of the divine characteristics. Freedom is misinterpreted and misused by many, owing to the point in evolution of the mass of humanity, but it is a fundamental, divine principle; and where principles are involved the Hierarchy knows no compromise. There is no spiritual principle behind any of the activities of the Axis Powers, behind German activity or Japanese aggression. Therefore, the Hierarchy does *not* stand with power or strength behind any of their efforts.

3. *Humanity as a whole.* The men, women and children of the world are all implicated in and affected by this universal war. The effects reach into the most isolated village, the most extensive desert and the highest mountain top, as well as into the cities and congested areas of all the nations. No one is exempt from the consequences of this present catastrophe. The bulk of humanity are universal and innocent sufferers. The majority scarcely realise what it is all about; they view this great historical climax from the purely self-centered angle and from the point of view of how it affects them as individuals and their nation as a whole. An increasing number are coming to realise that this war must be fought to a successful finish because there is no peace or hope or right world relationships as long as two nations—one in the Western hemisphere and the other in the Eastern—can precipitate disaster upon countless millions. A minority are realising that the war has precipitated the condensed evil of the ages and that humanity is faced with the oppor-

tunity of erasing past errors, ancient selfishness and in-
grained wickedness, and of inaugurating a new and better
world. In this new world there will be freedom of approach
to God, opportunity for individual expression, freedom to
live in right relations and scope for creative living. A few—
a very few—know that this is a climaxing point in an ancient
conflict between Christ with His Hierarchy of Masters, and
"spiritual wickedness in high places." A mere handful of
knowers and disciples know, past all controversy and discussion, that, heading up those unhappy lands—Germany and
Japan—are ancient leaders who have again sought to bring
planetary disaster and to deflect the ends and the aims of
the Great White Lodge.

Among all these are thousands who stand bewildered,
sensing the truth but feeling helpless in the face of the
gigantic horror which the evil gang now ruling Germany
has precipitated upon humanity. They tend to right thinking
but are still the prey of the unscrupulous and the selfish.
When their thinking has been guided into right lines
through a process of right presentation of the situation,
they will constitute a powerful asset to the Forces of Light.

Such is the situation with which the Hierarchy and
humanity is today faced. The strength of the Forces of
Light is growing; the power of the Forces of Darkness may
be waning but is still vastly strong—upon the physical plane.
Their main hold is upon the minds of men and that is
exceedingly potent and unweakened, for it is aided by the
mild, unthinking person, by the bewildered, the pacifist,
the appeaser and the isolationist. The idealism of this group
is turned to the aid of Germany by the skilful evil workers.
The German armies are still unbeaten; central Europe is a
mighty fortress, dominated by the arch enemy of mankind,
sitting on his mountain-top. There, symbolically, he is to
be found, the initiator into evil conditions, and into slavery.
The armies of the Lord stand poised, and victory will be
theirs when there is complete unity of purpose, concentrated attention upon right human relations, and a

spread of idealistic aspiration to all who are fighting this battle for freedom. For this unity of purpose all the enlightened people of the world must work. It is not yet adequately present.

Let us now turn to the work of the Hierarchy and to the event for which all initiates and disciples are now preparing—the coming Wesak Festival.

THE TASK OF IMPLEMENTING THE WILL-TO-GOOD

May 1944

How is the Hierarchy working at this time? In what manner are the Masters aiding the work of the Forces of Light? Can something of moment and of lasting significance happen at this coming May Full Moon? How do the Masters look at the world situation? What are Their plans? Can these plans be materialised? And what can the individual disciple, initiate and world disciple accomplish in the face of humanity's dilemma?

These are all normal and intelligent questions and can be answered partially, though not fully, owing to three reasons:

1. The outcome of the coming climaxing conflict depends on humanity itself. A greater effort is required, particularly in America—an effort to see the issues clearly, to understand the causes of this war, and a determination to take those steps—through propaganda and discussion—which will clarify the minds of the masses. Into these age-long causes I cannot here go; there is not time to do more than enumerate certain of them

   a. Universal and ancient selfishness, materialism, aggression, and national prides. Of these faults all nations have been guilty.
   b. A sense of separateness of which the border issue between such nations as Russia and Poland is symbolic. The need of humanity and its general well-being comes

eternally first. Nations and their ephemeral disputes are of secondary interest.

c. A tendency—centuries old—among the Germanic peoples to dominate, to take what is not their own, to regard themselves as unique, superior, and as embodying a super-race; there is also a fixed determination, on behalf of their own interests, to plunge other nations and races into war. Today they have achieved a planetary war.

2.   There are factors present in this battle between evil and good which are so deeply esoteric and hidden from the understanding of the most advanced human being that it is useless for me to enlarge upon their existence. They are concerned with the ability of the mind, or of the mind principle, to react to truth or to lies; the mystery of this reaction is hidden in the evolutionary process itself. A point can be reached in human development where acceptance of deception is impossible and clear thinking is normal. The potency of glamour (which holds so many people in prison) is related to this mystery. Glamour holds not those who are mentally and emotionally undeveloped; they are complete realists and see life in its bare outlines and baldly. The highly developed are not subject to glamour; they also think realistically but this time with true mental perception and not instinctively. The thinking man, in his process of training, but who is still largely governed by his emotions, is exceedingly prone to glamour, and very often to the glamour of a sentimental so-called loving attitude. These people do not realise that love is a process of determining action on the basis of the ultimate good of the individual or the group, and that the immediate reactions of the personality are secondary. In this conflict the Hierarchy is concerned with the final issue, with the future welfare and the ultimate well-being of humanity. They are not so concerned with the immediate suffering and pain of the personalities involved. Is this a hard saying? A tiny replica of this correct attitude can be found in the influence, words and actions of those wise parents, those far-sighted guides

of youth, who see the need of discipline if their children are in the future to be rightly oriented, and to live correctly. The temporary discomfort of the discipline and the rebellion of the children do not in any way condition such parents. They see ahead.

3. The conflict at present involving humanity has its source not only in human weakness and selfishness, but in a situation which has existed for ages between the Great White Lodge of Masters and the Lodge of Black Adepts. This started in Atlantean times and must now be fought out to a finish. With the details of this struggle (fought on mental levels) you have no concern, except in so far as you and the rest of mankind react to lies or to truth. Two streams of mental energy or of thought-directed ideas impinge powerfully at this time upon the human consciousness. One is embodied in the lying propaganda emanating from the Axis Powers and affecting potently not only their own peoples but the selfish politicians, the intolerant and the racially conditioned people, and the well-intentioned but short-sighted appeasers and pacifists. The second stream is embodied in the idealism, the humanitarianism, and the clear presentation of the factual situation which characterise the best minds in every nation and which condition the thinking of the leaders of the United Nations; this stream has, for instance, conditioned the attitude and the changed orientation of the U. S. S. R., and has brought them to a position of cooperation and to a relinquishing of some of their separative ideas.

The leader of the conflict against evil in high places is the Christ, the Head of the Hierarchy. What is the attitude of the Christ at this time? In all reverence, and as one of His humblest friends and personal workers, I am permitted to tell you a little of His position as He nears the great event in May of this year. He knows Himself to be the inner spiritual Commander of the Armies of the Lord. His is the responsibility of awakening the souls of men to their presented opportunity and to the need of bringing

to an end this ancient conflict between the Lords of Evi
and the Messengers of Light. His has been the problem o
teaching humanity that, in order to demonstrate true love
and to provide scope and opportunity for a civilisation ir
which love, brotherhood and right human relations are gov
erning factors, those essential steps must be taken whicl
will accomplish this.

He said when He was on earth two thousand years ago
"I came not to bring peace, but a sword." The sword o
the spirit is wielded by the Hierarchy, and by its mean:
cosmic evil is arrested; the sword of discrimination is wielded
by the initiates and the disciples of the world, and by it.
means the distinction between good and evil, with a conse
quent presentation of free choice between the two, has beer
laid before humanity, and the lines of demarcation have
been made abundantly clear in this world war. It hac
been the hope of the Christ and the longing of all the
Masters that men would see clearly and make free anc
right choice, so that—without physical plane warfare—they
would bring about the needed changes and the ending of
wrong conditions. But the conflict descended on to the
physical plane and the sword of material war (symbolically
speaking) was taken up by humanity.

Forget not (particularly those of you who are outraged
by physical conflict through your pacifist inclinations) that
in the West, it was Germany which first of all took the
sword in hand, marching into Poland and bringing misery
devastation and cruelty to a smaller and much weaker
nation, thus forcing France and Great Britain to fulfill
their pledged obligations to that little nation and to declare
war upon the aggressor. It was Japan who brought war
into the Eastern hemisphere. The Forces of Light were
left with no alternative but to fight in defense of freedom.

Prior to the war, the Hierarchy did what it could to
change the trend of human living and thinking, awakening
the consciences of the intelligent, stimulating the activity
of the humanitarians and impressing the minds of Their
disciples in order to arouse goodwill, a driving desire for

right human relations and peaceful conditions. But the movement was not strong enough; the sword appeared on earth and mankind was plunged into war.

Since then the work of impressing the minds of the world disciples and of those whom they can influence has been along the lines of clarifying the issues, making plain that for which we fight, and arousing men and women to take such action as will, once and for all, end the possibility of a similar world cataclysm.

The activities of our Master, the Christ, fall into three categories:

1. Stiffening the will to fight on behalf of the spiritual issues and for the great humanitarian aims of the Hierarchy.
2. Impressing the minds of diplomats, thinkers and lovers of mankind to work out now certain post-war plans which will entirely change our present civilisation and bring about the new.
3. Arousing the minds of the masses and turning them— each in his own place and manner—into a more religious channel. The growth of spiritual desire and aspiration is phenomenal today, could you but see the indications as the workers on the inner side do.

Our Master, the Christ, is also at this time carrying forward three major activities. I can tell you briefly what they are, but only the disciples of the world will grasp the true implications.

He is, first of all, occupied with the process of deflecting the will-energy, emanating from Shamballa, in such a way that it will not be seized upon and misused by the Axis Powers in order to stiffen their peoples into increased opposition to the Forces of Light. It must be rechannelled and used to stiffen the purpose of the United Nations to carry the war to a finish of victory and of triumph, to increase the will-to-unity of all the allied peoples and to make firm the intention of the post-war planners that freedom, educational facilities, truth and right living shall be the lot of the incoming generation. This necessitates on the part of the Christ a concentration for which we have no equivalent word and a purely spiritual endeavour (a monadic effort) of which we have no faintest idea.

Secondly, He is working within the confines of the Hierarchy itself, preparing His disciples, the Masters, for certain great post-war events. For the war *will* end. The Restoration of the Mysteries, the initiation of those disciples who have stood firm and unafraid during the war, the enlargement of Their ashrams, owing to the almost unforeseen development of the spiritual sense among the world aspirants who would not normally have become disciples during this incarnation, and also the externalisation of Their ashrams during the next one hundred years, preparatory to the reappearance of the Hierarchy upon earth, are some of His present hierarchical responsibilities. These involve a tremendous expenditure of force, of second ray energy, just as His first activity demands an unusual expenditure of first ray power—something which even He, in His high place, is only now learning to handle, as a pledged Disciple of Sanat Kumara.

His third activity is the effort to offset the growing hate in the world, to strengthen the trend towards unity, and to show people everywhere the danger of separateness. A growing and (from the worldly point of view) reasonable hatred of the German people and of the Japanese is steadily rising. This hate they have brought upon themselves. Hate ever lacks discrimination. The great Law of Spiritual Retribution requires that justice be meted out, but hatred will close the eyes of justice. The law must be administered, and the world will see the expression of that same law, stated in the words, "Whatsoever a man soweth, that shall he also reap." But the materialistic law of hate and of separation must be negated and offset. The problem with which the Christ is faced is wellnigh—from the human angle—insoluble. He will require the united effort of all men of goodwill to stem the rising tide of hate—the floodgates of which were opened by Germany when she began her attacks upon the

Jews; she is now in danger of drowning in the waters which she has set loose. There is also a rising tendency to separation among certain of the Allied Nations, with which the Christ must deal. Several of them are as houses divided against themselves. Such are Poland, France, Yugoslavia and Greece. How can their differences be reconciled?

The hate of those who have suffered at the hands of the Axis Powers, or as a result of war conditions, must be offset. How can this be done? Such are some of the problems with which the Christ is wrestling. He must work through His disciples, and They must be trained. He must work through the stimulation of the hearts of the intelligent people and of the humanitarians everywhere. He must pour out the life-giving energy of the Christ-life on a wide scale throughout the entire world, and do so in the midst of those conditions wherein human receptivity and sensitivity are at their lowest point, owing to the numbness which comes through intense suffering. He stands in His place unmoved and unafraid, with clear perception of the truth and spiritual insight into the true situation. In collaboration with His great Brother, the Buddha, He is preparing for the next step.

Today the Hierarchy is facing a climaxing activity. From the Full Moon of May, 1944, until the Full Moon of May, 1945, the Members of the Hierarchy will unitedly be putting forth Their maximum effort to close the door upon the Forces of Evil, to direct the Shamballa energy (now let loose upon the world) so that its *destructive* aspect may be transmuted or directed towards the stimulation which will result in the rebuilding of the world. This will then affect not only the Members of the Hierarchy, but all on Earth who respond to hierarchical impression. Have the following statement in mind:

> The focussed and concentrated work of the Hierarchy at the time of the Full Moon of May, 1944 is—by Their united effort, Their blended thought and Their illumined will power, under the trained guidance of

the Buddha and the Christ—to withdraw the energy
of the will-to-separation and aggression (a distortion
of first ray energy) away from the Forces of Evil and
channel it again, via the Hierarchy; it will then demonstrate as the Will-to-Good, and this will express itself
via the men of goodwill on Earth. This requires a great
Act of Absorption by the Hierarchy.

The Buddha will start the process at the time of His appearance, through the use of a great first ray mantram.
This can be used only by someone of His initiate standing
and in collaboration with the Lord of the World. He will
thereby deflect the Shamballa force which the Adepts of
the Black Lodge have turned loose into the Axis nations;
this has been made possible by their receptivity to the will-
to-power. He will "corral" it (if I may use such a colloquial
and inappropriate term) and will place it at the disposal of
the Christ. The reception and the acceptance of this first
ray energy will require a tremendous effort upon the part
of the Christ, the Custodian of the energy of the second
Ray of Love-Wisdom. It is for this "reception" that He
started to prepare at the time of the April Full Moon.

I have told you elsewhere that this direct impact of the
Shamballa energy upon humanity very seldom occurs. It
has been loosed only three times during the entire history
of the human kingdom. At other times, it makes its impact
directly upon the Hierarchy, and is then transmuted or
stepped down so that humanity can take it. The three times
it has been directed, unimpeded and untransmuted, towards
humanity are:

1. At the time of the individualisation of animal-man
   when the mind principle was implanted. This was
   the birth hour of the human soul.
2. In Atlantean days when the power of the Black
   Lodge was so great that defeat faced the Hierarchy
   and the destruction of the human soul. Shamballa
   then interfered, and the world of that time was

destroyed. This period is recognised in modern history as the time of the Great Flood.

3. Today, once again, the Powers of Darkness are attempting to destroy humanity and the spiritual values. The power of Shamballa was let loose, destroying old forms—political, social and religious— but at the same time this power was seized upon by the evil forces to destroy the souls of men, to precipitate war and to destroy the cities and all our centres of civilisation and culture. The first phase or form of destruction was directed by the disciples, the aspirants and the clear thinking people of the world, and this was needed and very good. The old social, political and religious forms were stultifying the human soul and handicapping all progress. The second phase or form of destruction was directed by evil, and was focussed through those nations who· had succumbed to the glamour of superiority, to the temptation of material aggression and to intolerant racial hatreds, implemented by cruelty and barbarism.

The time has now come when this divine energy must express itself through the second aspect of the will-to-good, and not through the first aspect, the will-to-power. Mankind has had to be shown that it is not yet ready for power, because the will-to-good is not adequately strong to balance this first aspect of the will.

This then is the task of the Christ and of the Buddha at the time of the May Full Moon—to channel and redirect the Shamballa force. If They can do this, the result will be a new realisation and accomplishment of the will-to-good by the new group of world servers, under the receptive guidance of the world disciples and a responsive activity of the men and women of goodwill.

Therefore, get this clearly in mind, so that your cooperation can be intelligent and rightly directed.

First, *at the time of the May Full Moon,* the Buddha

will sound out a great mantram and become the "absorbing Agent" of the first ray force. He will use the magnetic power of the second ray to attract this force to Himself and will hold it steady, prior to redirecting it. The Christ will then—on behalf of the Hierarchy—become the "receiving Agent" of this potent energy, and the seven groups of Masters Who work with the human and sub-human kingdoms will (in response to His demand) become the "directing Agents" for the sevenfold expression of this force.

Second, *at the time of the June Full Moon,* the Hierarchy, under the guidance of the Christ, will let loose this will-to-good upon humanity, producing seven great results, according to the seven subrays of this first Ray of Will or Power:

1. Power will be given to the disciples of the world and the initiates among men, so that they can direct efficiently and wisely the coming process of rebuilding.

2. The will-to-love will stimulate the men of goodwill everywhere so that hatred will gradually be overcome and men will seek to live together cooperatively. This will take some time, but the inner urge is there and subject to stimulation.

3. The will-to-action will lead intelligent people throughout the world to inaugurate those activities which will lay the foundation for a new, better and happier world.

4. The will-to-cooperate will steadily increase also. Men will desire and demand right human relations—a result more general than that produced by the activity of the first three aspects of this ray, but which will be a natural outcome of this activity.

5. The will-to-know and to think correctly and creatively will become an outstanding characteristic of the masses. Knowledge is the first step towards wisdom.

6. The will-to-persist (which is an aspect of devotion and idealism) will become a human characteristic—a sublimation of the basic instinct of self-preservation. This will

lead to a persistent belief in the ideals presented by the Hierarchy, and the demonstration of immortality.

7. The will-to-organise will further a building process which will be carried forward under the direct inspiration of the Hierarchy. The medium will be the potency of the will-to-good of the new group of world servers and the responsive goodwill of mankind.

I have expressed in these few simple terms the results of the planned determination of the two Great Lords which must take shape and emerge at the time of the May and June Full Moons. What they succeed in doing will take years to demonstrate, but the end is inevitable once the right direction of the will-to-good has been achieved. This demonstration is dependent, however, upon two things:

1. The focussed work of the Christ and of the Hierarchy during the coming year, until May 1945.
2. The reflective thinking and careful planning of the new group of world servers during the same period.

Much outer activity upon a planetary scale will not be possible till 1945, but much can then become possible if hierarchical requirements are met. A year of preparation for the tremendous task of implementing the will-to-good and of producing a better civilisation and way of life is short indeed.

The Christ has gone into retreat for a month and cannot be reached even by the Masters until May 5th. He is in closest consultation with the Buddha and with the Lord of the World. This great Triangle of Potencies—the Lord of Will or Power, the Lord of Wisdom, and the Lord of Love—are today entirely preoccupied with the task of bringing the war to an end, and therefore with the task of neutralising the destroyer aspect of the first ray. This They will do by implementing the will-to-good by means of the wisdom of which the Buddha is the experienced Custodian, and also by laying down those plans whereby the Christ may—via the Hierarchy and the New Group of World

Servers—bring about that "loving understanding" (eso-terically understood and bearing little resemblance to what is usually understood by those words) in the hearts of men. When this Triangle of Energies has synchronised its efforts, then at the May Full Moon, the great task of leading human-ity into the light of a new day can be begun.

In the meantime, the Masters and Their ashrams are likewise getting ready to implement these plans and are endeavouring to inspire Their disciples with the same vision and objectives, so that they too may be prepared to play their due part.

Such, my brothers, is the situation as regards the posi-tion of humanity and the intentions and work of the Hier-archy. What then is the work which you can and must do?

I have for years indicated certain lines of activity which we, the Teachers and Guides on the inner side of life, would have all aspirants and disciples follow. The plans outlined by me during the past ten years are definitely a part of the hierarchical program and are being presented in their spe-cific forms by the other Masters. There is little that I can add. There is nothing which I tell you at this time that you do not already know. Do I need to ask you to work indi-vidually and in the place where you are for national and world unity? Must I plead with you to do what you can to heal divisions, and thus render effective that basic integ-rity which should unite the three major world powers through which the Hierarchy is attempting to work? Do I need to enjoin the necessity to counteract hate with justice, understanding and mercy? Have I to continue explaining the need for the complete triumph of the Forces of Light, for the triumphant progress of the armies of the United Nations, and for that triumph to be won first of all on spiritual levels and then carried through—with commonsense and per-sistence—on to the physical side of life, as well as in the intervening mental world? Do I need to ask for the control of emotions in the general interest, and for the consecration of time, energy and money to the enormous task of human salvage?

On these points I shall not dwell. Nothing is here gained by reiteration except the growing burden of a responsibility which you can shoulder to your eternal happiness or discard to your shame and eventual karmic reaction. Only this will I say: Get rid of selfishness, provincialism and insularity. Think in terms of the one humanity. Let your lives count in the scale of useful and needed service. Leave off saying and thinking those things which are critical of others—other people and other allied nations. See the issues of this conflict clearly, and let no false and glamorous sentiment lead you to favour weakness towards the Axis Powers at this unique and critical moment. The form or forms of their tyranny must be broken and due payment made in all justice and discrimination to an outraged world. But the souls that implemented that tyranny must—through sore trial and right spiritual direction—be again led to walk in the light. The children of the Axis nations must not be penalised for the wickedness or the weakness of their fathers; they must be educated in new and better ways and loved into right understanding of their relationships.

For two complete generations there must be a peace which will be unbroken because behind it and protecting it will stand the Armies of the Lord. At the close of that time, if the educational work done has been adequate, sane, wise and sound, then these Armies can rest from their labours and the sword be turned into the ploughshare. If this program of supervision, education and spiritual direction is not thus enforced, the war that would then take place would wipe out humanity—as happened once before in human history.

I would here refer you to a parable, spoken in terms of far-sighted vision and warning by the Christ centuries ago, anent the man who cleaned house, casting out the devils; when it was all swept and garnished, it remained empty (as symbol of unused opportunity and ignored responsibility) and then, as the Lord of Light put it, "the last state of that man was worse than the first." The sweeping and cleansing has been going on for five long years, the final stages of this destroying but cleansing process are now being taken. Then, my brothers, what?

I have told you over the years what we seek to have you do: Rally to the aid of the new group of world servers, hard pressed in this day of battle. Spread goodwill—to humanity as a whole, learning steadily to think in terms of that whole; uphold those activities which benefit the whole and do not favour one particular nation, even if it is your own. Work today for victory and for the annihilation of evil. Work tomorrow for justice and for the restoration of security. When there is security, readjustment, the obliteration of the aggressor leaders, protection and restoration of the weak and the oppressed, plus right living conditions and wise education for the youth of the world, then peace will come but not till then. Let the soporific of beautiful peace talk die out and let sane methods of establishing goodwill and right human relations precede the discussion of peace. The world talked itself into a dreamy state of idealistic rhapsody about peace between the first phase of this world war and the present one. This must not again occur and it is the task of the intelligent humanitarian to prevent it.

For the work to be done during the next twelve months (and then continued during the ensuing years), I make one last appeal. Stand with fixed intent, implementing the massed intent of the unthinking, the terrified and the distressed and weak. Cooperate with the new group of world servers in every land. Let the Full Moons of May and June constitute high points of spiritual attainment which can and will condition your daily life and service during the ensuing year. Let nothing deter you. Nothing from any quarter causes the Christ to deviate from His planned purpose; just in so far as His purposes coincide with your soul purpose, move outward into a wider field of service. If you feel no response to world need and no call to serve, then beware and seek a deeper measure of soul contact and spiritual relationship. Every word spoken or written at this time by an aspirant or a disciple is of a definite potency—either good or bad.

You know about the new group of world servers. The

work of the men and women of goodwill has been presented to you. The request for the forming of triangles of light and of goodwill has been placed clearly before you. The need for clear thinking is plain. The Hierarchy asks for your aid and your support in the arena of world affairs. I have myself laid my plans before you. There the program must be left to be carried out by you if you choose. For a quarter of a century (since 1919) I have taught you. I ask now for your cooperation in our mutual responsibility—the helping of humanity.

May He Whom we all love and serve, the Master of all Masters and the undying Friend of Mankind shed His light upon your way and evoke your trust, your understanding and your help in His task—climaxing this year—of leading humanity into the light of a new day.

THE CYCLE OF CONFERENCES

March 1945

The three months of March, April and May in this year mark a moment in time of major significance in our planetary history. I refer to the Easter Full Moon, celebrated on March 28th, the Wesak Full Moon, which falls this year on April 27th, and the Full Moon of June— Christ's "Unique Occasion" as it has been called—which falls on May 26th. From the standpoint of both the Hierarchy and Humanity, the events during these few weeks of spiritual and mundane import (focussed through these three Festival Moons of *Aries, Taurus* and *Gemini*) will be of stupendous effect. What is done during this time by the Members of the spiritual Hierarchy of our planet (Who face a major test of Their hierarchical *power,* not a test of Their love), what is accomplished by the disciples working in the world at this time, and also by the new group of world servers, can and will determine the destiny of man for centuries to come. Even those who have no knowledge of occult matters or of human fate or of the effective enterprise of human free will (esoterically understood) stand today with bated breath, waiting to see what will happen and towards which goal or goals human thinking and planning will be directed.

The masses of mankind everywhere have only one desire—tranquility. I use not the word "peace," because it has such a misleading connotation. Thinking men and women in every country stand with massed intent, determined, if possible, to take those steps which will ensure peace on Earth, through the expression of goodwill. Note that phrasing. The working disciples throughout the world are struggling with every means at their disposal to spread the gospel of sacrifice, because only upon sacrifice can world stability be safely founded—the sacrifice of selfishness. In those words is summed up the demand being made on those whose responsibility it is to determine policies (national and international) and to take those steps which will establish right human relations. The Hierarchy stands—no longer watching and waiting, but acting today with impelling wisdom and fixed decision in order to strengthen the hands of Their workers in every field of human activity (political, educational and religious) so that they may take right action and correctly influence human thinking.

A powerful first ray activity—the activity of will or purpose—is swinging into action. The Christ, as the Leader of the Forces of Light, has empowered the Ashrams of the Masters upon this first Ray of Power to strengthen the hands of all disciples in the field of government and of political arrangement in every nation; to enlighten, if possible, the various national legislatures by whatever means may be needed, so that the potency of their words, the wisdom of their planning, and the breadth of their thinking may prove so effective that the "Cycle of Conferences and of Councils," now being initiated by the statesmen of the world, may be under the direct guidance (again if possible) of Those in the Council Chamber at Shamballa Who *know* what is the Will of God. The selfishness of the little minds in the various legislatures of the world must in some way be offset. That is the problem. I wonder if you can grasp the significance of this happening? Down the ages, individual statesmen and rulers have from time to time been responsive to the influence of that spiritually supreme Council; but it has been the responsiveness of the *individual* disciple who has worked alone and unaided and who has faced, (or experienced) defeat as often, if not oftener, than he has experienced victory. Today, in the planning now going forward in connection with the various international conferences and councils of which you all know, the spiritual effort (for the first time in human history) is to bring all of them, *as functioning groups,* under the direct impact of the energy which motivates and actuates that place where the Will of God is known and the purposes of divinity are defined and projected. This means that each of the coming world conferences (and there will necessarily be many) will have a greater and far more extensive effect than would otherwise be the case; it means, however, that the risks involved and the clash of minds will also be far greater. This is a point which you should bear in mind as you study and read reports of these various conferences.

Forget not that divine energy must make its impact upon human minds; these minds are the only available instrument—in their aggregated effect—through which the Will of God can express itself; they are necessarily responsive to the stimulating and energising results of that impact, and this will evoke results suited to the type of mind affected. Response will be compatible with the quality and the intention of those minds. Where goodwill is present, and where there is unselfish intention and a broad point of view, those qualities will be strengthened and endowed with potency; where selfishness rules, where isolationism and separativeness are present, and where there is the intention to gain individual and national ends instead of those international purposes which will profit all humanity, those qualities will equally gain in strength.

Two momentous, but preliminary, conferences have already taken place, thus inaugurating this new cycle of *group functioning.* The League of Nations was an abortive effort—

well intentioned but relatively useless, as later happenings proved. One of these initial conferences was held at Yalta. There, three men, constituting a basic triangle, met with goodwill to all and endeavoured to lay the ground for coming world happenings.

All true movements conditioning long cycles in world affairs have at their centre a triangle through which energy can flow and certain definite purposes can be worked out. Little is understood, as yet, anent the nature of the task to be done or the type of men who work in first ray groups and Ashrams, and in Whose hands the political destiny of man rests at any one time. The whole subject of discipleship has been distorted by theological definitions, based upon sweetness of character, which often works singularly for ineffectiveness. The long cycle of ecclesiastical rule has biased human thinking so that the nature of spiritual strength and effectiveness is interpreted in terms of religion and in the terminology of churchianity (I did not say, of Christianity), or in the phraseology of a marked pacifism or a dominating, religious, temporal control. The long rule of the various churches is over. This should be grasped. They have done their work—in the early stages very good work, in the middle stages a necessary consolidating work, and in the modern stage a crystallising and reactionary work. The rule of the churches is over, but *not* the precepts of Christianity or the example of the Christ. He is, however, responsible for a newer and more effective presentation of the coming world religion, and for that the churches should prepare, if they have enough illumination to recognise their need and His effort to meet that need.

Today a balance must be reached, and this will take place through the medium of an enlightened statesmanship and through a political activity which will be based increasingly upon the good of the whole of humanity, and not upon benefiting any one nation in particular. This balance will not be expressed in religious terms and in so-called spiritual terminology. It will express itself through group work, through conferences, through Leagues of Nations, organised parties and legislation. All of this will be the result of an intensive activity of the Masters and of Their disciples upon the first Ray of Will or Power. The quality of their work will be to express the will-to-good; they see the world in large terms. To the uninitiate, they may at times seem isolated in their actions and over-powerful in the decisions which they reach and which they then proclaim to the world—much to the irritation of the little-minded and of those who interpret freedom in terms of their individual, unenlightened point of view. They are, however, working under spiritual direction as much as any religious leader and this will increasingly be recognised. History will justify their actions, because they will have given a trend to world affairs and to human thinking which will work out in a clearer perception of necessity. What they do will evoke discussion and ofttimes disagreement, as have the decisions of the Yalta triangle of workers. But they are so constituted that they do not resent this; they know that the discussion evoked and the criticisms raised will reveal the inherent smallness and separative instincts of their opponents, and—at the same time—will evoke the banding together of those who see behind the apparently high-handed initial activity an effort to precipitate with clarity the issues with which humanity is faced. Thus humanity can be brought to understanding. These are the things which the triangle at Yalta attempted to do. These they may not have consciously recognised as the work asked of them on account of their discipleship, but they automatically worked this way because they correctly sensed human need. They were and are handicapped by the fact of their own humanity, which makes them liable to make mistakes, but they are far more handicapped by the facts of human selfishness and national greed and by the general low level of human attainment—viewing humanity as one whole.

Having made the issues clear, as they see them, having evoked the enthusiasm of the men of goodwill in the world, and the violent criticism of those who think in terms of partisanship, nationalism, and prejudice, the experiment of the conference in Mexico City was undertaken with success. It was realised that there was an ascertainable measure of hemispheric unity upon which statesmen could count, and thus a foundation could be created for the far more difficult international conference to be held in San Francisco at the time of the Wesak, the Full Moon of the Buddha. Not for nothing is this conference being held during the five days of the Wesak Full Moon. It will be a time of supreme difficulty, in which the Forces of Light will face what I call "the forces of selfishness and separativeness."

Subjectively speaking, the conference will be under the direct influence of the Hierarchy. The consequent stimulation of both the selfish and the unselfish aspects will evoke a tremendous emotional and mental potency. It is therefore essential that all aspirants and disciples throw the weight of their spiritual development and the light of their souls on the side of the Forces which are attempting to plan for the good of humanity, and who regard the welfare of the whole as of far greater importance than any national situation or demand.

Forget not that the Forces of Evil are still powerful, particularly on the physical plane, and that there are many channels through which they can work. Germany is defeated, but is still capable of a final effort of destructiveness and violence. Japan is well on the way to defeat, but is still powerful. The hierarchy of evil on the inner side is being pushed back by the Forces of Light, but its grip on humanity has not relaxed. It is through ignorance that these forces can still attain much power—the ignorance of humanity itself. Nations and people are still ignorant of the true nature of each other; the world is full of distrust and suspicion. Humanity as a whole knows little about Russia, for instance. The true significance of Its ideology is misunderstood because of the initial mistakes of those who engineered the revolution; the license of unruly men in the early days gave onlooking humanity a wrong slant on what was happening. But those days are over. In the fires of suffering and through deepened understanding, this great and composite nation will advance towards a demonstration of brotherhood which may yet set an example to the entire world. China needs a full literacy; her citizens as a whole know nothing of other nations; on a higher turn of the spiral, that educational supremacy which distinguished an oligarchy of learning in the days of China's ancient glory will again distinguish the masses of her people. The great continent of Europe and the British peoples are still unaware of the real significance of the Western hemisphere and of the United States—with its exuberant youthfulness. They find it as irritating as their deeper maturity and wide experience proves irritating to Americans. Americans, both in the northern and in the southern hemispheres, are still basically ignorant of the history of the nations from which they spring, because they have laid the emphasis upon their relatively brief history and have been brought up on a biased and oft prejudiced picture of European culture and of British aims. This ignorance throughout the world plays right into the hands of the Forces of Evil and—beaten as they now are on the physical plane—they will give more violent battle to world goodwill on the planes of emotional decision, and on mental levels to those ideologies which are of benefit to the whole of humanity.

Physical plane methods having resulted only in the complete devastation of Europe and in casualties which (if civilian men, women and children are included) amount to untold millions, the forces of evil will now endeavour to utilise *the character* of humanity as a whole (at its present total point of development) to hinder the Forces of Light, prevent the attainment of world tranquility and world understanding, and thus delay the day of their own final defeat. This defeat, when accomplished, must include the three worlds of human evolution—mental, emotional and physical. For long these evil forces have used psychology in order to reach the ends they had in view, and have used it with amazing success; they are still using it, and can be depended upon to employ its methods to the uttermost. They use the press and the radio in order to distort human thinking;

they present half-truths, impute false motives, rake up past grievances, foretell (with foreboding) imminent difficulties; they foster ancient prejudices and hatreds, and emphasise religious and national differences. In spite of much shouting, demanding and proposed organisation, there is no truly free press anywhere; particularly is it absent in the United States, where parties and publishers dictate newspaper policies. The main reason why there is no really free press is based on two factors: first, the fact that humanity is not yet free from its predetermined reasonings, its basic ignorances of factual history, or of nations and their psychology; humanity is still controlled by racial and national bias and by prejudice. Secondly, the fact that all this is nurtured and kept alive by the forces of evil, working upon the inner side of human affairs and dealing mainly with the psychological angle because it is so exceedingly potent. This they will increasingly do as this planetary war draws to a close; they will seek to offset the work of the Hierarchy, to hamper the activities of the new group of world servers and to cloud the issues involved to such a degree that the men of goodwill everywhere will be bewildered and will fail to see the clear outlines of the factual situation or distinguish between what is true and what is false. Forget not, the forces of evil are exceedingly clever.

It is necessary also to remind ourselves that, having won the war against aggression and barbarity upon the physical plane (and it is won), humanity has now earned the right to carry that accomplishment through to psychological and actual mental victory, and to do this *together* and with the mustered aid of enlightened men and women from every country—hence the inauguration of this Cycle of Conferences and Councils. This cycle will prove long or short, according to the release of the will-to-good from the spiritual world, in response to the massed intent of the men and women of goodwill everywhere.

As the destroying aspect of the Will of God nears the accomplishing of divine purpose, the will-to-good can emerge with clarity and dominate human affairs. Out of the immensity of planetary evil, demonstrated through the destructive war of the past few years (1914-1945), great and permanent good can come; the spiritual Hierarchy stands ready to evoke the good latent behind the work of destruction which has been done, but this can be so only if the goodwill of humanity itself is employed with adequate invocative power. If this goodwill finds expression, two things can occur: first, certain potencies and forces can be released upon the earth which will aid men's effort to attain right human relations, with its resultant effect—peace; secondly, the forces of evil will be so potently defeated that never again will they be able to wreak such universal destruction upon earth.

Years ago I said that the war which may follow this one would be waged in the field of the world religions. Such a war will not work out, however, in a similar period of extreme carnage and blood; it will be fought largely with mental weapons and in the world of thought; it will involve also the emotional realm, from the standpoint of idealistic fanaticism. This inherent fanaticism (found ever in reactionary groups) will fight against the appearance of the coming world religion and the spread of esotericism. For this struggle certain of the well-organised churches, through their conservative elements (their most powerful elements), are already girding themselves. Those sensitive to the new spiritual impacts are still far from powerful; that which is new always faces the supreme difficulty of superseding and overcoming that which is old and established. Fanaticism, entrenched theological positions, and materialistic selfishness are to be found actively organised in the churches in all continents and of all denominations. They can be expected to fight for their established ecclesiastical order, their material profit and their temporal rule, and already are making the needed preparations.

The coming struggle will emerge within the churches themselves; it will also be precipitated by the enlightened elements who exist in fair numbers already, and are rapidly growing in strength through the impact of human necessity.

The fight will then spread to thinking men and women everywhere who—in a protesting revolt—have denied orthodox churchianity and theology. They are not irreligious but have, through pain and sorrow, learned (without ecclesiastical help) that the spiritual values are the only values which can salvage humanity, that the Hierarchy stands, and that Christ—as the symbol of peace and the Leader of the Forces of Light—is not a negligible force but one that is evoking response from the hearts of men everywhere. *True religion will come to be interpreted in terms of the will-to-good and its practical expression, goodwill.* The coming world conferences and the international councils will give indication of the strength of this new spiritual response (on the part of humanity) to the overshadowing spiritual Potencies awaiting the invocative cry of mankind. When that cry arises, these divine energies will precipitate themselves into the realm of human thinking and planning. Men will then find themselves gifted with renewed strength and with the needed insight which will enable them to drive out the entrenched materialistic forces and the power of selfish interests—banded together to prevent human freedom. If the conferences to be held in the near future demonstrate that mankind is truly striving to bring about right human relations, the forces of evil can then be driven back; the Forces of Light will then take control.

The problem facing the Hierarchy is how to further these desirable ends without infringing on human freedom of thought and action. It is with this problem that the great Council of the spiritual realm, of the Kingdom of God, is dealing at this time, and it will provide the subject of Their discussions and final decision until the middle of June. When the sun begins to move southward again, Their decisions will have been made on the basis of human demand. Humanity will by then have indicated the strength and nature of its goodwill; it will have sounded the "word of invocation"—reaching up into the spiritual realm like a breathing forth of the very soul of humanity; it will have expressed a measure of its willingness to sacrifice in order to stabilise human living, and to rid the world of separativeness and of the abuses which culminated in this war; it will at least have set the stage for the blue-printing and planning which the Cycle of Conferences and Councils will undertake. On the side of the Hierarchy and in response to human demand (in degree and in kind, according to *the quality* of the demand), the Hierarchy will play its part and aid in making possible that which men dream, vision, and for which they plan today.

Let us consider for a minute what the Hierarchy stands ready to do and what its Members will plan and formulate during the Easter Festival this month, during the Wesak Festival in April, and during the Festival of the Christ at the end of May. It might be said that the Hierarchy, in conjunction with the great Council of the Will of God at Shamballa, will divide Their work into three parts, each governing three phases of the coming restoration of humanity to civilised and cultured living on a new and higher turn of the spiral. They will deal with the problem of spiritual freedom, as it embodies itself in the Four Freedoms, and with the problem of right human relations, as it will express itself through international relations, national parties and general human affairs. It is not for me to tell you what humanity, through its statesmen and leaders, will plan to do at the coming conferences. It is my task to mobilise the new group of world servers and the men and women of goodwill so that they may stand as a great "army of implacable spiritual will" behind the participants in these conferences and councils, enabling them to think with clarity about the issues involved and thus (through this clear thinking) affect telepathically the minds of men; this involves the use of a power seldom employed as yet on the side of righteous endeavour, though already widely used by the materialistic leaders of the forces of evil.

It is the task of the Hierarchy to find and reach the enlightened men and women in all the churches, all the political parties, all the organisations—social, economic, and educational—so that their united purpose will be clear. This

They will do through the medium of Their active, working disciples in the world. Thus They will pave the way for the true freedom of mankind—a freedom which is as yet a dream and a hope in even the most democratic countries.

But behind all this activity, watched over by the spiritual Guides of the race but determined and implemented by humanity itself, will be found the focussed attention of the Hierarchy. This spiritual tension which exists among Them is far more potent than any of you suspect; it is part of Their preparatory work to make available certain spiritual forces and powers which—though complementary or supplementary to the self-initiated effort of mankind—will make that effort successful. What humanity has now to do, and is already doing to a certain degree, is to arrive at a right orientation as regards human affairs. Let us therefore look at the three phases of this preparatory work now going on, and endeavour to gauge what will be the results if these energies and potencies are released through the invocative demand of men.

The Forces of Restoration

There is first of all the phase, now in progress, which will culminate at the time of the Easter Full Moon. This is dedicated to planning for an inflow of the *Forces of Restoration*. Do not misunderstand these words. The Hierarchy is *not* occupied with the restoration of the old order, with the state of life prior to the war, or with the renewal of the theologies (religious, political and social) which have governed the past and which have been largely responsible for the war. The restoration referred to is psychological in nature, but will work out in the restoration of the will-to-live and the will-to-good. It will consequently be foundational, and will guarantee the new civilisation and culture. This is a very different matter.

These Forces of Restoration are concerned with human vision, human integrity and human relations as they underlie the entire problem of the brotherhood of man. These

energies, if released upon the Earth, will render futile the
efforts of the old order (in politics, religion and education)
to restore what was and to bring back that which existed
prior to the war. They will endeavour to offset two tendencies which will have to be taken into momentous consideration during the coming cycle of conferences:

    a. The tendency to crystallise, to cherish that which has
        gone (and gone forever, let us hope) and to over-
        estimate that which is old, worn-out and, if I may
        use the word, stagnant.
    b. The tendency to over-fatigue and to complete col-
        lapse—once the war is over. This tendency is due
        to the weight of the war and to the physical and
        psychological strain under which mankind has la-
        boured for so many years.

Great danger to the future of the race lies in these two
tendencies; the Hierarchy is determined to offset them as
far as possible, whilst the forces of evil are eagerly trying to
foster and nurture them. They are also dangers which the
intelligent leaders of the race equally recognise. This recognition will make them slow in arriving at final decisions,
because they will realise the need for a cycle of restoration
before final and lasting decisions are made. They will therefore work for a slower moving forward and for a more careful
and even prolonged investigation of the situation and of
future possibilities than may seem desirable to the impatient.

    These new and living restorative forces are under the
direction and the control of One Whom we might call
(speaking symbolically, yet factually) the *Spirit of Resurrection*. It is this living spiritual Entity, working temporarily
under the direction of the Christ, Who will restore livingness
to men's spiritual aims and *life* to their planning; Who will
engender anew the vitality needed to implement the trends
of the New Age and Who will guide humanity out of the
dark cave of death, isolation and selfishness into the light
of the new day. It is this resurrection life which will be
poured into humanity at Easter time this year, to some

degree, but which—during the next three Easter periods— can be poured in in full measure, if the men and women of goodwill will think clearly, speak forcefully, demand spiritually and implement the inner plans with intelligence.

On a planetary scale, and not just in reference to mankind, this Spirit of Resurrection is the opponent and the antagonist of the Spirit of Death. Physical death takes place only when the psychological and mental vitality of the individual, of a nation, or of humanity drops below a certain level. Humanity has been responding to the processes of dying during the last 150 years; psychologically, mankind has been ruled by selfishness, and selfishness is the potent seed of death—material death, psychological death and mental death. This is seen well demonstrated in the German nation. Think this statement out, and then recognise that similar seeds and similar areas of death (though to a lesser degree) exist in every nation—even in the younger nations of the world. Hence the war; hence the destruction of all the outer garments of civilisation.

But the work of the Angel of Death, awful as it may seem as it demonstrates today on a planetary scale—but beneficent as we know it to be in intent and in purpose— will give place to that of the Spirit of Resurrection.

It is the planning of this restoration and this resurrection activity which is now under consideration by the Hierarchy, having been handed over to Them because They are closer to man than are Those Who function in the Council Chamber at Shamballa. It must be remembered that this Spirit of Resurrection is a Member of that Council and Their chosen Emissary. He (if one may be permitted to personalise the impersonal) is in truth the "Sun of Righteousness" Who can now arise "with healing in His wings"; Who can carry this life-giving energy which counteracts death, this vision which gives incentive to life, and this hope which can restore all nations. At the Full Moon of March, let the demand go out for the appearance of this life-giving Spirit. Let it go forth with such intensity that the Hierarchy will be called into active response and will immediately release the potency of this Spirit into the hearts of men everywhere.

All of these spiritual forces, working as they are at this time under the direction of the Leader of the Forces of Light, the Christ, are closely related and their activity is most intimately synchronised. In a deeply occult sense, they are all working *together*, because in the human family there are those who are at every stage of responsiveness. This triple work of the Hierarchy, therefore, proceeds simultaneously—from the standpoint of time. The Forces of Restoration are —on a small scale—evoking response from the members of the new group of world servers and from disciples everywhere. As their psychological "morale" stiffens and their will-to-live and their will-to-good is strengthened, an immediate effect will be felt on a larger scale; the work of the Spirit of Resurrection will intensify, and is already making its presence felt. More and more people are beginning to be forward-looking and to hope with greater conviction and courage for a better world set-up; their hitherto wishful thinking and their emotional desire are slowly giving place to a more practical attitude; their clear thinking and their fixed determination are far more active and their plans better laid because both their thinking and their planning are today based on facts; they are also beginning to recognise those factors and conditions which must *not* be restored, and this is a point of major importance.

At the stage which we are now passing through, these responsive people fall into three categories:

The visionary dreamer or the well-intentioned but impractical person whose ideas and world plans and suggestions as to the new world order litter the desks of world leaders and of those groups and organisations who are attempting practically to blueprint the future. Their dreams and ideas deal with projects for which the world of today is not ready and will not be ready for several thousand years. It is an easy thing for them to present impossible Utopias which have not the faintest relation to things which are needed today and which could be made possible. The name of these people is legion, and at this time they constitute a definite hindrance. A vision of the impossible is not the type of vision which will keep the people from perishing. Because of an inability to compromise and to face up to things as they are, these people and those whom they influence are landed in despair and disillusionment.

The intelligent people of the world who are actuated by the spirit of goodwill and by the conviction that things must be changed. They are often staggered by the magnitude of the task to be undertaken, and this frequently leads them to take one of three positions:

a. They fall into the depths of pessimism. It is a pessimism based on a real ability to sense the scope of the problem and to assess the resources available. This may land them in non-activity.
b. They may leave the settling of the problem to the trained statesmen, diplomats and politicians, standing ready to help when—but only when—decision has been made. This leads to a shifting of responsibility. Yet, because the war involved the people of all lands and masses of population, so must the reconstruction of the world.
c. They may assume responsibility, ventilate the abuses which must be put right, discuss proposed plans and, from their particular angle of vision, set to work to bring about, to the best of their ability, right human relations. This attitude of responsibility and consequent activity may lead to mistakes, but in the aggregate of the endeavour it will meet the demand for right action in an emergency—this time a world emergency.

Those *partisan and nationally minded persons* who will attempt to exploit the world situation for their own immediate ends and for the benefiting of their particular nation or group. These people, and they are found in every nation, are selfishly motivated; they do not care for humanity as a whole and have no liking or interest in anything or anyone but their political party and the reactionary interests of some national group. They see in the present world situation a grand opportunity to engineer moves which will benefit an individual, a class or a nation. In doing this, they frequently have a wide grasp of affairs and are keen politicians, but all they know is to be used and so implemented that it attains their narrow ends, no matter at what cost to the rest of the world. These people are usually a large majority. Their attitude leads inevitably to trouble and hinders the work of restoration; it handicaps those who are seeking to establish the entire human family in a sounder way of life than heretofore, and to give a saner and wiser motivation to international relationships. These are the people who are the most to be feared at the coming conference at San Francisco. The isolationists in all nations, particularly in the United States, French national idealism, and the obsession of certain factors in the Polish race over boundaries will need watching, as these attitudes can be exploited by the evil and selfish interests which (behind the scenes) are seeking to prevent the world attaining that equilibrium which will permit tranquillity. These three groups, however, indicate the successful operation of the Forces of Restoration. These are tentatively beginning their work and preparing the way for a much fuller expression of the intentions of the Spirit of Resurrection, after the coming Full Moon of March and in the three years which lie ahead.

The Forces of Enlightenment

A realisation of the need of humanity, and a careful appraisal of that which must be done to meet that need, have awakened the men of goodwill to responsiveness to the Forces of Restoration; this has led to an insistent demand that the second phase of the hierarchial work be set in motion. This phase is directed towards those activities and the development of that invocative spirit which will bring the Forces of Enlightenment into contact with humanity and lead to activity on their part. These forces can function fully and until 1949 hold sway over the minds of men, *if* the people of the world can be organised to stand with massed intent behind that type of statesmanship which is seeking the greatest good of the greatest number, which sees the world as one great interdependent whole, and which refuses to be sidetracked by the clamouring of the selfish little minds or by the demands of the reactionary forces to be found in all lands.

These Forces of Enlightenment are always present on Earth on a small scale, influencing the minds of the new group of world servers, the selfless workers for humanity, and the thinkers in every school of thought, working in every field of human betterment; they work upon and through all who truly love their fellowmen. They are unable to influence the minds of the closed egocentric person; they can do little with the separative isolationist; they are ineffectual where the theologian of all groups—political, religious or social—is concerned, and they can do little with the type of mind that is concentrated upon personal or group problems (*their* group, expressing *their* ideas and working *their* way) and who fail to see themselves or the group in relation to the whole of humanity.

Today, however, a community of suffering and a general recognition that the causes of war are to be found in selfishness and in inherent cruelty has greatly widened people's approach to reality and to possibility, as they exist today. Churchmen, statesmen and leaders of important world groups are admitting the failure of their church, or their legislative bodies, or their policies to bring about world order and world tranquillity. They are seeking earnestly for new ways in government, new modes of suitable living, and for a method whereby right human relations can be established. They present a field of expression to the Forces of Enlightenment and offer Them opportunity to change the ways of human thinking; they are being mobilised by the light-bearing energies upon the planet so that wisdom, understanding and skill in action may distinguish the activities of men in the immediate future.

The organiser of these Forces at this time is the Buddha. He is the symbol of enlightenment or of illumination. Countless millions down the ages have recognised Him as a Light-bearer from on high. His *Four Noble Truths* exposed the causes of human trouble and pointed to the cure. His message can be paraphrased in the following words: Cease to identify yourselves with material things; gain a proper sense of the spiritual values; cease regarding possessions and earthly existence as of major importance; follow the *Noble Eightfold Path* which is the path of right relations—right relations to God and to each other—and thus be happy. The steps on this Path are:

Right Values	Right Aspiration
Right Speech	Right Conduct
Right Mode of Living	Right Effort
Right Thinking	Right Rapture or true Happiness

His ancient message is as new today as it was when He spoke His words on earth; a recognition of its truth and value is desperately needed, and the following of the "eight right ways of living" will enable humanity to find liberation. It is on the foundation of His teaching that the Christ raised the superstructure of the brotherhood of man to form an expression of the Love of God. Today, as it views the crumbling, devastated world, mankind has a fresh opportunity to reject selfish, materialistic motives and philosophy and to begin those processes which will—steadily and gradually—bring about its liberation. It will then be possible for men to tread the Lighted Way which leads back to the divine Source of light and love.

The Buddha could *point* to the goal and indicate the Way because He had achieved full enlightenment; the Christ gave us an *example* of One Who has reached the same goal; the Buddha left the world after reaching illumination; the Christ returned to us, proclaiming Himself as the Light of the World, and showed us how we too could learn to tread the Lighted Way.

The Buddha, Whose Festival is held ever at the Full Moon of May (or of *Taurus,* falling this year during the last week in April), acts today as the agent of that great Life in Whom we live and move and have our being, Who is Himself the true Light of the World and the planetary Enlightener. I refer to the Ancient of Days (as He is called in the *Old Testament*), to the God of Love, to Sanat Kumara, the Eternal Youth, the One Who holds all men in life and Who is carrying His whole creation along the path of evolution to its consummation—a consummation of which we have not as yet the faintest idea. Year after year, ever since the Buddha achieved His goal of illumination, an effort has been made to increase the flow of enlightenment into the world and to throw the light of wisdom, experience and understanding (as it is called) into the minds of men. At each Full Moon of May this has been the effort of the spiritual Forces which are working out the Will of God. A supreme effort will be made by Them this year, during the five days of the Full Moon (April 25-30), and a major test of the effectiveness of Their activity will be given at the San Francisco Conference. This I would ask you to remember, and for this I beg you to mobilise.

A great Triangle of Force will be called into play during those five days as the nucleus through which the Forces of Enlightenment will work. The three Lives controlling the energy which it is hoped can be released for the illumining of men's minds are:

1. The Lord of the World, the Light of Life Itself.
2. The Buddha, the Lord of Wisdom, bringing spiritual light to the Hierarchy and revealing what is the divine purpose.
3. The Christ, the Lord of Love, presenting the demand of humanity and acting as the distributing Agent for the Forces of Enlightenment.

The Forces of Light, upon the physical plane, have driven the forces of evil and of darkness backward, and are bringing the war to an end through the defeat of the Axis Nations.

But another great "division" of those Forces (if I may symbolically use a military term) is being mobilised and can be brought into active service at the *Full Moon of May* (*Taurus*) *if* the demand is strong enough, is mentally powerful and adequately focussed. These Forces work entirely upon the level of the mind and with the minds of men; it is their task to bring the battle between the Forces of Light and the Forces of Darkness to an end—not only physically, but through the inauguration of an era of right thinking. This will end the present cycle of emotional distress, of agony, of glamour and illusion, and of materialistic desires which today form the pattern of men's lives. This has to be done by means of the spiritual will, working as enlightenment upon the mental plane and demonstrating as wisdom, and as skill in action, motivated by loving understanding. These three aspects of light—mental enlightenment, the illumination which wisdom confers, and loving understanding—all find their perfect expression in the Lord of the World (Whom the orthodox call God) and in His reflections, the Buddha and the Christ—the One Who brought Illumination to the world and the Other Who demonstrated the actuality of the Love of God. These three great expressions of divinity (One so divine that we can only know Him through His representatives) can be called into a new and most potent activity through right invocation at the time of the Full Moon of May. Those who can carry out this great act of invocation are the spiritually minded people everywhere, the enlightened statesmen, the religious leaders, and the men and women of goodwill, *if* they can stand with massed intent, particularly throughout the entire month of April. Their assistance can also be invoked by the dire need of men, women and children everywhere who can voice no cry, for they know not where to turn, but whose appeal is heard and noted.

Their work, however, must be focussed through and implemented by the world intelligentsia, by leading "lovers of humanity," working in the various organisations and groups dedicated to human betterment, and by representative unselfish people. It is *they* who must receive the inflow of "lighted wisdom" and of loving understanding; today this can be made possible in a manner never known before. The success of the effort now being spiritually planned is dependent upon the ability of mankind to use the light they already have, in order to establish right relations in their families, in their communities, in their nation and in the world.

This matter of being in a position to receive, and then be the agents of, enlightenment is an intensely practical matter. It is hoped that the response will be so real that it will constitute a great and uniform activity which will leave no single *thinking* person untouched, which will put the responsibility of establishing right human relations upon the shoulders of the men and women of goodwill, and not on the shoulders of the unthinking, undeveloped and suffering masses. This is a major point to bear in mind. If the thinking and executive people of the world can have their minds "illumined" by the spirit of wisdom and understanding, they can act as distributors of that light through enlightened planning and legislation, and thus affect the entire world. This is the immediate opportunity ahead, and when I say "immediate" I refer to the coming five days of the Wesak Festival. This should have a pronounced effect upon the San Francisco Conference. I also refer to the next five years, with their five Wesak Festivals on five May Full Moons.

This year will mark a climaxing effort in the long relation of the Buddha to humanity. Year by year, since He left the earth, He has come back to humanity, bringing light and blessing. Year by year, He has released this light and has presented opportunity to the Forces of Enlightenment to strengthen Their hold upon the minds of men. The success of Their effort has been so great that it has led to the crescendo of knowledge, to the glory of modern science and to the widespread education which has distinguished the past five hundred years. *Knowledge* is the hallmark of our civilisation; it has often been knowledge misapplied and dedicated to the selfishness of men, but it has been an impersonal thing personally applied; this must end. Now another phase of that light can begin to demonstrate as the result of the past, and that is *Wisdom*. Wisdom is the enlightened application of knowledge, through love, to the affairs of men. It is understanding, pouring out everywhere as the result of experience.

I call you, therefore, everyone, to a great service of demand and of invocation on behalf of humanity—a demand for the inflow of light upon the decisions of men. I would ask you to request and expect the needed enlightenment for those who have to make decision on behalf of men everywhere. Your individual enlightenment has nothing to do with this demand. It is a selfless motive which is required and which must lie behind your individual and group demand. You are demanding enlightenment and illumined perception for those who have to guide the destiny of races, nations and world groups. On their shoulders lies the responsibility to take wise action, based on world understanding, in the interests of international cooperation, and in the establishment of right human relations.

Throughout the month of April, until May first, the realisation of this is a major duty. To the support of the Forces of Enlightenment I call all today. As individuals, you must work for an open and receptive mind, free from prejudice or national bias; as individuals, you need to think in broader terms and of the one world and the one humanity. The mass of right-thinking and convinced demand which you, who seek to serve the Christ, can throw behind the men legislating for the world, can bring great results and can release the Forces of Enlightenment in a new and potent manner.

Concentration upon the work to be done is of such importance and will call for such practical activities that I will write no more at this time. I desire to keep the immediate issue clear. We will deal later with the *Forces of Reconstruction*. I would like to close this message with some words which I wrote many years ago. They express the needed attitude and orientation:

> I ask you to drop your antagonisms and your antipathies, your hatreds and your racial differences, and attempt to think in terms of the one family, the one Life and the one humanity.

AN EASTER MESSAGE

Easter Day 1945

On this day, we recall to our minds the fact of Resurrection—a universal and eternally recurring resurrection. I would like to talk with you anent the Christ, about His work as head of the Hierarchy, and about the rebuilding which humanity must undertake and which the Hierarchy is seeking to impulse at this time. A great period of reconstruction is planned. Here are the two words around which I wish to create my theme: *Resurrection* and *Reconstruction*. It will be a reconstruction implemented by Those Who *know* the meaning of resurrection, and it will involve a resurrection of humanity through the medium of its intelligentsia and men and women of goodwill. These two groups (the Hierarchy and Humanity) will need to be brought into a closer rapport, and this is entirely possible if the followers of the Christ realise their opportunity and shoulder their responsibilities. I would point out that when I use the phrase "followers of the Christ" I refer to all those who love their fellowmen, irrespective of creed or religion. Only upon this basic premise can a hopeful future be founded.

I do not care whether or not those who read my words accept the occult teaching of a spiritual and planetary Hierarchy over which the Christ presides, or whether they think in terms of Christ and His disciples. The essential recognition for which I plead is that this great group of spiritual Individuals, Who receive so general a recognition throughout the world and in all the great religions, should be regarded as *active*. The Christian view of the Christ is built upon that which He enacted for us two thousand years ago and through which He symbolically indicated to us the way which all aspirants must go. It portrays a picture of a waiting, quiescent Christ, living in some vague and far away heaven, "resting on His laurels" and practically doing nothing very much until such time as the sons of men of every race and creed acclaim Him as Saviour; this they must do both as individuals and as representing the organised Christian Church. It is a picture of a listening, observing Christ, animated by pity and compassion, but Who has done all He could and now waits for us to do our part; it is also a picture of One Who waits to see what humanity, as a whole, will accept theologically. In the mind of the narrow, fundamentalist theologian, Christ is seen as presiding over a peaceful place called Heaven, into which the elect are welcomed; He is also seen as consigning all who remain aware of their own spiritual integrity and responsibility, who refuse to be gathered into organised churches or who go idly or wickedly through life, to some vague place of eternal punishment. To this vast multitude (probably the majority) His love and compassion apparently do not reach, and His heart remains untouched. It appears that He cares not whether they suffer eternally or attain complete annihilation.

This surely cannot be so. None of these pictures is accurate or adequate; they are not true in any sense of the word. This is being realised by the more intelligent of the world thinkers, and from the time of this *Full Moon of June* (*Gemini,* celebrated this year the last week of May) a different message must be sent out by the churches of Christendom, if they are to meet the need of mankind and so aid in the work of reconstruction which lies ahead. They cannot stop this work, but the churches could be ignored if an inability to think with clarity is shown and if they are not freed from theological narrowness.

Resurrection is the keynote of nature; death is not. Death is only the ante-chamber of resurrection. Resurrection is the clue to the world of meaning, and is the funda-

mental theme of all the world religions—past, present and
the future. Resurrection of the spirit in man, in all forms
in all kingdoms, is the objective of the entire evolutionary
process and this involves liberation from materialism and
selfishness. In that resurrection, evolution and death are
only preparatory and familiar stages. The note and message
sounded by the Christ when last on Earth was resurrection
but so morbid has been mankind and so enveloped in
glamour and illusion, that His death has been permitted to
sidestep understanding; consequently, for centuries, the em
phasis has been laid upon death, and only on Easter Day
or in the cemeteries is the resurrection acclaimed. This
must change. It is not helpful to a progressive understanding
of the eternal verities to have this condition perpetuated
The Hierarchy is today dedicated to bringing about this
change and thus altering the approach of mankind to the
world of the unseen and to the spiritual realities.

Before, however, They could do anything, our present
civilisation had to die. During the coming century, the
meaning of the resurrection will be unfolded and the new
age will reveal its true significance. The first step will be
the emergence of humanity from the death of its civilisation
of its old ideas and modes of living, the relinquishing of
its materialistic goals and its damning selfishness, and it
moving into the clear light of the resurrection life. I am
not here speaking in symbolical or mystical terms. I am
dealing with facts—facts as real and as imminent as the
coming Cycle of Conferences, and facts for which the past
two hundred years have prepared humanity. This prepara
tion has culminated in the restlessness of the twentieth
century and has led to the horror of this world war, 1914
1945 through which we have been passing.

The true work of *The Cycle of Conferences* about which
I wrote earlier will only be inaugurated at San Francisco
There the stage will be set for those processes which will
usher in an era of relative tranquillity; thus the door of
the dark cave of materialism will be opened and the stone
rolled from the door of the sepulchre which has too long

entombed mankind. Then will follow those steps which will lead to a new and better life and which will indicate the expression of the spirit of resurrection. These facts (so near to manifestation) are physical facts; they will demonstrate as such *if* the disciples of the world recognise what it is that the Christ desires, and *if* the men and women of goodwill implement their response to His wishes.

Speaking symbolically, the first step after the advent of the spirit of the resurrection will be similar to that in the Biblical story. Mary, that woman of sorrow, of experience and of aspiration, stands (as ever in the symbolism of the world) as the symbol of materialism. Humanity must say with her, "They have taken away my Lord and I know not where they have laid Him." But—she said it to the Lord Himself, not recognising Him and realising only her own deep need and despair. So must it be again. Humanity—materialistic, suffering, facing the future with despair and agony, but still aspiring—must go forth from the cave of matter, seeking the Christ and at first not recognising Him or the work that He is attempting to do. The churches—materialistic, hide-bound and submerged in their theological concepts, seeking political power or possessions, emphasising stone buildings and cathedrals whilst neglecting "the Temple of God, not made with hands, eternal in the heavens"—are occupied with the symbols and not with the reality. Now they must learn to recognise that the Lord is not with them and they too must go forth, as Mary did, and seek Him anew. If they will do so, they will surely find Him and again become His messengers.

The fact of the resurrection will be demonstrated during the next few centuries, and the Living Christ will walk among men and lead them onward towards the Mount of Ascension. The Pentecost will become truth. All men will come under the tide of inspiration from on high, and though they may speak with many tongues, they will all understand each other.

What I have to say to you, I intend to divide into two parts:

The Work of the Christ Today
The Coming Work of Reconstruction

These two convey the same basic ideas and thus complement each other. They proclaim the fact that all that truly concerns us is that which takes place upon Earth in line with the "blueprints" which guide the work of the Christ. (When I use the phrase "concerns us" I refer to man's physical, emotional and mental reactions). They proclaim the fact that every state of consciousness is anchored within humanity and that all are factual here and now, did men but know it. They proclaim also the truth that Christ has never left us for a distant heaven of nebulous outlines, but that He is ever within our reach. They proclaim also the fact that His interest, His arduous labours on our behalf and the activities of His working disciples, the Masters of the Wisdom and the Lords of Compassion, are with us, here and now. They proclaim that we are *not* alone, but that the Forces of Light and of Enlightenment are constantly working; that the strength and the wisdom of Those who *know* are being mobilised to aid mankind, and that nothing can now arrest or prevent the contact between that intelligent aspiring centre, called humanity, and the inner spiritual group, the Hierarchy.

The Work of the Christ Today

Forget not one important point. The Hierarchy itself is the result of human activity and aspiration; it has been created by humanity. Its members are human beings who have lived, suffered, achieved, failed, attained success, endured death and passed through the experience of resurrection. They are the same in nature as are those who struggle today with the processes of disintegration but who—nevertheless—have in them the seed of resurrection. All states of consciousness are known to Them and They have mastered all of them; They have mastered them as men, thus guaranteeing to humanity the same ultimate achievement. We are apt to look upon the members of the Hierarchy as different radically from humanity, forgetting that the Hierarchy is a community of successful men, Who earlier submitted Themselves to the purificatory fires of daily living, working out their own salvation as men and women of affairs, as business men, as husbands and wives, farmers and rulers and that they know life, therefore, in all its phases and gradation. They have surmounted the experiences of life; Their great Master is the Christ; They have passed through the initiations of the new birth, the baptism, the transfiguration, the final crucifixion and the resurrection. But they still are men and differ from the Christ only in the fact that He, the first of our humanity to attain divinity, the Eldest in a great family of brothers (as St. Paul expresses it), the Master of the Masters and the Teacher of angels and of men was deemed so pure, so holy and so enlightened that He was permitted to embody for us the great cosmic principle of love; He thus revealed to us, for the first time, the nature of the heart of God.

These perfected men, therefore, exist; They are more than men because the divine spirit in them registers all stages of consciousness and awareness—subhuman, human and superhuman. This inclusive development enables them to work with men, to contact humanity at need, and to know how to lead us forward to the phases of resurrection.

There is no need for me to enlarge at this point upon the world that They are attempting to aid and to salvage. The state of humanity today is known to all truly thinking people. Devastation, crucifixion, slaughter and death are widespread; sorrow, pain, disillusionment and pessimism are conditioning the thinking and the reactions of millions, whilst the plight of the unthinking but helpless masses has reached an inconceivable height of misery. The ignorance, lack of understanding, and selfishness of men everywhere, particularly in the countries which have escaped the ravages of war, aggravate the situation. Nevertheless with serenity and confidence, the Hierarchy today faces its arduous task.

One aspect of Their work and attitude I would like to touch upon, for it is apt to cause misunderstanding among those with narrow vision and (if I may describe them) with constricted, though loving, hearts. I refer to the attitude taken by the Hierarchy during the past years of war. This attitude has caused some to find in it cause for criticism. Let me be explicit and also bring in the time equation. I can well do so, because it was through my writings that the position of the Hierarchy was affirmed and publicly stated.

In 1932, I wrote a series of pamphlets which were intended to mobilise the disciples of the world under the name of the New Group of World Servers and to arouse the men and women of goodwill in a final effort to awaken humanity to the need for change. I endeavoured to institute a worldwide house cleaning and to incite men to take the steps which were needed to avert war—a war which the Hierarchy saw coming closer, day by day. In a way unrealised and undreamt of by the average man, the Forces of Evil were in a most potent manner emerging from their ancient lair; they were intent upon seeking those whom they could mould and obsess, and thus hurry mankind towards disaster. They found minds responsive to their evil promptings in *every* country; they found also that it was possible to take possession of two countries, Japan and Germany and—to a very much less extent—of Italy.

The Hierarchy, foreseeing this, attempted to offset their efforts. They made appeal to the spiritually minded people of the world; Their appeal reached millions and culminated in May, 1936, in a planetary effort wherein the Great Invocation was used upon a large scale in most of the countries of the world. For another three years Their labour of love continued; They struggled to save humanity and to arouse men to their imminent peril; They endeavoured to arrest the selfishness of humanity and to produce a new and fresh orientation to the spiritual values, and thus avert war. They failed. The men and women of goodwill and the spiritually minded people could not appreciate the true nature of the impending danger. Some recognised it and did their utmost; a few worked hard, trusting to the wisdom of those who knew and asked their aid; most of them were disturbed and worried, but none of them appreciated properly *the double danger* with which humanity was faced: the danger arising out of human selfishness and greed, plus the danger which was nearing the Earth through the agency of the combined forces of evil. These forces were organised by beings of most evil and expert experience and were preparing to obsess and ultimately possess the negative German people, ruled by a group of men of such positive selfishness and aggressive materialistic spirit that they could easily become the agents of the subjective evil forces.

In September, 1939, supreme wickedness broke loose upon earth. Because the Hierarchy could not and would not infringe upon human free will, the evil which humanity itself had engendered manifested itself, and that to which certain nations and certain individuals had responded appeared, and thus World War II started. Rampant evil took possession of the earth through the medium of the Axis nations. The Germans marched into Poland. This country was the recipient of the first impact because of her national selfishness, her suppression of the lower classes, her exaltation of a Fascist-minded aristocracy and her hatred of the Jews. The United Nations then began slowly to organise under the impression of the Forces of Light. The war was on.

What, under these circumstances was the Hierarchy to do? Full opportunity had been given to humanity to arrest the descent of evil into manifestation. Voices of leaders and humanitarians everywhere were proclaiming the need for reform. On which side should the Hierarchy throw its weight and its influence? Should it take sides at all, or should it be neutral? Should it remain aloof and take the position of the onlooker, the observer? Should it stand superior to the deeds of mankind and await the decision of the battle to be fought? Should it conform to the sentimental ideas of the church-trained public and talk "Peace, peace" when there was no peace, and present a negative aspect of love-to-all-peoples whilst hatred strode rampant over the earth?

It must be remembered that if this war had resembled other wars down the centuries, and had simply been a fight between human groups and nations, the Hierarchy would have remained outside the conflict and left mankind to fight a conclusive victory on the merits of its fighting units. But this time a great deal more was involved and this the Hierarchy knew. This war has not only been an aggressive conflict between nations or of hate between the exponents of differing ideologies but something far more serious. The Hierarchy knew that extremely powerful forces were taking advantage of human stupidity to intrude into world affairs, and that potent groups of evil beings were organised to exploit the existing world situation. They knew also that the combination of ancient evil with men's selfishness would inevitably prove too strong for even the United Nations, if they were left unassisted to meet the Axis Powers and the Lords of Evil emerging from their hiding place. So the Hierarchy took its stand upon the side of the United Nations and let it be known that it had done so. In doing this, definite physical steps were taken to aid the Forces of Light; men and leaders were carefully chosen and picked disciples were placed in positions of power and of authority. The leaders of the United Nations and of their armies are not Godless men, as are the leaders of the Axis Powers; they are men of rectitude and of spiritual and humanitarian purpose and are able thus to work—consciously or unconsciously—under the inspiration of the Hierarchy. This has been amply demonstrated. On account of this decision of the Hierarchy, Christ became automatically the Leader of these Forces.

His work has been greatly hindered by the sweet sentimentality of the unthinking Christian and by the well-meaning, but oft unintelligent, pacifist. Both these groups would sacrifice the future of humanity to temporary methods of "being nice" or "being kind" or taking gentle measures. The forces of evil, stalking the world today, do not understand such measures. The cry of such people that "God loves all men" is true—eternally and forever true. It is one of the unalterable facts of existence itself. God loves—without distinction and irrespective of race or creed. To that Great Life naught matters but humanity and its perfecting, because upon humanity depends the salvation of all the kingdoms in nature. But this statement (made in time and space and as it concerns the form aspect and not the spirit in man) is frequently misleading, and the simple-minded are apt to forget that the Christ said, "He that is not with me is against me."

Men fail also to realise the potency of the thought wielded by Those who work under and with the Christ. Thought is pure divine energy, impersonal and—like the sun—it pours down upon the worthy and the unworthy, unless definitely and deliberately directed. The Hierarchy was therefore faced with the problem and the necessity of seeing that pure impersonal thought energy did *not* find its way into the ranks of those fighting human freedoms, for it stimulates the minds and the mental processes of the good and the bad alike. This danger They deliberately offset by directing Their thought to the forces fighting under the leaders of the United Nations and by openly taking Their stand upon the side of right human relations. They did not dare to do otherwise, for—in their place and given circumstances—the leaders of the forces of evil have proved themselves cleverer and more calculating than those fighting for human freedom. It is this distinction and its necessity that some kindly and well-intentioned but ignorant Christian thinkers often overlook.

The work of Christ in relation to the war has also been handicapped by the commercially minded in all nations, particularly in the neutral countries, who have profited by the war, as well as by "big business" interests in many lands. These are focussed at this time through certain monied groups in every powerful nation, particularly in the United States. He has been hindered also by those individuals who seek to exploit the plight of suffering humanity to their own financial advantage.

Therefore, when the war broke out and humanity chose to fight and the forces of evil were let loose upon our planet, the Hierarchy ceased its efforts to bring peace through goodwill and openly sided with those fighting to drive evil back whence it came, and to defeat the Axis nations. Because of this decision on Their part, unthinking people claim that the statements of those who represent the Hierarchy on earth have been contradictory and that the actions of the Hierarchy have not been compatible with their preconceived ideas of how love should be demonstrated. For the past five years, therefore, the efforts of the Christ and of His followers, the Masters of the Wisdom, have been directed towards clarifying the true issues in the minds of men, towards indicating the lines along which right action should be taken, and towards unifying inter-allied policies. They have been occupied with banding together the men of goodwill throughout the world in preparation for the Cycle of Conferences and the coming world readjustments. They have sought to protect the sufferers, organising methods of relief, guiding the minds of army leaders, and arousing public opinion to take those steps which will eventually lead to right human relations. Temporarily, the German people and the Japanese have been left to their fate and to the tender mercies of the armies of evil; the present debacle in Germany is a testimony as to what evil can bring upon those who follow it. With all these modes of strengthening the Forces of Light and of extricating humanity from the descended evil, the Hierarchy has also been occupied with lines of activity which may not be disclosed, because they concern the handling of the subjective forces of evil. The potency of these forces will be realised if the length of time which the war has lasted is considered and also the fact that two nations have been able to withstand—until the past few months—an entire world of nations united against them.

This is a phenomenal fact in itself and a witness to the

strength of the evil group—objective and subjective—which has sought to gain dominance over mankind. Had the Hierarchy not taken sides with the United Nations and thrown the power of its thought into the battle, victory might still be a long way off. Today it is well-nigh in our hands.

As I said elsewhere, it is a fallacy to believe, as some do, that the main trend of Christ's work is through the medium of the churches or the world religions. He necessarily works through them when conditions permit and there is a living nucleus of true spirituality within them, or when their invocative appeal is potent enough to reach Him. He uses all possible channels whereby the consciousness of man may be enlarged and right orientation may be brought about. It is, however, truer to say that it is as World Teacher that He consistently works, and that the churches are but one of the teaching avenues He employs. All that enlightens the minds of men, all propaganda that tends to bring about right human relations, all modes of acquiring real knowledge, all methods of transmuting knowledge into wisdom and understanding, all that expands the consciousness of humanity and of all subhuman states of awareness and sensitivity, all that dispels glamour and illusion and that disrupts crystallisation and disturbs all static conditions, come under the realistic activities of the department within the Hierarchy which He supervises. He is limited by the quality and the calibre of the invocative appeal of humanity and that, in its turn, is conditioned by the point in evolution attained.

In the Middle Ages of history, and earlier, it was the churches and the schools of philosophy which provided the major avenues for His activity, but it is not so today; this is a point which the churches and organised religion would do well to remember. There is now a shift of His emphasis and attention into two new fields of endeavour: first, into the field of world-wide education, and secondly, into the sphere of implementing intelligently those activities which come under the department of government in its three aspects of statesmanship, politics and legislature. The common people are today awakening to the importance and responsibility of government; it is therefore realised by the Hierarchy that before the cycle of true democracy (as it essentially exists and will eventually demonstrate) can come into being, the education of the masses in cooperative statesmanship, in economic stabilisation through right sharing, and in clean, political interplay is imperatively necessary. The long divorce between religion and politics *must* be ended, and this can now come about because of the high level of the human *mass* intelligence and the fact that science has made all men so close that what happens in some remote area of the earth's surface is a matter of general interest within a few minutes. Time and space are now negated.

The Coming Work of Reconstruction

I have referred to the coming Full Moon of June as "Christ's Unique Occasion." (*The Reappearance of the Christ,* Chapter II.)   Just what is entailed in that statement I am not empowered to say, but I can cast some light upon one phase of it. It has long been a legend (and who shall say it is not a fact?) that at each Full Moon of June, Christ repeats and preaches again to the assembled world (to the hearts and minds of men) the last sermon of the Buddha, thus linking the full enlightenment of the pre-Christian era and the wisdom of the Buddha to the cycle of the distribution of the energy of love, for which Christ is responsible.

This year the message of the past and of the present will be augmented, enhanced and supplemented by the enunciating of the new note, word or theme which will distinguish the New Age and characterise the coming civilisation and culture. It will climax all the past and lay the seeds for the future. The significance of this statement lies in the fact that telepathically and with the entire force of the Hierarchy behind Him, plus the potency of Those to Whom is committed the expression of the Will of God (later to be implemented by the Hierarchy under the direction of the Christ), the World Teacher will, in His Own right, make certain statements and use certain word-formulas which will create the nucleus of the thoughtform and present the blueprint around which and upon which the New Age will be developed. For this moment the thinking and the planning of the enlightened aspirants of the world have made—consciously, but mostly unconsciously—long preparation. They have, through their efforts, provided the mass of thought substance which the coming pronouncement will affect. Christ will bring this into proper form for the creative activity of the New Group of World Servers working in every nation and in every religious, social, economic and political group.

Christ's pronouncement will be embodied in certain Stanzas, of which those already given are a small part. Only He can use these Words of Power in their proper manner, connotation and emphasis; only an inadequate paraphrase of certain sentences found in that pronouncement can be given to humanity, and this paraphrase can be used only *when the war is over and not before.* This means that they can be employed only when both Germany and Japan are under the complete control of the United Nations, through whom the Hierarchy has been working. This will not imply the attainment of complete peace, but it will mean the end of all aggressive fighting and all organised resistance, leading to a period of relative tranquillity.

Standing in His Own place at a central point in Asia, remote from the throngs and the impact of humanity, Christ will bless the world at the exact moment of the Full Moon of June. He will then repeat the Buddha's last words or sermon, as well as the Beatitudes which He uttered when on earth and which have been so inadequately and misleadingly translated—a translation based upon the memory of what He said but not upon direct dictation. To these two messages, the Christ will add a new one, imbued with power for the future. That part of what He says in which it is possible for men to participate will be used for years to come in the place of the two Stanzas of the Great Invocation which have been used for nine years.

Behind the Christ, focussing with intensity today and preparing for a great act of spiritual cooperation at the time of the June Full Moon, stands the Hierarchy. Together with Him, They will invoke a group of spiritual Forces which (for lack of a better name) we will call the *Forces of Reconstruction.*

I would ask you to have clearly in your minds the three groups of spiritual energies which—at the time of the three Full Moons of April, May and June—will be released into activity and which will aid humanity in its major task of rebuilding the new and better world:

The Forces of Restoration. These will work to restore morale and psychological health, thus implementing the resurrection of humanity from the death cycle through which it has been passing. The restoration of men's mental condition to a wholesome and happier approach to life is the primary objective. These forces will bring about the emergence of the new civilisation—which is definitely man's creative work.

The Forces of Enlightenment. These, when let loose upon Earth, will produce a clear grasp of the Plan which the Hierarchy desires to see work out, a revelation of the issues involved in their right and possible sequence; and they will also give a sense of proportion to human thinking, plus an appreciation of the spiritual values which should determine the objective policies. These Forces will salvage the cultural gains of the past (a past which is dead and gone and of which little should again be restored) and will implement (upon the few foundational cultures of the past) that new and better culture which will be distinctive of the New Age.

The Forces of Reconstruction. These will usher in an era of pronounced creative activity and will bring about the rebuilding of the tangible world upon the new lines. This the total destruction of the old forms will necessitate. It is this great group of Forces which will be set in motion by the Christ at the June Full Moon; the focus of Their work will definitely be upon the physical plane. Their task is to precipitate and bring into manifestation that which the work of the Forces of Restoration and of Enlightenment have made subjectively possible.

These Forces might be regarded as embodying and making declarative the "new materialism." This is a statement warranting our closest consideration. It is essential that we bear in mind, as we face the activities of the future process of rebuilding, that matter and substance and their fusion into living forms are aspects of divinity; it has been the prostitution of matter to selfish ends and for separative purposes which has been responsible for the misery, the suffering, the failure and the evil which have characterised the career of mankind down the ages and which precipitated this world war. Today humanity is being given a fresh opportunity to build again on sounder and more constructive lines that better civilisation which is the dream of those who love their fellowmen, and to attain a new aptitude in handling substance. If men can demonstrate a gained wisdom in the creation of a form which will house the spirit of resurrection and express the enlightenment gained by the bitter experience of the past, then humanity will rise again.

The unique opportunity which confronts the Christ as His great hour draws near is that of unifying, synthesising and integrating all these forces into one great and potent downpouring of spiritual energy. These energies involve the activities of the Spirit of Resurrection, the inspiration of the Buddha as He this year conveys the strength of the One in Whom we live and move and have our being, and that which the Christ Himself will set in motion in response to the invocative appeal of the new group of world servers, the men of goodwill and the "massed intent" of the inarticulate masses. It is essential that we try to grasp the unity of this hierarchical effort.

The energy which will lead to the restoration of human aspiration, right idealism and fixed humanitarian intention is that distributed by the Forces of Restoration which were set in motion this year, at the time of the Easter Full Moon, under the direction of the Masters of the Wisdom and the supervision of the Christ. They will concern themselves with the reorientation of the human psyche and with the inevitable consequences of that reorientation—the acquiring of the vision which will bring about right human relations. This will be largely done by the spiritual people in the world, by aspirants, working disciples and (where possible) through the spiritually minded people in the churches and humanitarian and esoteric groups.

The energy which will lead to intelligent activity and to correct mental planning I have called that of the Forces of Enlightenment; once these have been released, it becomes the responsibility of the new group of world servers to direct them. Then through the enlightened plans of the world intelligentsia and prominent humanitarians and racial server , it will be possible to establish those spiritual principles and that correct cooperative relationship which should distinguish human affairs in the future. Those who will be directly affected, if the plans go as desired, are the big educational systems, the world-wide propaganda institutions, and all those agencies which work to educate and direct public thinking and mould public opinion.

The energy which I have called the Forces of Reconstruction will be more general in their application, and they will affect the masses of men through the work of the men and women of goodwill. I have therefore outlined a planned distribution of the three great streams of divine energy which will be set in motion at the three current Full Moons—one already past and two to come:

The energy of restoration, at the time of the April Full Moon

The energy of enlightenment, at the time of the Wesak or May Full Moon

The energy of reconstruction, at the time of the June Full Moon.

The inspiring sources of these spiritual agencies are, first of all, the Spirit of Resurrection (an extra-planetary Being), then the Lord of the World, working through the Buddha, and finally the Christ Himself. These Three will work through the Hierarchy, the new group of world servers, and the men and women of goodwill. Such is the general plan proposed by Those Who stand—with enlightened spiritual purpose—ready at this time to lead humanity out of darkness into light, from the unreal to the real, and from death to immortality. That most ancient of prayers comes today to have its deepest spiritual significance. Let me repeat it in the order in which today it gains meaning:

> Lead us, O Lord, from death to Immortality;
> From darkness to Light;
> From the unreal to the Real.

The beauty of this synthesis and the wonder of this opportunity are surely apparent as we study what is here written and consider these aspects of the divine Plan. Great Forces, under potent spiritual leadership, are standing ready to precipitate Themselves into this human world of chaos, confusion, aspiration and bewilderment. These groups of energies are ready to focus and distribute themselves, and the Hierarchy is closer to mankind than ever before; the new group of world servers are also "standing attentive to direction" in every country in the world, united in their idealism, in their humanitarian objectives, in their sensitivity to spiritual impression, in their united subjective purpose, in their love of their fellowmen, and in their dedication to selfless service; the men and women of goodwill are also to be found everywhere, ready to be guided into constructive activity, and to be the agents (gradually trained and educated) for the establishment of what has never yet truly existed—right human relations.

Thus, from the highest spiritual Being upon our planet, through the graded spiritual groups of enlightened and perfected men who work upon the inner side of life, on into the outer world of daily living, where thinking, loving men and women serve, the tide of the new life sweeps. The Plan is ready for immediate application and intelligent implementing; the workers are there, and the power to work is adequate to the need. The three Full Moons which we have been considering are simply the three points in time through which the needed power is to be released.

Here, my brothers, is a picture of possibility. I seek to present it to you today because of world need; here is the ground for a sound, optimistic approach to the future; here is the assurance that the world can be rebuilt, that constructive action can be successfully taken, that enlightenment will increasingly make its presence obvious, and that humanity will indeed rise out of its unhappy past into a new world of understanding, of tranquillity, of cooperation and of renewed spiritual impulse.

It will not be easy. The spiritual energies which will be released will inevitably evoke opposition. Selfishness and hate, with their secondary effects of greed, cruelty and nationalism, are not dead nor will they die for a long time to come. In the post-war world these conditions must be ignored and the new group of world servers and the men and women of goodwill must work together for an enlightened education, for a cooperative economic life, for right human relations in all departments of human experience, for clean political activity, for disinterested service, and for a world religion which will restore Christ to His rightful place in the hearts of men, which will take the pomp, the materialism and the politics out of the churches, and which will unify the spiritual intention of all the religions to be found in both hemispheres. This is a vast program, but the number of enlightened men and women is also very great, and the power at their disposal ensures the ultimate triumph of their spiritual idealism.

The major need is to bring these people into a much closer relationship, to take those steps which will enable them to realise that they are an integral part of a group of directed and intelligent world servers, and yet to leave them free to work in their own way, each in his own place and chosen field of service, and to see all these phases of the work as supplementary to all others and as the working out of a divine Plan, originating in the Hierarchy of spiritual Lives. Their work will be consciously carried out under the direct guidance of Christ and His disciples.

Long patience will be needed. Mistakes will be made. There will be periods of indecision, of ineffective action and of negative yet deep discouragement. Workers will be prone to attitudes of despair, and at times the task will appear to them to demand too much, to be too difficult and the forces opposing what they seek to do too strong. But behind all the reconstruction with which humanity is faced is the potency of inevitable resurrection, the constant flow of enlightened thinking into and directing the mass consciousness, plus a growing realisation that humanity is *not* alone, that the spiritual values are the only real values, and that the *Hierarchy stands*, immovable in its spiritual strength, steadily oriented towards world salvation, and acting ever under the direction of that great divine yet human Leader, the Christ. The Christ has passed through all human experiences, and has never left us; with His disciples, the Masters of the Wisdom, He is drawing closer to humanity decade after decade; when He said at the Ascension Initiation, "Lo, I am with you always even until the end of the age," He meant no vague or general idea of helping humanity from some distant locality called "the Throne of God in Heaven." He meant just what He said—that He was staying with us. The *fact* of His Presence upon earth in physical form is known today by many hundreds of thousands, and will eventually be realised by as many millions.

Therefore, my brothers, believe in the reality of the work to be done by these great spiritual Potencies, invoked during the three Full Moons of April, May and June. Go forth to the task of helping humanity, of establishing goodwill, of bringing about right human relations and of restoring a true spiritual perspective, with undaunted courage, sure faith and the firm conviction that mankind is *not* alone.

May the blessing of the Christ and of the Hierarchy rest upon all true servers and may they stand tranquil in the midst of strife.

THE GREAT INVOCATION
Stanza Three

April 17, 1945

As this world catastrophe draws to its inevitable close and the Forces of Light triumph over the forces of evil, the time of restoration opens up. For each of you this indicates a renewed time of service and of activity. I send you herewith the final Stanza of the Great Invocation, as I promised.* I gave you the first about nine years ago and the second during the course of the war. I would ask you to use it daily and as many times a day as you can remember to do so; you will thus create a seed thought or a clear-cut thoughtform which will make the launching of this Invocation among the masses of men a successful venture when the right time comes. That time is not yet.

This Great Invocation can be expressed in the following words:

> From the point of Light within the Mind of God
> Let light stream forth into the minds of men.
> Let Light descend on Earth.
>
> From the point of Love within the Heart of God
> Let love stream forth into the hearts of men.
> May Christ return to Earth.
>
> From the centre where the Will of God is known
> Let purpose guide the little wills of men—
> The purpose which the Masters know and serve.
>
> From the centre which we call the race of men
> Let the Plan of Love and Light work out
> And may it seal the door where evil dwells.
>
> Let Light and Love and Power restore the Plan on Earth.

---

* Reprinted from Discipleship in the New Age, Vol. II pp. 148-151, to preserve the historical sequence of the issuing of the three Stanzas of the Great Invocation.

It has been difficult to translate into understandable and adequate phrases, the very ancient word-forms which the Christ will employ. These word-forms are only seven in number, and they will constitute His complete, new utterance. I have only been able to give their general significance. Nothing else was possible, but even in this longer form, they will be potent in their invocative appeal, *if* said with mental intensity and ardent purpose. The points of emphasis upon which I would ask you to dwell (once it is permissible to use the phrases) are two in number:

1. *May Christ return to earth.* This return must *not* be understood in its usual connotation and its well-known mystical, Christian sense. Christ has never left the earth. What is referred to is the externalisation of the Hierarchy and its exoteric appearance on earth. The Hierarchy will eventually, under its Head, the Christ, function openly and visibly on earth. This will happen when the purpose of the divine will and the plan which will implement it is better understood and the period of adjustment, of world enlightenment and of reconstruction has made real headway. This period begins at the San Francisco Conference (hence its major importance) and will move very slowly at first. It will take time but the Hierarchy thinks not in terms of years and of brief cycles (though long to humanity), but in terms of events and the expansion of consciousness.

2. *May it seal the door where evil dwells.* The sealing up of the evil forces, released during this war, will take place within the immediate future. It will be soon. The evil referred to has nothing to do with the evil inclinations, the selfish instincts and the separativeness found in the hearts and minds of human beings. These they must overcome and eliminate for themselves. But the reduction to impotency of the loosed forces of evil which took advantage of the world situation, which obsessed the German people and directed the Japanese people, and which worked through barbarity, murder, sadism, lying propaganda and which prostituted science to achieve their ends, requires the imposition

of a power beyond the human. This must be invoked and the invocation will meet with speedy response. These evil potencies will be occultly "sealed" within their own place; what this exactly means has naught to do with humanity. Men today must learn the lessons of the past, profit from the discipline of the war and deal—each in his own life and community—with the weaknesses and errors to which he may find himself prone.

I would here recall to you what I said last year anent this final Stanza of the Invocation.

I am preparing to present to you for wide distribution throughout the world, the last stanza of the Great Invocation. It is by no means easy to translate the words of this stanza in terms which will make it of general appeal and not simply of importance to convinced esotericists. . . . It can be so presented that the masses everywhere, the general public will be prompted to take it up and will use it widely; they will do this on a relatively larger scale than the intuitional, the spiritually minded or even the men of goodwill. A far wider public will comprehend it. I will give A.A.B. this stanza at the earliest possible moment; this will be conditioned by world affairs and by my understanding of a certain esoteric appropriateness in the setting of a time cycle. If plans mature as desired by the Hierarchy, the new stanza can receive distribution at the time of the Full Moon of June 1945, as far as the Occident is concerned, and considerably later for the Orient. Prior to these set points in time, the stanza can be used by all esoteric school members, after being used for one clear month by my group, dating that month from the time that the most distant members of the group receive it.

I seek to have this Invocation go forth on the power generated by my Ashram and by all of you affiliated with my Ashram; the Ashrams of the Master K.H. and the Master M. are likewise deeply committed to participation in this work.

I would ask you also to read and re-read the two Instructions which you are at this time receiving—one dealing with the Cycle of Conferences and other with The Work of the Christ. (*The Reappearance of the Christ,* Chapter IV.) Master their contents and let the blueprint of the hierarchical plan take shape in your minds. Then you can do your share in implementing it and will be able to recognise those who in other groups and in different lands are also a vital part of hierarchical effort.

THE RELEASE OF ATOMIC ENERGY

August 9, 1945

I would like at this time to touch upon the greatest spiritual event which has taken place since the fourth kingdom of nature, the human kingdom, appeared. I refer to the release of atomic energy, as related in the newspapers this week, August 6, 1945, in connection with the bombing of Japan.

Some years ago I told you that the new era would be ushered in by the scientists of the world and that the inauguration of the kingdom of God on Earth would be heralded by means of successful scientific investigation. By this first step in the releasing of the energy of the atom this has been accomplished, and my prophecy has been justified during this momentous year of our Lord 1945. Let me make one or two statements anent this discovery, leaving you to make your own application and deductions. Little as to the true nature of this happening is as yet known, and still less is understood. Certain ideas and suggested thoughts may be of real value here and enable you to see this stupendous event in better perspective.

1. It was the imminence of this "release" of energy which was one of the major subjective factors in the precipitation of this last phase of the war. This world war started in 1914, but its last and most important phase began in 1939.

Up till then it was a world war. After that date, and because the forces of evil took advantage of the state of war and belligerency existing on the planet, the real war began, involving the entire three worlds of human evolution and a consequent activity of the Hierarchy. Man's attention is normally focussed on the externalities of living. Nevertheless, all great discoveries, such as those made in connection with astronomy or in relation to the laws of nature or involving such a revelation as that of radio-activity or the epoch-making event announced this week concerning the first steps taken in the harnessing of cosmic energy, are ever the result of inner pressure emanating from Forces and Lives found in high Places. Such inner pressures themselves function under the laws of the Spirit and not just under what you call natural laws; they are the result of the impelling work of certain great Lives, working in connection with the third aspect of divinity, that of active intelligence, and are concerned with the substance or matter aspect of manifestation. Such activities are motivated from Shamballa. This activity is set in motion by these Lives, working on Their high plane, and it gradually causes a reaction in the various departments of the Hierarchy, particularly those working under third, fifth and seventh ray Masters. Eventually, disciples upon the physical levels of activity become aware of the inner ferment, and this happens either consciously or unconsciously. They become "impressed," and the scientific work is then started and carried through into the stages of experimentation and final success.

One point should here be remembered, and that is that this phase applies to both the great White Lodge and the Black Lodge—the one dedicated to the beneficent task of purifying and aiding all lives in the three worlds of material evolution and to the release of the soul in form, and the other to the retardation of the evolutionary process and to the continuous crystallising of the material forms which hide and veil the *anima mundi*. Both groups have been profoundly interested and implicated in this matter of the release of energy from the atom and the liberation of its inner aspect, but their motives and objectives were widely different.

2. The imminence of this release—inevitable and under direction—produced an enormous tension in hierarchical circles because (to express the idea colloquially) a race was on between the Dark Forces and the Forces of Light to acquire possession of the techniques necessary to bring about this liberation of needed energy. Had the Dark Forces triumphed, and had the Axis Powers obtained possession of the needed scientific formulas, it would have led to a major planetary disaster. The released energy would have been used first of all to bring about the complete destruction of all opposing the forces of evil, and then it would have been prostituted to the preservation of an increasingly materialistic and non-idealistic civilisation. Germany could not be trusted with this power, for all her motives were compelling wrong.

You might here fall back on the trite religious platitude that the innate good in humanity and mankind's inherent divinity would eventually have triumphed, because naught can finally overcome the universal trend to good. You are prone to forget that if the evil forces possess potencies which can destroy form in the three worlds on such a wide scale that the souls of advanced aspirants and disciples, and those of initiates seeking incarnation, cannot come into outer expression during a particular world crisis, then you have direfully affected the time-schedule of the evolutionary process; you will have greatly delayed (perhaps for millennia of years) the manifestation of the kingdom of God. The time had come for that manifestation, and hence the powerful activity of the dark forces.

This attempt to hinder the planned progress constituted a definite menace and indicated a supreme danger and problem. The evil forces were closer to success than any of you have ever dreamed. They were so close to success in 1942 that there were four months when the members of the spiritual Hierarchy had made every possible arrangement to withdraw from human contact for an indefinite and unforeseen period of time; the plans for a closer contact with the evolutionary process in the three worlds and the effort to blend and fuse the two divine centres, the Hierarchy and Humanity, into one working, collaborating whole seemed doomed to destruction. Their fusion would have meant the appearance of the Kingdom of God on earth; the obstacles to this fusion, owing to the active tension of the dark forces, seemed at that time insuperable; we believed that man would go down to defeat, owing to his selfishness and his misuse of the principle of free will. We made all preparations to withdraw, and yet at the same time we struggled to get humanity to choose rightly and to see the issues clearly.

The necessity to withdraw was averted. I may not say in what manner, beyond telling you that the Lords of Liberation took certain unexpected steps. This They were led to do owing to the invocative powers of humanity, used consciously by all those upon the side of the will-to-good and unconsciously by all men of goodwill. Owing to these steps, the efforts of those fighting in the realm of science for the establishing of true knowledge and right human relations were aided. The trend of the power to know and to discover (a definite form of energy) was *deflected away* from the demanding evocative minds of those seeking to destroy the world of men, leading to a form of mental paralysis. Those seeking to emphasise the right values and to save humanity were simultaneously stimulated to the point of success.

In these very few words I have disposed of a stupendous world event, and in this brief paragraph I have summed up the working out of a specialised divine activity.

3.   When the sun moved northward that year (1942), the great White Lodge knew that the battle had been won. Their preparations were halted and the Masters then organised for renewed effort (through Their disciples) to bring about those conditions wherein that which was new and that which was in line with loving divine purpose could freely move forward. The war was not won by the surrender of

Germany. That was only the outer result of inner happenings. The war was won by the Forces of Light when the mental potency of the forces of evil was overcome and the "energy of the future" was directed or impelled by Those Who were seeking the higher human values and the spiritual good of mankind. Four factors lie behind the momentous happening of the release of this form of atomic energy, through the medium of what is erroneously and unscientifically called the "splitting of the atom." There are other factors, but you may find the following four of real interest:

a. There was a clearly directed inflow of extra-planetary energy released by the Lords of Liberation, to Whom invocation had been successfully made; through the impact of this energy upon the atomic substance being dealt with by the investigating scientists, changes were brought about which enabled them to achieve success. The experiments being carried forward were therefore both subjective and objective.

b. A concerted effort was made by a number of disciples who were working in fifth and seventh ray ashrams, and this enabled them to impress lesser disciples in the scientific field and helped them to surmount the wellnigh insuperable difficulties with which they were confronted.

c. There was also a weakening of the tension which had hitherto successfully held the forces of evil together, and a growing inability of the evil group at the head of the Axis Powers to surmount the incidental war fatigue. This brought about, first of all, a steady deterioration of their minds, and then of their brains and nervous systems. None of the men involved in the direction of the Axis effort in Europe is today normal psychologically; they are all suffering from some form of physical deterioration, and this has been a real factor in their defeat, though one that may be difficult for you to realise. It is not so in the case of the Japanese, whose psychological make-up is totally dif-

ferent, as are their nervous systems, which are of fourth
rootrace quality. They will be and are being defeated
by physical war measures and by the destruction physically of their war potential and the death of the form
aspect. This destruction . . . . . . and the consequent release of their imprisoned souls, is a necessary happening; it is the justification of the use of the
atomic bomb upon the Japanese population. The first
use of this released energy has been destructive, but I
would remind you that it has been the destruction of
forms and not the destruction of spiritual values and
the death of the human spirit—as was the goal of the
Axis effort.

Forget not that all success (both good and bad) is
dependent upon the sustaining of the point of tension. This point of tension involves the dynamic
focussing of all mental, emotional and physical energies
at a central point of planned activity. This, by the way,
is the objective of all true meditation work. It is in
this act of tension that the German people failed. This
cost them the war; their tension broke because the
group of evil forces who were impressing the negative
German people were unable to attain the point of
tension which the Hierarchy could reach when it was
reinforced through the action of the Lords of Liberation.

d. Another factor was the constant, invocative demand and
the prayers (articulate and inarticulate) of humanity itself. Men, impelled largely by fear and the innate
mobilising of the human spirit against slavery, reached
such a pitch of demanding energy that a channel was
created which greatly facilitated the work of the Hierarchy, under the direct influence of the Lords of Liberation.

4.   The release of the energy of the atom is as yet in an
extremely embryonic stage; humanity little knows the extent
or the nature of the energies which have been tapped and
released. There are many types of atoms, constituting

the "world substance"; each can release its own type of force; this is one of the secrets which the new age will in time reveal, but a good and sound beginning has been made. I would call your attention to the words, "the liberation of energy." It is *liberation* which is the keynote of the new era, just as it has ever been the keynote of the spiritually oriented aspirant. This liberation has started by the release of an aspect of matter and the freeing of some of the soul forces within the atom. This has been, for matter itself, a great and potent initiation, paralleling those initiations which liberate or release the souls of men.

In this process of planetary initiation humanity has carried its work as the world saviour down into the world of substance, and has affected those primary units of life of which all forms are made.

5. You will now understand the meaning of the words used by so many of you in the second of the Great Invocations:
The hour of service of the saving force has now arrived.
This "saving force" is the energy which science has released into the world for the destruction, first of all, of those who continue (if they do) to defy the Forces of Light working through the United Nations. Then—as time goes on— this liberated energy will usher in the new civilisation, the new and better world and the finer, more spiritual conditions. The highest dreams of those who love their fellowmen can become practical possibilities through the right use of this liberated energy, if the real values are taught, emphasised and applied to daily living. This "saving force" has now been made available by science, and my earlier prophecy substantiated.*

---

* See *A Treatise on White Magic*, published in 1934, beginning on page 333, where the following statements appear:
It might be noted here that three great discoveries are imminent and during the next two generations will revolutionise modern thought and life.
One is already sensed and is the subject of experiment and investigation, the releasing of the energy of the atom. This will completely change the economic and political situation in the world, for the latter is largely dependent upon the former. Our mechanical civilisation will be simplified, and an era ushered in which will be free from the incubus of money (its possession and its non-possession), and the human family will recognise universally its status as a bridging kingdom between the three lower kingdoms of nature and the fifth or spiritual kingdom. There will be time and

As I said above, the first use of this energy has been material destruction; this was inevitable and desirable; old forms (obstructing the good) have had to be destroyed; the wrecking and disappearance of that which is bad and undesirable must ever precede the building of the good and desirable and the longed-for emergence of that which is new and better.

The constructive use of this energy and its harnessing for the betterment of humanity is its real purpose; this living energy of substance itself, hitherto shut up within the atom and imprisoned in these ultimate forms of life, can be turned wholly into that which is good and can bring about such a revolutionising of the modes of human experience that (from one angle alone) it will necessitate and bring about an entirely new economic world structure.

It lies in the hands of the United Nations to protect this released energy from misuse and to see that its power is not prostituted to selfish ends and purely material purposes. It is a "saving force" and has in it the potency of rebuilding, of rehabilitation and of reconstruction. Its right use can abolish destitution, bring civilised comfort (and not useless luxury) to all upon our planet; its expression in forms of right living, if motivated by right human relations, will produce beauty, warmth, colour, the abolition of the present forms of disease, the withdrawal of mankind from all activities which involve living or working underground, and will bring to an end all human slavery, all need to work or fight for possessions and things, and will render possible a state of life which will leave man free to pursue the higher aims of the Spirit. The prostituting of life to the task of providing the bare necessities or to

---

freedom for a soul culture which will supersede our modern methods of education, and the significance of soul powers and the development of the superhuman consciousness will engross the attention of educators and students everywhere.

A second discovery will grow out of the present investigations as to light and colour.

The third development, which will be the last probably to take place, will be more strictly in the realm of what the occultists call magic. It will grow out of the study of sound and the effect of sound, and will put into man's hands a tremendous instrument in the world of creation.

making it possible for a few rich and privileged people to have too much when others have too little, will come to an end; men everywhere can now be released into a state of life which will give them leisure and time to follow spiritual objectives, to realise richer cultural life, and to attain a broader mental perspective.

But, my brothers, men will fight to prevent this; the reactionary groups in every country will neither recognise the need for, nor desire this new world order which the liberation of cosmic energy (even on this initial tiny scale) can make possible; the vested interests, the big cartels, trusts and monopolies that controlled the past few decades, preceding this world war, will mobilise their resources and fight to the death to prevent the extinction of their sources of income; they will not permit, if they can help it, the passing of the control of this illimitable power into the hands of the masses, to whom it rightly belongs. The selfish interests among the big stockholders, the banking firms and the wealthy organised churches will oppose all change, except in so far as it will benefit them and bring more financial gain to their coffers.

Signs of this opposition can already be seen in the utterances of certain powerful men who are today encouraging a gloomy outlook in London and in Washington and elsewhere; the Vatican, that wealthy and reactionary ecclesiastical organisation, has already expressed its disfavour, because that Church knows—as do all the vested and monied interests—that their days are numbered, provided humanity governs its decisions during the next fifty years by the idea of the greatest *good* to the greatest number. World decisions must therefore, in the future, be based upon a steady determination to further right human relations and to prevent selfish control, financial or ecclesiastical, by any group of men, anywhere, in any country. We believe the determination of Great Britain, the United States, and Canada, who are in possession of the secrets, is along these lines.

These few suggestions will give you much food for thought and real ground for happy, confident, forward thinking. Organise now for the goodwill work. The future of the world lies in the hands of the men of goodwill and in those who have unselfish purpose everywhere. This release of energy will eventually make money, as we know it, of no moment whatsoever; money has proved itself (owing to man's limitations) a producer of evil and the sower of dissension and discontent in the world. This new released energy can prove itself a "saving force" for all mankind, releasing from poverty, ugliness, degradation, slavery and despair; it will destroy the great monopolies, take the curse out of labour, and open the door into that golden age for which all men wait. It will level all the artificial layers of modern society and liberate men from the constant anxiety and gruelling toil which have been responsible for so much disease and death. When these new and better conditions are established, then men will be free to live and move in beauty and to seek the "Lighted Way."

SECTION FOUR

STAGES IN THE EXTERNALISATION OF THE HIERARCHY

STAGES IN THE EXTERNALISATION

The Subjective Basis of the New World Religion

Introductory Statements   December 1919

Those thoughtforms which will materialise as the religion of the New Age already exist on the mental plane and are in process of precipitation upon the physical plane. Their lineaments can already be discerned. The wise Guides of the race, working under the Christ and having in view the need of the public for a form, seek at this time to hold just as much as may be of the old form and lineaments, as much, that is, as is consistent with evolution and progress. In the West, what the Great Ones seek to break is not the form of Christianity but the grip of the Churches on the minds of the masses. The old forms of thought and of interpretation are now too restricted and too tightening in their hold upon the imprisoned and struggling life. That life must break forth. It cannot be confined by the ancient restrictions. Yet at this time there does not exist the need for an utterly new venture or for an entirely new presentation of truth. Nature and evolution move with gentle gradations and not with breaks and uncorrelated manifestations in the world of forms. In all the progressing developments, the old outlines can be seen—enlarged, purified and more beautiful, yet recognisable as the old form on a higher turn of the spiral. It is not the freak cults, nor the widely divergent sects, nor the bands of advanced religious revolutionaries who can meet the crying need of the many enquirers today. What is required is the re-vivification of the old forms, and their infusion with fresh life; the old organisations must be awakened to the hour of opportunity and must change from static organisations to living organisms. The old rituals must be revived and brought up to date (in the esoteric sense of the word) and the religious students of the world must be graduated into a higher school, given the occult interpretations, and taught that, after all, the truth has been present all the time, but hidden and misinterpreted.

It is surely easier to swing the masses into step and give them the newer light of truth if that light is poured on to familiar ground. All must be given the chance to see and hear, and be offered the opportunity to weigh and judge the significance of reality. It is not just the two or three of supreme importance, or who have the nerve to take the needed forward steps, who must receive prime consideration, but the truth must be stepped down and adapted in such a way that the advanced minds, the enquiring minds, and the reactionary masses may have opportunity proffered them, to the measure of their receptivity. Did not the greatest of all the Great Ones do this Himself in the synagogue and with His disciples in Judean days?

The aspirants and disciples of the world must realise that the hour has struck, and that the forces of the Christ are being marshalled for a supreme endeavour. These forces include both the human and the angel evolutions. It might be of use if I were to give you some idea of the scheme of preparation for the transition period between the old age and the new as it is in process of completion in the Council Chamber of the Great Lord. Your acceptance and understanding of it and of its symbolic implications are dependent upon your capacity to assimilate truth, to use your intuition, and thus to assist in the work itself when the right time comes.

One event is already in process of manifesting. The Christ and His disciples, the Masters of Wisdom and the Great Companions, are approaching nearer to the physical plane. The work of mental preparation for that event, and

the construction of the thoughtform of the advent or second
Coming, has now been completed. There remains the precipitation of that event, its appearance on astral levels and
its materialisation on the physical plane. I would ask all
of you who read these words anent the second Coming, to
reserve opinion as to the exact nature of that event. Keep
the concept *impersonal* and link not that appearance to a
personality or to an individual. If you make the mistake of
attaching the meaning to an individual, you will limit your
understanding and fail in right recognition of group purpose. The work of pouring out the principle of love (which
is the Christ principle) and of lifting the masses in their
consciousness to the pitch where they can understand and
welcome that love-principle is the main work of the new
age, and it will inaugurate the age of brotherhood and mould
humanity into the likeness of the Christ. That the oriental
peoples may call this great Official by another name than
that of "The Christ" has no bearing on reality and alters
not the fact of His influence and His esoteric coming.

Certain of the Masters have the work under Their control, and through Their grouped disciples are already actively
engaged in the work of preparation. The Master Morya,
the Master K.H. and the Master Jesus are the three working
at this time in closest cooperation with the Christ. With
them work the Master Hilarion, He Whom you call the
Master D.K., and another Master Who is specially linked
with the work of preparation in the sacred land of India.
One of the English Masters is also exceptionally active, and
the Master in America is laying His plans toward an active
participation in the work. These consecrated Workers form
a nucleus around the Christ and direct much of the preparatory work. It is not possible for me to tell you the lines of
Their activity; I can but give you evidence which may later
be demonstrated as true. These Masters are definitely preparing Themselves for the task of outer activity and are
intensifying Their work on the astral plane. To this fact
can be traced the interest people are now showing in occultism and in the work of the Masters; more and more people

re becoming sensitive to and conscious of Their presence, nd more and more are finding their way into the groups f disciples.

The Master Morya is at this time acting as the inspirer f the great national executives throughout the world. E'en hose whose ideals coincide not with yours are being welded nto the world plan, and much of their immediate work s organising the individual nations and welding them into n homogeneous whole, preparatory to their entrance into he great international thoughtform. All who work with far ision and all who hold before any seething and bewildered ation an ideal *for the whole* are under His wide inspiration. nternationalism is the aim of His endeavour. With Him orks the great Angel or Deva of the spiritual plane, referred o in the *Treatise on Cosmic Fire* as the Lord Agni; He eeks to touch with the hidden spiritual fire the head centres f all intuitive statesmen. Three great groups of angels— he gold, the flame coloured and the white and gold—work n mental levels with those lesser angels or devas who vitalise houghtforms and who keep alive the thoughts of the Guides f the race for the benefit of humanity.

The Master K.H., the Chohan on the teaching ray and Ie Who will be the next world teacher, is already active n His line of endeavour. He is attempting to transmute he thoughtform of religious dogma, to permeate the hurches with the idea of the Coming, and bring to a sor- owing world the vision of the Great Helper, the Christ. He orks with the rose devas and with the blue devas on astral evels, with the wise help of the great guardian Angel of hat plane, called (in Hindu terminology) the Lord Varuna. The activity of the astral plane is being much intensified and he angels of devotion, in whom the aspect of divine love s pre-eminent, work with the astral bodies of all those who re ready to strengthen and redirect their spiritual aspiration nd desire. They are the angels who guard the sanctuaries f all the churches, cathedrals, temples and mosques of the orld. They are now increasing the momentum of their ibration for the raising of the consciousness of the attendant congregations. The Master K.H. works also with the prelate of the great Catholic Churches—Greek, Roman and Anglican —with the leaders of the Protestant communions, with the foremost workers in the field of education, and also through and with, the dominant demagogues and organisers of the people. His interests lie with all those who, with unselfish intent, strive after the ideal, and who live for the helping of others.

The Master Jesus works especially with the masses of the Christian people who inhabit the occidental countries and who gather in the churches. He is distinctively a great leader, an organiser, and a wise general executive. A special group of devas work under His command, and His connection with all true church leaders and executives is very close. He acts ceaselessly on the inner esoteric council of the churches, and with Him the groups of violet angels cooperate. In church matters He Himself carries out the behests of the Christ, saving Him much and working as His intermediary. This will seem logical to you, for His destiny is closely interwoven with the Christian Church and it marks the culmination of His work for the West. No one knows or understands so fully and wisely as He the problems of the Western culture, nor the needs of the people who carry forward the destiny of Christianity.

The Master Hilarion is actively occupied in the field of America, stimulating the intuitive perception of its people. He has under observation all those who are true psychics and who develop their powers for the good of the community. He controls and transmutes the great active movements which endeavour to strip the veil from the world of the unseen. He impresses the minds of those whose vision will justify His effort. And He has much to do with various psychical research movements throughout the world. With the aid of certain groups of angels, He works to open up the world of departed souls to the seeker, and much that has of late convinced the materialistic world of life beyond has emanated from Him.

He Whom you call the Master D.K. works much with

those who heal with pure altruism; He occupies Himself with those who are active in the laboratories of the world, with great philanthropic world movements such as the Red Cross, and with the rapidly developing welfare movements. His work also embraces teaching, and He does much at this time to train the various disciples of the world, taking the disciples of many of the Masters and so relieving Them temporarily, in this hour of crisis, from Their teaching responsibilities. Many of the healing angels, such as those referred to in the Bible, cooperate with Him.

The Master Who works in and for India labours with the minds of the politicians, educators and religious dreamers and idealists. He strengthens the efforts of all those who work for the liberation of the submerged masses, provided their methods are constructive and not destructive, and that the gains desired are not furthered at the expense of any part of the human family. He labours not to exalt one section of the populace at the expense of another, but works towards brotherhood and the right understanding of the requirements of all souls, be they far advanced along the path, or just starting upon their planetary pilgrimage under the Law of Rebirth.

One of the English Masters has in hand the definite guidance of the Anglo-Saxon peoples towards a joint destiny. The future for the Anglo-Saxon is great and not yet has the highest flow of the tide of its civilisation been reached. History holds much glory for England and America when they work together for world good, not supplanting each other or interfering with each other's empire but working in the fullest unison for the preservation of the peace of the world and the right handling of world problems in the field of economics and of education.

As the seventh Ray of Organisation and of ceremonial work is now coming into prominence and manifestation, the work of the Master on that ray is that of synthesising, on the physical plane, all parts of the plan. The Master Rakoczi takes of the general plan as it is outlined in the inner Council Chamber and approximates it to the possible.

He might be regarded as acting as the General Manager for the carrying out of the plans of the executive council of the Christ.

It might be of interest here to point out that when He comes Whom angels and men await, and Whose work it is to inaugurate the new age and so complete the work He began in Palestine two thousand years ago, He will bring with Him some of the great Angels, as well as certain of the Masters. The angels have ever been active in Biblical history, and will again enter into the lives of human beings with more power than has lately been the case. The call has gone out for them again to approach humanity, and with their heightened vibration and superior knowledge unite their forces with those of the Christ and His disciples for the helping of the race. They have, for instance, much to communicate anent colour and sound, and the effect of these two forces on the etheric bodies of men and animals and flowers. When what they have to impart is apprehended by the race, physical ills and sickness will be offset. The group of violet angels or devas who work on the four etheric levels will be especially active and they will work in the four main groups of men who are in incarnation at any given time. Four rays dominate at any period, with one of the four more potent than the other three. You have this idea symbolised in the four castes in India and you will find also that these four castes are found universally throughout the planet.

These four groups of angels are a band of servers, pledged to the service of the Christ, and their work is to contact men and to teach them along certain lines.

a.   They will teach humanity to see etherically, and this they will do by heightening human vibration by interaction with their own.

b.   They will give instruction in the effect of colour in the healing of disease, and particularly the efficiency of violet light in lessening human ills and in curing those physical plane sicknesses which originate in the etheric body.

They will also demonstrate to the materialistic thinkers of the world the fact that the superconscious world exists and that angels and men who are out of incarnation and possess no physical bodies can be contacted and known.

They will train human beings in the knowledge of superhuman physics so that weight shall be for them transmuted. Motion will become more rapid, speed will be accompanied by noiselessness and smoothness, and hence fatigue will be eliminated. In the human control of etheric levels lies the overcoming of fatigue and the power to transcend time. Until this prophecy is a fact and recognised as such, the meaning of the above words will remain obscure.

They will teach humanity how rightly to nourish the body and to draw from the surrounding ethers the requisite food. Man will concentrate his attention upon the etheric body and the work and health of the physical body will become increasingly automatic.

They will also teach human beings as individuals and as a race to expand their consciousness to include the superphysical. In the accomplishment of this, the separating web (the veil of the temple) which divides the physical plane from the unseen world will be recognised as a fact in nature by the scientist. Its purpose will be acknowledged. Eventually it will be destroyed, by man discovering how to penetrate it. The date is imminent.

Through the increasing sensitivity of men and through the steady thinning of the separating veil, more and more during the coming years will the telepathic faculties of men and their power to respond to inner inspiration be developed and demonstrated. By the growth of intuitional telepathy and the increasing comprehension of the power of colour and sound will the work of the Christ and of the Great Ones be contacted and understood, and the peoples released from the thralldom of the past and enabled to enter into the liberty of the Kingdom of God.

Religious Organisations in the New Age

Let us now return to our consideration of the spread of the deepened religious ideals and the growth of the new religious organisms. In the process of transmuting the old form and so releasing the imprisoned life, there are two things which are steadily held in view by the Guides of our evolution:

First, that the general public serves or is dominated by the concrete mind and is unable to grasp abstractions. It is the form which matters to them the most, for they are conservative and cling to the familiar. The church is intended to serve the masses and is not intended to be of use (except as a field of service) to the esotericists of the world, for they heed not the form to the same extent, having contacted somewhat the inner compelling life.

Secondly, the church movement, like all else, is but a temporary expedient and serves but as a transient resting place for the evolving life. Eventually, there will appear the Church Universal, and its definite outlines will appear towards the close of this century. In this connection, forget not the wise prophecy of H.P.B. as touching events at the close of this century. This Church will be nurtured into activity by the Christ and His disciples when the outpouring of the Christ principle, the true second Coming, has been accomplished. No date for the advent do I set, but the time will not be long.

The Christian church in its many branches can serve as a St. John the Baptist, as a voice crying in the wilderness, and as a nucleus through which world illumination may be accomplished. I indicate the hope. I do not assert a fact. Its work is intended to be the holding of a broad platform. The church must show a wide tolerance, and teach no revolutionary doctrines or cling to any reactionary ideas. The church as a teaching factor should take the great basic doctrines and (shattering the old forms in which they are expressed and held) show their true and inner spiritual significance. The prime work of the church is to *teach,* and *teach ceaselessly,* preserving the outer appearance in order to reach the many who are accustomed to church usages. Teachers must be trained; Bible knowledge must be spread; the sacraments must be mystically interpreted, and the power of the church to heal must be demonstrated.

The three main channels through which the preparation for the new age is going on might be regarded as the Church, the Masonic Fraternity and the educational field. All of them are as yet in relatively static condition, and all are as yet failing to meet the need and to respond to the inner pressure. But in all of these three movements, disciples of the Great Ones are to be found and they are steadily gathering momentum and will before long enter upon their designated task.

The *Masonic Movement* when it can be divorced from politics and social ends and from its present paralysing condition of inertia, will meet the need of those who can, and should, wield power. It is the custodian of the law; it is the home of the Mysteries and the seat of initiation. It holds in its symbolism the ritual of Deity, and the way of salvation is pictorially preserved in its work. The methods of Deity are demonstrated in its Temples, and under the All-seeing Eye the work can go forward. It is a far more occult organisation than can be realised, and is intended to be the training school for the coming advanced occultists. In its ceremonials lies hid the wielding of the forces connected with the growth and life of the kingdoms of nature and the unfoldment of the divine aspects in man. In the comprehension of its symbolism will come the power to cooperate with the divine plan. It meets the need of those who work on the first Ray of Will or Power.

The Church finds its mission in the helping of the devotee, in aiding the great public which is innately religious and of good will. It hides in its heart those who vibrate to

the great love ray, the second Ray of Love-Wisdom. Chris
Himself works through it and by its means seeks to contac
the vast Christian public. It is the leaven in His hands t
leaven the whole lump, and being in a form comprehende
by the people, it can touch the great masses of seeking souls

By means of the *educational work* of the world, th
Great Lord seeks to reach those of the intelligent public wh
cannot be reached by means of ceremonial and symbolism
as in Masonry, or by religious means and ritual, as in th
Church. It touches the masses and those in whom the in
telligence aspect predominates to the lessening of the othe
two aspects. It aids those men who are predominantly o
the third Ray of Intelligent Activity.

In all these bodies there are to be found esoteric group
who are the custodians of the inner teaching and whos
uniformity in aspiration and in technique is one. Thes
inner groups consist of occult students and of those who ar
in direct or occasional touch with the Masters and of thos
whose souls are in sufficient control so that the will of th
Hierarchy may be communicated and gradually filter dow
to the channel of the physical brain. These groups whic
constitute the true inner esoteric group are many, but thei
membership is yet small, for the fact that a student ma
belong to any of the outer esoteric groups so-called is n
indication of his true esoteric status. When the few who ar
the true esoteric students of the world know the differenc
between etheric and astral forms, between mental clair
audience and clairvoyance and their astral counterparts, be
tween the elementals of thought and the elementals of na
ture, then will the Christ and His church have a rea
esoteric group on the physical plane and the outer organisa
tions receive the needed stimulation. That is why it is neces
sary to work with the students at this time and train them i
the nature of true occultism. When we understand bette
the significance of time in prevision, and of force in move
ment, and when we comprehend more fully the laws tha
control the subtler bodies, and through them therefore th
laws that function on the planes whereon those bodies ex

press themselves, then will there be more intelligent and more useful work offered in cooperation with the Occult Hierarchy.

In the esoteric group, which is composed of the true spiritual esotericists found in all exoteric occult groups, in the church, by whatever name it may be called, and in Masonry you have the three paths leading to initiation. As yet they are not used, and one of the things that will eventuate—when the new universal religion has sway and the nature of esotericism is understood—will be the utilisation of the banded esoteric organisms, the Masonic organism and the Church organism as initiating centres. These three groups converge as their inner sanctuaries are approached. There is no dissociation between the One Universal Church, the sacred inner Lodge of all true Masons, and the innermost circles of the esoteric societies. Three types of men have their need met, three major rays are expressed, and the three paths to the Master are trodden, leading all three to the same portal and the same Hierophant.

It must not be forgotten that only those souls who are on the Probationary Path or the Path of Discipleship will form the nucleus of the coming world religion. It exists on the inner planes for the purpose of gathering out of all the churches those who have reached the point in evolution where they can consciously and of their own free will place their feet upon that PATH which leads to the centre of peace; who can in full awareness turn their eyes upon the Great Lord, and transmute the life of worldly endeavour into the life of service. The first detachment gathered into the coming Church will be found to be a part of the present great band of servers. These have, down the ages, been associated with the Christ in His work. Remember always the fact of the work He did in connection with the last advent, and remember likewise that in the turning of the cyclic wheel, in the evolution of the spiral, similar conditions will eventuate, the same needs arise, and the same egos incarnate that were present in the days of old in Palestine. The numbers of those associated with Him will be greatly increased, for all who knew Him in earlier incarnations in the ancient East, all whom He cured or taught, all who contacted Him or in any way incurred karma with Him or with the Master Jesus, will have the opportunity to cooperate at this time. Each sincere aspirant who is closely connected with the present Church organisations, who feels a close link with the Christ and who loves Him, can be practically sure that in Palestine they saw Him, knew Him and mayhap served and loved Him.

The sacraments, properly understood, serve to strengthen this link and realisation, and such a one as that of Baptism (when entered upon with understanding) will draw forth oft a response from the Great Lord Himself. It is almost as if a golden strand were directed from His heart to the heart of the servant—a strand unbreakable and unfathomable and which, with each administration of any of the holy rites in the succession of lives, becomes stronger, broader and brighter. Eventually these many strands will become reabsorbed into their source when the Body of the Christ—one of the seven Heavenly Men on the second or monadic plane—is completed in full expression, for each one linked to Him becomes, in a vital sense, a cell in His Body. This the initiate Paul truly sensed and knew. Via this strand passes the power to strengthen, to stimulate, to vivify and to bless, and this is the true apostolic succession. All true disciples are priests unto the Lord.

There is no question therefore that the work to be done in familiarising the general public with the nature of the Mysteries is of paramount importance at this time. These Mysteries will be restored to outer expression through the medium of the Church and the Masonic Fraternity, if those groups leave off being organisations with material purpose, and become organisms with living objectives. When the Great One comes with His disciples and initiates we shall have (after a period of intensive work on the physical plane beginning around the year 1940) the restoration of the Mysteries and their exoteric presentation, as a consequence of the first initiation. Why can this be so? Because the Christ, as you know, is the Hierophant of the first and second initiations and He will, if the preparatory work is faithfully and well done, administer the first initiation in the inner sanctuaries of those two bodies. Many faithful workers will, during His period of work on earth, take this first initiation, and some few will take the second. The race has now reached a point where many souls are on the Probationary Path and need but the heightening of their vibration (made possible by His Presence) to reach the portal of the Path itself.

And now what is it that you all can do? What is the condition surrounding the aspirants of the world today? We have a world full of unrest, a world full of pain, sorrow and strife, a world in which the emotional bodies of humanity are in a condition of tremendous disturbance, a world in which animals, men, women and children suffer, agonise and die; a world in which hunger, sin, sickness, famine, rapine, and murder stalk unarrested; a world in which the forms of religion exist but the life has gone, in which science is prostituted to the ends of money and hate, and in which the produce of the earth is not for the sustenance of the race but for the nourishing of the purses of the few; a world in which faith is oft the subject of scoffing, in which unselfishness is regarded as the attribute of a fool, and in which love is exploited in its lowest expression, sex. Is this the atmosphere in which the Christ and His disciples can breathe? Is this a condition in which They can find harmonious influences? Is this a state of affairs in which They can work and live? Are the vibrations extant upon this planet similar to Theirs and to which They can respond? We know that it is not so and that much must be done to facilitate Their work. What then can we do?

First, teach the law of evolution and its inevitable corollary, perfected men. Men must be taught that such Great Souls exist, and exist entirely to serve Their fellow-men. The public must be familiarised with Their names and attributes, with Their work and purpose, and men must be told that They are coming forth for the salvation of the world.

Secondly, disciples and aspirants must on every hand live harmoniously and *love*. The violent vibrations of our surroundings must be stilled by a strong counter vibration of love, remembering ever that as we work on the side of evolution, the power of the Godhead itself is with us, available for use. Naught can withstand the steady pressures of love and harmony when they are applied long enough. It is not spasmodic efforts that count. It is the long-sustained, unvarying pressure which eventually breaks down opposition and the walls of separativeness.

Thirdly, esoteric organisations must stand for all that tends to unity. All types of work, all the exterior efforts of the many organisations must meet with loving cooperation and assistance. We stand in a world of endeavor as focal points for love. Our objective is the helping of the Great Ones and the rendering to Them of that intelligent assistance which will make Their plans for humanity materialise. Through us, They choose to work for the uplift of the world, and through the esoteric groups there must be the putting forth of that intensified spiritual effort which will stem the tide of evil and avert the possible difficulties that lurk in the darkness of the present chaos. The living organism of aspirants and disciples can provide a centre of peace, power and love, of practical help and spiritual uplift such as the world has not hitherto seen. Such is the hope. See you to it.

Definite work must also be done in healing, in exorcising, in curing mental and astral diseases, and it must be demonstrated to the world that the ancient power to heal still lies in the hands of those who consistently follow the Christ. Those who use this power *only* for the sake of the little ones, taking and seeking no personal reward, can manifest the ancient way to heal which has small resemblance to the modern methods of the mental schools.

Preparation too must be given to the developing of the higher psychic powers, and through the trained expression of those powers can proof be given to the scientists of the world of the latent forces in man which can be utilised by those who wisely and sanely follow in the footsteps of the

Christ, the greatest Psychic of all time. Hospitals and schools will appear under the direct guidance of the Masters; Teachers Who can heal will come forth, and others will appear who will train the minds of the pupils to be responsive to direct inspiration from above. The faculty of the intuition must be developed scientifically.

Finally, Church members and members of the Masonic fraternities must familiarise themselves with the inner significance of the various rites, ceremonies, colours and rituals, and with the work performed upon the floor of the temple. They must know why such and such things are done in due order and the reason for the various precedences, the words, gestures and acts.

Should there be a real and true response to these practical suggestions, it may be possible for the work to go forward more rapidly than at present seems possible. Much trouble and stress may be averted if the aspirants of the world measure up to their proffered opportunity and make due sacrifice and effort. Much preliminary work has to be done. There must be much heavy work, ploughing the soil and weeding out that which is undesirable.

This may take seven years. The work to be done in that period will be silent educational work, and the diligent propaganda that the Church and analogous organisations can do. Classes must be held by the occultists of the world in which the teaching is stepped down to meet the need of the little ones; the broad platform upon which the Church should stand should be proclaimed, and instruction should be given in the meaning of its ceremonies and teachings. Then will follow seven years of germination of the seed sown, a period of growth and developing influences. This brings us to the period of thirteen years from now for the cycle of fourteen began the year before I proffered you these suggestions. Should the work progress as desired, it may mark the time of the near appearing of the Great Lord and the close sound of His feet.

These Servers who watch on the inner side, the disciples and initiates engaged in this work, watch with loving care all who struggle in the thick of the fray. They are like the Headquarters Staff who follow the battle from a secure eminence. In Their security lies your ultimate success, for They hold in Their hands the solution of many problems and apply the solution when the battle goes contrary. One thing always I appeal to you to remember, for it is of vital importance. It is the fact that in the destruction of the form lies hid the secret of all evolutionary growth. This is not a truism. You can see it in constant expression. The Masters utilise the form (a form of Church organisation, a Masonic Fraternity, an esoteric group) as much as may be. They seek to work through it, imprisoning the life within the confining walls for just as long as the purpose is served and the race is instructed through that form. Then comes the time when the form may no longer serve the intent, when the structure atrophies, crystallises, and becomes vulnerable and easily destroyed. So it goes, and a new form takes its place Watch and see if this is not ever so. In the infancy of the race the forms for long endured. Evolution moved more slowly. But now on this upward trend the form has but short duration. It lives vitally for but a brief period; with rapidity it moves through its cycle; with rapidity it disintegrates and is succeeded by another. This rapidity will increase and not decrease as the consciousness, or inner expanding realised life of the race, vibrates to a more rapid rate of rhythm.

This will be tremendously increased during the vital and unusual cycle upon which we entered in 1918, which will be tremendously speeded up in 1925, and will climax in a peculiar sense in 1934. We shall then enter upon three years of excessive endeavour in an effort to hasten the Coming and to prepare mankind for the great day of opportunity. You who know of these times and can interpret them aright in the light of the illumined intuition, must unite together for the rendering of Service and for the helping of the Brotherhood, of which the Christ is the divine Leader, and of which the Masters, the initiates, disciples and aspirants are the working and living organism on the physical plane.

The Externalisation of the Ashrams

January 1946

In these words I refer to an aspect of the amazing enterprise upon which the Hierarchy is embarked within this cycle: Its appearance, expression and activity upon the physical plane for the first time since it withdrew into the subjective side of life and focussed itself on the mental plane (instead of the physical) during the days of ancient Atlantis and after the war between the Lords of the Shining Countenance and Lords of the Dark Face, as *The Secret Doctrine* calls it. For millions of years, as a result of the triumph of evil in those days, the Hierarchy has stood in silence behind world events, occupied with the following work—a work which will eventually be carried on exoterically instead of esoterically:

1. The Hierarchy stands as a wall between humanity and excessive evil. Forget not that as humanity is thus protected that protection extends to all the subhuman kingdoms, of which the fourth kingdom, the human, is the Macrocosm. The excessive evil, emanating from cosmic sources, requires the trained skill of the Hierarchy and the fiat of Shamballa to prevent it flooding over disastrously.

2. The Hierarchy works constantly at the task of awakening the consciousness aspect in all forms, so that it is awakened, expanded and intelligently employed.

3. The Hierarchy directs world events, as far as mankind will permit (for the free will and free decision of mankind may not be ignored), so that the unfolding consciousness may express itself through developing and adequate social, political, religious and economic world forms. They give direction; They throw a light; They impress those who are in contact with Them, and through the inflow of ideas and through revelation They definitely influence the tide of human affairs.

4. The Hierarchy directs and controls, more than is realised, the unfolding cyclic cultures and their resultant civilisations. These can then provide adequate forms, temporarily

useful for the emerging soul of humanity. The format of cultures and civilisations receives special attention.

5. The Hierarchy receives and transmits energies and consequent forces from Shamballa, with resultant effects within the Hierarchy itself, and also with effects upon humanity and upon the soul of all things to be found in all kingdoms.

6. The Hierarchy receives that esoteric "Fire of God" which brings to an end cycles, ideologies, organisations and civilisations when the due and right time comes. This They do in order to make place for that which is better and which will prove adequate and not limiting to the awakening consciousness and the emerging life.

7. The Hierarchy prepares men for initiation by:

   a. Receiving them into the Ashrams of the Masters.
   b. Offering Their disciples opportunity to serve in relation to the emerging Plan.
   c. Inaugurating through the means of the disciples of the period those new presentations of the training needed for initiation. Each *major* cycle receives new forms of the same ancient, yet basic, teaching. This present one is such a cycle, and much of my own work is in connection with this.

All of these activities and functions of the Hierarchy are well known to many of you theoretically, and to some at first hand—which is a good and useful thing to recognise. These activities have all been carried on "behind the veil" and are, of course, only a very small part of the total work of the Hierarchy. Much of it would be entirely incomprehensible to you. However, if the disciples of this modern world, and the initiates, can measure up to their present and presented opportunity, it should be possible for all of this not only to be carried forward in the full light of day, but with the co-operation and the understanding acceptance of the intelligent people everywhere, and also with the devoted acquiescence (though blind acceptance) of the man in the street.

Something of this, something of the new activities which will be brought to the attention of disciples in physical bodies, something of the scope of the undertaking of externalisation, something of what all of you can do to prepare the way for this major change, and something of the tremendous difficulties involved, I am seeking to convey to you, if I can.

One of the things now occupying the attention of the Masters is the externalisation of their ashrams on the outer plane. This is preparatory to later envisioned developments. If this can be done then other developments may be possible. An extension of the ashram is desired. It was with this in view that I inaugurated a new activity in May 1941 and chose so many of my disciples resident in New York. I also began to give out the teaching on the stages of discipleship (*Discipleship in the New Age,* Vol. I, Section III) and suggested that the group members meet together for one full afternoon around the time of the full moon each month, and to do this in a quiet and unhurried spirit. I desired that they spend the entire afternoon in conference, mutual understanding, discussion of group problems as these affect group service, and—above all—make an attempt (through deep united meditation and the pooling of knowledge) to approach closer to the Hierarchy. This would aid them to work together as a group for world aiding and to do it *together.* I asked them to study the relation which exists between a Master and His disciples.

These groups, indicated for externalisation, exist on the inner side as part of one inner Group; they must be externalised for service purposes. The fact that this externalisation is possible indicates certain developments which are the result of the past, of the unfoldment of humanity's developing powers to recognise Reality, of the invocative cry of the masses everywhere, plus the directed invocation of the spiritual people of the world, and the effect of the world war (1914-1945). All these factors have wrought a great destruction in the materialistic world and have produced a very real expansion in the human consciousness; also, as one of the Masters, unknown to you, remarked at a meeting of Members of the Hierarchy a few weeks ago, "One of the gates is open; those who are ready can come in, but we now can go through it also, and can go to them in a new sense and more directly. May Shamballa help us."

It is realised by all in the Hierarchy that the major test connected with a higher initiation confronts Them. Disciples should attempt to realise the tremendous sacrifice involved in this outward move of the Hierarchy into secular existence. The higher the state of initiation, the harder it will be for the initiate concerned. It is, for instance, less of an effort for me to contact you than it would be for some of the Chohans, such as the Masters M. and K.H. I am nearer to you, because I am still utilising the same physical body in which I took the fifth initiation, nearly ninety years ago. Chohans have taken a still higher initiation and are focal points of powerful Ashrams; Their task of adjustment is very much harder. Their invocative appeal to the Lord of the World in His Council Chamber at Shamballa has been mounting for some time. It has been called "The Appeal for Alignment" because the Members of the Hierarchy feel and know that this great return to Earth which has been arranged for the Hierarchy after so long an absence, will call for a fuller expression of the spiritual will than even They realise; They know that it will require the cooperation of Shamballa as well as the cooperation of humanity.

What I have to say about the externalisation of the Hierarchy and its Ashrams could well be divided for the sake of clarity into the following points which will form the basis of the instruction. We shall attempt to follow this outline.

> Hierarchical Adjustment and Alignment:
>> Within Itself.
>> In connection with the Council Chamber of Sanat Kumara. Little can be said about this.
>> In relation with humanity.

You will note that this involves the three planetary centres.

Hierarchical preparation at the Wesak Festival.

The Mode of Approach towards Externalisation.
   Steps in the externalisation process.
   Approach via certain Ashrams.
   In the consciousness of the disciple in physical expression.
   Through dissemination of information of a preparatory nature.

The Externalisation itself. This involves:
   The Return of the Christ.
   The Ashrams concerned at the Coming.
   The organisation of the implicated Ashrams into due form on earth.
   The externalisation of the Ashrams.
   Adjustment of the Ashrams and the Masters to exoteric living.

It will involve also adjustment by disciples and aspirants to the increased stimulation, and the enunciation of certain basic statements.

The Work of the Externalised Ashrams.
   Creating and vitalising the new world religion.
   The gradual reorganising of the social order.
   The public inauguration of the system of initiation.
   The exoteric training of disciples and of humanity in this new cycle.

We can begin on our first point, but only those students who are an integral part of the Hierarchy and in active communication with some Ashram can profit in any measure by information on this subject. For example, those of you who are affiliated with my Ashram (or that of another of the Masters), and going through your preliminary training and functioning on the periphery of the hierarchical centre can get a general idea and develop (if you attempt to do so) an intuitive perception of the proposed hierarchical integrity and future functioning.

Resent not my words "functioning on the periphery," for they indicate great opportunity for service. The Masters need many such as you on the outskirts of Their Ashrams to aid in hierarchical endeavour, because you can reach the general public more easily than They can do, and you can step down the teaching far more adequately than could more advanced disciples. You and disciples like you are a definite part of the Hierarchy; as you function in an Ashram you have a most useful place, and I would beg you to have this ever in mind. I will, therefore, give you whatever information I can and which is permissible, but shall of necessity have to leave much unsaid.

Hierarchical Adjustment and Alignment

What do I mean by the use of the word "adjustment" in connection with the Hierarchy? Adjustment to karma, to the personality, to the soul, to circumstances in the three worlds, to the impact of astral forces, or to the thought currents of those not oriented to the Kingdom of God, does not constitute part of the training of Those Who are beyond the third degree of initiation. Initiates on and beyond that level have transcended reaction along these lines, whilst those below the third initiation are in process of rapid adjustment. I use the word 'adjustment' here definitely in the sense of *reorientation,* and in this sense much can be noted.

For aeons and for countless cycles, the Hierarchy has functioned withdrawn into a silence on the higher levels of the mental plane and on the buddhic levels where contact has had to be made with Them by those disciples who have, by discipline, development and service, fitted themselves to establish such a relationship. This reorientation and emergence into physical plane publicity is going to demand much from the Members of the Hierarchy. Just as it has not been easy for me to establish and retain contact with you even when you have established the right to such a contact, so—for Them—it is going to be still more difficult to be in touch with those who are not even disciples.

For aeons and for cycles, the Members of the Hierarchy have been submitting Themselves to the needed training in order to react correctly when fuller contact has been established by Shamballa with the Hierarchy. I would have you note the phrasing here. That contact has now been established as a result of the inflow of certain extra-planetary forces and by an "act of determined direction," emanating from the Council Chamber of the Lord of the World. Misunderstand me not. The Hierarchy has always been in touch with the "Place of Purpose" (as it has been called) through the medium of its Chohans and its senior Directors, such as the Christ, the Manu and the Lord of Civilisation. These great Beings have steadily revealed this purpose to the Members of the Hierarchy so that They have been able to grasp and work out the emerging Plan. But even to the Masters the Shamballa force has had to be stepped down, just as the force of the Hierarchy requires modifying for the average disciple and aspirant, if they are to respond constructively to it.

Today, however, things are somewhat changed. New inflowing energies and the partial "sealing" of evil in its own place (a sealing which will be progressively effective) have made a closer relationship possible. The Masters are somewhat freer from certain of the arduous labours of the past cycles. Some of the available inflowing Shamballa forces are being absorbed *directly* by humanity and by certain of the subhuman kingdoms, particularly the mineral kingdom. This latter absorption will lead eventually, when complete, to those volcanic episodes and those basic earthquakes which will change the face of the earth by the time the sixth rootrace comes into manifestation. It is this direct inflow to the kingdoms functioning exoterically in the three worlds which has relieved and will to some extent relieve the otherwise overpowering pressure upon the Hierarchy, and will also act as a great aligning antahkarana between the three planetary centres. It is to this alignment I refer in this instruction—the alignment of the three centres upon this planet and the adjustments that this necessitates and inevitably enforces.

For the sake of humanity in the first place, and secondarily for the development of the subhuman kingdoms, the Hierarchy has made certain difficult adjustments and alignments between the planetary centres, and these have been compulsory in their effects. Therefore, bear in mind that the adjustments which the Hierarchy may impose upon itself bear small resemblance to the adjustments which you have to make in relation to your personality life. They are all hallmarked by the idea of service to the whole. The Hierarchy in its true sense has no personality through which to express itself, and this greatly complicates the problems which have to be faced as it contemplates exoteric manifestation and work.

Adjustments and Alignments within the Hierarchy

What, in the last analysis, is this Hierarchy? It is a great salvaging corps of dedicated, liberated Units of Life, working in group formation with all forms and lives in all kingdoms and with all souls particularly. As the Hierarchy so works, its emphasis is solely on *the consciousness aspect* of all forms; its present agency of salvage and of service is the mind, as it expresses itself through the minds of all humanitarians, all aspirants, all disciples (of all rays and degrees) and of all initiates; the Hierarchy also can express itself through the medium of thought currents and ideas and through them impose its hierarchical concepts upon the embryonic minds of the general and average public; and it also directs the educational work of all nations, so that the undeveloped masses can become—in due turn—the intelligent general public.

The Hierarchy works, as you know, in or through three major departments, each possessing its full Personnel, and under three Great Lords. I have dealt with this in some detail in *Initiation, Human and Solar,* as well as elsewhere in my writings; more information at this point is needless and of no real service to you.

The Hierarchy works also through the seven major Ashrams and their affiliated Ashrams, and these "seven which are the forty-nine" represent in their totality the seven rays with their subrays, and are the custodians, transmitters and distributors of the seven ray energies to the seven planetary centres and—via these seven centres—to those in the fourth kingdom in nature (as they gradually unfold over the aeons) and then, via these, to the seven centres in individual man. Such is the synthesis.

The seven major centres or Ashrams within the Hierarchy are each presided over by Masters of Chohan rank; the seven subsidiary centres or Ashrams are presided over by Masters and Adepts (of the fifth and fourth initiations), aided by initiates of the third degree and certain picked and senior disciples. Several of the seven affiliated Ashrams are, as yet, incomplete as regards personnel, but vacancies are rapidly being filled as the spiritual effects of the world war (1914-1945) make themselves felt. These effects are very real and have been a source of great encouragement to hierarchical workers.

Before the Hierarchy can emerge (as is the intention), the relation between a major Ashram and its subsidiary Ashrams must be firmly established, whilst that between a major Ashram and other major Ashrams has to be brought more definitely and unquestionably closer to Shamballa, and under the influence of that great first ray centre. The energy which will align and adjust the subsidiary forty-nine Ashrams is that of the second Ray of Love-Wisdom. That, however, which will bring about a similar adjusting and aligning impetus in the seven major Ashrams is the energy of the first Ray of Will or Power. I have here given you a most important item of occult information, but one which is of no importance to you individually; it serves, however, to present proof of the significant occult relation between the three planetary centres. Just as the third planetary centre, Humanity, has now reached a point of intelligent development so that a closer rapport can be set up between it and the Hierarchy, so the Hierarchy also has moved forward as a unit so that a closer corresponding rapport can also be set up between It and Shamballa. Just as the rapport between the Hierarchy and Humanity is established via aspirants, disciples and initiates in physical existence who are responding to the love-wisdom of the universe in some measure and who work via the intelligent people in incarnation primarily, so rapport between Shamballa and the Hierarchy is being more closely established via the senior Ashrams, and not via the secondary ones. You have, therefore, a situation which might be depicted somewhat as follows:

I. First Planetary Centre ....Shamballa
        working through
    1. The seven Rays or the seven Spirits before the Throne.
    2. Certain great Intermediaries.
    3. The Council Chamber of the Lord of the World.

II. Second Planetary Centre ....Hierarchy
        working through
    1. The seven major Chohans and Their Ashrams.
    2. The forty-nine Masters of the secondary Ashrams.
    3. The sumtotal of the secondary Ashrams.

III. Third Planetary Centre ....Humanity
        working through
    1. Disciples in manifestation—of the seven ray types.
    2. The new group of world servers.
    3. The sumtotal of humanitarians, educators and men of goodwill.

This is but a rough picture and one which is not totally correct; it will, however, show you certain direct lines of contact and of relationship which *are* true and which will suffice to give you a vague and general idea of the new alignment being set up between the three major planetary centres, requiring new adjustments.

At this particular time, the emphasis of the needed alignments and adjustments with which the Hierarchy is faced is being placed upon activity *within the Hierarchy Itself*. The secondary Ashrams are being stimulated; new ones are being gradually formed, for there are not as yet forty-nine minor Ashrams; vacancies in the major Ashrams are being filled as rapidly as possible from the ranks of those working in minor Ashrams and the places of these latter are being taken by accepted disciples who are being fitted for this work through experience, difficulties and the tension of world service. All these changes necessitate much adjustment. The interior work of hierarchical alignment is in the charge of the Chohans of the Major Ashrams, whilst the task of superintending the interior adjustments incident to new alignments and the admission of new personnel is being watched over and directed by the forty-nine Masters who are in charge of minor Ashrams—either Ashrams with what is regarded as a full complement of workers, or Ashrams in process of attaining that full complement, or embryonic Ashrams of which there are already quite a few.

One of the results of this hierarchical alignment and adjustment will be the establishment, for the first time, of a fluid interplay and movement between the three planetary centres. Chohans are today passing out of the Hierarchy into the Council Chamber of the Lord of the World, or on to one or other of the Seven Paths; senior Masters in charge of Ashrams are taking higher grades of initiation and taking the rank of Chohans; initiates above the third degree are rapidly taking the fourth and fifth initiations and becoming Masters (taking both initiations in one life) , and their places are being taken by lesser initiates; these, in their turn, have been training disciples to take their places, until in this process of substitution and replacement we arrive at the door which symbolically stands between humanity and the Hierarchy, and today stands wide open, so that *accepted disciples* are taking initiation, *pledged disciples* are being accepted, and *accepting disciples* are taking their pledges.

Thus a great and new movement is proceeding and a tremendously increased interplay and interaction is taking place. This will go on until A.D. 2025. During the years intervening between now and then very great changes will be seen taking place, and at the great General Assembly of the Hierarchy—held as usual every century—in 2025 the date in all probability will be set for the first stage of the externalisation of the Hierarchy. The present cycle (from now until that date) is called technically "The Stage of the Forerunner". It is preparatory in nature, testing in its methods, and intended to be revelatory in its techniques and results. You can see therefore that Chohans, Masters, initiates, world disciples, disciples and aspirants affiliated with the Hierarchy are all at this time passing through a cycle of great activity.

In the adjustment necessitated by the rapidly advancing alignment, the Members of the Hierarchy are fitting Themselves for the objective work of public expression. This entails far more difficulty than you might imagine or anticipate, because it entails the development of that form of "resistance to the pull of the lower vibration" of which you can know nothing, for that lower vibration is a necessary aspect of your normal expression—little as you may like to realise this. You need to realise that there is nothing in the Masters or higher initiates which can respond to any vibration of this nature. Though They cannot absorb it or react to it or re-develop it again, it can cause Them the acutest discomfort and pain; that is the reason why the Son of God was called in The Old Testament a "man of sorrows and acquainted with grief". This did not in reality refer to His sufferings for poor miserable humanity (as orthodox theology so selfishly interprets it) but to the fact that He had to submit Himself to contact with humanity. The Hierarchy is therefore, along all lines (many of which I may not indicate or upon which I may not enlarge), preparing Itself for the experience of physical manifestation; It is also endeavouring to "create" the needed responsive apparatus which will be of such a nature that

Members of the Hierarchy may function with the minimum of difficulty on earth and will experience the least possible measure of handicap; They will thus be enabled to give full time and attention to the work to be done by Them in physical manifestation.

They are endeavouring also to establish a closer telepathic rapport and a more intimate (though strictly impersonal) relationship with Their disciples on all rays, so that there can be a free interplay of thought and a consequent better hierarchical integrity and one which—no matter what may happen in the three worlds—cannot be disrupted or in any way lessened.

Although for Them no astral plane exists and glamour is entirely non-existent, They have to learn to do a most peculiar thing: to work on the astral plane (because it exists for humanity and for the animal kingdom) , to traverse this region of glamour and then to "demonstrate light in dissipating fog" in a manner for which there has hitherto been no call. None of this information may make much sense to you, but I am simply seeking to go on record for the sake of those who will come after you. There is little more that I may give you anent adjustment and alignment within the Hierarchy. It is rapidly proceeding, and just in so far as disciples demonstrate upon the outer physical plane and in the three worlds their affiliation with an Ashram will they share in this dual process. Are you prepared for this?

In Connection with the Council Chamber of Sanat Kumara, the Lord of the World

As this subject concerns one of the seven goals towards which the Masters aim after They have attained the fifth initiation, it will be obvious to you that there is little that I can say about it. One of the seven Paths for which the Way of the Higher Evolution prepares the senior initiates is the Path of Earth Service. This Path, as you know, keeps the Masters attached to service in the three worlds for a period much longer than the average. It involves tremendous sacrifice. Just as the disciple has to live a dual life, with one part of his reflective nature and awareness centred in the life of the Hierarchy and the other part of his mental responsiveness equally centred on life in the three worlds, and this simultaneously, so the Master, when He chooses this Path, forms a constituent part of the Council Chamber of the Lord of the World and at the same time works consciously in the three worlds, via the Hierarchy (of which He remains also a part), and with the human and subhuman kingdoms in nature. As evolution proceeds, He will work increasingly via humanity because humanity will be shouldering its responsibilities as the Macrocosm of the lesser microcosm. This dual activity entails much specialised training, and as the initiatory process becomes exoteric and men everywhere recognise it and participate in it, the training which Members of the Hierarchy also undergo will not be so secret and mysterious as it is today. But the time has not yet come to publicise it.

Only certain further generalisations are here possible, some of which are already known to you because they are so broad that their inclusions and implications are obvious. This, for instance, concerns the "centre where the Will of God is known". Here at Shamballa work Those Who have unified Their personality will and Their spiritual will with the universal will, and such a unification inevitably brings knowledge. It is, however, not knowledge as you understand it. It is a blend of wisdom based on knowledge, understanding based on intuitive perception, and identification based on alignment, esoterically comprehended. For this peculiar condition or awareness we have no word in any language, and only the utilisation (the trained utilisation) of the abstract mind can possibly convey to you even an embryonic factual conception. But that type of imaginative conception will become more common during the next two centuries, and my words here will therefore serve an ultimate purpose. Those Who form the Council Chamber of the Great Lord are under no misapprehension as to His will because They see it *whole*. Paul, the initiate, hints at this when writing one of the Epistles; he is in touch then with certain Members of the Hierarchy and is concerned with the theme of Love, which is the fundamental hierarchical theme and motive. He says to Them: "Now we see through a glass darkly, but then face to face; now we know in part, but then shall we know even as we are known." He there points towards the future progress of the Hierarchy—a progress which remains as yet only a vague promise, lacking form and shape. But he wrote for initiates to whom love was a growing, vital concern, and to whom love and its practice meant light and the basic motif of all living, divine activity. It is not possible to reveal the will of God and the motivating Purpose of His manifesting Self, except to Those Who have demonstrated perfected love and Who register no sense of disunion or the faintest reaction to separateness.

At Shamballa, the Great Lives Who function there not only see manifestation whole and apart from all the limitations of time, but They *feel* all the major evolutionary impulses which are bringing the developing world into line with the divine Will. They embody those impulses not in terms of progressive movement, but in terms of one great divine and spiritual reaction. This idea can perhaps be best understood by you in terms of the Eternal AUM which is the symbol of the Eternal NOW. You have been told, and it has been demonstrated, that the AUM is composed of one major Sound, three minor sounds, and seven subsidiary vibratory tones. So it is with the Will of God which is embodied and held in synthesis by the Members of the Council Chamber. To Them, as They "hold the Will of God in solution, it is one clear note; as They see that Will in motion, it is three abiding chords, carrying outwards into all the worlds the Purpose of the ONE Who for aeons will abide; as They impel that Will to demonstrate, it is seven vibratory tones, drawing out into the reflected worlds the structure of the Plan. And thus the note, the chords and tone produce the Plan, reveal the Purpose and indicate God's Will." This is a quotation from certain of the ancient Archives which constitute the study of the Masters; they relate to the nature of Shamballa, its work and emanating energies.

Shamballa, as it constitutes the synthesis of understanding where our Earth is concerned, is also the centre where the highest Will of the Solar Logos is imposed upon the Will of our planetary Logos, Who is, as you know, only a centre in His greater body of manifestation. With this item of information you can have no possible concern; the Masters Themselves are only learning the Will of the planetary Logos; the objective of effort in Shamballa is, however, the apprehension of solar Purpose, the Plan of which is working out on the highest levels of our planetary system, just as the Will, Purpose and Plan of Shamballa work out on the three lowest levels of our planetary system. Again, this item of information serves only to indicate hierarchical objectives, and those objectives extend away from time and space into the Mind of God Himself.

There are certain synonyms which here may serve to develop your synthetic thinking and so bring in a definite measure of enlightenment.

SHAMBALLA	HIERARCHY	HUMANITY
Synthesis	Unity	Separation
Will	Purpose	Plan
Life	Soul	Appearance
Spirit	Consciousness	Substance
Livingness	Organism	Organisation
Apprehension	Polarisation	Focus of Activity
Power	Momentum	Action
Energy	Distribution	Forces
Direction	Transmission	Reception
Head	Heart	Throat

It will be apparent to you how little you can understand of the Shamballa intention when you realise that it is not easy for you to see any true distinction between unity and synthesis and, at the same time, how impossible it is for me to make the distinction clear. All I can say is that synthesis *is,* whilst unity is achieved and is the reward of action and effort. As you progress upon the Path of Initiation the meaning of unity clarifies. As you direct yourself towards the Way of the Higher Evolution synthesis emerges. More than that it would be useless for me to say.

This problem of the apparently impenetrable darkness of intention as grasped by Shamballa, of meaning, of inscrutability, of a spiritual imperviousness which *holds,* in spite of all fluctuations in the three worlds of human evolution and the remaining two of superhuman unfoldment, provides a situation to which the Hierarchy has to make adjustment through alignment. You are, in your small way, making your adjustment to the Hierarchy through a steady construction of the antahkarana, and in so doing are aiding in the construction of the antahkarana which unites Humanity and the Hierarchy—the first few strands of which were established through the sacrifices of certain of the Sons of God when the Hierarchy was founded on Earth. Today, the Hierarchy is working at the establishing of the linking strands between Itself and Shamballa, and good progress has already been made. It might be said here that for the past seven hundred years the chain of Hierarchy has been complete; by this I mean that the planetary rainbow bridge uniting the three major centres has existed. The task ahead of all these three major centres, working in alignment through adjustment, is to strengthen and beautify (if I may so express it), to electrify this bridge, thus producing full planetary intercommunication between the three centres and the four minor centres, so that "the weight of the Will of God, the momentum of the Purpose of Sanat Kumara and the Plan of His Representatives may progress unimpeded from point to point, from sphere to sphere and from glory to glory."

It is this complete establishment of relationship between Shamballa, the Hierarchy and Humanity which brought about the planetary crisis through which the world has just passed and, from some standpoints, is still passing.

Shamballa, as I have told you, can now reach Humanity, the third major centre, directly, and therefore has two points of planetary contact: the first, via the Hierarchy, as has been for long the case, and secondly, in a straight line, carrying energy direct to Humanity, without any transmission and consequent modifying of impact, as has also been the case hitherto. When this direct line of spiritual, dynamic, electrical energy made its first impact on earth (after the Great Council held in 1825), it first of all awakened men's thinking in a new and comprehensive way, producing the great ideologies; it aroused their massed desire, and registered obstruction on the physical plane. It found its course impeded and discovered it was faced with barriers. This energy from Shamballa, being an aspect of the ray of the destroyer, proceeded to "burn up" in the fires of destruction, all such hindrances upon the planes in the three worlds. This was the deeply esoteric and unrecognised cause of the war—the beneficent bringing to an end of the impediments to the free flow of spiritual energy down into the third centre; this was the factor which called "evil from its hidden place" and brought the opposing forces to the surface of existence, prior to their "sealing". To the extent that this was so, mankind in the World War (1914-1945) was the unhappy victim of spiritual circumstance; however, from the angle of man's historical past, humanity was the engineer of its own fate; but it took both the esoteric activity of Shamballa and the exoteric activity of humanity over a millennia of years to precipitate the conditions which made this new alignment possible and brought about the sealing (still being carried slowly forward), and plunged mankind into the vortex of war. This impelling downpouring energy from the highest centre penetrated not only to the heart of humanity, but into the very depths of the mineral kingdom, implicating also the animal and the vegetable expressions of divine life.

Because of this direct impact between Shamballa and Humanity, by-passing the Hierarchy, the Hierarchy was left free for the work of rehabilitation and salvaging, for reconstruction and for the application of the regenerative forces of resurrection. The Hierarchy needed and welcomed this interlude and recognised it as an essential aspect of the Plan.

The "cycle of Shamballa impact" is now over; the appeal of humanity to the Christ and His Hierarchy has again refocussed the energy of Shamballa via the Hierarchy, and the direct work of the Hierarchy with Humanity can again take on fresh meaning, can be re-established on new and somewhat different lines, and thus definitely bring in that "new heaven and new earth" for which men have so long waited. This will take time, but the new energies and their emerging qualities are adequate to the task, and will alleviate much and bring about great changes in due course of time. You will note, therefore, that the Hierarchy has been faced with three adjustments as the result of being deliberately "put out of alignment," though only temporarily, with both Shamballa and Humanity. This was symbolised for us at the Crucifixion when the Saviour hung pendant between heaven and earth. These adjustments are:

1. Adjustment to those extra-planetary energies which were released into the highest centre. This was made possible by two factors:

   a. The direct impact between Shamballa and Humanity or between will and intelligence. This is an important point to recognise.
   b. The temporary quiescence of the love principle, as the Hierarchy waited for the results and effects of this direct impact upon the earth.

This was effectively carried out with much destruction in the world of forms.

2. Adjustment to certain basic changes within the Hierarchy Itself in preparation for the process of externalisation which was begun this century.

3. Adjustment to a disciplined and reoriented humanity,

working today in the dark, it is needless to say, groping along unknown ways, appealing to the Hierarchy for more light and understanding, but awakened and alert for changes.

These adjustments are proceeding with rapidity; the technique being employed is realignment, through a definite action of the Will, as far as Shamballa is concerned, and by an outpouring of Love, as far as humanity is concerned. This Act of the Will is carried out by the three Heads of Departments in the Hierarchy, under the guidance of the Christ and by the Chohans of the seven major Ashrams. They constitute a group of ten to Whom this task has been committed, for the reason that They are the only Members of the Hierarchy Who possess the needed qualifications and in Whom the Will aspect is adequately developed. The task of pouring out the Love principle in a new and dynamic manner is being carried out by all the Masters and by all initiates who have taken the third initiation. This stream of love will focus itself each coming Full Moon in a special act or demonstration of love.

You will note also how fully occupied the Hierarchy is with work, preparatory to emergence, and with those plans and activities which will lead to renewed interior activity, based *not* on lack of previous unity and integrity, but on the absorption of new energies, made available via Shamballa, of these extra-planetary forces to which I have earlier referred. This task of reorganisation prior to moving outward, will be completed by May, 1946. Then the task of the new alignment with humanity will be started and the great work undertaken which will proceed for several hundred years.

In Relation with Humanity

I shall not deal here with the work to be done in centuries to come in and through humanity, which is the goal of all these adjustments—at least as far as your present interest is concerned. I shall touch only upon the activities of the Hierarchy as it establishes—on a more powerful basis—a more direct contact with mankind. Since 1925 the Hierarchy has directed Its thoughts to men, but It has not vitalised, as It will eventually do, the religious movements or churches in all lands, or the educational work in all countries, or any of the activities which are concerned with the aiding of humanity through welfare movements. It was felt that it was necessary for mankind to show the Hierarchy, as well as themselves, the nature of the impulses towards love and selflessness which may have been already established, and to do this free of hierarchical prompting and influence, and in this way demonstrating that they possessed that which might be depended upon as innate and as present in a living, creative manner. The demonstration has been *good*; humanity *has* shown creative love, of which goodwill and humanitarian efforts are the lowest aspects. The showing has been better than was anticipated, and this new and vital re-alignment between the Hierarchy and Humanity becomes now beautifully possible and can be carried forward without danger. The Hierarchy is now the Custodian of far greater power than heretofore, on account of Its adjustment to Shamballa.

This hierarchical readjustment to humanity is being carried out at this time in the Ashrams by the setting up of magnetic centres which, through their directed activity, will influence humanity in the coming large scale process of reorientation. In studying this, you must remember that these are not centres or concentrations of forces, but *groups of disciples* whose quality is oriented towards mankind and whose potency of thought will act magnetically upon aspirants and humanitarians and, through them and their goodwill activities, will reach and impress men everywhere. The adjustment being at this time undertaken, therefore, is between hierarchical groups and groups of men and women upon earth; it is intended, as you have been told, that Humanity itself will be the world-saviour, working with the aid of the Hierarchy—as yet invisibly behind the scenes. When this interim work of salvage is accomplished, then the Hierarchy will externalise Itself.

You can imagine the adjustments, therefore, going on in all the Ashrams in preparation for all this and—though I touch not upon it—you can imagine the general effect of these inter-hierarchical adjustments and alignments upon disciples and aspirants upon the earth; they are the first, needless to say, who will respond to this activity. As all this is taking place in the present difficult period of world rehabilitation, the immensity of the problem involved and the quality of the tension are abnormal. It is not easy for disciples today; of this the Hierarchy is well aware. This fact also involves for Them still another aspect of hierarchical adjustment. They have—for the sake of the work to be done—to establish a closer alignment between the inner Ashrams and the outer groups, between Themselves and Their senior disciples carrying the burden of the outer world service; this alignment has also to be extended between senior disciples and initiates and the workers on earth.

The pureness of the motives animating the Hierarchy will constantly emerge with greater clarity in your minds, as you attempt to understand, even in a small measure, Their problems. There are other problems of which you can know nothing—problems related to the new energies pouring into our planet, impersonally and dynamically; problems of fresh tensions, incident to stronger and new alignments; problems concerned with human enlightenments and reactions in the face of the darkness which evil initiated; problems of increased personnel, disturbing the rhythm but necessitated by the demand for workers; problems connected with the growth and training of the Members of the Hierarchy upon the Way of the Higher Evolution; other problems incident to the planetary crisis, to the Initiation of the Lord of the World Himself, and to the amazing demonstration of the success of the evolutionary process up to the present time. This success has been proven by the alignment for direct interplay of the three major planetary centres—Shamballa, the Hierarchy and Humanity.

HIERARCHICAL PREPARATION AT THE WESAK FESTIVAL

April-May 1946

I have delayed writing my usual Wesak message until this late date because of a certain event in the Hierarchy which was maturing and which necessitated my entire attention. This event was connected with the Wesak Festival and involved among other matters the formation of a new Ashram in which the Wisdom aspect would be of particular importance and not the Love aspect; this Ashram would also be related in a peculiar manner to the Buddha. It had to be formed at this time in order to be the recipient, and then the custodian, of certain "endowments" which the Buddha will bring at the time of the May Full Moon. The endowments concern the will-to-good of the Lord of the World, the Ancient of Days, though they do *not* concern goodwill as *you* understand that phrase. This Ashram, when duly formed and established, will enable the Members of the Hierarchy to respond to this aspect of the divine Purpose— the Purpose which as you know lies behind and implements the Plan; this Ashram, related to the Buddha, will be specifically under the close supervision of the Christ, and also of the Lord of Civilisation—at this time the Master R. They are the only two Members of the Hierarchy able to register the divine Purpose (in regard to its immediate objectives) in such a manner that the entire Hierarchy can be informed and can then work unitedly and intelligently at its implementation. More than this I may not tell you about this particular hierarchical move, affecting as it does both Shamballa and the Hierarchy.

This Wesak Festival is of supreme importance because it is the first Festival since the war ended, because it takes place at a time when a definite orientation of the Hierarchy will take place, and because a fresh tide of spiritual impulse and directed second ray energy will flood the entire Hierarchy; the work, therefore, to be done by the Hierarchy will be far more effective. This you may anticipate and upon this you can count.

But—as you may well have surmised—it is the Full Moon of June which is (this year) the season of prime and outstanding importance; it is in many ways easier for Western believers and esotericists to tune in and participate in the activities of the Hierarchy when closely connected with the Christ than it is in those related to the Buddha. The main intention in these early stages of keeping the Eastern Festival of Wesak is to familiarise the Western world with the fact of the presence of the Buddha and with His activities in connection with humanity. Such great progress has, however, taken place in the spiritual development of humanity that the Buddha need no longer continue with His task unless He so desires—and then only for a period of years, known to Him and the Lord of the World. He could cease His annual contact with the Hierarchy at this time, if He so chose, owing to the direct contact now established between the Hierarchy and Shamballa. This, however, He does not immediately choose to do. For a few decades longer He will cooperate with the Christ in widening the channel of contact between Shamballa, the Hierarchy and Humanity. After that, He will "proceed to His Own place" in the solar Hierarchy and will no longer visit the Himalayas annually, as has been His custom for so many centuries. The Eastern Festival of Wesak (Vaisaka) and the Christian day of remembrance, Good Friday, will fade out of the consciousness of humanity in due time; they are both festivals related to aspects of the first Ray of Power or Will. The abolition of the fear of death and the establishment of a close relation of the Hierarchy with Shamballa will render obsolete these ancient ceremonial rites.

In this message I would like to consider with you primarily the Festival of the Christ, held at the time of the Full Moon of June, and the work of the Christ as He prepares Himself for the fulfillment of His true mission on Earth. The Christian Church has so distorted that mission and ruthlessly perverted the intention for which He originally manifested that a consideration of that mission is deeply needed and should be revolutionary in its effects. Starting with St. Paul, the theologians interpreted His words in such a manner that they served to bridge the gap between the spiritual future of the world and the Jewish dispensation which should have been passing out. So effective has been their work that the teachings of the loving, simple Son of God have been largely ignored; the failure of Christianity can be traced to its Jewish background (emphasised by St. Paul), which made it full of propaganda instead of loving action, which taught the blood sacrifice instead of loving service, and which emphasised the existence of a wrathful God, needing to be placated by death, and which embodied the threats of the Old Testament Jehovah in the Christian teaching of hell fire.

This situation is one which the Christ is seeking to alter; it has been in preparation for His instituting a new and more correct presentation of divine truth that I have sought —with love and understanding—to point out the faults of the world religions, with their obsolete theologies and their lack of love, and to indicate the evils of Judaism. The present world faiths must return to their early simplicity, and orthodox Judaism, with its deep-seated hate, must slowly disappear; all must be changed in preparation for the revelation which Christ will bring.

The first things which the Christ will do, beginning with this Full Moon of June, will be to prepare all people everywhere (if possible through their regenerated, religious institutions) for the revelation for which all humanity waits.

It is this revelation which lies behind all the activities which now engross the attention of the Hierarchy. There have been many revelations of divine purpose down the ages, each of which uniquely altered the point of view and the pattern of living for men everywhere. There was the ancient revelation, given through the people of India, as to the existence of the Self and the Not-Self—a revelation which is now coming to have meaning through the teaching of modern psychology; there was the revelation of the Ten Commandments, given through the Jews and—because of the negativity shown then and today by the Jews—given in a negative and not a positive form. The Christ endeavoured to offset and bring to an end the need for the Ten Commandments, by giving us the eleventh commandment; this, if kept, would entail the keeping of all the others. There was the revelation which Christ Himself gave, summing it up for us in His life of service, in the love which He preached and in His constant repudiation of theological Judaism (the Sadducees and the Pharisees). This difficulty with Judaism still persists and is symbolised for us in the failure to recognise the Messiah when He came to them in their own country and let it be known that He came to the whole world and not to the Jews alone.

For this new revelation the Christ is preparing as are all the members of the Hierarchy, from the highest Chohan down to the humblest accepted disciple; it is for this that all the ashrams are getting ready; it is for this also that (in a weak and feeble manner) Christian people, those of the other world faiths, and spiritually minded people are likewise preparing.

Therefore, we have isolated (if I may use such a word) three activities to which the Christ is at this time dedicated:

1. The reorganisation of the world religions—if in any way possible—so that their out-of-date theologies, their narrow-minded emphasis and their ridiculous belief that they know what is in the Mind of God may be offset, in order that the churches may eventually be the recipients of spiritual inspiration.

2. The gradual dissolution—again if in any way possible—of the orthodox Jewish faith, with its obsolete teaching, its separative emphasis, its hatred of the Gentiles and its failure to recognise the Christ. In saying this I do not fail to recognise those Jews throughout the world who acknowledge the evils and who are not orthodox in their thinking; they belong to the aristocracy of spiritual belief to which the Hierarchy itself belongs.

3. Preparation for a revelation which will inaugurate the new era and set the note for the new world religion.

To these three efforts of the Hierarchy, superintended by the Christ, another two must be added, of perhaps even greater importance. The first one is the reaction of the Hierarchy itself to the new relationship established between It and Shamballa and to that new, direct and potent channel which has lately been induced by the efforts of the Hierarchy and human invocativeness. The second activity is one leading towards a much closer relation between the Hierarchy and Humanity; this will lead eventually to the externalisation of certain of the Ashrams, and later to the appearance of the Hierarchy on earth, bringing the new revelation.

These various efforts may appear to the casual reader as relatively unimportant. This is a superficial point of view and one which meets with little sympathy from the Hierarchy. That the Jews should be rid of fear is of major importance; that they should know and recognise the Christ as the Messiah, and therefore find for themselves that the religion they follow is destructive of many of the finer values, is likewise of major importance; that orthodox Judaism, along with all the other faiths, should realise that there is no desire to make them Christian (in the ordinary sense of the term), but that they should all move towards some loving synthesis and eliminate their mutual antagonisms and rivalries is equally urgent, and this statement includes the Christian faiths as well. That the Vatican cease its political scheming, its exploitation of the masses and its emphasis upon ignorance is as important; that the manifold divisions of the Protestant churches be bridged is imperative. If none of these things happen, humanity is headed towards a religious war which will make the past war appear like child's play; antagonisms and hatreds will embroil entire populations and the politicians of all the nations will take full advantage of the situation to precipitate a war which may well prove the end of humanity. There are no hatreds so great or so deep as those fostered by religion.

The Christ, therefore, has to add to all the many objectives which occupy His attention still another—the effort to avert a final war. This incipient war is contrary to the will-to-good of the Lord of the World and any world plan; it *can* be averted by goodwill. This is the most important statement in this message, as far as humanity is concerned.

Great and stirring events are imminent, and they will take place when the effect of the new Invocation is more pronounced and its use more general. This is primarily the responsibility of those who are affiliated with the three movements which demonstrate the part I have sought to take in the world preparation. These are: The Arcane School, and this refers primarily to the books for which I am responsible; the Triangles, which constitutes a deeply esoteric mode of working, yet one of extreme simplicity; and the Goodwill movement, which has in it a factor of major importance in that this movement (embracing already as it does many, many thousands) seeks to promote right human relations with its acute and immediate appeal to the masses; it is this that the masses want essentially, and is oft what lies behind the things which they do and the plans which they make, so often ignorantly and disastrously.

You will note that my outstanding theme is that of *world planning;* this is the main preoccupation of the Hierarchy. This planning falls into two categories, and for these the Christ is responsible. These are:

1. The esoteric preparation for the physical appearance or the material emergence of the Hierarchy on earth; with this activity the Buddha is definitely associated as it is connected with His final service to mankind.

2. The establishing, by all means available, of right human relations; this, as it is achieved, will swing the Ashrams gradually into external activity as need arises, and it involves the constant cooperation of the Masters.

Since 1931 I have hinted at much of this, and my activities (carried forward with these things in view) have followed the sequence outlined below:

1. I attempted to reach certain people in order to see how far an ashram could function in external form on earth. It has proved only a partial success and the results of my experiment have been given in the book, *Discipleship in the New Age*. The effects of the experiment upon the individuals involved have not proved encouraging; the effect upon the esotericists and aspirants of the world has been most successful and has greatly enhanced the sense of reality, so essential to the recognition of the hitherto unseen Hierarchy.

2. I published books which gave the new esoteric teaching, founded on the past, of service today, and indicative of the future. In those books I isolated for the new generation of esoteric students the "truths" which were true, extracting them from the mass of imaginative thinking and consequent formulation of thoughtforms which esotericists (since the time of H.P.B.) have so consistently created and presented to the enquiring public as truths. I indicated the new truths which were of significance for the future and for which the truths of the past were a needed foundation, and gave enough in outline and in "seed" concepts to show the lines along which the new world religion, the new political regimes and the new social order could be set up. I gave you the blueprints. I enunciated these as principles, leaving men free—as must ever be the case—to work out the details according to their contributing civilisations and their peculiar national cultures, which should unitedly create a beautiful whole and not provide barriers of separativeness as is today the case. I finally brought to the attention of the public the idea that the externalisation of the Hierarchy was a major hierarchical project, for which due preparation would have to be made.

3. The world war then reached a final stage; the first stage was from 1914-1918; it then proceeded in a subterranean

fashion, only to erupt once more in 1939, continuing with extreme fierceness and cruelty till 1945, when the power to continue the fight ended and the atomic bomb wrote *finis* to the world chapter of disaster. That atomic bomb (though used only twice destructively) ended the resistance of the powers of evil because its potency is predominantly etheric. Its uses are twofold at this time:

a. As the forerunner of that release of energy which will change the mode of human living and inaugurate the new age wherein we shall not have civilisations and their emerging cultures but a world culture and an emerging civilisation, thus demonstrating the true synthesis which underlies humanity. The atomic bomb emerged from a first ray Ashram, working in conjunction with a fifth ray group; from the long range point of view, its intent was and is purely beneficent.

b. As a means in the hands of the United Nations to enforce the outer forms of peace, and thus give time for teaching on peace and on the growth of goodwill to take effect. The atomic bomb does not belong to the three nations who perfected it and who own the secrets at present—the United States of America, Great Britain and Canada. It belongs to the United Nations for use (or let us rather hope, simply for threatened use) when aggressive action on the part of any nation rears its ugly head. It does not essentially matter whether that aggression is the gesture of any particular nation or group of nations or whether it is generated by the political groups of any powerful religious organisation, such as the Church of Rome, who are as yet unable to leave politics alone and attend to the business for which all religions are responsible—leading human beings closer to the God of Love.

4.   The world war now being ostensibly over and the work of restoration, leading to resurrection, being slowly implemented, the work of the Hierarchy is to foster that enthusiasm

in the hearts of people everywhere which will enable them to work wholeheartedly *for* right human relations and the spread of that simple but tonic quality, goodwill. It is enthusiasm in the spiritual sense which is lacking today, even among those who see the Mind of Christ and the Plans of the Hierarchy as existing in factual usefulness; those who have for years read my teachings on goodwill with real belief in what I say but who evidence no willingness to sacrifice time or money, block the growth of the movement. It is the task of the Hierarchy to promote goodwill as the first step in Their plans, and it is that quality which is today closest to the heart of Christ; "goodwill to men," or rather among men, was the primary stage in the threefold promise made by the angels at His Birth:

a. Goodwill, leading to right human relations, leading to
b. Peace on Earth, leading to
c. Glory to God.

Analysed, these words simply mean that goodwill will result in right human relations in that centre which we call *Humanity;* this will produce the possibility of that peace which characterises the *Hierarchy* appearing on earth, and leading to the glory of God, which animates the activity of *Shamballa,* the centre where the Will of God is known. Therefore, intelligent relationship, practical love and the full expression of the divine will are bound to occur, if the correct sequence of activities is followed. At present, even the first of them remains a hope. The factors of the failure of the religious and political groups and the apathy of the mass of men have greatly complicated the task of the Hierarchy.

5. My personal work has been to bring all this to the attention of the general public through my interpretation of the *Problems of Humanity* and bring it to the point where simplicity of purpose, an inspiring and flaming ardour and a minimum of organisation may implement the new presentation of goodwill as it affects and changes the sov-

ereign world religions which are forgetful of the words of the Christ, "My kingdom is not of this world"; as it permeates into the political conferences of world statesmen and rulers, and as it governs the decisions of science and economics. In so doing and in the direful task of pointing out mistakes and errors of ancient standing, wrong and disastrous attitudes and human separativeness, an inevitable opposition has been evoked; had there been none, my efforts would have been futile. I have said naught that is not true and I retract no single word which I have said. There are many who prefer the esoteric truths anent the antahkarana, the world constitution, the doctrine of man, the Law of Rebirth and the many intricate teachings related to world planning. These they have received in full measure from me. There are others who desire information anent the Hierarchy, the work and standing of the Masters, the training to be given to disciples and initiates. This again they have received. I have now dealt in the past few years with world abuses and the problems with which humanity is faced in this period of restoration—of God's plan for man, and not of former conditions.

It is interesting to note that when the Hierarchy seeks to meet the need of the masses for better conditions, and to aid in the changing of ecclesiastical and political abuses, men are apt then to withdraw their interest because the task is hard, or to repudiate the statements anent that which is evil because (from their point of view) it is not possible for the Hierarchy to find fault or take a stand against wrong, just as many repudiated the fact that the Hierarchy took its stand, during the war, upon the side of the Forces fighting for the freedom of humanity and refused in any way to endorse those fighting on the side of darkness.

The Hierarchy is a great fighting body today, fighting for the souls of men, fighting all that blocks the expansion of the human consciousness, fighting all that limits human freedom (I said not license) and fighting to remove those factors and barriers which militate against the return of the Christ and the emergence of the Hierarchy as a fully functioning body on earth. There is nothing weak, vacillating, sentimental or neutral in the attitude of the Hierarchy; this must be grasped by humanity, and the strength and insight as well as the love of the Hierarchy must be counted upon.

I have in the above remarks enumerated for you certain of the objectives facing the Hierarchy at this time and involving the personal attention of the Christ; they all have a potent and beneficent effect upon humanity. Let me enumerate them in concise form, because it is essential that there be clear perception of the emerging values on the part of workers of all grades and kinds in the world, for otherwise perception is not possible. To each point enumerated I will append in a few brief words the reason why it is regarded as important:

1. The Reorganisation of the World Religions.
   Reasons
   a. To make way for the World Religion, universal religion.
   b. To return humanity to the simplicity which is in Christ.
   c. To rid the world of theology and ecclesiasticism.

2. The Gradual Dissolution of Orthodox Judaism.
   Reasons
   a. Because of its presentation of a wrathful Jehovah, caring only for his chosen people. This is a basic evil. The Lord of the World, the God in whom we live and move and have our being, is totally otherwise.
   b. Because of its separativeness.
   c. Because it is so ancient that its teachings are largely obsolete.
   d. Because when the Jews become spiritual they will greatly benefit mankind, for they are found in every land.

3. Preparation for a New Revelation.
   Reasons
   a. Because where there is no vision the people perish.

    b. Because human expectancy indicates its emerging presence.

    c. Because the new Invocation will inevitably bring it to us.

4.   The Reaction of the Hierarchy to Shamballa.
    Reasons
    a. Produces a direct channel.
    b. Conditions the inflow of power energy.
    c. Relates the will-to-good to goodwill.
    d. Creates new constructive tensions and new ashrams.

5.   A Closer Relation of the Hierarchy to Humanity.
    Reasons
    a. Produces (in the near future) the externalisation of certain ashrams.
    b. Leads to the reappearance of the Hierarchy on earth.
    c. Recognises that man's point of development warrants this.
    d. Presents a nearing opportunity for revelation.

6.   An Effort to avert War.
    Reasons
    a. Because the next war would annihilate the greater part of the human race.
    b. Because, having a religious basis, the hate involved would be greater far than anything hitherto known.
    c. Because Shamballa would be involved, and this has never been the case.

You can see therefore how critical, spiritually, are these times, and how urgent is the task which confronts the Hierarchy and its workers on earth. The war may be over in the physical sense, but great issues are still involved and undetermined and can lead either to peace or to a renewal of those conditions in which wars are generated and which, once generated, cannot be avoided.

It is with all these foregoing factors in mind that we

approach the next two great Festivals: the *Wesak Festival* and *Christ's Unique Occasion*. One point I must make here, and I make it with great joy: this year 1946 marks the beginning of a cycle in which humanity is more closely involved in the Festivals than ever before and in which they can take a much more important part than ever before. The Wesak Festival has long been kept in many countries and—as time goes on and the instruction of the masses proceeds—the meeting held at the time of the May Full Moon will assume great importance, but *its keynote will be changed*. What the new keynote will be has not yet been announced, and will not be for 35 years. As I earlier pointed out, its significance, and that of Good Friday, belong to the past and their usefulness is nearly finished. It is the intention of the Buddha and the Christ that in each country there should eventually be someone who will act as Their Representative at the time of the two Festivals, so that the distribution of spiritual energy from the first great Aspect or Ray will be direct from the Buddha (and later Shamballa) to the Christ, and then from the Christ to those disciples in every country who can be overshadowed, and so act as channels for the direct current of energy.

The same procedure will be followed at the time of the Full Moon of June, except that Shamballa will not be so involved, and with the difference that at the May Festival it will be a first ray disciple who will be overshadowed, and at the June Festival a second ray disciple will represent the Christ in every land. This can mean either the soul or the personality ray of the disciple.

It has not been possible to organise this development this year, but next year a beginning can be made, even if only three or four countries can work under this inspiration. The effects of this development will be far-reaching, though not immediately apparent to the onlooker.

This year, at the great Festival in the Himalayas at which the Buddha will appear as usual, He has let it be known that His main duty is to bring the initial inflow of the threefold energy which the Invocation invokes and will continue to invoke for many decades. From the Mind of God, Light will flow through Him to the waiting world of men—that human centre whose eternal mission is to bring light to all created lives. From the Heart of God, He will bring to the Hierarchy, via the Christ, that deep unending inflow of Love which will make it possible for the Hierarchy to perform its hard task and externalise itself. It is not possible for human beings to realise the sacrifice and the hardship which this emergence will entail, and only a vast inflow of divine love can make it possible.

An effort also will be made to relate Shamballa, "the Centre where the Will of God is known," directly to the new group of world servers, via those Ashrams which are working along the lines of outer, practical goodwill. The reception of this energising will-to-good should produce a definite "stepping-up" or increase of goodwill and enable the Goodwill movement to proceed with greater momentum this coming autumn and winter; it will take the entire summer for the needed assimilation by those engineering this movement all over the world.

The absorption of the Love which flows from the Heart of God to the Hierarchy will necessarily have widespread effects; however, one of the most immediate will affect the Triangles and increase the potency of the network of light and of goodwill, already in existence. You can see, therefore, from all the above, how much closer the Buddha is coming this year to humanity. He now finds it possible to permit human beings to know His specific objective; this has never before been the case. It is the result of war and the efforts of the Hierarchy to bring out in the human being certain ennobling qualities and spiritual reactions which the stress of war could evoke. This year will mark a unique and peculiar opportunity, based on the fact that there has not yet been time for people to slip back into the old ways of thinking or for the setting up of any reactionary structures. This may not be the case next year and therefore it would be wise to take as full advantage as possible of the coming Festivals. Those who have faith and vision are asked o link up (imaginatively, because anything else would scarcely be possible) with the Buddha, then offer themselves as channels for the spiritual potencies which He will bring.

The Festival of June which is so uniquely Christ's, and which emphasises His relationship to humanity, in reality covers three whole days, each with a different keynote:

1. The keynote of *Love* in its hierarchical sense—free from sentiment, emotion and personal emphasis—a love that sacrifices and understands, that acts with strength and decision, and that works on behalf of the whole and not in the interests of any group or individual.

2. The keynote of *Resurrection,* emphasising the new note of livingness, of the living Christ and of that "life more abundantly" which the war has made possible by forcing a return to the real values.

3. The keynote of *Contact,* of a closer relation between Christ and His people, between the Hierarchy and Humanity.

The word "keynote" has been deliberately chosen and signifies *the sound* which preceded each major inflow at the May Festival; these energies will be released at a solemn ceremony on each of the three days. At each ceremony the Christ will say the new Invocation alone, and then the united Hierarchy will intone the stanza alone, invoking light, love and the will-to-good (one on each of the three days). Those disciples or initiates who happen to be interested and watching the Triangles or the Goodwill movement will have them in their minds as they say the first and third stanzas, and the new group of world servers will receive some attention when the second stanza is chanted.

I would call your attention, therefore, to the interest shown by the Hierarchy in the embryonic efforts in which you are engaged and which I started; I would point out, however, that the attention paid is not exclusive, but that wherever two or three are gathered together in the name of the Master of the Hierarchy, energy will flow; that wherever goodwill is a goal and evokes effort in no matter what form, the energy of the will-to-good will make itself felt, and that the new group of world servers is a far larger group than just the few known to you. Today its numbers are several million.

The result of this solemn three days of invocation will be followed by a climaxing day wherein the Hierarchy will unitedly, and led by the Christ, pronounce the entire Invocation, prefacing each stanza with its appropriate keynote, again sounded in unison. These notes you cannot know, but if, for instance, a very large number of the new group of world servers were brought together, their united OM might approximate the appropriate keynote.

It will be apparent to you, therefore, that in the new cycle now beginning with the climaxing of the war and the formation of the United Nations, the Festivals of May and June not only become more closely linked, but the procedure has been changed and the effect on humanity intensified. I would have all who care to meet together at these Festivals to try and do so subjectively (wherever they may find themselves) and to participate intelligently in the ordained ceremonies. I would ask all to think imaginatively and to act *as if* they were accepted disciples or at least on the periphery of some ashram. I am asking you to take part in these two ceremonies with a full play of the imagination; these ceremonies will later be externalised at some centre in every country. A trained nucleus and a devoted band of believers is in process of being gathered together (though only as yet in the consciousness of the Hierarchy), and though at the present time there will be no outer ceremonies or any knowledge as to who will be chosen in the various lands to represent the Hierarchy, in deed and in truth, the first step towards human participation is being made this year.

The knowledge of this will give purpose and fixed intention to all of you who have for years kept these festivals. In truth, I bring you the invitation of the Hierarchy to share in Their ancient work, and not—as in the past—to play the part of interested onlookers. I would warn you that, if you do succeed in any measure of participation, it will be necessary to guard yourselves from overstimulation and to take steps wisely to use, on behalf of humanity, the energy with which you may be charged.

This knowledge will be particularly useful to those who are occupied with any of the groups and organisations which are responsive to hierarchical interests. True participation may lead to the sudden conviction of the reality of that which I have told you; faith and belief and commonsense will then no longer be needed, and you will *know*.

I have here told you the things which the Christ has planned for the immediate future. I have told you also some of the things which He and the Masters must do as preparatory steps to the new world which can and will supersede the old unhappy world that lies immediately behind us. I have chosen to speak to you of these activities in which it is now possible for you to share, with the exception of those which affect the relation between Shamballa and the Hierarchy. However, those who are initiates of the third degree (and there are quite a few working on the earth among men at this time) can share in all of them.

This is an intensely practical message and calls for your renewed pledge to serve humanity and to find your way into an Ashram where that service may be directed. It calls for sacrifice until it hurts, and where it touches you the most; it calls for a joyous sense of unity with that station of power and light which we call the Hierarchy and which stands ready—as never before—to share with humanity that power and that light to the limit of human capacity to use it.

I beg you, in closing, to aid in two matters which are of importance to Him Whom all disciples, initiates and spiritual men have loved and followed for nearly three thousand years, the Christ. (I am referring here to His appearance as Shri Krishna and as one other who was little known but who did a great work in still earlier centuries.) It is work in preparation for His coming.

I beg you to shoulder the responsibility of distributing the Invocation on as large a scale as possible and in every country. It is of great potency, and when used by men of all faiths can aid in the process of averting war. I ask you also to make possible the wide distribution of the book *The Problems of Humanity* which I have written, for they strengthen the hands of those who are already seeking to deal with these problems and they bring the need to the attention of the unawakened. This will require sacrifice, for it calls for the expenditure of money; even the Hierarchy works through normal channels and needs money, and even the Christ has need of financial resources in order to reach the needy sons of men. I ask your aid and I await your decision.

That He Whom we serve may be nearer to all of us than ever before, that the work of establishing right human relations may proceed apace, and that light and love may stream forth from Shamballa and the Hierarchy over all of you who love your fellowmen is the earnest wish, accompanied by my blessing, for you at this season of the will-to-good.*

Mode of Approach Toward Externalisation (August 1946)

One of the most important things emerging from the theme of this amazing and imminent event (the reappearance of the Hierarchy on the physical plane) is the factor of the developments and the adjustments going on within

---

* NOTE: *The Tibetan has asked me to make clear that when he is speaking of the Christ he is referring to His official name as Head of the Hierarchy. The Christ works for all men, irrespective of their faith; He does not belong to the Christian world any more than to the Buddhist, the Mohammedan or any other faith. There is no need for any man to join the Christian Church in order to be affiliated with Christ. The requirements are to love your fellowmen, lead a disciplined life, recognise the divinity in all faiths and all beings, and rule your daily life with Love.*

A. A. B.

he Hierarchy Itself in preparation for this happening. Incidentally, I would here point out that what will take place, and what is already tentatively taking place, is *the externalisation of the Ashrams.* The great official departments, such as the teaching department or that of emerging civilisations, will not at this time reappear. Their activities will still, for a long time, be retained within the Hierarchy upon Its own plane. The first step is the appearance of certain Ashrams, controlled by certain Masters, upon the physical plane, evoking general recognition and guaranteeing to the public the *fact* of the Hierarchy and the restoration of the Mysteries. Later, if these steps prove successful, other and more important reappearances will be possible, beginning with the return of the Christ.

But in the meantime, great and momentous happenings are taking place within the Hierarchy and in relation to Its Membership. Disciples upon the periphery of any Ashram are apt to be unobservant of the training and attitudes of Those Who are senior to them in an Ashram; they frequently overlook the fact that They too—from the Christ down to the humblest initiate—are in process of steady and increasing hierarchical discipline, training and instruction. Because the senior disciples and initiates have reached a goal which has seemed for long quite unattainable to the average aspirant, it is assumed that they have attained; the fact that they have only passed a milestone upon the endless Way of Bliss is entirely forgotten. But, owing to the impulsion of life itself, progress ever continues; knowledge must ever be transmuted into wisdom; love must ever be accompanied by divine will; planning must ever give way to divine purpose; light must ever be succeeded· by life; from the Hierarchy, the initiate must pass to Shamballa, and from Shamballa he will follow one or other of the seven Paths; the Path of Evolution gives place to the Way of the Higher Evolution; planetary recognitions eventually expand into solar contacts; the Christ-consciousness eventually unfolds into something so all-inclusive that we have as yet no word for it or any need of words; recognition of the Father and of monadic being causes all lesser recognitions to fade out, and soul-consciousness and progressive life in form are no longer goals but are left far behind.

In spite of all this, it is necessary to remember that the gain of all experience for ever persists, nothing is ever lost; that which life in form has conferred is still in the possession of the immortal spiritual entity; that which the soul-consciousness has enfolded and included is still the rich endowment of Being, centred now in the Monad; hierarchical experience is merged into the purposes of the Council Chamber at Shamballa, but ability to work in the Hierarchy ever lasts because the hierarchical constitution and institution condition all manifestation—for what reason this is so, no one knows, but so is the divine Will.

In synthesis and in the all-inclusive awareness of the great Life which enfolds all that is, everything (except what we know as evil) is persistent and for ever endures.

You will have noted (if you are true students of what I have given out to the world) that information anent the Hierarchy has fallen into three major categories:

1. The work of the Hierarchy in relation to man and to the three worlds of human evolution.
2. The interior constitution of the Hierarchy and its internal activity.
3. Its superior relation to Shamballa and to extra planetary livingness.

A great deal that has been conveyed to you in the two final categories has been merged by you into an interested but totally impractical realisation that the Hierarchy apparently has a life of its own which proceeds independently of humanity and that it also has its own goals and objectives which are no concern of yours. These deductions are dependent upon your domination by the separative mind, for in reality the work and the activity proceeding in all three centres—Shamballa, the Hierarchy and Humanity—are merged, fused and interdependent; they are all mutually evocative and invocative.

The fact, for instance, that the Hierarchy is approaching closer to humanity and will eventually make an appearance upon the physical plane is due, not only to hierarchical intent, but to the demand of mankind and to the strong vibration and note which humanity has set up. To that extent, humanity controls some of the activities of the Hierarchy and thus precipitates action. At the same time, all that is happening can be traced to Shamballa, is inherent in divine purpose and is impulsed and impelled by Shamballa energy, distributed throughout the planet, via the Hierarchy in the majority of cases. Both the Hierarchy and Humanity are brought under the influence of extra-planetary forces which make their impact upon the planet, via Shamballa. Therefore, a great interdependence emerges, of which the head, heart and solar plexus centres in the individual man's etheric body are symbols; their unified relation keeps the man functioning and demonstrating as a coherent whole at a particular level of consciousness. It is essential that students endeavour to grasp this, and so develop within themselves at least the rudiments of this synthetic unified grasp of living conditions and of a vital situation.

These instructions can aid all earnest aspirants and disciples to develop this type of understanding with as much speed and accuracy as possible. It is distinctive of the hierarchical type of mind: concerned with itself as a divine group, conscious of the pull and evocative power of the highest centre, Shamballa, responsive to the demands of humanity, and sensitive to the "call" of that third major centre through which the life of the planetary Logos expresses itself. The consciousness of the Master is therefore preoccupied with three main lines of responsibility, but only one of them is innate within the living organism of which He is a part; that aspect of His life is invocative in two directions: towards Shamballa and towards Humanity; to Him, the other two centres are evocative.

Today, human beings as a whole are so loudly invoca-

tive that the entire trend of the life of the Hierarchy and
Its plans to date have been subjected to change, to post
ponement as far as certain interior and purely hierarchical
determinations are concerned, and to a hastening of certain
plans which were slated (if I may use such a word) to take
place several centuries later than this but which—owing to
the unexpected preparedness of humanity—can take place
not prematurely really, but securely and in the fullness of
time; this fullness of time, as regards the particular planning
with which we are dealing, is from now until the year 2025
A.D.—a brief period of time indeed in which to see the
consummation of the larger purpose of the planetary Logos
working through the three major centres within His body
of manifestation. This purpose was threefold in nature:

1.   It involved the ability of Those in the Council Cham
ber at Shamballa to react to and absorb certain extra
planetary energies and to use them in an intra-planetary
sense. It had not been anticipated by the Directing Agents
of these forces that our planetary Logos would achieve a cer
tain goal so early in time and space as He has.

2.   It involved a great expansion, numerically and in the
consciousness of the Hierarchy. This predicates a great
influx of intiates and disciples and a tremendous inflow of
what is esoterically called "angelic essence" from the deva
kingdom, under the direction of certain great Devas who
have affiliated during the past two hundred years with the
Hierarchy. This again had not been expected so early.
The result of this happening has been that the door of
initiation through which mankind passes stands wider open
(symbolically speaking) than ever before, and at the same
time, the Masters are passing with greater rapidity on to
the Way of the Higher Evolution; this is due to the fact
that initiates are fitting themselves so rapidly to take Their
places, and disciples are moving on into initiate position
so fast, that a great pressing forward has become legitimate.

3.   It involved, finally, a great awakening in the human
family and a major spiritual reorientation. This again had

been believed possible of accomplishment when the sun passed into Capricorn about 2300 years hence. But—it has already taken place and necessarily has brought about a basic adjustment in the plans of the Hierarchy and a renewed emphasis upon the purpose, as registered in Shamballa.

This, being factual, and the time ripe for decision, has caused an intra-planetary ferment and great activity in the three major centres. In the last analysis (and this is the factor of supreme importance) this development—this unexpected right absorption of spiritual energy, and this seizing of spiritual opportunity—is due to humanity itself; above everything else, it is the readiness of mankind for that which is new, and humanity's determination to create a new and better world, adapted more adequately to their "renewed" spiritual nature, that is responsible for all the activity.

In this section of our training themes (if I may call them so) we shall deal primarily with the response and the subsequent activity of the Hierarchy in relation to humanity. This will take the form of a new Approach and a reappearance exoterically.

It would be wise, therefore, to keep the following ideas constantly in mind; I will enumerate them sequentially and for the sake of clarity:

1. The work of the Hierarchy, throughout the ages, has been fundamentally threefold in nature:

a. A constant effort to set up a closer and more understanding relation with Shamballa. This involves:

An unfoldment of the will aspect in conjunction with a full use of intelligent love.
A constant adaptation of the developing Plan to the emerging, energising Purpose.
An increasing ability to transmit energy from Shamballa to the three worlds, from the cosmic etheric levels to the cosmic dense physical planes.

b. To unfold—within the periphery of the hierarchical center—a life, a plan and a technique which will train all who find their way into an Ashram, which is in itself an aspect of the life of the Hierarchy. This ancient and intelligent effort has created and conditioned what you know as the Hierarchy. However, it is constantly subject to change in response to new situations and developments.

c. To represent, finally, within the Hierarchy, the qualities of all the seven Rays, through the medium of the seven major Ashrams and their allied and subsidiary Ashrams

There are many other aspects of the hierarchical constitution and objectives, but these three are the ones with which we are at this time the most concerned.

2.   Today, the relation of Shamballa to the Hierarchy is closer than at any previous time, owing to the following factors:

a. The one-pointed work and plan—pursued by the three great departments in the Hierarchy (the department of the Manu, that of the Christ, and that of the Lord of Civilisation) —in which the three Leaders have unitedly acted as a Triangle of transmission between the Council Chamber of the Lord of the World and the Hierarchy. They are, all three, Members of the Council, though none of Them is yet working at the very centre of affairs; in order to be of greater service in Their own sphere, They have taken Their stand upon the periphery of the Council's influence.

b. The invocative work carried out both consciously and unconsciously by humanity itself, which has been of such a potency that it has penetrated beyond the ring-pass-not (symbolically understood) of the Hierarchy to Shamballa itself, and has evoked response. This invocative work reached a high point of potency as a result of the world war (1914-1945) and its note and appeal are still persistent.

c. The rapid development of integration among advanced people, which has forced many on to the Path of Discipleship, and therefore into certain of the Ashrams, and has likewise enabled many disciples to take initiation.

3. The recognition by a very much larger number of the general public of the *fact* of the Hierarchy; this has established a new type of relation between the Hierarchy and humanity. Hitherto the relation was dependent upon recognition, by advanced aspirants, of the nature of their position in relation to the Hierarchy; today, the recognition of thousands who are not in any way advanced aspirants or in any sense prepared for affiliation with the Hierarchy has created a new type of problem; it connotes to the Hierarchy a promising development, though at the same time an embarrassing one, requiring as it does a different mode of adjustment to human demands than that entailed by the admittance of disciples to Their Ashrams; it requires the attention of certain disciples and initiates in all the Ashrams and the ability of the Hierarchy to penetrate and dissipate the thick cloud of inchoate thoughtforms which the bewildered, interested and curious public have created anent Them.

4. The use by the Hierarchy of the destroyer aspect of divinity, the first Ray, in such a manner that it is in fact a creative factor and one which, in the last analysis, not only releases the life from its previous limitations, but also calls in—under the Law of Balance—the building activity of the second Ray. The work of destruction is now practically accomplished and over, and the work of the Builders is beginning.

5. The new group of world servers has been created as an

intermediate body between the Hierarchy and the general public. This group is divided into two lesser groups:

a. Those disciples and workers who are already integrated into some one of the Ashrams.

b. Intelligent and humanitarian aspirants and workers in world affairs and in all departments.

These two groups unitedly form a transmitting agency through which the Hierarchy can reach the mass of men with the new concepts, the techniques of the new civilisation and the basic propositions under which humanity will move forward into greater light.

6.   The recognition by humanity of its major problems, and the increasing ability of the general public to view these problems in terms of One Humanity, of the whole. This ability indicates to the Hierarchy the position of Humanity upon the Path at this time and the readiness of mankind for the new revelation—to be followed later by the restoration of the Mysteries.

7.   The new orientation of the human family within itself to the concept of the *One Humanity* and the intensely alert spiritual demand which is today distinctive of mankind everywhere, and which has forced the Hierarchy to come to certain basic decisions and to readjust Itself to a much closer cooperation with the human centre of life and purpose.

It is interesting to note (though it is of no immediate moment) that the work of destruction initiated by the Hierarchy during the past one hundred and seventy-five years (therefore since the year 1775) has in it the seeds—as yet a very long way from any germination—of the final act of destruction which will take place when the Hierarchy will be so completely fused and blended with Humanity that the hierarchical form will no longer be required. The three major centres will then become the two, and the Hierarchy will disappear and only Shamballa and Humanity will remain, only spirit or life, and substance as an expression of intelligent love will be left. This corresponds to the experience of the individual initiate at the fourth initiation, when the causal body, the soul body, disappears and only the monad and its expression, the personality (a fusion of soul and form) are left. This event of final dissolution will take place only at the close of our planetary existence, when the door to individualisation is finally closed for a pralayic period and the Way of the Higher Evolution will be more closely trodden than the Path of Initiation.

Therefore, my brothers, the closer relation of the Hierarchy to Shamballa, the stimulation of its own interior life, and the readiness of humanity for revelation and for certain unexpected development, will condition the cycle into which we are now entering. This is, therefore, the most amazing period in the history of humanity. Added to this, it must be borne in mind that we are entering another greater round of the Zodiac, and this coincides with the lesser zodiacal activity because Aquarius governs the greater immediate cycle of 25,000 years and is also the sign into which the sun is now moving for a period of 2300 years—a most amazing happening and full of import in our planetary history; it is a coincidence of which our planetary Logos is well aware and of which He is making full and intelligent use. It is a cycle also wherein, for the first time, the three major planetary centres—Shamballa, Hierarchy and Humanity—are in direct and unimpeded relation, for today the alignment is correct and adjusted for the first time in planetary history. Even if this be only temporarily so, something has been initiated, the effects of which will never be lost. It is a cycle also in which the planetary Logos, having successfully taken initiation and thus affected His entire planetary life, has also established certain extra-planetary relationships which are necessarily incomprehensible to you and of no moment whatsoever to the individual human being, but which will eventually create a situation in which our planet will become a sacred planet. This process, as it unfolds and develops, will have a potent subjective and deeply spiritual effect upon every kingdom in nature and in the realm also of super-nature.

Let us now proceed with our consideration of our theme, after our study of these basic premises.

Steps in the Externalisation Process

For some time, ever since 1425 A.D., (a date to which I referred earlier) the Hierarchy has been aware that the time would come when this projected move would take place. Preparations have gone steadily forward. A point to be remembered is that this impulsed intention (emanating in the first place from Shamballa) came as a major disturb-ance to the rhythm of many tens of thousands of years; it has been a basic conditioning factor. The Masters, however, Who will make the move outwards into contact with the world are not the Ones Who registered the initial impulse from Shamballa, nor are the three Heads of the great depart-ments the same. The earlier Masters initiated the needed steps of preparation, and the work has gone steadily forward since.

You might well ask what were these steps and along what lines has the preparation gone? The first steps con-cerned internal preparation. Though the Masters of the Wisdom have all passed through the human experience and are simply men who have achieved a relative measure of per-fection, there are aspects of physical contact which They have completely transcended and utterly negated. There is nothing in the three worlds with which They have any affinity, except the affinity of life and the impulse of love for all beings. Recovery of certain facilities of activity has been deemed necessary. For instance, the five senses, where a Master is concerned, exist and are used at need, but the contact established and maintained with disciples and senior aspirants in the world (through whom They primarily work) is largely telepathic; hearing and sight, as you understand their uses, are not involved. The science of impression, with its greatly increased effectiveness over individual contact through the senses, has entirely superseded the more strictly human method. Except in the case of Masters working on the physical plane and in a physical body, the outer physical senses are in abeyance; for the majority of Masters Who still use these senses, the use is strictly limited; Their work is still almost entirely subjective and the mode of telepathic interplay and of impression is practically all the means which They employ to reach Their working agents. Therefore, the recovery of past usages of a more physical nature has been one of the preparatory moves.

Another has been the achievement of a wide culture and understanding of the current civilisation which will be coming into activity and control when the intended project is carried out. You have been told—and told correctly—that the Masters do not trouble Themselves to attain proficiency in all educational subjects—in modern history, for instance, or the newest scientific procedures, or in the use of foreign languages. In all Their Ashrams there are those who can supply Them with any specified knowledge which They may need at any given time or for any specific purpose. This will still remain true of Those Who have attained the rank of Master, but it is not true of all the senior initiates, many of whom, as they passed into higher grades and under instruction from a Master, have retained their worldly knowledge, besides specialising in certain strictly mundane approaches to worldly affairs. For instance, there are adepts who are authorities upon modern financial matters, and these initiates of the fourth degree are competently preparing to institute later those newer techniques and modes of financial interplay which will supersede the present disastrous methods; they will inaugurate a system of barter and exchange, of which modern money is the travestied symbol. This newer method of financial relationships will be comprehensively human and it will supersede big business and private enterprise. It will at the same time, however, retain those phases of modern enterprise which will draw out the initiative and the resourcefulness of the individual. Other initiates have specialised in the various languages, and two of them are authorities in basic English; this is the form of the English language which will eventually take the place of other languages in all forms of international and business intercourse without in any way obliterating the individual national languages in daily use in any country.

Two things must be realised as the interested student considers this event of externalisation:

1.   The senior Members of the Hierarchy will not at first be the ones who will make the needed approach. Under Their direction and Their close supervision, this approach will be made—in the early stages—by initiates of and under the degree of the third initiation, and also by those disciples who will be chosen and designated to implement Their efforts and so will work under Their direction. It is only in the later stages, and when the time has come for the return into recognised physical expression of the Christ, leading to the definite restoration of the Mysteries, that certain of the senior Members of the Hierarchy will appear and take outer and recognisable physical control of world affairs. The time for this will be dependent necessarily upon the success of the steps taken by the members of the Hierarchy who are not so advanced.

2.   Members of the Hierarchy, whether working in the early stages or later when the true externalisation takes place, will work as members of the human family and not as proclaimed members of the kingdom of God or of souls, known to us as the Hierarchy; they will appear in office of some kind or another; they will be the current politicians, business men, financiers, religious teachers or churchmen; they will be scientists and philosophers, college professors and educators; they will be the mayors of cities and the custodians of all public ethical movements. The spiritual forcefulness of their lives, their clear, pure wisdom, the sanity and the modern acceptableness of their proposed measures in any department in which they choose to function, will be so

convincing that little impediment will be set in the way of their undertakings.

At the present stage of preparation, the task of the disciple who is charged with laying the foundation for the New Age methods and with the labour of getting ready for the first group of Ashram members, is hard indeed. He stands for so much that is deemed visionary and impossible; the difficulties which confront him seem impossible; he teaches truths whose first effect is necessarily destructive, because he endeavours to rid humanity of old forms of religious, economic and political doctrine; his impersonality—which recognises faults as well as virtues—enrages many and often those from whom he had expected understanding and a true impartiality; his failure to be impressed or attentive to old rites and ceremonies, to ancient and obsolete but precious ideas, and his constant warfare on conditioning glamours and illusions meet, in these early stages, with little encouragement. He works frequently alone and usually with little recognition and lacks time for his own personal hierarchical contacts; he is not necessarily connected with any so-called esoteric groups and—if he is—his task is that much harder; only advanced disciples with a full and concious constant contact with their particular Ashram are able to work in this way. Occult bodies and esoteric groups are, at this time, the most glamoured of any of the world groups; the work of any disciple in such groups is bound, in the early stages, to be destructive. The present occult groups which came into existence prior to 1919 will eventually all disappear; the members who are true and sound, broad-minded and sane, and rightly oriented and dedicated, will find their way into esoteric bodies which are free from dogmatism and doctrines and which are recipients of hierarchical life.

The preparatory work of externalisation, therefore, falls into three phases or stages, as far as relation to mankind is concerned:

First. The present stage in which a few isolated disciples and initiates, scattered all over the world, are doing the important task of destruction, plus the enunciation of principles. They are preparing the way for the first organised body of disciples and initiates who—coming from certain Ashrams—will proceed with the next phase of the work.

Second. The stage of the first real externalisation upon a large and organised scale will succeed upon the above endeavours. These disciples and initiates will be the real Builders of the new world, of the new civilisation; they will assume leadership in most countries and take high office in all departments of human life. This they will do by the free choice of the people and by virtue of their advanced and proven merit. By this means, gradually the Hierarchy will take over the control upon the physical plane—subjectively as well as objectively—of the direction of human affairs. This direction will be in virtue of their known and approved capacity and will not involve the imposition of any hierarchical control or authority; it will simply signify the free recognition by free people of certain spiritual qualities and effective activities which they believe signify that these men are adequate to the demanded job, and whom they therefore choose as directing agents in the new and coming world. Freedom of choice under the authority of a spiritual livingness which demonstrates competency will be distinctive of the attitude of the general public. Men will be put into high office and into positions of power not because they are disciples or initiates, but because they are wise and intelligent servants of the public, with an internal awareness, a deeply religious and inclusive consciousness, and a well-trained mind with an obedient brain.

This stage of hierarchical appearance is dependent upon the effective service of the first group of isolated and hardworking disciples who are the senior members of the new group of world servers and who are today working among the sons of men. This second group will take over from them, and theirs will be the task of instituting a more unified preparation for the return of the Christ. The first group prepare humanity for the possibility; the second group definitely prepare for the return itself. They will build for a future which will arise out of the wreckage of the past, which wreckage they will remove; they will instill certain basic concepts anent right human relations into men's minds. Their immediate group work, when they are coming into power and recognition, will consist of a sweetening and a clarification of the political situation and the presentation of those ideas which will eventually lead to a fusion of those principles which govern a democracy and which also condition the hierarchical method—which is somewhat different; this effort will produce a third political situation which will not be entirely dependent upon the choices of an unintelligent public or on the control which the hierarchical technique evidently involves. The mode of this new type of political guidance will later appear.

This second group will implement the new religion; by the time they come into control the old theological activities will have been completely broken; Judaism will be fast disappearing; Buddhism will be spreading and becoming increasingly dogmatic; Christianity will be in a state of chaotic divisions and upheavals. When this takes place and the situation is acute enough, the Master Jesus will take certain initial steps towards reassuming control of His Church; the Buddha will send two trained disciples to reform Buddhism; other steps will also be taken in this department of religions and of education, over which the Christ rules, and He will move to restore the ancient spiritual landmarks, to eliminate that which is nonessential, and to reorganise the entire religious field—again in preparation for the restoration of the Mysteries. These Mysteries, when restored, will unify all faiths.

Groups of spiritually-minded financiers who are conscious members of an Ashram will take hold of the world economic situation and bring about great and needed changes. All these activities, built upon the preparatory work of the first group, are also preparatory in nature.

Third. The stage wherein Christ and the Masters of

the Wisdom can make public appearance and begin to work publicly, openly and outwardly in the world of men. The time of Their coming will be dependent upon the success of the work undertaken by the first two groups; it is not possible for me to prophesy anent this matter. So many factors are involved: the earnest work of the two groups, the readiness and the willingness of mankind to learn, the rapidity with which the forces of restoration and of resurrection can rehabilitate the world, the responsiveness of advanced humanitarians and intelligentsia to the opportunity to rebuild, to recreate and to reorganise the factors which the new culture and the new civilisation will demand. Even the Hierarchy Itself, with all Its sources of information, does not know how long this will take, but They are ready to move at any time.

In the meantime, as the first group struggles with the immediate problem in the outer world, and the second group—still within the confines of the Hierarchy Itself—makes due interior preparation and applies to its chosen membership the needed training and the desired reorientation, the Christ and the Masters are occupied with the task of preparing for the restoration of the Mysteries. This restoration will fall into three phases and will cover and include in its symbolism all phases of human unfoldment. The story of mankind will be pictorialised. These three phases correspond broadly and in a general sense to the three degrees of the Blue Lodge in Masonry. The analogy is not entirely accurate, owing to the unavoidable degeneracy of Masonry, but with the restoration of the Mysteries, Masonry also will come into its own. These phases are:

1.   The stage of a general recognition of light in all departments of human living. This is inferred in the first stanza of the new Invocation. If the ritual of the E. A. is studied in the light of this information the significance will emerge. The poor and destitute candidate emerges into the light.
2.   The stage of complete economic reorientation; in this, humanity is relieved of all economic anxiety and is free to

receive its due wages and the right reward of all service rendered in the building of the Temple of the Lord; this building proceeds with rapidity.

3.   The stage wherein the reward of light is received and the reward of service rendered; spiritual status is recognised through the medium of what is regarded as a major initiation, for which the first two initiatory degrees are only preparatory. This first great initiation will be objectively staged and the general public will recognise it as the major rite and ritual of the new religious institution of the period. This is the stage where the forces of resurrection are active, when the Lord is with His people and Christ has returned to earth. Religion is then recognised as an attitude governing all phases of human experience.

Approach, via Certain Ashrams

Students must not proceed on the assumption that in the process of externalisation there is a general moving forward of the entire Hierarchy onto the physical plane. Such is not the case. The whole effort is as yet (and will be for some time) experimental, and only a few of the Ashrams and a certain number of the trained disciples and initiates will be involved at first. It still remains to be proved how ready humanity is for this attempt. The Christian concept of the return of a triumphant Christ, coming in the clouds of heaven to Jerusalem, there to reign for a thousand years, is true in one way and utterly false as to design, location and method. Christ will return; the Jerusalem referred to (literally "the place of peace") is not the chief city of a small country called Palestine or the Holy Land; the word is simply symbolic of a peaceful world—a world which, through its own self-initiated efforts, has attained a general quietude and has acquired a certain measure of right human relations. His coming in the air might be interpreted literally to mean that at the right time He will come by plane from the place on earth where He has been for many generations, watching over the sons of men; the words "every eye shall see Him" might mean that, by the time He comes, television will have been perfected and He will then be seen, by its means, from even the most distant spot on earth. To the orthodox Christian, the above will sound like the rankest blasphemy, but the question immediately arises: Why should it be blasphemy for Him to use modern methods? Whilst on earth before, He conformed to the customs of His time. "Riding on the clouds of Heaven" may sound more picturesque and apparently require a greater expression of divinity, but why use such a means when a plane will equally well fulfill the purpose and carry the prophecy to completion? A great deal of reactionary stupidity will have to be eliminated before He can come, and it will be as the new generation assert their hold over human thinking. But it is not the event or the stage of Christ's appearing with which we are now dealing, but with the preparatory stages and with the task of fitting the world (which means, in this case, preparing the human consciousness) for the presence in physical activity and manifestation of the Hierarchy—in full force and with its esoteric equipment.

In the early stages, the task of preparation is arduous and difficult. Things will be relatively easy for the senior Members of the Hierarchy when They find the right time for Their appearance. In the meantime, the world disciples have to take the world—as it is at this time—and slowly and laboriously instill the new ideas, incite to better methods of human relations, help dissipate the aftermath of war, hold before the eyes of distraught humanity the new vision of hope and of spiritual enlightenment, offset the scheming of reactionary and conservative politicians and churchmen, and teach the youth of the age the new modes of living, indicating to them the better values, and thus slowly and gradually bringing in the new order.

Among the seven major Ashrams and their subsidiary and affiliated Ashrams only a few have undertaken to send their disciples and their initiates *at this time* to carry out this initiatory task. The three major Ashrams so engaged are:

1. The Ashram of the Master K. H. This is the second ray Ashram and—with that of the Master M.—the most powerful in the Hierarchy; it controls the building forces.
2. The first ray Ashram, that of the Master M. He is the custodian of the principle of synthesis, the work of which is that of organic fusion, and this is ever needed to supplement that of the building agents.
3. The Ashram of a Master on the fifth ray, the custodian, among other things, of science and of that which relates and brings into expression the duality of spirit-matter. This Ashram has an important part to play in the work of preparation, for it is through the scientific use of energy that the world will be rebuilt and the factual nature of the Hierarchy be proved.

Through the pressure of education (second ray energy), through the growth of the concept of synthesis (first ray energy), and through the correct use of energy (fifth ray energy), this world can be brought into a condition of preparedness for the externalisation of the Hierarchy.

The efforts of the disciples coming from the Ashram of K. H. will be largely directed towards the general public, but they will work primarily through educators in all countries and through those concerned with the teaching of religion. Educators touch those preparing for all types of activity. The task will be necessarily slow, particularly at first, but the second ray endowment of these disciples (as that of all disciples on this ray) is a steady persistence which brooks no discouragement, even when discouragement makes its appearance. Such disciples refuse to discontinue their effort or to change the spiritually-ordained plans, even when the obstacles to accomplishment seem insuperable. Disciples will come deliberately into incarnation and will take office in institutions of higher learning and in the churches, and will exert such pressure that old and obsolete methods, ancient outworn theologies and selfish and competitive techniques will be ended and the sciences of cooperation, of right human relations and of correct adjustment to life through meditation and right vision will supersede the present methods of learning; this will lead to no damage to the acquisition of academic knowledge or the right apprehension of spiritual truth. The vision will be different and the goals of a higher order, but the best that is now taught along the lines of art, religion and science will still be available; they will, however, be presented with a greater enlightenment and a better emphasis. They will meet the people's need. The churches, being today headed towards failure and lacking vision, will eventually and inevitably crash upon the rocks of unwarranted and abused authority, yet out of the wreckage will emerge those true and spiritually enlightened churchmen who—with vision and sure knowledge, free from dogmatism and hating ecclesiastical authority—will develop the new world religion.

Paralleling these activities (and disciples on this ray are already taking the needed steps) will come that of the disciples and initiates who are working under the direction of the Master M. Their work lies in the field of right human relations and in the production of that synthesis of effort which will create a new intuitional consciousness and—consequently—a changing political consciousness and situation in which the family of nations will stand together for certain basic values. These are fundamentally three in number:

1. The freedom of the individual. These freedoms have been voiced for us in the words of that great first ray disciple, Franklin D. Roosevelt. They are the four essential freedoms.
2. Right international interplay, necessitating finally the abolition of war.
3. Clean political regimes, free from graft, selfish ambition and dirty political manoeuvering.

In the achievement of these ends (and only major issues will be considered, leaving the lesser and unimportant effects to be dealt with later) the disciples of synthesis and the instigators of right political relationships will work in close cooperation with disciples upon the second ray whose task it is to educate the general public in the truer values. A trained and enlightened public, shouldering right responsibility, will elect only those men whose vision is in line with the new ethics, the new science of right human relations, and who recognise as a basic political tenet the equality of all men—an equality founded on a universal and basic divinity.

Allied to the efforts of these two groups of disciples and initiates will be those disciples on the fifth ray, whose task it will be to lead mankind into *the benefits* of the atomic age. The occultist has ever proclaimed that the field wherein the Hierarchy works is that of energy; they have taught that there is nothing in existence but energy in some form or other, and that all we see, all with which we daily work (including our own material natures, mental, emotional and physical), and all that produces phenomena is energy in relation to forces, or forces as they are directed by energy.

This the emerging group of disciples will incontrovertibly prove; by their efforts the new civilisation will be created, in which humanity will have time for freedom, for the deeper educational considerations and for a political activity of the spiritual kind; science will produce a world wherein labour (as we now know it) will be abolished and every phase of man's life will be implemented by science—not in order to make him more comfortable or more like a robot or more selfish, but as an aspect and outgrowth of true freedom; men will be free to think, to establish new modes of cultural interests, and free also to unfold the higher abstract mind and to interpret its conclusions through the medium of the trained lower concrete mind.

The united work of these three groups of disciples and initiates prepares the way for the externalisation of the Hierarchy; this preparation is already under way and taking definite form, though as yet the efforts are embryonic and the workers very few in number. A beginning *has* nevertheless been made and great changes will take place during the next twenty-five years; these will indicate the general structure of the new world of culture, will emphasise as normal the higher concepts of the so-called "visionary" world planner and lay the foundation for the work of the other Ashrams, when the time for an expanded effort arrives.

When the three major Ashrams have done their work, and this work—in spite of the difference of ray—is largely educational, then the other Ashrams will slowly send in their representatives to cooperate and to continue with the task. The first Ashram to do so will be that of the third ray; by the time disciples appear from that Ashram the world will be ready for an all-over financial adjustment; the "principle of sharing" will be a recognised motivating concept of the new civilisation. This will not involve beautiful, sweet and humanitarian attitudes. The world will still be full of selfish and self-seeking people, but public opinion will be such that certain fundamental ideals will motivate business, being forced upon business by public opinion; the fact that the new general ideas will in many cases be governed by the expediency of interplay will not basically matter. It is the sharing that is of importance. When the "adjuster of finances" (as an advanced disciple from this Ashram is called in the Hierarchy) appears, he will find conditions greatly changed from those now prevalent, and this to the following extent:

1. The principle of barter and of exchange (to the benefit of all concerned) will control.
2. Owing to the development of atomic energy on behalf of human welfare, national currencies will have been largely superseded, not only by a system of barter but by a universal monetary exchange—representative of the bartered goods when they are relatively small and unimportant—and by a planned scale of related values. National material assets and the needed commodities will all be provided for under an entirely new system.
3. Private enterprise will still exist, but will be regulated; the great public utilities, the major material

resources and the sources of planetary wealth—iron, steel, oil and wheat, for instance—will be owned in the first place by a governing, controlling international group; they will, however, be prepared for international consumption by national groups chosen by the people and under international direction.

Upon this subject I have no time to give, and besides this, anything I could say would be regarded as visionary and impractical in a world which has not yet been subjected to the educational processes of the disciples and initiates on the first, second and fifth rays or to the fundamental changes which the new generation of young people (now growing up) will shortly inaugurate.

Upon this threefold condition of the basic control of the products of the planet, these third ray disciples, working under the senior initiates above mentioned, will build the new structure of material relationships—a most difficult task, owing to the evil "pull" of the substantial assets and the continued control, even though greatly lessened, of human selfishness. This "pull" is regarded esoterically as evil because it embodies the principle of imprisonment and has, for untold aeons, engrossed the attention of the human being, to the exclusion of all true values.

Later, disciples and initiates of the seventh ray and of the sixth ray will come into physical incarnation. The only Ashram which will be then unrepresented—and this for a long time—will be the fourth. As the fourth ray is, however, the constant ray of the human family, its influence is consistently present, and this Ashram is equally constantly aware of and influential in human affairs; it will come into full expression when the intuition of the human being, emanating as an energy from the fourth or buddhic plane, has been evoked by the human soul and is a recognised asset in human consciousness. The fourth ray will come into manifestation before many generations have passed, but only from the angle of its incarnating Monad, and not from the angle of its active Ashram.

Once the contact—in physical manifestation and physical recognition—has been established, a system of "appearances and of abstractions" will be instituted by the Hierarchy, producing what might be regarded as a circulation of its life and representatives between the two major planetary centres, the Hierarchy and Humanity. According to the need upon the physical planet, and upon the acceptance of certain designs, will an Ashram be prominently active or relatively inactive.

The ancient activities of the Hierarchy will still persist—the activities of preparing disciples and initiates for initiation and for participating consciously in hierarchical effort; the Schools of the Mysteries (as outlined by me in *Letters on Occult Meditation*) will come into being and practice, but this will be temporarily a secondary activity; the full expression of ashramic energy will be directed to practical world affairs and to the education of the general public, and not in the early stages to esoteric matters. In the last analysis, there is for the Master and His disciples no such thing as esotericism, except in so far as Shamballa is concerned. There is only definite and planned work with the consciousness of all forms, and—where humanity is involved—this is regarded as a process of education, leading to an expansion of perception and the changing of acquired academic knowledge into an overshadowing and conditioning wisdom. The implementing of human affairs to bring about this unfoldment in consciousness is in the hands of disciples who are undergoing the process themselves, and it is not in the hands of the Masters, Whose consciousness is fully expanded—a consciousness entering a higher and greatly different phase, connected with Being and Life and the purposes of Shamballa.

Approach Towards Externalisation in the Disciple's Consciousness

I find it necessary here to make one point clear. The disciples sent out from the various ashrams do not arrive on earth conscious of a high mission or knowing well the nature of the task to which they have been subjectively assigned. In the case of certain disciples who will be of special world prominence and who are of initiate rank, they may attain to a conviction of mission (if I may call it so) in their extreme youth and thus be oriented towards their life task from the very start; that conviction will grow and deepen and clarify as the years go by. But it must be remembered that the majority of disciples will not so react. They will come into incarnation with certain gifts and innate talents and with certain firmly rooted ideas, endowed with irrevocable ideals and a brain which is responsive to a well-developed mind. They will, normally and through natural trends and predilections, find their way into that field of human activity wherein they are intended to work and in which they are to bring about certain basic changes in line with hierarchical intent. This hierarchical intent will usually be unknown to them (though this may not always be the case), but the work to be done will seem to them impelling and necessary and something which they must do at all costs. They will find their way into politics, into the educational movements and into science; they will work as humanitarians, as social workers and in the field of finance, but they will follow these lines of activity through natural inclination and not because they are being "obedient" to instruction from some Master. They will be successful in their endeavour because the potency of the Hierarchy will be behind them, and there is much that the inner Ashram can accomplish for its outer working disciples in the way of opening doors, implementing efforts and arranging contacts, and other facilities; this is all done, however, without any evidence of the inner impulsion. Recognition of the inner effort will be dependent upon the status in the Ashram of the disciple. When the disciple is a very advanced one, he may become aware of his high mission and know it to be no fanatical and self-initiated intention, but a definite task undertaken in response to ashramic planning. Such cases will usually be the exception and not the rule, particularly in the early stages. Such hierarchical workers will gather around them lesser disciples who will work along the same lines, through community of interest but not through recognition of similar instructions—a very different thing. In the one case, the consciousness of mission is developed through periods of definite planning with the Ashram and in consultation with the Master or His senior workers. In the more usual case, the disciple re-acts and works in response to impression, being at this stage totally unaware from whence the impression comes; he regards it as an activity of his own mind acting as a directing agent in all the planned activities, the life theme and purpose which are his service dynamic.

One major characteristic is, however, present in all these working disciples and aspirants; this is a wide humanitarianism and a determination to aid in the cause of human welfare. One interesting distinction will later emerge and condition the new age in contradistinction to past and present methods. Disciples and aspirants will not be dedicated to purely humanitarian and welfare work. That will be a motive and not an objective in work. They will not give up their days and efforts solely to the relief of human necessity. All phases of human living—politics, finance and science, as well as religion—will be recognised to be their immediate and spectacular task, but the motivation in the future will not be primarily business success or personality ambition but the impulse to subordinate these to the general effort and to aid humanity as a whole, with a long range vision.

It is this growing spirit of humanitarianism which will lie behind all movements towards world socialisation in the various nations. This movement is symptomatic of a change in the orientation of man's thinking, and therein lies its major value. It is not indicative of a new technique of government in reality, and this particular phase of it is ephemeral; it is at the same time foundational to the new world order which will emerge out of all these experiments which human thinking is at this time evolving.

These are the things which will be in the consciousness of disciples commissioned by the Hierarchy to bring about the needed changes and the new orientation, and not any recognition of Masters and Their orders or of any hierarchical and ashramic background.

Whilst in incarnation such disciples stand free to serve one-pointedly and wholeheartedly that section or phase of human effort in which their lot and life-trend appear to cast them. They may be quite unconscious of any spiritual objective (so-called today) except the recognition that they love their fellowmen; this love will condition all they do and will motivate their every effort.

From the standpoint of the Master, they can be reached, impressed and directed, and most definitely they are so reached; from their own standpoint they are simply busy, energetic people, gifted with a good mind, profoundly interested in their chosen life task and proving themselves capable of effective work along some particular line, able to influence and direct others in similar activity and definitely bringing about changes in the branch of human endeavour with which they are concerned, thus lifting underlying principles on to higher levels. This is straight hierarchical work. It affects on broad lines the consciousness of humanity.

These disciples may be conscious that their effort and their thinking are part of a forward-moving evolutionary endeavour; to that extent they are mission-conscious, but the value of this attitude is that it relates them, in consciousness, to many others, similarly motivated and conscious of a similar vision. It is of course wise to remember that all such disciples are pronounced ray types and are integrated personalities in the highest sense of the word. They will work on earth as high grade personalities, under the impact of strong motives which emanate from the soul in response to impression from the Ashram, but of this, in their physical brains, they know nothing and care less. Part of their effectiveness in service is due to the fact that they are not preoccupied with soul contact and with the idea of academic service. Their eyes are on the job to be done, their hearts are with their fellowmen, and their heads are busy with methods, techniques and practices which will raise the entire level of endeavour in their chosen field. Hence their inevitable success.

Disciples who are intensely interested in personal responsiveness to the soul, who work diligently at the problem of soul contact, who are busy with the art of serving consciously and who make service a goal, who are keenly alive to the fact of the Ashram and to the Master, will *not* be asked to do this work of preparing for the externalisation of the Hierarchy. Advanced disciples who are stabilised in the Ashram, and who are so used to the Master that He assumes in their consciousness no undue prominence, can be trusted to work along right lines in the world and do the work of preparation. They cannot be sidetracked or deflected from one-pointed attention to the task in hand by any soul call or urge; hence they are free to do the intended work.

The situation, therefore, in relation to the consciousness of disciples in the intensely difficult, though interesting, period with which humanity is faced could be summed up in the following statements:

1.   The disciple is not motivated by any desire to externalise the Hierarchy or to see the Ashram with which he is affiliated functioning physically on the outer plane. He may be totally unaware of this hierarchical intention. If he is aware of this underlying purpose, it is entirely secondary in his consciousness. The good of humanity and a stabilised spiritual future for mankind are his major life incentives.

2.   The disciple is strictly humanitarian in his outlook. He works for the One Humanity and though aware possibly that he is affiliated with the Hierarchy, his loyalties, his service and his life intention are directed entirely to the cause of human betterment. In this attitude he is coming to resemble the Masters Whose life directive is not hierarchical possibilities but adherence to the purposes of Shamballa, in action, in relationships and to the Plan for all living units in the three worlds.

3.   The intuition of the disciple is alert and active; the new ideas and the vital fresh concepts are foremost in his mind.

He almost automatically repudiates the reactionary and conservative thinking of the past and—without fanaticism and undue emphasis—he lives, talks and instructs along the new lines of right human relations.

4.   The disciple, occupied with hierarchical plans for the future, has a completely open mind as regards the growth of true psychic powers. He deplores and represses all negative conditions and forms of thinking as he contacts them in his environment, but he encourages the growth of all forms of higher sensory perception which expand the human consciousness and enrich its content.

5.   According to his hierarchical status, he will become increasingly a channel of power in the world. His own ashramic life will deepen as his world service develops. The statement in the Bible (or rather injuction) to "take root downward and bear fruit upward" has for him a deeply occult significance.

I am not here touching upon the growth of a disciple *as a disciple*, or on his individual progress on the Path; I am considering the type of consciousness with which he faces the task which confronts him. Unless he fulfills within himself the requirements enumerated in this section of our study, he will not be one of the workers in this interlude between the old age and the new.

The Dissemination of Information of a Preparatory Nature

Those who do the work of reaching humanity with the needed information fall into two main groups:

1. Disciples and convinced aspirants who are today working in the field of occultism.
2. Those disciples and initiates who will emerge from the three Ashrams and whose work is largely to act as the vanguard of the Hierarchy and precede it into outer manifestation. This will begin in the year 1975, if the disciples now active will do their work adequately.

Much has already been done in familiarising the general public with the concept of the Hierarchy. Much of it has been done in such a manner as to bring the whole subject into disrepute, as well you know. The groups now occupied with the dissemination of occult teaching would be well-advised to change their methods if—beneath their pronounced ignorance and their love of the spectacular—there lies a true belief and a real humanitarian desire. Information anent the Hierarchy should take the following lines:

1.   Emphasis should be laid on the evolution of humanity with peculiar attention to its goal, perfection. This is not the idealistic perfection of the visionary mystic, but the control of the instrument, man in incarnation, by the indwelling and overshadowing soul. The constitution of man should be increasingly taught.

2.   The relation of the individual soul to all souls should be taught, and with it the recognition that the long-awaited kingdom of God is simply the appearance of soul-controlled men on earth in everyday life and at all stages of that control.

3.   From a recognition of this relationship, the fact of the spiritual Hierarchy can then be deduced and *the normality* of its existence emphasised. The fact will appear that the Kingdom has always been present but has remained unrecognised, owing to the relatively few people who express, as yet, its quality.

4.   When this recognition has become general, the idea (by this time permanently present in the human consciousness everywhere) and good sense also will testify to the fact of the presence of Those Who have achieved the goal; Their demonstration of divinity will be regarded as normal, as constituting a universal objective, and as the guarantee of humanity's future achievement; degrees of this divine expression can then be pointed out, ranging from that of the probationary disciple, through disciples, to Those Who have achieved mastery, and up to and inclusive of the Christ.

5.   Thus gradually the idea or concept of the existence, in bodily presence, of the Masters will be inculcated and stead-

ily accepted; a new attitude to the Christ will be developed which will be inclusive of all the best that the past has given to us but which will integrate men into a more sane and acceptable approach to the entire problem.

6. The time will come when the fact of the presence on earth of the Christ as Head of the Hierarchy and the Director of the Kingdom of God will be accepted; men will also realise the truth of the present revolutionary statement that at no time has He ever left the earth.

7. Emphasis will also increasingly be laid upon the unfolding Plan, and men will be brought to its recognition through a study of the evolution of the human family, through a close consideration of historical processes, and through a comparative analysis of ancient and modern civilisations and cultures. The thread of purpose will be noted and followed through, century after century, integrating not only history into one complete story of the revelation of divine qualities through the medium of humanity, but integrating with it and into it all world philosophies, the central theme of all creative art, the symbolism of architecture and the conclusions of science.

This approach of the central fact of human evolution—the steady growth of divinity and the revelation through man of divine powers—will offset the fanciful, fantastic presentation of the Hierarchy which has coloured all the occult movements and the various Theosophical and Rosicrucian presentations. The subject will be presented in a manner acceptable and reasonable. It will not be a slower process, but the reverse. The results of the old and foolish way of introducing the subject has greatly retarded the intended work. Men, however, in the future, will accept with rapidity and thankfully what is reasonable and which has its roots in the past, can be proven by history, and which presents a true and possible hope for the future.

It can be expected that the orthodox Christian will at first reject the theories about the Christ which occultism presents; at the same time, this same orthodox Christian will find it increasingly difficult to induce the intelligent masses of people to accept the impossible Deity and the feeble Christ which historical Christianity has endorsed. A Christ Who is present and living, Who is known to those who follow Him, Who is a strong and able executive and not a sweet and sentimental sufferer, Who has never left us but Who has worked for two thousand years through the medium of His disciples, the inspired men and women of all faiths, all religions and all religious persuasions; Who has no use for fanaticism or hysterical devotion but Who loves all men persistently, intelligently and optimistically, Who sees divinity in them all and Who comprehends the techniques of the evolutionary development of the human consciousness (mental, emotional and physical, producing civilisations and cultures appropriate to a particular point in evolution) —these ideas the intelligent public can and will accept.

They will prepare and work for conditions in the world in which Christ can move freely among men, in bodily Presence; He need not then remain in His present retreat in Central Asia. They can and will accept with ease the unity of all faiths when the relationship of the Buddha and the Christ is correctly presented; then the picture of a Christ demanding a unique position, to the exclusion of all other sons of God, will fade out in the wonder of the true apostolic succession, in which many sons of God, on different rays, of differing nationalities and with varying missions, are to be seen historically leading humanity along the path of divine unfoldment and nearer to God, the Source.

Temporarily, the fact of God Immanent will engross the attention of all true spiritual teachers, and the fact of that divine immanence making itself felt in perfection through the Christ and other divine Representatives will for a time relegate the teaching on God Transcendent into the background. Undue emphasis has been placed on this major truth, to the exclusion of the nearer and more practical truth of God in every man and in every form in every kingdom in nature; much evil has eventuated by the failure to lay the emphasis upon God Immanent. Later on, when the truth of the Christ indwelling every man and revealed in perfection through the historical Christ and His great Brothers down the ages has been accepted, the teaching of God Transcendent, which is the secret mystery in the custody of Shamballa, will be revealed and emphasised. The two halves of a perfect Whole will then be recognised by humanity.

The key to the Hierarchy and Its reappearance on earth in physical form, and the consequent materialisation of the kingdom of God among men, is *the simple truth of God Immanent.* It is the clue to the evolutionary process, and the eternal hope of all forms in all kingdoms in nature. This is the central truth, the convincing truth, and the revealing truth which will underlie all information anent the Hierarchy, and this the coming generation of disciples will distribute. If this truth is factual and possible of demonstration, then the fact of the Hierarchy is proved and the authenticity of the eternal existence of the kingdom of God on earth is established.

THE RETURN OF THE CHRIST *

May 1947

Year after year I have written you (and all who care to listen) a message which has often been prophetic, always related to the fundamental spiritual union of the East and the West, of the Buddha and the Christ, and which has consistently laid emphasis upon the immediate spiritual opportunity. Every year I have prepared these messages with great care, and in their synthesis there emerges (if you have read them in order and intelligently) a picture of the spiritual life of the world. It is a picture which involves the knowable past, which concerns the immediate present, and carries forward into a future of spiritual unfoldment, transcending in

---

* Part of this message and the one following it on page 612 appear in chapters III and VII of *The Reappearance of the Christ.* Chronologically they belong in the historical sequence here given.

expression all that has hitherto been known, because it has ever been based on the reality, *on the fact of God Immanent.*

God Transcendent, greater, vaster and more inclusive than His created world, is universally recognised and has been generally emphasised; all faiths can say with Shri Krishna (speaking as God, the Creator) that "having pervaded the whole universe with a fragment of Myself, I remain." This God Transcendent has dominated the religious thinking of millions of simple and spiritually-minded people down the centuries which have elapsed since humanity began to press forward towards divinity.

Slowly, there is dawning upon the awakening consciousness of humanity, the great parallelling truth of God Immanent—divinely "pervading" all forms, conditioning from within all kingdoms in nature, expressing innate divinity through human beings and—two thousand years ago—portraying the nature of that divine Immanence in the Person of the Christ. Today, as an outcome of this unfolding divine Presence, there is entering into the minds of men everywhere a new concept: that of Christ in us, the hope of Glory. There is a growing and developing belief that Christ *is* in us, as He was in the Master Jesus, and this belief will alter world affairs and mankind's entire attitude to life.

The wonder of that Life lived two thousand years ago is still with us and has lost none of its freshness; it is an eternal inspiration, hope, encouragement and example. The love He demonstrated still holds the thinking world in thrall, even though relatively few have really attempted to demonstrate the same quality of love as He did—a love that leads unerringly to world service, to complete self-forgetfulness and to radiant, magnetic living. The words He spoke were few and simple, and all men can understand them, but their significance has largely been lost in the intricate legalities and discussions of St. Paul, and the lengthy disputations of theological commentators since He lived and left us—or apparently left us.

Yet—today Christ is nearer to humanity than at any other time in human history; He is closer than the most aspiring and hopeful disciple knows, and can draw closer still if what I here propose to write is understood and brought to the attention of men everywhere. For Christ belongs to humanity, to the world of men, and not only to the churches and faiths throughout the world.

Around Him—in that High Place on Earth where He has His abiding place—are gathered today all His great Disciples, the Masters of the Wisdom, and all Those liberated Sons of God Who, down the ages, have passed from darkness to Light, from the unreal to the Real, and from death to Immortality; They stand ready to carry out His bidding and to obey the Master of all the Masters and the Teacher alike of Angels and of men. The Exponents and the Representatives of all the world faiths are there waiting—under His guidance—to reveal to all those who today struggle in the maelstrom of world affairs, and who seek to solve the world crisis, that *they are not alone.* God Transcendent is working through the Christ and the Spiritual Hierarchy to bring relief; God Immanent in all men is standing on the verge of certain stupendous Recognitions.

The great Apostolic Succession of the Knowers of God is poised today for renewed activity—a Succession of Those Who have lived on earth, accepted the fact of God Transcendent, discovered the reality of God Immanent, portrayed in Their Own lives the divine characteristics of the Christ life and (because They lived on earth as He did and *does*) have "entered for us within the veil, leaving us an example that we too should follow His steps," and Theirs. We too belong eventually in that great Succession.

You may wonder why, at this hour of the Festival of the Buddha, I am writing to you anent His great Brother, the Christ. I am doing it with deliberation because the eyes of all spiritual Knowers are fixed upon Him, because the Buddha Himself is standing behind Him in humble recognition of the divine task which He is on the verge of consummating, and because of the imminence of that spiritual accomplishment. I write thus because not only are all those who are functioning consciously in the Kingdom of God aware of His plans, but because those great spiritual Beings Who live and dwell in the "Father's House," in the "centre where the Will of God is known," are also mobilised and organised to assist His work. The spiritual line of succession from the throne of the Ancient of Days down to the humblest disciple (gathered with others at the feet of the Christ) is today focussed on the task of helping humanity.

The great moment for which He has so patiently waited has almost arrived; the "end of the age" to which He referred when speaking to His small group of disciples—"Lo! I am with you all the days even unto the end of the age"—has come and today He stands and waits, knowing that the hour has come when He will "see of the travail of His soul and be satisfied." May I repeat: Right through the spiritual succession of the Sons of God there is naught to be seen and felt but expectancy and preparation.

From the Father's House (the Shamballa of the esotericist) the fiat has gone forth: "The hour has come." From the kingdom of God where reigns the Christ, the answer has been flung back: "Father, Thy will be done"; down in our struggling, bewildered, unhappy world of men, the cry is ceaselessly rising: "May Christ return to Earth." Thus in the three great spiritual centres—the Father's House, the Kingdom of God, and awakening Humanity—there is but one Purpose, one idea and one united expectancy. . . .

I write here in no fanatical or adventist spirit; I speak not as a speculative theologian or an exponent of one phase of religious wishful thinking. I speak because the time is ripe and because the appeal of simple faithful hearts has penetrated to the highest spiritual sphere and set in motion energies and forces which cannot now be stopped; I speak because the invocative cry of distressed humanity is today of such a volume and sound that—united to the wisdom and the knowledge of the spiritual Hierarchy—it has given rise to certain activities in the Father's House. These will result in the glory of God, in the transformation of the divine will-to-good into human goodwill and resultant peace on Earth.

A new chapter in the great book of spiritual living is about to be written; a new expansion of consciousness is an imminent happening; a fresh recognition of divine attentiveness is now possible to humanity, and a revealing expectancy will prove the accuracy of the Biblical statement, "every eye shall see Him." The religious livingness or spiritual history of mankind can be summarised for us by a series of recognitions —recognition of Those Who, down the ages, have constituted the Apostolic Succession, culminating for us in the great religious leaders who have come out among us since 700 B.C. and founded the great modern world faiths, and—above all else—in the Christ Himself Who embodied the perfection of God Immanent, plus awareness of God Transcendent; recognition of those major spiritual concepts of love, life and relationship which have hovered ever in the background of man's thinking and which are now on the verge of right expression; recognition of the true brotherhood of man, *based on the one divine life, working through the one soul and expressing itself through the one humanity;* recognition, therefore, of relationship both to the divine life throughout the world and to mankind itself. It is this developing spiritual attitude which will lead to right human relations and eventual world peace.

Today another recognition is becoming possible. It is the recognition everywhere of the imminent return of Christ (if such a phrase can be true of One Who has never left us) and of the new spiritual opportunities which this event will make possible.

The basis for this recognition lies in the deep-seated conviction, innate in the human consciousness, that some great Teacher, some Saviour, Revealer, Lawgiver or divine Representative *must* come forth from the world of spiritual realities, because of human need and human demand. Always, down the centuries, at the hour of man's greatest need and in response to his voiced demand, a divine Son of God *has* come forth and under many different names. Then the Christ came and apparently left us, with His work unfinished and His vision for mankind not yet consummated. For two thousand years it has seemed as if all His work had been blocked, frustrated, and of no avail—for the growth of the churches during the centuries is no guarantee of the spiritual success at which He aimed. It needed more than theological interpretations and the numerical growth of the world religions (including Christianity and Buddhism) to prove His world mission successfully carried forward. It all seemed impossible, necessitating three conditions; in these a test of His work could be attempted; today these three conditions are proven facts.

First: a general planetary situation which has (unfortunately owing to man's selfishness) proved to be so catastrophic in nature that humanity has been forced to recognise the cause and source of the disaster; secondly, a spiritual awakening which would have its impulse in the deepest depths of man's consciousness, and such is the case today as a result of the world war (1914-1945) ; thirdly, a steadily mounting invocative cry, prayer or demand, directed toward high spiritual sources, no matter by what names such sources may be called.

Today, all these three conditions have been fulfilled and humanity faces renewed opportunity. The disaster which has overtaken mankind is universal and widespread; no one has escaped, and all men are involved in some way or another—physically, economically and socially. The spiritual awakening of men everywhere (within or without the world faiths, and largely outside of them) is general and complete, and a turning to God is to be seen on every hand. Finally, these two causes have aroused—as never before—the invocative cry of humanity; it is clearer, purer and more selfless than at any other time in human history, because it is based on clearer thinking and common distress. True religion is again emerging in the hearts of men in every land; this recognition of a divine hope and background may possibly take people back into the churches and world faiths, but *it will most certainly take them back to God.*

Religion is the name, surely, which we give to the invocative appeal of humanity which leads to the evocative response of the Spirit of God. This Spirit works in every human heart and in all groups. It works through the spiritual Hierarchy of the planet; it impels the Head of the Hierarchy, the Christ, to take action, and the action which He is taking will lead to His return, with His disciples.

I wonder if you appreciate the import of what I have just said? The idea of the return of Christ is a most familiar one, and the concept of a returning Son of God in response to human need has its place in the teaching of the majority of the world faiths. Ever since He apparently departed to the sphere where the faithful have put Him, little groups of these people have reasoned themselves into the belief that on such and such a date He will come back, and ever their prophecies and expectancies have been doomed to failure. He has not come. Such people have been laughed at by the crowd and rebuked by the intelligent. Their eyes have not seen Him and there has been no tangible indication of His Presence. Today, I tell you that He will come; that plans for His coming are already set on foot, but I set no date or hour. The time is known only to the two or three, but "in such an hour as ye think not, He will come." (Matt. XXIV. 44)

I tell you, first of all, a truth hard for the orthodox thinker of any faith to accept: *He cannot return because He has always been here upon our Earth,* watching over the spiritual destiny of humanity; He has never left us, but in physical body and securely concealed (though not hidden), He has guided the affairs of the spiritual Hierarchy, of His disciples and workers who are unitedly pledged with Him to Earth Service. He can only *reappear.* It is a spiritual fact that those who have passed from the cave of the tomb into the fullness of the resurrection life can be seen, and at the same time evade the vision of the believer; seeing and recognition are two very different things, and one of the great recognitions of mankind in the near future is the recognition that always He has been with us and shared with us the familiar usefulness and peculiar characteristics of our civilisation and its many gifts to man.

The early signs of His approach with His disciples can already be discerned by those who note and rightly interpret the signs of the times. There is (among these signs) the coming together spiritually of those who love their fellow-men. This is in reality the organising of the outer physical army of the Lord—an army which has no weapons but those of love, of right speech and right human relations. This unknown organisation has proceeded with phenomenal speed during the aftermath of war, because humanity is sick of hate and of controversy.

The general staff of the Christ is already active in the form of the New Group of World Servers; they are as potent a body of forerunners as has ever preceded a great world Figure into the arena of mankind's living. Their work and influence is already seen and felt in every land, and nothing can destroy that which they have accomplished. The spiritual and organising effect of sound in the form of expressed and voiced invocation has been also attempted since 1935, and the energy of the invocative cry of humanity has been directed into those channels which reach from Earth to that High Place where dwells the Christ. From there, it has been transmitted on to those still higher spheres where the attention of the Lord of the World, the Ancient of Days, the Father of all, plus the Creative Energies and Living Beings Who dwell there with Him, can be focussed on humanity and those steps can be taken which will embody more rapidly the Purposes of God.

For the first time in human history, the demand of the people of the Earth is so potent and so in line with divine direction in time and space that the end is inevitably sure; the looked-for spiritual Representative must come forth, and this time He will not come alone but will be accompanied by Those Whose lives and words will evoke recognition in every department of human thinking. The symbolic prophecies found in all the world Scriptures anent this imminent event will prove their veracity; their symbolism will nevertheless elicit re-interpretation, and circumstances and happenings will not necessarily be exactly as the Scripures would appear to indicate. For instance, He will come indeed "in the clouds of the air" as the Christian Scriptures say (Matt. XXIV. 64), but of what great interest is that when millions come and go in the clouds each hour of the day and of the night? I mention this as one of the outstanding prophecies and one of the most familiar; it is, however, one which means little in our modern civilisation. The fact that is of importance is that He will come.

The Wesak Festival has been held, down the centuries, in the well-known valley in the Himalayas (if the faithful would only believe it) in order:

1. To substantiate the fact of Christ's physical existence among us ever since His so-called departure.
2. To prove (on the physical plane) the factual solidarity of the Eastern and Western approaches to God. Both the Christ and the Buddha are then present.
3. To form a rallying-point and a meeting-place for those who annually—in synthesis and symbolically—link up and represent the Father's House, the Kingdom of God, and Humanity.
4. To demonstrate the nature of the work of Christ as the great and chosen Intermediary, standing as the Representative of the spiritual Hierarchy and as the Leader of the new group of world servers, and in His Person voicing their demand for the recognition of the factual existence of the Kingdom of God here and now.

Perhaps one of the major messages I have for all of you who read my words is this great truth and fact of the physical Presence on Earth at this time of the Christ, of His group of Disciples and Executives, of Their representative activities on behalf of mankind and of Their close relationship. This relationship comes out at certain of the great spiritual Festivals where relationship includes not only the Kingdom of God but also the Father and the Father's Home. There is the Festival of Easter; the Festival of the Buddha

Who, in physical Presence, expresses the spiritual solidarity of our planet; and the Festival in June, peculiarly the Festival of the Christ, when He—as Leader of the new group of world servers—employs the new Invocation on behalf of all men of goodwill in all lands; at the same time, He gathers up the inchoate and unexpressed demands of those masses who seek a new and better way of life. They want love in daily living, right human relations, and an understanding of the underlying Plan.

It is these physical happenings which are of moment, and not the vague hopes and promises of the theological faiths. It is the physical Presence upon our planet of such recognised spiritual Figures as the Lord of the World, the Ancient of Days; the seven Spirits Who are before the throne of God; of the Buddha, the spiritual leader of the East, and the Christ, the spiritual leader of the West, which I bring at this climaxing time to your attention. To you I say that the vague belief in Their existence, the dreamy speculations as to Their work and Their interest in human welfare, and the unconvinced, yet hopeful, wishful thinking of believers (and also unbelievers), will soon give place to certain knowledge, to visual recognition, to provable signs of executive work, and to the reorganisation (by men of unusual potency) of the political, religious, economic and social life of the planet.

All this will not come as the result of some proclamation or some stupendous planetary event which will force human beings everywhere to say: Lo! He is there! Lo! Here are the signs of His divinity! for that would evoke only antagonism and laughter, resistance or fanatical credulity. It will come as a recognition of potency in leadership, through dynamic but logical changes in world affairs, and through action taken by the masses of the people from the depths of their own consciousness.

Many years ago I indicated that the Christ would come in three ways, or rather, that the fact of His Presence could be proved in three distinctive phases.

I said then that the first move which the Hierarchy

would make would be the stimulation of the spiritual consciousness in man, the evocation of humanity's spiritual
demands on a large scale, and the nurturing—on a worldwide
scale—of the Christ consciousness in the human heart. This
has already been done, and with most effective results. Of
the factual nature of this process the vociferous demands of
men of goodwill, of welfare workers and of those pledged to
international cooperation, to the relief of world distress
and to the establishment of right human relations are the
undeniable expression. That phase of the preparatory work
which is indicative of His coming has now reached a stage
where nothing can arrest its progress or slow down its momentum. In spite of appearances, this uprising of the Christ-
consciousness has been successful, and what may appear as
reverse activity is of no importance in the long run, and
only of a temporary nature.

The second move of the Hierarchy, I told you, would
be the impressing of the minds of enlightened men everywhere by spiritual ideas embodying the new truths, by the
"descent" (if I may so call it) of the new concepts which
will govern human living, and by the over-shadowing of all
world disciples and the new group of world servers by the
Christ Himself. You will recall how, in the Bible story,
Christ symbolically evoked the recognition of John the
Baptist and imparted the things of the Kingdom of God
to the disciples who walked to Emmaus, though they recognised not their Companion. This planned move of the
Hierarchy is also progressing well; men and women everywhere and in every department of life are enunciating those
new truths which should in the future guide human living;
they are building those new organisations, movements and
groups—large or small—which will familiarise the mass of
men with the reality of the need and the mode of meeting it.
This they are doing because they are driven thereto by
the warmth of their hearts and their loving response to
human distress; without formulating it thus to themselves,
they are nevertheless working to bring into visibility the
Kingdom of God on earth. No denial of these facts is pos-

sible, in view of the multiplicity of this type of organisations, books and speeches.

Thirdly, I told you that Christ might come in person and walk among men as He did before. This has not yet taken place, but plans are being laid which will enable Him to do so. Those plans do not involve the birth of some nice child in some nice home on earth; they will not produce the wild claims and the credulous recognition of the well-meaning and the unintelligent, as is so frequently the case today, nor will someone appear and say: This is the Christ. He is here or He is there. I would point out to you, however, that the widespread appearance of such tales and claims, though undesirable, misleading and wrong, nevertheless demonstrates human expectancy of the imminence of His coming. Belief in His coming is basic in the human consciousness. How He will come, in what manner, I may not and should not say. The exact moment has not yet arrived, nor has the method of His appearance been determined. The factual nature of the two earlier and preparatory moves, already made by the Hierarchy under His direction, are the guarantee that He *will* come and that—when He does—mankind will be ready.

For a brief moment, I would like to summarise certain aspects of the work He set in motion two thousand years ago, because it holds the clue to His future work. Some of it is well known to you, for it has been emphasised by the world faiths and particularly by teachers of the Christian faith. But all of them have made His work appear difficult for man to grasp, and the undue emphasis laid upon His divinity (an emphasis which He Himself never made) has made it appear that He and He only, and no one else, could possibly do the same things. Theologians have forgotten that He Himself stated that "greater things shall ye do, because I go unto the Father" (John XIV. 12). He here indicates that this passing to the Father's House would result in such an inflow of spiritual strength, insight and creative accomplishment in men, that their deeds would surpass His. Because of the distortion of His teaching and its remote relation to man,

we have not yet done those "greater things." Some day
we assuredly will, and—along certain lines—we already have.
Let me relate some of the things He did which we can do,
and which He will aid.

1.   For the first time in human history, the love of God
was embodied in a man, and Christ inaugurated the era
of love. That expression of divine love is still in the making;
the world is not yet full of love and few there are that
understand the true meaning of the word. But—speaking
symbolically—when the United Nations has emerged into
factual and actual power, the welfare of the world will then
be assured. What is that welfare but love in action? What
are right human relations but love among men, groups and
nations? What is international cooperation but love on a
world scale? Those are the things which the love of God
in Christ expressed, and those are the things which we are
working here today to bring into being. We are attempting
to do it on a vast scale, and this in spite of opposition—an
opposition which can only temporarily succeed, such is the
potency of the awakened spirit of man. These are the things
which the Hierarchy, in its already successful procedures, is
aiding and will continue to aid.

2.   Christ taught also that the Kingdom of God is on Earth
and told us to seek that Kingdom first and let all things
go for its sake. That Kingdom has ever been with us, composed of all those who, down the ages, have sought spiritual
goals, liberated themselves from the limitations of the
physical body, emotional controls and the obstructive mind.
Its citizens are those who today (unknown to the majority) live in physical bodies, work for the welfare of humanity,
use love instead of emotion as their general technique, and
compose that great body of "illumined Minds" which guide
the destiny of the world. The Kingdom of God is not something which will descend on earth when men are good
enough! It is something which is functioning efficiently
today and demanding recognition. It is an organised body
which is already evoking recognition from those people who

do seek first the Kingdom of God and discover thereby that the Kingdom they seek is already here. Christ and His disciples are known by many to be physically present on Earth and the Kingdom which They rule, with its laws and modes of activity are familiar to many, and have been throughout the centuries.

Christ is the World Healer and Saviour. He works because He is the embodied soul of all Reality. He works today, as he worked in Palestine two thousand years ago, through groups. There He worked through the three beloved disciples, through the twelve apostles, through the chosen seventy, and the interested five hundred. . . . Now He works through His Masters and Their groups, and thereby greatly intensifies His efforts. He can and will work through all groups just in so far as they fit themselves for planned service, for the distribution of love, and come into conscious alignment with the great potency of the inner groups.

Esotericists, occult students, Rosicrucians and Theosophists have always proclaimed the physical Presence of the Christ, but have so distorted the teaching by dogmatic assertions on unimportant details and by ridiculous claims, that they have evoked little recognition of the underlying truth, nor have they portrayed a Kingdom which is attractive. Yet that Kingdom exists and is not a place of disciplines or golden harps and peopled by unintelligent fanatics, but a field of service and a place where every man has full scope for the exercise of his divinity in human service.

3.   At the Transfiguration, Christ revealed the glory which is innate in all men. The triple lower nature—physical, emotional and mental—is there shown as prostrate before the glory which was revealed. In that moment, wherein Christ Immanent was in the physical form, wherein humanity was represented by the three apostles, a Voice came from the Father's Home in recognition of the revealed divinity and the Sonship of the Transfigured Christ. On this innate divinity, upon this recognised Sonship, is the brotherhood of all men based—one life, one glory which shall be re-

vealed, and one divine relationship. Today, on a large scale (even when by-passing the implications of divinity) the glory of man and his fundamental relationships are already a fact in the human consciousness. Accompanying those characteristics which as yet remain deplorable and which would appear to negate all claims to divinity, is the wonder of man's achievement, of his triumph over nature. The glory of scientific attainment and the magnificent evidence of creative art—both modern and ancient—leave no room to question man's divinity. Here then are the "greater things" of which Christ spoke, and here again is the triumph of the Christ within the human heart.

Why this triumph of the Christ consciousness must always be spoken of in terms of religion, of church-going and of orthodox belief is one of the incredible triumphs of the forces of evil. To be a citizen of the Kingdom of God does *not* mean that one must necessarily be a member of some one of the orthodox churches. The divine Christ in the human heart can express itself in many different departments of human living—in politics, in the arts, in economic expression and in true social living, in science and in religion. It might be wise here to remember that the only time it is recorded that Christ (as an adult) visited the Temple of the Jews, He created a disturbance! Humanity *is* passing from glory to glory and, in the long panorama of history, this is strikingly observable. The glory is today revealed in every department of human activity, and the Transfiguration of those who are on the crest of the human wave of civilisation is very close at hand.

4. Finally, in the triumph of the Crucifixion or (as it is more accurately called in the East) the Great Renunciation, Christ, for the first time, anchored on earth a tenuous thread of the divine Will, as it issued from the Father's House (Shamballa), passed into the understanding custody of the Kingdom of God, and through the medium of the Christ was brought to the attention of mankind. Through the instrumentality of certain great Sons of God the three divine aspects or characteristics of the divine Trinity—will,

love and intelligence—have become a part of human thinking and aspiration. Christians are apt to forget that the crisis in the final hours of the Christ was not in those spent upon the Cross, but during those spent in the Garden of Gethsemane, when His will—in agony and almost despair—was submerged in that of the Father. "Father," He said, "not my will but Thine be done." (Luke XXII. 42.)

Something new, yet planned for from the very depth of time, happened then in that quiet garden; Christ, representing mankind, anchored or established the Father's will on earth and made it possible for intelligent humanity to carry it out. Hitherto, that Will had been known in the Father's House; it had been recognised and adapted to world need by the Spiritual Hierarchy, working under the Christ, and thus took shape as the divine Plan. Today, because of what Christ did in His moment of crisis hundreds of years ago, humanity can add its efforts to the working out of that Plan. The will-to-good of the Father's House can become the goodwill of the Kingdom of God and be transformed into right human relations by intelligent humanity. Thus the direct line or thread of God's will reaches now from the highest place to the lowest point and can, in due time, become a *cable of ascension* for the sons of men and of descent for the loving, living spirit of God.

I would have you forget distance, remoteness and vagueness and realise that I am talking of exact and literal happenings on our planet. I am dealing with recognitions and occurrences and with factual events which are the conscious possession of many. *The Christ of history and the Christ in the human heart are planetary facts.*

There is one aspect of this return of the Christ which is never touched upon and to which no reference is ever made. I, a humble disciple of the Christ, would like here to speak of it. It is the factor of what this coming out again among men, this return to outer everyday activity, will mean to the Christ as He faces it. How will He feel when the hour of His appearance arrives?

There is a great initiation spoken of in the New Testament, to which we have given the name of the Ascension. Of it we know nothing. Only a few items of information are brought to us in the Gospel story: the fact of the mountain top, of attendant watchers, and of the words of Christ, assuring them that He was not leaving them. Then the clouds received Him out of their sight. There were none present who could go further with Him. Their consciousness could not penetrate to the place where He had chosen to go; they even misinterpreted His words and only in a vague and mystical sense has humanity ever understood His disappearance or the significance of His persistent but unobserved Presence. The watchers were assured by two of the Knowers of God Who were also present that He would come again in like manner. He ascended. The clouds received Him and today the clouds which cover our planet are waiting to reveal Him.

He is now waiting to descend. This descent into our unhappy world of men can present Him with no alluring picture. From the quiet mountain retreat where He has waited, guided and watched over humanity, and where He has trained His disciples, initiates and the new group of world servers, He must come forth and take His place prominently on the world stage, and take His part in the great drama which is there being played. This time, He will play His part, not in obscurity as He previously did. but before the eyes of the entire world. Because of the smallness of our little planet, and because of the prevalence of the radio, television and the rapidity of communication, His part will be watched by all, and the prospect must surely, for Him, hold certain horror, must present its tests and major adjustments, plus painful and unavoidable experience. He does not come as the omnipotent God of man's ignorant creation, but as the Christ, the Founder of the Kingdom of God on Earth, to complete the work He started, and again to demonstrate divinity in far more difficult circumstances.

The Christ suffers, however, far more from those in

His Own household than from those in the outer world; His work is more impeded by the advanced aspirant than by the intelligent thinker. It was not the cruelty of the outer world of men which caused the depths of sorrow to the Christ; it was His Own disciples, plus the massed sorrow—spread over the entire cycle of living—past, present and future—of humanity.

He comes to correct the mistakes and the misrepresentations of those who have dared to interpret His simple words in terms of their own ignorance, and to recognise those whose faithful service has made His return possible. He too is facing a major test, preparatory to a great initiation, and when He has passed the test and fulfilled His task He will pass to a still more exalted position in the Father's House or to some distant place of service where only the most exalted can follow Him; His present position will then be taken by the One Whom He has prepared and trained.

But before all this can happen He must again enter the public arena, play His part in world affairs and prove the scope of His mission. He will gather around Him, in the flesh, His chosen associates and advisors; these will not be the ones who gathered around Him in those earlier simpler days, but those members of our human family who today recognise Him and are preparing to work with Him as far as in them lies. It is a different world to which He is now planning to return and this is largely due to the intellectual development of the mass of men. This presents Him with stupendous difficulties, for the intellects of men must now be reached and not just their hearts (as in the earlier days) , if the Will of God is to be intelligently carried out on Earth. His major task is surely the establishing of right human relations in every department of human living. I would ask you to use your divine imagination and endeavour to think out what must be the implications of the task which confronts Him; I would ask you to ponder on the difficulties which He must inevitably face—the difficulty, above all, of mass intellectual wrong emphasis.

He, the Representative of the love of God, is asked to work again in the world arena wherein His earlier message has been negated, forgotten or misinterpreted for two thousand years, and wherein hate and separativeness have distinguished all men everywhere. This will plunge Him into a foreign atmosphere and into a situation wherein all His divine resources will be needed and will be tried to the uttermost. The generally accepted idea that He will return as a triumphant warrior, omnipotent and irresistible, has surely no basis in fact. That He will ultimately lead His people, humanity, into Jerusalem *is* a fact, founded on a secure foundation; but it will not be into a Jewish city called Jerusalem, but into "the place of peace" (as the word Jerusalem means). A careful consideration of the world situation today, and a dedicated use of the imagination, will reveal to the sincere thinker how appalling is the task which He has undertaken. But He has again "set His face to go up to Jerusalem" (Luke IX. 51); He will again appear and guide mankind into a civilisation and a state of consciousness in which right human relations and world-wide cooperation for the good of all will be the universal keynote. He will—through the new group of world servers and the men of goodwill—complete His association with the Will of God (His Father's business) in such a manner that the eternal will-to-good will be translated by humanity into goodwill and right relations. Then His task will be done; He will be free again to leave us, this time not to return, but to leave the world of men in the hands of that great spiritual Server Who will be the new Head of the Hierarchy, the Church Invisible.

The question now arises: In what way can we be of service? How can we aid during this preparatory stage?

On this point I have but little to say. The whole idea of His return is so familiar to you in its anticipatory nature (though not in the factual details as I have hinted them to you) that I find it hard to say anything practical or which will arrest your attention.

What the members of the spiritual Hierarchy are doing is much indeed; those disciples who are in conscious touch with the Masters of the Wisdom—or, if you prefer the term, with the senior disciples of the Christ—are working day and night in order to establish such confidence, correct attitudes and understanding of the divine spiritual "push" or enterprise that His way will be made easier. They and their groups of lesser disciples, aspirants and students of the realities stand unitedly behind the Christ and can thus enable Him to accomplish His purpose. Their major realisation is that of a cyclic crisis in the spiritual life of our planet; it is one which has been anticipated in the Father's House (Shamballa) for thousands of years. They have registered the fact that, for the first time in human history, all the three spiritual centres or groups through which God works are unitedly focussed on the same objective. Shamballa, the Spiritual Hierarchy, and Humanity (the Father's House, the Kingdom of God, and the world of men) are all striving in one vast movement for an intensification of the Light of the World. This Light will irradiate in a fashion unknown before, not only the Father's House, which is the source of all our planetary light, but also the spiritual centre from which have come all Those Teachers and World Saviours Who have stood before men and said, as did Hermes, the Buddha and the Christ: "I am the Light of the World." This light will now flood the world of men, bringing illumination to men's minds and light into the dark places of human living.

It is light and—above all else—"life more abundantly" which Christ will bring, and until He brings it we know not what it signifies; we cannot realise the revelation which this will entail and the new possibilities which will open before us. But through Him, light and life are on their way, to be interpreted and applied in terms of goodwill and of right human relations. For this the spiritual Hierarchy is preparing. This time the Christ will not come alone, for His co-workers will come with Him. His experience and Theirs will be the reverse of the previous one, for this time every eye will see Him, every ear will hear Him, and every mind will pass judgment upon Him.

Therefore I say that you can freely aid in the reconstruction work which the Christ proposes, if you will familiarise yourselves and all men whom you can contact with the following facts:

1. That the return of Christ is imminent.
2. That the Christ, immanent in every heart, can be evoked in recognition of His appearance.
3. That the circumstances of His return are only symbolically related in the world Scriptures; this may produce a vital change in the preconceived ideas of humanity.
4. That the major required preparation is a world at peace; however, that peace must be based on an educated goodwill, which will lead inevitably to right human relations, and therefore to the establishment (figuratively speaking) of lines of light between nation and nation, religion and religion, group and group, and man and man.

If you can succeed in presenting these four ideas to the world at large, thus overcoming the intelligent criticism that all that is said is too vague, prophetic, and visionary, you will do much. It is possible, surely, that the ancient truism, "the mind is the slayer of the real" may be fundamentally true where the mass of humanity is concerned, and that the purely intellectual approach (which rejects the vision and refuses to accept the unprovable) may be far more at fault than the anticipations of the Knowers of God and the expectant multitude.

The intelligence of divinity is vested in the spiritual Hierarchy, and that Hierarchy is today composed of Those Who have united in Themselves both the intellect and the intuition, the practical and the apparently impractical, the factual way of life and the way of the man who sees a vision. There are also the people who must be found in the market place of daily life; these are the people who must be trained in the divine recognitions which are essentially physical plane responses to the new expansions of consciousness. The Christ Who will return will not be like the Christ Who (apparently) departed. He will *not* be a "man of sorrows"; He will *not* be a silent, pensive figure; He will be the enunciator of spiritual statements which will not necessitate interpretation (and give rise to misinterpretation) because He will be present to indicate the true meaning.

He has been for two thousand years the supreme Head of the Church Invisible, the spiritual Hierarchy, composed of disciples of all faiths. He recognises and loves those who are not Christian but who retain their allegiance to their Founders—the Buddha, Mohammed, and others. He cares not what the faith is, if the objective is love of God and of humanity. If men look for the Christ Who left His disciples centuries ago they will fail to recognise the Christ Who is in process of returning. The Christ has no religious barriers in His consciousness. It matters not to Him of what faith a man may call himself.

The Son of God is on His way and He cometh not alone. His advance guard is already here and the Plan which they must follow is already made and clear. Let recognition be the aim.

PREPARATION FOR THE REAPPEARANCE OF THE CHRIST

June 1947

I have much to say here as a sequence to my previous communication to you—and here I am speaking to all aspirants and disciples. The opportunity is so great at this time that I seek to face you with your choices, leaving you free to make up your own minds. What you decide will, however, *affect definitely the remainder of your life activity*. Herein lies your challenge. What I have to say is of a relatively simple nature—so simple that it may seem to you as in the nature of an anti-climax. Yet simple as the problem may be, it is most difficult to solve. Your reaction to what I have to say will depend upon the nature of your sense of values, and not upon any capacity for abstruse reasoning. The average human aspirant and the intelligent human being are apt to emphasise the present complexity of human affairs and events; these they believe are engulfing men in every land. They thus provide—for themselves—an answerable alibi.

The emphasis of what I have to say is related to the message which I recently sent out re the Return of the Christ. That message carried its own challenge and the questions which it aroused in every sincere human heart are:

1. How can I personally meet this challenge?
2. What can I specifically do?
3. What are the steps which I and every aspirant should take?

These questions mean one thing to one person and another thing to another. Some of the replies will emerge as you read what I have to say. I am writing here for people who are disciples of the Christ, but my words can convey meaning to all sincere thinkers and Christian believers.

The complexities and difficulties of this post-war period are very great. The closer an aspirant is to the source of spiritual light and power, the more difficult is his problem, and at the same time the clearer will be his understanding of the facts. Looking away from the detail of the foreground, which ever assumes undue proportions, and divorcing oneself from those details as they deluge one's daily life with perplexities and anxieties, the problem is relatively simple and twofold in nature.

First of all, the outer, physical war is only just over; two years is a short time since the firing ceased and no country has as yet recovered from its dire effects. There is no true intercourse between nations and no true understanding. Today the United States permits the raising of funds in order to arm the Zionists against Great Britain, an ally and a friendly power; it is authorising propaganda against Russia, also an allied and friendly power. There is no true effort anywhere (carried on with fixed determination and right compromise) to bring to an end those economic conditions which are the major cause of war and which are responsible for breeding hatred among nations.

Secondly (and of still more importance from the angle of the spiritual values, though less easily perceived), the Forces of Evil are still active; they may have been driven back, but they are still powerful; they are still subtly working and are still striving for a firmer foothold; they are still cleverly feeding world anxiety and world insecurity in order to create another point of world tension.

Until these two sources of world tension are recognised and correctly handled, the life of the aspirant, and still more of the disciple, is exceedingly hard. You may retort (and truly) that the life of all who suffered through the war, the fate of the starving people who are still taking the brunt of the attack in Europe—the inhabitants of Great Britain, Italy, China, Poland, and the Balkans, plus Germany and Japan, who are responsible for the difficulty, and all who are engulfed in the results of Germany's attack upon the world—is hard beyond endurance, and must therefore be shared by all aspirants and disciples. That is indeed true. But the more advanced thinkers and workers have far more than the general fate to endure. They—if they open their hearts and minds—participate not only in the difficulties confronting the mass of men everywhere, but they are also aware of the spiritual possibilities ahead, of the task to be completed in sealing "the door where evil dwells," and of the stupendous and unique circumstances which are faced by those who recognise and accept the imminent return of the Christ.

As the disciple confronts both the inner and the outer events and possibilities, he is apt to register a sense of complete frustration; he longs to help, but knows not what to do; his grasp of the menacing difficulties, his analysis of his resources and of those with whom he works, and his clarity of perception as to the forces ranged against him, make him feel inclined to sit back and say: What is the use of any effort I can make? Why not let the two forces of good and evil, of the Black Lodge and the Spiritual Hierarchy, fight it out alone? Why not permit the pressure of the evolutionary current, eventually and at long last, to bring cessation to the fight and the triumph of the good? Why attempt to do it *now?*

These are natural reactions when considering the present field of conflict, the prevalent greed and the international and racial antagonisms, and the selfish motives which control so many national units, plus the dull apathy of the masses, and in particular, the growing suspicion and distrust between the United States and Russia—a situation in which both groups are almost equally to blame. This war-generating situation is fostered behind the scenes by the highly clever and strongly anti-communistic power of the Roman Catholic Church, with its organised political plans—plans which are growing notably in the United States. To these, the intelligent thinker adds the reactionary activities in every land, and the fight for oil which governs the policies of Russia, the United States and Great Britain. To these factors must be added today the struggle between Hindu and Moslem for the control of India, and the fight over Palestine—fomented by the Zionists, and *not* by the Jews as a whole—a fight in which the Zionists prevented the displaced Jewish persons (only 20% of the whole) from discovering how welcome they are in many countries throughout the world; a fight which has greed and *not* any love of Palestine behind it, and which is governed by financial interests and *not* by the humanitarian spirit which the Zionists claim and which would force them to accept the offers made by Great Britain, Canada, Chile, Belgium and many other lands.

These factors, when realised by thinking men and women, produce a deep discouragement and a sense of futility and hopelessness. Instead, they should be faced

with courage, with truth and understanding, as well a
with the willingness to speak factually, with simplicity and
with love in the effort to expose the truth and clarify the
problems which must be solved. The opposing forces of
entrenched evil must be routed before He for Whom
all men wait, the Christ, can come.

The knowledge that He is ready and anxious publicly
to appear to His loved humanity only adds to the sense of
general frustration, and another very vital question arises.
For what period of time must we endure, struggle and fight.
The reply comes with clarity; He will come unfailingly when
a measure of peace has been restored, when the principle of
sharing is at least in process of controlling economic affairs
and when the churches have begun to clean house. Then
He can and will come; then the Kingdom of God will be
publicly recognised and will no longer be a thing of dream
and of ideals.

Aspirants are prone to ask the question as to why the
Christ does not come—in the pomp and ceremony which
the churches ascribe to the event—and by His coming demonstrate His divine power, prove convincingly the authority
and the potency of God, and thus end the cycle of agony
and distress. The answers to this are many. It must be
remembered that *the main objective of the Christ will no
be to demonstrate power but to make public the already
existent Kingdom of God.* Again, when He came before
He was unrecognised, and is there any guarantee that this
time it would be different? You may ask why would He not
be recognised? Because men's eyes are blinded with the tears
of self-pity and not of contrition; because the hearts of men
are still corroded with a selfishness which the agony of war
has *not* cured; because the standards of value are the same
as in the corrupt Roman Empire which saw His first appearance, only in those days these standards were localised
and not universal; because those who could recognise Him
and who hope and long for His coming are not willing to
make the needed sacrifices, and thus ensure the success of
His advent.

Another factor militating against His being recognised, and one which will probably surprise you, is the fact that there are so many exceedingly good people in the world today, so many selfless workers and disciples and so many truly saintly people, that the spiritual competition would call forth a degree of holiness on His part which would negate His appropriation of a physical body of a calibre which would enable Him to manifest among men. This was *not* the case two thousand years ago; it is, however, the case today, so great is human advancement and the success of the evolutionary process. To enable Him today to walk among men requires a world which will have in it enough effective workers and spiritually-minded people to change the atmosphere of our planet; then and only then, the Christ can and will, come. I am not, however, presenting you with an impossibility.

Modern esotericism and the success of scientific, spiritual living are now so widely recognised that the consciousness of men everywhere has been profoundly affected; this will be increasingly so as the hope of His coming and the preparation for it spread among men. The situation indicates no divine frustration (of which that of the world disciples might be the reflection), nor does it indicate any inability to appear. Rather, it indicates the wonder of the divinity in man and the success of the divine plan for man. Divinity, however, awaits the expression of man's free will.

Another answer is that when Christ comes forth from the Place of Power, bringing His disciples, the Masters of the Wisdom, with Him, that Place of Love and Power will be situated on earth, and will be publicly recognised; the effects of that appearance and of that recognition will be terrific, calling forth an equally terrific onslaught and effort by the Forces of Evil—*unless* humanity itself has first sealed "the door where evil dwells." This must be done by *the establishing of right human relations*.

Still another reply, upon which I would ask you to ponder, is that Christ and the spiritual Hierarchy never— no matter what the incentive may be—infringe upon the divine right of humanity to achieve freedom by fighting for freedom, individually, nationally and internationally. When true freedom covers the earth, we shall see the end of tyranny, politically and religiously. I refer here not to modern democracy, which is at present a philosophy of wishful thinking, but to that state of the realm in which the people themselves will rule; these people will not tolerate authoritarianism in any church, or totalitarianism in any political system or government; they will not accept or permit the rule of any body of men who undertake to tell them what they must believe in order to be saved, or what government they must accept. I say not that these desirable objectives must be accomplished facts on earth before Christ comes. I *do* say that this attitude to religion and politics must be generally accepted as necessary to all men, and that steps must have been successfully taken in the direction of right human relations.

These are the things which the new group of world servers, the disciples, the aspirants and the men of goodwill everywhere must believe and teach in preparation for His coming.

There is, therefore, nothing to offset the sense of frustration (which is undeniably present and based on factual conditions) but the acceptance and the development of a state of mind which will be founded on a belief in the veracity of the historical records which bear witness to many advents at crucial times in human affairs, and to many world Saviours —of Whom the Christ was the greatest. The right and constructive attitude must also be based on an innate recognition of the existence of the Christ and of His Presence with us at all times; it must be grounded in the knowledge that the war—with all its unspeakable horrors, its cruelties and its cataclysmic disasters—was but the broom of the Father of all, sweeping away obstructions in the path of His returning Son. It would have been well-nigh impossible to prepare for the coming in the face of the pre-war conditions. Upon these facts the new group of world servers must today take their stand. They must recognise the obstructing factors, but must also refuse to be frustrated by them; they must be aware of the hindrances (many of them financial and based on material greed), and then employ such skill in action and such business acumen that these hindrances will be overcome; they must walk clear-eyed through world difficulties and—holding His five-pointed star before them—pass unscathed and successful through the midst of all frustrating factors.

I seek not here to deal with the usual spiritual frustrations or wish to waste time with the ordinary platitudes and the well understood replies, which do not aid because they remain platitudes and are not translated into action. I shall deal here with only two factors which condition the present opportunity; these can be regarded as so completely hindering that, unless they are removed, there will be a long delay before Christ can return. They are:

1. The inertia of the average aspirant or spiritually-minded man.
2. The lack of money for the work of preparation.

Both these hindrances are fundamentally based on one and the same thing: *materialism*—one on the materialism of *physical* effort, and the other on that of a world attitude.

Let us keep these themes simple and down on the level at which most people work and think today; let us be intensely practical and force ourselves to look at conditions as they are, thus arriving at a better knowledge of ourselves and of our motives.

1. *The Inertia of the Average Spiritually-Minded Man*

The average aspirant, man of goodwill, or disciple, is constantly aware of the challenge of the times and the opportunity which spiritual events may offer. The desire to do good and to accomplish spiritual ends is ceaselessly gnawing away within his consciousness. No one who loves his fellowmen, who has a dream of seeing the Kingdom of

God materialise on earth, or who is conscious of the awakening of the masses—slow though it may be—to the higher spiritual values, but is thoroughly dissatisfied. He realises that what he contributes of help to these desirable objectives is little indeed. He knows that his spiritual life is a side issue; it is something which he keeps carefully to himself and which he is frequently afraid to mention to his nearest and his dearest; he tries to dovetail his spiritual efforts into his ordinary outer life, struggling to find time and opportunity for it in a gentle, futile and innocuous manner. He finds himself helpless before the task of organising and re-arranging his affairs so that the spiritual way of living may dominate; he searches for alibis for himself and eventually rationalises himself so successfully that he ends by deciding that he is doing the best he can in the given circumstances. The truth is that he is doing so little that probably one hour out of the twenty-four (or perhaps two) would cover the time given to the Master's work; he hides behind the alibi that his home obligations prevent his doing more, and he does not realise that—given tact and loving understanding—his home environment can and must be the field in which he triumphs; he forgets that *there exist no circumstances in which the spirit of man can be defeated* or in which the aspirant cannot meditate, think, talk and prepare the way for the coming of the Christ, provided he cares enough and knows the meaning of sacrifice and silence. *Circumstances and environment offer no true obstacle to the spiritual life.*

Perhaps he hides behind the alibi of poor health, and frequently behind that of imaginary ills. He gives so much time to the care of himself that the hours which could be given to the Master's work are directly and seriously curtailed; he is so preoccupied with feeling tired, or tending a cold, or with fancied heart difficulties, that his "body consciousness" steadily develops until it eventually dominates his life; it is then too late to do anything. This is particularly the case with people who have reached their fiftieth year or over; the trouble then is predominantly with women. It is an alibi which it is hard not to use, for many feel tired and ailing and this, as the years go by, is apt to get worse. The only cure for the creeping inertia is to ignore the body and take your joy in the livingness of service. This leads to a longer life. I speak here not of definite disease or of serious physical liabilities; to these right care and attention must be duly given; I speak to the thousands of ailing men and women who are preoccupied with taking care of themselves, and so waste hours of the time which could be given to the service of humanity. I ask those who are seeking to tread the Path of Discipleship to release those many hours spent in needless self-care into the service of the Hierarchy.

Still another alibi leading to inertia is *the fear* people have of speaking about the things of the Kingdom of God to others; they are afraid of being rebuffed, or of being thought peculiar, or of intruding. They therefore preserve silence, lose opportunity, and never discover how ready people are for the discussion of realities, for the comfort and hope which the thought of Christ's return can bring, or for the sharing of spiritual light. This is essentially a form of spiritual cowardice, but it is so widespread that it is responsible for the loss of millions of hours of world service.

There are, brother of mine, other alibis, but the three above noted are the most common; the release of the majority of aspirants from these hindering conditions would bring to the service of the Christ (to use the language of the labour union) so many man-hours and so much overtime endeavour that the task of those who admit no alibis would be greatly lightened and the coming of the Christ would be much nearer than it is today. What we call inertia is not simply psychological in nature. *The qualities of matter* or substance itself are involved. Inertia is the slowest and the lowest aspect of material substance and is called in the Eastern philosophy, the quality of tamas. It has to be transmuted into a higher quality, that of activity or (giving it its technical term) its rajasic quality, and this leads later on to the highest quality of rhythm or sattva. To the rhythm of life under which the Christ and the Spiritual Hierarchy operate, and which vibrates in harmony with human need and hierarchical response, I call you not. I do, however, call you to demonstrate the quality of activity and to refuse to hide behind alibis. It is essential that all aspirants recognise that in the place where they now are, among the people who are their karmic associates, and with the psychological and physical equipment with which they are endowed, they can and must work. I shall not labour this subject. There is no possible coercion or undue pressure exerted in the service of the Hierarchy. The situation is clear and simple. There are at the present time three great activities going on:

First, the activity to be felt in the "centre where the will of God is known," that will-to-good which has carried all creation on toward a greater glory and a steadily deepening, intelligent responsiveness; this today is creatively endeavouring to bring in the new world order, the order of the Kingdom of God under the *physical* supervision of the Christ. This might be regarded as the externalisation of the spiritual Hierarchy of our planet. Of this, the return of the Christ to *visible* activity will be the sign and the symbol.

Secondly, the critical activity which is conditioning the spiritual Hierarchy, from the Christ Himself down to the lowest aspirant to be found on the periphery of that centre where the love of God has full play. *There* it is fully realised that (in the words of St. Paul) "the whole creation groaneth and travaileth in pain together until now, waiting for the manifestation of the Sons of God". It is for that manifestation that They now prepare, these "Sons of God Who are the Sons of Men"; it is for this coming forth to outer active service that They are already—one by one—entering into outer activity upon the physical plane. They are not recognised for what They are, but They go about the Father's business, demonstrating goodwill, seeking to enlarge the horizon of humanity, and thus prepare the way for the One Whom They serve, the Christ, the Master of all the Masters and the Teacher alike of angels and of men.

Thirdly, there is humanity itself, "the centre which we call the race of men"—a centre at present full of chaos, turmoil and confusion, a humanity full of pain, bewilderment, disturbance, yet mentally aware of infinite possibilities, emotionally fighting for that plan which seems to them to be the best, but with no sense of coherency or any realisation that it must be the *one world for the one humanity*. They desire simply emotional peace, security in which to live and work, and a vision of a future which will satisfy some inchoate sense of divine persistence. They are physically ill, deprived for the most part of the essentials of normal wholesome living, wracked with the sense of financial insecurity and—consciously or unconsciously—invoking the Father of all on behalf of themselves and of the rest of the world.

The solution is the return of the Christ. This is the ascertained will of God; it is the desire of Christ Himself and of His disciples, the Masters of the Wisdom; it is the unrealised demand of men in all lands. Where there is unification of purpose, of spiritual intention and of realised need, then there is only one thing which can arrest that return, and that is the failure of mankind to prepare the stage for that stupendous event, to clear the highways, familiarise the people with the idea, and bring about the required measure of peace on Earth—a peace based upon right human relations.

2.   *The Lack of Money for the Work of Preparation*

We come now to the second of the major hindrances: the lack of financial support for the Christ's workers and disciples in all lands as they endeavour to release spiritual energy and bring a new order out of the present world chaos. This is perhaps *the* major difficulty, and it appears at times an insuperable one; it involves the problem of true financial trusteeship and the deflection of adequate sums of money into channels which will definitely aid in the work of preparation for the return of the Christ. It is for this reason that I closed the previous section of this article with the words "right human relations."

The problem is therefore a peculiarly hard one, for the

spiritual workers of the world have not only to train people to *give* according to the need and their means, but in many cases they have first of all to provide them with a motive so magnetic in its appeal that they must perforce give; they have also to provide the trust, foundation and organisation through which the money given may be administered. This presents them with a most impressively difficult task and one which is responsible for the present impasse. The impasse is not, however, based only on the novelty of raising funds in preparation for the return of the Christ, but it is based also on the trained selfishness of the majority of those who own the world's wealth and who—even if they give—do so because it fosters prestige or indicates financial success. It must be remembered here that every generalisation presupposes exceptions.

Generalising, and therefore over-simplifying the subject, we can assume that money finds its way into four main channels of expenditures:

1. *Into the myriad homes of the world* in the form of wages, salaries or inherited wealth. All this is at present most unevenly balanced, producing extreme riches and extreme poverty.

2. *Into great capitalistic systems* and monopolies to be found as towering structures in most lands. Whether this capital is owned by the government, or by a municipality, or by a handful of wealthy men or by the great labour unions matters not. Little of it is yet spent in reality for the betterment of human living, or for the inculcation of the values which will lead to right human relations.

3. *Into the churches and religious groups* throughout the world. Here (again speaking in general terms and at the same time recognising the existence of a small spiritually-minded minority) the money is deflected into the material aspects of the work, into

the multiplying and preservation of ecclesiastical structures, into salaries and general overhead, and only a percentage of it really goes into the teaching of the people, into a living demonstration of the fact of His return—for centuries a definite doctrine of the churches. That return has been anticipated down the ages, and might have occurred ere now had the churches and religious organisations everywhere done their duty.

4. *Into philanthropic, educational and medical work.* All of this has been exceedingly good and greatly needed, and the debt of the world to the public-spirited men who have made these institutions possible is great indeed. All of this has been a step in the right direction and an expression of the divine will-to-good. It is, however, frequently money misused and misdirected and the values developed have been largely institutional and concrete. They have been limited by the separative tenets of the donors or the religious prejudices of those who control the disbursement of the funds. In the quarreling over ideas, religious theories and ideologies, the true assistance of the One Humanity is overlooked.

The fact remains that had the directing agencies through whose hands the money of the world is channelled any vision of the spiritual realities, of the one humanity and the one world, and had their objective been the stimulation of right human relations, the mass of men everywhere would be responding to a vision very different from the present one; we would not be faced as we are today with the expenditures—running into countless billions—necessitated by the need to restore *physically,* not only the physical bodies of countless millions of men, but entire cities, transportation systems and centres responsible for the reorganisation of human living.

Equally, it can be said that if the spiritual values and the spiritual responsibilities attached to money (in large quantities or in small) had been properly appreciated and taught in homes and schools, we would not have had the appalling statistics of the money spent, prior to the war in every country in the world (and spent today in the Western Hemisphere), on candy, liquor, cigarettes, recreation, unnecessary clothes and luxuries. These statistics run into hundreds of millions of dollars every year. A quota of this money, necessitating the minimum of sacrifice, would enable the disciples of the Christ and the New Group of World Servers to prepare the way for His coming and to educate the minds and hearts of men in every land in right human relations.

Money—as with all else in human living—has been tainted by selfishness and grabbed for selfish individual or national ends. Of this, the world war (1914-1945) is the proof, for although there was much talk of "saving the world for democracy" and "fighting a war to end war," the main motive was self-protection and self-preservation, the hope of gain, the satisfaction of ancient hatreds, and the regaining of territory. The two years which have elapsed since the war have proved this to be so. The United Nations is occupied with rapacious demands from all sides, with the angling of the nations for place and power, and for the possession of the natural resources of the Earth—coal, oil, etc., and also with the underground activities of the great Powers and of the capitalists which they all create.

Yet all the time, the one humanity—no matter what the place of residence, what the colour of the skin, or what the religious beliefs—is clamouring for peace, justice and a sense of security. All this, the right use of money and a realisation on the part of many of their financial responsibility (a responsibility based on the spiritual values) would rapidly give them. With the exception of a few great far-sighted philanthropists, and of a mere handful of enlightened statesmen, churchmen and educators, this sense of financial responsibility is to be found nowhere.

The time has now come when money must be re-valued and its usefulness channelled into new directions. The voice of the people must prevail, but it must be a people educated in the true values, in the significances of a right culture, and in the need for right human relations. It is therefore essentially a question of right education and correct training in world citizenship—a thing that has not yet been undertaken. Who can give this training? Russia would gladly train the world in the ideals of communism, and would gather all the money in the world into the coffers of the proletariat, eventually producing the greatest capitalistic system the world has ever seen. Great Britain would gladly train the world in the British concepts of justice and fair play and world trade, and would do it more cleverly than any other nation because of vast experience. The United States would also gladly undertake to force the American brand of democracy upon the world, using her vast capital and resources in so doing, and gathering into her banks the financial results of her widespread financial dealings, preserving them safely by the threat of the atomic bomb and the shaking of the mailed fist over the rest of the world. France will keep Europe in a state of unrest as she seeks to regain her lost prestige and garner all she can from the victory of the other allied nations. Thus, my brother, the story goes—each nation fighting for itself and rating each other in terms of resources and finance. In the meantime, humanity starves, remains uneducated, is brought up on false values and the wrong use of money; until these things are being righted, the return of the Christ is not possible.

In the face of this disturbing financial situation, what is the answer to the problem? There are men and women to be found in every land, every government, every church and religion, and every educational foundation who have the answer. What hope is there for them and for the work with which they have been entrusted? How can the people of the world, the men of goodwill and of spiritual vision help? Is there anything they can do to change the thinking of the world in regard to money, and to deflect it into channels where it will be rightly used? The answer lies within these people themselves.

There are two groups who can do much: those already using the financial resources of the world, if they will catch the new vision and also see the handwriting on the wall which is bringing the old order down in destruction; and secondly, the mass of the good, kindly people in all classes and spheres of influence.

The power of the little man and of the unimportant citizen is not yet truly grasped, yet there is a vast opportunity before them if they have the courage and the patience to do the needed work.

These men and women of goodwill and spiritual inclination must reject the thought of their relative uselessness, insignificance and futility, and realise that now (in the critical and crucial moment that has come) they *can* work potently. The Forces of Evil *are* defeated, though not yet "sealed" behind the door where humanity can put them and which the *New Testament* foretold would happen. The world is in the balance again. Evil is seeking every avenue available for a new approach but—and this I say with confidence and insistence—the little people of the world, enlightened and selfless in their viewpoint, exist in sufficient numbers to make their power felt—if they will. There are millions of spiritually-minded men and women in every country who, when they come to the point of approaching in mass formation this question of money, can permanently rechannel it. There are writers and thinkers in all lands who can add their powerful help, and who will if correctly approached. There are esoteric students and devoted church people to whom appeal can be made for aid in preparing the way for the return of the Christ, particularly if the aid required is the expenditure of money and time for the establishing of right human relations and the growth and spread of goodwill.

A great campaign to raise money is not demanded, but the selfless work of thousands of apparently unimportant people is required. I would say, my brothers, that the most needed quality is *courage;* it takes courage to put aside diffidence, shyness and the dislike of presenting a point of view, particularly a point of view connected with money. It is here that the majority fail. It is relatively easy today to raise money for the Red Cross, for hospitals and for educational institutions. It is exceedingly difficult to raise money for the spread of goodwill, or to secure financial sources and the right use of money for forward looking ideas, such as the return of the Christ. Therefore I say that *the first prerequisite is courage.*

The second requirement for the workers of the Christ is to make those sacrifices and arrangements which will enable them to give to the limit of their capacity; there must not be simply a trained ability to present the subject, but each worker must practice what he preaches. If, for instance, the millions of people who love the Christ and seek to serve His cause gave at least a tiny sum of money each year, there would be adequate funds for His work; the needed trusts and the spiritually-minded trustees would then automatically appear. The difficulty is not with the organising of the money and work; it lies with the seeming inability of people to give. For one reason or another, they give little or nothing, even when interested in such a cause as that of the return of the Christ; fear, or the love of purchasing, or the desire to give presents, or failure to realise that many small sums mount up into very large sums—all these things militate against financial generosity, and the reason always seems adequate. Therefore, *the second prerequisite is for everyone to give as they can.*

Thirdly, the metaphysical schools and the esoteric groups have given much thought to this business of directing money into channels which appeal to them. The question is often asked: Why do the Unity School of thought, the Christian Science Church, and many New Thought movements always manage to accumulate the required funds, whilst other groups, and particularly the esoteric groups, do not? Why do truly spiritual workers seem unable to materialise what they need? The answer is a simple one. Those groups and workers who are the closest to the spiritual ideal are as a house divided against itself. Their main interest is on abstract spiritual levels, and they have not apparently grasped the fact that the physical plane, when motivated from the spiritual levels, is of equal importance. The large metaphysical schools are focussed on making a *material* demonstration, and so great is their emphasis and so one-pointed is their approach that they get what they demand; they have to learn that the demand and its answer must be the result of spiritual purpose, and that that which is demanded must not be for the use of the separated self or for a separative organisation or church. In the new age which is upon us, prior to the return of the Christ, the demand for financial support must be for the bringing about of right human relations and goodwill, and not for the growth of any particular organisation. The organisations so demanding must work with the minimum of overhead and central plant, and the workers for the minimum yet reasonable salary. Not many such organisations exist to-day, but the few now functioning can set an example which will be rapidly followed, as the desire for the return of the Christ grows. Therefore *the third prerequisite is the service of the one humanity.*

The fourth prerequisite must be the careful presentation of the cause for which the financial support is required. People may have the courage to speak, but an intelligent presentation is of equal importance. The major point to be emphasised in the preparatory work for the return of Christ is the establishing of right human relations. This has already been started by men of goodwill all over the world, under their many names, and here I have done naught but indicate another motive for presentation.

We come now to *the fifth prerequisite: a vital and sure belief in humanity as a whole.* There must be no pessimism as to the future of mankind or distress over the disappearance of the old order. *The good, the true and the beautiful* is on its way, and for it mankind is responsible, and not some outer divine intervention. Humanity is sound and rapidly awakening. We are passing through the stage where everything is being proclaimed from the housetops—as the Christ stated would be the case—and as we listen or read of the flood of filth, crime, sensual pleasure or luxury buying, we are apt to be discouraged; it is wise to remember that it is wholesome for all this to come to the surface and for us all to know about it. It is like the psychological cleansing of the subconscious to which individuals submit themselves, and it presages the inauguration of a new and better day.

There is work to do, and the men of goodwill, of spiritual instinct, and of truly Christian training must do it. They must inaugurate the era of the use of money for the spiritual Hierarchy, and carry that need into the realms of invocation. Invocation is the highest type of prayer there is, and a new form of divine appeal which a knowledge of meditation has now made possible. To this end I will give you a short form of spiritual demand which I would ask you all to use in the place of any prayer, meditation or invocation for money which you may have hitherto used. It is short and powerful, but requires a unified group or a truly integrated personality to use it. . . . . .

I have naught to add in the way of an appeal for funds, courage or understanding. If the courage of the Christ, as He faces return to this physical outer world, if the need of humanity for right human relations, and the sacrificing work of the disciples of the Christ are not enough to fire you and to energise you and those whom you can reach, there is nothing that I can say which will be of any use.

WORK IN THE COMING DECADES

April 1948

This is the last *Wesak Message* which I intend to give you. In 1949, I shall have completed thirty years of carefully planned and meticulously outlined work; this work I undertook under cyclic law (related to the periodical giving out of the esoteric teaching) in order to aid humanity and the work of the Hierarchy, to both of which I happen to belong.

On November 19th, 1919, I made my first contact with A.A.B. (much to her distress and dismay), and I have worked steadily with her ever since. The books which I then planned have been well-nigh finished; the various phases of the work which were a part of the preparation for the reappearance of the Christ have taken form and should go forward with gathering momentum during the next twenty years.

The two major ideas which it was my task to bring to the attention of humanity everywhere throughout the world have been securely anchored (if I may be permitted to use such a term), and these constitute by far the most important aspect of the work which I have done. These formulated ideas are:

1. The announcement of the existence (hitherto un-recognised) of the *New Group of World Servers.* This is an effective group of workers, intermediate between Humanity and the Spiritual Hierarchy of the planet.
2. The statement, sent out lately, in connection with the *Reappearance of the Christ,* and for the immediate consolidation of the work of preparation.

All else that I have done in the service of the Hierarchy is of secondary importance to these two statements of spiritual *fact.*

The fifth volume of *A Treatise on the Seven Rays* re-mains to be finished, as does the second volume of *Disciple-ship in the New Age;* there is nothing else; what remains, therefore, can easily be accomplished before my term of thirty years comes to an end. Other work awaits me under the reorganisation of all the hierarchical efforts incident to the reappearance of the Christ and the closer relationship which will then be established between humanity and the Hierarchy. The work of hierarchical reorganisation is at present largely internal and concerns not humanity at this time.

I have made it entirely clear to all of you what is the work which you should do and I have no intention (in this final message) of pleading with you to do it—beyond asking you to *carry on where I leave off.* I refer of course to my exoteric work.

That the work which I am now doing was definitely ending in 1949 was quite unknown to A.A.B. and has no relation whatsoever to the fact that her health is precarious. It has, however, some relation to the fact that she has resumed more active work as a disciple in the Ashram of her own Master, after twenty-eight years of service in mine. Before I began the work of the past three decades, I knew exactly the time I had in which to bring about the results desired by the Hierarchy; all has been meticulously carried out under a most clearly visioned plan.

First, there was the necessity to find the nucleus of people through whom I had to work; the first step was therefore the writing of certain books which would carry the new teaching, and act therefore as a selective agent for the discovery of those who would work in the new emerging cycle.

The starting of the Arcane School by A.A.B. was only incidental to this objective; its aim is to train those disciples who can implement the Plan and thus prepare for the re-appearance of the Christ; the Arcane School can therefore provide a trained body of workers.

Ten years after that, I began to expand the range of contacts, and the teaching began to reach thinkers on continents other than the American. As a result, I began to form my own Ashram and to find people in all countries who were disciples, qualified as such, but who needed the impact of the influence of a second ray Ashram. When this was done, the major part of the second decade of my work became possible, and I therefore wrote a pamphlet entitled *The New Group of World Servers*. In it I called attention to the fact that there existed upon the Earth, in every nation, men and women who (in some form or another) recognised the spiritual Hierarchy of the planet, who had a quality of non-separateness, definitely present or else rapidly developing, and who were gathered together in no limiting organisation but primarily by their trend of thought and the habit of their activity. They constituted a group who were subjectively, spiritually, practically and openly creating a new form of human relationship. This new relation resulted in mutual understanding and a mental cooperation which recognised no barriers or national limitations. On the inner side of spiritual incentive and endeavour, they work today as one group; on the outer side of world affairs, they may not be aware of each other physically, or arrive at any open contact, yet they are animated by the same principles and are carrying forward—in all nations and in every great department of human thinking and planning—a similar work.

In this decade of my work, two major activities were inaugurated: the creation of the Triangles and the formation of Men of Goodwill,* and these are just on the verge of a major creative activity. They constitute an effort to energise and relate members and adherents of the new group of world servers (and particularly in the organisation of men of goodwill), to find and mobilise the groups formed by the new group of world servers throughout the world, so as to bring added strength to all of them by swinging into a massed effort men of prayer, men of good intention, and those who believe in the divine will-to-good, plus those who implement it through love—no matter what they mean by that vague term. Thus *a nucleus of a great synthesis* was brought about in this second decade, and it will have lasting effects upon human living and design. Owing to planetary frustration and the enhanced activity of the Forces of Evil, the work of the Triangles and of the men of goodwill has been more slowly formulated than had been originally expected, but this has been through no fault of theirs; this period of frustration will be over before very long and a greatly increased momentum will be the result. For this increased response upon the part of the public, you should now lay your plans.

In the third and final decade of my work, the time and opportunity came to announce, in a new and more emphatic manner, what all the world religions have proclaimed, that—with due preparation and the establishment of a pronounced tendency towards right human relations—the time had come when the Christ could again appear and take His rightful place as World Teacher. The emphasis has never before been

* Since 1951 this work has been carried forward under the title of World Goodwill.

laid upon the needed work of preparation. The results of this pronouncement have not yet had time to make themselves felt, but the next ten years will reveal the full import of what has been done.

With that pronouncement my planned work was brought to a finish; the book* which will indicate the proximity of this happening and the lines along which the new world religion will be promoted is now in the press. I would call your attention to the fact that the general concept of a World Saviour (always attached to the office of the Christ, no matter by what name the exalted Son of God may be called in any world cycle) is in reality closely related to the far more important function of World Teacher. People love to be saved, for it ignores their own immediate responsibility, which teaching definitely emphasises. It must be remembered that it is the teaching given by the Christ which saves humanity—not any symbolic death upon a cross. *Men must save themselves by their reaction and their response to the teaching given in its purity by the Christ;* this is a point which should be forcefully instilled by all of you; it is not man-made interpretations which save a man, but his self-initiated application of his own understanding of the teaching. This must be brought today to the consciousness of as many human beings as the followers of the Christ can reach.

Here you have a brief account of the work which I undertook on behalf of the Hierarchy and for the Christ, Whom I most reverently regard as my Master. This work has not been unsuccessfully carried forward; many of you who read these words have done what you could to help and of this I am not unmindful nor is the Hierarchy ungrateful. Perhaps—with a still clearer picture in your minds—you will find yourselves able to do still more.

I intend to indicate (still briefly) what should be done in the next two decades, but would like first of all to touch upon the state of the world and refer to its condition, because they have both handicapped hierarchical effort and particularly what I sought to do (which was a major hierarchical

---

* *The Reappearance of the Christ.*

enterprise), and yet at the same time they have cleared the way in a most extra-ordinary manner for the appearance of the Christ.

When I began my exoteric work in 1919, I had not expected to be frustrated by the second world war, or rather by the final phase of World War I. The Hierarchy had hoped that the lesson had been severe enough to force those changes which were essential to the future of mankind. But humanity had not learned the needed lessons. As I have often told you, the Hierarchy—because of the divine principle of free will in humanity—cannot foretell how men will act in times of crisis; the Hierarchy cannot enforce the good way of life against normal human desire, for this good way of action must come from out the very depths of human thinking and feeling, and must emerge as a free and non-supervised endeavour; the Hierarchy may not take those possible steps which will prevent men making mistakes, for it is through those mistakes that men learn "by the means of evil that good is best," as your great initiate-poet has expressed it. All that the Hierarchy can do is to present the needed teaching which will direct man's thinking along right lines, to point the way of true relationships, and at the same time demonstrate objectively the nature of the bad way. This the Hierarchy has always done. As a spiritual group, They can and do set Their faces against selfishness, greed, and against all that seeks to imprison the human spirit and impair its freedom. To illustrate—the Hierarchy demonstrated against the totalitarianism which the two great Powers, Germany and Japan expressed when they precipitated the second world war. This They still do and will continue to do when any aspect of totalitarian greed and aggressiveness in any form (subtle and undeclared or openly demonstrated) attempts to limit the freedom of the individual, the free spiritual man, no matter what his point in evolution.

Toward the end of the second decade of my work, totalitarianism reared anew its most evil head, and perforce the Hierarchy took sides against this primary principle of evil, though never against any group of human beings. Please note this. The point I seek to make is that the Hierarchy is inflexibly against any demonstration of the principle of non-freedom, no matter what form it takes, but *is ever on the side of humanity*. The spirit of evil which animated German actions evoked every possible opposition from the Forces of Light and from their source, the Hierarchy. Today this totalitarian evil is expressing itself through the planning of the Russian oligarchy, through the Zionist movement, and through all groups which seek to fetter and imprison the spirit of man; but the people under the sway of this evil influence and the scheming of these evil groups are never regarded in any light different to that of the rest of mankind. They are looked upon as glamoured, or as weak and ignorant (which they undoubtedly are), but they are never separated off in the thinking and planning of the Hierarchy from the rest of mankind. The evil must not be permitted or allowed to triumph, but the unhappy and glamoured exponents of this evil are loved, along with the rest of mankind. This is a point which is hard for the illogical thinker to understand, but it expresses most truly the attitude of the Christ and of all who serve His cause.

With the focussed entrance of greed and of totalitarian ruthlessness into the world arena, much that I had planned and much that all of you were attempting to do, met with frustration; the work of all disciples was in many ways greatly hindered and handicapped, though *not* from the long range vision, but only from the angle of short range action. I would ask you to have this in mind. The vision stands even when immediate action is blocked.

Today it would appear, from all the indications and from the dominant world trends, that the still unconquered greed of certain of the more powerful nations is undeniably rampant, and that we are therefore facing another period of frustration and of major world difficulty. Feeling against Russia is running high among the Western Powers and is largely her own fault, though it is primarily based upon two main factors—one of them bad and the other good.

The bad reaction is based on the same old triplicity of

fear, greed and jealousy and—from the angle of those three phases of selfishness—is entirely justified. That fact, in itself, supplies a major difficulty. Think this out.

The good reaction is based on the frustration of the idea or concept of developing a unified peaceful world—a world in which there would be no war and in which men could live at peace with each other and in security, and in which men everywhere could work, relatively unopposed, towards right human relations. This super-world and this unified humanity is a true ideal, but is not a feasible project.

Spiritual workers should face the various world alternatives:

1. An all-dominant Russia, whose regime would cover the planet, enforcing her *totalitarian* interpretation of communistic doctrine (there is a right and true interpretation), refusing freedom to the individual in the interest of the State, and—because of a low opinion of the human masses—everywhere standardising her interpretation of democracy.

2. A world in which all nations live in an armed armistice, in which distrust is forever rampant and in which science is prostituted to the art of destruction. In this world an explosion must and will eventually take place which will destroy humanity as once before it was destroyed, according to the Bible and the other world Scriptures and the hierarchical records.

3. A world in which the United States proves itself to be the controlling factor, after wiping out Russia, which she can well do if she acts now. It will be a predominantly capitalistic world, run by several nations but headed by the United States. A capitalistic nation is not necessarily wrong; capital has its place, and Russia (the enemy of capitalism) is by no means free from capitalistic bias. The motives of the United States are very mixed motives: greed of money or its equivalent, such as oil, and at the same time sincerely good intentions for the establishment of human freedom in a democratic world—modelled, of course, on American democracy. Other motives are an appreciation of the armed fist and, at

the same time, a longing for economic sharing and for that essential kindness which is such a strong American characteristic—a mass characteristic. These mixed motives will produce eventually a very confused world, one in which it will be found that humanity has learned very little as the result of the World War (1914-1945) and is acquiescent to the cycle of well-intentioned money control.

4.   A world divided into "blocs" for mutual aid and economic sharing. Of this, the proposed treaty between Great Britain, France and the Benelux countries is a tentative sample, though tainted by objectionable motives, from the angle of the Hierarchy. Fear is the major factor producing this treaty, but it has in it nevertheless the seeds of hope. There is nothing intrinsically wrong in any group of nations standing together for mutual aid and economic cooperation. The wrong factor comes in when they stand *united against* any other group of nations, and therefore against any group of human beings. It is this attitude, engineered and fostered by Russia, which has lead to the relatively new concept of *blocs against*. Along this line, and with this attitude of antagonistic groupings, only disaster can lie.

Blocs in themselves can be good and proper if they follow lines of natural cleavages, of language differences and of cultural distinctions. They can be essentially right if they are formed for economic, educational, religious and social aims and can therefore provide no true cause for alarm. Such blocs would be cultural and not militaristic, economic and not greedy, and they could provide a normal and progressive movement away from the separative nationalism of the past and towards the distant creation of the One World, and the One Humanity. This will some day be seen, but the time is not yet. Mankind is not ready for some super-government, nor can it yet provide the unselfish and trained statesmen that such a government would require. As yet, there are more seeds of danger in this concept than there are of helpfulness. Nevertheless, it is a dream which will some day materialise, after the creation and the functioning of blocs have proved how men should work and live together.

The United Nations is still the hope of the world and can remain so; it is a great field of experimentation, but is suffering today from an initial error. That error was the admitting of a totalitarian Power into its nations. For seven long and terrible years the Forces of Light had been fighting totalitarianism. In the early days of the post-war period the Nations compromised with principles and admitted Russia to the United Nations. Had they proceeded to unite all the other nations of the world on the sure ground of economic reform, of needed national reorganisation and of regional groups (a better term than "blocs"), Russia would have been forced to conform, for her very existence would have been at stake. An initial error can lead to much trouble, and it is this type of trouble which the United Nations today faces.

I have here given you the possibilities with which the work is challenged and confronted, and again I must refuse to foretell what will happen. It is not permitted. I have felt it necessary to summarise the situation because it is in this world that you and all men of goodwill will have to work for the next twenty years; this period of settlement will not be an easy one in which the disciples of the Christ have to prepare for His appearance. The two decades ahead of you are those in which you must bring to fruition the seeds which I have planted. Though I shall not be actively and outwardly working with you or communicating with you as I have done over the past thirty years, you will have my books (which will then be finished) and the relation which I now hold to you and to all the activities which I have helped you to inaugurate will remain basically the same; it will be more subjective but many in the world today know the means of reaching me.

The Christ, Whom I serve as a disciple, and the spiritual Hierarchy, of which I am a member, are drawing steadily nearer to humanity; in the past I have used the statement to reassure you, "The Hierarchy stands"; today I say to you, *"The Hierarchy is near."*

The work that must be done in the two coming decades is as follows, and I shall not enlarge upon it because you have been trained to do it; you know what to do and the responsibility is yours—as will be my unfailing help.

1.   Prepare men for the reappearance of the Christ. This is your first and greatest duty. The most important part of that work is teaching men—on a large scale—to use the Invocation so that it becomes a world prayer and focusses the invocative demand of humanity.

2.   Enlarge the work of the Triangles so that, subjectively and etherically, light and goodwill may envelop the earth.

3.   Promote ceaselessly the work of World Goodwill, so that every nation may have its group of men and women dedicated to the establishing of right human relations. You have the nucleus, and expansion must be undertaken. You have the principle of goodwill present throughout the world; the task will be heavy indeed but far from impossible.

4.   Undertake the constant distribution of my books, which contain much of the teaching for the New Age. In the last analysis, the books are your working tools and the instruments whereby you will train your workers. See that they are kept in steady circulation.

5.   Endeavour to make the Wesak Festival (at the time of the May Full Moon) a universal festival and known to be of value to all men of all faiths. It is the festival in which the two divine Leaders, of the East and of the West, collaborate together and work in the closest spiritual union; the Christ and the Buddha use this festival each year as the point of inspiration for the coming year's work. See that you do likewise. The spiritual energies are then uniquely available.

6.   Discover the members of the new group of world servers, whenever possible, and strengthen their hands. Look for them in every nation and expressing many lines of thought and points of view. Remember always that in doctrine and dogma, and in techniques and methods, they may differ widely from you, but in love of their fellowmen, in practical goodwill and in devotion to the establishing of right human relations they stand with you, they are your equals, and can probably teach you much.

And now: What shall I say to you in closing, my comrades, my brothers and my co-disciples? I have said to you so much over the past years that there is little left to say; you have all you need wherewith to carry on the work, impulsed from the Hierarchy, through what I have attempted to do. I can only say that I have confidence in you and that I expect no slackening of effort from you. You are dedicated and consecrated and will remain so, for the closeness of the Hierarchy and the nearness of the Christ indicate to you increased sources of strength.

May the blessing of the One Whom we all serve rest upon you all and upon all disciples everywhere, and may you do your full share in helping men to pass from darkness into light and from death to immortality.

THE ASHRAMS CONCERNED AT THE COMING

June 1948

The Full Moon is upon us and the thoughts of the world (to a far larger extent than you realise) are directed towards the Christ. It is upon His concerns that I speak to you today, inextricably bound up, as they are, with the concerns of humanity, and this by His Own choice. Many today in all lands are turning their thoughts consciously to Him; others are aware of a vague turning towards some divine Person or Power Who must and should help mankind in its hour of need. There is a rising, an ascension of the spirit of man everywhere which is better known to us than to you, whose values and reactions are not so spiritual. The strength, the power and the special energies which He received at that dramatic moment when He, the Buddha and the Lord of the World created a Triangle of Light at the time of the Wesak Festival, will be released by Him at the hour of the Full Moon of June. This Light has been concentrated upon the "centre which we call the race of men," but it has not yet been released. At the Full Moon it will be poured out all over the Earth. During the interim between reception and distribution, it has been transformed into the energy of goodwill and into that light which will illumine the minds of men.

The Great Invocation—now being used by so many—has greatly facilitated the receptivity of men; the creative appearance of effective goodwill can, however, be some time in manifesting. Nevertheless, nothing can arrest its subtle working and its eventual widespread appearance, on a scale great enough to be effective throughout the whole world. This greatly to be desired expression of divine purpose will be fulfilled *if* humanity (as a whole) stands in steady expectancy, wise activity, and makes broad and brotherly decisions. As I have often told you, the final decisions in world affairs have to be made through mankind's deliberate choice; no compulsion is ever exerted by the Hierarchy or by the disciples of the Christ to force men to take some desirable action. Man's free will *must* be preserved. In an unique manner, men are today facing a period of the freeing of the human soul, or a period of its imprisonment indefinitely; the right decision will lead to the Kingdom of God, and the other to a retrogression which will deify the past and prolong past wrong action.

This outpouring of spiritual energy passes through the groups or (to use a technical word which is relatively unimportant) through the Ashrams of all the Masters of the Wisdom, the Disciples of the Christ. It is then transformed or transmuted by them so as to meet adequately the needs of the different types of people who compose humanity and who are represented in the Ashrams by different Masters. Through all the Masters and through all disciples this energy passes, so that all—at their many different stages—may receive the needed stimulation. They precipitate certain specialised aspects of this newly received energy, and they therefore will be peculiarly active in the coming period.

Five of the Masters and Their five Ashrams are primarily involved in this preparatory work. There is first of all the Ashram of the Master K.H., which is the presiding Ashram in this work, owing to the fact that it is a second ray Ashram, and therefore upon the same line of spiritual energy and descent as the Christ Himself. Another reason is that the

Master K. H. will assume the role of World Teacher in the distant future when the Christ moves on to higher and more important work than dealing with the consciousness of humanity. Next comes the Master Morya and His Ashram, because the whole procedure is projected from Shamballa, and He is in close touch with that dynamic centre. The Master R., as the Lord of Civilisation, is necessarily closely involved in this preparatory work, and also because He is what has been called the Regent of Europe. Another Ashram is also very deeply concerned in this work; I have, at times, referred to the Master Who was responsible for the organisation of Labour. This work He began to do in the latter part of the nineteenth century, but left it to carry forward of its own momentum when Russia entered the field and laid an undue emphasis upon the proletariat during the revolution and in the later years of the first quarter of the twentieth century. I (D. K.) am the fifth Master concerned in this special work and am, as it were, the liaison officer between those active and conscious disciples who are working in the world of outer affairs and those directly responsible to the Christ for the desired work of preparation. Certain disciples from these five Ashrams or groups have been (and will be) especially trained for the work of contacting the public.

The stimulation which can be given will be released at the coming Full Moon. The five specialised energies are as follows:

1. *The Energy of Love-Wisdom.* This energy always has an effect upon every type of human being in the world. Its effect is to stimulate the tendency towards goodwill and to produce a mental development which can transmute the knowledge—garnered down the ages—into wisdom. It is wisdom which is needed today. Those who are now attempting to foster goodwill in themselves and others will be stimulated into wise action. You can see, therefore, that the outpouring of this energy is the first and greatest need. It *can* reach mankind because the Founders of all the world religions (I refer not to their many diversifications) are banded together in

unison with the Christ, Their Lord and Master; through Their united and directed effort, these energies will flow. Forget not that Christ represents the energy of love and the Buddha that of wisdom.

2. *The Energy of Will or Power.* The outpouring of this energy, owing to the "little wills" of the majority of men and the developed strenuous wills of certain present world Leaders, will not have as wide or potent an effect or contact as may the others. Its inflow will, however, serve to bring about a "fixed intention" on the part of many to work ceaselessly for true peace and understanding. These people will therefore aid in the task of implementing goodwill. It will, nevertheless, strengthen the will of the selfish, ambitious and obstinate men who are in positions of power and influence, and produce increased trouble—at least temporarily. The salvation of the world and the production of the needed security will be brought about in the long run by the mass of men everywhere, in all lands; it will be the result of an intensified educational process. Humanity, as yet, does not know how to handle wisely the energy of the will-to-power, and it is largely this that has handicapped the manifestation of the will-to-good. The Shamballa force is too strong for those who are naturally will-ful. In the case of certain potent men, this energy reaches them directly, and is not stepped down for them through contact with the Hierarchy of Love; it naturally expresses itself in the political fields and in the realm of governments, through rulers, officials, statesmen and politicians. When the "little wills" of the intelligentsia, of those who serve the public in some capacity or other, and those above all who are working in some connection with the United Nations, become strengthened, stimulated and focussed on goodwill, the union of the two energies of Love-Wisdom and of Will can bring about the needed changes in the planetary life. This is not an immediate happening, but it is not a visioning of the impossible.

3. *The Energy of Active Intelligence.* This third type of energy is the easiest one for modern humanity to receive—which is perhaps a sad commentary upon man's aspirations.

The proof of this lies in the fact that much of this type of energy (through the selfish perception and desires of mankind) has been *crystallised into money*. Human intelligence has served on the side of materialism and not on the side of the spiritual values. Money is the concretised expression of the third type of spiritual energy. This particular expression appeared first in the ancient and equally materialistic system of barter and exchange; then, in later civilisations (predominantly including ours) we have the appearance of money, made first from the products of the mineral kingdom, and then later came paper money, made from the products of the vegetable kingdom. This has culminated in the modern preoccupation with money. There is very deep occult meaning to be found in the statement in the *New Testament* that "the love of money is the root of all evil". It is largely money and selfishness which lie behind the present disastrous economic situation. Great financiers are in reality those in whom the receipt of money, or of this type of energy, constitutes the line of least resistance, plus the will to make vast fortunes, which cannot be gainsaid. They will to make a fortune; they bring their intelligence to bear upon their goal, and naught can stop them. Many of them are purely selfish; some regard their money as a trust to be used for others and are amazingly generous in a philanthropic and humanitarian sense. These men are receptive to the first type of energy, and frequently all the three types find a channel through them, and the world is greatly benefited; such men are nevertheless very rare. It still remains for the crystallised aspect of this third energy—money—to be used on a large scale for the furtherance of the work of the Hierarchy. It is at this point and in connection with money that the great test of goodwill should demonstrate.

4. *The energy which produces order.* This is the energy of the seventh ray or power of divinity. At this time, its major expression will come through the relationships and adjustments required between capital and labour, and labour will be primarily involved. This energy is being assimilated in the Ashram of the Master Whom I mentioned above; at the

inception of the industrial era He was responsible for the formation of the labour movement—a movement bringing into relation the workers of the world. It is interesting to have in mind that today labour functions internationally; it is a group which learns with rapidity and has in it the seeds of vast good; it is probably the group which will place goodwill in the forefront of human thinking—upon a pinnacle of thought. This Master to Whom I refer belongs to the Ashram of the Master R. He relieves Him of this phase of the work to be done.

5. *The energy of right human relations.* This energy is a subsidiary expression of the energy of Love-Wisdom—the first of the great outpouring energies. It emanates, therefore, from the subsidiary Ashram for which I am responsible. I have written and taught much about it, and with some success. "Right human relations" is not simply goodwill, as people seem to think; it is a product or result of goodwill and the instigator of constructive changes between individuals, communities and nations. About it I need not write, for you have enough teaching from me to guide you. Your daily actions will be those of goodwill, directed towards the establishing of right human relations *if* you are rightly oriented *within* the race of men and *towards* the spiritual Hierarchy.

These energies—along with others at this time far less potent and therefore of only secondary importance—will greatly stimulate the hearts and minds of men. It is the task of the Members of the Hierarchy to distribute these energies (once they are released by the Christ) to the working disciples on the physical plane and to the myriad aspirants in training or discipleship and to the members of the New Group of World Servers. Members of the New Group of World Servers consist of those who are completely dedicated to the service of humanity and to the establishing of right human relations under hierarchical impression; aspirants and quite a few disciples have diversified interests and only serve part time. To all these groups is committed the task of implementing the work and directing the energies for which the Christ is responsible. The objectives of the Hierarchy in this divine act of massed impression and stimulation are briefly three, as follows:

1. To bring about those conditions which will make the coming of the Christ possible. The blended influence of these energies will bring about what may at first appear to be undesirable results, because the remaining opposition of the Forces of Evil is still active and must be overcome; this may necessitate drastic measures, but great good will eventually appear.

2. To prepare the minds of men so that they may be ready for the influence of the Avatar about Whom the Scriptures speak. He is called the Avatar of Synthesis and His influence will be spread through the work and the activity of the Christ.

It must be remembered that synthesis is an aspect of the first divine characteristic, the Will, or rather, the Will-to-Good. This energy or influence, which the Christ Himself will wield (and for which He has been long preparing Himself), produces cohesion, a drawing together and a tendency to fusion and union. The separateness of humanity, and its selfishness, had reached such vast proportions, and its effects were so completely dominated by the Forces of Evil, that—in response to the massed inchoate demand of humanity—the Hierarchy called for spiritual interposition. The endless selfish propaganda, in speech or in writing, most of it materialistic, nationalistic and basically untrue and wrongly motivated, became such a clamour that it reached to spheres usually impervious to the sounds of earth; the Avatar of Synthesis was called in to aid.

The main objective and the immediate task of the Christ is to bring to an end the separateness which exists between man and man, family and family, community and community and nation and nation. This is a simple statement, and one that can be understood easily by the most ignorant; it is simple also in that it provides a practical objective and task for the smallest and the most unimportant of the sons of men; all can cooperate if they will. It is nevertheless a task which has required the mobilising of the entire planetary Hierarchy, and the assistance also of a great Being Who would normally work on levels of consciousness higher than those on which Christ and His disciples labour.

3. To stimulate the aspiration in the hearts of men so that human receptivity to the good, the beautiful and the true may be greatly increased. These energies will bring in the new creative era, which will sweep into expression as soon as world tension has subsided; then men will be free to think and to create the new forms for the new ideals; then they will bring into manifestation in words, in colour, in music and in sculptured forms the new revelation and the new world which the coming of Christ will inaugurate.

It will be obvious (if you have considered my words with care) that a great spiritual movement is under way—perhaps the greatest of all time, if we except the great spiritual crisis which brought the fourth kingdom into being, the human kingdom. I have mentioned above only three of the most important results for which the Hierarchy hopes. Humanity is deemed to have reached a point in evolution where much can be done, because the minds of men—for the first time on a worldwide scale—are sensitive to spiritual impression; the opportunity of the moment is unique, because minds everywhere are showing themselves superlatively receptive to both good and evil. Men are not today governed so much by blind impulse as by considered thought. There have always been small groups and rare souls who have demonstrated the capacity to respond to spiritual impression. The line of least resistance for the masses is the selfish impulse, and there lies the major point of attack by the Forces of Light.

The totalitarian powers have always realised and exploited this capacity of human beings to be responsive to good or bad impression. By impressing certain doctrines, certain principles and certain beliefs on their people, and by withholding the truth or the facts and ignoring the realities, they contrive to swing their people into an acceptance which means—for the controlling initiators—immense power.

Other nations, the so-called democracies, are in a state of great confusion, split into political, religious and social parties, listening to the teaching, the dreams and the plans of every person who has an idea and thrusts himself forward into the public consciousness, having no true or good policy, tainted by selfishness (personal or national, and sometimes both), and demanding the settlement of material affairs with small attention—if any—to the recognised spiritual goals and values.

There is fortunately a growing body of those of all faiths, or of no religious faith, to be found in every continent and nation who are aware of the stirring of this spiritual movement—linking humanity and the Hierarchy. This is due to their reaction to spiritual hope, to the expectancy and to the curiously widespread belief that divine intervention is possible and at hand. As the momentum of this spiritual activity develops, so will the responsiveness among men develop, and *if* the reaction is that which is hoped for it will be the masses everywhere who will slowly unite to bring about the conditions needed for the reappearance of the Prince of Peace, bringing with Him the potency and the benediction of the Avatar of Synthesis. The number of these semi-enlightened people is growing fast; desperation is hastening their response to help from on high, and in due time their numbers will be so great that totalitarianism, as well as chaotic democracy, will not be able to stand against them.

This is no mystical or visionary dream with which I am presenting you. It involves hard business sense *on the physical plane,* a practical commonsense, a cessation of the constant presentation of a beautiful future in a mythical heaven of idleness and uselessness. The bringing in of the Kingdom of God, the preparation for the coming of the Christ and the salvaging of mankind demand courage, organisation business acumen, psychology and persistence; it needs trained workers and much money; it calls for carefully considered programmes, possessing long range vision, plus sensible modern procedures. It is to this that all with true vision and a love of humanity are called today; it means the spreading of an intelligently cultivated goodwill and the fostering of those conditions, attitudes and points of view which will inevitably bring about right human relations.

I would call your careful attention to one most important matter. The moment that a point of balance is reached, the moment that those who stand for separateness and materialism, for totalitarianism or for any *imposed* regime (and consequently an evil unity), and those who stand for the freedom of the human soul, for the rights of the individual, for brotherhood and right human relations, are equal in force, in position and in influence, *then* the doors of the Hierarchy (symbolically speaking) will open, and the Christ with His disciples will come. This balance has to reach a point upon mental levels; it has to be reached by those who can think, who can influence, and in whose hands lies the responsibility for what the masses below the mental level know and believe. The unskilled labourer, the numerous people who never think, who are only young in the experience of incarnation, and the multitudes who evade thought even when they are capable of it, lie in the hands of two vast and dominant groups: the totalitarians and the democracies.

The consequences of attaining a point of balance are very close today. Organised evil is not in power; organised good is still quite ineffective, largely owing to the failure of the religions of the world to give a true picture of Christ's mission; therefore the struggle for control is with us *now*. If the forces of evil, plus the groups of men who seek control of the human spirit (no matter in what country they are found, and they can be found in every single country without exception), become dominant, the doors of evil will open and the life of man will lose its meaning; death will settle down upon our planet—death both spiritual and mental. If the forces of good, the work of the new group of world servers, and the activities of men of goodwill everywhere prevail, the doors of the spiritual Hierarchy will open and—to use a Biblical phrase—the Hosts of the Lord will issue forth. *The Christ Will Come.*

ORGANISING THE ASHRAMS INTO FORM ON EARTH

June 1949

I would ask you, at the time of this Full Moon of June to spend a little time in visualising the situation which is likely to come about on Earth if and when (as a result of the preparatory work done by and for humanity), the Hierarchy is externalised or manifests itself as a definite and recognised organisation upon the physical plane. What will happen in the world if and when the Masters of the Wisdom function objectively and physically among people in—for instance—our great cities? For millions of years, They have worked behind the scenes, utilising the minds, brains and physical equipment of Their disciples in order to carry out Their beneficent purposes. Such workers under hierarchical inspiration are by no means mediumistic in their nature, but have established a right relationship with their own souls and with the Master of their Ashram. They are responsive to hierarchical impression; they know the plans which the Masters are endeavouring to carry out, and their cooperation is willingly and consciously given; they are left entirely free to work as they see fit—after due recognition of the information and the inspiration given.

Will this system of working on behalf of humanity come to an end? In what manner will the effective and needed changes be made? How will the proposed organisation take place? Of how much of these changes and organisation will average humanity be aware? These and many similar questions almost automatically arise in your minds, and it is essentially necessary that the creative imagination of the advanced man, of aspirants, of probationary disciples (as well as that of the working disciple), does not run riot, creating those thoughtforms which could intervene between the true vision and the work to be done, and interfere therefore with the needed manifestation. It is exceedingly important that the following facts should be realised: the thinking of those who are preparing humanity for the reappearance of the Christ must be most closely guarded and controlled; wishful thinking and the formulation of plans in line with ordinary human methods and techniques must not be permitted at this time. The first lesson, therefore, which you have to learn in this work of preparation, is *controlled thought and sensitivity to hierarchical impression.*

The sole task which confronts you and all aspirants and disciples, is to prepare humanity for two events:

1. The organisation of certain of the Masters' Ashrams in the different countries of the world wherein they can render effective service.
2. The reappearance of the Christ at a date somewhat later than the externalisation of the Ashrams and their physical plane organisation.

How, where, when and in what manner the Masters will make Their appearance is none of your affair. Their plans are laid, and They look for and expect no unthinking and unintelligent obstructions and assumptions from those to whom the task of preparation is committed. They have seen to it that the teaching of the New Age has been given to aspirants and disciples in the world, for distribution; They are rapidly admitting new disciples into Their Ashrams, and as fast as is desirable and permissible (for the Hierarchy works ever under law) They are passing them into the halls of initiation.

At the same time, competent disciples are searching the world for sensitive and willing aspirants; these disciples are laying their emphasis upon intelligence and spiritual freedom, working out as free and understanding cooperation;

these disciples will not be sidetracked by the devotion—unin-
telligently expressed—of the neophyte upon the occult way.
It is occult students for whom search is now being made, and
not mystics; it is for clear-thinking men and women that
the call has gone forth, and not for the fanatic or for the
person who sees nothing but the ideal, and who is unable
to work successfully with situations and *things as they are*,
and who cannot, therefore, apply the necessary and unavoidable compromise.

The coming or the advent of the Hierarchy on earth
will not bring the sudden and the beneficent changes which
the enthusiastic desire. Every necessary evolutionary move
is always a slow move. At no time will the Hierarchy infringe the natural processes of evolutionary growth or the
normally slow development of the various kingdoms in
nature towards divine expression. The Masters will, however, take advantage of all the points attained by these kingdoms, and They will (at certain critical times) utilise the
more advanced specimens of the natural types—in a selective
process—in order to bring in something new, better or different. This applies to the human kingdom just as much
as it does to the vegetable, for instance. There is a line of
thought for you in this statement.

One major technique employed by the Hierarchy is a
constantly applied stimulation. Of this, the effect of the sun
upon all life-forms is a symbol. It must however be remembered that the Masters have, therefore, to apply such stimulation scientifically, working first in one direction and then in
another, modifying the stimulation and the inpouring stream
of energy to meet a need; this They do in order to produce
the desired result, and to bring to fruition that which is
latent within the individual. They work with seven major
types of energy; five of these are now in full use and two
of them are rapidly coming into effective service. It must
be borne in mind that I am here referring to the use of
stimulating, vivifying, fructifying and mutable energies
under what is called (esoterically) "scientific impression."
These energies are:

1. *The energy of prana;* this is the life-giving energy from the Sun which deals out both life and death, health and disease, according to the quality of the substance or material form upon which it makes its impact. This impact and its results are today entirely automatic in application and effectiveness, and are regarded as functioning "below the threshhold of the consciousness" of humanity, and necessarily of the Hierarchy. Its rhythm is established and its effects are well known and proven. The direction of this energy will eventually be in the hands of that great planetary centre, Humanity; therefore, to mankind will then be committed the responsibility for its distribution to the subhuman kingdoms in nature.

2. *The energy of the emotions* or that of the astral plane. This energy is today in a condition of extra-ordinary activity, producing basic changes upon all sides, stimulating desire (both good and bad), and governing, via the solar plexus centre, all that lies below the diaphragm in the human vehicle of expression upon etheric and physical levels. This, when combined with a powerful inflow of the energy of prana, produces and stimulates every aspect of the animal magnetism with which every physical form is equipped; when combined with the energy of mind, it produces a magnetic personality, and this in both the good and the bad sense.

3. *The energy of the mental plane.* This is rapidly coming into an unique potency and its effects today are reaching down into the very depths of humanity, thus bringing to the surface the mental capacity which is latent in and hitherto unused by the masses of men everywhere. It can be described as pouring into the human consciousness by means of four divisions of mental energy:

  a. The energy of ideological thought.
  b. The energy of religious formulations; these are

in process of creating great changes in the minds of men concerning the religious concepts of the world and the new spiritual values.

c. The energy which is today producing the struggle for freedom and liberation from environing conditions. This may express itself as the world fight (at this time) for the freedom of the will of men, as it expresses itself in the press, in speech, in government, or in the struggle for a deepened spiritual life for man. This "energy of liberation" was sensed, registered and voiced for humanity by Franklin D. Roosevelt in *The Four Freedoms,* so much discussed by men today; he thereby laid the foundation for the new civilisation and the new world culture.

d. The energy of the spiritual Hierarchy of the planet, as it is applied today by the Hierarchy in the transmutation of the sad and sorry past of humanity into the glorious prospect of the New Era. This is, as you may well imagine, a sevenfold energy, emanating from and directed by the seven major Ashrams, under the direction of the Christ and of the senior Masters and Chohans, deciding in council the method, the extent and the quality of the distribution of the energy involved; They decide also where it should make its impact so as to achieve the best and the most constructive results. It is with this sevenfold energy that the Hierarchy will work in preparation for its physical plane manifestation and for the reappearance of the Christ.

4. *The energy of humanity itself,* organised and directed by the advanced thinkers and workers in all and every (and this I reiterate) branch of human executive work; in every educational process and in all political regimes. I would most definitely emphasise the widespread nature of this energy contact because esoteric students have very frequently

the erroneous idea that the Hierarchy works only through the medium of esoteric and so-called occult groups. The more advanced a man may be, the more sensitive to impress he becomes, and the human race has now reached a point of sensitivity never before attained. This has happened through the agency of the energies listed above. Disciples and aspirants and the intelligentsia everywhere and in every land are today—consciously or unconsciously—responsive to these four energies; the closer they are affiliated with some Ashram in the Hierarchy, the more the sevenfold hierarchical energies can be distributed to the rest of the human family. It is therefore in this field that the major hierarchical endeavour will—during the next fifty years—express itself. Here, consequently, lies the fundamental problem confronting the Hierarchy, for these energies must be most carefully directed and their resultant impact be most scientifically considered if over-stimulation is to be avoided.

5. *The energy of the second aspect of divinity,* vaguely called by the mystics of the past era "the Christ consciousness." This naturally focusses through the Christ Himself, standing as the Representative in the Hierarchy of the solar energy of love-wisdom. It is a form of peculiar, magnetic energy of which mankind today knows little; nevertheless, upon this energy much speculation has been permitted and many false thoughtforms have been built. It is a dangerous energy because of its exceeding potency and also because this inflowing energy has to use the vehicle of the substance of the three lower worlds, and its area of influence is on the three lower planes of human existence. This at first necessarily produces conflict, and its first major conflict is now impending. I have dealt with this conflict elsewhere when discussing with you the fourth Ray of Harmony through Conflict.* The use of this second fundamental energy (which is the primary energy of our present solar system, focussing

---

* *A Treatise on the Seven Rays,* Volume V.

upon our planetary life) presents to Christ Himself a great
test of His skill in action; its use constitutes the major test
or task which faces Him when He reappears and has the
responsibility of releasing its potencies on earth. The task of
all disciples is consequently *to promote wisdom,* and this
they must learn to do under the influence of the Buddha.
He taught the primary lesson of mental discrimination and
detachment—two basic qualities which must be called into
activity during this amazing preparatory period with which
all aspirants are today confronted.

These are, therefore, the points which all groups of
disciples and spiritual workers must learn to present to
seeking humanity. They concern the creating and the vitalising of the new world religion. This theme lies at the root
of all that is new: discrimination between the mental approach and the soul approach, thus learning that true detachment which was symbolically but erroneously applied by
all monastic orders throughout the world (both occidental
and oriental) during the past few centuries, applied therefore in time and space but having no relation to the inner
spiritual import. The true monastic spirit and discipline
will emerge later in the historical processes of humanity.

6. *The energy of the first divine aspect* (that of will or
power) now being applied with the most scrupulous care
by Shamballa. This energy of the will is—as you have been
taught—the potency of the life in all beings; it has in the
past only been permitted to make contact with "the substance
of humanity" via the Hierarchy. Lately, direct impact has
been permitted experimentally and of this the world war
(1914-1945) was the first evidence, clarifying issues, presenting opportunity, purifying human thinking and destroying
the old and worn-out civilisation. It is an exceedingly dangerous energy and cannot be applied in fuller measure until
the race of men has learned to respond more adequately to
the energy of the second aspect of love-wisdom, and therefore to the rule of the Kingdom of God.

7. There remains another energy which can only be applied very much later on and only if the activity of the six preceding energies fulfill their purpose. With it we cannot here deal, for the future is too uncertain, and in any case, it will only come into activity in the middle of the Aquarian Age.

These energies, along with the five specialised energies referred to in my June (1948) Full Moon Message will swing into great activity as the years slip away. The year 1952 will see the five specialised energies assuming great potency.

I would again call your attention to the fact that the evocative power of the Great Invocation (now used by so many hundreds of thousands) and the *sound* of its mantric rhythm is increasingly responsible for this work; a great deal of the resultant effectiveness is due to the fact that humanity is using this mantram in steadily increasing numbers, and this—combined with its scientific use by the Hierarchy—is very fruitful in results. It is well here to bear in mind that (to quote an old sentence by one of the Masters) *"where the focus is, so will be the anchorage where descending potencies under mantric inspiration are concerned."* This means that, due to the effort of countless thousands of men and women everywhere, energies hitherto unable to penetrate deeper into substance than the hierarchical substance and the levels of the higher mental plane can now, for the first time, be successfully anchored on dense physical levels or at least upon etheric levels. This is a fact and is far more important than you are perhaps able to appreciate.

I have earlier told you that the five Masters concerned with the initial stages of the organisation of the Hierarchy on earth are the Master K.H., the Master Morya, the Master R., the Master Who started the labour movement in the modern world, and myself, the so-called Master D.K.

The division of labour is here of great interest. In my June message for 1948, I referred to the five specialised energies which were at that time released to carry forward their impersonal task. Each of these energies is concerned with the desired organisation, for it must ever be remembered that though the organisation which we are considering is concerned with the *interior* or subjective work of the Hierarchy, the repercussions and the resultant effects will take place on earth, with physical plane effects, because the old occult truism "as above, so below" will be rapidly and objectively demonstrated. This result and the effects produced will constitute one of the modes whereby the Hierarchy will prove its factual presence on earth.

The Ashram of the Master K.H. is already assuming an increased stimulating potency, but it will nevertheless be one of the last to manifest objectively on the physical plane. The mission of that Ashram is to produce the energy which will make possible and definite the reappearance of the Christ. That reappearance is the major pre-occupation of the Master K.H. and His group of initiates and disciples. The first step taken by the Ashram was embodied—as far as all of you are concerned—in the pamphlet entitled *The Reappearance of the Christ* (Wesak Message, May 1947). To this must be added the vitalisation and the stimulation of the two-thousand-year-old thoughtform which men, down the centuries, have created in anticipation of His coming or advent. The movement toward expectancy and preparation is now rapidly gaining momentum. This was the first concrete result of the combined desire of this second ray Ashram. However, the work being done in this Ashram is more definitely concerned with three lines of activity. These are:

1. The preparation of the many combined Ashrams, leading to externalisation.
2. The formulation of the techniques and disciplines which will be of service to the initiate or disciple who is making the primary effort to function objectively, to work *before* the screen of life and not *behind* the scenes, as hitherto, and to develop that

"resistant capacity" which is needed to withstand the violent impacts of physical plane living.

3. The mental and spiritual registration of the plans of the Christ, and the consequent development of that skill in action which will permit these plans to materialise correctly.

Within the second ray Ashram of the Master K. H. and His affiliated groups (such as the Ashram for which I am responsible) it is the energy of wisdom which is being effectively used. It might be said that this dual energy, hitherto a fused and blended energy, is today working as a true duality. The energy of wisdom is active within all the Ashrams (on all rays and under all the Masters); the energy of love is directed primarily towards the third great planetary centre, Humanity, stimulating the aura of that mass of living units so that their "magnetic appeal will be the outstanding quality of their divine approach." The directing Agents for this dual activity are the Master K. H. and a chosen group of His senior initiates and disciples, of whom I am not one, because I have another task committed to me.

The Master K. H. is therefore constantly in close association with the Christ, the Head of the Hierarchy. Christ is today, with the aid of the Lord of the World and the Buddha, preparing Himself for the most difficult task with which He has ever been confronted. It is not a matter of the Christ issuing forth from the High Place where He is today to be found, and suddenly appearing among men; it is not a case of His taking infant form and growing into His work with advancing years; it is not a case of His being instantly recognised and acclaimed by millions of miserable human beings awaiting liberation. None of these ideas or hopes forms any part of His plan, nor are they possible. No Member of the Hierarchy, and certainly not its Supreme Head, attempts to bring about results which are doomed to failure; presented thus, they would be bound to fail, because the point of sensitivity of humanity makes failure inevitable—if success is expected along these most ordinary lines.

Skill in action, wise and understanding judgment, the adaptation of present affairs to the desired future, the coordination of the work to be done, and the clear enunciation of the platform upon which the new teaching must be founded, plus the survey (if I may so express it) of the foundations upon which the new structure of the coming civilisation must be founded—it is with these things that the Christ is at this time concerned. You can realise, therefore, the tremendous and cooperative activity with which the Master K. H. and His Ashram are concerned. The stimulation of that activity comes from two directions: necessarily from Shamballa, from the Buddha and from the Avatar of Synthesis, and increasingly from the world of men, as expectancy, hope and demand combine to make their united appeal.

The Ashram or group centre through which the Master Morya works is also exceedingly busy. It is obvious to you that as this is a first ray Ashram, the energy coming from the Avatar of Synthesis will make its primary impact upon this Ashram, which provides the line of least resistance. There, it is scientifically stepped down or broken down prior to distribution to the Ashrams of the five Masters engaged in the work of preparation.

The highest aspect possible of assimilation by the Hierarchy is directed by the Masters towards the Christ and is used by Him in His individual and planned preparatory work. Though He demonstrated when here before that His mission or work had a group or brotherhood objective, it is well known in hierarchical circles that first ray synthesis is something higher still than unity, and that even the Christ has somewhat to grasp anent this new potency—coming both from Shamballa or from the Father (as the Christ used to call that emanating source), and also from extra-planetary sources. Above all, He has the difficult task of training or adapting His physical vehicle so that it can assimilate this extra-ordinary high potency and, at the same time, keep it in a condition in which He can move outward on the physical plane among men.

The Christian Church has laid so much emphasis on Christ's unique position as the one and only Son of God that great error has crept in and has been fostered for centuries; Christ Himself foresaw the possibility of this error and tried to offset it by pointing out that we are all the "Sons of God" and that "greater things than I do shall you do"—a statement which no commentators have ever understood or adequately explained. The occult fact is that there is no being on Earth, from the very lowest form of life to the very highest, who is not moving onward towards a greater and finer expression of divinity, and Christ Himself is no exception to this universal evolutionary law. He is therefore, at this time and because He is preparing to raise the entire human family nearer to God, laying Himself open to certain powerful inflowing energies, absorbing into Himself streams of spiritual force, and undergoing a dynamic stimulation which is entirely new to Him; this constitutes His testing for the exalted initiation which now confronts Him; it constitutes also the sacrifice He is making in order to complete His work on Earth and bring a new salvation to humanity.

The Christ is working, therefore, in very close cooperation with the Master Morya, and also with the Manu (one of the three Heads of the Hierarchy), and these three—the Christ, the Manu and the Master Morya—create a triangle of energies into which (and through which) the energy of the Avatar of Synthesis can pour, finding right direction under Their combined efforts.

On the physical plane, the initiates and the disciples working in the Ashram of the Master Morya are primarily occupied with the expression of synthesis in the world of politics and of government, and with offsetting wrong approaches to synthesis, seeking to preserve freedom in unity. It is a subjective synthesis for which they work—a synthesis which will express itself in an outer differentiation. This synthesis will define the many aspects of the essential, basic unity which, working out under the stimulation of the energy of synthesis, will bring about eventual peace and understanding on earth—a peace which will preserve individual and national cultures, but which will subordinate them to the good of the whole of humanity.

We come now to the preparatory work being done by the Master Who started what is called by you "the labour movement." This is regarded by the Hierarchy as one of the most successful attempts in all history to awaken the masses of men (in the brackets called middle class and lower class) to general betterment, and thus set up a momentum which would, occultly speaking, "swing them into light."

Along with the development of the labour movement, mass education came into being, with the result that—from the angle of developed intelligence—the entire level of conscious awareness was universally raised. There is still much illiteracy, but the average citizen in all the western democracies and in the Soviet Union is as well educated as the intellectual man in the Middle Ages. You have, in this activity, an outstanding instance of how the Masters work, for (to the average onlooker) the labour movement arose from within the masses and the working classes; it was a spontaneous development, based upon the thinking and the teaching of a mere handful of men who were regarded primarily as agitators and trouble makers; they were in reality a group of disciples (many of them unconscious of their esoteric status) who were cooperating with the Law of Evolution and also with the hierarchical Plan. They were not particularly advanced disciples, but they were *affiliated* with some Ashram (according to their ray), and were therefore subject to impression. Had they been advanced disciples or initiates, their work would have been futile, for their presentation of the Plan would not have been adapted to the level of the intelligence of the then totally uneducated masses composing labour.

This Master works primarily with the intelligentsia, and He is therefore a third ray Master—upon the Ray of Active Intelligence. His Ashram is occupied with the problems of industry, and the goal of all the thinking, all the planning and all the work of impressing receptive minds is directed towards spiritualising the concepts of the labour party in every country, and of industrialists, thus turning them towards the goal of right sharing, as a major step towards right human relations. This Master therefore co-operates with the Master R.—Who is the Head of the third ray Ashram, and Who is also one of the Triangle of Forces which controls the greater Ashram of the Hierarchy Itself. The Ashram of this Master (Who has always withheld His name from public knowledge) is a lesser Ashram within the major third ray Ashram, just as my Ashram lies within the ring-pass-not of the Ashram of the Master K. H. This Master is necessarily an Englishman, for the industrial revolution started nearly one hundred years ago in England, and the potency of the work done is related to its mass effect and to the results achieved in every land by labour and its methods. All the great labour organisations, national and international, are loosely knit together subjectively, because in each group this Master has His disciples who are working constantly to hold the movement in line with the divine Plan. It is well to bear in mind that all great movements on earth demonstrate both good and evil; the evil has to be subdued and dissipated, or relegated to its right proportional place, before that which is good and in line with hierarchical planning can find true expression. What is true of the individual is true also of groups. Before the soul can express itself through the medium of the personality, that personality has to be subdued, controlled, purified and dedicated to service. It is this controlling, subduing process which is going on now, and it is vociferously fought by the selfish and ambitious elements.

Nevertheless, the work of this Master is outstandingly successful in preparing the intellectual principle of the masses for eventual right recognition of the Christ. A right sense of values is being developed, and in the right direction of this potent labour group in every land lies the foundation of the new civilisation.

The Ashram of this Master is therefore occupied with worldwide economic problems, and also with a direct attack upon the basic materialism to be found in the modern world. The problems of barter and exchange, the significance of money, the value of gold (a basic symbol of the third Ray of Active Intelligence), the production of right attitudes towards material living, and the entire process of right distribution are among the many problems dealt with in this Ashram; the work done is enormous and of great importance in preparing men's mind for the return of the Christ and for the New Age which He will inaugurate. Capitalists and labour leaders, financial experts and thinking workers, and members of all the differing ideologies which are prevalent in the world today are to be found actively working within this Ashram. Many of them are what the orthodox religious man or the hide-bound occult student would regard as non-spiritual, yet all of them are in reality deeply spiritual in the correct sense, but they care not for labels, for schools of thought nor for academic, esoteric teaching. They exemplify within themselves a livingness which is the hallmark of discipleship.

The time has come when the first and major principle governing true esotericism must be grasped as conditioning all hierarchical workers: *Right Motive.*

The time has come when the quality of ashramic work is recognised, first of all, as being: *Selfless Service.*

The time has come when men everywhere must realise that entry into a Master's Ashram is dependent upon *Intelligence,* plus right motive and service.

When these three factors are present in any human being, the Masters know that good material is presented to Them for training. Today the world is full of such men and women, and in them lies the dominant hope of the future.

One more point I would like to discuss. Through the work of this Master and His Ashram the "sealing of the door where evil dwells" will come about, because it is essentially this group which (if I dare so express it) is coping

with raw materialism and the false values which it engenders.
The door has to be sealed by a vast mass of coordinated
human forces, and not by one or two enlightened men.
This fact must be grasped by you. The energy of love-
wisdom, the energy of the second ray, can and will bring
in the Kingdom of God; the energy of the divine will can
and will galvanise with its dynamic potency the entire human
family to the point where a group transition will take
place from the fourth into the fifth kingdom. It is nevertheless this third ray energy, as wielded in the Ashram of
this English Master, under the direction of the Mahachohan,
the Lord of Civilisation, which will force a right attitude
toward materialism, which will bring about a balance between the material values and the spiritual, and which
will eventually thrust back into futility the Forces of Evil
which have for so long distracted the world of men. I am
choosing my words with care.

You will note, therefore, how the three divine aspects
are united in one great movement to bring in the Kingdom
of God, and that the first step towards this longed-for consummation is the appearance of the Masters upon the physical plane, and then, somewhat later, the reappearance of
the Christ.

We now come to a consideration of the vast Ashram
controlled by the Master R. He is the Lord of Civilisation
and His is the task of bringing in the new civilisation for
which all men wait. It is a third ray Ashram, and therefore
enfolds within its ring-pass-not all the Ashrams to be found
upon the third Ray of Active Intelligence, upon the fifth
Ray of Concrete Science and upon the seventh Ray of Ceremonial Order. All these Ashrams are working under the
general direction of the Master R. He works primarily
through the Masters of these three types of ray energy. He
Himself at this time is occupied with seventh ray energy,
which is the order-producing energy upon our planet.

This is the Ray of Ceremonial Order, and through the
activity of its energy, when correctly directed and used, a
right rhythm is being imposed upon all aspects of human

living. An effort is being constantly made to arrest the ugly chaos of the present and to produce the ordered beauty of the future. The major weapon now being used by the combined Forces of Evil is chaos, disruption, lack of established security, and consequent fear. The potency of these evil forces is exceedingly great because they belong to no one group of people and to all the ideologies. The chaos produced by indifference, the chaos produced by uncertainty, the chaos produced by fear, by starvation, by insecurity, by watching others suffer innocently, and the chaos produced by the warring and conflicting ambitious elements in every nation (*without exception*) —these are the factors with which the Master R. is attempting to deal; the task is one of supreme difficulty. The entire rhythm of international thinking has to be altered, and that constitutes a slow and arduous task; the evil personalities which, in every country, are responsible for the chaos and uncertainty, have eventually to be replaced by those who can work in cooperation with the rhythm of the seventh ray, and thus produce ordered beauty.

The task is further complicated by the fact that in the substitution of order for chaos, national cultures must be preserved and the outline of the new civilisation presented to the people. This major Ashram is therefore confronted with two elements in every land and nation: those people who hold on to the bad old things of the past, and those who work for the extreme opposite of this point of view and for that which is new. Under the influence of this seventh ray energy *balance has to be brought about* and preserved, so that the "noble middle way" of right action and of right human relations can be safely trodden. The task of the Master R. is, however, lightened by the fact that the seventh ray is now coming into activity and its potency is increasing year by year. His task is also aided by the intelligent work done by the Ashram of the English Master Who works consistently with the awakening and the arising masses.

Every October and every March, the Master R. gathers

together His council of helpers, the Masters and the senior initiates in the Ashrams of the third, the fifth and the seventh rays. Though He is the Head of the third Ray of Aspect and is in control, therefore, of the two Rays of Attribute mentioned above, He does not Himself wield these forces, because He is One of the three Heads of the Hierarchy and His work cannot be confined to the activity of any one ray. He works through the Ashrams of these rays, but He Himself works primarily in cooperation with the Christ and the Manu.

Now we come to the work which I (D. K.), a second ray Master, am attempting to do. With what energies am I working? What is the goal towards which I am striving under the direction of the three great Lords of the Hierarchy? I am working with the energy of right human relations; this is a definite and integral part of the energy of the second ray. It is a magnetic type of energy and draws men together for betterment and for right understanding. It is also related in a peculiar way to the energy of the first Ray of Will or Power. Perhaps this will be clearer to you if I point out that the will-to-good is an aspect of the Ray of Will, but that goodwill is an attribute of the second Ray of Love-Wisdom, thus relating that ray to the first ray.

There is no need for me to enlarge upon the work which I am doing in and through my Ashram; you know it well, for I have frequently outlined it, and my books present the goal adequately for this generation.

In this particular though relatively short cycle, my Ashram is in a key position. It is closely linked to the first ray Ashram of the Master Morya, through the work of Men of Goodwill and through all goodwill movements in the world at this time. Goodwill is essentially an expression of the second Ray of Love Wisdom, and is therefore an aspect of all the Ashrams in that great second ray Ashram, the Hierarchy. But all goodwill work is today being galvanised also into violent activity through the dynamic energy of the first ray, expressing the will-to-good.

You have, therefore, this dynamic type of energy channelled through the Ashram for which I am responsible. This Ashram works also in close cooperation with that of the Master R. because the *intelligent* activity of the energy of goodwill is our objective, and its expression through intelligence, applied with wisdom and with skill in action, is the task demanded of all men and women of goodwill throughout the world. When the Labour Movement is swept by the energy of goodwill, basic changes in world affairs will take place. I would ask all workers for goodwill to attempt to reach labour in all countries with these ideas, correctly presented.

I have tried here to give you some idea of the synthesis of this hierarchical work for humanity, and thereby give to all men and women of goodwill the needed courage to go forward.

You ask me (and rightly) of what use is all this information to men and to the aspirant who is trying to serve? The one thing which humanity needs today is the realisation that there *IS* a Plan which is definitely working out through all world happenings, and that all that has occurred in man's historical past, and all that has happened lately, is assuredly in line with that Plan. Necessarily also, if such a Plan exists, it pre-supposes Those Who are responsible for the originating of the Plan and for its successful carrying forward. From the standpoint of average humanity, who think in terms of earthly happiness, the Plan should be something joyful and something which would make material life easier. To the spiritual Hierarchy, the Plan involves those arrangements or circumstances which will raise and expand the consciousness of mankind and enable men, therefore, to discover the spiritual values *for themselves* and to make the needed changes *of their own free will,* and thus produce the demanded betterment of the environment, consistent with the unfolding spiritual recognition.

Nothing of true value is to be gained by any arbitrary or autocratic activity on the part of the spiritual Hierarchy. That is one of the lessons to be learnt, as the work of the totalitarian powers—in the past and today—and its effects are noted. Under the totalitarian system, freedom is curtailed or abolished, the free will of the individual is denied and prevented expression, the individual is regarded as the appurtenance of the all-powerful State and held in that position by police regimentation; individual development is of value only in so far as the interests of the State are served, but the individual himself—as an independent divine unit of humanity—is non-existent, from the totalitarian point of view. Would you, therefore, have the spiritual Hierarchy of our planet work along totalitarian lines, enforcing peace and comfort, taking steps to arrest evil by force and working for the material well-being of men? Or would you have the Masters lead humanity itself, through right understanding, to take the needed action, even if it involves trial and error and a much slower process? Would you have mankind standing on its own feet as intelligent agents of the divine Plan? Or would you have them treated as irresponsible children who must be energetically protected against themselves? Is it not better for the rapidly awakening intelligence and activity of men (in every land) to be trained to recognise the essential unity of all human beings, and so be led to take the action needed which will endorse that unity, which will work for the entire group of human beings in all lands everywhere, and which will also and at the same time preserve the individual and the national cultures, alongside a universal civilisation and a world-wide system of divine recognition? It is toward this general freedom and the intelligent activity of the free individual that the Hierarchy is steadily and successfully working; the concept of unity and of united activity for the good of all is far more widely grasped and understood than you perhaps realise. The totalitarian approach works toward an imposed unity and one which will include all peoples and bind them down to a uniformity of belief—politically, economically and socially—and which will and does basically ignore the spiritual values, putting the State in the place of that divine spiritual centre where spiritual reality is to be found.

The method of the Hierarchy is to work through individuals and through groups for the production of such a widespread spiritual recognition that men everywhere will accept as factual the inner government of the planet, and will work together for the founding of the Kingdom of God in objective manifestation on Earth—and not in some distant time and some vague heaven. This is no mystical or impossible dream, but is simply the recognition and the externalisation of that which has been for ever present, which definitely took objective form when Christ was with us two thousand years ago, and which will proceed to universal recognition when He is with us again in the immediate future.

Therefore, all who work and struggle for the good of humanity and under the direction of the Hierarchy, take heart and renew your courage. The Hierarchy not only *stands* (as oft I have told you), but It is approaching daily and yearly closer to humanity. The power of the focussed spiritual unity of the Hierarchy can be felt today in many ways; it is largely responsible for the patient effort of all humanitarian workers and of all who vision unity in the face of great odds, and in spite of the fatigued lethargy and the pessimism which conditions, too hard for human endurance, have imposed upon men's minds. The Hierarchy stands and works. The Masters are working according to Plan— a Plan which is founded in the past history of the race and can there be traced; a Plan which necessitated because of human selfishness, the drastic horror of the war (1914-1945); a Plan which today can and will bridge the gulf which now exists between the unsatisfactory, selfish and material past and that new future which will demonstrate a large measure of world unity, and which will steadily and with skill in action substitute the spiritual values for those which have hitherto held sway.

The guarantee of this is the developing intelligence of men everywhere fighting blindly for freedom and for understanding, and receiving ever the inner assurance, knowledge and aid of Those Who are working out (as always) those situations and conditions wherein mankind can best arrive at divine expression.

THE EFFECTS OF THE EXTERNALISATION

September 1949

In my previous instruction upon this theme I dealt with the various energies which would be brought into activity or utilised when the Masters emerged from the silence in which They have guarded Themselves for so many thousands of years. The point to be grasped is that the energies with which I dealt will be used in a new and more vital manner. These enegies are ever present and ever active, but they swing into activity sequentially and under law and order, and some are more prominent at one time than others; they act vitally and energetically in the needed programme which the plans of the Hierarchy may entail in any particular cycle.

These energies bring about what we idly call the "events" of the day; they condition our passing civilisations and are so much a part of the world in which we live and move and have our being that events, as expressions of directed energies, mean little to us, except in so far as they may affect adversely our personalities. They connote simply a way of life in any specific time. These energies were started on their activities in the very night of time; they established—each of them—their needed cyclic rhythm; they are responsible for the activity of substance on matter or of the action of the vital or etheric body upon matter; they are the lowest formulated expression of the creative Intelligence, embodying the principle of life or livingness because they essentially are life itself and life in action. Forget not that dense matter is not a principle; it is only that which is responsive to the creative principle.

When, however, the externalisation of the Hierarchy begins to take place (and it will be spread over quite a long period of time), the impact of these substantial energies on matter will be radically altered because they will be—for the first time in history—directed from etheric levels, from the etheric body of the planet in the three worlds; hitherto, these energies have been directed from the buddhic plane which is the lowest of the cosmic etheric levels. Fundamentally, direction will still be from the buddhic plane, but the detailed and focussed direction will be given from within the three worlds and upon the physical plane; this will be the task of the externalised Ashrams, organised to function openly.

It was the knowledge that this important development was imminent which made the Hierarchy in the last century widen the area or the scope of its teaching activity and thus bring to the consciousness of modern man the knowledge of what occultism essentially means. The keynotes upon which the occult philosophy is built are:

1. There is naught in manifestation except organised energy
2. Energy follows or conforms itself to thought
3. The occultist works in energy and with energies.

The thought of God brought the universe of energies into organised form upon the highest of the seven planes, or upon the first cosmic etheric level. These energies have for untold aeons been directed from the fourth or lowest of the cosmic etheric planes, the plane which we call the buddhic and regard as the first definitely spiritual plane, in our usually erroneous thought; this direction has been under impression from Shamballa, and the Masters have "manipulated these energies in conformity with the Plan, which is the blueprint of the Purpose."

In the great Approach of the Hierarchy to humanity and its imminent appearance upon the physical plane, the centre of direction will also necessarily approach still nearer, and—as a result of the future hierarchical manifestation—centres of energy direction will be found wherever the ashram of a Master is located in any part of the world. This is a statement of profound significance; it is an indication of hierarchical policy and a mode whereby modern science (working as it does with energies) can be brought into cooperative association and relation with an ashram upon the physical plane knowing it for what it is—an entirely new departure.

Earlier I stated that the physical plane areas or localities which constitute the present modern exits for energies, through which directed energies can pass to carry out the creative process, are five in number: New York, London, Geneva, Darjeeling and Tokyo. These five form a five-pointed star of interlocking energies, symbolic of the major divisions of our modern civilisation. I would have you bear in mind that all that I am here giving you anent energy is in relation to the human kingdom and to nothing else; I am not relating these energies to the other kingdoms in nature; I am here concerned with physical plane utilisation of energy through the power of directed thinking and on behalf of the evolution and well-being of mankind. At each one of these five centres one of the Masters will be found present, with His ashram, and a vortex of spiritual forces will there be organised to hasten and materialise the plans of the Christ for the new and coming world cycle.

The organising of these five centres will be done slowly and gradually. A senior disciple will appear and will work quietly at the foundation work, gathering around him the needed agents, aspirants and assistants. All these workers at any particular centre will be trained to think, and the effort now present in the educational and social world to force men to think for themselves is a general part of this training process. Until a man can do his own thinking and deciding, he cannot be an intelligent, willing and understanding co-operator, working with an ashram and controlling and directing the creative process. If the new heavens and the new earth are to be a fact in manifestation and in reality, it means a great re-creating process must get under way, and this is the concept lying behind the teaching anent the five centres on Earth and the part which they will play in rebuilding and reorganising the world.

As the next few years bring into focus the hierarchical intention, disciples and aspirants must look for those men and those few women who will be working as a group along spiritual lines in or near one or other of these five localities.

Initial opposition to the founding of these centres of clear thinking men and women, working freely and understandingly with one of the Masters or senior initiates, is already unhappily present; it is to be found in the narrowness, the biassed information and the lack of freedom of the totalitarian schools of thought. This was inevitable, for the Black Lodge ever endeavours to parallel, offset and undo the work of the White Lodge, and hitherto quite successfully. But the cycle of success is slowly closing because the energy of goodwill, emanated by the Will-to-Good, is rapidly becoming effective.

In London, in New York, in Geneva and Darjeeling and in Tokyo, a Master will eventually be found, organising a major energy centre; at the same time His Ashram will continue to function upon buddhic levels, for the entire personnel has not been alerted for externalisation. The Ashram will therefore be working on two levels—and yet that is not a correct statement of fact, as there are no levels, as well you know, but only states of consciousness. Ask me not how this can be; ponder on the relation of this dual and simultaneous appearance by attempting to grasp the nature of the manifested form of the planetary Logos in the Person of Sanat Kumara. Sanat Kumara is not the personality of the planetary Logos, for personality as you understand it is not existent in His case. It is not the soul of the planetary Logos, because that soul is the anima mundi and the soul of all forms in all kingdoms. Sanat Kumara, the Eternal Youth, can be seen by Those Who have the right, presiding, for instance, over the Council in Shamballa, yet at the same time He is present as the life and the informing intelligence upon and within our planet.

You have therefore five points where the externalisation of the Ashrams will take place and eventually be focussed. From these points, as time elapses, other Ashrams, subsidiary in nature, will be found emerging, sponsored and founded by disciples and initiates from these five Ashrams, and representing the three major rays and two minor rays. To start with, they will be founded through the presence in these localities of some senior or world disciple; it must be remembered that the forerunner of all movements which appear upon the physical plane is an educational propaganda, therefore some disciple upon the second ray will come into action, first of all, in all these five points; he will be followed by a disciple upon the seventh ray. All world movements are, as well you know, externalisations of subjective ideas and concepts and of phases of formulated thinking; and the appearance of the Hierarchy upon earth in tangible form is no exception to this rule.

Disciples in these ashrams have been in training for nearly one hundred and fifty years to do this work; some have managed to keep the originating idea and impulse clear and untainted by their own thinking, and have adhered—even in their own intimate thoughts—to the hierarchical programme, as presented to them by their Masters or the senior initiates. Others have not possessed so clear a reasoning faculty or so active an intuitive perception and—whilst grasping certain major concepts such as world unity or hierarchical gradations and control—have distorted the truth and produced the many ideologies which have wracked the world during the past century; even this distortion is, however, being turned to good, for it produced a redoubled effort on the part of the Hierarchy to offset it; it led to an increased forcing process by means of which many earnest and willing aspirants reached the grade of accepted disciple; it produced also a ferment of thought in the world which has served to awaken the mentality of the masses to possibilities and to horizons hitherto only visioned by advanced and initiate thinkers. The man in the street today has absorbed ideologies to an unforeseen extent, and the attempt to make him an active factor in our modern civilisation is not too harmful in view of the time element, as divinely conceived, and from the point of view of the staunch and basic integrity of the divine human being.

Time and divinity, events and instinctual goodness, will in the long run triumph. The intermediate agonies are distressing but not final, and they are not triumphant from the angle of the dark Forces. These Forces face (as a result of the war and of the resurrecting human spirit) a vista of nearing and inevitable defeat.

Already the centres in London and in New York are showing signs of life, and disciples are active in both places and along all lines of human expression. The centre in Geneva is also active, but not so thoroughly and inclusively; it waits for a greater calm and a firmer sense of security in Europe.

The centre in Darjeeling is what is termed occultly "vibrating", but this is in response to the relative nearness and propinquity of the Himalayan Brotherhood; whilst in Tokyo there is small activity as yet, and what there is is of no great moment. The work at this centre will actually be brought into being through the work of the Triangles. By that I do not mean that it will be a centre of the Triangle work, but that the concentrated meditative activity of the people engaged in the Triangle activities will magnetically draw out that which must appear when a centre is organised. They are in fact creating the needed atmosphere, and that is ever a preliminary step. Once the atmosphere or the air in which to breathe and move is existent, then the living form can appear.

Objectively, therefore, the second ray work of teaching is the first to be organised. Subjectively, the first ray workers are already active, for the work of the first ray with its disturbing and destroying activity prepares the way; pain and disruption ever precede birth, and the agents of the first ray have been working for nearly two hundred years. The agents of the second ray started their preparation around the year 1825 and moved outward in force soon after 1860. From that date on, great concepts and new ideas, and the modern ideologies and arguments for and against aspects of the truth, have characterised modern thought and produced the present mental chaos and the many conflicting schools and ideologies, with their attendant movements and organisations; out of all these, order and truth and the new civilisation will emerge. This civilisation will emerge as the result of mass thinking; it will no longer be a civilisation "imposed" by an oligarchy of any kind. This will be a new phenomenon and one for which the Hierarchy has had to wait, prior to reappearing. Had the Hierarchy come before this era of thought and of massed discussion and the fight to further creative ideas, the tenets and the truths for which the Hierarchy stands could be regarded as being also "imposed" upon humanity, and therefore as infringing human freedom. This will not now be the case, and the Hierarchy will come forth into exoteric manifestation because humanity has, of its own free will, developed a quality analogous to that of the Hierarchy and therefore magnetic to that spiritual organisation. Goodwill will draw forth from its holy secret hiding place the Exponents of Love, and thus the new world will come into being.

These subsidiary ashrams are already being attempted in various parts of the world. It is necessary for you to remember that the members of these ashrams will not all be on the teaching line, but will be composed of disciples upon many rays; the attempt to form coherent and integrated ashrams is based upon the recognition of the initial difficulty of the various ray aspirants to comprehend each other's point of view and mode of working, and to think in the many differing terms and modes of thought. There are, however, three fundamental requirements which must condition and colour all the ashrams, no matter what the ray:

1. An internal group unity, conducive to a synthesis of understanding between the various ashrams. There spring out of a unified group objective a sense of loyalty to the Hierarchy and a uniformly disciplined life. I said *uniform,* brother of mine, for the discipline is that of spiritual inclination and an inspired intention which produces a similarity in the living-

ness of the units in the ashram; this is, of course, diversified by the ray quality of the aspirants and disciples and by *personality tradition*. Ponder on those last two words.

2.   Similarity of objective. By that I mean an apprehension and appreciation of the hierarchical Plan and of the contribution each ashram has to make for its materialisation on earth; to this must be added an united ashramic similarity of instinctual and intuitive telepathic rapport with the senior Members of the ashram—the Masters and initiates of high degree, and through Them—with the Christ. I would here call to your attention that the mental inclination of all the esotericists in the world for the past one hundred years has been directed towards individual rapport with a Master, and this because of the necessity of discovering the ashram with which the aspirant must make contact.

This attitude has now widened in its approach mentally, by the many diversified disciples in the many different ashrams, into a group movement or a group inclination towards the Christ, the major and most important factor in the implementation of the hierarchical Plan. This mental approach is not the same thing as the constant aspirational preoccupation of the earnest Christian follower with the thought of Christ. It is something quite different.

It is a unified group endeavour, generated in each ashram and fostered by all alike, to bring the entire group—as a band of world servers—into the aura of the thought currents of the Christ, as He formulates His ideas, creates the thought-form needed prior to manifestation, and makes His arrangements for His reappearing. This is not the same thing as establishing a telepathic rapport between an individual disciple and the Christ, for that is not needed or desirable. The unity of aim, the desire to serve, the recognition of the present focussed intention of the Hierarchy (under the guidance of the Christ), become an invocative, magnetic state of group consciousness; this evokes from the Christ and His informed Masters an identification of Their united thought with the group aspiration. This is the higher spiritual correspondence of what is called in the three worlds *kama-manas*.

This is not, I realise, an easy thing to understand when divorced from the usual Christian concept of the relation of Christ to the individual aspirant. The idea may perhaps be clarified for you by reminding yourselves that some of you who read these words know me and have found your way into my ashram, under the guidance of your own soul and my ready recognition. Others all over the world, through their spiritual intuition and their desire to serve and to know, have brought into their recognised area of consciousness the teaching which is given in my books. Their relation to me is symbolic of the type of relation which disciples and aspirants can and do establish with the Christ. Though the analogy is far from perfect, it is possible to recognise the correspondence in its many gradations of reciprocal sensitivity.

3.   A fundamental and basic similarity of sympathetic response by the units in all ashrams to the needs of humanity, to the quality of the programme for their development which the objective demands, and to the nature of goodwill and understanding (intelligently applied) ; all these qualities are not handicapped by undue emotional sensitivity.

These three conditions will be found in all the ashrams and will unite the members within any ashram to those in other ashrams in a measure or rhythm of telepathic relation. From this unified and central position a rapidly deepening telepathic relation will inevitably be established and sustained *by the group,* with the ashram and with the Christ, on the one hand, and with humanity, on the other. With this as a foundational and conditioning quality, the work can proceed as required.

You will note, therefore, why I have so consistently emphasised, during the past thirty years of teaching, the necessity for the development of a truly spiritual and psychic sensitivity, plus the unfoldment of the faculty of a scientific telepathic rapport. I have thereby laid the foundation of the Science of Impression, with the illumined and rightly oriented mind as the interpreter, the analyser and the transmitter.

ASHRAMIC ADJUSTMENT TO EXOTERIC LIVING

October 1949

We now come to another point in our study of this subject: This concerns one of the most difficult problems confronting the Masters at this time; it presents also an unique problem to the Christ. The daily physical life of the Masters, of the Christ, and of those Members of the Hierarchy (initiates and accepted disciples) Who function in physical bodies, has had its orientation upon the subjective levels of life; the majority of Them, and particularly the senior Members of the Hierarchy, do not as a rule intermingle largely with the public or walk the streets of our great cities. They work as I do from my retreat in the Himalayas, and from there I have influenced and helped far more people than I could possibly have reached had I walked daily in the midst of the noise and chaos of human affairs. I lead a normal and, I believe, useful life as the senior executive in a large lamasery, but my main work has lain elsewhere—widespread in the world of men; I reach this vast number of human beings through the medium of the books which I have written, through the groups which I have started and impulsed, such as Men of Goodwill and the Triangles, and through my disciples who talk and spread the truth as I have sought to present it.

So it has been with the work of all the Masters, except two or three Who have undergone special training in order to do some special preparatory work for the externalisation of the Hierarchy. The English Master is one of these, and another Master also Who works, relatively unknown, in North America. I have referred to Him before as the Master P—though that is not, in reality, His initial.

This rule of solitariness or of withdrawing applies to all the Masters and to the Christ, for it is in the solitude of the mind, and as far as possible in the solitude of physical location, that the various branches of the great White Lodge have chosen to work ever since Atlantean days. It is not the solitude of a separative spirit, but the solitude that comes from the ability to be non-separative, and from the faculty of identification with the soul of all beings and of all forms. This can best be accomplished in the intense quiet of those "protected" areas where the Masters in the various branches of the Brotherhood have chosen to dwell. This solitude and physical isolation enables Them to work almost entirely from the level of the buddhic or intuitional plane, perfecting the Science of Impression, influencing and working through those minds which are susceptible to Their mental impression. This applies equally to Masters in physical vehicles and to Those Who have "no anchorage" in the three worlds; it applies also to disciples who are in or out of the body, according to their destiny, immediate karma or form of service. St. Paul, for instance, was in the initiate stage of learning rightly to withdraw and to work in what Patanjali calls "isolated unity" when he spoke of himself once as "being caught up into the third heaven" and there learning the untold beauties of the divine life.

The problem, therefore, before the Masters and Their disciples is to work (when the externalisation takes place) in the midst of physical plane existence, no longer withdrawn, isolated and protected, but functioning openly in the middle of events and physical realities and all the diversity of contacts which the three worlds present. It is perhaps helpful to remember that when the Christ was in physical presence on earth two thousand years ago, the population of the world was relatively small compared to that today; contact between peoples was practically nil, and where it existed was usually of a strictly military or commercial nature, with a somewhat exclusive interchange of scholastic ideas and personnel between the rare centres of learning. It was easy in those days to withdraw into the desert and to disappear into the unfrequented place and to recharge and revitalise the spirit, to touch again closely the Sources of inspiration on the higher levels of consciousness, and thus reorient the working instrument in the three worlds to the higher field of contact and inspiration. Much of this can be noted in the Gospel story of the life of Christ and of the Master Jesus.

When the Christ reappears and the Hierarchy exter-
nalises itself on earth, conditions will be totally different;
there are today no empty spaces; the population of the world
is enormously enlarged and is growing from year to year; no
locality is isolated or unattainable; the jungles are open territory to the explorer and to the numerous commercial agents;
vast cities cover the planet and oceans are traversed by multitudes of ships; the airways of the world are travelled by millions of passengers annually; the land is divided into minute
sections by railroads, highways, speedways and myriads of
lesser roads and streets. In fact, every living unit in the world
is in touch with thousands of other units and can—through
the many means of information—be in touch with millions;
the news presses grind out the news from hour to hour and
the eyes of millions are ceaselessly glued to the printed page
at all hours of the day or night; the ears of other millions are
daily and hourly attuned to the voice of the radio. Only the
inner perceptive sense remains inactive, for only advanced
humanity lives constantly in touch with the world of spiritual
perception and intention.

The conditions, therefore, confronting the Hierarchy
constitute a serious and drastic problem. As far as we can, we
will attempt to consider these conditions, for some understanding of the problem is necessary if right work is to be
done.

Necessarily, the problem is one of a change in the orientation of perception but not necessarily in modes of living or
in any definitely physical plane adjustments. Hierarchical
orientation has for some centuries been one of a very strict
internal consolidation, in order that the magnetic aura of the
Hierarchy may unfailingly respond to impression from Shamballa, and also be of so potent a nature that it can form a
protective screen around the human family. Forget not the
nature of the protective service which the Masters have assumed on behalf of mankind, standing between humanity
and the emanations and influences and the magnetic aura of
the Black Lodge.

This internal consolidation has been greatly strengthened during the past one hundred years. Because of this, and because of the resultant clarity of impression and of the potent out-going influence, the Plan for humanity—as a Whole—was imparted with emphasis to disciples in the Ashrams, and by them was formulated clearly and presented to humanity.

H.P.B. (one of the first working disciples to go forth on the externalisation impulse and with first ray energy driving him) gave the background of the Plan, under impression from me; the more detailed structure and the sweep of the hierarchical intention have been given by me in the books which A.A.B. has introduced under her own name to the public (in so doing acting under my instructions). For the first time in human history, the purpose of past events—historical and psychological—can be clearly noted as the foundation for all present happenings, thus bringing the mysterious Law of Karma in an easy manner to public attention. The present can also be seen, indicating the way of the future and revealing clearly the Will-to-Good which is animating the entire evolutionary process—a process in which humanity (again for the first time) is intelligently participating and cooperating. It is this cooperative participation, even if unconsciously rendered, which has made it possible for the Hierarchy to grasp the opportunity to bring to an end the long silence which has persisted since Atlantean days; the Masters can now begin to undertake to renew an ancient "sharing of the secrets," and to prepare humanity for a civilisation which will be distinguished by a constant intellectual perception of truth, and which will cooperate with the externalised Ashrams in the various parts of the world.

The internal consolidation is now being somewhat loosened, if I may use such an inadequate expression, and a majority of the Members of the Hierarchy are withdrawing Their close attention from reception of impression from Shamballa and are now orienting Themselves—in an entirely new and directed manner—to the fourth kingdom in nature. At the same time, a very powerful minority of Masters are entering into a much closer association with the Council of Sanat Kumara.

In this way the potent and dynamic influence of Shamballa will be strengthened instead of lessened by the reorientation of the majority of the Masters and initiates. These statements have, of course, implications which will not be understood by you and which will necessarily pass unnoticed; you will respond, however, to the realisation that the minority—in renewed and closer contact with Shamballa—have to master the technique of relationship; this will entail much use of the sacrificial will. The reason is that They are (on a higher turn of the spiral) submitting to a forcing process which will make great demands upon Them, but which will serve to release the majority to a new and more potent form of immediate Earth service. In other words: a few of the Masters and higher initiates are undergoing a special and applied stimulation and are undertaking work for which the united Ashrams, in their higher brackets, have hitherto been responsible. This subjects Them to a great strain and forces Them to use the will aspect of Their divine natures in entirely new and unknown ways. They relinquish much, in order to enable the entire Hierarchy to give far more in radiance, guidance, and magnetic invocative strength than has even before been the case.

The majority of the Masters and initiates, in Their turn, also relinquish much in order to work exoterically among men. They subject Themselves voluntarily to an active stimulation from the senior "contacting minority" but relinquish the "joy of Shamballic contact". Temporarily, the training which the majority have been receiving in "cosmic orientation," in the use of the will-to-be (a meaningless phrase to you), and in the "bliss of receptivity to the will-to-good of Sanat Kumara" is given up. The entire attitude of the group of Masters, initiates and disciples who are to be responsible for the externalisation of the Hierarchy and for the preparation for the reappearance of the Christ is focussed upon the expert use of the Science of Contact. This time, the science is used upon a wide and telepathic scale, with the souls of men, and upon the technique of expressing spiritually the nature of "isolated unity" in the cities, jungles and *the massed inhabited* areas of the earth. This involves, as you can well imagine, the use of an expert ability to remain untouched by the evil rampant upon the physical plane, and yet to remain in complete sympathetic and understanding contact with all humanity and with all events that affect humanity. It was prophecy which impelled the Christ to say, when last in public appearance among men, that His disciples were "in the world and yet not of the world"; Christ depicted in simple yet profoundly revealing terms the life of the Members of His Ashrams (the entire Hierarchy) when again He would walk with Them in the plain sight of humanity. He pictured Them as one with the Father (the Council of Life in Shamballa) , and yet as one with Him (as the hierarchical Head) , and as one also with all that breathes and that inhabits form. I advise all disciples who seek to cooperate with the impending activity of the Hierarchy to study with care the seventeenth chapter of the Gospel of St. John; this was written by that disciple of love, under the influence of the energy emanating from the buddhic vehicle of the Christ, which is also—as you have been told—identical with the buddhic vehicle of the Buddha. The identity of the two vehicles is symbolic of the entire teaching anent "isolated unity" and divine participation, which the Masters in Their Ashrams are teaching Their disciples of all grades, these days, as the first step toward the externalisation of Their activities.

An intensive training process, therefore, is being carried out in every ashram and along identical lines, resulting in the "isolation," occultly understood, of certain Masters and initiates. They have been thus isolated in order that They may work more readily and easily with Shamballa; They can thus form a dynamic and galvanic storehouse of energy (the energy of the divine Will) and thus make it available for the use of the other Members of the Hierarchy, as They stand in "isolated unity" upon the highways of Earth, and thus are "in the world and yet not of the world". The learning of this lesson calls into activity the sacrificial will of both the hierarchical groups; this remains the binding cord between Them and that aspect of the antahkarana along which energy can flow in a new and electric fashion from Shamballa, via the hierarchical minority referred to above, and into the large group of Masters and initiates and disciples to whom is committed the task of consolidation. All this constitutes—for the Members of the Hierarchy—a definite process of testing out and of trial, prior to and preparatory to some of the higher initiations.

Again, the Members of the Hierarchy are not only sensitive to impression from the two other planetary centres (Shamballa and Humanity), but They are acutely aware of the Forces of Evil which are fighting furiously against the externalisation of the spiritual work. The energy which cosmic evil generates is active along three main channels:

1.   From the centre of cosmic evil upon the cosmic astral plane. Of this centre you can know nothing, and its emanations and its magnetic aura can only be understood and recognised or interpreted by the senior Masters and by initiates of still higher rank. As the potency of the astral plane (which is so familiar to us all) weakens, and glamour and illusion are negated by a rapid spiritualising of humanity, the power of cosmic evil will correspondingly weaken and the Forces of Evil will be unable to reach the planet with their present easy effort. It is against the impact of this emanating evil that the Hierarchy stands in protection of humanity. Hitherto it has been the task of Shamballa, working through the Hierarchy, to protect humanity from the "intention to destroy" of the cosmic Forces of Evil, but—in the coming cycle and as a result of the triumph of the Forces of Light in the world war—the potency of Shamballa can be combined with that of the "protecting Agents of Light."

2.   From the Black Lodge which is the externalisation of the centre of cosmic evil on Earth. Just as the White Lodge is the representative or correspondence of the cosmic centre of light upon Sirius (the true Great White Lodge), so the Black Lodge is also representative of ancient and cosmic evil. The Black Lodge is also far more advanced in externalisation than is the White Lodge, because materialism and matter are,

for it, the line of least resistance. The Black Lodge is therefore far more firmly anchored upon the physical plane than is the Hierarchy. It requires a much greater effort for the White Lodge to "clothe itself in matter and work and walk on material levels" than for the Black Lodge. Owing, however, to the spiritual growth of mankind and to the steady, even if slow, orientation of mankind to the spiritual Hierarchy, the time has come when the Hierarchy *can* materialise and meet the enemy of good upon an even footing; the Hierarchy need not be further handicapped by working in substance whilst the Forces of Evil work both in substance and in matter. Once the reappearance of the Christ and of the Hierarchy is an accomplished fact, these Forces of Evil face sure defeat. The reason for this is that the trend of human living and thought is turning steadily towards the subjective spiritual values, even if these values are interpreted in terms of material wellbeing at present and of better living conditions for all—with peace and security also for all. The Black Lodge or the planetary centre of evil works almost entirely upon the astral plane, and is impressed directly and guided in detail from the cosmic astral plane.

3.   From the negative or purely material forces of the planet, which are not necessarily either good or bad but which have been used instinctually and oft unconsciously by humanity for purely material ends, and are therefore basically antispiritual and subject to the influence of human desire—a desire oriented towards selfishness, and therefore towards separateness. This form of evil is being combated today by the New Group of World Servers. Of this battle you know something because every thinking man and woman is immediately implicated.

I have spoken of the evil present in the planet in very simple terms, and there are phases of it to which I have not referred; the interlocking and inter-penetrating of the grades of evil are far more numerous and intricate than you surmise.

In summing up, I would say that the present re-orientation of the Hierarchy, in relation both to Shamballa and to

Humanity, ushers in the cycle of complete defeat of cosmic evil upon our planet, leaving only an isolated and weakened Black Lodge to die a slow death; this permits the purification of human desire to such an extent that "matter will be redeemed by the sacrificial will of Those Who know, by the will-to-good of Those Who are, and by the goodwill of those sons of men who have turned their faces to the light and who in turn reflect that light."

As all disciples know, one of the problems with which they are constantly confronted is an extreme sensitivity to the thought currents of those with whom they are immediately in contact. The more advanced the disciple, the greater is his problem. The theory that if one lives and works on a high level of consciousness one is immune to that which emanates from the lower level does not in practice hold good. The occult law proclaims that the greater can always include the lesser, and just as that is true of the planetary Logos (Who is the sumtotal of all lesser forms within His manifested universe) , so the same law applies also to all human beings. The disciple, therefore, can always include that which emanates from those who are below him on the ladder of evolution. The more a disciple is under the influence of the Law of Love, the more easily does he tune in and absorb the thoughts and register the desires of those around him, and particularly of those who are tied to him in the bonds of affection and of karmic relation. As disciples proceed from initiation to initiation, the will aspect fortifies the intellect and directs the expression of the energy of love, and thus the problem lessens, for the initiate learns certain protective rules which are *not* available to the neophyte. The latter must learn, first of all, how to identify himself with others, as the basis of a *higher* identification which conditions the senior initiates in the scale of being.

The preparation of the Members of the Ashrams found within the Hierarchy, Who must emerge from Their retreats and live among men in the ordinary intercourse of daily life, has necessitated much discussion and instituted a drastic training system within the Ashrams. Into the nature of this training I cannot enter, for it differs for disciples upon the various rays and the theme is too large at this point for our purpose. The problem has been how to preserve the sympathetic, sensitive rapport and to lay the basis for the higher, inclusive identification, and yet at the same time preserve a spiritual detachment which will enable the disciple to do his needed work, unhampered and unimpeded by the distress, the anxiety or the thought activity evoked by the minds and the desires of those with whom he is working.

The necessary detachment cannot be based upon the innate instinct of self-preservation, even when that is carried into the realm of the soul; it must be motivated by an occult absorption in the task, and implemented by the will which keeps the channel of contact open between the disciple and the ashram and between the disciple and his sphere of activity; this channel must be kept entirely clear of all lower identifications. This might be termed a method of eliminating all tendencies to register anything save a wise apprehension of the point in evolution of those contacted; a sound appreciation of the problem to be faced on their behalf, and a process of directing the needed energy of love in such a manner that the stream of projected love not only aids the recipient, but protects the disciple from undue contact; it will then evoke in the person to be helped, or the group to be aided, no reciprocal personality expression; instead, it lifts the entire quality of the personality life or the group life on the purificatory way on to higher levels of awareness.

A great part of the work to be done by the disciples who are emerging from the ashrams, and will continue thus to emerge, is of a purificatory nature at this time, and increasingly so for the rest of this century. On the Path of Probation, the aspirant is taught to purify himself and his three vehicles of contact; upon acceptance into an ashram, a large measure of the needed purification has been achieved. From then on, no emphasis should be laid by the disciple on the purification of his own nature, for this would produce too close and intimate a self-focus and tend to an overstimulation of the personality vehicles. But the lessons learnt upon the

Probationary Path will be found by him to be simply the foundation for the Science of Purification or—if I may use a word made familiar to you through the war experience—of De-contamination. This will be brought into full expression by the working disciples who will be responsible for the preparation of the world for the reappearance. This purificatory process falls into the following stages:

1.   The stage wherein the tainted area, the hidden evil, or the diseased factors are recognised and duly contacted in order to ascertain the extent of the purificatory measures required. This is a point of danger for the disciple.

2.   The process of discovering the magnetic areas, magnetised in past centuries, and even aeons, by Members of the Hierarchy. This is done so as to make available the transmission of energies there stored. In the cycle which is now close at hand, these magnetic centres will be largely tapped or utilised by the world disciples responsible for the purificatory work.

3.   The stage wherein the disciple withdraws his attention from the source of difficulty and concentrates upon certain mantric usages and certain hierarchical formulas, thus setting loose the energies needed to destroy the germs of evil, latent or active, thus eliminating certain materialistic tendencies, and *strengthening the soul of all that is to be purified* and the life to be found within every form. It is wise to remember that, for instance, as the Master works with His disciples and strengthens the life within them and evokes their soul into potency from latency, every form and every atom within their various bodies is equally energised and aided. It is this fundamental process which will guide the disciples and the initiates in the coming work of world purification.

4.   The stage of withdrawing of the purifying energies; this is to be followed by a period of stabilising the purified form and starting the life and soul within it on a new cycle of spiritual growth.

I have worded all this in such a manner that it will be evident that the work to be done is not confined only to humanity, but also to the forms of life in the other kingdoms in nature.

The study of this *Science of Applied Purification* is one which is engrossing the attention of all the ashrams at this time; disciples in the first ray ashram, in the second ray ashram and in the seventh ray ashram are peculiarly active along these lines, for the destruction of evil is the work of the first ray, and in so destroying its effects purity is achieved; the fostering of good then becomes possible and is the work of the second ray, of the Builders; and the bringing of spiritual energy into contact with substance, and consequently with matter, is the unique work of the seventh ray because it is now in manifestation. The rays which are active and in manifestation at this time and in this cycle are there in conformity to the Plan and in preparation for the externalisation of the Hierarchy and the reappearance of the Christ. These rays are particularly involved, and therefore the initiates and the disciples in the ashrams of the Masters are also particularly implicated.

The Science of Applied Purification is also the *Science of Applied Energy,* with the specific objective in view of "eliminating the undesirable and that which hinders the entrance of the light, and thus providing space and entry for the desired, for the good, the beautiful and the true". In the application of this science there is of course no infringement of the human prerogative of free will. This ancient science is concerned primarily with the purification and with the redemption of matter, and it is entirely in the hands of human beings, under the direction of the Hierarchy. This direction may be consciously or unconsciously registered. *The Science of Redemption* (to which I have several times earlier referred) is in reality the applied art of esotericism and of spiritual living which is already being taught to mankind; they are steadily learning to redeem the bodies through which they function. It is in reality the art or science of relationship between the Life and the lives, as H.P.B. expresses it.

As far as the other kingdoms in nature are concerned, the purification is applied by the Hierarchy, through the medium of human beings, and this can be seen in process at this time. This present activity, carried on now largely unconsciously, will be redoubled and carried forward consciously by trained initiates and disciples, working through and with aspirants. It is this that is now being studied in the various hierarchical ashrams, and when applied—after 1975—will bring about great and important changes in world living.

Another matter to which the Hierarchy is at this time attending, in view of the coming adjustments required, is the discovery of aspirants and those who are close to accepted discipleship in all lands, in order that the language problem will present little difficulty. Having discovered such people, Their next step is to subject them to a process of training in telepathic susceptibility, so that they will be sensitive to hierarchical impression. At the same time, their intuition will require stimulation but—as the intuition is useless and inaccessible without a high grade intelligence—all these people must be sought for upon mental levels. The possession of the abstract mind is not sufficient. It is useful, in that it guarantees the ability of the aspirant to construct the antahkarana; it is nevertheless quite possible to possess a well developed *abstract consciousness* and yet to be quite devoid of all intuitive perception.

For example, this is the major limitation of Z . . . He is a *sound* abstract thinker and they are somewhat rare, being usually impractical idealists. He is not, however, the least intuitive as yet. He could easily be—given certain needed surrenders.

Basically speaking, the intuition is not the revealer of esoteric truths. They come along another line of spiritual perception. The intuition is essentially the organ of *group perception* and that which eventually elevates the personality to its rightful position as the agent of the Soul *in the group*

Z . . . has a sound theory as to group attitudes and group work, and he will be exceedingly surprised at these comments of mine. But—as long as he insulates himself from warm group contacts and fails to seek (in the name of service) the love of the group, and as long as he fails to recognise error and his own part in any current mistakes whenever they occur, and as long as he transfers responsibility to others when he is himself to blame, he will fail to register intuitive information, because his personality reactions will intervene. He must not be deceived by the fact that people like him on the platform; that *is* group work, but not essentially working *with* the group. He must learn that at present he is the onlooker at the group and as yet not a part of it, and that he is primarily focussed on "delivering the goods" (if I may use your American phrase) to his personality and its acclaim, and not to the group. This will be hard for him to realise and he must be given time. He wants to make good, spiritually and esoterically, but needs to grasp the fact that this is done through love and understanding and not through the intellect. He is insulated by his own strong desire to make good, according to his own theories and to his personality, thus proving to himself the grasp his soul may have over that personality. This creates barriers, but the insulating and separating wall between him and his co-workers is very thin and could easily be "rent in twain," *if* his pride would permit and if he would descend to a recognition of equality with all the group with whom he is associated, and with the most unimportant members of that group; this he does not yet do—in spite of what he believes about himself.

The searchlight of the Hierarchy is sweeping the planet at this time singling out men and women, here and there, from the mass of men. They indicate esoteric possibility, and in their lives love of humanity and love of the Christ is a basic and fundamental factor.

The ordinary devoted person, who constantly pledges and dedicates himself to the Christ or to the Masters in a spirit of adoration, will *not* be chosen for this specific training. Their own attitudes and development come violently between them and their objective. The man who forgets about himself, and who is more interested in helping unhappy human beings, but who is nevertheless staunchly convinced of the factor of the unseen worlds, is the man for whom search is at this time being made.

When these men and women are found, the work of the discovering initiate is to see to it that information comes to the aspirant in some form or another anent the hierarchical Plan, concerning the reappearance of the Christ (under some name familiar to the aspirant's religious background), and about the fundamental and needed occult truths—with particular emphasis upon the Law of Cause and Effect, and secondarily upon the Law of Rebirth. The Law of Cause and Effect is of far greater importance than the Law of Rebirth, because it necessitates *action* upon the part of the aspirant, and that action inevitably conditions the future. There is nothing he can do about the Law of Rebirth but submit to it and be grateful that opportunity continues to present itself .

As regards the many other adjustments which Members of the Hierarchy in all Their many differing grades will have to make in what might be called Their personality lives and habits, I have naught to say. I know well the questions which will arise in your minds, and I would like to touch upon one or two of them. For instance, some of you are asking:

1. How will these Members of the Hierarchy in Their various grades appear on earth? Will They come through the methods of ordinary birth, of childhood and maturity? Some initiates may follow this ordinary pattern, some are already passing through it today and are in the stages of infancy and adolescence; to them will be given a large share of the preparatory work. Some will not pass through these relatively limiting phases, but will pass back and forth between the outer world and the world of hierarchical endeavour; they will be sometimes present in physical bodies and sometimes not. This method of activity will not be possible as long as

the present rules of national and civilian identification, of passports and of drastic airport and seaport inspection are required by the authorities; such people as these "transitting initiates" would not be able to identify themselves. This form of appearance is therefore postponed for some time. Some of the Masters will create what is called in the language of the East the "mayavirupa"—a vehicle of expression which is built of atomic physical and astral substance and of concrete mental substance. This They can create at will, use at will and cause to vanish at will; Their problem is not, therefore, so acute in the matter of appearing and of reappearing as is that of the initiate who cannot thus create to suit his purpose and his service.

2. Will all the Members of the Hierarchy make Their appearance at the same time? Certainly not. The appearing of these initiates and Masters will begin with isolated members appearing and living among men, coming forth one by one, doing the required work, returning through the portals of apparent death to the inner subjective Ashram, and then again appearing by one or other of the methods mentioned above. This process has been going on for some time and began around the year 1860. The work of these disciples in the human consciousness is already being recognised, and already they have succeeded in changing the consciousness and the thinking of many millions. Their ideas are already permeating world thinking. I would remind you also (for your encouragement) that I myself am among this number of working initiates (for, in the last analysis, that is all that any Master is), and that I, from my physical anchorage, i.e., my physical body and my location in northern India, and in collaborating with a disciple, A.A.B., and also with F.B., have done much to bring certain concepts (old and yet new in their presentation) to the consciousness of humanity. I have also done much to stimulate from latency to potency the instinctual goodwill of men. I mention this for this is not a unique achievement; there are many other Masters Who—with Their

disciples—are to be found today actively functioning in human affairs and struggling, under adverse conditions, to change the trend of human thinking from a frank materialism to a genuine spiritual aspiration.

There are many other questions arising in the minds of my readers, and the less advanced they are the greater the questioning and the greater the emphasis upon the materialistic, and therefore non-important, aspects of this entire subject. With them I have no intention of dealing, though I know well what they are, and so does A.A.B. They are of no vitality, and will answer themselves in due time.

When the task of the preparation of men's minds is further advanced, when the knowledge of the existence of the Masters and Their hierarchical endeavour and of the united Hierarchy of our planet are a commonly recognised truth, and when active goodwill is recognised as a real national asset in all lands, then the speed of the externalisation of the Hierarchy will be greatly increased; then the five spiritual centres will begin to take definite form, and will call also for recognition; the groups there working will be known, and they will also be in close touch with each other. From that time on, the network of initiates and disciples under the direction of the Masters will be world-wide, and in every field of human expression the opinion of these men and women, and of the Masters presiding at the five centres and in Their affiliated groups, will be regarded as of immense value by all governmental, economic and social organisations.

Then—under a great wave of spiritual inspiration—the divine spirit of expectancy for the reappearance of the Christ will sweep through the world; it will then be regarded as credible and creditable, and His coming will provide the germ for all world hope; the reason for this will be that the most respected, enlightened and cultured people on the planet will be looking for Him. And then, my brothers, He will come, bringing new energies of love and compassion and implementing the spirit of fresh enlightenment; to these important events must also be added the new revelation for which all men wait and to which they will be able to respond, owing to the needed and new stimulation.

Many who are reading this section of my instructions will be disappointed (so futile and silly is the human mind in so many cases) because I do not choose to consider now the means whereby the Members of the Hierarchy will adjust Themselves to modern living conditions, as to what food They will eat and whether They will marry or not marry. One thing only will I say: They will take modern life and what it means and will proceed to demonstrate how that life (the normal product of the evolutionary process) can be lived divinely; They will express the highest ideal of marriage (I would here remind you that many of the Masters are married and have raised families) and demonstrate the principle which underlies the perpetuation of the race of men; They will also show how all life is one life, that the form nature is ever a sacrificial unity in the vast scheme of divine manifestation; They will show us also that whatever we do, whether we eat or drink, all must be done under correct, temperate and natural law and in a spirit of loving understanding, and ever to the glory of God. They will express ordered, temperate living in all things, and will demonstrate also the possibility of the existence of people on earth who have no wrong inclinations and no bad qualities in their natures. They will stand forth as living examples of goodwill, of true love, of intelligent applied wisdom, of high good nature and humour, and of normalcy. They may indeed be so normal that recognition of what They are may escape notice.

They will, finally, demonstrate to all around Them the significance of right motive, the beauty of selfless service and a vivid intellectual perception. This, my brothers, is such a platitudinous statement, from the point of view of the nice well-meaning person, that its value may escape your attention. Yet it is a statement that, any initiate will tell you, warrants your closest attention and consideration—a consideration which must be followed by an effort to express these same qualities upon your way towards the Door of Initiation.

The Work of the Externalised Ashrams

The barest outline must here suffice. I have dealt with the proposed work of the externalised Ashrams at some length in the foregoing pages and also in several of my other books,* and a more detailed presentation will not be possible at this time. The approaching externalisation will bring about an increased stimulation which will necessarily affect disciples and aspirants and will involve a period of adjustment to this higher vibration. Adjustment to the increased livingness will be facilitated by the enunciation of certain basic statements for the guidance of disciples, aspirants and people of goodwill.

Specifically, the externalised Ashrams will be active along four major lines:

1. Creating and vitalising the new world religion.
2. The gradual reorganising of the social order—an order free from oppression, the persecution of minorities, materialism and pride.
3. The public inauguration of the system of initiation. This will involve the growth and comprehension of symbolism.
4. The exoteric training of disciples and of humanity in this new cycle.

Meanwhile, what is it that you, my brothers, must do in this interim period? What is your work and your goal? Let me emphasise one or two points:

The material goal which all who love their fellowmen and serve the Hierarchy must ever have in mind and at

---

* *Letters on Occult Meditation,* Letters VIII and IX.
  A Treatise on Cosmic Fire, Pages 747-760.
  A Treatise on the Seven Rays, Vol. V: (*The Rays and the Initiations*).

heart *is the defeat of totalitarianism.* I do not say the defeat of Communism, but the defeat of that evil process which involves *the imposition of ideas,* and which can be the method of the democratic nations and of the churches everywhere, just as much as it is the method of the U.S.S.R. This we call totalitarianism. I would ask you to have this distinction clearly in your minds. Your material goal is the defeat of all that infringes human free will and which keeps humanity in ignorance; it applies equally to any established system— Catholic or Protestant—which *imposes* its concepts and its will upon its adherents. Totalitarianism is the basis of evil today; it is found in all systems of government, of education; it is found in the home and in the community. I refer not here to the laws which make group relations sound, possible and right; such laws are essential to community and national well-being and are not totalitarian in nature. I refer to the imposition of the will of the few upon the total mass of the people. The defeat of this undesirable tendency everywhere is your definite material goal.

Your spiritual goal is the establishing of the Kingdom of God. One of the first steps towards this is to prepare men's minds to accept the *fact* that the reappearance of the Christ is imminent. You must tell men everywhere that the Masters and Their groups of disciples are actively working to bring order out of chaos. You must tell them that there IS a Plan, and that nothing can possibly arrest the working out of that Plan. You must tell them that the Hierarchy stands, and that It has stood for thousands of years, and is the expression of the accumulated wisdom of the ages. You must tell them above all else that God is love, that the Hierarchy is love, and that Christ is coming because He loves humanity.

This is the message which you must give at this time. And with this responsibility I leave you. *Work,* my brothers.

Training for new age discipleship is provided by the *Arcane School.* The principles of the Ageless Wisdom are presented through esoteric meditation, study and service as a *way of life.*

Write to the publishers for information

INDEX

A

A.U.M., symbolism and composition, 533

Abstract mind, nature of, 98

Abstractions, inability to grasp, 510

Accidents to individuals, causes, 62-63

Act of the Will carried out, 538

Adepts, Atlantean, 122

Adoration, nature of, 268

Adrenal glands, 119

Aggression, material, abandonment for spiritual objectives, 182-183

Agni, Lord, work, 505

Airplanes, Atlantean, 122

Alignment and correct relation of three spiritual centres, 274-275

Alignments within Hierarchy, 522, 526-531, 535

Americans, northern and southern, ignorance of Europe, 451

Angel of Death, work replaced by work of Spirit of Resurrection, 458

Angel of the Presence—
  comparison with Avatar, 293
  contrast with Dweller on Threshold, 293-294
  definition, 137
  embodiments, 292-293

"Angelic essence", inflow from deva kingdom, 562

Angels—
  "fall", 118
  work, 505, 506, 507, 508-509
  See also Devas.

Anglo-Saxon peoples, destiny, 507

Anima mundi, nature of, study, 59

Animal-men, transition into human family, 47-49

Antahkarana—
  channel for energy from Shamballa, 687-688
  construction, agency of abstract mind, 694
  uniting humanity and Hierarchy, 535
  world building, aid to, 64

Apostolic succession, true, 514, 590, 593-594

Approach—
  Great—
    first, 409
    preparation for by Hierarchy, results, 395-396
    second, 409-410
    third, preparation for, 413, 415
  greatest of all time, 387, 389
  to God, new, on its way, 406

Approaches—
  divine, study, 56
  Great Cyclic, symbol and guarantee, 406
  three great, 394-396

Aquarian Age—
  characteristics outstanding, 36
  civilisation, germ, nurture, 35
  culture and civilisation, germ, protection, 39
  emphases, contrast with Piscean, 3
  increasing expression of at-one-ment, 168
  of brotherhood and understanding, 225
  synthesis and light, 36
  truths, newer, 30

Aquarius—
  expression of group consciousness, transmission, 155
  governs cycles of 25,00 and 2,300 years, 567

Arcane School—
  aim and accomplishment, 633
  founding and work, purposes, 322-323

Aristotle, group work, 28

Art—
  creative, central theme, integration, 589
  creative, evidence of man's divinity, 605
  of invocation, 324

Aryan Root Race, basis, 124

"As if", acting, 556

Ascension initiation of Christ, 487

Ashram—
  active or relatively inactive according to need, 582
  each, contribution to externalisation, 680

Fusion—Continued
of—
Hierarchy and humanity, results, 398
inner spiritual way of life and outer cultural activity, 193
personality and soul, 360-361
Shamballa and Hierarchy, results, 408
Will, Love, and Intelligence of God, 275

G

Gandhi, appraisal, 368
Geneva, function in creative process, 675, 676, 678
German—
nation, death, 458
people, glamour, 231, 356, 424
people, negativity, 345, 425, 428, 496
obsession, 474, 475, 489
Germanic peoples, psychology, 432
Germany—
energy centres, 85
evil leaders, 258, 326, 425
reactions to Shamballa force, 133
surrender, outer result of inner happenings, 494-495
Gethsemane, Father's will anchored on Earth, 606
Glamour—
concern of group of Trained Observers, 38
non-existent, 531
of German people, 231, 356, 424
of propaganda and world illusion, 217
work with, 36, 41
world, conquest, 64, 359, 360, 361, 362
world, root of catastrophe, 354
Goals, material and spiritual, of disciples, 700-701
God—
concepts of in human consciousness, history, 410-414
definitions, new, 406
fact, basic truth, 289
Heart, Love from, effects, 554
immanent, fact, concept, acceptance, 415, 590-591
kingdom, definitions, 603-604
Light, 406
Love—
embodied in man, 603
expression and focus, Full Moon, 1942, 362

expression in Right Human Relations, 603
major cyclic approach to earth, 72
Revealers, source, 406-407
Messengers and Representatives to aid and guide humanity, 264
Mind, Light from, effects, 554
purposes, directed, origin, 407
response to cry, never failing, 264
soul, revelation, 288
transcendence, definition and significance, 290-292
Transcendent, seen, known, and approached, 355-356
Transcendent, teaching regarding, 590-591
Will—
attractive power, embodiment, 359
beneficent demonstration, 72
embodied and held in synthesis, 533
execution, 270-271
expression and focus, Full Moon, 1942, 362
expression of Self, importance, 447
focus, place, 407
for humanity, 398
held in custody, 269
in operation, techniques, 345
indication, 533
knowledge of, 446
loving understanding as it affects humanity, 161
purpose, 161
to produce changes in consciousness, results, 107
unfoldment, 264-265
Wisdom of, Messengers source, 407
Good—
and bad, emergence into prominence, benefits, 423-424
true, and beautiful on its way, due to humanity, 630
Good Friday, significance nearly finished, 553
Goodwill—
action, results in New Age, 679
activating on physical plane, 280
active, recognition as real national asset, 698
distinction from will-to-good, 669
education of public in, results, 321-322
effective, creative appearance, manifestation, delay, 643
energy, 670, 676

New—Continued
  Group of World Servers—Cont.
    tasks, 177-178, 334, 398-400
    training by Christ, 607
    work in true democracy, 53
    vision, new idealism, and new life technique needed, 310
  World Order, 185-187, 190-193, 230, 241, 499
  World Religion. *See* Religion, New World.
New York, function in creative process, 675, 676, 678
The Next Three Years, pamphlet, 22-24
1918, entrance of cycle, 518
1919—
  first contact of Master D.K. with A.A.B., 631
  prior to, occult groups, disappearance, 571
1925—
  conclave of Masters, results, 106
  Great Council, 389
  importance, 518
1932, mobilisation of disciples, 474
1934, climax of cycle, 518
1936—
  failure, causes, 394-395
  planetary effort, 474
1939, war, 475, 491
1942—
  decisive year in conflict, 326
  June Full Moon, test, 361-362
  widespread goodwill or postponement, prophecy, 97
1945, San Francisco Conference, 464, 466
1945-1948, work, 461
1946—
  beginning of cycle, 553
  completion of task of reorganisation, 538, 638
1946-2025, consummation of purpose of Logos, 562
1949, completion of collaboration of Master D.K. and Alice Bailey, 631
1975—
  purificatory work, 694
  scientific recognition of fact of soul, 58
  true peace, accompaniments, 325
  vanguard of Hierarchy preceding it into outer manifestation, 587
Nirmanakayas, responsive to extra-solar reservoirs, 156
Noble Eightfold Path, 463

Noble Middle Way, trodden, 668
Normality, return to, danger, 369-370

O

O.M.—
  Ray, 145
  use, 144-145, 146
Obsession, definition, 307-308
Occult—
  bodies and esoteric groups, glamoured, 571
  life, scientific aspect, 104
  philosophy, keynotes, 674
  withdrawal of Piscean atoms, 3
Occultism, definition, 337
Occultists, advanced, future, training school, 511
Old Testament, theme, 124
Oligarchy of illumined minds, government by, 52
"One in Whom we Live and Move"—
  body, centres, 72-73
  life of, cause of impacts, 109
One world for one humanity, 623
Opinion, public, influencing, 379-385
Opposites, pairs—
  in consciousness, origin, 41
  problem in disciple's life, 136-137
Order, production, energy, 646-647
Overshadowing—
  by Avatar of Synthesis, 303, 306, 307
  by Christ, 307, 601
  disciples at Wesak, future, 553
  for leadership, 260
  in answer to invocation, 268
Over-stimulation, danger, 557

P

P., Master, work in North America, 682
Pacifism, no place in Hierarchy, 232
Pacifists—
  sweet sentimentality obstruction to work of Forces of Light, 476-477
  world, arguments, 179
Pain—
  purifying agent, 116
  uses, recognition, 155
Patanjali, teaching avatar, 298
Path—
  of Earth Service, 531-532
  of World Saviour, 269
  of World Service, 269
  to God, fact of, 405

Ray—Continued
  seventh—Continued
    rhythm, cooperation with, 668-669
  sixth, disciples and initiates, incarnation, 581
  third—
    Ashram, adjustment of finances, 580-581
    avenue of aid by Christ preparatory to New Age, 512
    energy, achievements, 667
    traits and use in preparing for Reappearance, 645-646
Rays, five, represented in externalisation, 677
Reactionary stupidity, elimination, 576
Reality, living substance, relationship to, future, 416-417
Reappearance of Christ—
  Angels accompanying Christ, work, 508-509
  bringing new energies of love and revelation, 698-699
  fact spread by disciples, necessity, 701
  painful to Himself, 607
  plans being laid, 602, 609-612
  preparation for—
    injunction, 641
    lack of money, 623-631
    united group endeavour, 680
    work of Master D.K. and Alice Bailey, 631-632
  statement of fact and of preparatory work, 632
  See also Christ; Coming One.
Rebuilding and reorganisation, five centres concerned, 675-677
Reconstruction—
  by first- and second-Ray workers, 335
  participation, preparation for, 382-383
  work—
    basis, 379-382
    coming, 472, 480-491
    practical steps, 320-332
    preparation for, 313-318
Re-creating process needed, 675
Redemption of matter, 693
Reflection on outer plane of more critical inner conditions, 352
Rehabilitation, scope, 341
Reincarnation, basic law of nature, 232
Relationship, principle, stimulation, 106, 108

Religion—
  and politics, divorce, cessation, 480
  definitions, 57, 596-597
  in New Age, 54-56
  in post-war world, 191, 192-193
  new—
    implementation and reformation, 573
    of Great Approaches, 401, 406
    of Invocation and Evocation, 401
  new world—
    achievements, prophecy, 400
    anchoring, 387-388, 400, 402
    attitude of humanity leading to, 409
    basis in truths, 404-406, 416
    characteristics, 418-422
    creation and vitalisation, 658, 700
    development, 578
    foundations, opportunity for laying, 390
    implements and aims, 401
    keynote, 418
    nucleus, 513
    preparation for, 448
    subjective basis, 502-518
    theme, initiation, 348
    theme, prophecy, 344, 414
    war against by fanatics, 453-454
  old forms, re-vivification and infusion of new life, 502-503
  orthodox, condition during world war, 355-356
  orthodox, past achievements, 400-401
  recognised in New Age, 575
  true, emerging in hearts of men, 596
  true, interpretation in future, 454
  work of seed group, 54-56
  world, motivation by invocation, 150
  world, platform, 55-56
Religions—
  form, deterioration, 402-403
  world, failure, 651
  world, reorganisation, 551
Religious—
  ideals, deepened, spread, 510
  organisations in New Age, 510-518
  problem, 200-203
  unity, progress toward, 54
  war of future, 453
Renaissance, inspiration, 49

* United Nations, a coalition of nations formed early in 1942 to oppose the Axis powers.

** United Nations, an organisation formed April-June, 1945, in San Francisco to maintain peace.